MANAGING ORGANIZATIONS
FUNCTIONS AND BEHAVIORS

MANAGING ORGANIZATIONS
FUNCTIONS AND BEHAVIORS

CHARLES D. PRINGLE
James Madison University

DANIEL F. JENNINGS
Baylor University

JUSTIN G. LONGENECKER
Baylor University, Professor Emeritus

Merrill Publishing Company
A Bell & Howell Information Company
Columbus Toronto London Melbourne

Cover photo: Photography and Photo Research,
Carlye Calvin

Published by Merrill Publishing Company
A Bell & Howell Information Company
Columbus, Ohio 43216

This book was set in Meridien.

Administrative Editor: Tim McEwen
Production Coordinator: Linda Bayma
Art Coordinator: Patrick Welch
Cover Designer: Cathy Watterson
Text Designer: Cynthia Brunk
Copy Editor: Dan Duffee

Photo credits: All photos copyrighted by individuals or
companies listed. Alan Bagg, p. 53; Darryl Baird, p. 1;
Merrill Publishing/photographs by Kevin Fitzsimons,
pp. 177, 323; Tom Krouse, p. 515; and Terry Tietz,
p. 431.

Library of Congress Catalog Card Number: 87-72203
International Standard Book Number: 0-675-20813-0
Printed in the United States of America
1 2 3 4 5 6 7 8 9—92 91 90 89 88

To Anne Marie, Kay, and Frances

PREFACE

Managers play key roles in organizations and in society. The more productive and effective organizations are, the higher is a society's standard of living. Although organizational effectiveness reflects a number of key factors, none is more important than the performance of the organization's managers. This book focuses on the work of managers.

Regardless of your particular field of study, *Managing Organizations* will provide an excellent starting point toward developing a successful career that will involve both managing and being managed. In this book, you will learn how organizations operate and what managers can do to improve operating effectiveness. These basic principles can be applied to schools, churches, government agencies, and hospitals, as well as to business organizations.

Philosophy

We have designed the text to reflect the theory of management as well as its actual practice. Each chapter is based on sound theoretical concepts and reports the latest relevant academic research. Liberally integrated into the discussion are examples of real managers in actual organizational situations. These examples bring the theory and research to life. From the first to the last page of *Managing Organizations,* you will find evidence of our belief that management theory and practice are inextricably intertwined.

Organization

The text is organized to present a topical coverage and includes a framework of six important areas of management. Part One, "Introduction to Management," contains two chapters and gives you an overview of the manager's job and traces the evolution of management theory from its conception to the present. Part Two, "Management Planning and Decision Making," has five chapters and deals with how managers analyze the environment, set objectives, develop strategy, implement operational plans, acquire information, and make decisions. In Part Three, "Organizing for Effective Performance," five chapters introduce you to the concepts of how jobs are designed, how organizations should be structured and staffed, how organizations must change periodically, and how the informal aspects of an organization affect its operations. The behavioral aspects of management—motivating, leading, managing work groups, and communicating—are covered in the four chapters of Part Four, "Leading and Motivating." Part Five, "Controlling Performance," focuses on financial and behavioral controls, as well as on the key areas of operations management, social responsibility, and ethics. Finally, Part Six, "Opportunities in Management," has two chapters that provide you with the international aspects of management and the management of your own career.

Overall, our coverage of the managerial functions, organizational behavior, organization theory, quantitative techniques, operations management, social responsibility, ethics, and the international arena is consistent with the accreditation recommendations of the American Assembly of Collegiate Schools of Business (AACSB) and includes timely references. Almost three-fourths of the references date from the 1980s and over half date from 1983.

Features

Each chapter begins with a statement of *learning objectives* (one for each major section in the text) and an outline to provide an overview of the chapter's content and purpose. A *summary* is provided at the end of the chapter along with a list of the *key concepts* covered in the discussion. End-of-the-chapter *questions* are designed to test your understanding of the chapter's major concepts, and a *supplementary reading list* steers you to additional sources of relevant information. To help you apply the concepts you have studied, each chapter concludes with one or two *cases* that require you to use what you have learned to analyze a realistic situation. The majority of the cases are based on real-world companies (often disguised) with the remainder being hypothetical cases written to illustrate particular points. At the end of the text is a *glossary* of key concepts to help you succinctly define central words and phrases.

Boxed inserts on current issues are used to relate incidents and situations found in the real world to the concepts and ideas presented in the text.

Supplemental Material

A complete instructional package is available to assist you in mastering management concepts. These include a computerized management simulation game, an instructor's manual to accompany the simulation, a study guide, an instructor's manual to accompany the text, a computerized test bank, and transparencies.

The computerized management game is called *Management: A Simulation* and was prepared by Dr. Paul Cretien and Dr. Dan Jennings. The game simulates an imaginary pharmaceutical firm in a dynamic business environment. Students act as management teams to produce and market multiple products. The players experience both positive and negative outcomes from various management decisions. An instructor's manual is available to accompany the simulation game.

The study guide, prepared by Charles Williams, contains a study checklist on how to master the material for exams, a synopsis of each chapter, and self-tests to test your knowledge of learning objectives, concepts, and chapter contents. Answers are provided for the self-tests.

The instructor's manual, also prepared by Charles Williams, includes explanations of each chapter's learning objectives and key concepts. Lecture outlines, teaching notes, and answers to discussion questions are also included.

The computerized test bank was prepared by Betty Pritchard and contains approximately 2,100 questions that are true-false and multiple choice. The test bank is available in either printed or microcomputer versions. Transparencies taken from the figures and tables in the text are also available.

ACKNOWLEDGMENTS

A project of this magnitude requires the help of numerous individuals, and we have been particularly fortunate in this respect. Everyone in Merrill's production, art, and design departments is to be commended for their creativity and hard work. Special acknowledgment goes to our production editor, Linda H. Bayma, who was not only highly supportive and cooperative, but also managed to keep our work focused and on schedule. The copyediting skills of Dan Duffee added significantly to the clarity of our writing.

We are grateful for the valuable suggestions of the many individuals responding to our survey and to those who reviewed *Managing Organizations*. They are:

Jennifer Bailey
Towson State University

C. A. Bell
University of Pittsburgh—Johnstown

Lester R. Bittel
James Madison University

Joseph Comer
Towson State University

John Crim
Columbus College

Michael Currid
Susquehanna University

John de Young
Cumberland County College

Philip B. DuBose
James Madison University

Theodore A. Dumstorf
East Tennessee State University

William B. Fox III
Farleigh Dickinson University

Allen Gulezian
Central Washington University

George B. Harmon
Marymount College

Joseph C. Hope
Seattle Pacific University

Henry F. Houser
Auburn University

Donald F. Kuratko
Ball State University

Timothy A. Matherly
Florida State University

Charles McGee
Clarion University

Vincent P. McNally, Jr.
St. Joseph's University

James L. Nimnicht
Eastern Washington University

Steve Norton
Indiana University at South Bend

Eugene Owens
Western Washington University

Dennis Patzig
James Madison University

James G. Pesek
Clarion University

E. Leroy Plumlee
Western Washington University

Donna Randall
Washington State University

Norman Scarborough
Presbyterian College

Joy Throckmorton
Indiana State University

Robert Vichas
Old Dominion University

Paul L. Wilkens
Florida State University

Ronald M. Ziggi
Memphis State University

Dean Robert E. Holmes of James Madison University and Dean Richard C. Scott of Baylor's Hankamer School of Business have created an environment that is conducive to research and writing and we thank them. Dr. R. Duane Ireland of Baylor's Management Department has been most supportive.

Several colleagues at Baylor University offered encouragement and support. The insights of Dale Allen, Van Gray, Mike Umble, Tammy Hunt, Van Miller, and Jack Wimer are appreciated.

Emily Ketcham, Patti Moore, and Sandy Tighe are thanked for typing the manuscript.

Finally, without the support, patience, understanding, and encouragement of our wives and families, this book would never have gotten past the planning stage. Thank you Anne Marie and Erin; Kay, Courtney, and Christopher; and Frances. This book is dedicated to you.

Charles D. Pringle
Daniel F. Jennings
Justin G. Longenecker

CONTENTS

MANAGING ORGANIZATIONS
FUNCTIONS AND BEHAVIORS

PART ONE

INTRODUCTION TO MANAGEMENT

THE FIELD OF MANAGEMENT

Types of Managers ☐ The Distinctive Skill of Management

THE MANAGER'S JOB: AN OVERVIEW

Managerial Behavior Patterns ☐ Managerial Skills ☐ Transferability of Managerial Skills ☐ Differences in Managerial Work ☐ Roles of the Manager ☐ Functions of the Manager

THE CHALLENGE OF MANAGEMENT

Major Issues Facing Management ☐ Management and Productivity

Summary ☐ Key Concepts ☐ Discussion Questions ☐ Notes ☐ Supplementary Reading

CASE: A Day in the Life of James Marks

This chapter will enable you to

☐ Define management and identify the unique features of managerial activities.

☐ Become familiar with the manager's job, including managerial behavior patterns, the skills required for effective management, differences in managerial work, and the manager's multiple roles.

☐ Identify and discuss the basic managerial functions.

☐ Discuss the significant challenges facing management today.

CHAPTER 1
MANAGEMENT: AN OVERVIEW

Organizations pervade our lives. Most of us are born in hospitals. We are educated in schools. The clothes we wear are created by clothing manufacturers and sold to us by retail outlets. Our food is produced on farms, processed by manufacturers, and sold to supermarket chains. Your television was designed, built, and assembled by an organization; the programs come from such companies as CBS, ESPN, or HBO; and the electricity to power the set will be produced by a local utility. This book was produced by a publisher.

All of these organizations require management, and the relative effectiveness of that management determines the quality of the product or service produced. Managerial effectiveness is a prime determinant of the success of every organization. Successful firms usually grow and expand, thereby creating more jobs. The more successful organizations are, the more society benefits through full employment and a high standard of living.

The topic of this book is *management*. You will learn what managers do, and you will become familiar with various theories, techniques, and tools designed to increase managerial effectiveness. This knowledge is useful for anyone who works in, deals with, or belongs to a formal organization.

If you are interested in a managerial career, this book is a starting point. As you may have already guessed, the demand for managerial talent far exceeds the supply of good managers. This book, in itself, will not make you a "good manager," but it will acquaint you with the underlying theory and the actual practice of management. As such, it will provide you with a start toward developing a successful career that will involve both managing and being managed.

IS MANAGEMENT IMPORTANT?

Consider these comments recently found in the news media:

> Although the [nuclear power] industry has made thousands of design and engineering improvements since Three Mile Island, 10 percent of America's reactors are currently shut down for nonroutine problems, many of them due to bad management.

> Following a $250 million trading loss in one week created largely by one employee's unauthorized trades of mortgage-backed securities, a spokesperson for the affected stock-brokerage firm commented: "It's poor supervision; we know that."

> The B-1 [bomber] program is behind schedule and unfinished because of management deficiencies at all levels. . . .

> If we really want to strengthen American schools, our current fixation on teachers is not the most efficient way to begin. . . . For greater leverage on the schools we'd be smart to pay closer attention to the schools' principals. . . . A great school almost always boasts a crackerjack principal. . . .

> We've got this really strange thing in our country where we like to blame the American workers for the fact that we're not competitive. Now let's assume we had a losing football team. Can you imagine anyone blaming the players? You'd get folks on the coach and the quarterback in a hurry. But in industry, ahhh, it's always the workers. Never forget that the worker does not create his product, he doesn't design his product, he doesn't determine how it's put together. All he does is assemble it. All these other things that determine success or failure are done before it gets to him. [statement by H. Ross Perot]

SOURCE: These comments, in order of appearance, were found in: "America's Big Risk," *Newsweek*, 27 April 1987, p. 58; "Merrill Lynch Takes a Bath," *Newsweek*, 11 May 1987, p. 53; "B-1 Problems Blamed On Bad Management," *Harrisonburg (Va.) Daily News-Record*, 5 March 1987; Chester E. Finn, Jr., "Better Principals, Not Just Teachers," *The Wall Street Journal*, 18 February 1987; and David Remnick, "H. Ross Perot to GM: 'I'll Drive.' GM to H. Ross Perot: 'Oh, Yeah?' " *The Washington Post Magazine*, 19 April 1987, p. 28.

THE FIELD OF MANAGEMENT

Management is the process of acquiring and combining human, financial, informational, and physical resources to attain the organization's primary goal of producing a product or service desired by some segment of society. This process is essential to the functioning of all organizations, profit and nonprofit: essential resources must be acquired and combined in some way to produce an output. A hospital administrator, for instance, must staff a hospital with physicians, nurses, and technicians; provide modern equipment for diagnosis, treatment, and recovery; and raise funds from patients, private donors, and the government. These resources must then be combined to produce healed patients. The same general process, illustrated in Figure 1–1, applies to the production of an automobile, an audit of accounting records, the issuance of a government regulation, or the education of a student.

The manager provides the dynamic force or direction necessary to acquire static resources and combine them into a functioning, productive organization. He or she is the individual in charge and is expected to get results and to see that things happen as they should.

Types of Managers

The manager may carry any one of many different titles. At the top, a manager is identified by such titles as *chairman of the board, president,* or *chief executive officer* (CEO). At somewhat lower levels, a manager is called *vice-president* (an

FIGURE 1–1 The managerial process

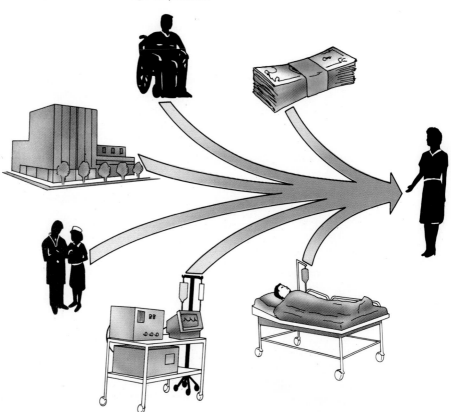

FIGURE 1–2 Management activities at three different levels

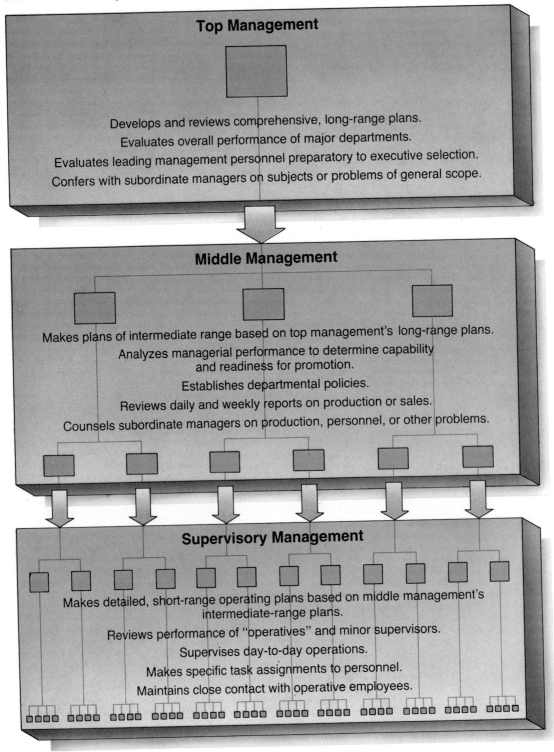

Top Management

Develops and reviews comprehensive, long-range plans.
Evaluates overall performance of major departments.
Evaluates leading management personnel preparatory to executive selection.
Confers with subordinate managers on subjects or problems of general scope.

Middle Management

Makes plans of intermediate range based on top management's long-range plans.
Analyzes managerial performance to determine capability
and readiness for promotion.
Establishes departmental policies.
Reviews daily and weekly reports on production or sales.
Counsels subordinate managers on production, personnel, or other problems.

Supervisory Management

Makes detailed, short-range operating plans based on middle management's
intermediate-range plans.
Reviews performance of "operatives" and minor supervisors.
Supervises day-to-day operations.
Makes specific task assignments to personnel.
Maintains close contact with operative employees.

infinite variety), *divisional manager,* or *regional manager.* At the lowest managerial levels, such titles as *department manager, assistant department manager, supervisor,* and *office manager* appear. In each instance, the title is expected to give some indication of the function and level of the manager.

Figure 1–2 indicates some of the activities performed at the top, middle, and supervisory levels of management. This statement of activities reveals some of the similarities and differences in focus and outlook at these levels. Each level, for instance, has the responsibility for planning and evaluating performance, but the types of plans and the focus of the performance evaluation differ significantly from level to level.

The Distinctive Skill of Management

We have come to recognize that management and the abilities of the manager are separate and distinct from the activities and abilities required of operating personnel. At one time, it was customary to promote the most proficient worker when filling a management vacancy. Although this procedure had much to recommend, it ignored the fact that ability to direct the work of others is substantially different from that of doing one's own work.

As an example, consider the case of a professor who accepted an offer to become the head of a large department at another university. The offer was based primarily upon the professor's impressive research and publication record. Once the professor took over the new administrative position, however, it quickly became apparent to the members of the department that expertise in research did not necessarily qualify one to manage a department. While unanswered department correspondence piled up, scheduling deadlines passed

EDUCATION AND THE FAST TRACK

Business Week recently selected fifty "fast track" managers who were 35 years old or younger as a sample of the most successful young managers in the U.S. Of these fifty, forty-one had earned graduate degrees: thirty-five had master of business administration (MBA) degrees, four had master's degrees in other areas, and two had law degrees.

In the public sector, *Management* magazine selected its TOP 40—America's top forty public servants in the federal government who were 40 years old or younger. Of this group (with an average age of 34), 68 percent held master's degrees, professional credentials (law, engineering), or Ph.D.'s.

SOURCE: "Is There a Future CEO in This Bunch?" *Business Week,* 10 November 1986, pp. 97–104; and Tierney R. Bates, "The Big Thrill," *Management* 6, no. 2 (1987): 9–14.

unnoticed, and meetings of department heads went unattended, the professor stayed ensconced in an office at home turning out more articles!

Likewise, the characteristics and abilities that make a good sales representative or a successful accountant do not necessarily make a good sales manager or a successful head accountant. Operative workers are basically responsible for performing their own jobs satisfactorily, whereas managers are responsible not only for their own jobs but also for the job performance of subordinates.

THE MANAGER'S JOB: AN OVERVIEW

The practice of management is both a science and an art. In recent decades, management has become a branch of knowledge concerned with establishing and systematizing facts, principles, and methods through experiments and hypotheses. To the extent this has been accomplished—and you will see some evidence of this accomplishment throughout the text—management is scientific. Few scholars would claim, however, that management is exclusively a science. Our knowledge of planning, organizing, leading, controlling, and so on remains incomplete. To the extent our knowledge is deficient, management continues to be an art, dependent upon personal aptitudes, skills, applications, and intuition.

In this section, we will examine the manager's job from a number of different perspectives: managerial behavior patterns, the skills required for effective management, differences in managerial work, the multiple roles of the manager, and the functions of the manager. These are simply alternative ways of viewing managerial work. Taken together, they give us a more complete view of the manager's job than would a single perspective.

Managerial Behavior Patterns

Observation of managers in action reveals that most managers are extremely busy. Recent surveys reveal that the chief executives of major firms work an average of eleven to twelve hours per weekday, plus about ten hours over the weekend. Over half of the executives in one survey travel seven or more days per month.[1] Vacations tend to be infrequent and of short duration. These executives often spend lunch periods on business; sometimes they eat sandwiches at their desks and sometimes they have business lunches with customers, public officials, or staff members. As a chairman of a New York advertising agency said, "A chief executive doesn't take time off if he wishes to remain chief executive."[2] This view is supported by scholars:[3]

It should be remembered that the brain works continuously. Unlike physical job-related work which ends at quitting time, managers may continue to think about job-related problems long after they leave the job and perhaps, even while they are asleep. . . . Certainly, measuring managers' activities on the job is not going to present a full picture of the work.

That a manager works hard and spends long hours on the job tells little about the patterning of managerial activities. We might surmise that an efficient manager would take one project at a time, complete it, and move on to the next project. Studies of managers in action, however, have shown that the systematic, orderly executive seldom exists in the real world.[4] Rather, the manager's activities are characterized by "brevity, variety, and fragmentation."[5] One study of managers in Great Britain revealed that they could not explicitly state what they wanted to achieve in their jobs, perhaps because of "the episodic and fragmented patterns of their days. . . ."[6]

The characteristic of brevity is particularly pronounced at lower levels of the organization. In separate studies, Guest and Ponder found extreme brevity in activities at the foreman level, with an average duration of forty-eight seconds in the former study and about two minutes in the latter.[7] A study of 1,476 lower-level managers in New York City government indicated that they spent one to three hours each, per week, on fourteen different tasks, and less than one hour each, weekly, on forty-three other tasks.[8]

Yet such brevity of attention does not necessarily imply inefficiency. John P. Kotter indicates that managers face two fundamental challenges: (1) knowing what to do in the face of great uncertainty and (2) getting it done with a diverse set of people despite having little direct control over most of them. Managers cope with these challenges in two ways: *agenda setting* and *network building.*[9]

Effective managers, according to Kotter, set agendas comprised of "loosely connected goals and plans that address their long-, medium-, and

THE EXECUTIVE'S VARIED ACTIVITIES

In Henry Mintzberg's study of chief executives, he found that they averaged thirty-six written and sixteen verbal contacts each day.

> A subordinate calls to report a fire in one of the facilities; then the mail, much of it insignificant, is processed; a subordinate interrupts to tell of an impending crisis with a public group; a retiring employee is ushered in to receive a plaque; later there is a discussion of bidding on a multimillion-dollar contract; after that, the manager complains that office space in one department is being wasted. Throughout each working day the manager encounters this great variety of activity. Most surprising, the significant activity is interspersed with the trivial in no particular pattern. Hence the manager must be prepared to shift moods quickly and frequently.

SOURCE: Henry Mintzberg, *The Nature of Managerial Work,* p. 31. Copyright © 1973 by Henry Mintzberg. Reprinted by permission of Harper & Row, Publishers, Inc.

short-term responsibilities."[10] This framework allows the manager to react to the seemingly inefficient daily flow of events in an opportunistic and efficient manner.

Successful managers also build a network of relationships with people whose cooperation will be necessary to satisfy the executives' agendas. These networks allow the managers to gain information, make suggestions, and attain objectives through short yet meaningful conversations. Kotter's conclusions regarding network building were reinforced by a study of fifty-two managers in three diverse organizations. The researchers found a significant relationship between managerial success and two networking activities: interacting with outsiders and socializing or politicking with other employees.[11]

A survey of undergraduate students, conducted by a career consulting firm, found that the college students were unaware of the importance of network building in work organizations. The students perceived little connection between success and such social behavior as getting along with the boss, having a helpful adviser, or playing office politics.[12]

Managerial Skills

Robert L. Katz suggests that managerial positions require three types of basic skills: *technical, human relations,* and *conceptual.*[13] Although managerial positions differ in the technical skill required, most necessitate some technical ability. A laboratory supervisor, for example, needs to understand the nature of laboratory tests conducted under his or her supervision. A controller requires a knowledge of accounting. Even at top levels, knowledge of the industry is required, particularly in smaller companies where extensive staff assistance is unavailable.

Competence in interpersonal relations is an important asset to the administrator because a manager accomplishes work through the efforts of others. A manager must blend the efforts of subordinate managers who frequently differ in backgrounds, areas of specialization, and viewpoints. The ability to integrate diverse interests and simultaneously preserve the loyalty and enthusiasm of team members contributes directly to organizational effectiveness.

Conceptual skills are essential if the manager is to be able to discern problems, devise solutions, analyze data, and exercise judgment. These tasks are often intellectually demanding because problems do not always lend themselves to easy solutions. In strategic planning, financial administration, designing control systems, and other areas, the issues may call for the very best thinking.

The need for these skills varies from position to position, as illustrated in Figure 1–3. At lower levels, managers direct routine work and can perform successfully with minimum conceptual ability as long as they have the appropriate technical knowledge and human relations skills. As more complex activities are planned and directed, the demand for conceptual skills increases and the need for technical skills decreases. The focus of the manager's human re-

FIGURE 1–3 Skills required at different managerial levels

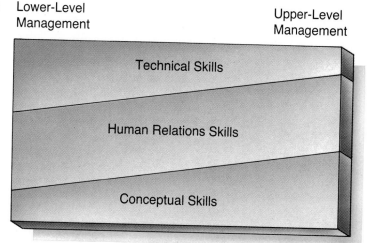

lations skills changes as he or she is promoted upward. At lower levels, the manager requires leadership ability within his or her own unit. At higher levels, skills in intergroup relationships—being able to resolve interdepartmental conflict and promote cooperation—become increasingly important.

Transferability of Managerial Skills

That managerial skills are somewhat transferable from one organizational setting to another is clear from the example of George Schultz. Over a period of two decades, Schultz served as dean of the Graduate School of Business at the University of Chicago, as secretary of the treasury in the Nixon administration, as president of the Bechtel Group (a worldwide construction company), and as secretary of state in the Reagan administration. Those positions differed greatly, but all required managerial skill.

Other examples can be cited to demonstrate the limited transferability of managerial skills. In 1983, James J. Morgan resigned as executive vice-president for marketing at Philip Morris USA to become chairman and chief executive of Atari, a manufacturer of home computers and video games. Although the transition from the cigarette industry to computers would be difficult, Morgan and Atari thought his expertise in consumer product marketing was transferable. Less than a year later, after overseeing huge financial losses, Morgan left Atari. Some observers commented that Morgan's background in the cigarette industry might have been appropriate for a move to a traditional consumer products firm, such as Procter & Gamble, but it did not prepare him well for the fast-paced world of home computers.[14]

How transferable are managerial skills? Robert H. Hayes comments that "managers who are truly able to jump into different situations and run them effectively are very, very rare."[15] John Kotter points out that the successful general managers he has studied have spent years in a single organization,

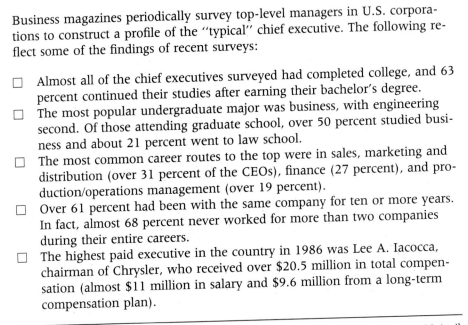

THE CHIEF EXECUTIVE OFFICER

Business magazines periodically survey top-level managers in U.S. corporations to construct a profile of the "typical" chief executive. The following reflect some of the findings of recent surveys:

☐ Almost all of the chief executives surveyed had completed college, and 63 percent continued their studies after earning their bachelor's degree.

☐ The most popular undergraduate major was business, with engineering second. Of those attending graduate school, over 50 percent studied business and about 21 percent went to law school.

☐ The most common career routes to the top were in sales, marketing and distribution (over 31 percent of the CEOs), finance (27 percent), and production/operations management (over 19 percent).

☐ Over 61 percent had been with the same company for ten or more years. In fact, almost 68 percent never worked for more than two companies during their entire careers.

☐ The highest paid executive in the country in 1986 was Lee A. Iacocca, chairman of Chrysler, who received over $20.5 million in total compensation (almost $11 million in salary and $9.6 million from a long-term compensation plan).

SOURCE: Maggie McComas, "Atop the Fortune 500: A Survey of the C.E.O.s," *Fortune,* 28 April 1986, pp. 26–31; and "Executive Pay: Who Got What in '86," *Business Week,* 4 May 1987, pp. 50–94.

acquiring knowledge about the company and its industry. During those years, the executive develops an extensive network of relationships with key people, both inside and outside the firm. Such relationships and detailed knowledge of the organization are rarely transferable to other firms.[16] Robert L. Katz suggests that the transferability of managerial skills is possible only in large organizations where the manager has extensive staff assistance and highly competent technical operators throughout the organization.[17] A new manager in such a setting could rely on other individuals for the daily operations of the organization while he or she concentrated on planning and goal setting.

Research evidence indicates that companies in either growth industries or declining industries perform more effectively when at least 20 percent of managers in the top levels were hired from outside the business within the past three years. Insiders, the researchers conclude, are less likely to recognize when a strategy is losing its effectiveness and when the status quo needs to be abandoned. In mature businesses, on the other hand, where the need for innovative thinking is less essential, insiders who know the business well are likely to be more effective.[18]

Differences in Managerial Work

Although all managerial jobs have certain elements in common, even managerial jobs at the same hierarchical level can differ considerably. Rosemary Stewart, a British researcher, suggests that managerial jobs vary along three lines:[19]

1. The *behavioral demands* made upon the manager by subordinates, peers, superiors, external contacts, and so on—these are the things that the manager must do.
2. The internal and external *constraints* that limit the manager's behavior— these include monetary and personnel constraints, provisions in the union contract, the organization's technology, and so on.
3. The *choices* that a manager has in doing a job differently from another manager—these include the freedom to choose which aspects of the job to emphasize, which to delegate to subordinates, and which to ignore.

These three variables (shown in Figure 1–4) provide a means of identifying the nature and difficulty of various managerial jobs. If we can develop systematic ways of distinguishing among managerial jobs, our efforts to select and prepare people for management will be vastly improved.[20]

Roles of the Manager

Another way to understand the nature of complex managerial work is to identify the manager's multiple *roles*. This use of activity categories helps us to see the tremendous variety that characterizes the manager's job. Although identification of specific roles is somewhat arbitrary, one of the better known categorizations is given here.[21] These ten roles, grouped into three general categories, are also shown in Figure 1–5.

Interpersonal Roles

□ *Figurehead* As symbolic head of an organization, the manager must perform duties of a legal or ceremonial nature. Examples of such activities are welcoming official visitors and signing letters to retiring employees.

□ *Leader* In performing this widely recognized role, the manager guides and motivates subordinates.

□ *Liaison* This role is concerned primarily with horizontal relationships. The manager establishes a web of external relationships, getting to know peers and building a relationship of mutual assistance.

FIGURE 1–4 A model for understanding managerial jobs and behavior

Informational Roles

□ *Monitor* The manager receives information and analyses related to both operations and external events. Keeping up with trends and learning about new ideas also fall within this area.

□ *Disseminator* This role entails the transmission of information received from outside to members of the organization. The manager who calls a staff meeting following a business trip is playing the disseminator role.

□ *Spokesperson* The manager speaks on behalf of the organization. An example is the manager's speech to the trade association or press.

Decisional Roles

□ *Entrepreneur* In initiating change, the manager performs an entrepreneurial role. A decision to launch a computer feasibility study is an example.

□ *Disturbance Handler* Unexpected problems or disturbances—loss of an im-

FIGURE 1–5   Roles of the manager

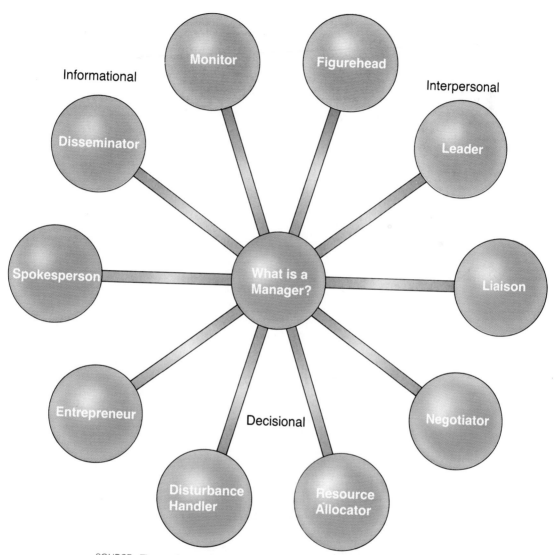

SOURCE: These roles are described by Henry Mintzberg in THE NATURE OF MANAGERIAL WORK (New York: Harper & Row, Publishers, Inc., 1973), chapter 4.

portant customer or feud between two subordinates, for example—require the manager to play a disturbance-handler role.

□ *Resource Allocator*   As a resource allocator, a manager determines the distribution of organizational resources such as money, time, and equipment. A manager's approval of a budget or establishment of a personal time schedule involves the allocation of resources.

□ *Negotiator*   As a negotiator, a manager bargains with customers or other outsiders or insiders. Representing the organization in labor negotiations or bargaining with a key employee illustrates the negotiator role.

A number of different roles may be evident in a given situation. In the study of lower-level managers in New York City government, managers engaged in eight of these ten roles. (The roles of spokesperson and figurehead were reserved for higher-level managers.)[22] Another study of 228 managers at all levels indicated that the roles of disseminator, figurehead, negotiator, liaison, and spokesperson were more important at the higher managerial levels. Supervisors rated the leader role as more important for successful job performance than did either middle or top managers. Overall, the study supported Mintzberg's suggestion that managers at all levels perform similar roles but with differing emphases.[23]

Functions of the Manager

Another approach to analysis of management activity identifies certain basic *management functions*. In attempting to classify, in this manner, what the manager does, we are seeking some fundamental categories that permit a logical grouping of managerial activities according to their purpose and nature. A number of basic functions are widely recognized, even though there is some variation in labeling them.

In this book, the following so-called classical functions will provide the framework for our analysis of management activities:

□ Planning and decision making
□ Organizing for effective performance
□ Leading and motivating
□ Controlling performance

This particular classification scheme is used to structure the text because:[24]

> The classical functions still represent the most useful way of conceptualizing the manager's job, especially for management education. . . . The classical functions provide clear and discrete methods of classifying the thousands of different activities that managers carry out and the techniques they use in terms of the functions they perform for the achievement of organizational goals.

Planning and Decision Making. Managerial planning involves thought and decision concerning a proposed course of action. The plan may be concerned with not only a decision to take action but also such aspects as "who," "when," and "how."

The first step in the planning process is setting organizational objectives. These objectives provide direction for the organization and also serve as a basis for teamwork among organizational components and individuals. Attaining the objectives requires strategic planning; that is, devising a basic approach or

DO YOU HAVE WHAT IT TAKES TO BE A MANAGER?

Successful managers come in all shapes, sizes, ages, and temperaments. Hence, generalizing about the "typical" successful manager is risky. Many successful managers, however, possess the following characteristics:

- ☐ Great amounts of energy
- ☐ A desire for variety rather than routine
- ☐ An ability to make decisions
- ☐ A need for achievement
- ☐ A need for power
- ☐ Excellent human relations skills, including an ability to work with others and an ability to communicate well

strategy to reach the organization's objectives. The strategy for the organization is typically broken down and supplemented with policies—guidelines for administrative action—and specific operating plans for particular organizational units. Middle- and lower-level managers, guided by top management's strategy, formulate more specific goals and plans for their particular divisions or departments. This interlocking set of policies and plans serves as a program of action for managers at all organizational levels.

Although decision making is involved in planning, motivating, and the other managerial functions, this activity is often considered so important that it is emphasized as a separate function. Basically, decision making is a conscious choice from among two or more courses of action. Ideally, the manager makes this choice by identifying the problem or opportunity being faced, searching for possible solutions, evaluating the alternatives, and choosing and implementing one or more of the alternatives.

Because the future is uncertain, the manager uses various types of tools to reduce the risk and subjectivity of decision making. Management information systems, for instance, are designed to provide data on internal operations and the external environment. In some situations, data analysis is aided by quantitative techniques using mathematical models.

Organizing for Effective Performance. Implementing plans requires an organization. Viewed broadly, organizing includes providing for physical facilities, capital, and personnel. Building an organization also concerns determining relationships among functions, jobs, and personnel. Each of these is a part of the creation of the organizational machine that is designed to accomplish some objective.

This organizing might be visualized as breaking down an overall objective into the specific functions and assignments necessary for the accomplishment of that objective. This involves creating jobs and specifying job content and then grouping jobs and activities into departments and divisions. Organizing is concerned with the relationships among these units and the jobs within the units and, more broadly, with the fit between the organization's overall structure and its external environment.

Leading and Motivating. The organizational machine must be activated to carry out management plans. The functions of leading and motivating set the organization in motion.

A major responsibility of managers at all organizational levels is to direct and inspire the work of others. High-performing employees can make the difference between a marginal organization and a highly effective one. Through leadership, a manager secures the cooperation of others in accomplishing an objective. And, in motivating, the manager encourages subordinates to strive persistently for high job performance. These functions require the manager to understand individual and group behavior and to communicate clearly.

Controlling Performance. Controlling performance means monitoring the organization to ensure the achievement of objectives and the completion of plans. Perhaps the most obvious feature of controlling is the comparison of organizational or individual performance with pre-established standards, or expected results. If deviations from standards are revealed, it is the manager's responsibility to take corrective action, by getting performance back up to the time schedule, getting quality up to par, or making other adjustments necessary to meet the expectations previously established. Corrective action takes many forms, such as improving work processes, motivating subordinates, correcting communication breakdowns, revising decision-making procedures, or modifying the organization's structure.

A Synthesis. The approaches we have taken to viewing managerial work are not unrelated. For instance, consider the function of managerial planning. Planning requires the use of conceptual skills and, later, human relations skills in communicating those plans to others. The final plans will reflect the constraints under which the manager must operate and the demands made by peers, superiors, and subordinates. While planning, the manager may well become a liaison in discussing the plans with managers of other units which may be affected; a monitor in collecting and interpreting information from the environment and other parts of the organization; an entrepreneur in initiating change for the organization; and a resource allocator in determining the allocation of financial and human resources necessary for carrying out the plan. Hence, we have viewed the manager's job from alternative, but highly related, perspectives.

THE CHALLENGE OF MANAGEMENT

Major Issues Facing Management

The issues that most concern American managers are revealed by their responses to survey questions from such publications as *Business Week, Fortune,* and *The Wall Street Journal.* The responses of executives indicate that management's major problems fall into three main categories:

☐ *Human resources*—including such issues as hiring highly qualified workers, training them well, placing them in the appropriate jobs, motivating them, and evaluating their performance accurately.

☐ *Organizational behavior*—including the executives' desire for better communication in their organizations, closer teamwork, less conflict, and greater employee involvement in decision making.

☐ *Costs and product quality*—including problems that involve the cost of producing goods and services, international competition in the areas of labor costs and product quality, and the costs of government regulation.

These major problems are all exacerbated by the increasing complexity of the environment. Managers face not only domestic but worldwide competition in virtually every industry. Technological change is occurring at a rapidly increasing rate. And government regulation continues to influence virtually every aspect of organizational policy and behavior. Managing in such an environment is indeed a demanding activity.

All of the problems mentioned are a part of a larger challenge managers worldwide face today—the challenge of increasing productivity:[25]

> Although there's no free lunch, one thing comes awfully close: productivity. When it's growing, business can do the impossible. Companies can hand out raises, slash prices, and increase profits—sometimes all at once. Productivity transforms luxuries once reserved for society's elite into ordinary household items.

Management and Productivity

Productivity is a measure of economic output per unit of investment, as shown in Figure 1–6. When an organization can produce more of a product or service without lowering its quality and for the same unit of investment, an increase in productivity is the result. Or, if an organization can produce the same output as before and at a lower unit of investment, an increase in productivity is the result.

Economic and, to a large extent, social progress depend upon an upward trend in productivity. In the twenty years following World War II, output per

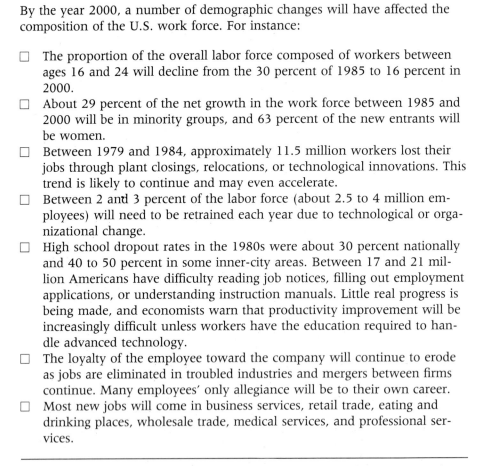

SOME HUMAN RESOURCE TRENDS

By the year 2000, a number of demographic changes will have affected the composition of the U.S. work force. For instance:

☐ The proportion of the overall labor force composed of workers between ages 16 and 24 will decline from the 30 percent of 1985 to 16 percent in 2000.

☐ About 29 percent of the net growth in the work force between 1985 and 2000 will be in minority groups, and 63 percent of the new entrants will be women.

☐ Between 1979 and 1984, approximately 11.5 million workers lost their jobs through plant closings, relocations, or technological innovations. This trend is likely to continue and may even accelerate.

☐ Between 2 and 3 percent of the labor force (about 2.5 to 4 million employees) will need to be retrained each year due to technological or organizational change.

☐ High school dropout rates in the 1980s were about 30 percent nationally and 40 to 50 percent in some inner-city areas. Between 17 and 21 million Americans have difficulty reading job notices, filling out employment applications, or understanding instruction manuals. Little real progress is being made, and economists warn that productivity improvement will be increasingly difficult unless workers have the education required to handle advanced technology.

☐ The loyalty of the employee toward the company will continue to erode as jobs are eliminated in troubled industries and mergers between firms continue. Many employees' only allegiance will be to their own career.

☐ Most new jobs will come in business services, retail trade, eating and drinking places, wholesale trade, medical services, and professional services.

SOURCE: "Change in America," *Chronicle of Higher Education,* 17 September 1986, p. 1; "Altering the Face of Work," *The Washington Post,* 30 November 1986; "The End of Corporate Loyalty?" *Business Week,* 4 August 1986, pp. 42–49; and "Productivity: Why It's the No. 1 Underachiever," *Business Week,* 20 April 1986, pp. 54–55.

worker in the United States increased by 3.2 percent annually. But, beginning in 1965, this figure declined to an average annual increase of only 1.9 percent. Between 1978 and 1985, the average increase was only 0.7 percent. In 1986, productivity failed to increase at all, for the first time in six years.

A number of factors external to organizations affect productivity. Often cited are a declining work ethic, a tax system that discourages the savings

FIGURE 1–6 Productivity

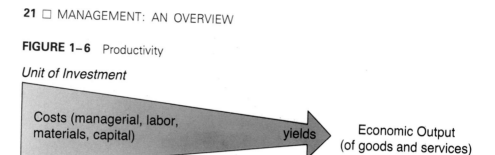

needed for new investment, and government regulations that divert resources from productive endeavors. Many observers, though, think that American managers are ultimately responsible for the problem. Economist Lester Thurow, for example, believes the problem lies in three areas:[26]

□ American firms employ more managers and white-collar workers than can be economically justified.
□ Managers have failed to generate an environment in which labor can play an active role in increasing productivity.
□ Managers emphasize short-run returns on investment at the expense of long-range research and development.

In truth, the U.S. productivity problem has multiple causes—both internal and external to organizations. Although managers cannot be expected to solve all of these problems, they do have the ability to improve productivity through many types of decisions. Managers must provide appropriate motivational appeals to organization members and design jobs to encourage enthusiastic and effective performance. Capital and labor must be combined in the right proportions. In serving a changing environment, managers must introduce new product and service innovations and apply new technologies to production processes. The quality of these and many other decisions depends on the quality of management insight and the wisdom of management choices. In the final analysis, productivity may be regarded "as a measure of management's efficiency, or lack of efficiency, in employing all the necessary resources—natural, human, and financial."[27]

This chapter has presented an overview of the field of management and the manager's job. Chapter 2 adds perspective to this view as it traces the evolution of management thought from its early days to contemporary times.

SUMMARY

Management is the process of acquiring and combining human, financial, informational, and physical resources to attain the organization's primary goal of producing a product or service desired by some segment of society. This process is essential to all organizations, profit and nonprofit alike. The abilities required of a manager differ significantly from those required of operating personnel.

Examination of the managerial job reveals that most managers are extremely busy and engage in activities characterized by brevity, variety, and fragmentation; effective management requires *technical, human relations,* and *conceptual* skills; managerial jobs differ along a number of dimensions involving *demands, constraints,* and *choices;* and managers play a variety of *roles* in their work.

A useful approach to analysis of management activity identifies certain basic management *functions.* Regardless of the type of organization or the level of the manager, most managers must engage in certain activities. Although the nature of the function varies among settings and levels, managers must *plan and make decisions, organize* for effective performance, *lead and motivate* subordinates, and *control* performance.

Managing effectively in a rapidly changing environment is a demanding task. Although managers face many challenges, perhaps the greatest is how to increase organizational *productivity.* To the extent that management is successful in improving productivity, society will benefit both economically and socially.

KEY CONCEPTS

Management

Agenda setting

Network building

Technical skills

Human relations skills

Conceptual skills

Managerial roles

Management functions

Productivity

DISCUSSION QUESTIONS

1. How is the process of management similar in both profit and nonprofit organizations? How is it different?
2. Why do managers seem to have such fragmented work schedules? Does it reflect a lack of planning?
3. Explain how *agenda setting* and *network building* are related to managerial effectiveness.
4. What is the relative importance of *technical* skills, *human relations* skills, and *conceptual* skills at the top-management level versus the first-line supervisory level?
5. Are the management skills of an individual universal; that is, are they transferable from setting to setting without any significant loss of effectiveness?
6. How does identification of the manager's *multiple roles* help one understand the complexity of the management process?
7. What is the relationship between *managerial functions* and *managerial roles?*

8. What relationships exist between the functions of *planning and decision making* and *organizing for effective performance?* Between *planning and decision making* and *controlling performance?*
9. What are some of the major issues facing management today?
10. What is meant by the phrase *"productivity* is a measure of management's efficiency"?

NOTES

1. Amanda Bennett, "Early to Bed . . . ," *The Wall Street Journal: A Special Report—Executive Style,* 20 March 1987, p. 22D; "Long Hours Greet Managers Who Make It to the Top," *The Wall Street Journal,* 10 June 1986; Maggie McComas, "Atop the Fortune 500: A Survey of the C.E.O.s," *Fortune,* 28 April 1986, p. 28; "Top Executives Work 57 Hours a Week: Survey," *The Houston Post,* 2 January 1985; and "The Organization Man, Cont'd," *Newsweek,* 27 October 1980, p. 96.
2. "Even Bosses Unwind; at Least Some Do, Some of the Time," *The Wall Street Journal,* 5 August 1986.
3. Stephen J. Carroll and Dennis J. Gillen, "Are the Classical Management Functions Useful in Describing Managerial Work?" *Academy of Management Review* 12 (January 1987): 43.
4. Examples of studies of managerial behavior are the following: Robert Dubin, "Business Behavior *Behaviorally* Viewed," in *Social Science Approaches to Business Behavior,* ed. George B. Strother (Homewood, Ill.: Richard D. Irwin, 1962), pp. 11–15; Rosemary Stewart, *Managers and Their Jobs* (London: Macmillan, 1968); and Henry Mintzberg, *The Nature of Managerial Work* (New York: Harper & Row, 1973). The Mintzberg study is particularly useful because it reports extensive observations over time of managers at work and also provides excellent summaries of related research.
5. Mintzberg, *Managerial Work,* p. 31.
6. Rosemary Stewart, "Managerial Agendas—Reactive or Proactive?" *Organizational Dynamics* 8 (Autumn 1979): 45.
7. These studies are summarized in Mintzberg, *Managerial Work,* p. 34.
8. Peter Allan, "Managers at Work: A Large-Scale Study of the Managerial Job in New York City Government," *Academy of Management Journal* 24 (September 1981): 613–19.
9. John P. Kotter, "What Effective General Managers Really Do," *Harvard Business Review* 60 (November-December 1982): 156–67.
10. Ibid., p. 160.
11. Fred Luthans, Stuart A. Rosenkrantz, and Harry W. Hennessey, "What Do Successful Managers Really Do? An Observation Study of Managerial Activities," *Journal of Applied Behavioral Science* 21, no. 3 (1985): 255–70.
12. "Today's College Kids are Naive About the Workplace, a Study Concludes," *The Wall Street Journal,* 12 May 1987.
13. Robert L. Katz, "Skills of an Effective Administrator," *Harvard Business Review* 52 (September-October 1974): 90–112.
14. "Atari Turns to a Marketing Magician," *Business Week,* 25 July 1983, p. 26; and "Jim Morgan's Unhappy 10 Months at Atari," *Business Week,* 23 July 1984, pp. 90–91.

15. Sherry Siegel, "Competing Through Manufacturing: Robert Hayes on Revitalizing America," *Management Review* 74 (March 1985): 22.
16. John P. Kotter, "General Managers Are Not Generalists," *Organizational Dynamics* 10 (Spring 1982): 16–17.
17. Katz, "Skills of an Effective Administrator," p. 101.
18. "Should Companies Groom New Leaders or Buy Them?" *Business Week,* 22 September 1986, pp. 94–96.
19. Rosemary Stewart, "A Model for Understanding Managerial Jobs and Behaviors," *Academy of Management Review* 7 (January 1982): 9–11; and Rosemary Stewart, "To Understand the Manager's Job: Consider Demands, Constraints, Choices," *Organizational Dynamics* 4 (Spring 1976): 27.
20. Peter D. Couch, "Learning to be a Middle Manager," *Business Horizons* 22 (February 1979): 35.
21. Abridged and adapted from chapter 4 in *The Nature of Managerial Work* by Henry Mintzberg. Copyright © 1973 by Henry Mintzberg. Reprinted by permission of Harper & Row, Publishers, Inc.
22. Allan, "Managers at Work," pp. 613–19.
23. Cynthia M. Pavett and Alan W. Lau, "Managerial Work: The Influence of Hierarchical Level and Functional Specialty," *Academy of Management Journal* 26 (March 1983): 175.
24. Carroll and Gillen, "Are the Classical Management Functions Useful . . . ?" p. 48.
25. "Productivity: Why It's the No. 1 Underachiever," *Business Week,* 20 April 1986, p. 54.
26. Lester C. Thurow, "White-Collar Overhead," *Across the Board* 23 (November 1986): 25–32; Lester C. Thurow, "Revitalizing American Industry: Managing in a Competitive World Economy," *California Management Review* 27 (Fall 1984): 9–39; and Lester C. Thurow,"Where Management Fails," *Newsweek,* 7 December 1981, p. 78.
27. Richard C. Gerstenberg, quoted in "Management Itself Holds the Key," *Business Week,* 9 September 1972, p. 142.

SUPPLEMENTARY READING

Bartolomé, Fernando, and Laurent, André. "The Manager: Master and Servant of Power." *Harvard Business Review* 64 (November-December 1986): 77–81.
Bittel, Lester R., and Ramsey, Jackson E. "The Limited, Traditional World of Supervisors." *Harvard Business Review* 60 (July-August 1982): 23–36.
Drucker, Peter F. "Management: The Problems of Success." *Academy of Management Executive* 1 (February 1987): 13–19.
Gabarro, John J. "When a New Manager Takes Charge." *Harvard Business Review* 63 (May-June 1985): 110–23.
Hales, Colin P. "What Do Managers Do? A Critical Review of the Evidence." *Journal of Management Studies* 23 (January 1986): 88–115.
Kerr, Steven; Hill, Kenneth D.; and Broedling, Laurie. "The First-Line Supervisor: Phasing Out or Here to Stay?" *Academy of Management Review* 11 (January 1986): 103–17.

Klein, Janice A., and Posey, Pamela A. "Good Supervisors are Good Supervisors—Anywhere." *Harvard Business Review* 64 (November-December 1986): 125–28.

Koprowski, Eugene J. "Exploring the Meaning of 'Good' Management." *Academy of Management Review* 6 (July 1981): 459–67.

Kotter, John P. "General Managers Are Not Generalists." *Organizational Dynamics* 10 (Spring 1982): 5–19.

————. "What Effective General Managers Really Do." *Harvard Business Review* 60 (November-December 1982): 156–67.

Levinson, Harry. "Criteria for Choosing Chief Executives." *Harvard Business Review* 58 (July-August 1980): 113–20.

Maister, David H. "The One-Firm Firm: What Makes It Successful." *Sloan Management Review* 27 (Fall 1985): 3–13.

Mintzberg, Henry. "The Manager's Job: Folklore and Fact." *Harvard Business Review* 53 (July-August 1975): 49–61.

Peace, William H. "I Thought I Knew What Good Management Was." *Harvard Business Review* 64 (March-April 1986): 59–65.

Sasser, W. Earl, Jr., and Leonard, Frank S. "Let First-Level Supervisors Do Their Job." *Harvard Business Review* 58 (March-April 1980): 113–21.

Skinner, Wickham. "The Productivity Paradox." *Harvard Business Review* 64 (July-August 1986): 55–59.

Villeré, Maurice F. "Are Organizational Vegetables Growing Where You Work?" *Business Horizons* 28 (November-December 1985): 47–54.

A DAY IN THE LIFE OF JAMES MARKS

James Marks absentmindedly pulled his Lincoln Town Car to a halt in its reserved parking space next to the main entrance of Corley-Marks, Inc. James was wondering what was bothering old "Butch" Bowers. Butch usually handled the front gate security chores with a smile and a friendly greeting. This morning he barely spoke. James hoped that Sally Bowers and the children were fine. He decided to phone the guard shack later and check with Butch.

James stopped and chatted with several employees en route to his office. He made a point of mentioning Miss Maxwell's new hairdo and kidding Mike Baena about the latest Celtic win. Another day at the salt mines, James thought . . . and he loved it!

Mildred Balke, the administrative assistant for Personnel, reminded James that today was the deadline for the first draft of his forthcoming speech. James shook his head; he had completely forgotten his promise to give an hour talk to the student Management and Marketing Club at the nearby state university. Such a topic— "What is it that managers do?"

James sorted through his IN box trying to assess the day's paperwork burden. There was that study again from Marketing trying to justify the reorganization of sales territories. He could just hear Pete Gentry down in Manpower jumping all over their numbers. James concluded that this whole sales territory thing had gone far enough. He decided to schedule a meeting for the next afternoon to resolve the issue.

James spent the next hour or two

Case prepared by Professor Paul R. Reed of Sam Houston State University.

reading correspondence, leafing through the latest trade publications, and talking on the phone to various subordinates. Things seemed to be going well throughout the organization.

James managed to write a letter of appreciation for Bill Blythe in Legal and get halfway through Herb Earl's performance appraisal. He seemed to have difficulty keeping his mind from drifting towards the soon-to-be-introduced Model 730, a sure winner. He wondered if the Marketing Department was right in recommending multiple channels of distribution. And the colors seemed a little too loud. Then there was the question of what to do after the 730. Vern Birkholz over in Finance had wondered the other day if the company had too many "eggs in one basket." Maybe he was right. Diversifying might reduce risk and improve cash flow. For the next 15 minutes, James considered the notion from various angles.

He lost his train of thought when Susan Jones's call was put through. As James suspected, the subject was about another EEO complaint, this one about sexual harassment over in Shipping. Susan's solution to fire the accused supervisor didn't sound right to James. He suggested she form a committee of both sexes to establish policies to handle similar future situations more adequately. He told Susan that he had read about one company's grievance system in the latest issue of *Personnel Journal* and suggested that she find the article.

Susan's call was followed by Bill Sweeney's from Personnel. Apparently, Butch Bowers's change in personality had stemmed from worry over the birth of his sixth child. Both Sally and the baby were doing fine. Sweeney was instructed to send flowers and make sure that Butch was given two or three days off with pay when his wife and infant were released from the hospital.

About 11 A.M., James left the office and went out to the shop floor. He slowly moved down the walkway between the work sites, nodding and speaking briefly with several of the workers. When he arrived at Line 5, the foreman escorted him over to one of the large new grinding machines. Its operator, Todd Cromwell, showed James how he had perfected a method of polishing the connections on the underside of the Model 730. James was clearly impressed by the improvement in the connection seal. He told the foreman to adopt the new idea for the whole assembly line and made a mental note to make sure that Todd's future paychecks reflected the company's appreciation.

It was almost 1 P.M. when James arrived at the country club for the monthly get-together with the local area's executive council. He initially had thought these meetings were a waste of time but changed his mind as he saw the value of establishing friendly ties with nearby CEOs. The sharing of information had cut costs and solved problems in several areas. The speaker at this meeting discussed the impact of the new immigration law upon hiring and related record-keeping. James could foresee another federal agency muddying the waters.

James returned to the office before 3 o'clock and saw the note placed conspicuously in the middle of his desk. It read: "Your speech outline for your state university talk?" He sat down heavily in his chair and decided that he had better quit procrastinating. Just what could he tell these young students?

Question

1. Based upon this thumbnail sketch of James's day, prepare a brief outline for the state university talk.

THE CLASSICAL SCHOOL OF MANAGEMENT THOUGHT

Scientific Management □ Administrative Management □ Bureaucratic Management □ A Synthesis of Classical Thought

THE BRIDGE FROM CLASSICAL TO CONTEMPORARY MANAGEMENT

The Hawthorne Studies □ Mary Parker Follett's Work □ Chester I. Barnard's Work

CONTEMPORARY MANAGEMENT

Open Systems Theory □ Contingency Management □ Our Approach to Management

Summary □ Key Concepts □ Discussion Questions □ Notes □ Supplementary Reading

CASE: Worry at Wernett's

This chapter will enable you to

□ Describe the classical school of management thought and its objectives.

□ Understand how later management researchers and theorists expanded the classical concept of management to include human behavior in organizations.

□ View organizations as open systems with interrelated subsystems.

□ Explain the modern contingency approach to management and its current state of development.

CHAPTER 2
HISTORICAL TRENDS IN MANAGEMENT THOUGHT AND PRACTICE

An understanding of current management thought and practice requires a historical perspective. The management process is as old as history itself. The construction of the Great Pyramids, for instance, was a project of such complexity that it could not possibly have been completed without superb managerial planning and supervision. Yet, even though management has been practiced for centuries, a systematic analysis of the field and the development of a theory of management did not begin until about 1900.

A detailed description of management thought even since the turn of the twentieth century would fill a very large book.[1] Hence, this chapter will examine only the major highlights in the evolution of management in the twentieth century. Our discussion will follow the diagram shown in Figure 2–1, beginning with the classical school of management thought.

THE CLASSICAL SCHOOL OF MANAGEMENT THOUGHT

Classical (meaning "historically important") *management thought* was a compilation of three separate, but related, fields of endeavor—(1) *scientific management,* (2) *administrative management,* and (3) *bureaucratic management.*[2] Each field is closely associated with the work of a particular person, and our discussion will focus on the contributions of these three individuals.

FIGURE 2–1 Major trends in the development of management thought

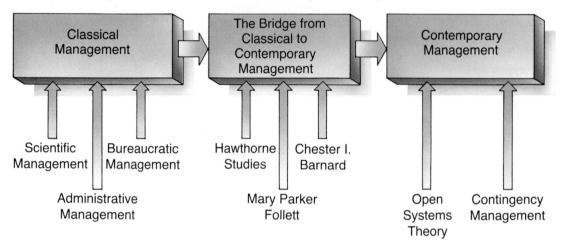

Scientific Management

Any description of classical management thought must begin with Frederick W. Taylor (1856–1915), the "father of scientific management." As Drucker has stated: "Taylor was the first man in history who actually studied work seriously. This is his historical importance."[3]

Job design, at the beginning of this century, can best be described as casual. Workers performed tasks according to tradition and subjective judgment, and managers gave little systematic thought to techniques for improving worker efficiency. Scientific management grew out of Taylor's questioning these traditional ways of managing work as he progressed from a machinist to shop superintendent in the Midvale Steel Company in the 1880s. For the next thirty years, as a consultant, and later as a manager with Bethlehem Steel Company, Taylor refined his approach to work analysis and wrote about his ideas.[4]

The basic goal of scientific management was to increase employee productivity through a systematic, or "scientific," analysis of the employee's work. This research and experimentation with the task would culminate in the "one best way" to perform the job. Workers who were appropriate for the task would then be selected, given detailed instructions in the new method, and required to perform exactly in the manner prescribed.

Workers who followed the prescribed methods earned wages which were significantly higher than they had received before. Taylor felt that economic incentives served as the major motivator of industrial workers. Employees would be willing to follow the "one best way," Taylor reasoned, if high wages were tied to high production. Management, in turn, would be pleased because, even with the higher wages, labor costs per unit would be lower than before, thanks to increased worker productivity.

Taylor, then, saw scientific management as the systematic—or scientific—investigation of all the facts and elements connected with the work being managed. It was the very opposite of management by tradition and rule of thumb. Much of his work—such as job analysis, careful selection of workers, and employee training—serves as the foundation for modern personnel management. His scientific approach to problem solving also can be found in more modern forms today, as we will see in the discussion of the managerial decision-making process in chapters 6 and 7.

Many criticisms were made of the work of Taylor and the scientific management movement.[5] Some people objected to the dehumanization potential of scientific management. The work of an employee was analyzed as one might analyze the operation of a machine, and the goal was maximization of efficiency of this human "machine." Although Taylor exhibited a sense of fairness toward employees and a desire to see them share the benefits of higher productivity, the potential for misuse of scientific management was exploited by other managers.

In fact, the scientific management movement fell into such disrepute that Congress undertook an investigation of it. In 1912, Taylor appeared before an investigating committee of the House of Representatives and gave a careful exposition of scientific management as he understood and practiced it. He vigorously defended the basic concepts of scientific management against the attacks of those who felt that these concepts had served to exploit and take advantage of labor. In spite of these criticisms of Taylor's work, it does stand as a pioneer, revolutionary approach to management that makes its creator one of the outstanding figures in management history.*

Administrative Management

While Taylor focused on the planning of work and management techniques for the supervisor, across the Atlantic a French business executive analyzed management from a top-level perspective. Henri Fayol's (1841–1925) analysis was based on his lengthy experience as the managing director of a large coal mining business and resulted in the publication of *General and Industrial Management* in 1916.[6] This work made two significant contributions to management thought: (1) the delineation of the *functions*—or duties—of a manager and (2) the establishment of a set of *principles*—or guidelines—which managers might apply as they performed their functions.

Fayol felt that management consisted of five essential functions: *planning, organizing, commanding, coordinating,* and *controlling* (shown in diagrammatic

---

*Taylor was, of course, only one of many contributors to the development of a scientific approach to management. Other pioneers included Henry L. Gantt, Frank and Lillian Gilbreth, Harrington Emerson, Wallace Clark, and Henry R. Towne, to name but a few.

SCHMIDT AND THE PIG IRON EXPERIMENT

Taylor and his associates studied a group of 75 men at Bethlehem Steel Company who loaded pig iron (each pig weighed about 92 pounds) onto railroad cars. Based on "scientific" calculations of the distance the men had to walk to the railroad car, how fast they walked, how often they should rest, and so on, Taylor determined that, instead of the 12½ tons per day each man was loading, 47½ tons was actually a "proper day's work."

In order to demonstrate the accuracy of his calculations, Taylor selected a physically fit worker to act as an experimental subject. This worker has become known to management history as "Schmidt." As Taylor described the scene:

The task before us, then, narrowed itself down to getting Schmidt to handle 47 tons of pig iron per day and making him glad to do it. This was done as follows. Schmidt was called out from among the gang of pig-iron handlers and talked to somewhat in this way:

"Schmidt, are you a high-priced man?"

"Vell, I don't know vat you mean."

"Oh yes, you do. What I want to know is whether you are a high-priced man or not."

"Vell, I don't know vat you mean."

"Oh, come now, you answer my questions. What I want to find out is whether you are a high-priced man or one of these cheap fellows here. What I want to find out is whether you want to earn $1.85 a day or whether you are satisfied with $1.15, just the same as all those cheap fellows are getting."

"Did I vant $1.85 a day? Vas dot a high-priced man? Vell, yes, I vas a high-priced man."

"Oh, you're aggravating me. Of course you want $1.85 a day—everyone wants it! You know perfectly well that that has very little to do with your being a high-priced man. For goodness sake answer my questions, and don't waste any more of my time. Now come over here. You see that pile of pig iron?"

"Yes."

"You see that car?"

"Yes."

"Well, if you are a high-priced man, you will load that pig iron on that car to-morrow for $1.85. Now do wake up and answer my question. Tell me whether you are a high-priced man or not."

"Vell—did I got $1.85 for loading dot pig iron on dot car tomorrow?"

"Yes, of course you do, and you get $1.85 for loading a pile like that every day right through the year. That is what a high-priced man does, and you know it just as well as I do."

"Vell, dot's all right. I could load dot pig iron on the car tomorrow for $1.85, and I get it every day, don't I?"

"Certainly you do—certainly you do."

"Vell, den, I vas a high-priced man."

"Now, hold on, hold on. You know just as well as I do that a high-priced man has to do exactly as he's told from morning till night. You have seen this man here before, haven't you?"

"No, I never saw him."

"Well, if you are a high-priced man, you will do exactly as this man tells you to-morrow, from morning till night. When he tells you to pick up a pig and walk, you pick it up and you walk, and when he tells you to sit down and rest, you sit down. You do that right straight through the day. And what's more, no back talk. Now a high-priced man does just what he's told to do, and no back talk. Do you understand that? When this man tells you to walk, you walk; when he tells you to sit down, you sit down, and you don't talk back at him. Now you come on to work here to-morrow morning and I'll know before night whether you are really a high-priced man or not. . . ."

Schmidt started to work, and all day long, and at regular intervals, was told by the man who stood over him with a watch, "Now pick up a pig and walk. Now sit down and rest. Now walk—now rest," etc. He worked when he was told to work, and rested when he was told to rest, and at half-past five in the afternoon had his 47½ tons loaded on the car. And he practically never failed to work at this pace and do the task that was set him during the three years that the writer was at Bethlehem. And throughout this time he averaged a little more than $1.85 per day, whereas before he had never received over $1.15 per day, which was the ruling rate of wages at that time in Bethlehem. That is, he received 60 per cent higher wages than were paid to other men who were not working on task work. One man after another was picked out and trained to handle pig iron at the rate of 47½ tons per day until all of the pig iron was handled at this rate, and the men were receiving 60 per cent more wages than other workmen around them.

This example illustrates the essence of productivity. Over the three-year period, the average number of tons loaded daily by each worker rose 280 percent, while the average cost to the company of loading one ton of pig iron dropped 58 percent.

Some controversy exists over the accuracy of Taylor's account of the pig-iron experiment. Charles D. Wrege and Amedeo G. Perroni in their article "Taylor's Pig-Tale: A Historical Analysis of Frederick W. Taylor's Pig-Iron Experiment" (*Academy of Management Journal* 17 [March 1974]: 6–27) present various pieces of evidence which bolster their claim that Taylor's story is more fiction than fact. Yet in another analysis, Edwin A. Locke in his article "The Ideas of Frederick W. Taylor: An Evaluation" (*Academy of Management Review* 7 [January 1982]: 14–27) argues that Taylor's account is historically accurate in most of its details. Whether true or false, Taylor's views on worker productivity have had a significant impact on contemporary management thought.

SOURCE: Frederick Winslow Taylor, *The Principles of Scientific Management* (New York: W. W. Norton & Co., 1911), pp. 44–47.

FIGURE 2–2 Fayol's five essential functions of management

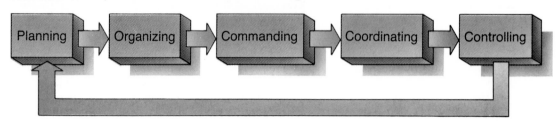

form in Figure 2–2). Planning was the act of forecasting the future—up to ten years in advance—and then preparing to deal with the forecasted events. The organization, according to Fayol, should have an overall general plan from which department managers could derive plans for their own areas of responsibility. Once planning was accomplished, the manager should organize by acquiring the necessary material and human resources and by structuring the human resources into jobs, departments, and so on in order to carry out the organization's plans.

Planning and organizing were basic preparations for the operating functions: commanding consisted of setting the human resources in motion toward the organization's objectives; coordinating involved harmonizing and uniting all activities; and controlling served to make certain that all operations were proceeding according to plan.

As the manager engaged in these functions, a number of principles were useful in guiding managerial behavior. Fayol formulated fourteen such principles, some of which are shown in Figure 2–3. Because management deals with

FIGURE 2–3 Selected principles of management from Fayol

> *Division of Work*—specialization of labor, in managerial and nonmanagerial jobs, increases organizational productivity.
>
> *Authority and Responsibility*—authority is the right of a manager to give orders and require conformity to those orders. Responsibility goes with and must match authority.
>
> *Unity of Command*—each employee should receive orders from only one superior.
>
> *Subordination of Individual Interest to General Interest*—the interests of one employee or a group of employees must be subordinated to the overall interests of the organization.
>
> *Scalar Chain*—the scalar chain is the line of authority, from superior to subordinate, running from the top to the bottom of the organization. This chain should be the channel used for communication and decision making.
>
> *Equity*—all employees should be treated with fairness, kindness, and justice.

SOURCE: Henri Fayol, *General and Industrial Management,* trans. Constance Storrs (London: Pitman Publishing, 1949), pp. 19–42 (the explanations of the principles have been paraphrased).

people in a wide variety of circumstances, these principles had to be flexible and adaptable to varying situations, and the process of applying them would be more of an art than a science.

Much of Fayol's work seems relatively self-evident and obvious to readers today, and changing conditions and ideas have made other parts of his work obsolete. But some of Fayol's writings have had significant impact on modern management thought. Even today, for example, the functions of planning, organizing, and controlling are major areas of research and teaching in collegiate schools of business and public administration. As another example, the principle of equity has become so important to organizations that much of it has been formalized into law in the United States. Certainly, Fayol's place in history as the first management theoretician remains secure.

Bureaucratic Management

At the same time that Fayol and Taylor were independently developing their ideas, a German intellectual, Max Weber (1864–1920), was analyzing the basis for managerial authority in organizations. From this analysis originated the concept of *bureaucracy* to describe a rational organization that performed its task with high efficiency. The basic elements of this system of management are shown in Figure 2–4.

Weber's purpose, however, was not to prescribe an ideal type of organization but to analyze how bureaucracy permitted leaders (or managers) to

FIGURE 2–4 Elements of a bureaucracy

1. A specific division of labor among organizational members exists. Each member's authority and responsibility are clearly defined.
2. A well-defined chain of command is present. All positions are organized into a hierarchy. Each lower position is under the control and supervision of a higher one. There is a right of appeal and an established grievance procedure from lower to higher positions.
3. Members of the organization are selected on the basis of adequate technical training which can be demonstrated through educational qualifications or examination.
4. Promotion is based on seniority or achievement, or both, and is dependent on the judgment of superiors.
5. All administrative acts, decisions, and rules are recorded in writing even when oral discussion is traditional.
6. The managers of the organization should not be the owners.
7. All organizational members are subject to strict and systematic discipline and control in the conduct of their duties.

SOURCE: Max Weber, *The Theory of Social and Economic Organization,* trans. and ed. A. M. Henderson and Talcott Parsons (New York: The Free Press, 1947), 329–34 (the elements have been paraphrased).

dominate subordinates. In a bureaucracy, the manager's right to give orders was based on "rational-legal authority," meaning that managers obtained their positions of authority through a procedure (e.g., formal selection and promotion) that the members of the organization considered legitimate.[7]

Today, of course, the word *bureaucracy* conjures up visions of red tape, excruciating slowness of operations, and inefficiency. This connotation, however, is quite unlike the meaning Weber intended. One translation of his work indicates that he felt a bureaucracy, managed by competent individuals hired solely on the basis of their qualifications, was "capable of attaining the highest degree of efficiency."[8] The primary reason for the superiority of this management system lay in the organization's technical knowledge, regardless of whether the organization existed in a capitalistic or socialistic economy.[9]

Weber's ideas, of course, are reflected in large contemporary organizations. Indeed, managing an organization consisting of thousands of employees could not be accomplished without a rational organizational system. Although the extremes to which bureaucracy has often led have been decried, and bureaucratic principles have often proved inefficient in rapidly changing situations, Weber certainly deserves to be recognized as the founder of organization theory.

A Synthesis of Classical Thought

Although these three theorists worked independently without knowledge of one another's contributions and wrote from different perspectives and cultures, they shared the same goal. Their basic intent was to make organizations operate more efficiently and productively. Whether the organization is a small business or a mammoth corporation, rational, scientific procedures should be applied to its operations.

The work of these theorists, and the work of others we have been unable to mention, reflected certain assumptions about human beings. Among these assumptions were the following:[10]

1. Human beings act rationally.
2. Individuals need clear job limits to avoid confusion. They cannot work out the relationships among their jobs without detailed guidance from their superiors.
3. Management involves primarily the formal, official activities of individuals and should be administered without regard to their personal problems or characteristics.
4. People do not like to work and, hence, need to be closely supervised.

In the next section, we shall see how management thinkers began to move away from these assumptions.

THE BRIDGE FROM CLASSICAL TO CONTEMPORARY MANAGEMENT

A large number of events, theorists, and writings could be included in this section. At the risk of excluding a number of important ideas, we have elected to focus on three areas which well illustrate the movement of management thought away from the classical assumptions.

The Hawthorne Studies

The Hawthorne Studies refer to a series of experiments conducted in the Western Electric Company's Hawthorne plant in Chicago and Cicero, Illinois, beginning in 1924.[11] The studies, carried out initially by researchers from the National Academy of Sciences, were designed to discover the relationship between the level of illumination in the workplace and the production level of employees. The underlying assumption, that at some level of lighting workers would be most productive, had obvious roots in scientific management.

In one phase of the experiments, workers were divided into two groups—a test group and a control group. Lighting affecting the test group was increased from twenty-four to forty-six to seventy foot-candles, while control group lighting was held constant. It was assumed that output of the test group would show some increase in contrast to that of the control group. Results were surprising, however, because production of both groups increased in roughly the same proportion!

In another experiment, lighting of a test group was reduced from ten to three foot-candles, while lighting of the control group was held constant. Rather than declining, however, test group output increased—as did that of the control group! At a later stage, illumination was reduced until it reached the level of moonlight (.06 of a foot-candle), but not until then did output drop appreciably.

Certainly, "rational" behavior was not being observed. The employees involved were aware that their performance was being recorded, and the researchers assumed that they were reacting to being observed and to the attention they were receiving. The results were so confusing that the researchers were prepared to abandon the project until a group of faculty members from Harvard University agreed to act as consultants to the study. The leaders of this new research team, Elton Mayo (1880–1949) and Fritz J. Roethlisberger (1898–1974), were to leave an enduring mark on the field of management thought.

Through interviews, observation, and experimentation (such as the Bank Wiring Room study described in the accompanying box), the researchers began to conclude that the human element in production was more significant than had been realized. Workers' personal problems affected their work performance. Additionally, workers brought to their jobs various social needs which led them to form informal groups, characterized by elaborate sets of norms.

BANK WIRING OBSERVATION ROOM STUDY

A later phase of the Hawthorne Studies focused upon a group of fourteen workmen engaged in wiring certain types of telephone equipment. They were paid on an incentive basis so that the more they produced, the more they earned. Contrary to "rational" economic need predictions, however, most of the workers produced significantly below their capacity even though they did not appear to be fatigued and seemed to have some free time during the work day.

Further investigation revealed that the workers had established their own informal production standard—or norm—for a "fair day's work." Reasons for the norm were voiced by two of the workers as follows:

> No one can turn out the [standard that management has set] consistently. Well, occasionally some of them do. Now since the layoff started there's been a few fellows down there who have been turning out around 7,300 a day. . . . I think it is foolishness to do it because I don't think it will do them any good, and it is likely to do the rest of us a lot of harm. . . . If they start turning out around 7,300 a day over a period of weeks and if three of them do it, then they can lay one of the men off, because three men working at that speed can do as much as four men working at the present rate.
>
> You know, the supervisors came around and told us that . . . if we would turn out more work we would make more money, but we can't see it that way. Probably what would happen is that our [standard] would be raised, and then we would just be turning out more work for the same money. I can't see that.

This informal standard was enforced through "binging"—the administration of a fist to the offending "rate buster's" arm—ridicule, sarcasm, and other techniques. Rather than being motivated by management's incentive system, the workers seemed more concerned with being accepted by their fellow workers. The activities which determined the production of the group were not formal, but informal—devised by the employees themselves.

SOURCE: Quotes are from F. J. Roethlisberger and William J. Dickson, *Management and the Worker* (Cambridge: Harvard University Press, 1939), pp. 417–18.

The researchers began to view the organization as a social system, which brought together the formal organization with its hierarchy and rules and the informal organization based on human interactions and sentiments. Although the technical aspects of efficiency and productivity were important, they should be balanced by a concern for human beings and their needs. As Wren has so aptly put it:

In short, the outcome of the Hawthorne research was a call for a new mix of managerial skills. These skills were ones which were crucial to handling human situations: first, diagnostic skills in understanding human behavior, and second, interpersonal skills in counseling, motivating, leading, and communicating with workers. Technical skills alone were not enough to cope with the behavior discovered at the Hawthorne Works.[12]

The Hawthorne Studies have been widely criticized on a number of grounds: among them, inappropriate research methodology, misinterpretation of results, biased samples of workers, and overemphasis on social factors with an accompanying underemphasis on the actual work being performed and the employees' economic incentives.[13] Yet, despite these faults, this series of studies modified the rational/technical assumptions of the classical school by emphasizing the importance of the human element in management.

Mary Parker Follett's Work

The emphasis on human behavior in the workplace received further impetus from the writings of Mary Parker Follett (1868–1933), an American political philosopher. Throughout her work is an emphasis on the *group* as the primary building block of organizations. It was only through relationships with others in groups, she believed, that an individual could find his or her true identity and be fully creative.[14]

In a larger sense, an organization was a group. Members of the organization, whether managers or workers, were members of the same group and, hence, shared common interests. The attainment of the common interests of the organization's members became a "collective responsibility," and as the members worked together, the group attained an *integrative unity,* or "oneness."[15]

Unlike in Weber's bureaucratic model, it was not the responsibility of the manager to give orders but rather to define and articulate the group's common purpose. Rather than work *for* the manager, the workers worked *with* the manager, and all alike took their orders from the *situation* they faced.[16] "Our job is not how to get people to obey orders, but how to devise methods by which we can best *discover* the order integral to a particular situation."[17] Responding to the situation were individuals who, on the basis of their knowledge and expertise and in recognition of their common interest, would control their tasks to meet the overall objective. Control, in Follett's view, was not vertical (i.e., from above) but a cooperative, horizontal process.[18]

These ideas, although more theoretical than pragmatic, reflected Follett's optimistic view of individuals. In work organizations, people would demonstrate integrity and responsibility as they cooperatively sought to attain their common goals. The concepts that each individual is an integral part of the organization, that shared goals are desirable, and that each member can effectively participate in organizational decision making underlie the work of more

SOLVING CONFLICT THROUGH INTEGRATION

In Mary Parker Follett's view, conflict is best solved through integration:

> Compromise is the accepted, the approved, way of ending controversy. Yet no one really wants to compromise, because that means a giving up of something. Is there then any other method of ending conflict? There is a way beginning now to be recognized at least, and even occasionally followed: when two desires are *integrated*, that means that a solution has been found in which both desires have found a place, that neither side has had to sacrifice anything. Let us take some very simple illustration. In the Harvard Library one day, in one of the smaller rooms, someone wanted the window open; I wanted it shut. We opened the window in the next room where no one was sitting. This was not a compromise because there was no curtailing of desire; we both got what we really wanted. For I did not want a closed room, I simply did not want the north wind to blow directly on me; likewise the other occupant did not want that particular window open, he merely wanted more air in the room.

SOURCE: Mary Parker Follett, "Constructive Conflict," in *Dynamic Administration: The Collected Papers of Mary Parker Follett,* ed. Henry C. Metcalf and L. Urwick (New York: Harper & Row, Publishers, 1940), p. 32.

modern writers such as Douglas McGregor, Rensis Likert, and Chris Argyris. These concepts, too, are reflected in the present field of organization development, discussed in chapter 11.

Chester I. Barnard's Work

Perhaps no practicing executive has contributed more to the study of management than did Chester I. Barnard (1886–1961), president of New Jersey Bell Telephone Company. His book *The Functions of the Executive* developed his perspective on management and organizations.

Barnard believed that a manager had three essential functions.[19] The first was to provide a system of organizational communication. By this, Barnard meant that the manager was responsible for: defining the organization's structure; staffing it with loyal, responsible, able managers; and maintaining, informally, a general condition of compatibility among executive personnel. The second function involved recruiting and hiring personnel to staff the nonmanagerial ranks within the organization. Finally, the executive was to formulate and define the purpose and objectives of the organization.

The basic challenge the manager faced, Barnard felt, was how to induce individuals to cooperate in attaining the organization's objectives. To accomplish this, the manager must offer positive incentives to the organization's members or reduce negative burdens (such as lowering the work required).[20] If suitable incentives were unavailable, the only alternative was to change the worker's attitudes so that the available incentives would be effective.

Barnard recognized that potential incentives included the following: (1) money and material things; (2) opportunities for distinction, prestige, personal power, or attainment of a dominating position; (3) desirable working conditions; (4) satisfaction of personal ideals; (5) an attractive social situation; (6) familiar working conditions, practices, and attitudes; (7) opportunity for the feeling of participation in the course of events; and (8) opportunity for communication, camaraderie, and mutual support. Which of these to use and in what manner was the question. He emphasized that "the difficulties of securing the means of offering incentives, of avoiding conflict of incentives, and of making effective persuasive efforts, are inherently great; and . . . the determination of the precise combinations of incentives and of persuasion that will be both effective and feasible is a matter of great delicacy."[21] Management's goal was to synthesize the organization's need for efficiency with the satisfaction of the employees' needs.

Perhaps Barnard's major contribution, however, came in his conceptualization of an organization as a "system of consciously coordinated activities or forces of two or more persons."[22] Within this system, composed of the coordinated efforts and activities of human beings, each part was related to every other part in a significant way. If the system had many parts, they might well be grouped into subsidiary or partial systems. The system, as a whole, differed in quantity and quality from the sum of its parts.

The organizational system itself, Barnard indicated, included more than its employees. Suppliers furnishing supplies, customers making purchases, or investors contributing capital were also included in the organizational system. In fact, an organization could not be understood without reference to those groups and individuals who, although not employees, interacted with the organization and influenced it through their behavior.

Overall, Barnard's work focused on the manager's role as a professional, moral leader who was able to elicit the cooperative efforts of individuals to enhance the effectiveness of their organization and their own well-being. He

IMPORTANCE OF EFFORT

To try and fail is at least to learn; to fail to try is to suffer the inestimable loss of what might have been.

SOURCE: Chester I. Barnard, *The Functions of the Executive* (Cambridge, Mass.: Harvard University Press, 1938), p. v.

was the first management theorist to examine the organization as a system, using concepts from the field of biology. The power of the systems view was not immediately evident to other management theorists, however, and did not achieve general recognition until the 1960s, as we shall see in the following section.

CONTEMPORARY MANAGEMENT

The remainder of this book is devoted to contemporary management thought and practice. In this section we will lay a foundation for what is to follow by examining two current perspectives from which management is viewed.

Open Systems Theory

In contemporary management theory, an organization is visualized as a *system*—an entity composed of parts or subsystems. Within this system, managers serve as the decision-making or regulating subsystem.

The Systems Concept.   A system is a set of components that are related in the accomplishment of some purpose. Examples of systems abound. A physical organism, for instance, is composed of circulatory, muscular, skeletal, and nervous subsystems—all of which function together to sustain life. An automobile consists of pistons, spark plugs, axles, wheels, and so on, which work in unison to propel the car.

In the study of management, our principal concern is *organizational systems;* that is, systems composed of human beings, money, materials, information, equipment, and so on, which are related in the accomplishment of some goal or goals. Such systems differ significantly from biological or physical systems, which have identifiable structures, even when they are not functioning. An organizational system, however, has no structure apart from its functioning.[23] The basic structure of an organizational system is the patterned activities of individuals.[24] A building without people, even though it contains machinery and equipment and has a logo painted on its side, is not an organizational system any more than is a desert ghost town.

Organizational systems are essentially social systems composed of human beings who interact with one another in patterned activities. As Katz and Kahn have written, "The cement that holds social systems together is essentially psychological rather than biological. Social systems are anchored in the attitudes, perceptions, beliefs, motivations, habits, and expectations of human beings."[25]

Elements of Organizational Systems.   Organizational systems share certain elements. These include *input, process, output,* and *feedback,* as indicated in Figure 2–5. The inputs in a manufacturing firm, for instance, consist of raw ma-

FIGURE 2–5 Elements of an organizational system

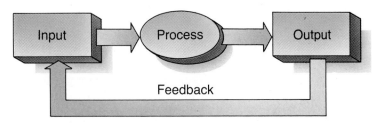

terials, technical knowledge, labor, equipment, information, and financing, all of which are combined under managerial direction into a process that results in a finished output or product. Consumer acceptance of the product results in a financial return (feedback) to the firm, which reactivates the cycle. Low sales, on the other hand, indicate that a change in the input or process is necessary

IMPROVING FEEDBACK

Increasingly, organizational systems are establishing special programs to enhance the flow of meaningful feedback from their environment. Note the following examples:

☐ The top executive of the Campbell Soup Company (which produces not only soup but also such products as Prego spaghetti sauces, Pepperidge Farm baked products, Swanson and Le Menu frozen dinners, Mrs. Paul's frozen foods, Vlasic pickles, and Godiva chocolates) sends his managers to the kitchens of 300 different homes across the nation to learn how customers pepare their meals. Additionally, he requires his executives to do their own grocery shopping so that they might keep in tune with the marketplace. He, too, may be found buying his family's groceries in the local supermarket each Saturday.

☐ When the Pontiac Division of General Motors Corporation introduced its Fiero sports car to the market, fifty assembly-line workers volunteered to survey five Fiero customers each for a year. The employees called the customers every three months to learn what they liked and disliked about the new car. The goal was to relay relevant information to the assembly plant to correct problems immediately. By contrast, the traditional form of feedback, through dealers' service departments, would have taken several months.

SOURCE: Based on "Campbell Soup's Recipe for Growth: Offering Something for Every Palate," *Business Week* 24 (December 1984): p. 66; and "A GM Plant with a Hot Line Between Workers and Buyers," *Business Week* 11 (June 1984): p. 165.

to produce a more acceptable output. Through cycles such as these, organizations maintain their existence. And many organizations outlive by decades and even centuries those human beings who founded them.

Organizational systems, then, are *open* to their environment. They import inputs, export outputs, and interpret the feedback they receive from the environment. What happens in the environment affects them, and as the environment changes, management must monitor the changes and adapt the organization to the new situation. For instance, as enrollments of full-time freshmen in colleges declined, many schools responded by offering evening classes to older, part-time students, by emphasizing continuing education, and by establishing degree programs "on-site" at major companies.

Although all organizations are open to their environment, the degree of openness varies. Some systems are designed to be relatively closed—a maximum security prison, for example—while others are deliberately quite open— a state legislature, for instance. Some managers believe that increasing the openness of their systems can be beneficial. Companies such as IBM, for instance, established panels of outsiders to evaluate technological trends and assess the potential of new opportunities. Such advisory boards help keep management informed of new developments in the environment and are able to advise without feeling constrained by corporate policy.[26]

Components of Organizational Systems.   Organizational systems consist of a number of interrelated *subsystems*. Major subsystems of a university, for example, are the school of business, the school of engineering, the athletic program, the bookstore, and so on. Corporate subsystems include the marketing department, production department, personnel department, and others. Each of these subsystems has a purpose which, if attained, aids the larger system in reaching its overall goals. Each subsystem, in attaining its purpose, must mesh its activities with the activities of the other subsystems. Within a system, there is no provision for an autonomous subsystem.

Although we commonly equate organizational subsystems with departments or divisions, it is also possible to view subsystems in a considerably broader context, as shown in Figure 2–6. In this conceptualization, organizations are viewed as goal-directed entities consisting of people. To achieve organizational goals, people must perform tasks, using technical knowledge and equipment, and they must work together in structured relationships. However, human beings are not mere robots—they will, and indeed must, enter into social relationships, both formal (job-related) and informal (non-job-related). The task of the managerial subsystem is to coordinate all of these subsystems and plan future activities.

Because the subsystems are interrelated, it follows that a major change in any single subsystem cannot be confined to that subsystem alone. Such a change will also have a significant impact on related subsystems. The most dramatic example in recent years is the introduction of computer networks into organizations (i.e., a change in the technical subsystem). This electronic linking

INTERRELATED SUBSYSTEMS

Chinese soldiers stationed in the Xisha Islands in the South China Sea unwittingly upset their island's natural system by their desire to eat eggs for breakfast. To satisfy their appetites, the soldiers had chickens brought in from the mainland. The chickens, however, began to wander into the bush where they were attacked by rats, some weighing over two pounds. To protect the chickens, cats were imported to kill the rats. The rats were soon gone, so the cats turned to the rare seabirds on the islands. Dogs had to be flown in to control the cats. Once the cat problem was solved, the dogs began to spend their time fighting and barking. The soldiers were still trying to remedy that problem when this report appeared in the *China Daily*.

SOURCE: Based on "Fowl Play on Isles Led to Menu Mania," *The Houston Post*, 18 April 1982.

of employees' work stations has an impact far beyond that of simply storing, processing, and transmitting information more efficiently.

Computer networking, for instance, can change the organization's structural subsystem. Some employees who formerly performed most of their work at a central office can now work at home or on the road. Traditional departmental barriers may become less important as electronic communication allows individuals to participate in project groups based on their expertise or relevance to the decision rather than their departmental office or location. The psychosocial subsystem may also undergo significant modification if employees become increasingly isolated from traditional interpersonal relationships and

FIGURE 2–6   Major organizational subsystems

Goal subsystem:	People with a purpose.
Technical subsystem:	People using knowledge techniques, equipment, and facilities.
Structural subsystem:	People working together on integrated activities.
Psychosocial subsystem:	People in social relationships.
Managerial subsystem:	People coordinating the other subsystems by planning and controlling the overall endeavor.

SOURCE: Adapted from Fremont E. Kast and James E. Rosenzweig, "Evolution of Organization and Management Theory," in *Contingency Views of Organization and Management*, Part 1, ed. Kast and Rosenzweig (Chicago: Science Research Associates, 1973) p. 13.

existing groups are replaced by new, electronic groups. Members of the managerial subsystem may find that standard operating procedures must be modified, that the traditional chain of command may no longer be as effective, and that new leadership skills may be required as communication becomes computer mediated. Finally, even physical changes in the shape of offices, furniture, and buildings are occurring to accommodate the new technology.[27]

Value of the Open Systems Approach. There are two overriding lessons for the manager contained in open systems theory. The first is that no organization exists in a vacuum. The environment constrains what the manager can do, but it also offers opportunities and potentialities. Managers must be aware of and understand environmental events and trends because the organization's well-being and even survival depend upon appropriate adaptation to change.

The second lesson of the systems approach is its stress on the interrelatedness of the parts of an organization. A manager is often tempted to see organizational problems and activities in isolation. In an extreme case, a manager may concentrate upon the efficient functioning of his or her own department and give only secondary attention to its relationships with other parts of the organization. Any neglect of important relationships results in some degree of inefficiency.

Contingency Management

Today's manager, although perhaps well-schooled in the need to monitor the environment and in understanding how different subsystems within the organization must mesh for overall effectiveness, also requires more specific guidance. Early managers were guided by such principles as Taylor's view that workers could be motivated primarily by economic reward and Fayol's belief that each worker should have only one boss. The behavioral sciences, too, postulated certain managerial principles. Among them, at various times, were such statements as "the most effective leaders are those who are equally interested in their subordinates' job satisfaction and in task accomplishment" and "human beings are motivated more by recognition, responsibility, and achievement than by pay, working conditions, or status."

The difficulty with these principles is simply that they are not universal; they work in some situations but not in others. The crucial point, of course, is to determine the circumstances under which certain managerial action will yield a particular set of results. The knowledge compiled in this area has become known as the field of *contingency management.*

To date, the development of contingency principles is still relatively limited.[28] Contingency concepts have their strongest empirical support in such areas as organization design and leadership. Other areas, such as decision making, have only recently become the focus of formal contingency-based research.

Although not yet well developed, the contingency concept is intuitively appealing. Even Little League baseball coaches know that shouting at one player for missing a fly ball will motivate him or her to practice harder while shouting at another player for the same error will cause that individual to withdraw psychologically from the team and begin to miss practice. Not all techniques work with different individuals in the same setting, nor do all work with the same individual in different settings. Contingency management is realistic in recognizing that management is more complex than earlier theorists believed it to be.

Our Approach to Management

Elements of each of the schools of thought just reviewed influence our approach to contemporary management. For instance, chapter 7 is devoted to the mathematical management-science approach to decision making, an outgrowth of Taylor's scientific management. Weber's ideas on organization structure will reappear in chapter 8, and Follett's emphasis on the self-actualization of human beings will be incorporated into chapters on human resource management (chapter 10) and organization development (chapter 11). And, of course, contingency concepts will be discussed throughout the book where appropriate. Finally, the basic open systems approach serves as the foundation for much of our analysis. This will quickly become evident in the following chapter, which examines the environment of organizations.

SUMMARY

Although the management process is as old as history itself, a systematic analysis of the field and the development of a theory of management did not begin until this century. In the early 1900s, theorists and practitioners of the *classical school* analyzed how to make organizations operate more efficiently and productively. An American manager and engineer, Frederick W. Taylor, developed the field of *scientific management,* which systematically analyzed a worker's task to discover the "one best way" to perform it. Henri Fayol, a French business executive, identified the basic *functions* performed by managers and established a set of *principles* to guide them. The question of managerial authority in organizations was addressed by Max Weber, a German sociologist, who developed the concept of *bureaucracy.*

A broader view of management, which indicated the importance and complexity of human behavior in organizations, was ushered in by the Hawthorne Studies. The emphasis on the human element in management received further impetus from the writings of Mary Parker Follett, an American political philosopher. An American business executive, Chester I. Barnard, enlarged upon these bases and developed a view of the organization as a *system,* composed of the coordinated efforts and activities of individuals.

Contemporary theorists have expanded upon this perspective to develop *open systems theory.* Organizations are viewed as systems made up of human beings, money, materials, information, equipment, and so on, which are related in the accomplishment of some goal or goals. Organizational systems are, of necessity, *open* to their environment, importing inputs, exporting outputs, and interpreting the feedback received from the environment. Within the organizational system exist a number of *interrelated subsystems*. Each has a purpose which, if attained, aids the larger system in reaching its overall goals. A change in any single subsystem will have ramifications for other related subsystems.

The current state of the managerial art is reflected in *contingency management*. Rather than relying on universal principles of management, this approach focuses on the situational factors that affect the managerial process. The crucial point is to determine the circumstances under which certain managerial actions will yield a particular set of results. Although not yet well developed, contingency management is realistic in recognizing the complexities of modern organizations.

KEY CONCEPTS

Classical school of management thought	Hawthorne Studies
Scientific management	Mary Parker Follett
Frederick W. Taylor	Chester I. Barnard
Administrative management	System
Henri Fayol	Organizational system
Managerial functions	Feedback
Management principles	Subsystem
Bureaucratic management	Interrelated subsystems
Max Weber	Contingency management
Bureaucracy	

DISCUSSION QUESTIONS

1. What was the major contribution of Frederick W. Taylor to management thought?
2. Henri Fayol's *general* theory of management was based on his own *specific* experience as a manager. What might an advocate of the contingency approach say about Fayol's method of theory building?
3. According to Weber, how did a manager in a bureaucracy obtain the right to give orders to subordinates?
4. Explain why it can be said that the three classical theorists discussed in the chapter shared the same goal.

5. How did the conclusions of the Hawthorne Studies modify some of the assumptions held by early management theorists?
6. Explain Mary Parker Follett's view of the individual.
7. According to Chester I. Barnard, what was the basic challenge the manager faced? How was the manager to meet this challenge?
8. Explain the *open systems* concept. What are the benefits to the manager of viewing the organization in this way?
9. Identify the major *subsystems* of your college or university.
10. What is the purpose of the *managerial subsystem* in an organization?
11. The *contingency* approach to management stresses the existence of significant variables in given situations. What are some variables that might affect proper management practice?

NOTES

1. One of the best—and most readable—sources on management history is Daniel A. Wren, *The Evolution of Management Thought,* 2d ed. (New York: Wiley & Sons, 1979).
2. This categorization is based on Fremont E. Kast and James E. Rosenzweig, *Contingency Views of Organization and Management* (Chicago: Science Research Associates, 1973), pp. 2–6.
3. Peter F. Drucker, "The Coming Rediscovery of Scientific Management," *The Conference Board Record* 13 (June 176): 26.
4. For a collection of Taylor's writings, see Frederick Winslow Taylor, *Scientific Management* (New York: Harper & Row, 1947).
5. For an excellent contemporary criticism of Taylor and his work, see Edwin A. Locke, "The Ideas of Frederick W. Taylor: An Evaluation," *Academy of Management Review* 7 (January 1982): 14–24.
6. Henri Fayol, *General and Industrial Management,* trans. Constance Storrs (London: Pitman Publishing, 1949).
7. Richard M. Weiss, "Weber on Bureaucracy: Management Consultant or Political Theorist," *Academy of Management Review* 8 (April 1983): 242–48; and John H. Jackson and Cyril P. Morgan, *Organization Theory: A Macro Perspective for Management,* 2d ed. (Englewood Cliffs, N.J.: Prentice-Hall, 1982): pp. 72–4.
8. Max Weber, *The Theory of Social and Economic Organization,* trans. and ed. A. M. Henderson and Talcott Parsons (New York: Oxford University Press, 1947), p. 337.
9. Ibid., pp. 337–38.
10. These assumptions are adapted from a more complete list of assumptions identified by Joseph L. Massie, "Management Theory," in *Handbook of Organizations,* ed. James G. March (Chicago: Rand McNally, 1965), p. 405.
11. Descriptions of the Western Electric experiments, including both the illumination and other phases, may be found in F. J. Roethlisberger and William J. Dickson, *Management and the Worker* (Cambridge: Harvard University Press, 1946); F. J. Roethlisberger, *Management and Morale* (Cambridge: Harvard University Press, 1941), chapter 2; and Stuart Chase, *Men at Work* (New York: Harcourt Brace Jovanovich, 1945), chapter 2.

12. Wren, *Evolution of Management Thought,* p. 313.

13. For a representative criticism, see Alex Carey, "The Hawthorne Studies: A Radical Criticism," *American Sociological Review* 32 (June 1967): 403–16; for a response to the criticism, see Jon M. Shepard, "On Alex Carey's Radical Criticism of the Hawthorne Studies," *Academy of Management Journal* 14 (March 1971): 23–32; for more recent criticisms, see Berkeley Rice, "The Hawthorne Effect: Persistence of a Flawed Theory," *Psychology Today* 16 (February 1982): 70–74; and Ronald G. Greenwood, Alfred A. Bolton, and Regina A. Greenwood, "Hawthorne a Half Century Later: Relay Assembly Participants Remember," *Journal of Management* 9 (Fall/Winter 1983): 217-31.

14. Mary Parker Follett, *The New State: Group Organization the Solution of Popular Government* (London: Longmans, Green, 1918), and *Creative Experience* (London: Longmans, Green, 1924).

15. Mary Parker Follett, "Business as an Integrative Unity," in *Dynamic Administration: The Collected Papers of Mary Parker Follett,* ed. Henry C. Metcalf and L. Urwick (New York: Harper & Row, 1940), pp. 71–94.

16. Mary Parker Follett, "The Giving of Orders," in *Dynamic Administration: The Collected Papers of Mary Parker Follett,* ed. Henry C. Metcalf and L. Urwick (New York: Harper & Row, 1940), pp. 50–70.

17. Ibid., p. 59.

18. Wren, *Evolution of Management Thought,* p. 332; and L. D. Parker, "Control in Organizational Life: The Contribution of Mary Parker Follett," *Academy of Management Review* 9 (October 1984): 738–41.

19. Chester I. Barnard, *The Functions of the Executive* (Cambridge, Mass.: Harvard University Press, 1938), pp. 217–34.

20. Ibid., pp. 140–60.

21. Ibid., p. 158.

22. Ibid., p. 73. See pp. 65–81 for the entire discussion of the organization as a system.

23. Daniel Katz and Robert L. Kahn, *The Social Psychology of Organizations,* 2d ed. (New York: Wiley, 1978), p. 36.

24. Ibid., p. 20.

25. Ibid., p. 37.

26. "An Advisory Council to Back up the Board," *Business Week,* 12 November 1979, p. 131.

27. See Sara Kiesler, "The Hidden Messages in Computer Networks," *Harvard Business Review* 64 (January-February 1986): 46–60; Frank Blackler and Colin Brown, "Evaluation and the Impact of Information Technologies on People in Organizations," *Human Relations* 38 (March 1985): 213–31; "Offices of the Future," *Newsweek,* 14 May 1984, pp. 72–75B; and Shoshana Zuboff, "New Worlds of Computer-Mediated Work," *Harvard Business Review* 60 (September-October 1982): 142–52.

28. Justin G. Longenecker and Charles D. Pringle, "The Illusion of Contingency Theory as a General Theory," *Academy of Management Review* 3 (July 1978): 679–83.

SUPPLEMENTARY READING

Barnard, Chester I. *The Functions of the Executive.* Cambridge, Mass.: Harvard University Press, 1938.

Breeze, John D. "Harvest From the Archives: The Search for Fayol and Carlioz." *Journal of Management* 11 (Spring 1985): 43–54.

Chang, Y. N. "Early Chinese Management Thought." *California Management Review* 19 (Winter 1976): 71–76.

Follett, Mary Parker. *Dynamic Administration: The Collected Papers of Mary Parker Follett.* Edited by Henry C. Metcalf and L. Urwick. New York: Harper & Row, 1940.

Fry, Louis W. "The Maligned F. W. Taylor: A Reply to His Many Critics." *Academy of Management Review* 1 (July 1976): 124–29.

Greenwood, Ronald G.; Bolton, Alfred A.; and Greenwood, Regina A. "Hawthorne a Half Century Later: Relay Assembly Participants Remember." *Journal of Management* 9 (Fall/Winter 1983): 217–31.

Katz, Daniel, and Kahn, Robert L. *The Social Psychology of Organizations,* 2d ed., chapter 2. New York: Wiley, 1978.

Kiesler, Sara. "The Hidden Messages in Computer Networks." *Harvard Business Review* 64 (January-February 1986): 46–60.

Koontz, Harold. "The Management Theory Jungle Revisited." *Academy of Management Review* 5 (April 1980) 175–87.

Locke, Edwin A. "The Ideas of Frederick W. Taylor: An Evaluation." *Academy of Management Review* 7 (January 1982): 14–24.

Massie, Joseph L. "Management Theory." In *Handbook of Organizations,* chapter 9, edited by James G. March. Chicago: Rand McNally, 1965.

Parker, L. D. "Control in Organizational Life: The Contribution of Mary Parker Follett." *Academy of Management Review* 9 (October 1984): 736–45.

Roethlisberger, F. J., and Dickson, William J. *Management and the Worker.* Cambridge, Mass.: Harvard University Press, 1939.

Von Bertalanffy, Ludwig. "The History and Status of General Systems Theory." *Academy of Management Journal* 15 (December 1972): 407–26.

Weber, Max. "Bureaucracy." In *From Max Weber: Essays in Sociology,* chapter 8, translated and edited by H. H. Gerth and C. Wright Mills. New York: Oxford University Press, 1946.

————. *The Theory of Social and Economic Organization.* Translated and edited by A. M. Henderson and Talcott Parsons. New York: Oxford University Press, 1947.

Weiss, Richard M. "Weber on Bureaucracy: Management Consultant or Political Theorist?" *Academy of Management Review* 8 (April 1983): 242–48.

Wren, Daniel A. "Scientific Management in the U.S.S.R., with Particular Reference to the Contribution of Walter N. Polakov." *Academy of Management Review* 5 (January 1980): 1–11.

————. *The Evolution of Management Thought.* 2d ed. New York: Wiley, 1979.

WORRY AT WERNETT'S

Jeanne Jones felt confused and frustrated as she walked slowly toward the Receiving Department, pondering the impossible order her boss had issued only moments before. Not only the sheer impossibility of carrying out the order, but also serious doubts as to the legitimacy of the directive had driven Jeanne into her current quandary.

Having been appointed assistant buyer in Women's Sportswear at Wernett's Department Store only three months earlier, she had established a smooth and rewarding working relationship with Helen Fabian, the department's buyer and one of the store's "rising stars." Since the Christmas selling season had begun, however, the air of compatibility had dissipated as Helen had grown increasingly tense and grouchy.

About one-fourth of the store's annual sales came during the weeks between Thanksgiving and Christmas. Since a buyer's income and opportunities for promotion depended upon being able to exceed last year's sales, the Christmas selling season was of paramount importance.

Under the leadership of Helen Fabian, sales in Women's Sportswear had consistently exceeded last year's sales by 20 percent since January. This increase had risen to about 23 percent the first two weeks of the Christmas season. But this record—easily one of the best among the store's eighty buyers—did not seem to satisfy Helen.

Only a few minutes ago, she had called Jeanne into her office. "Jeanne, our sales this week are up over last year's by about twenty-three percent. We should be able to

do better than that, however. On the way back from lunch, I stopped at the loading docks and saw our overdue shipment of suede blazers arriving. If we could get those onto the selling floor by this evening, I think we could beat last year's figures for this week by close to thirty percent. I'd like you to go see Charlie Barnoski, the head of Receiving, and get him to move those blazers up to the front of the receiving line so we can get them on the floor before the evening rush."

As Jeanne walked reluctantly toward Receiving, she pondered her predicament. The store's policy on receiving was quite clear. All goods were checked against purchase orders for quantity, quality, size, and color; marked with price tags; and sent to the selling floor *in the order they arrived at the store.* Although temporary help was hired during the Christmas season to increase the size of the Receiving Department staff, the average time period between the arrival of the goods at the store and their actual display on the selling floor was three days. Obviously this period was too long for Helen!

Now, as she arrived at receiving, Jeanne dreaded having to request an exception to store policy, especially since she had never even met Charlie Barnoski.

Questions

1. Analyze this situation from a systems viewpoint:
   a. What is the rationale behind the store's receiving policy?
   b. What are the systems implications of Helen Fabian's order to Jeanne?

2. What should Jeanne do?

Prepared with the assistance of Anne Marie Pringle.

PART TWO

MANAGEMENT PLANNING AND DECISION MAKING

THE ORGANIZATION AND ITS ENVIRONMENT

The Environmental Interface □ The General Environment □ The Specific Environment □ Failure to Monitor the Environment

ELEMENTS OF THE GENERAL ENVIRONMENT

The Economic Sector □ The Technological Sector □ The Social Sector □ The Governmental Sector

ELEMENTS OF THE SPECIFIC ENVIRONMENT

Customers □ Competitors □ Suppliers □ Regulatory Groups □ Technologies □ Human Resources

BOUNDARY-SPANNING MANAGEMENT

Nature of Environmental Scanning □ Dynamic vs. Stable Environments □ Coping with Change

Summary □ Key Concepts □ Discussion Questions □ Notes □ Supplementary Reading

CASES: Silver Dollar Concessions □ Western College

This chapter will enable you to

□ Show the importance of the interface between organizations and their environments.

□ Understand the significance of an organization's general and specific environments.

□ Identify important elements of an organization's general and specific environments.

□ Recognize the nature and importance of boundary spanning, including the process of environmental scanning.

□ Understand how managers cope with the uncertainty of a changing environment.

CHAPTER 3
MANAGEMENT AND THE
ENVIRONMENT

All types of human organizations are open systems. Thus, they interact with their respective environments and are subject to constraints imposed by those environments. For example, hospitals, business firms, churches, and government offices are open systems. Managers attempt to match their distinctive competencies (strengths and weaknesses of the organization) with various environmental trends (opportunities and threats). Managerial practices change as managers respond to environmental changes. The soaring cost of liability insurance during 1985–1986 forced many organizations either to raise prices or to accept smaller profits, eliminate products and services, and change their operations. Changes in inflation, interest rates, and oil prices cause managers to think how to decrease costs, increase productivity, and adapt to customer needs.

The first section of this chapter discusses the relationship of organizations, as open systems, to their environment. Attention then shifts to the nature of our contemporary environment—particularly to changes occurring in economic conditions, technology, social institutions, and government relationships. Subsequent sections examine management responsibilities related to the boundary area and to environmental scanning. In the final section of the chapter, we examine how managers cope with environmental change and uncertainty. If organizations are to achieve success, their managers must adequately monitor and control the interface between the organization and its environment.

THE ORGANIZATION AND ITS ENVIRONMENT

The Environmental Interface

As explained in the preceding chapter, an open system interacts with its *environment*—any condition or element that is not part of the organization itself. Figure 3–1 shows some of the elements of this complex environment and implies the varied types of interactions involved.

Interactions with some environmental elements (customers, for instance) have more immediate significance to an organization than do interactions with others (trade associations, for example). Furthermore, an element such as a labor union may be extremely important to an organization that is undergoing a strike and yet largely irrelevant to another organization, such as a family-owned pharmacy. A number of theorists have helped us understand the differing impact of environmental elements on varying organizations by distinguishing between *general* and *specific* environments.[1]

The General Environment

The general environment comprises both elements (such as the government) and conditions (such as inflation) that are of concern to all organizations. Although these elements and conditions are potentially relevant to any organization, most organizations are not affected by all of them on a daily basis.[2]

Because the impact of the general environment on a particular organization may be, at first, only indirect, managers often fail to detect important changes in the environment. In the early 1970s, for example, some traditional watchmaking companies failed to understand the impact of seemingly unre-

FIGURE 3–1 The organization's environment

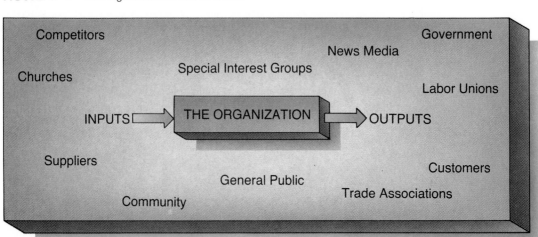

lated developments in the semiconductor industry. Other watchmakers, particularly those in Japan, perceived that advances in semiconductor technology would be transferable to the watch industry, permitting the manufacture of low-cost but highly accurate digital watches.[3] Although the environment eventually changed once again and digital watches gave way to the quartz analog, many watchmakers missed the substantial profits that were made on the millions of digital watches sold during the late 1970s.[4]

The Specific Environment

In contrast to the general environment, an organization's specific environment comprises elements that directly affect that organization's operations. Although all organizations share a common general environment, each organization has a unique specific environment. An example is the specific environment of a department store (Figure 3–2).

FIGURE 3–2 Specific environment of a department store

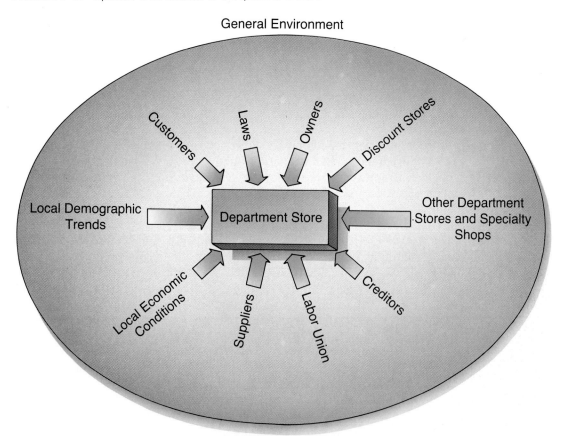

The department store's products, prices, decor, location, and type of employees reflect various elements of the store's specific environment. Of course, certain elements of the specific environment are more important at times than are others. Construction of a discount store across the street, for instance, will require certain immediate responses from the department store's management. Managers of a store in financial difficulty will be concerned primarily about creditors and cutting costs.

Events that occur in the general environment may eventually affect one or more elements of the specific environment. Then the store itself will be affected. For instance, the generalized move of Americans to the suburbs a few decades ago ultimately translated into the migration of a specific store's actual customers and its competitors to shopping areas away from the central business district. Stores, such as Sears, Roebuck, that detected and acted upon the general environmental trend in its infancy beat other stores to the competitive punch by closing their downtown locations and building new stores in suburban areas. One of these competitors was Montgomery Ward, which failed to discern the trend until its customer traffic and growth began to decline precipitously.

Failure to Monitor the Environment

With the large number of elements in an organization's environment and the complex interactions among these elements, it is not surprising that managers often fail to read the environment correctly. Yet, there are reasons besides complexity for management's failure to discern significant changes in the environment.

Complacency, based on past success, can lull a manager to sleep. In 1984, Tandy Corporation's Radio Shack stores were the leader in the $34 billion (retail) U.S. consumer-electronics market. Tandy's formula was to buy cheap in the Far East and then sell high using Radio Shack's Realistic labels. This formula produced annual earnings gains as well as gross profit margins of 30 percent. Such results are double those obtained by the average specialty retailer. In 1985, electronic "superstores" operated by such companies as Federated Group and Highland Appliance began to undercut Radio Shack's prices while offering brand-name goods. Even as these competitive actions became obvious, Tandy would not admit that many customers would rather own a Sony or RCA product than a Realistic product. In fiscal 1985, Tandy's earnings dropped 33 percent to $189 million, and Radio Shack stores were no longer number one.[5]

Perhaps a more common reason for the failure to monitor environmental trends is management's preoccupation with internal operating problems. Minimizing internal frictions, achieving economy of performance, and coordinating the activities of subsystems are tasks that absorb a manager's time and energy. Operational problems constantly demand solutions. A manager understandably tends to concentrate on the functioning of the system, overlooking the seriousness of changes in the environment. Hence, open systems are often operated as if they were closed.

ELEMENTS OF THE GENERAL ENVIRONMENT

The general environment of an organization consists of four sectors: economic, technological, social, and governmental. These sectors interact with one another as they affect the organization (Figure 3–3). There are a number of elements in each of the four sectors that are involved in this interaction process.[6]

The Economic Sector

Both the present and future state of the economy can affect an organization's performance. Elements of the economic sector include:

- ☐ the business cycle (the economy can be in a depression, recovery, or prosperity phase)
- ☐ inflationary trends
- ☐ interest rates
- ☐ material shortages

Each of these elements can either help or hinder the organization as it attempts to attain its objectives. For example, recessions often lead to unemployment, which causes lower sales for firms that produce discretionary goods. Periods of economic prosperity, on the other hand, can lead to an increased level of sales.

FIGURE 3–3   The general environment

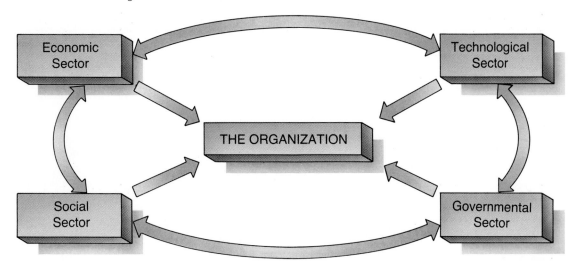

THE COST OF COMPLACENCY

Some firms are complacent with respect to their competitive position. For example, Dow Chemical Company continued to rely on basic commodity chemicals such as chlorine and ethylene rather than attempting to enter the highly profitable specialty chemical market. These commodity chemicals, which accounted for all but a fraction of Dow's earnings, were sold by the ton and delivered by the tankerful.

In 1984, Arab competitors flooded the world with lower-priced commodity chemicals, forcing Dow to close many of their plants and seek specialty-chemical acquisitions. During Dow's fiscal year of 1985, $600 million of unneeded plants and other assets were written off while Dow experienced its worst financial performance in decades.

SOURCE: Based on "Dow Chemical's Drive To Change Its Market—And Its Image," *Business Week,* 9 June 1986, pp. 92–96.

The high inflation of the late 1970s and early 1980s created a relentless cycle of wages pushing up prices pushing up wages. Yet low inflation can also cause concern. In situations where inflation is low, managers are unable to cover their inefficiencies with price increases—managers can sometimes mask failure by having profits fattened by inflation. Managers must learn to cut costs,

MANAGING IN THE NEW ECONOMY

The CEO of H. J. Heinz, Anthony O'Reilly, describes how corporate managers can perform in a changed economy:

> Create trim, supple organizations that can compete effectively in an acutely cost-conscious environment. Push employees to increase productivity. Do not simply accept the blessing of cheaper oil, but maximize its benefits. Think about what the customers need. Look well beyond the current quarter. Above all, be flexible enough to adjust when circumstances demand.

SOURCE: "America's New Economy: How To Manage In It," *Fortune,* 23 June 1986, p. 23.

raise productivity, and adapt swiftly to customer needs during periods of low inflation.

High interest rates may make needed plant additions too costly, but low interest rates will spur economic growth and allow companies to refinance profit-draining debt. Finally, material shortages disrupt the way the firm does business and cause cost increases.

Changes in the economic sector may be good for one company but bad for others. The declining oil prices of 1985 reduced the cost of fuel and raw materials by millions of dollars for such energy-intensive industries as airlines and chemicals. On the other hand, industries whose performances were dependent on the energy business experienced considerable losses. Panhandle Eastern (a gas pipeliner and exploration company), Hughes Tool and Armco (makers of oil-field equipment), NL Industries (in oil-field services and equipment), and InterFirst Corporation (a bank with energy loans) were companies that had sizable losses during that period.[7]

The Technological Sector

Technology involves the art and science employed to produce and distribute goods and services. A changing technology affects the firm's raw materials, products, services, and operations by providing opportunities for enhancing performance or creating threats to the firm's existence.

American firms are using changes in their manufacturing technologies as a key factor in global competitiveness. For example, IBM, General Electric, General Motors, and General Dynamics are spending billions of dollars for future factory automation. Table 3–1 describes the estimated investment of computer-aided manufacturing items for all U.S. firms in 1990. Smaller firms are also involved in retooling their manufacturing facilities. A survey indicated that more than a quarter of all firms planning to purchase robots in 1986 had annual sales below $10 million.[8]

TABLE 3–1 Estimated investments in plant-floor automation

Computer-aided Manufacturing Items	Investment (in millions of dollars)		
	1980	1985	1990 (est.)
1. Factory computers and software	$ 935	$ 2,861	$ 6,500
2. Robots and sensors	68	664	2,800
3. Automated test equipment	800	2,000	4,000
4. Materials handling systems	2,000	4,500	9,000
5. Machine tools and controls	3,000	4,800	7,000
6. Programmable controllers	50	550	3,000
Total spending	**$6,853**	**$15,375**	**$32,300**

SOURCE: "High Tech To The Rescue," *Business Week,* 16 June 1986, p. 102.

The Social Sector

The social sector encompasses the attitudes, or values, of people—customers, suppliers, and employees. These values create life-style changes that affect the demand for products and services and the way organizations relate to their employees. If an organization's management is to produce those goods and services that customers desire, then management must be aware and take into account these values.

Organizations have problems adapting to changes in values. There are many examples. When many managers urged urinalysis to discourage drug use, some employees argued that such tests violated their rights. Protest groups affected the public image of firms doing business in South Africa. Although Americans welcomed the jobs created by Japanese investments, there was resistance to Japanese management techniques.

The Governmental Sector

The governmental sector encompasses the regulatory, legal, and political entities that surround the organization. The amount of freedom that organizations have to pursue their own objectives is determined by the political and economic system, such as capitalism versus socialism. The political system influences the organization's objectives through various laws and regulations that can increase an organization's opportunities or threats.

Some examples of opportunities resulting from governmental actions include large purchases by government of goods and services, subsidies granted to business firms, trade tariffs and antidumping provisions imposed to protect

USING CUSTOMER VALUES TO COMPETE

Because the number of practicing dentists increased from 96,000 in 1965 to 135,000 in 1985 while the incidence of tooth decay dropped 50 percent (thanks to improved oral hygiene), competition among dentists has increased significantly. Since most dentists are equally competent, many of them are now competing with an appeal to the values of their clients. For instance, dentists are now stressing convenience—many have their offices open seven days a week, up to eleven hours each day. They allay anxieties by offering a friendly atmosphere in the office and by running ads stating that "we cater to cowards." Some dentists are even offering a free bike with every set of braces.

SOURCE: Based on "A Free Bike With Your Braces," *Newsweek,* 5 May 1986, p. 82.

against foreign competition, and removal of entry barriers to certain industries through deregulation.

The governmental sector can also negatively affect the financial performance of organizations. Such actions include provisions for environmental control, worker health and safety, product information and labeling, and merger limitation. At issue is whether the costs of regulation are justified by the benefits society receives from regulation.

The growth and pattern of regulation in the U.S. is changing. The Reagan administration reduced business regulation at the federal level, though increases occurred at the state level. In 1985, 250,000 bills were introduced in state governments, with 50,000 becoming law. In addition, 50,000 new regulations were proposed, with 35,000 being adopted.

The effects of the governmental sector can be pervasive. Every other sector in the general environment is influenced by governmental actions.[9]

ELEMENTS OF THE SPECIFIC ENVIRONMENT

In the preceding section, the general environment of an organization was described as consisting of four external sectors. While events occurring in these sectors create opportunities and threats for organizations in a general sense, their actual impact is somewhat unclear. Most organizations focus on the specific environment of their industry, which consists of a particular array of elements or competitive forces.

An organization's specific environment includes six external elements: customers, competitors, suppliers, regulatory groups, technologies, and human resources.[10]

Figure 3–1 described how an organization converts inputs into outputs. Inputs include labor, money, raw materials, information, and equipment. Outputs are the finished products or services of the organization. The six elements of the specific environment are an organization's input suppliers and output receivers. The relationship of the specific environment to the organization, as well as to the general environment, is depicted in Figure 3–4. The interaction between the organization and its specific environment is much closer than that between the organization and the general environment.

Customers

Customers are individuals and other organizations that exchange something of value to acquire an organization's products or services. Acquisition can be accomplished directly through the exchange of resources for products or services or indirectly through exchange with a supplier for service to a particular client group.[11]

FIGURE 3–4 The specific environment

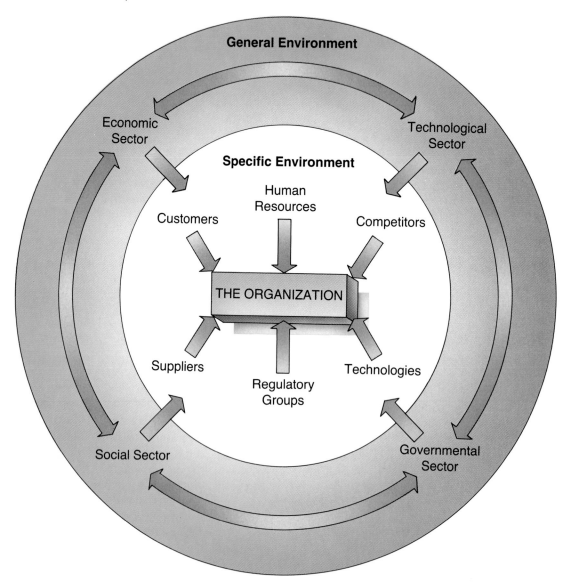

Competitors

Competitors are usually viewed as those organizations that offer similar products or services. Competition also occurs in other areas of the organization's specific environment. Firms compete for inputs and outputs. In addition, various competitive forces affect the organization. For example, customers can be a competitive force when they drive prices down, bargain for more services, or require higher quality. Customers may also adopt a strategy of backward integration, in which they acquire the capability to produce the same products or services that were previously purchased from others.

Suppliers become competitors when they reduce the quality of their products or services and when they threaten to raise prices. Suppliers may also adopt a strategy of forward integration, in which they acquire the capability to produce the same products or services that they purchase from others.

Organizations also face competition from new entrants into their market domain. For example, American automakers and semiconductor manufacturers have lost market share to Japanese firms entering U.S. markets.

Substitute products create competitive pressures because they limit profits in normal times and reduce bonanzas that firms can acquire during boom periods. NutraSweet, a sugar substitute, is an example of a substitute product that affected sugar producers.[12]

Suppliers

Organizations obtain their resources from suppliers. As stated earlier, suppliers provide labor, money, raw materials, information, and equipment to keep the organization functioning. Suppliers, as already stated, can become a competitive force.[13]

Regulatory Groups

Regulatory groups are the element in the specific environment that has the potential to influence or regulate the activities of the organization. These groups consist of both governmental agencies and special interest groups. Sometimes, the actions of business firms affect the health and safety of the general population as well as other organizations. For example, firms can pollute the environment, engage in deceptive trade practices, or use false advertising. Firms can also create monopoly conditions by acquiring their competitors. Governmental agencies that regulate organizations are created to control certain business practices. For instance, in the United States there are governmental agencies that protect the environment (Environmental Protection Agency), investigate trade practices (Federal Trade Commission), and regulate working conditions (Occupational Safety and Health Administration).

Special interest groups develop when individuals or organizations attempt to influence particular organizations. While these special interest groups have no regulatory power, considerable pressure can be applied. The leaders of the Moral Majority asserted that the 7-Eleven convenience stores owned by Southland Corporation sold pornographic material and urged a public boycott of the stores. Southland responded by removing the materials.

Technologies

The technologies of the specific environment are the means used to produce and distribute the organization's goods and services. The skill level required in an organization is influenced by the complexity of its technology. New technologies can create either opportunities or threats for each individual firm. IBM used technology as a competitive advantage against rival off-shore competitors who threatened IBM's lucrative personal computer (PC) business. IBM experienced market share losses because competitors could produce so-called clones that were cheaper. IBM responded by pioneering a fully automated plant that reduced the cost of manufacturing PCs.[14]

Human Resources

Employees are the human resources of an organization. Different organizations require different kinds and amounts of abilities in their employees. The fully automated IBM PC plant requires a wide range of skills. Other organizations do not require such a range of skills. For instance, stenciling logos on T-shirts requires employees with much lower ability.[15]

A deciding factor in where organizations locate is the skill available in local markets. GM, for example, had certain labor skill requirements that had to be available in the sites considered for its Saturn plant.

Unionization is also an important consideration. The presence of labor unions has to be considered because they represent a powerful factor in the human relations of an organization.

BOUNDARY-SPANNING MANAGEMENT

So far, we have examined the openness of organizational systems—that is, the way they interact with the world around them—and the changing nature of the environment. Because organizations are open and because environments change, managers must concern themselves with spanning *organizational boundaries,* the interface between organizations and their environment. This section analyzes the process by which managers monitor environmental change and adapt their organizations to maintain survival and growth.

Nature of Environmental Scanning

Organizations acquire knowledge about the environment by gathering, analyzing, and evaluating data about environmental events.[16] Peter Drucker has asserted that the most important events occurring outside an organization are not the trends themselves but rather the changes in the trends.[17] These changes ultimately determine the success or failure of an organization and its efforts. *Environmental scanning* involves how the organization searches its environment.

Managers have limited time and resources to learn about the elements of the general and specific environments. These elements differ with respect to importance and uncertainty for each organization. *Importance* concerns how much impact an element has on the performance of the organization. *Uncertainty* concerns the availability of information about a certain element.

VIDEO GAMES AND BOUNDARY SPANNING

Milton Bradley Company, a successful toy and game manufacturer for over 120 years, failed to read its environment accurately in the early 1980s and is now scanning for opportunities to correct the mistake.

In the late 1970s, Milton Bradley developed a television-connected game, but failed to market it because management felt that video games were a fad. Instead, they concentrated on hand-held electronic games. The choice was a major error—video games later captured more than 25 percent of all toy/game sales while hand-held electronic games gathered dust on store shelves.

By 1982, Milton Bradley found itself scanning the environment for a niche other than console video games or game cartridges—areas that were already too competitive. In mid-1982, Milton Bradley purchased General Consumer Electronics Corporation, a small company with a niche: it was the only company at that time to use black-and-white television monitors with color overlays for the screen in its video games. This made the games less expensive than those requiring color television, but the games were (theoretically at least) as attractive. The acquisition was disastrous. Milton Bradley lost $18 million in 1983 because of its lackluster performance in the video-game business.

By early 1984, Milton Bradley was acquired by Hasbro, a toy manufacturer that consistently increased its profits by sticking to the basics. Rather than offering electronic toys, Hasbro concentrated on conventional products such as GI Joe, Raggedy Ann and Andy, and stuffed animals based on the Muppets, Disney, and Peanuts characters. During the latter part of 1985, Hasbro (renamed Hasbro Bradley) successfully marketed a product line called Transformer—basic toys that can be converted into robots. Hasbro Bradley's stock increased from a 1984 low of $23 to $60 a share by December, 1984. Milton Bradley misread its environment and is now part of a company that did a better job of recognizing opportunities.

SOURCE: Based on "Milton Bradley: Playing Catch-up in the Video-game Market," *Business Week,* 24 May 1982, pp. 110–14; "Milton Bradley Agrees to Buy Video Game Firm," *The Dallas Morning News,* 18 July 1982; and "How to Transform a Toymaker," *Newsweek,* 17 December 1984, p. 72.

Researchers at the University of Georgia found that top managers will tend to direct their attention to the elements perceived to be relevant for organizational performance.[18] The element of the environment considered most significant depends upon the type of organization and the conditions of uncertainty facing the organization.

In a study of fifty medium-sized Southwest manufacturing firms with annual sales ranging from $2 to $500 million, researchers from Texas A&M University found that these organizations were most concerned with the customer element of the specific environment.[19] By contrast, a Baylor University study of forty-nine Texas savings-and-loan institutions, with assets ranging from $10 million to $3.4 billion, indicated that these firms were most concerned with regulatory groups.[20]

The emphasis on environmental scanning is still relatively new, and managers may not fully appreciate the relative importance of all of the environmental elements. One study of eighty-six firms suggests that scanning activities too often are devoted to understanding present conditions at the expense of understanding future trends:[21]

> Executives may ignore trends that appear to be irrelevant to their firms. There is significant danger associated with this behavior. History teaches that most new developments which threaten existing business practices and technologies do not come from traditional industries.

Dynamic vs. Stable Environments

The rate of environmental change is not a constant for all organizations and industries. To illustrate, environments do not change at the same pace for computer manufacturers, city libraries, hospitals, real estate brokers, and major airlines. Some are clearly more volatile than others. Environments may be described, therefore, as ranging from relatively stable to relatively dynamic, even though all are changing.

The requirement for environmental information increases as environments become more dynamic and less static.[22] As Figure 3–5 indicates, an uninformed manager may succeed in very stable situations. Two observations are important, however. First, the total environment, including the specific environment of most organizations, has been shifting in the direction of less stable and more dynamic and no doubt will continue to do so. Thus, the allowable margin for closed-system thinking is constantly narrowing. Second, the probability of success improves with the depth of environmental scanning. This holds true for any environment, although such information is most urgent in a highly dynamic environment.

A survey of 295 industrial corporations in the United States and Canada indicated that chief executive officers in complex, dynamic environments experienced the greatest difficulty in analyzing their environment, detecting trends, and deciding upon effective responses. The least difficulty was encoun-

FIGURE 3-5 Environmental dangers and environmental scanning

Environmental Conditions / Environmental Sensing Posture	Relatively Stable	Moderate Change and Innovation	Highly Dynamic
Internally Oriented	DANGER	EXTREME DANGER	PROBABLE FAILURE
Management Awareness of Environment		DANGER	EXTREME DANGER
Aggressive Search for Information and Continued Adaptation			DANGER

tered by those chief executive officers who were faced with simple, stable environments.[23]

Development of a system yielding a large amount of environmental information should improve the quality of decision making and avoid some of the glaring errors of managers who confine their attention to internal operations.

Coping with Change

Environmental scanning is a necessary first step, but it must be followed by appropriate decisions. Gathering information is not an end in itself but a means toward effective management—responding to or challenging conditions in the environment. When managers observe skyrocketing fuel costs, for example, they do more than file this information. They develop energy-conservation programs.

All organizations experience three primary problems as they adapt to environmental change: the entrepreneurial problem, the engineering problem, and the administrative problem. The *entrepreneurial problem* concerns how the organization develops innovations to improve its competitive position. The *engineering problem* concerns how technologies are created to implement the organization's response to the entrepreneurial problem. The *administrative prob-*

lem concerns how the solutions to the entrepreneurial and engineering problems are implemented in a way that allows the organization to adapt to future environmental challenges.[24]

In solving the three problems, top managers are the primary link between the organization and its environment. They can adjust organizational processes and structures and can also attempt to manipulate the organization's environment.[25] For example, managers of R. J. Reynolds are concerned that its lucrative cigarette market will shrink because of the social stigma of cigarette smoking. The chief executive officer of Reynolds is rapidly moving to broaden the base of the company, with such nonconsumer product divisions as Sea-Land, the nation's largest ocean shipper, and Aminoil, the nation's second largest oil and gas exploration company. Steps have been taken to enlarge the company's existing consumer products base by moving its Del Monte division into higher-margin foods, selling the Kentucky Fried Chicken division to PepsiCo, and energizing Heublein's wine and spirits businesses, as well as searching for other consumer products to acquire.[26]

Top managers can coordinate the activities of coping with change and reducing uncertainty by creating boundary-spanning roles between the internal elements of the organization and the elements of the external environment. *Boundary spanning* accomplishes two ends: (1) it allows the organization to detect changes in the external environment and (2) it permits the organization to be represented in the external environment.[27] For example, marketing personnel provide the means for detecting changes in the external environment when they monitor changes in consumer taste. In representing the organization to customers and others, marketing personnel send out information and influence public perception of the organization.

Many organizations are becoming increasingly proactive toward the environment. Corporations that previously relied on trade associations to represent their interests in Washington are now interested in national politics. For example, in 1961 there were 130 firms represented by registered lobbyists in Washington. Fifty of these 130 firms also had staffs with Washington addresses. By 1981, 650 firms utilized registered lobbyists, with 247 having their own staffs in the capital city.[28] Business firms are also increasing their political action committees (PACs). In 1974, 89 corporate PACs contributed $2.5 million to federal candidates, while in 1982, 1,310 such PACs contributed over $27 million.[29] Masters and Delaney reported that corporate PAC contributions exceeded labor donations by a significant amount in 1980.[30]

SUMMARY

Organizations are open systems; that is, systems which interact with their environments. This interaction involves exchanges with many external elements. The change and complexity of these environmental elements has major implications for organizational activities, decisions, and performance.

All organizations share a common *general environment* consisting of economic, technological, societal, and governmental sectors. Events occurring in the general environment often affect a particular organization's *specific environment,* those elements that directly influence the organization's operations. The elements of the specific environment include customers, competitors, suppliers, regulatory groups, technologies, and human resources. In coping with environmental changes, top managers make strategic choices linking the organization with its environment.

The *boundary,* or interface, between organizations and their environments is an area of importance to the process of management. To be effective, organizational managers must recognize environmental complexity, managerial complacency, or a preoccupation with internal operating problems.

The most effective *boundary-spanning* managers actively engage in *environmental scanning,* that is, in gathering information about conditions and changes in the environment. The process of gathering information differs in the extent to which it is formalized and instituted. The need for environmental scanning varies with the degree to which an environment is stable or dynamic. After gathering relevant information about the organizational environment, managers must plan, organize, and direct in terms of environmental knowledge. Organizations experience three primary problems as they adapt to environmental change: *entrepreneurial problems, engineering problems,* and *administrative problems.* In solving these adaptation problems, top managers are in a position to adjust organization processes and structure to environmental changes. Managers can also attempt to manipulate the organization's environment.

KEY CONCEPTS

Distinctive competencies	Boundary spanning
Open system	Environmental scanning
General environment	Dynamic environment
Specific environment	Stable environment
Environmental interface	

DISCUSSION QUESTIONS

1. Identify some of the important elements in your college's or university's *general* environment. Also identify some of the major elements in its *specific* environment.
2. In spite of the several examples in the chapter of firms that failed to monitor their environments, some managers persist in operating their organizations as if they were closed systems. How can this behavior be explained?

3. How is government regulation of business today different from that which existed prior to the 1960s?
4. Define *environmental scanning.*
5. Which of the environmental systems—regulatory, economic, social, technological—would be of greatest concern to a furniture manufacturer? To an electric power company?
6. Why might managers be more concerned with understanding present environmental trends than with future trends?
7. How would the environmental scanning conducted by an office of consumer affairs differ from that conducted by a corporate economist? Which is more important for a major corporation?
8. What environmental "scanning devices" might be used by a business firm to assist in developing social objectives?
9. Managers tend to scan certain elements of the specific environment more than others. Do you agree? Why?
10. How can managers use boundary-spanning roles to cope with environmental changes?
11. How effective was Milton Bradley in scanning its environment?
12. Other than public affairs departments and Washington influence, can you think of other ways in which organizations behave proactively toward the environment?

NOTES

1. See William R. Dill, "Environment as an Influence on Managerial Autonomy," *Administrative Science Quarterly* 2 (March 1958): 409–43; Robert B. Duncan, "Characteristics of Organizational Environments and Perceived Environmental Uncertainty," *Administrative Science Quarterly* 17 (September 1972): 313–27; and Richard H. Hall, *Organizations: Structure and Processes* (Englewood Cliffs, N.J.: Prentice-Hall, 1972).
2. Robert H. Miles, *Macro Organizational Behavior* (Santa Monica, Calif.: Goodyear, 1980), p. 195.
3. "Japanese Heat on the Watch Industry," *Business Week,* 5 May 1980, pp. 92–100.
4. Michael Ingrassia, "Digital Watches Out of Time," *Dallas Times Herald,* 4 January 1986.
5. "Burned By Superstores, Tandy Is Fighting Fire With Fire," *Business Week,* 28 October 1985, pp. 62–7.
6. Rosalie L. Tung, "Dimensions of Organizational Environments: An Exploratory Study of Their Impact on Organizational Structure," *Academy of Management Journal* 22 (March 1979): 672–93.
7. "Business Is Biting The Bullet," *Business Week,* 18 August 1986, p. 104.
8. "Retool or Die: Job Shops Get A Fix On The Future," *Business Week,* 16 June 1986, pp. 106–108.
9. William F. Glueck and Lawrence R. Jauch, *Business Policy and Strategic Management* (New York: McGraw-Hill, 1984), pp. 108–111. "State Regulators Rush In Where Washington No Longer Treads," *Business Week,* 19 September 1984, pp. 124–31.

10. Donald Jacobs, "Dependency and Vulnerability: An Exchange Approach to the Control of Organizations," *Administrative Science Quarterly* 4 (1974): 45–60.

11. Richard Osborn, James Hunt, and Lawrence Jauch, *Organization Theory: An Integrated Approach* (New York: Wiley, 1980), p. 176.

12. "Japan, U.S.A.," *Business Week,* 14 July 1986, pp. 45–46. Michael Porter, *Competitive Advantage* (New York: Free Press, 1985), pp. 4–22.

13. Osborn, Hunt, and Jauch, p. 177.

14. "IBM's No-Hands Assembly Line," *Fortune,* 15 September 1986, pp. 105–109; Richard Daft, *Organization Theory and Design,* 2nd ed. (St. Paul, Minn.: West, 1986), p. 52.

15. B. J. Hodge and William Anthony, *Organization Theory,* 2nd ed. (Boston: Allyn and Bacon, 1984), pp. 107–108.

16. Asterios Kefalas and Peter Schoderbek, "Application and Implementation: Scanning the Business Environment, Some Empirical Results," *Decision Sciences* 4 (1973): 63–74.

17. Peter Drucker, *Managing in Turbulent Times* (New York: Harper and Row, 1980), p. 68.

18. W. R. Bouton, W. M. Lindsay, S. G. Franklin, and L. W. Rue, "Strategic Planning: Determining the Impact of Environmental Characteristics and Uncertainty," *Academy of Management Journal* 25 (1982): 500–509.

19. Juhani Sormunen, Richard Daft, and Don Parks, "Environmental Uncertainty and the Frequency and Mode of Chief Executive Scanning," *Academy of Management Proceedings* (1984): 312.

20. Daniel Jennings and James Lumpkin, "A Relationship Between Strategic Momentum and Environmental Scanning: An Empirical Analysis," Baylor University working paper.

21. Neil H. Snyder, "Environmental Volatility, Scanning Intensity and Organization Performance," *Journal of Contemporary Business* 10 (2nd Quarter 1981): 16.

22. This proposition is supported by a study conducted by Kefalas and Schoderbek, "Application and Implementation: Scanning the Business Environment, Some Empirical Results."

23. Yezdi M. Godiwalla, Wayne A. Meinhart, and William D. Warde, "Environmental Scanning—Does It Help the Chief Executive?" *Long Range Planning* 13 (October 1980): 87–99.

24. Adapted from Raymond Miles and Charles Snow, *Environmental Strategy and Organizational Structure* (New York: McGraw-Hill, 1978), pp. 69–72; Jay Galbraith and Robert Kazanjian, *Strategy Implementation: Structure, Systems, and Processes,* 2nd ed. (St. Paul, Minn.: West, 1986), pp. 126–27.

25. John Child, "Organizational Structure, Environment, and Performance: The Role of Strategic Choice," *Sociology* 6 (1972): 1–21.

26. "The Consumer Drives R. J. Reynolds Again," *Business Week,* 4 June 1984, pp. 92–99.

27. James Thompson, *Organizations in Action* (New York: McGraw-Hill, 1967), pp. 20–24.

28. David Yoffie and Sigrid Bergenstein, "Creating Political Advantage: The Rise of the Corporate Political Entrepreneur," *California Management Review* 28 (Fall, 1985): 124–37.

29. Merick Masters and Barry Baysinger, "The Determinants of Funds Raised By Corporate Political Action Committees: An Empirical Examination," *Academy of Management Journal* 28 (September 1985): 654–64.

30. Merick Masters and John Delaney, "Interunion Variation in Congressional Campaign Support," *Industrial Relations* 33 (1984): 410–16.

SUPPLEMENTARY READING

Diffenbach, John. "Corporate Environmental Analysis in Large U.S. Corporations." *Long Range Planning* 16 (June 1983): 107–16.

Dollinger, Marc. "Environmental Boundary Spanning and Information Processing Effects on Organizational Performance." *Academy of Management Journal* 27 (June 1984): 351–68.

Engledow, Jack L., and Lenz, R. T. "Whatever Happened to Environmental Analysis?" *Long Range Planning* 18 (April 1985): 93–106.

Ghoshal, Sumantra, and Kim, Seok K. "Building Effective Intelligence Systems for Competitive Advantage." *Sloan Management Review* 28 (Fall 1986): 49–58.

Gilad, Tamar, and Gilad, Benjamin. "SMR Forum: Business Intelligence—The Quiet Revolution." *Sloan Management Review* 27 (Summer 1986): 53–61.

Hambrick, Donald. "Environmental Scanning and Organizational Strategy." *Strategic Management Journal* 3 (January-February 1982): 159–74.

Jain, Subhash C. "Environmental Scanning in U.S. Corporations." *Long Range Planning* 17 (April 1984): 117–28.

Javidan, Mansour. "The Impact of Environmental Uncertainty on Long-Range Planning Practices of the U.S. Savings and Loan Industry." *Strategic Management Journal* 5 (October-December 1984): 381–92.

Lenz, R. T., and Engledow, Jack L. "Environmental Analysis Units and Strategic Decision-making: A Field Study of Selected 'Leading-edge' Corporations." *Strategic Management Journal* 7 (January-February 1986): 69–89.

Yoffie, David B., and Bergenstein, Sigrid. "Creating Political Advantage: The Rise of the Corporate Political Entrepreneur." *California Management Review* 28 (Fall 1985): 124–139.

SILVER DOLLAR CONCESSIONS

Jim Pittman, an MBA student at a large state university, works with one of his professors in analyzing various organizations. Jim and his professor have just completed a study of Silver Dollar Concessions (SDC).

Mark Hughes formed SDC four years ago with two silent partners. Hughes had graduated from college with a degree in chemistry and had attended medical school for two years before starting SDC. As a medical student, he had attended a county fair and become interested in the various carnival games.

The carnival industry consists of companies that set up various games of skill and chance at county fairs. These gaming companies, which travel from site to site, have a dubious reputation in our society. The stereotypical "carnie" is viewed as an unsavory character, and games are thought to be run deceptively and dishonestly. Hughes believed that a company could prosper by using state-of-the-art gaming equipment, innovative ideas, a human-relations philosophy towards employees, and sound management principles. Hughes and his partners acquired a carnival game and two vehicles with an investment of $75,000 and began working county fairs.

Hughes has been successful in applying his concepts. SDC now has twenty games and twelve vehicles, employs up to sixty sales people during peak periods, and has a revenue of nearly $5 million. Before-tax profit margins average almost 40 percent. While SDC has prospered, other gaming companies have folded. Hughes has the opportunity to acquire the assets of two other companies at bargain prices. He is concerned, however, about how certain environmental factors might affect his company in the future. Pittman and his professor have developed a list of environmental elements that could have an impact on SDC.

Question

1. What environmental elements would you expect to be listed?

WESTERN COLLEGE

Western is a private, coeducational college of twenty-five hundred students located on a 96-acre tract near a major southern city. The college consists of three schools, Nursing, Liberal Arts, and Business Administration. The provost of the college, Dr. Thomas Gates, is the actual internal administrator. Dr. Richard Warren, the college president, serves mainly as a boundary spanner and fund raiser. Western's interface with its environment involves the following four areas: (1) student recruitment and admissions, (2) public relations and sports, (3) alumni affairs, and (4) placement of graduates.

The student recruitment and admissions office consists of six full-time admissions counselors and fifteen students. Each counselor is assigned a particular geographical area and visits the high schools in that area. The visits are followed up by letters promoting Western College. Newsletters are mailed both to high school seniors who show an interest in Western and to high school counselors. The students assigned to recruitment and admissions visit certain high schools and present a brief program about life at Western. During these visits, the students are accompanied by a full-time admissions counselor.

The public relations and sports area has a director of public relations and an athletic director. The public relations director has a staff of two that prepares press releases describing favorable accomplishments achieved by the college. Press releases are distributed to various news media. The public relations department sponsors a group of student musicians known as the Western Chorus. The main purpose of this group is to increase the public's awareness of the school by performing at churches, banquets, retreats, fellowships, and other social functions. Another group of Western students is used to host prospective students.

Western College, which has varsity teams competing in basketball, baseball, and track, is a member of an athletic conference. Varsity teams have received national recognition on occasion. Western also has a strong intramural sports program administered by the athletic department.

Each of the college's three schools mails a quarterly publication to its former students containing alumni information and news of that particular school. The publications department is responsible for developing layouts, artwork, printing, and distribution of these publications.

The alumni affairs office has a director and a staff of three. Various alumni clubs located around the country have been formed. Personnel in the alumni affairs office maintain frequent contact with former students through newsletters, alumni club meetings, and an annual homecoming event.

Placement of graduates is done mainly by the various department chairpersons. There is no on-campus placement center. Very few companies visit the campus. Data sheets are kept on seniors and sent to prospective employers upon request. The department chairs have almost the same power as other faculty members. Deans control expenditures and salary increases. The chairperson, selected from the tenured faculty members of the department, serves a two-year term, and not more than two consecutive terms. A chairperson is responsible for developing class offerings and faculty assignments, recruiting new faculty members, teaching two courses, and performing the various placement activities.

Questions

1. Identify the weakest boundary-spanning area.
2. How could this area be improved?
3. What benefits might result from these improvements?

ORGANIZATIONAL OBJECTIVES

Purpose—The Mission Statement ☐
Objectives and Goals ☐ The Value of
Organizational Objectives ☐ Organizations
and Coalitions

NATURE OF STRATEGIC PLANNING

Concept of Strategy ☐ Strategic Planning
vs. Operating Management ☐ Uncertainty
and Judgment ☐ Benefits of Strategic
Planning

MAKING STRATEGIC DECISIONS

Identifying Opportunities and Threats ☐
Determining Strengths and Weaknesses
☐ Developing Strategic Alternatives ☐
Adopting A Basic Strategy ☐
Implementing the Strategy ☐
Evaluating the Strategy ☐ A Different
Perspective: Logical Incrementalism

Summary ☐ Key Concepts ☐ Discussion
Questions ☐ Notes ☐ Supplementary
Reading

CASES: Teague Services ☐ Blue Bird
Sweepers, Inc.

This chapter will enable you to

☐ Understand why organizations exist and
why they compete in certain industries
by considering the organization's
objectives and the coalitions of interest
that are reflected in those objectives.

☐ Explain the importance of strategic
planning, how it differs from operating
management, and the various
elements involved in strategy
formulation.

☐ Visualize the processes involved in
formulating, implementing, and
evaluating organizational strategy.

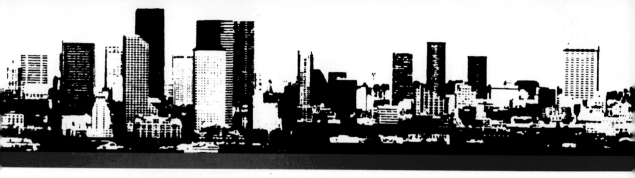

CHAPTER 4
STRATEGIC PLANNING

All organizations have objectives, strategies, and an existing mission, even if they are not consciously designed or communicated.[1] This chapter explains the nature of the mission statement, objectives, and strategies.

ORGANIZATIONAL OBJECTIVES

Purpose—The Mission Statement

Each organization is unique because of the values, beliefs, and philosophies of its stakeholders—the people and groups with an interest in the organization. This uniqueness is reflected in the organization's *mission statement*, "a broadly defined but enduring statement of purpose that distinguishes a business from other firms of its type and identifies the scope of its operations in product and market terms."[2]

Both profit and nonprofit organizations have mission statements, as shown in Figure 4–1. The mission statement of any business should provide answers to the following general questions: (1) What is our business? (2) What will it become? and (3) What should it become?

A well-defined mission statement is important in formulating and implementing strategies effectively. For example, Drucker states that organizational members develop an increased awareness of purpose when top managers de-

FIGURE 4–1   Sample mission statements

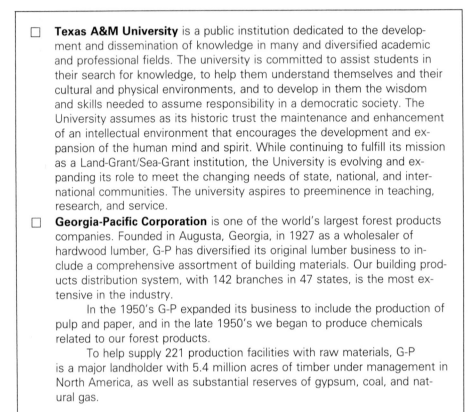

☐ **Texas A&M University** is a public institution dedicated to the development and dissemination of knowledge in many and diversified academic and professional fields. The university is committed to assist students in their search for knowledge, to help them understand themselves and their cultural and physical environments, and to develop in them the wisdom and skills needed to assume responsibility in a democratic society. The University assumes as its historic trust the maintenance and enhancement of an intellectual environment that encourages the development and expansion of the human mind and spirit. While continuing to fulfill its mission as a Land-Grant/Sea-Grant institution, the University is evolving and expanding its role to meet the changing needs of state, national, and international communities. The university aspires to preeminence in teaching, research, and service.

☐ **Georgia-Pacific Corporation** is one of the world's largest forest products companies. Founded in Augusta, Georgia, in 1927 as a wholesaler of hardwood lumber, G-P has diversified its original lumber business to include a comprehensive assortment of building materials. Our building products distribution system, with 142 branches in 47 states, is the most extensive in the industry.

In the 1950's G-P expanded its business to include the production of pulp and paper, and in the late 1950's we began to produce chemicals related to our forest products.

To help supply 221 production facilities with raw materials, G-P is a major landholder with 5.4 million acres of timber under management in North America, as well as substantial reserves of gypsum, coal, and natural gas.

SOURCE: Texas A&M University, *Bulletin and General Catalog,* 1986–1987, p. 81; Georgia Pacific Corporation, Annual Report, 1985, p. 1.

velop and communicate a clear mission statement.[3] Because many conglomerates of the 1960s had no clear concept of their purpose except "to make money" or "to grow," they expanded wildly by acquiring unrelated businesses and eventually experienced serious financial consequences.[4]

Effective mission statements require only infrequent modification. They should always be sufficiently flexible to meet major environmental changes.[5]

Objectives and Goals

Organizations come into existence as a result of purposeful action by one or more individuals. Once an organization has defined its purpose, the next step is to develop what it attempts to accomplish. Organizational objectives and goals are the results (or ends) that the organization wishes to accomplish within its mission. The terms *objectives* and *goals* are used in many different ways in management literature. Some authors use the terms interchangeably; some use *objectives* to refer to long-term results and *goals* to refer to short-term results. Some authors reverse those meanings. In this textbook, the terms are used synonymously throughout.

As Figure 4–2 indicates, objectives are an outgrowth of the organization's mission statement. Surveys indicate that most organizations have multiple objectives. One study of eighty-two organizations found that the number of goals any one company set ranged from one to eighteen, with the average company having five to six.[6] Too few goals may result in neglect of critical areas in the environment, while too many may overly disperse the efforts of employees.[7]

Goals may be either *short-range* or *long-range.* A survey of 228 companies headquartered in Texas indicated that the majority of firms established goals for three to five years into the future. Fewer than 7 percent set goals for periods in excess of ten years, and about 5 percent had no long-range goals at all (these were mostly small firms).[8] The planning horizon for an organization depends to a large extent upon its environment. Public utilities, which operate in a regulated, fairly predictable environment, often have longer range goals than construction companies, which face more dynamic, unpredictable environments.

As is evident in Figure 4–3, organizations establish goals in several areas. These goals reflect the organization's various stakeholders. For instance, many organizations set goals in such areas as customer service, return on stockholders' investment, treatment of employees, development of managers, and responsibility toward the local community.

FIGURE 4–2 Mission and objectives

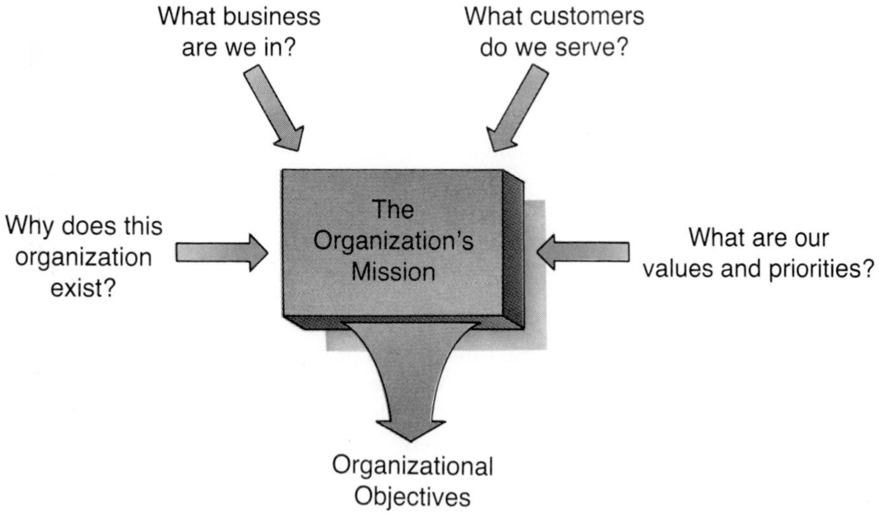

FIGURE 4-3 An example of organizational objectives

Objectives of Hewlett-Packard

Profit Objective	To achieve sufficient profit to finance our company growth and to provide the resources we need to achieve our other corporate objectives.
Customer Objectives	To provide products and services of the highest quality and the greatest possible value to our customers, thereby gaining and holding their respect and loyalty.
Technology Objective	To participate in those fields of interest that build upon our technology and customer base, that offer opportunities for continuing growth, and that enable us to make a needed and profitable contribution.
Growth Objective	To let our growth be limited only by our profits and our ability to develop and produce innovative products that satisfy real customer needs.
Employee Objective	To help HP people share in the company's success which they make possible; to provide employment security based on their performance; to ensure them a safe and pleasant work environment; to recognize their individual achievements; and to help them gain a sense of satisfaction and accomplishment from their work.
Management Objective	To foster initiative and creativity by allowing the individual great freedom of action in attaining well-defined objectives.
Society Objectives	To honor our obligations to society by being an economic, intellectual, and social asset to each nation and each community in which we operate.

Peter Drucker believes that objectives need to be set in all areas upon which the organization's survival depends. This, according to him, requires objectives in the areas described:[9]

A business must first be able to create a customer. There is, therefore, need for a *marketing objective*. Businesses must be able to innovate or else their competitors will obsolesce them. There is need for an *innovation objective*. All businesses depend on the three factors of production of the economist, that is, on the human *resource*, the *capital resource*, and *physical resources*. There must be objectives for their supply, their employment, and their development. The resources must be employed productively and their productivity has to grow if the business is to survive. There is need, therefore, for *productivity objectives*. Business exists in society and community and, therefore, has to discharge social responsibilities, at least to the point where it takes responsibility for its impact upon the environment. Therefore objectives in respect to the *social dimensions* of business are needed.

Finally, there is need for *profit*—otherwise none of the objectives can be attained. They all require effort, that is, cost. And they can be financed only out of the profits of a business. They all entail risks; they all, therefore, require a profit to cover the risk of potential losses.

Although nonbusiness organizations have no profit objective, they must nevertheless deal with the efficient use of scarce resources. Hospital administrators, for example, are expected to avoid waste in providing the best possible health care with the limited resources they have available. Their efficiency objective is comparable to the profit objective of a business organization.

A distinction must be made between *official* and *operative* objectives.[10] Official objectives are those that management espouses publicly. A state university president, for instance, may declare that a major goal of the university is to provide an education of the highest quality. The means to this end are termed operative goals—those objectives that the university actively pursues. These specify whether the university will emphasize the liberal arts or professional schools, whether resources will be allocated more heavily to graduate or undergraduate programs, and whether the faculty should emphasize teaching or research. Operative goals tell us what the organization is actually trying to do.

In some situations, operative goals may not be closely related to the organization's official statements. Take the public pronouncement of the university president above, for instance. In light of current enrollment trends, the overriding operative goal of the university may actually be to increase its enrollment, especially if its budget from the state is based on student head count. This goal is unlikely to be highly publicized, particularly if its attainment requires a relaxing of admissions standards.

The Value of Organizational Objectives

Objectives are vital to organizational success because they provide direction and are essential to managers in (1) identifying environmental opportunities, (2) guiding decision making, (3) facilitating teamwork, and (4) encouraging consistency.

Identifying Environmental Opportunities.   The environment presents both dangers and opportunities. By careful selection of objectives, management may exploit those opportunities and avoid those dangers. One value of organizational objectives, therefore, is proper orientation of the organization to its environment.

Guiding Decisions.   Objectives also provide a focus for policy making and other management decisions. Business decisions and policies—in production, sales, finance, and so on—should be directed to the achievement of the firm's objectives. As an example, suppose that a chemical manufacturer desires to lead not only in the production of standard chemicals but also in research and the introduction of new products. The company's personnel policies and practices must provide for the recruitment and retention of creative scientists for its research laboratories. Financial planning must permit the investment of large amounts in research and facilities over a long period of time before a dollar is ever realized from these investments. Production planning must be sufficiently flexible and imaginative to adapt to new production techniques and to assist in the development of production processes for new products. Marketing personnel must be able to assess and develop markets to permit exploitation of new discoveries originating in the laboratory.

Facilitating Teamwork.   Clearly formulated objectives enable all parts of an organization to work toward the same goal. Production and sales departments need not work at cross purposes if there is a common objective. If production policies call for a product of high quality, advertising will not stress price to the exclusion of quality. Nor will prices be set on the basis of a competitor's inferior line of products.

Encouraging Consistency.   Clear objectives also encourage a consistency in management, planning, and decision making over a period of time. Long-run goals provide caution against action that is merely expedient in the short run. Formulation of explicit objectives thus provides a stabilizing force in month-to-month and year-to-year management decisions. Mere implicit recognition of goals, however, involves the dangers of inconsistency, lack of coordination among departments, and temptation to compromise. If a student is not thoroughly committed to a college education, for example, the attraction of a good job or marriage may easily sidetrack that individual.

Organizations and Coalitions

In view of the numerous parties involved in the process of forming objectives, some writers have suggested that an organization should be thought of as a *coalition of interests*. In other words, organizational objectives in some way represent a consensus that has been hammered out in a manner acceptable to the various participants. Decisions are rarely the product of individual executives who have sufficient power to decide issues without regard for the views of others.

A variety of internal interests and external forces constrain the manager's choice of goals. It is unrealistic to think that a business manager sets objectives solely for the benefit of shareholders, totally apart from the consideration of other interests. This is simply impossible. Any manager who attempted to maximize profits by lowering wage rates or reducing quality would immediately experience severe opposition.

Managers, particularly top-level managers, play a unique role in the establishment of objectives. They must strike a balance among the various interests and participants. In other words, they must balance the pressures from the coalition members so that the continuing participation of each is assured.[11]

NATURE OF STRATEGIC PLANNING

While objectives are the ends that management hopes to attain, the means to those ends are the organization's *strategy*. *Strategic planning* is concerned with the development of broad or basic programs for the future, and it must be followed with planning of a more detailed nature.

Concept of Strategy

An important task of a top manager involves matching the strengths and weaknesses of the organization with opportunities and threats in the environment. The characteristics of the match constitute a strategy.[12]

Mintzberg describes strategy as a series of decisions.[13] In business firms, *strategic decisions* are concerned with such issues as breadth of product line, geographical scope, industry position, extent of vertical integration, and orientation toward growth. By making strategic decisions, top management determines the position of the firm relative to its environment. At any given time, the firm's orientation to the environment may be described as its *strategic posture*. Changes in this posture require redeployment of the firm's assets into new configurations. Strategic decisions express the firm's basic purposes and the direction it wishes to take in relating to and serving the society of which it is a part.

Many large corporations have adopted formal strategic planning during recent years. A study of 104 large manufacturing firms revealed that 90 percent engaged in some form of long-range planning. Surprisingly, two-fifths of those organizations had not instituted their formal planning programs until after 1975.[14] As environmental complexity and instability continue to increase, so will the adoption of more formal long-range planning processes.[15]

Strategic Planning vs. Operating Management

As stated earlier, strategic planning is concerned with the development of broad or basic programs for the future involving how top management adapts the organization to the environment. *Operating management* is involved with the day-to-day operation of the organization's business. It is concerned with producing and delivering the organization's goods or services as effectively and efficiently as possible.

Some management scholars and top managers have recently held that many organizations have not properly considered the capabilities and limita-

STRATEGIC PLANNING: OPERATING MANAGERS VS. PROFESSIONAL PLANNERS

An article in *Business Week* suggests that who does strategic planning in some U.S. corporations is changing. In such firms as GE, GM, and Eaton, line managers are replacing professional planners as strategists. Previously, a group of professionals with the distinct function of strategic planning had reported directly to a top manager. These professionals had become a powerful influence, and problems developed between the professional planners and operating managers. Strategies were not being properly implemented because the operating managers believed they had been bypassed during the formulation of strategy. Operating managers were made to feel as though they were second-class citizens by the professionals hired as strategic planners. Strategic planning was becoming less creative and more of a bureaucratic process: mechanical and routine, drawing further and further away from the realities of competitors and customers.

Both GM and GE decentralized the process of strategic planning by making their operating managers responsible for that function. GM now views the professional planner's role as being a catalyst for change rather than one of doing the planning. Professional planners have been transferred from headquarters to the "down-in-the-trenches" atmosphere of the operating divisions.

SOURCE: Based on "The New Breed of Strategic Planner," *Business Week,* 17 September 1984, pp. 62–66, 68. Also see Daniel H. Gray, "Uses and Misuses of Strategic Planning," *Harvard Business Review* 64 (January-February 1986): 89–97.

tions of the operations part of the business, especially in manufacturing, in formulating and implementing their strategic planning processes.[16] The functions of operational planning will be more fully discussed in chapter 5.

Uncertainty and Judgment

Of all the types of decisions required in business operation, strategic decisions involve the greatest uncertainty. Their complexity grows out of the possibility of their changing the firm's relationship to the environment. More routine decisions are based on the framework of the firm as given and are less uncertain. The environment, with its changing patterns, at times defies prediction and intelligent forecasting.

This does not mean that the strategist lacks any data whatsoever. It does mean that the issues are typically fuzzy and the best strategy unclear. As a result, the top-level manager must use more subjective judgment in strategy decisions than is required for more routine decisions.

Underlying strategic decisions is the need for the organization to develop a *distinctive competence,* that is, the ability to do some things particularly well in comparison to its competitors.[17] One survey of 247 managers in eighty-eight companies indicated that "top managers make deliberate choices to develop strategies and distinctive competences quite different from those of competing organizations, even though the environmental demands faced by companies within the same industry may be generally similar."[18] Some of the areas in which an organization may develop a distinctive competence are discussed in a later section of this chapter.

Benefits of Strategic Planning

When the new feature "Corporate Strategies" was introduced in *Business Week,* the publisher stated that strategic planning is a business concept which has become a "major thrust and emphasis" in the management of American corporations.[19] Strategic planning allows the top management to:[20]

> take advantage of key environmental opportunities, to minimize the impact of external threats, to capitalize upon internal strengths, and to overcome internal weaknesses. This approach to decision making can be an effective vehicle for generating synergy and *esprit de corps* among all managers and employees. This benefit alone can make the difference between a successful and an unsuccessful business.

CHRYSLER AND STRATEGIC PLANNING

Lee Iacocca's approach to turning Chrysler around is an outstanding example of how an organization can benefit from strategic planning. Facing severe internal weaknesses and external threats in 1979, Iacocca formulated and implemented a strategy to improve Chrysler's position. This strategic approach was a major reason for Chrysler's receiving federal government loan guarantees. In 1979, Chrysler experienced a net loss of $1.1 billion on sales of $11.4 billion. In 1985, net income was a positive $1.6 billion on sales of $21.3 billion.

SOURCE: Adapted from Lee Iacocca, "The Rescue and Resuscitation of Chrysler," *The Journal of Business Strategy* 4 (Summer 1983): 23–29; and "America's Most Valuable Companies," *Business Week,* 18 April 1986, pp. 64–5.

Organizations using strategic planning tend to be more successful and profitable than those that do not, according to a large number of studies.[21] For example, one study reported that up to 80 percent of possible improvement in an organization's profitability is achieved by changes in the firm's direction.[22] A longitudinal study of 101 retail, service, and manufacturing firms for a three-year period reported that firms using strategic planning tended to show significant improvements in sales, profitability, and productivity compared to firms without systematic planning activities.[23]

MAKING STRATEGIC DECISIONS

In formulating an organization's strategy, top managers often use a process similar to that described in Figure 4–4.

Identifying Opportunities and Threats

An important aspect of strategic planning is that top managers should formulate strategies (1) to take advantage of external opportunities and (2) to deter-

FIGURE 4–4 A process of making strategic decisions

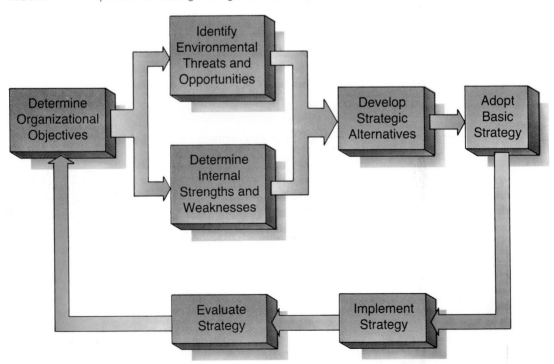

mine the risks and threats that the organization faces or will face. These opportunities and threats arise from both the elements of the specific environment and the elements of the general environment. Effective approaches for identifying these opportunities and threats were presented in chapter 3.

Determining Strengths and Weaknesses

Organizations perform various functions, including marketing, finance, production, personnel, and research and development. Internal strengths are the particular functions that an organization performs extremely well. Managers of successful organizations pursue strategies that capitalize on internal strengths. Deficiencies or weaknesses in functional areas can inhibit the organization's success.

There are innumerable functional interrelationships that can occur within an organization.[24] For example, marketing and production managers will face a limited number of options if the organization has severe financial problems. Yet a marketing staff that has achieved outstanding performance could inspire other functional areas to set higher goals.

Systematic methods for conducting strength-weakness assessments are not yet well developed.[25] An increasing number of organizations, though, are using the internal audits employed to identify the interrelationships that exist among the various functional areas to identify strengths and weaknesses as well.[26] The evaluation, in most cases, focuses on the following:

1. Financial capacity
2. Product/market position
3. Human resources
4. Physical plant and equipment
5. Technology base
6. Research and development programs
7. Production system
8. Marketing and distribution systems

The organization will have strengths in some of these areas, increasing the number of strategic alternatives available to it. These are areas in which an organization may wish to develop a distinctive competence. In other areas, it may be weak, reducing its possible options. Of particular consideration is the extent to which the firm's resources are already committed. Even though a firm may be strong in some areas, a prior long-term commitment of its resources may severely limit its strategic alternatives.

During the last decade, many corporations have become more analytical in considering the deployment of their resources. One popular analytical approach has been developed by the Boston Consulting Group. This approach can be visualized in terms of the matrix display illustrated in Figure 4–5, which

FIGURE 4–5 The business
portfolio matrix

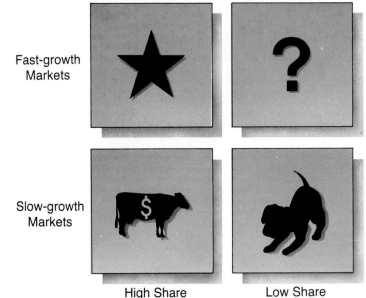

shows rate of growth for a market as a whole on the vertical axis and a company's share of that market on the horizontal axis.*

The market for microcomputers, for example, is "fast growth," while the market for candy is "slow growth." A major corporation operating in several different industries may have some divisions or segments of its business in each of the four quadrants. A multiproduct company, in other words, may simultaneously have "stars," "cows," "dogs," and "question marks."

A firm would naturally prefer to have stars instead of dogs! In considering the deployment or redeployment of its resources in the four quadrants of the matrix, management might reason somewhat as follows:

□ *Stars* (high share of fast-growth market): Inject additional money and attempt to gain an even larger share of the market.
□ *Question Marks* (low share of fast-growth market): Consider fighting for more market share but recognize danger of getting into a "cash trap."
□ *Cows* (high share of slow-growth market): Milk the "cash cows"—that is, remove money and reinvest in stars or possibly question marks.
□ *Dogs* (low share of slow-growth market): Eliminate them.

---

*The matrix described here was originally developed by Alan J. Zakon of the Boston Consulting Group and William W. Wommack, vice chairman of Mead Corporation, in 1967. This analytical approach has its critics. Many major corporations accept it, however, and the Boston Consulting Group has become the country's leader in business strategy consultation. For further reading on this and other analytical approaches, see Walter Kiechel, III, "Playing by the Rules of the Corporate Strategy Game," *Fortune,* 24 September 1979, 110–16.

SELF-SCRUTINY AT IBM

To combat a problem of reduced earnings, management at IBM introduced a strategic plan to identify external opportunities and improve internal weaknesses. Despite being a very profitable company, IBM experienced seven straight quarters of declining earnings and revenues from 1985 to 1986. Although economic conditions contributed to the situation, the problem resulted primarily from the company's becoming too bureaucratic and having a view of the world computer market that was out of date.

The chief executive of IBM, John Akers, announced a strategic plan to combat declining earnings. The plan included the following factors:

- □ a long-term strategy to diversify into high-margin software and services
- □ an intermediate-term strategy of introducing new products consisting of more powerful personal computers
- □ a three-part short-term strategy of (1) cutting costs to improve margins, (2) aggressive marketing to meet customer needs, and (3) streamlining management to eliminate layers of bureaucracy and to become more responsive to a changing environment.

SOURCE: Based on "How IBM Is Fighting Back," *Business Week*, 17 November 1986, pp. 15–157.

The underlying idea holds that an increase in a company's volume leads to reduction of production costs. This results, in turn, from the operation of what Bruce Henderson has termed the "experience curve." Practice tends to make perfect, and production costs reportedly decline 20 to 30 percent in real terms whenever experience is doubled. As a result of these forces, a company which increases its volume by expanding market share and/or by concentrating in fast-growth markets may be able to increase its efficiency and profitability. Although this is only one of various analytical methods, it illustrates the systematic corporate evaluation of resource deployment.[27]

The matrix has some limitations, as do all analytical techniques. One limitation is that viewing all businesses as either a star, question mark, cash cow, or dog may be an oversimplification. For example, some businesses are not easily classified because they may fall in the center of the matrix.

A second limitation is that the matrix does not consider change over time. Changes in market rate of growth or the organization's share of the market are examples. For instance, General Foods, at one time, managed its coffee business as a cash cow. But with the advent of automatic coffee makers in the home, that market became more volatile, resulting in the development of new varieties of ground coffees. General Foods' top management believed that though the company did not miss those opportunities, it was "a little late and not as aggressive in pursuing them because of the cash-cow concept."[28]

Developing Strategic Alternatives

Development of strategic alternatives involves an integration of data concerning environmental risks and opportunities with data concerning available resources. In the case of the going concern, one alternative is to continue doing what it is already doing. This approach is the simplest and may be the best, but only for a time. A corporation must eventually modify its strategy because of the inevitable changes in the environment. Other alternatives are needed for serious consideration and comparison with the status quo.

The development of strategic alternatives is a creative process that requires a vision of the various possibilities for meeting the needs of the industry. Courage is required to propose a drastic change because of the great uncertainty involved. Also, proposed changes in strategy tend to conflict with existing strategy, the accepted way of doing things. Changes pose difficulties, even

A TROUBLING ACQUISITION

One strategy that top managers use in improving their competitive advantage is to acquire other businesses. In some instances, acquisitions can be troublesome. For example, Mobil Corporation announced in 1978 that its acquisition of Montgomery Ward "provided the potential to fuel" Mobil's growth. Over the next four years, Montgomery Ward had losses amounting to nearly $400 million and required over $600 million in cash infusions and debt forgiveness.

Retail industry analysts reported that Montgomery Ward had the worst store location strategy among the three major retail chains. The majority of Ward's stores are in troublesome inner-city locations or second-rate malls, or they are low-profit freestanding stores. Ward's did not have a plan to become "anchors" in the best regional malls, and they are now having difficulty getting "upscale" customers to trade in their stores.

In this instance, Mobil failed to recognize the weaknesses of Montgomery Ward.

SOURCE: Based on "Mobil Tries To Make The Best of A Bad Buy," *Business Week*, 20 May 1985, p. 61.

in contemplation, because of traditional and comfortable patterns of thinking and operation.

Adopting a Basic Strategy

The decision as to which strategy to adopt is difficult and requires much subjective judgment. The difficulty in making this choice arises from the fuzzy nature of the problem, the existence of unknowns that will become known in the future, and the paucity of available information.

Individual managers possess personal values that also inevitably affect strategy determination. One manager may wish to gain or hold a given share of the market. Another may emphasize product specialization or social values. The importance of individual leadership is evident as we think of companies that have shown the "stamp" of their leaders—IBM, Chrysler, Polaroid, and Ford, for example. The opportunity and need for subjective judgment allow the introduction of personal values, philosophy, and ambitions.[29]

Whatever factors are included in the strategic decision, it is important that such a decision be made and that it be made clear to members of the organization. Otherwise, the company's direction is unclear, and the management team tends to move in various directions. Uncertainty appeared to characterize the W. T. Grant Company shortly before its collapse in 1975:[30]

> Worse yet, early on Grant seemingly could not make up its mind what kind of store it was. "There was a lot of dissension within the company whether we should go the K-Mart route or go after the Ward's and Penney position," says a former executive. "Ed Staley and Lou Lustenberger were at loggerheads over the issue, with the upshot being we took a position between the two and that consequently stood for nothing."

The strategic decision determines any changes to be made in the deployment of company resources. If a new strategy is to be followed, company assets must be recast into an appropriate mold for the new strategy. This often takes time because of the fixed nature of many assets, and rapid changes can be costly.

Redeployment of assets concerns more than financial and physical assets. Management groups, for example, have educational and experiential backgrounds that are related to existing strategy. Modification of that strategy may require changes in the management staff.

Implementing the Strategy

After the strategy has been formulated, it must then be implemented. A poorly implemented strategy can produce unsatisfactory results just as easily as a poorly formulated one.

Strategy formulation is an analytical and conceptual task, whereas implementation involves administrative and behavioral actions.[31] Middle- and

FIGURE 4–6 Strategic implementation process

Element	Activity
Structure, culture	Design the organization's structure and culture to match the strategy.
People	Ensure that middle- and lower-level managers have the right background, skills, and attributes to make the strategy work.
Rewards	Install a reward system for top-, middle-, and lower-level managers to ensure that desired behavior results.
Information	Design the necessary information processing system where useful, timely, and accurate information is distributed to all managers.
Control	Install a control system both to measure actual versus desired performance and to provide feedback to all managers.
Policies	Employ the right functional policies to make the strategy work.
Resources	Allocate resources to the functional and operating units in support of the strategies approved for those units.

SOURCE: Adapted from Jay Galbraith and Robert Kazanjian, *Strategy Implementation: Structure, Systems, and Process*, Second Edition (St. Paul, Minn.: West Publishing, 1986), pp. 97–100, 102–9.

lower-level managers put strategy into practice. Although top management must decide overall strategy, they need the support of middle and lower management to make the strategy successful. Every functional area of the firm is involved in implementing the strategy and accomplishing the desired objectives. Figure 4–6 describes the implementation process.

Evaluating the Strategy

An organization's competitive strategy needs to be periodically reevaluated to prevent deterioration and obsolescence of the basic strategic approach. An evaluation process consisting of three phases can be used by top management to evaluate existing strategy. These phases include:

☐ Reviewing the external opportunities and threats that are the basis of current strategies. The organization's external environment changes in various ways that can affect strategic decisions.

☐ Measuring organizational performance by comparing expected versus actual results of strategy implementation efforts. This evaluation process requires criteria that are measurable and verifiable. The organization's goals and objectives can be used for judging the effectiveness of both strategic decisions and their implementation as time goes by. Some common criteria used for evaluation purposes include market share, sales growth, and profitability.

□ Taking corrective action when deviations occur between expected and actual performance. For example, certain actions may be required, such as changing the organization's mission, revising objectives, altering the organization's structure, replacing key individuals, selling divisions, or acquiring new businesses. Note that taking corrective action does not always mean existing strategies will be discontinued or new strategies formulated. It does mean, however, that revised strategy formulation and implementation approaches should be considered.

A Different Perspective: Logical Incrementalism

A somewhat different view of strategic planning can be found in the perspective termed *logical incrementalism*.[32] According to this view, because of a rapidly changing environment, managers often have insufficient time and information to undertake a full, formal analysis of all possible strategic alternatives. Hence, they deal with events in an incremental fashion, as illustrated in the following example:[33]

> General Motors' top management only incrementally restructured its various car lines as it understood, step-by-step, the way in which the oil crisis and environmental demands would affect the viability of each existing divisional and dealership structure. In the aggregate these amounted to the greatest shift in balance and positioning among GM's automobile lines since Alfred P. Sloan.

The basic idea, of course, is that management sometimes does not know precisely its ultimate objective or its entire strategy. Bits and pieces of the strategy unfold incrementally as managers respond to a constantly changing environment. This incremental approach is necessitated by several factors, among them a lack of information about the environment, the difficulty of predicting the effect of various strategic decisions, and the resistance that major organizational changes usually encounter. Incremental movements allow the organization to experiment with various approaches, to learn, and to build awareness and commitment among those who must implement the decisions.

SUMMARY

An organization's *mission statement* distinguishes it from other organizations and identifies the scope of its operations. Objectives or goals are an outgrowth of the organization's mission statement and are developed for a number of areas to reflect its environment and stakeholders. Establishing objectives benefits an organization in several ways. For example, objectives provide a basis for decision making and for teamwork among departments and individuals. To some extent, organizational objectives reflect a consensus among the various internal and external participants.

Objectives are the ends that management hopes to attain, whereas the means to the ends are the organization's *strategy*. *Strategic planning* involves the decisions made by top managers as they attempt to match the internal strengths and weaknesses of the organization with external environmental opportunities and threats. Because of the uncertain future, and the complexity of planning, strategic planning necessitates subjective judgment. This judgment is consistently directed toward the development and maintenance of a *distinctive competence*—the ability of the organization to do some things better than its competitors. Strategic decisions involve choices concerning such factors as product/market scope, corporate growth, innovation, and geographic scope.

Developing a strategy for an organization involves a series of steps. These include identifying external opportunities and threats, determining internal strengths and weaknesses, developing alternatives, and then formulating a particular strategy. After formulation, strategies have to be implemented. Finally, the last step involves an evaluation of how actual accomplishments relate to the organization's desired objectives. Corrective action is needed when significant deviations occur. During periods of rapid environmental change, managers may follow a policy of *logical incrementalism,* that is, developing strategy in bits and pieces as they begin to understand the situation and secure the commitment of their subordinates.

KEY CONCEPTS

Mission statement	Coalition of interests
Short-term results	Strategic decisions
Long-term results	Operating decisions
Stakeholders	Experience curve
Multiple objectives	Strategy evaluation
Official objectives	Strategy formulation
Operative objectives	Strategy implementation
Planning horizon	Logical incrementalism

DISCUSSION QUESTIONS

1. What is the relationship between the organization's *mission statement* and its *objectives?*
2. Distinguish between *official* and *operative* goals. Give an example.
3. Why is it necessary for business organizations to have more than a profit objective?

4. In what way does a clearly stated objective enable all parts of an organization to work effectively together?
5. Define *organizational strategy* and explain its relationship to objectives.
6. What is the difference between strategic planning and operating management?
7. Compare and contrast strategy formulation and strategy implementation.
8. Why is it that a good strategy, selected carefully with proper consideration of all relevant variables, cannot be continued indefinitely?
9. What is meant by an organization's *distinctive competence?* Give examples of organizations which have attained distinctive competence in one or more areas.
10. How can the Boston Consulting Group's business portfolio matrix aid management in making strategic decisions? What are the limitations, if any, of this matrix?
11. Discuss how the phrase "taking corrective action" of the strategic evaluation process differs from strategy implementation.

NOTES

1. Fred R. David, *Fundamentals of Strategic Management* (Columbus, Ohio: Merrill, 1986), p. 58.
2. John A. Pearce II, "The Company Mission as a Strategic Tool," *Sloan Management Review* 23 (Spring 1982): 15.
3. Peter Drucker, *Management: Tasks, Responsibilities, and Practices* (New York: Harper & Row, 1974), p. 61.
4. Lester Digman, *Strategic Management: Concepts, Decisions, Cases* (Plano, Tex.: Business Publications, 1986), p. 47.
5. Daniel S. Cochran, Fred R. David, and C. Kendrick Gibson, "A Framework for Developing an Effective Mission Statement," *Journal of Business Strategies* 2 (Fall 1985): 4–17.
6. Y. K. Shetty, "New Look at Corporate Goals," *California Management Review* 22 (Winter 1979): 74.
7. Ibid.
8. Kamal M. Abouzeid, "Corporate Goal Identification and Achievement," *Managerial Planning* 29 (November-December 1980): 17–22.
9. Drucker, *Management: Tasks, Responsibilities, Practices,* p. 100. Reprinted by permission.
10. Charles Perrow, "The Analysis of Goals in Complex Organizations," *American Sociological Review* 26 (December 1961): 855.
11. For a more extensive review of this topic, see the following: Richard M. Cyert and James G. March, *A Behavioral Theory of the Firm* (Englewood Cliffs, N.J.: Prentice-Hall, 1963); and Edwin A. Murray, Jr., "Strategic Choice as a Negotiated Outcome," *Management Science* 24 (May 1978): 960–72. A model of how coalitions influence strategy in organizations is provided by V. K. Narayanan and Liam Fahey, "The Micro-Politics of Strategy Formulation," *Academy of Management Review* 7 (January 1982): 25–34. They conclude that effective strategic management involves not only emphasis on the content of the strategy but equal attention to the internal political processes within the organization.

12. Charles W. Hofer and Dan Schendel, *Strategy Formulation: Analytical Concepts* (St. Paul, Minn.: West, 1978), p. 4.

13. Henry Mintzberg, "Patterns in Strategy Formulation," *Management Science* 24 (1978), 936.

14. Noel Capon, John U. Farley, and James Hulbert, "International Diffusion of Corporate and Strategic Planning Practices," *Columbia Journal of World Business* 15 (Fall 1980): 5–6.

15. William M. Lindsay and Leslie W. Rue, "Impact of the Organization's Environment on the Long-Range Planning Process: A Contingency View," *Academy of Management Journal* 23 (September 1980): 385–404.

16. For a good discussion of this situation see the following: Steven C. Wheelwright, "Reflecting Corporate Strategy in Manufacturing Decisions," *Business Horizons* (February 1978): 57–66; and Wheelwright, "New Breed of Strategic Planner: Number-Crunching Professionals Are Giving Way to Line Managers," *Business Week*, 17 September 1984, pp. 62–68.

17. Charles C. Snow and Lawrence G. Hrebiniak, "Strategy, Distinctive Competence, and Organizational Performance," *Administrative Science Quarterly* 25 (June 1980): 317–36.

18. Ibid., p. 334.

19. "Publisher's Memo," *Business Week*, 9 January 1978, p. 5.

20. Ibid.

21. For a comprehensive overview of this area and some tentative explanations for conflicting findings, see Charles B. Shrader, Lew Taylor, and Dan R. Dalton, "Strategic Planning and Organizational Performance: A Critical Appraisal," *Journal of Management* 10 (Summer 1984): 149–71.

22. Sidney Schoeffler, R. Buzzell, and D. Heany, "Impact of Strategic Planning on Profit Performance," *Harvard Business Review* (March 1974): 137.

23. Richard B. Robinson, Jr., "The Importance of Outsiders in Small Firm Strategic Planning," *Academy of Management Journal* 25 (March 1982): 80.

24. David, *Fundamentals of Strategic Management*, p. 148.

25. Stanley Harper, "A Developmental Approach to Performance Appraisal," *Business Horizons* (September-October 1983): 69.

26. David, *Fundamentals of Strategic Management*, p. 150.

27. A popular alternative to this matrix is GE's nine-cell planning grid. A good discussion of this grid can be found in William F. Glueck and Lawrence R. Jauch, *Business Policy and Strategic Management* (New York: McGraw-Hill, 1984): 293–294. Various other matrices are presented in David, *Fundamentals of Strategic Management*, pp. 198–230.

28. Richard G. Hamermesh, "Making Planning Strategic," *Harvard Business Review* 64 (July-August 1986): 117.

29. For a discussion of the effect of one aspect of the CEO's personality on the organization's strategy, see Danny Miller, Manfred Kets De Vries, and Jean-Marie Toulouse, "Top Executive Locus of Control and Its Relationship to Strategy-Making, Structure, and Environment," *Academy of Management Journal* 25 (June 1982): 237–253.

30. "How W. T. Grant Lost $175 Million Last Year," *Business Week*, 24 February 1975, p. 75.

31. Jay Galbraith and Robert Kazanjian, *Strategy Implementation: Structure, Systems, and Process*, 2nd ed. (St. Paul, Minn.: West, 1986), p. 91.

32. James Brian Quinn, "Strategic Change: 'Logical Incrementalism,'" *Sloan Management Review* 20 (Fall 1978): 7–21; and "Managing Strategic Change," *Sloan Management Review* 21 (Summer 1980): 3–20.

33. Quinn, "Strategic Change," p. 10.

SUPPLEMENTARY READING

Barney, Jay. "Types of Competition and the Theory of Strategy: Toward An Integrative Framework." *Academy of Management Review* 11 (October 1986): 791–800.

Camerer, Colin. "Redirecting Research in Business Policy and Strategy." *Strategic Management Journal* 6 (January-March 1985): 1–95.

Drucker, Peter F. "Entrepreneurial Strategies." *California Management Review* 27 (Winter 1985): 9–25.

Fredrickson, James. "The Comprehensiveness of Strategic Decision Processes: Extensions, Observations, Future Directions." *Academy of Management Journal* 27 (June 1984): 445–466.

Ghemawat, Pankaj. "Building Strategy on the Experience Curve." *Harvard Business Review* 63 (March-April 1985): 143–49.

————. "Sustainable Advantage." *Harvard Business Review* 64 (September-October 1986): 53–58.

Ginter, Peter M.; Rucks, Andrew C.; and Duncan, W. Jack. "Planners' Perceptions of the Strategic Management Process." *Journal of Management Studies* 22 (November 1985): 581–96.

Gray, Daniel H. "Uses and Misuses of Strategic Planning." *Harvard Business Review* 64 (January-February 1986): 89–97.

Harrigan, Kathryn Rudie. *Strategic Flexibility: A Management Guide for Changing Times.* (Lexington, Mass.: Lexington Books, 1985).

Hayes, Robert H. "Strategic Planning—Forward in Reverse?" *Harvard Business Review* 63 (November-December 1985): 111–19.

Hitt, Michael A., and Ireland, R. Duane. "Relationships Among Corporate Level Distinctive Competencies, Diversification Strategy, Corporate Structure and Performance." *Journal of Management Studies* (July 1986): 401–16.

McGowan, William G. "What Business Are We Really In? The Question Revisited." *Sloan Management Review* 28 (Fall 1986): 59–62.

Mintzberg, Henry, and Waters, James A. "Of Strategies, Deliberate and Emergent." *Strategic Management Journal* 6 (July-September 1985): 257–72.

Narayanan, V. K., and Fahey, Liam. "The Micro-Politics of Strategy Formulation." *Academy of Management Review* 7 (January 1982): 25–34.

Nutt, Paul. "Tactics of Implementation." *Academy of Management Journal* 29 (June 1986): 230–261.

Shrivastava, Paul. "Is Strategic Management Ideological?" *Journal of Management* 12 (Fall 1986): 363–377.

Webster, Frederick, Jr. "Marketing Strategy in a Slow Growth Economy." *California Management Review* 28 (Spring 1986): 93–105.

Willard, Gary, and Cooper, Arnold. "Survivors of Industry Shake-Outs: the Case of the U.S. Color Television Set Industry." *Strategic Management Journal* 6 (October-December 1985): 299–318.

TEAGUE SERVICES

Henry Allen, President of Teague Services, has become concerned about the profitability of his company. Allen has just talked with his partners and is worried about what happened during the meeting. Driving home, Allen recalls how he started the business.

Henry Allen was an assistant football coach for one of the state's football powers and was active in many civic organizations. Several years ago, the owner of a large janitorial-supply firm had problems with the turnover of salespeople and approached Allen about becoming sales manager. After a series of meetings, Allen purchased the firm. He immediately provided quicker deliveries, better service, and good advice to his customers about tough cleaning jobs. The business grew rapidly, though Allen's prices were higher than his competitors'.

Allen hired a janitorial field representative, Bob Warren, from the state's largest janitorial supply firm and began bidding on janitorial supply contracts offered by government agencies and large companies. Allen discovered that these organizations were more interested in price than service and quality, and he adjusted accordingly. Allen was successful in offering contracts but found that they were vulnerable to price competition from other suppliers. One of the largest volume items specified for bids was liquid detergent. Allen learned that the manufacturer's markup on liquid detergents was very high. Warren

mentioned that he knew where to purchase the equipment and chemicals needed to manufacture a liquid detergent. Allen worked out a financial arrangement whereby Warren could become a part owner of Teague Services. Allen and Warren purchased equipment to manufacture liquid detergent and moved their company to a much larger and expensive warehouse. Allen was concerned that not all of the new space was being occupied. He approached Mack Burgess, who sold various types of packaging materials (tape, cartons, labels, and so forth) about buying into the company. Soon, Teague's warehouse was filled with packaging materials. Burgess had determined that prompt deliveries would allow Teague Services to increase their market share of packaging materials.

Burgess later mentioned to Warren that many of his customers had difficulty obtaining wooden shipping pallets. Burgess and Warren suggested that Allen offer this service. Charles Strong, who owned a small pallet-building operation and was experiencing working-capital problems, was offered the opportunity to buy into Teague Services. Strong quickly accepted. A larger building was rented for the pallet operation, and more equipment was purchased.

Several months after Strong invested in Teague Services, Allen became concerned. Overhead had greatly increased. Their detergent was not selling well despite a sizable investment in equipment, chemicals, and plastic bottles. The pallet business did not seem to be going anywhere. Their sales literature had so many different kinds of cleaning and packaging products listed that the customers seemed more confused than interested. Allen scheduled a meeting with his partners to discuss these issues.

At the meeting, Warren, Burgess, and Strong mentioned that Teague Services should begin selling office furniture and carpeting. Their argument was that many of their existing customers would purchase these items and that no inventory would be carried beyond sample books. Teague Services' wholesale buying power would be useful in offering these items. Allen became extremely nervous during and after the meeting.

Question

1. What special problems are encountered when more than one type of business is offered at once?

BLUE BIRD SWEEPERS, INC.

Marvin Ireland, president of Blue Bird Sweepers, has just received a telephone call from a large conglomerate regarding a possible takeover. Ireland would be allowed to remain in a management capacity. He feels that the offer will free him from many of the day-to-day burdens and allow him to consider "future opportunities" for the company. Ireland is troubled, however, because he believes that the offer is financially low. This fact, together with a high forecasted growth in the industry, makes Ireland reluctant to consider selling.

Background

Twenty years ago while an engineering student in college, Ireland began a lawn service with two friends. Ireland and his friends would attend classes in the morning and work on lawns in the afternoon. Later, the three partners purchased a small truck and trailer and began spraying insecticide for several of their commercial clients. This turned out to be a profitable investment and more than paid for itself in two months.

The commercial customers requested that the partners clean their parking lots. Ireland purchased a small sweeping truck and began sweeping the parking lots of local companies. This endeavor also proved highly profitable.

After graduating from college with an engineering degree, Ireland became convinced that a need existed for innovative street-sweeping machinery. His two partners were reluctant to become involved and bought out Ireland for twenty-five thousand dollars.

With those proceeds, Ireland moved to a large Midwestern city and began designing street-sweeping machinery. As a means of support, Ireland worked as a draftsman for an engineering firm during the day and designed his street-sweeping machine at night. While the design was being perfected, Ireland convinced one of the owners of the engineering firm to invest one hundred thousand dollars in a partnership to be named Blue Bird Sweepers. Ireland agreed to work ten years for the engineering firm at a certain salary if the street-cleaning venture failed. Ireland used the investment to build two street-sweeping machines that were considered innovations in the industry. Ireland succeeded in obtaining a cleaning contract from the city and then began selling machines to companies in other cities.

Ireland's partner convinced him to form a corporation with two divisions. One division would be responsible for manufacturing and selling the street sweepers, while the other division would contract to perform cleaning services for commercial, industrial, and municipal customers using the new machine. Ten years ago a public stock offering was held. Today, the firm's stock is sold over the counter at between $8 and $10 per share. Ireland owns 20 percent of the two million shares outstanding. His original partner in Blue Bird was killed in a hunting accident and willed his ownership to Ireland.

Present Situation

The machinery manufacturing division is located in modern facilities and sells its products both nationally and internationally. Annual sales are $15 million. The contract cleaning division now maintains a 70 percent market share in the large Midwestern city where Blue Bird originated. Annual sales of the contract cleaning division are five hundred thousand dollars. Profits last year were 15 percent of assets for the combined divisions.

Ireland manages with a very lean staff and performs many of the day-to-day functions himself. In addition to these daily tasks, Ireland monitors technological changes within the industry using a cost-benefit analysis. Many changes have quickly been adopted by Blue Bird. His board of directors has insisted that Ireland delegate more of his operating duties and function as a chief executive.

Ireland believes that while the industry is growing, the strong possibility for a revolutionary idea exists. He wants to work on a principle involving water flushing rather than sweeping. A simple yet innovative machine could be developed that cleans parking lots with a high pressure water flow.

Questions

1. What effects does Ireland's management style have on organizational growth and development?
2. If you were on the board of directors of Blue Bird, would you recommend accepting the offer?
3. If you were Blue Bird's president, Ireland, what would you do now, and why?

THE PLANNING PROCESS

Nature of Planning □ Integration of Plans □ Time Spans □ Standing Plans □ Managerial Attitudes □ Contributions of Subordinates

PREMISES OF PLANS AND CONTINGENCY PLANS

Planning Premises □ Contingency Planning

OPERATIONAL PLANNING TOOLS

Forecasting and Budgeting □ Management by Objectives □ Break-Even Analysis

Summary □ Key Concepts □ Discussion Questions □ Notes □ Supplementary Reading

CASES: Spice Company □ Delta Corporation

This chapter will enable you to

□ Understand the differences between operational planning and strategic planning.

□ Explain how business plans are developed and how planning contributions are made by various organizational members.

□ Describe the nature of contingency planning and understand the use of multiple scenarios.

□ Identify some of the planning techniques and tools used by managers.

CHAPTER 5
OPERATIONAL PLANNING

Planning does not stop when decisions are made about objectives and strategies. These basic concepts must be formed by management into an interlocking set of long-range and short-range operating plans. This chapter examines the planning process and the preparation of operating plans.

THE PLANNING PROCESS

Planning involves a series of steps, going from the general to the particular. As shown in Figure 5–1, *strategic planning* (the subject of chapter 4) includes the establishment of objectives and the determination of strategy. These steps reflect the basic mission of the organization. Figure 5–1 also shows that *operational planning* (the primary focus of this chapter) includes the formulation and integration of functional plans. These plans identify the specific programs and activities necessary to reach the broader objectives.

Nature of Planning

Planning involves systematic thought and decision making about a proposed course of action. It entails the selection of a given path to the future from the various possible alternatives. It is a continuing activity of management. Managers never reach a point at which they stop planning. This does not mean, however, that they never complete work on specific plans. The budget for a

FIGURE 5–1 The corporate planning process

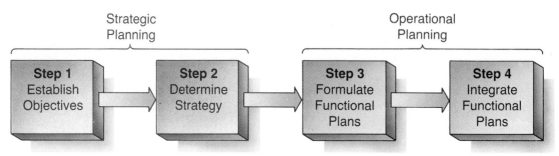

given year may be adopted, but the manager who approves it must immediately turn to other planning and must soon begin consideration of the budget for the following year.

Plans require decision making, a topic treated in chapter 6. Selection of a proposed course of action necessitates a decision in favor of this particular

TOP PRIORITY: PLANNING

Threats to organizational health and survival quickly focus attention on those factors managers consider most crucial. When William R. Haselton (a Ph.D. in chemistry) was promoted to the position of chief executive of St. Regis Paper Company in 1979, he expressed embarrassment about St. Regis's mediocre performance—seventeenth of twenty-one companies in the forest products industry.

Haselton's prescription was a carefully developed five-year plan.

"What," the reader may ask, "is so special about five-year plans? Doesn't every big company have them?" Maybe so, but taking them seriously is another matter. Make no mistake: Haselton is taking this one seriously. On the surface, he's a soft-spoken, mild-mannered man, but nobody who has dealt with him can ignore the steely determination underneath.

Success for such a plan depends on many factors, some of which (such as general economic conditions) are beyond management's control. Haselton's approach, however, indicates the high priority given to planning as one critical factor in the company's success.

SOURCE: Adapted from Jean A. Briggs, "Woodsman, Spare That Company," *Forbes* 125, no. 3 (February 4, 1980): 37–8.

course of action and a rejection of other possibilities. Decision making is not synonymous with planning, however, because decision making is also required in other functions of management.

Plans are directed to the accomplishment of some objective or to the solution of some problem. Overall planning is concerned with broad company objectives and strategies. Functional and divisional planning is directed to the achievement of subsidiary goals which contribute to realization of the company's fundamental objectives. At each level of the organization, some planning occurs that is concerned with the specific mission of that particular level.

Plans become more specific and shorter range as departmental managers engage in planning for their specific operations. As shown in Figure 5–2, production managers prepare production plans, marketing managers prepare marketing plans, and so on. The goals of each functional department are derived from or related to the overall goals and plans for the entire organization.

Integration of Plans

The open systems concept, explained in chapter 2, is relevant to several aspects of planning. The various functional operating plans, for example, should blend into an overall corporate plan or set of plans for a particular time period.

After functional plans are formulated, therefore, management must integrate them. This step produces a truly comprehensive plan rather than a set of contradictory plans. Each functional plan must be questioned as to its contribution to established objectives. Each must also be examined to determine its

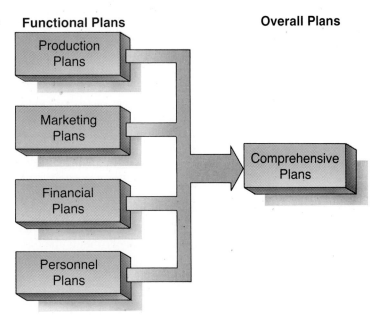

FIGURE 5–2 Functional plans and overall plans

FIGURE 5–3 Degrees of integration in planning

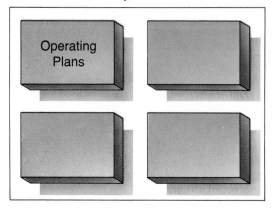

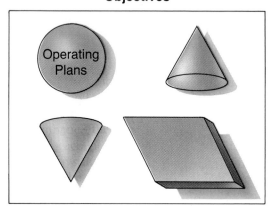

compatibility with other plans of the corporation. If each of six divisions proposes to spend $1 million and only $3 million is available, changes are imperative.

A second application of the systems concept is concerned with the relationship of operating plans—even well-integrated operating plans—to the basic objectives of the organization. The plans must "fit" the objectives, as illustrated in Figure 5–3. This may seem simple, but it does not happen automatically. Middle-level and lower-level managers sometimes follow plans that do not mesh with the "grand strategy" designed by top management.

Suppose, for example, that a corporation wishes to raise the quality level of the products it produces and sells or to sell custom-made products rather than standardized products. Such a decision may necessitate changes in recruitment, training, and compensation of sales personnel, in addition to many other types of change. Special effort is required to modify well-established practices and policies.

Comprehensive planning produces an internally consistent hierarchy of plans, starting with the broad plans for the total enterprise and including the supporting specific and detailed operational plans.

The concept of *suboptimization* is pertinent to the practice of planning for the entire system. It is possible for a given department to optimize its output by reducing the efficiency of other departments or other functions. Simultaneous optimization of all departments may be impossible. The ideal combination of plans calls for optimization of company-wide operations. This often necessitates suboptimization—that is, operating at less than ideal conditions in particular departments—in order that the overall operations of the entire company might be optimized.

Time Spans

Time spans for planning may range from less than one year to more than twenty. The time span tends to lengthen as one moves upward from lower to higher organizational levels. We do not expect credit managers, sales unit managers, machine shop managers, and other lower-level managers to develop long-range plans comparable to those for the organization as a whole. Instead, their planning is more tactical in nature and typically confined to meeting specific short-run objectives.

Figure 5–4 presents a planning model which makes a general distinction between the time frame for strategic planning and that for operational planning. A time horizon of three to fifteen years is suggested for the former and a

FIGURE 5–4 Time frames for planning

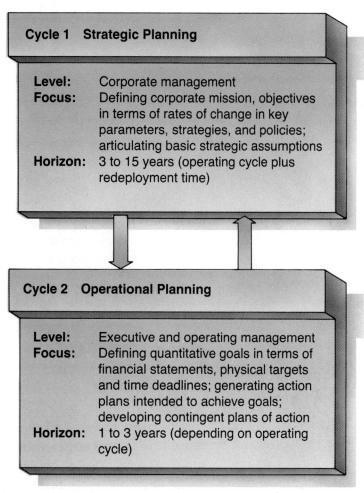

Cycle 1   Strategic Planning

Level: Corporate management
Focus: Defining corporate mission, objectives
              in terms of rates of change in key
              parameters, strategies, and policies;
              articulating basic strategic assumptions
Horizon: 3 to 15 years (operating cycle plus
              redeployment time)

Cycle 2   Operational Planning

Level: Executive and operating management
Focus: Defining quantitative goals in terms of
              financial statements, physical targets
              and time deadlines; generating action
              plans intended to achieve goals;
              developing contingent plans of action
Horizon: 1 to 3 years (depending on operating
              cycle)

SOURCE: John C. Camillus and John H. Grant, "Operational Planning: The Integration of Programming and Budgeting," *Academy of Management Review* 5 (July 1980): 375.

PLANNING AS A RITUAL

In any given case, there is no guarantee that planning will improve performance. Only *good* planning can improve what would otherwise occur. And the planning must be translated into action. The possibility of bad or ineffective planning is evident in these comments of Russell L. Ackoff:

> A good deal of corporate planning I have observed is like a ritual rain dance; it has no effect on the weather that follows, but those who engage in it think it does. Moreover, it seems to me that much of the advice and instruction related to corporate planning is directed at improving the dancing, not the weather.

SOURCE: Russell L. Ackoff, *Creating the Corporate Future: Plan or be Planned For* (New York: Wiley, 1981), p. ix.

time horizon of one to three years for the latter. The key element in determining the length of the operational planning cycle is the nature of the operating cycle. The operating cycle of a construction firm, for example, is much longer than the operating cycle of a food-processing firm.

Standing Plans

Not all plans are tied to specific periods—either long-range or short-range. Organizational policies, for example, may be described as standing plans. Although policies are subject to modification over time, they have greater continuity than operating plans.

A *policy* might be defined as a basic statement serving as a guide for administrative action. By saying it is a guide, there is an implication that the policy does not usually specify detailed answers to particular problems. The manager has some degree of freedom.* As an example, a policy that says "all divisional managers are responsible for the establishment and maintenance of a system of internal control within their divisions" does not dictate what form the system must take. It simply indicates that each division must have a system of internal control. The system's design rests with each divisional manager, who can tailor it to the particular needs of that division.

---

*A policy establishes general guidelines, in contrast to a *rule* (such as "no smoking"), which permits no discretion regarding action to be taken, and a *procedure,* which specifies a chronological sequence of activities.

Managerial Attitudes

Managers today face markets and competitive situations that are increasingly turbulent and changeable. A company and its management must "run fast" just to stay even with competition.

In striving for progress and even survival in such a fast-changing world, managers try to assess the future in order to meet it as rationally as possible. Planning is a practice that becomes increasingly attractive with growing uncertainties. As might be expected, most large organizations engage in formal planning. A survey of 500 large U.S. corporations discovered that 94 percent had some type of documented long-range plans.[1] The major question is not whether to plan but how to plan most effectively.

WHEN OPERATING PLANS DON'T WORK

In 1984, General Motors (GM) was the largest single user of computers outside of the U.S. government. Nevertheless, GM's top managers believed that computers were not being used effectively by the various functional areas. For example, the chairman, Roger Smith, stated that "design" computers could not communicate directly with "production" or "sales" computers. Smith envisioned that a computer system could be developed to link all of GM's functional areas together. Toward that end, GM acquired Electronic Data Systems (EDS), a firm specializing in organizing computers. H. Ross Perot, the largest shareholder of EDS, became a board member of GM. Industry analysts believed that Perot and Smith would together redesign GM's manufacturing system, in part by developing innovative operational planning techniques.

After two years, sales were declining, operating costs were a problem, competition from U.S. and foreign companies was extremely fierce, and Perot and Smith were feuding. Perot repeatedly criticized GM's management for receiving exorbitant salaries and for being out of touch with what was happening on the plant floor. Perot described GM as being a "lumbering dinosaur."

In late 1986, the GM board bought out Perot for $750 million to end the feud. Some GM managers privately agreed that inequities existed in the treatment of executives as compared with workers and that inefficiencies were prevalent. Other GM managers, however, viewed Perot's departure as being a positive move to eliminate a critic who was no longer constructive.

SOURCE: Adapted from Eric Gelman, Richard Manning, Daniel Pedersen, and Nikki Greenberg, "Wheels of the Future," *Newsweek,* 17 June 1985, pp. 65–72, and "GM's Woes Not Gone With Perot," *Dallas Morning News,* 7 December 1986.

In spite of its importance planning is perhaps the most easily neglected of all managerial functions. In a survey of long-range planning in multinational firms, executive respondents identified top management's preoccupation with current problems as having the greatest negative impact on planning effectiveness.[2] It is a rare manager who does not become too busy. The natural reaction is to devote time to those activities clamoring for attention. James G. March and Herbert Simon have even suggested a *Gresham's law of planning,* in which daily routine drives out planning.[3]

The negative effects of neglected planning are not always apparent in the short run. In fact, the organization may proceed from year to year with little outward indication of its weakness in planning. Eventually, however, management deficiencies in planning are revealed.

Contributions of Subordinates

In the past, top managers were viewed as the only planners for the organization. Information was funneled to them, and they did the planning. Recently, as discussed in chapter 4, several firms have decentralized the process of strategic management, making their operating managers responsible for planning. By delegating and decentralizing, planning is pushed downward through the organization. Specific plans are formulated by the divisions responsible for carrying out the work, within the framework of overall objectives and policies.

If managers wish to draw extensively upon the thinking of subordinates in planning, there are special ways to encourage such contributions. Subordinates may be asked to submit proposals or to criticize tentative plans. They may also be asked to serve on planning committees that work out plans for the entire organization.

PREMISES OF PLANS AND CONTINGENCY PLANS

Planning Premises

The planner is confronted with numerous uncertainties in the environment. He or she must make certain assumptions concerning these uncertainties. Will interest rates increase, remain stable, or fall? Will Congress modify present tax laws? Assumptions about such uncertainties constitute *planning premises,* or the bases upon which plans are constructed. Premises commonly concern economic conditions, government fiscal policy, competitors' plans, trends in raw materials and labor markets, and so on.

Contingency Planning

Difficulty in predicting future conditions has led some companies to a practice known as *contingency planning.* To some extent, planners have always experienced uncertainty, but the problem became increasingly serious during the

1970s. Planners found it uncommonly difficult to formulate dependable assumptions. Unforeseen changes undercut basic assumptions, and plans became obsolete. Some management groups met the problem by developing contingency plans—a set of plans for each of several circumstances. This process is portrayed in Figure 5–5.

FIGURE 5–5 A model for contingency planning

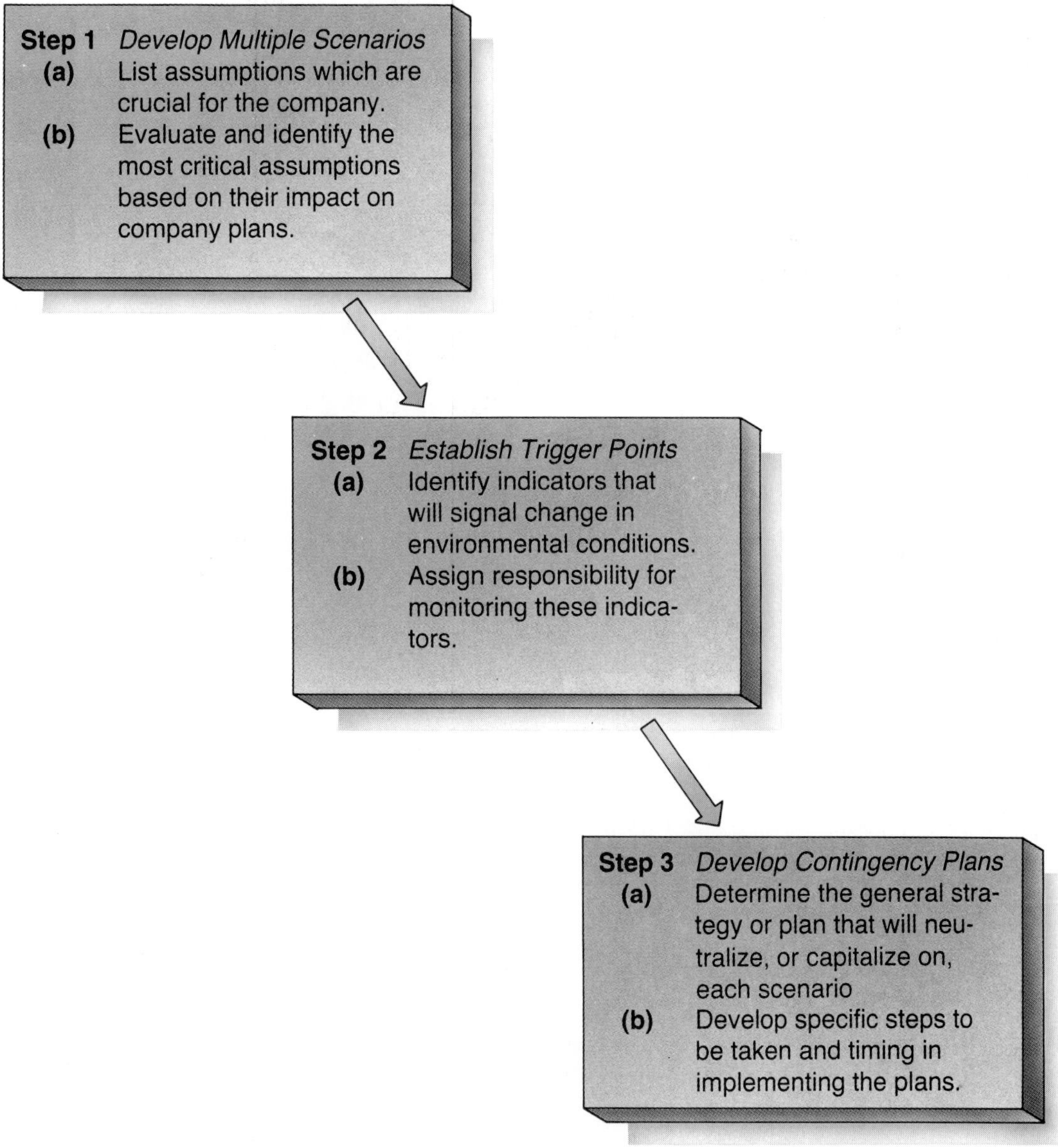

Step 1 *Develop Multiple Scenarios*
(a) List assumptions which are crucial for the company.
(b) Evaluate and identify the most critical assumptions based on their impact on company plans.

Step 2 *Establish Trigger Points*
(a) Identify indicators that will signal change in environmental conditions.
(b) Assign responsibility for monitoring these indicators.

Step 3 *Develop Contingency Plans*
(a) Determine the general strategy or plan that will neutralize, or capitalize on, each scenario
(b) Develop specific steps to be taken and timing in implementing the plans.

Planners develop *multiple scenarios* as they formulate a series of assumptions about the future.[4] One scenario, for example, may specify the economic conditions thought most likely to occur. Alternative scenarios might use a more optimistic assumption or a more pessimistic assumption. This use of multiple scenarios is not limited to assumptions about economic fluctuations and may express differing assumptions about weather, political elections, environmental regulations, shortages of raw materials, strikes, and so on.

Plans must be prepared to cover the various conditions specified in the multiple scenarios. Although the term *contingency plans* suggests a complete set of plans "on the shelf" for use as needed, they are often developed somewhat informally. Contingency plans may be general statements of action to be taken without completely specifying the intended operations. Contingency plans that are properly developed specify *trigger points*—events that call for implementation of particular contingency plans.

One benefit of contingency planning is the broader outlook provided for managers, who become more sensitive to various external forces. Probably the greatest drawback to contingency planning is the heavier administrative burden imposed on managers, who must prepare not one but multiple sets of plans. If the firm's environment is extremely unpredictable, however, the benefits may well justify the cost. Because of the administrative load, the customary practice is to develop the various contingency plans in less detail.

OPERATIONAL PLANNING TOOLS

A number of tools and techniques have been developed to make planning more systematic. This section discusses the primary tools available to management.

Forecasting and Budgeting

One of the mechanisms for translating business-level strategy (how will we effectively compete?) into departmental activities is the organization's Management Control System (MCS).[5] The relationships among MCS, strategic planning, and the various organizational departments are depicted in Figure 5–6. Two important elements of an MCS are forecasting and budgeting, which are discussed in this chapter. Other elements are developed in chapters 10 and 17.

Forecasting Techniques. Virtually any plan depends upon the availability of funds. An estimate of incoming funds, usually called the sales forecast, can be developed through a number of different techniques.[6]

Surveys are used by some organizations to determine the demand for their product or service during an upcoming fiscal period. Using statistical sampling

FIGURE 5–6 Forecasts and budgets in the strategic planning process

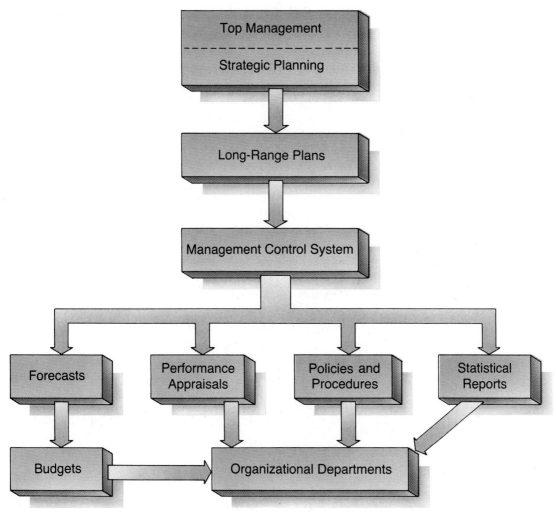

SOURCE: Adapted from Richard L. Daft and Norman B. Macintosh, "The Nature and Use of Formal Control Systems for Management Control and Strategy Implementation," *Journal of Management* 10 (Spring 1984): 60.

techniques, forecasters interview present and potential customers or clients over the telephone, in person, or through mailed questionnaires to determine their buying plans. This technique is useful in forecasting demand for consumer durable goods, such as automobiles or major appliances, or industrial goods, such as heavy equipment or machinery. In both cases, the buyer usually plans the purchase well in advance, because of its expense, and can estimate the probability of purchase with some accuracy. Some organizations conduct such surveys with their own personnel, while others hire research firms or use the results of national surveys such as those conducted by the Survey Research Center of the University of Michigan.

Some organizations combine the forecasts of their sales representatives into an overall demand forecast. Management assumes that sales representatives should be able to predict future customer purchases since they maintain close contact with customers. Sales representatives, however, may not be fully informed of the organization's upcoming sales promotion and advertising plans or of environmental developments that might affect future sales. Also, if the organization uses forecasts to establish sales quotas, the submitted forecasts may be too low. Most firms which use this technique, therefore, adjust each individual forecast to reflect predicted environmental developments and past forecasting error on the sales representative's part before combining the adjusted forecasts.

Statistical techniques may be used to forecast future sales from past sales data. In one version of this technique, actual sales figures for the past several years are statistically related to "predictor variables" such as product price, advertising expenditures, and per capita disposable income in the sales area for those years. Using the analytical tool of multiple regression, the forecaster can derive an equation which will predict sales for the upcoming year using estimates of next year's product price, advertising expenditures, per capita income, and so on. The validity of this approach, of course, depends upon the similarity between past trends and future conditions. Any significant departure from historical trends will weaken the forecast dramatically, and departures from historical trends seem to be occurring with increasing frequency. Because such departures are difficult to predict, one review of the evidence concludes that forecasts of two years or longer are "notoriously inaccurate."[7]

These techniques demonstrate some of the varied approaches available to forecasters. Use of more than one technique is recommended since a forecast based on two or more techniques has greater validity than one based on only a single estimate. Once the revenue forecast is developed, the organization can begin the budgeting process.

Budgeting Procedures. The revenue forecast is used to budget expenditures in such areas as production, labor, purchasing, and marketing. The budget is probably the most universal planning tool. As a plan of operation expressed in financial terms, the budget allocates resources in a manner intended to help the organization attain its objectives.

Most organizations use their fiscal year as the time period for budgeting. It is common practice to prepare the budget during the quarter preceding the start of the fiscal year, with final adoption just prior to the beginning of the new year. Before the beginning of each quarter, the budget for that quarter is often prepared in greater detail. During the year, the budget tends to become outdated because of changing conditions. For this reason, it is common practice to revise the budget periodically during the budgetary period. This technique is called a *rolling,* or *moving,* budget. Budgeting, in this sense, is a continuous process rather than a yearly event. Some organizations use *variable,* rather than *static,* budgets. While static budgets are based on a specific forecasted level of sales, variable budgets attempt to match planned expenditures to varying revenue levels.

Zero-base budgeting differs from the traditional *incremental budgeting.*[8] Incremental budgets are constructed on the foundation of past budgets, the costs and benefits of new activities are analyzed, and those activities with net benefits are added to the budget as are other increases required by inflation and other factors. Zero-base budgeting, on the other hand, begins with a "clean slate" each fiscal period. The cost and benefit of all activities—new and old—are examined, and the activities are then ranked in terms of overall importance to the organization.* The activities above a certain cut-off point are approved for the coming year.[9] In this manner, every dollar budgeted is justified in terms of attaining organizational goals, and major reallocations of resources can be made on a yearly basis. Planning is flexible rather than being locked into past activities and decisions.[10]

Some scholars are beginning to recommend that organizations use zero-base and incremental budgeting simultaneously, for different subsystems in the organization. The former is recommended because of its ability to deal with a changing environment. The latter is useful because it serves as one of the prime stabilizing processes in organizations.[11]

Management by Objectives

A tool that aids in translating broad organizational goals into specific, individual objectives is *management by objectives* (MBO). Formulated in 1954 by Drucker, MBO is currently used in a wide variety of organizations—profit and nonprofit, large and small.[12] Although its primary application is in planning, MBO concepts are also useful in motivation, management development, control, and performance appraisal.

MBO is a planning technique that involves lower-level employees in the process of goal setting. This approach is in sharp contrast to the more traditional approach, in which the superior unilaterally establishes goals for subordinates. The MBO process itself comprises the three basic steps illustrated in Figure 5–7.

Step 1.   MBO begins with a meeting between the manager and subordinate in which the two discuss individual objectives for the subordinate. These objectives should be commensurate with the larger goals of the organization and the unit in which the subordinate works. Such meetings occur throughout the

---

*Zero-base budgeting is applicable to operations over which management has some discretion. In business organizations, such operations would include marketing, research, engineering, capital expenditures, and so on. Not included would be such areas as direct labor and direct materials; such costs are budgeted through standard costing procedures.

FIGURE 5–7   The MBO process

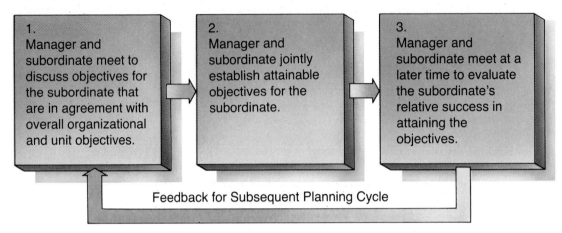

organization between all superiors and subordinates. The objectives discussed should be those which not only benefit the organization but also contribute to the professional development of the subordinate. The systems approach indicates that individual goals must be set within the framework of unit and organizational goals, since one manager's objectives may affect other individuals and units.

Step 2.   The manager and subordinate then jointly establish specific objectives for the subordinate. These objectives may be six-month goals, yearly goals, or tied to the completion of a major project. In some organizations formal "action plans" are developed to guide subordinates in attaining their goals.

   The objectives must be clearly stated and should be neither too difficult nor too easy to attain. Unreachable goals may cause the subordinate to give up in despair, while easy goals do not provide sufficient motivation or feelings of

THE NEED FOR JOINT PARTICIPATION

The desirability of joint participation between the manager and subordinate in setting the subordinate's goals was emphasized in the tragic accident of the space shuttle *Challenger* in 1986. Although the National Aeronautics and Space Administration (NASA) was one of the first government agencies to adopt MBO, hopelessly unrealistic objectives concerning launch schedules were given to subordinates, who then came under intense pressure to meet the schedules. Safety shortcuts were taken in a disastrous attempt to attain objectives that were virtually unattainable.

accomplishment once they have been reached. Each objective is usually assigned a weight—or priority—since the attainment of some goals may be more critical than others.

Each objective must be *verifiable*. That is, the manager and subordinate must be able to answer the question, "Has this goal been attained?" Hence, goals must be specified in exact terms. For instance, it would be inappropriate for a sales manager to set a goal of "increasing sales over the next six months." Instead, the manager might establish an objective of "increasing sales over the next six months by 8 percent while maintaining an average profit margin of 10 percent on all sales."

It is important that the goals be established jointly by the manager and subordinate. Goals dictated by the manager will not have full subordinate acceptance or commitment, and goals established without the manager's participation may be inappropriate to the unit. Also, nonparticipation by the superior may cause the subordinate to feel that the manager has little interest in the subordinate's development or in MBO in general.[13]

Step 3. If the mutually established objectives are clearly defined, verifiable, and reasonably attainable, the manager and subordinate should experience little difficulty in evaluating the subordinate's success in attaining the goals. The evaluation session should be constructive—not a forum for placing blame or finding fault. The last part of the session should be devoted to establishing goals for the next period.

Although established goals should not be changed without careful consideration, unforeseen environmental conditions can make some goals less realistic than they appeared earlier. In such cases, the goals should be modified by the manager and subordinate prior to the evaluation session. The evaluation must be based on the attainment of realistic goals.

Benefits of MBO. Knowledge of the relative effectiveness of MBO is quite limited. Although most experts believe that full implementation of an MBO program requires two to five years, the longest experimental study to date lasted only three years.[14] A review of 185 studies of MBO concludes that those studies which used the least sophisticated research methods were the most likely to show that MBO was effective. More rigorous research studies were less likely to arrive at that conclusion.[15]

Advocates of MBO claim, however, that a properly designed and implemented program should yield a number of benefits. Perhaps the most important is that each manager in the organization is required to plan for the future in some detail. Another major benefit is the subordinate's stronger commitment to his or her job goals as a result of participation in setting the goals. This commitment, in turn, should lead to increased job satisfaction and, perhaps, superior performance, since the individual knows exactly what is expected and in what direction to channel activities. Job ambiguity and perhaps even stress are therefore reduced.[16] Finally, communication between the manager and subordinate should be improved, and performance evaluation and control are facilitated by being conducted on a rational, objective basis.

Problems with MBO. Research has pinpointed a number of problems that arise in MBO programs.[17] A major complaint of managers, for instance, is that MBO increases the amount of paperwork—to report progress toward goal attainment—and consumes considerable time in the counseling of subordinates. MBO may also place heavy emphasis on quantitative goals at the expense of equally important qualitative goals. And, in one study, the positive effects of MBO diminished over time in the absence of a program designed to "reinforce" the importance of MBO to the participants.

A major weakness in MBO may be found in its implementation. In some firms, for example, superiors simply assign goals to subordinates. Nonattainment of goals may be punished, so that MBO becomes negative motivation—"either attain your goals or else." Also, superiors may not take the program seriously, and attainment of goals may not be properly rewarded. If all employees, regardless of performance, receive virtually the same percentage salary increase, they will perceive little relationship between goal attainment and rewards.[18]

Perhaps most crucial to the success of MBO is the wholehearted support of top management. Management can best demonstrate its support by introducing the program in a highly visible manner. The introduction should consist of a clear statement of the purposes of MBO, followed by detailed orientation and training in MBO concepts, including a workshop in which employees learn how to set moderately difficult, verifiable job goals. Top management can also reinforce the importance of the program periodically through group meetings, written support, refresher courses, and so on.

Break-Even Analysis

Break-even analysis is a useful tool for managers who are planning to add new product or service lines to their current offerings or for potential entrepreneurs who plan to open their own businesses. This tool helps the manager determine what level of operations is required to break even, that is, to reach the point at which total revenue equals total cost. A knowledge of the following cost and revenue concepts is essential to the understanding of break-even analysis:

Fixed costs	Costs that remain the same over the short run regardless of the organization's level of operations. Examples include property taxes, fire insurance premiums, and interest payments on debts.
Variable costs	Costs that vary with the level of operations. Raw materials costs, sales commissions, and direct labor costs are examples.

CHRYSLER'S REVISED BREAK-EVEN POINT

The resurgence of Chrysler, which lost $3.5 billion between 1978 and 1982, was partly made possible by lowering the firm's break-even point from an annual sales level of 2.4 million cars and trucks to about 1.2 million. The lower break-even point resulted from extensive white- and blue-collar layoffs, closing or consolidating twenty plants, and salary and benefit concessions from employees.

SOURCE: Based on "Chrysler? Profits? Iacocca Does It," *Newsweek,* 14 June 1982, p. 78.

Total cost	Fixed costs plus variable costs.
Total revenue	Total sales dollars, determined by multiplying product (or service) price by the quantity forecasted to be sold.
Break-even point	Level of operations at which total revenue equals total cost.

For example, assume that you are considering opening a small "submarine sandwich" shop in a large office building currently under construction. Several hundred people will be working in the building once it opens. You determine that fixed costs such as space rental, salaries, and insurance will be approximately $3,000 per month. The going price for submarine sandwiches is $3, and you estimate the cost of making the sandwich to be about $2. You plan to have the shop open for business five days a week from 10:00 A.M. to 4:00 P.M. How many sandwiches must be sold to break even?

The analysis of Figure 5–8 shows the relationships among the various costs and revenues and reveals the break-even point. Note that fixed costs are $3,000 no matter how many sandwiches are sold, while variable costs increase with the number of sandwiches sold, Hence, if there are no sales, total costs will be $3,000. If 6,600 sandwiches are sold, total cost is $16,200 ($3,000 of fixed costs plus $13,200 of variable costs—that is, 6,600 sandwiches at $2 a sandwich). Total cost for any level of monthly sales may be determined from the graph. The monthly capacity of 6,600 sandwiches is based on selling a maximum of fifty per hour for six hours twenty-two days per month.

Total revenue ranges from zero at no sales to $19,800 at capacity (6,600 sandwiches at $3 per). The total-revenue line intersects the total-cost line at sale of 3,000 sandwiches. Sale of 3,000 sandwiches, then, will bring in just enough revenue to cover total cost; this is the break-even point. Monthly sale of less than 3,000 sandwiches will result in a loss because the total-cost line is above the total-revenue line. Monthly sale of more than 3,000 sandwiches will result in a profit.

FIGURE 5–8 Analysis to find the break-even point

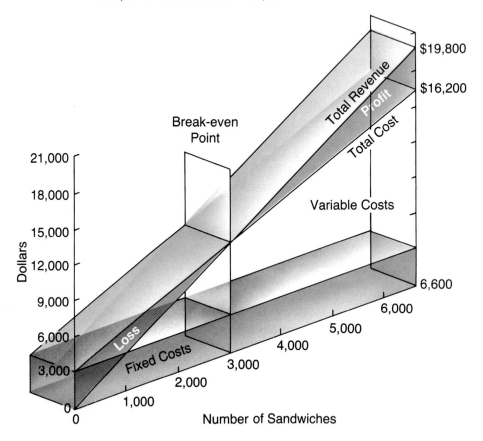

The same results can be determined by the following formula:

$$\text{Break-even point in units} = \frac{\text{Fixed costs}}{\text{Unit price} - \text{Variable costs}}$$

This translates into

$$3,000 \text{ units} = \frac{\$3,000}{\$3 - \$2}$$

This information must now be matched with a forecast of the demand for the product in order to determine if sales of 3,000 per month are realistic. Remember that any change in the estimated costs or the selling price will affect the break-even point. This type of analysis can be used to experiment with different pricing.

SUMMARY

Planning consists of the activities involved in choosing courses of action to achieve organizational objectives. In keeping with the open systems concept, functional plans must be formulated and integrated to fit the overall strategy and objectives of the organization. Both long-range and short-range plans are necessary, and some types of plans (such as policies) are regarded as standing plans because of their continuing nature. In spite of the importance and growing emphasis in the use of planning, management pressures frequently lead to its neglect.

Planning is a part of the activities of all management personnel. Some use is made of staff planners, who have the advantage of being able to devote their full attention to the analysis of business problems and the preparation of specific plans. Managers differ in the degree to which they use the thinking of subordinates in planning for the future.

In planning, it is necessary for management to adopt certain assumptions or *premises*—particularly with regard to external factors—that serve as bases for plans. Because of the growing difficulty of predicting future environmental conditions, some companies have adopted the practice of *contingency planning.* They develop *multiple scenarios* of the future and formulate a set of strategies and plans for each scenario.

Managers have available a number of tools and techniques to help them plan organizational operations. Forecasting techniques and budgeting procedures are almost universal planning tools. The forecast serves as the base from which the budget is developed. *Rolling* budgets and *variable* budgeting techniques are particularly useful for organizations in dynamic environments. Some business and government organizations have turned to *zero-base budgeting* in recent years in an attempt to match planned expenditures to specific organizational goals and make the budgeting process more flexible.

Another planning tool is *management by objectives* (MBO). MBO is an organization-wide program in which each manager and subordinate jointly establish job-related objectives for the subordinate. The objectives must be clear, verifiable, commensurate with overall organizational goals, and neither too easy nor too hard to attain.

Benefits claimed for MBO include improved planning, greater job commitment, increased job performance and satisfaction, and better superior-subordinate communication. Problems may result with a lack of top management support, a failure to set goals jointly, or a failure to provide adequate incentives for goal attainment.

Break-even analysis is used to determine the level of operations at which total revenue will equal total cost. This tool is useful to managers who are planning to add or delete product or service lines. The projected break-even point can be compared to a forecast of demand for the product or service in order to determine the feasibility of carrying the line.

KEY CONCEPTS

Comprehensive plans	Time horizon
Contingency planning	Verifiable goals
Suboptimization	Zero-base budgeting
Functional planning	Variable budgets
Multiple scenarios	Variable costs
Gresham's law of planning	Fixed costs

DISCUSSION QUESTIONS

1. Explain the relationship of the open systems concept to planning.
2. What determines the length of the time period covered by business planning?
3. With the uncertainties confronting most businesses, how can you justify attempts at long-range planning?
4. Explain why planning is of greater importance than other managerial functions.
5. What is meant by *contingency planning?*
6. What are *multiple scenarios?* Why are they used?
7. In *management by objectives,* what sort of objectives are the manager and subordinate supposed to establish?
8. Why should the manager and subordinate establish the objectives together?
9. What are some problems associated with MBO that management should attempt to avoid?
10. What are some forecasting techniques that can be used?
11. How does *zero-base budgeting* differ from the traditional incremental budgeting process?
12. What are some of the limitations of break-even analysis?
13. Tri-Star makes trophies for various sporting events. The company sells a standard-sized trophy for $25 per unit and has a variable cost of $10 per unit. With a fixed cost of $15,000, how many units must Tri-Star sell to break even?·Construct a graph indicating the break-even point.

NOTES

1. James S. Ang and Jess H. Chua, "Long Range Planning in Large United States Corporations—A Survey," *Long Range Planning* 12 (April 1979): 99.
2. George A. Steiner and Hans Schollhammer, "Pitfalls in Multinational Long-Range Planning," *Long-Range Planning* 8 (April 1975): 8.
3. James G. March and Herbert A. Simon, *Organizations* (New York: Wiley, 1958), p. 185.
4. For a discussion of how Royal Dutch/Shell uses scenario analysis, see Pierre Wack, "Scenarios: Uncharted Waters Ahead," *Harvard Business Review* 63 (September-October 1985): 73–89; and "Scenarios: Shooting the Rapids," *Harvard Business Review* 63 (November-December 1985): 139–50.

5. James Todd, "Management Control Systems: A Key Link Between Strategy, Structure, and Employee Performance," *Organizational Dynamics* (Spring 1977): 65–78.

6. An excellent overview of forecasting techniques may be found in David M. Georgoff and Robert G. Murdick, "Manager's Guide to Forecasting," *Harvard Business Review* 64 (January-February 1986): 110–20.

7. Robin M. Hogarth and Spyros Makridakis, "Forecasting and Planning: An Evaluation," *Management Science* 27 (February 1981): 122.

8. Peter A. Pyhrr, *Zero-Base Budgeting* (New York: Wiley, 1973).

9. For a summary of the problems involved in implementing zero-base budgeting programs in organizations, see Stanton C. Lindquist and R. Bryant Mills, "Whatever Happened to Zero-Base Budgeting?" *Managerial Planning* 29 (January-February 1981): 31–35.

10. Peter A. Pyhrr, "Zero-Base Budgeting: Where to Use it and How to Begin," *S.A.M. Advanced Management Journal* 41 (Summer 1976): 4–14.

11. John J. Williams, "Designing a Budgeting System with Planned Confusion," *California Management Review* 24 (Winter 1981): 75–85.

12. Peter F. Drucker, *The Practice of Management* (New York: Harper & Row, 1954). For a report on the development of MBO and its early use at General Electric, see Ronald G. Greenwood, "Management by Objectives: As Developed by Peter Drucker, Assisted by Harold Smiddy," *Academy of Management Review* 6 (April 1981): 225–30.

13. See, for instance, John C. Aplin, Jr., and Peter P. Schoderbek, "MBO: Requisites for Success in the Public Sector," *Human Resource Management* 15 (Summer 1976): 30–36.

14. John M. Ivancevich, "Change in Performance in a Management by Objectives Program," *Administrative Science Quarterly* 19 (December 1974): 563–74.

15. Jack N. Kondrasuk, "Studies in MBO Effectiveness," *Academy of Management Review* 6 (July 1981): 419–30.

16. James C. Quick, "Dyadic Goal Setting and Role Stress: A Field Study," *Academy of Management Journal* 22 (June 1979): 241–52.

17. See, for instance, Anthony P. Raia, "A Second Look at Management Goals and Controls," *California Management Review* 8 (Summer 1966): 49–58; Ivancevich, "Changes in Performance," pp. 563–74; and Perry D. Moore and Ted Staton, "Management by Objectives in American Cities," *Public Personnel Management* 10 (Summer 1981): 223–32.

18. An analysis of the ethical issues involved in the MBO process may be found in Charles D. Pringle and Justin G. Longenecker, "The Ethics of MBO," *Academy of Management Review* 7 (April 1982): 305–12.

SUPPLEMENTARY READING

Banks, Robert L., and **Wheelwright, Steven C.** "Operations vs. Strategy: Trading Tomorrow for Today." *Harvard Business Review* 57 (May-June 1979): 112–20.

Camillus, John C., and **Grant, John H.** "Operational Planning: The Integration of Programming and Budgeting." *Academy of Management Review* 5 (July 1980): 369–79.

Dean, Burton V., and Cowen, Scott S. "Zero-Base Budgeting in the Private Sector." *Business Horizons* 22 (August 1979): 73–83.

Greenwood, Ronald G. "Management by Objectives: As Developed by Peter Drucker, Assisted by Harold Smiddy." *Academy of Management Review* 6 (April 1981): 225–30.

Hitt, Michael A.; Ireland, R. Duane; and Stadter, George. "Functional Importance and Company Performance: Moderating Effects of Grand Strategy and Industry Type." *Strategic Management Journal* 3 (May-June 1982): 315–30.

King, William. "Evaluating Strategic Planning Systems." *Strategic Management Journal* 4 (January-February 1983): 263–77.

Kondrasuk, Jack N. "Studies in MBO Effectiveness." *Academy of Management Review* 6 (July 1981): 419–30.

Miesing, Paul, and Wolfe, Joseph. "The Art And Science of Planning At The Business Unit Level." *Management Science* 31 (June 1985): 773–80.

Mintzberg, Henry. "What Is Planning Anyway?" *Strategic Management Journal* 2 (March-April 1981): 319–24.

Pringle, Charles D., and Longenecker, Justin G. "The Ethics of MBO." *Academy of Management Review* 7 (April 1982): 305–12.

Ramanujam, Vasudevan; Venkatraman, N.; and Camillus, John. "Multi-Objective Assessment of Effectiveness of Strategic Planning: A Discriminant Analysis Approach." *Academy of Management Journal* 29 (June 1986): 347–72.

Robinson, John. "Paradoxes In Planning." *Long Range Planning* 19 (December 1986): 21–34.

SPICE COMPANY

Spice Company was unprofitable last year on a sales volume of $3 million. The company's fixed expenses amount to $1.2 million per year, and variable expenses last year amounted to $2.1 million. The sales manager wants to redesign the package in which the company's product is displayed. The sales manager reports that it will cost $150,000 to design the new product and that sales will be increased by 15 percent during next year. But it is unlikely that the new design will have any effect on sales beyond the next year.

Questions

1. What is the company's break-even point?
2. Assuming that the package redesign is adopted, what is the company's new break-even point?
3. Should the package redesign be undertaken?

DELTA CORPORATION

Bill Joiner carefully studied the draft of performance objectives he had received in the mail from one of his new sales representatives, Ralph Stone. He pondered what steps he should take next and wondered just what approach he should take in reviewing the objectives with Stone.

Bill Joiner was the Florida district sales manager for Delta Corporation, a national distributor of construction tools and equipment. Joiner's primary responsibility was the supervision of a seven-man field sales force covering the state of Florida.

Stone had joined Delta two months earlier. This would therefore be the first

time that Joiner would go through the cycle of the MBO program with him. At Delta, subordinates drafted new objectives and reviewed them with their superiors every six months.

Bill remembered that the company had stressed the importance of mutual understanding and agreement between subordinate and superior as the keystone of the MBO program. He wondered what action he should take in response to Ralph Stone's first attempt at drafting objectives (Exhibit 1).

SOURCE; Fred E. Schuster, CONTEMPORARY ISSUES IN HUMAN RESOURCES MANAGEMENT; CASES & READINGS, © 1980, pp. 455–456. Reprinted by permission of Prentice-Hall, Inc., Englewood Cliffs, New Jersey.

Questions

1. How did Ralph Stone set his objectives?
2. Are there any problems with the approach he used?
3. Analyze each of the goals Ralph has set.

EXHIBIT 1 Delta Corporation MBO worksheet

Name: Ralph Stone	**Department:** Fla. District Sales
Title: Field Sales Rep.	**Supervisor:** Wm. Joiner

Objectives	Target Date for Completion
1. Significantly increase market share of the Delta product line in my territory	continuing
2. Develop additional contacts within my present customers' organizations as well as prospecting for new business with firms we do not now service	daily
3. Strengthen my knowledge of the Delta product line	(as soon as possible)
4. Achieve a total sales volume of $326,000 for all products this quarter	June 30
5. Improve customer relations	continuing
6. Develop my management potential by completing at least one evening course this year at Florida Atlantic University	December 31

MANAGERIAL DECISION MAKING

Types of Decisions ☐ Managerial Decision-
Making Styles

INFORMATION FOR DECISION MAKING

Computer Information Systems ☐ The
System's Shape ☐ Management of the
System ☐ Expert Support Systems

THE DYNAMICS OF DECISION MAKING

Rational Decision Making ☐ Bounded
Rationality

CREATIVITY IN DECISION MAKING

What Is Creativity? ☐ Enhancing
Organizational Creativity

Summary ☐ Key Concepts ☐ Discussion
Questions ☐ Notes ☐ Supplementary
Reading

CASES: Delta Manufacturing Company
☐ Then and Now

This chapter will enable you to

☐   Explain decision making and the types
of decisions that managers face.

☐   Understand how a computer
information system aids managers in
making decisions.

☐   Describe and analyze how managers
actually make decisions and the
constraints under which they must
operate.

☐   Discuss organizational creativity and
how it may be enhanced.

CHAPTER 6
INFORMATION AND DECISION MAKING

The *decision-making process* is a part of management. Decision making is not always easy or pleasant, however. In organizational settings, there is a tempting tendency to postpone decisions, to wait for further developments, to engage in additional study. Of course, such a procedure is often logical. Yet there comes a time when choice is necessary. Effective managers distinguish themselves by their ability to reach logical decisions at such times.

H. Ross Perot, who founded Electronic Data Systems (EDS) and then sold it to General Motors, commented on the contrast between decision making at EDS and at GM shortly before leaving his position on the GM board of directors:[1]

> The first EDSer to see a snake kills it. At GM, first thing you do is organize a committee on snakes. Then, you bring in a consultant who knows a lot about snakes. Third thing you do is talk about it for a year.

MANAGERIAL DECISION MAKING

Managerial decision making involves a conscious choice. By making such a choice, a manager comes to a conclusion and selects a particular course of action from two or more alternatives. "The objective in making a decision . . . is to choose from among the most promising alternatives the one (or ones)

THE COMPOSITE DECISION

One of the most successful new car introductions in recent years was Ford's Taurus (as well as its sister, the Mercury Sable). Perhaps more than any automobile today, the Taurus represents the product of a composite decision.

Representatives from the planning, design, engineering, and manufacturing departments worked together as a group from the very beginning, rather than in traditional fashion—first product planning, then design, then engineering, and then manufacturing, with each working in isolation from the others. Considerable input was also gathered from the marketing department, assembly line workers, and Ford's suppliers.

SOURCE: Based on "How Ford Hit the Bull's-Eye with Taurus," *Business Week*, 30 June 1986, pp. 69–70.

that will produce the largest number of desirable consequences and the smallest number of unwanted consequences."[2]

In defining decision making, there is a tendency to focus upon the final moment in which the manager selects a course of action. A decision is announced, for example, that a new branch plant will be built in a particular city. Management has obviously made a decision. This concentration upon the final choice, however, tends to obscure the fact that decision making is in reality a process in which the choice of a particular solution is only the final step. The various stages of decision making include steps of investigation and analysis as well as the final choice of alternatives.

Managers make decisions because they have been delegated the necessary authority to make choices of this type. They are presumed to have the right to make decisions pertaining to the organization and activities subject to their direction. Their decision-making authority is not absolute, however. Behavioral scientists have stressed the numerous organizational influences at work in reaching a given decision. Many managers and even nonmanagerial personnel often affect the final choice. Herbert A. Simon refers to the *composite* decision and suggests that almost no decision made in an organization is the task of a single individual.[3]

Types of Decisions

A simple classification of decisions along a continuum ranging from *routine* to *nonroutine*—as shown in Figure 6–1—provides a useful distinction for study of managerial decision making. As can be seen, most decisions involve situations

FIGURE 6–1 A continuum of managerial decisions

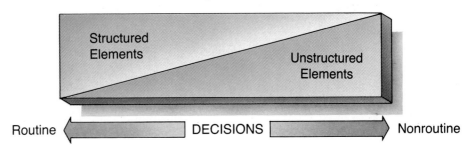

which contain both structured (that is, well-defined) and unstructured (that is, ill-defined) elements.

Decisions near the routine end of the continuum focus on well-structured situations. Such decisions recur frequently, involve standard decision procedures, and entail a minimum of uncertainty. Common examples include payroll processing, reordering standard inventory items, paying suppliers, and so on. The decision maker can usually rely upon policies, rules, past precedents, standardized methods of processing, or computational techniques. Probably 90 percent of management decisions are largely routine, although any manager's experience is significant in determining whether a specific decision is routine.

Decisions at the opposite—or nonroutine—end of the continuum deal with unstructured situations of a novel, nonrecurring nature. Their complexity is compounded by incomplete knowledge and the absence of accepted methods of resolution. Nonroutine decisions include not only the major corporate decisions, such as merger or acquisition, but also more restricted ones, such as adoption of a new advertising theme or motivation of a particular employee. A significant characteristic of such decisions is that no alternative can be proved to be the "best" possible solution to a particular problem. A much higher degree of subjective judgment and even intuition are involved in nonroutine decisions.

One of the most important lessons a manager can learn is that virtually all important—and most minor—decisions are made under conditions of ambiguity. Ambiguous situations may be characterized by *"lack of familiarity* (newness); *complexity* (interactions of events too difficult to analyze completely); or *contradictory situations* where different elements suggest different structures."[4] Even the most sophisticated mathematical decision models, the most elaborate computer systems, and the most complete market research cannot remove the element of ambiguity from managerial decision making. At best, they can reduce it somewhat. As one source suggests, you as a manager "should take adequate precautions by ensuring a sufficient number of alternative courses of action if your intended course turns out to be the wrong course."[5]

Managerial Decision-Making Styles

A dozen managers, each faced with the same unstructured problem, would likely use twelve widely divergent methods—or styles—to analyze the problem and formulate a solution. This variance in decision-making styles reflects differences among managers in the way they perceive, organize, and understand their environment. These differences stem from dissimilar work backgrounds, educational experiences, social influences, value systems, and psychological attributes.

Decision-making styles have been classified in many different ways. One recent classification suggests the following four basic styles:[6]

□ *Decisive*—refers to a manager who processes a minimum amount of information to arrive at one firm conclusion. This individual is concerned with action, results, speed, and efficiency. Long, detailed reports will be sent back, ignored, or given to someone else to summarize.

□ *Flexible*—characterizes a manager who prefers concise reports containing a wide variety of briefly stated alternatives from which to choose. Rather than planning highly structured solutions, this manager prefers that solutions evolve as he or she gains acceptance from others.

□ *Hierarchical*—describes a manager who carefully analyzes large amounts of information to arrive at one "best" solution. He or she values perfection, precision, and thoroughness. Brief or summarized reports are viewed as inadequate.

□ *Integrative*—refers to a manager who uses masses of information to generate many possible solutions simultaneously (rather than sequentially as flexible managers do). This manager constantly alters and improves his or her plans and shuns brief reports in favor of complex analyses from varying points of view.

The effectiveness of any particular decision-making style depends on the specific situation the manager is facing.

Wickham Skinner and W. Earl Sasser, in their analysis of managerial decision-making styles, conclude that successful decision makers are inconsistent in the way they attack problems, varying their approach to fit the problem situation.[7] One problem, for example, may require analysis at a high conceptual level, while another may require a review of operational details. In one situation, a manager may consult subordinates in solving a particular problem. In another situation, the same manager may arrive at the decision alone. Unsuccessful decision makers, on the other hand, generally approach each problem in the same predictable style. An adaptable contingency style is apparently more effective than a single, unvarying approach to decision making.

INFORMATION FOR DECISION MAKING

"It is a capital mistake to theorize before one has data," wrote Sir Arthur Conan Doyle in his *Adventures of Sherlock Holmes*. His statement could easily be applied today to the manager faced with a multitude of decisions. The importance of pertinent, timely information for decision making cannot be overlooked.

Information has been called "the raw material of which decisions are made." And, just as in manufacturing, a direct correlation exists between the quality of the raw material and the quality of the resultant product. In today's world of giant conglomerates and far-flung overseas operations, a manager without adequate, reliable information is completely lost.

Computer Information Systems

A manager receives some of the information needed for decision making through the firm's *computer information system* (CIS), a system that collects data related both to internal operations and the external environment and then transforms the data into usable information. Not all—not even most—information reaches the manager through this channel. Top managers particularly seem to rely on discussions with others for significant amounts of information, and scheduled committee meetings provide especially rich sources of information.[8] Less formal channels, such as social activities, business luncheons, telephone calls, strolls through the workplace, and periodicals also serve as information sources. Clearly, though, computers are providing increasing amounts of information to managers, and managers are using computers more and more to analyze data as a basis for decision making. In 1987, for example, *The Wall Street Journal* reported that 93 percent of senior executives used a personal computer, and 60 percent of the top managers surveyed used their computers for planning and decision support.[9]

The System's Shape

A CIS has two basic parts, as shown in Figure 6–2. During the 1960s and much of the 1970s, the emphasis in most organizations was on such *transaction processing functions* as payroll, accounts receivable and payable, and inventory record keeping. These functions were usually processed on large mainframe computers situated in centralized electronic data-processing departments.

During the 1980s, however, technological advances in hardware (physical equipment) and software (computer programs) have made it possible for virtually any manager to have access to computer power through a decision support system. A *decision support system* allows a manager to access and manipulate data from various sources in creative ways, including retrieving and combining data from different data bases inside or outside the organization,

FIGURE 6-2 Computer
information system

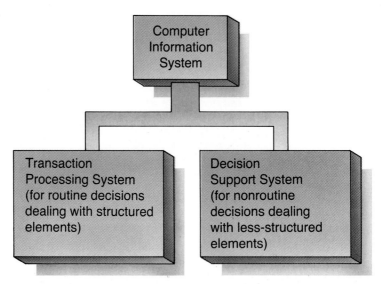

simulating the outcomes of various decisions, and displaying data in a variety
of tabular or graphic forms.[10]

In practice, a decision support system resembles the diagram in Figure
6–3. Managers with personal computers at their desks are able to access, via
modems, a central data base. A central data base allows managers of two separate departments to share the same information without having to store it in
two different places. It also protects the integrity of the data by allowing only
those managers who have approval to have access to certain information.

Additionally, managers may also maintain their own data bases, tailored
to their particular jobs. Either or both sets of data can be manipulated and
analyzed through either a general-purpose program package purchased from a
software company or a dedicated package designed for a manager's particular
use.

Many organizations have *networked*, or electronically linked, the firm's
computers. Networking permits data to be jointly used throughout the organization, facilitates the sharing of expensive printers or high-capacity hard disks,
and allows users to send electronic messages to one another. It is even possible,
through external networks, to link an organization's CIS to suppliers, distributors, and customers.

Management of the System

As information-processing applications proliferate, management is becoming
increasingly concerned about integrating the various computers and accompanying software into a system. Without well-designed policies, "the natural ten-

FIGURE 6–3 Simplified view of decision support system with a central data base

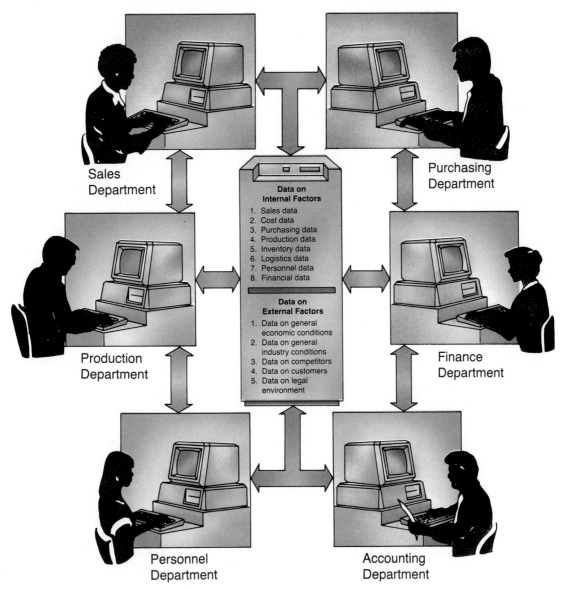

dency will be for users to acquire hardware and software without any consideration of overall corporate goals."[11]

The days when a central electronic data-processing department could control all information processing in an organization are over. Some organizations, however, have gone to the other extreme, allowing managers to buy whatever equipment or software they desire as long as they use their own

THE CIS AND STRATEGIC DECISION MAKING

The design of an organization's CIS should be supportive of the organization's strategy. Progressive companies use information technology to gain a competitive advantage. For instance, Merrill Lynch used a complex technology interface of communications and data processing between its brokerage offices and its bank to devise the Cash Management Account, which eliminated traditional boundaries between the banking and securities industries. As a result, Merrill Lynch gained about 450,000 new accounts and $60 million in annual fees.

In a far different industry, Akzo Coatings, a Dutch paint manufacturer, used information technology to reduce the anxiety of body shop customers (who worry about the cost of repairing their damaged cars) and body shop owners (who fear they will underestimate the costs of repairs). Akzo developed and now sells a computerized system that gives body shops instant access to spare-parts costs, repair procedures, and labor-cost guidelines for 2,000 car models. Shop employees simply enter a description of the car, the parts, and the repairs needed into a personal computer and instantly receive a repair cost calculation. This use of information technology gave Akzo a two-year lead over its competition.

SOURCE: Based on Robert I. Benjamin, John F. Rockart, Michael S. Scott Morton, and John Wyman, "Information Technology: A Strategic Opportunity," *Sloan Management Review* 25 (Spring 1984): 6; Henry C. Lucas, "Utilizing Information Technology: Guidelines for Managers," *Sloan Management Review* 28 (Fall 1986): 40; and "Information Power," *Business Week*, 14 October 1985, p. 111.

budgets. The outcome of such a system is a plethora of hardware and software that may serve individual managers well but overall is unworkable. For example, a manager in one department may learn a word processing or spreadsheet program but upon being transferred to another department may have to learn an entirely new system.

What is needed is an organization-wide set of policies and standards that permit individual departments to design systems that will meet their users' needs without violating compatibility requirements. The benefits of such a coordinated system are clear: the firm can purchase hardware and software at volume discounts, large numbers of employees can be trained to use standard systems, users can move freely from one department to another, and all of the computers can be electronically connected to form a network for the electronic transmission of data.[12]

Expert Support Systems

As a part of the field of artificial intelligence, computer programs called *expert support systems* (ESS) are being developed to help managers solve difficult problems through specialized symbolic reasoning. The scheme of an ESS is shown in Figure 6–4.

The *user interface* allows the computer system to communicate with the manager. Programmed into the computer is a knowledge base of facts and rules related to a problem and a set of reasoning methods, termed an *inference engine*. The reasoning methods interact with the knowledge base. Both can be added to as the problem evolves.[13]

For example, suppose you wished to find the single person on earth whose height and weight were closest to yours. A conventional computer program would compare you one-by-one with each of the five billion people on earth to find the closest match. This process would require about seven minutes on the largest of supercomputers. An ESS, however, could find the answer in about 75/1000 of a second, because the computer's memory would have been programmed to "reason" through a graphical map on which one axis is weight and the other is height. Each person on earth would be represented by a dot, so as soon as your height and weight were entered, the system would plot your height-weight coordinates and immediately identify the closest dot.[14]

FIGURE 6–4   Expert systems architecture

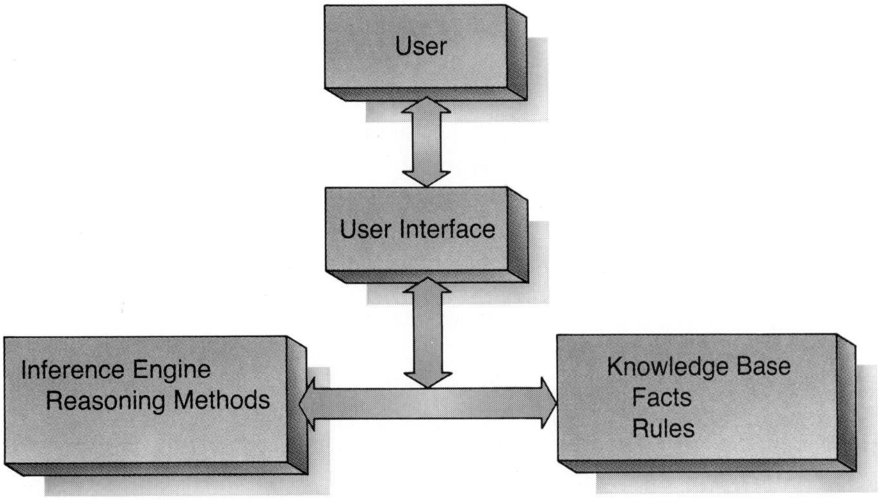

SOURCE: Reprinted from "Expert Systems: The Next Challenge for Managers," by Fred L. Luconi, Thomas W. Malone, and Michael S. Scott Morton, *Sloan Management Review* 27 (Summer 1986): 7, by permission of the publisher. Copyright © 1986 by the Sloan Management Review Association. All rights reserved.

Through this ability to "think," such systems may enable managers to make probabilistic decisions on the basis of incomplete and contradictory data and to retrieve all related facts when only a single piece of information is called up.[15] Expert support systems are now only in their primitive stage, but many organizations are already attempting to develop them in ways that will offer a distinct competitive advantage.

THE DYNAMICS OF DECISION MAKING

In chapter 4, we examined the making of strategic decisions. Now we turn to a more generic analysis of managerial decision making. Although decisions are required in determining strategy, they are also necessary in many other managerial functions—leading, motivating, controlling, staffing, structuring, and so on.

Rational Decision Making

A rational approach to decision making involves a series of steps to reach a problem solution, as illustrated in Figure 6–5. Recognition and proper identification of a problem constitute the first step in decision making.

Identification of Problem. A problem has often been defined as a discrepancy between what exists and what is desired. The same situation that one manager considers a problem may be perceived as an opportunity by another manager. In any case, problems or opportunities surface in various ways. Sometimes they explode in the face of management—a key supervisor resigns or a government contract is canceled. In other cases, imagination and perception are required to detect the problem, because problems often do not appear in convenient forms. Some years ago, Donald G. Fisher, who was in the San Francisco real estate business, bought a pair of Levi cords. When he found that the pair was the wrong size, he asked his wife to exchange them for a pair in the same style but the proper size. When she could not find his size in that

FIGURE 6–5 A model of the decision-making process

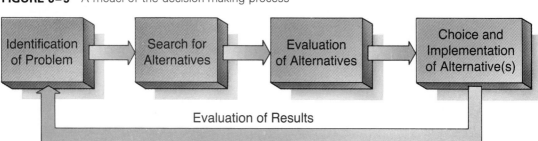

style, Mr. Fisher perceived an opportunity. He opened a store that carried every style and size that Levi Strauss made. The company that grew out of that single store became known as The Gap.[16]

Experience is often useful in helping a manager discover problems. One study of thirty-three upper-level managers in major organizations indicated that 80 percent of them were aware of a problem's existence before such formal indicators as financial figures reflected it and before a superior or subordinate presented it to them.[17]

Occasionally, managers waste time developing solutions to "problems" which are only symptoms of deeper problems. What appears to be a problem may not be the problem at all. A high rate of employee turnover, for instance, may be less a problem than a symptom of underlying defects in promotion policies, wages, or working conditions. Management must constantly strive, then, to sift from superficial difficulties the true problems that require investigation and solution. The way a decision maker perceives the problem is a major determinant of the alternative solutions that he or she will consider using.

Search for Alternatives.　Consideration of the various possible solutions or alternative courses of action constitutes the second stage of decision making. Richard M. Cyert and James. G. March theorize that managers begin their search for alternatives by identifying familiar alternatives employed in previous situations. If these alternatives seem unsuitable, then less familiar possibilities are explored.[18] Nonroutine decisions, then, often require imagination and creative thinking.

In searching for solutions, decision makers face certain constraints that limit their spheres of discretion. These constraints are barriers which preclude certain choices that would otherwise be possible. The two most immediate constraints involve time and money. Decisions must generally be made by a specific date, and unlimited funds are not available for many otherwise desirable alternatives. Other constraints may be imposed by top management, government regulations, technological limitations, economic conditions, the abilities and interests of the firm's employees, and so on.

Evaluation of Alternatives.　Evaluating the alternatives generated requires the manager to predict an uncertain future. Possible pros and cons must be considered. The manager may attempt to assign probabilities of future occurrence—based on past experience, formal forecasts, or subjective judgment—to the more pertinent factors.

At this stage, intuition may influence the decision process. Intuition "is that psychological function which transmits perceptions in an unconscious way."[19] One study reveals that senior-level managers use intuition in several different ways and in various stages of the decision-making process.[20] For instance, experienced managers can often intuitively sense when a problem exists. Intuition may also be used in its best-known form as an unconscious process in which managers integrate ideas that do not at first appear to be related (often termed the "aha!" experience). At the final stage of the decision process, intuition may be used by experienced managers as a check on the results of formal decision analysis models. To use intuition effectively, a manager must have extensive experience in problem analysis and decision making in his or her particular industry. Intuition is not a random guess, nor is it the opposite of rationality.

During the evaluation stage, the manager must also realize that various alternatives may have differing impacts on various parts of the organization. Special interests of specific departments and individuals tend to interfere with the process by which facts are investigated and decisions reached. A decision favorable for the firm as a whole may strengthen or weaken the positions of different departments. To protect and enhance their various positions, therefore, rival managers often compete with each other, bargain, build alliances with others, and in sometimes devious ways attempt to influence outcomes. The evaluation process, then, must include the power struggles among various factions in the organization.

The manager must also be aware that decisions at higher levels in the organization automatically trigger the need for specific operational decisions to be made at lower levels. A hospital administrator's decision to open a new intensive care unit, for example, initiates a series of decisions concerning what kinds of equipment will be needed, where it should be purchased, what types of personnel will be required, how these personnel will be organized, and so on.

Choice and Implementation of Alternative(s). The climax of the decision-making process arrives when the manager exercises the final judgment. The manager may have gone step by step through an analysis of the problem and the proposed solutions, but the moment arrives when choice is necessary.

If the choice is based upon a careful analysis, the manager is lauded as decisive. Indecision often indicates an unwillingness to face the situation. By choosing, one commits oneself to a given position. In some decisions, a reputation is at stake, and the decision maker may risk disagreement and misunderstanding. Decision making can thus be a lonely, agonizing process to some managers.

The act of choice does not end the decision-making process. Forthright expression of the decision once it is made can help clear the air of uncertainty. Explanations to those affected may be desirable if the reasoning supporting the particular course of action is not clear. This step is often necessary to gain the requisite understanding and support.

Finally, the manager spends a great deal of time in implementing decisions—in seeing that they are carried out. This requires an ability to secure the cooperation of others in seeing that plans are followed. The success or failure of a decision is largely determined by how well it is implemented. Evaluation of the relative success of the implemented decision involves the managerial function of control, which is discussed in chapter 17.

SUNK COSTS AND THE FUTURE

Have you ever gone to a movie that you had been eagerly anticipating and, within the first ten minutes, realized that the movie was not only lousy but also was unlikely to get any better? What did you do? According to a rational approach to decision making, you should have left the theatre at that point. But, in fact, many of us do not; we reason that we just paid $5.00 for admission plus $3.00 for refreshments and we hate to waste that money. Furthermore, we just drove through thirty minutes of heavy traffic to get to the theatre, and all of that effort would be for naught if we did not see the entire movie.

The point, of course, is that sunk costs (that is, costs already incurred) should be irrelevant in making decisions concerning future courses of action. Whether we leave the movie now or see it through to the bitter end, we will still have incurred the financial costs of $8.00, plus the psychic costs of wading through traffic. So why not go do something worthwhile with that last hour and a half rather than spend it watching a terrible movie?

NOTE: The reasons why managers stick with some courses of action longer than they ought to (often termed "escalating commitment to a course of action") are reported in Barry M. Staw and Jerry Ross, "Knowing When to Pull the Plug," *Harvard Business Review* 65 (March-April 1987): 68–74.

Bounded Rationality

Even taking into consideration practical constraints, *objective rationality* in decision making is an unattainable goal. The manager, operating from a unique perceptual perspective—influenced by his or her training, education, and experience—often identifies and understands only part of a complex problem. Identification of possible alternatives is limited by the manager's habits, incomplete understanding of the organization's goals, deficiencies in knowledge, and inadequate information. The manager, then, operates under conditions of *bounded rationality*, viewing a complex situation in an oversimplified way, taking into account only those few factors of which he or she is aware, understands, and regards as relevant.

Since neither the problem nor the alternative solutions are completely identified, it should not be surprising that the final decision does not—except by accident—yield a *maximum* return to the organization. Managers must instead settle for a satisfactory return. In other words, they cannot maximize; they must *satisfice*, that is, select a course of action that they believe will be satisfactory or "good enough."[21] As Lee Iacocca, chairman of Chrysler, once put it, "I have always found that if I move with 75 percent or more of the facts I usually never regret it. It's the guys that drive you crazy who wait to have everything perfect."[22]

Research indicates that managers are often more action-oriented than contemplative. A study of managers in fourteen companies operating in four countries concludes that:[23]

> Managing a response effectively requires that the manager get on with the job, rather than engage in a prolonged search for the ideal. Although managers found it difficult to interpret the uncertainties that surrounded them, they found that interacting with a problem was the most efficient route to a solution. This interaction led to an increased understanding of the situation that was greater than that which could be achieved through deskwork alone.

CREATIVITY IN DECISION MAKING

What Is Creativity?

Successful decision makers are creative. Creativity involves the development of new ideas, new combinations of existing knowledge, and new approaches to problem solving. Rather than taking an obvious explanation, the creative person is always questioning, probing for a deeper understanding, and seeking a better way.

In recent years, the term *entrepreneur* has gained popular usage in referring to creative people who take risks by starting their own businesses.* But entrepreneurs exist in businesses of all sizes and ages. At the heart of all entrepreneurial activity is innovation—the implementation of creative ideas. Innovative change can occur in small or large organizations. The individual manager's role in innovative change can range from creating new ideas and approaches to fostering an internal environment in which the creativity of subordinates is enhanced.

A mental block must first be overcome to encourage a person's creativity. As Herbert Simon points out, "As long as we refer to acts of creativity with awe and emphasize their unfathomability, we are unlikely to achieve an understanding of their processes."[24] Creativity is not a mysterious process: it is an outgrowth of training and experience stored as knowledge. This knowledge, combined with a sensitivity to opportunity, an understanding of future trends and developments, and a willingness to be adventurous, produces creative problem solving.[25]

---

*One author uses the term *intrapreneur* to refer to an entrepreneurial type who is an employee— rather than the owner/founder—of a company. See Gifford Pinchot III, *Intrapreneuring, or Why You Don't Have to Leave the Corporation to Become an Entrepreneur* (New York: Harper & Row, 1985).

Enhancing Organizational Creativity

The following suggestions are some of the ways in which organizational creativity can be enhanced. There are many other effective techniques.[26] Regardless of the technique, consistently innovative organizations are amply rewarded in the marketplace.

Foster a Supportive Environment. James Brian Quinn, in a study of innovative large companies on three continents, concludes that "continuous innovation occurs largely because top executives appreciate innovation and manage their company's value system and atmosphere to support it."[27] Such executives project a vision of excellence; that is, they expect their organizations to be industry leaders in innovation. Such vision, if supported through appropriate resource allocation, can attract quality employees and give focus to their entrepreneurial drives.[28]

Any person who has worked at different times in a stagnant, bureaucratic organization and in a progressive, innovative organization clearly understands the importance of a supportive environment. In the former situation, employees with creative ideas are flatly informed that their proposals will not work, and their bosses may even read them policies or rules that prohibit the proposed behavior. On the other hand, in the latter situation the employee's boss often responds to creative ideas with "let's find a way to make this work!"

Establish a New Venture Division. Because the bureaucracy of large organizations can stifle creativity, many companies form new venture divisions to nurture innovative ideas. A *new venture division* is a small organizational unit guided by entrepreneurial managers. Though autonomous of the corporation's daily operations, the unit receives long-term financial and technological support from that parent company.[29] One of the pioneers of this concept is 3M Company. To attain its goal of having one-fourth of its annual sales revenue come from new products, 3M allows any employee who has an idea for a new product not supported by his or her supervisor to go to any other division in the company to seek funding. If the idea is funded, a team of volunteers from various disciplines forms a business development group. If the product becomes a success, the team is rewarded; if it fails, all members of the group are guaranteed a job at their previous level in the organization. To encourage creativity, failure must not be disparaged.

Use Nominal Groups to Generate New Ideas. The *nominal group technique* (NGT) can be used to generate new ideas from individuals with varied backgrounds and perceptions without the distractions associated with such traditional interacting groups as committees.[30] The term *nominal* refers to a group of people working in the presence of one another without interacting.

Interacting groups can stifle the generation of new ideas in a number of ways: domination by one person, pressure to conform, negative prejudgment

CREATIVITY IS HARD WORK!

As Thomas Alva Edison, who held 1,093 patents, stated: "Genius is one percent inspiration and ninety-nine percent perspiration." Indeed, evidence indicates that highly creative people work extraordinarily hard: Einstein produced 248 publications; Picasso turned out an average of over 200 works per year; Mozart wrote over 600 compositions before dying at age 35; Bach dictated his final composition (well over his 1,000th) on his deathbed at 65; and twentieth-century U.S. Nobel laureates in science wrote an average of over one dozen publications before turning 30, four times what ordinary scientists write in their entire careers.

SOURCE: Based on Daniel Q. Haney, "Key to Creativity May Be Drive—Not Intelligence," *The Houston Post*, 6 February 1985.

of new ideas, and pursuit of only a single train of thought (since the initial stages of a discussion may focus thoughts in one particular direction).[31] To overcome these weaknesses, the NGT has each group member formulate ideas by writing each idea on a separate card without speaking to the other group members. The purpose is to stimulate "creative tension" within the group members by placing them in the presence of others who are silently working. If one member observes other members industriously writing down alternative solutions, then he or she will be encouraged to formulate a list of alternative solutions.

Then, each group member, one at a time, reads aloud the alternatives on the card. Each alternative is recorded on a blackboard or tear sheet as it is read aloud. No comments are permitted as the alternatives are read and recorded.

Since discussion is at first prohibited, the problems associated with committees are unlikely to occur. In one comparative study, for example, nominal groups generated significantly more alternative solutions (an average of thirteen) to a problem than did traditional interacting groups (an average of 8.4).[32]

Train Employees to Become More Creative. There is some evidence that a person's creative potential can be developed through training. For example, after undergoing two days of intensive training in creative problem solving, a group of thirty-two engineers, engineering managers, and technicians showed evidence of improved creativity. They spent more time in different modes of thinking, they were more open to different ideas, and they made fewer negative judgments about new ideas.[33] Many companies, such as General Electric and Arco Petroleum, are so convinced that such training works that they sponsor creativity workshops for their employees.[34]

SUMMARY

Managerial decision making is an integral part of the management process. It involves a *conscious choice* from among two or more alternative courses of action. The decisions that managers face vary from *routine* to *nonroutine*, with the latter being characterized by incomplete knowledge, ambiguous information, and the absence of accepted methods of resolution. The approach—or style— used to solve such nonroutine problems varies among managers and depends upon each manager's background, perceptions, and psychological attributes.

Managers receive information for decision making in a variety of forms. The most formal information channel is the firm's *computer information system* (CIS), which collects data on internal operations and the external environment and then transforms the data into usable information. Although computers were traditionally used for *transaction processing functions* (such as payroll), recent technological advances have made it possible for managers to have direct access to computer power through a *decision support system*. Such systems allow managers to access and manipulate data from various sources in creative ways, usually via a personal computer that also provides access to a central data base. An organization's CIS requires careful management to ensure that compatibility and electronic networking requirements are met. Recent advances in artificial intelligence have brought the potential of *expert support systems* closer to managers' offices.

The decision-making process begins with the *identification of a problem* and then proceeds to a search for possible solutions or *alternative courses of action*. The selection of feasible alternatives is bounded by a number of practical and psychological constraints. The alternatives that are identified must be carefully *evaluated*, and the evaluation should lead logically to the *choice and implementation of one or more alternatives*. Because managers often have an incomplete understanding of the problem and its alternative solutions, decision makers, of necessity, *satisfice* rather than *maximize*.

Successful decision makers are creative, and creativity is essential to organizational innovation. Organizations can stimulate creativity in decision making in a number of ways, including fostering a supportive environment, establishing a new venture division, using nominal groups to generate new ideas, and training employees to become more creative.

KEY CONCEPTS

Routine decision	Decision support system
Nonroutine decision	Networking
Decision-making style	Expert support system
Computer information system	Intuition

Sunk costs

Bounded rationality

Maximizing

Satisficing

Creativity

Entrepreneur

New venture division

Nominal group technique

DISCUSSION QUESTIONS

1. Why are most important managerial decisions actually *composite* decisions?
2. Give an example of a *nonroutine decision* that must be made under conditions of ambiguity. Can the ambiguity be removed?
3. Explain the distinction between the transaction processing and the decision support functions of a CIS.
4. What are the advantages to managers of having their own *decision support systems* rather than having to rely on a centralized data processing center?
5. What are the advantages of electronic networking?
6. "Problems, problems—all I have is problems!" These words of one manager indicate a sharp awareness of problems. In what way could *problem identification* be difficult?
7. What are the principal difficulties that hamper the development of *alternatives* in decision making?
8. If the preceding steps in decision making are taken, why is the final step of *choosing an alternative* difficult?
9. If a manager is effective as a decision maker, does this indicate that he or she is a good manager?
10. Why do not even the most thoroughly considered decisions yield *maximum returns* to the organization?
11. Explain how the concept of *satisficing* might apply in the decision to purchase a computer for use in a large business corporation.
12. Assume that your university is trying to identify ways to increase its enrollment. How might the number of creative suggestions from the members of the committee on student enrollment be enhanced?

NOTES

1. "Ross Perot's Crusade," *Business Week*, 6 October 1986, p. 61.
2. E. Frank Harrison, *The Managerial Decision-Making Process* (Boston: Houghton Mifflin Co., 1975), p. 32.
3. Herbert A. Simon, *Administrative Behavior* (New York: Macmillan, 1957).
4. Martin L. Gimpl and Stephen R. Dakin, "Management and Magic," *California Management Review* 27 (Fall 1984): 132.
5. Ibid., p. 135.
6. Phillip L. Hunsaker and Johanna S. Hunsaker, "Decision Styles—In Theory, in Practice," *Organizational Dynamics* 10 (Autumn 1981): 23–36.
7. Wickham Skinner and W. Earl Sasser, "Managers with Impact: Versatile and Inconsistent," *Harvard Business Review* 55 (November-December 1977): 140–48.

8. Jack William Jones and Raymond McLeon, Jr., "The Structure of Executive Information Systems: An Exploratory Analysis," *Decision Sciences* 17 (Spring 1986): 220–49; and Henry Mintzberg, *The Nature of Managerial Work* (New York: Harper & Row, 1973).

9. "Executives' Computers," *The Wall Street Journal*, 23 February 1987.

10. Bernard C. Reimann, "Decision Support Systems: Strategic Management Tools for the Eighties," *Business Horizons* 28 (September/October 1985): 72.

11. Henry C. Lucas, "Utilizing Information Technology: Guidelines for Managers," *Sloan Management Review* 28 (Fall 1986): 41.

12. Thomas P. Gerrity and John F. Rockart, "End-User Computing: Are You a Leader or a Laggard?", *Sloan Management Review* 27 (Summer 1986): 33–4.

13. Fred L. Luconi, Thomas W. Malone, and Michael S. Scott Morton, "Expert Systems: The Next Challenge for Managers," *Sloan Management Review* 27 (Summer 1986): 4.

14. "Computers That Come Awfully Close to Thinking," *Business Week*, 2 June 1986, pp. 93–4.

15. Ibid., pp. 92–6.

16. Trish Hall, "For a Company Chief, When There's a Whim There's Often a Way," *The Wall Street Journal*, 1 October 1984.

17. Marjorie A. Lyles and Ian I. Mitroff, "Organizational Problem Formulation: An Empirical Study," *Administrative Science Quarterly* 25 (March 1980): 109.

18. R. M. Cyert and J. G. March, *A Behavioral Theory of the Firm* (Englewood Cliffs, N.J.: Prentice-Hall, 1963), pp. 120–22.

19. Carl G. Jung, *Psychological Types*, trans. H. Godwin Baynes (New York: Harcourt, Brace, 1924), p. 568.

20. Daniel J. Isenberg, "How Senior Managers Think," *Harvard Business Review* 62 (November-December 1984): 85–86.

21. Herbert A. Simon, *Administrative Behavior*, 3d ed. (New York: The Free Press, 1976).

22. " 'No Free Lunches'," *Newsweek*, 8 October 1984, p. 71.

23. R. Jeffery Ellis, "Improving Management Response in Turbulent Times," *Sloan Management Review* 23 (Winter 1982): 3.

24. Herbert A. Simon, "How Managers Express Their Creativity," *The McKinsey Quarterly* (Autumn 1986): 67.

25. Ibid., 67–78.

26. An excellent list of suggestions can be found in James Brian Quinn, "Managing Innovation: Controlled Chaos," *Harvard Business Review* 63 (May-June 1985): 73–84.

27. Ibid., p. 77.

28. Ibid., p. 78.

29. Robert A. Burgelman, "Managing the New Venture Division: Research Findings and Implications for Strategic Management,"*Strategic Management Journal* 6 (January-March 1985): 39–54.

30. The nominal group technique was devised by Andrew H. Van de Ven and Andre L. Delbecq. The technique is described in a number of sources; one of the clearest statements may be found in Van de Ven and Delbecq, "Nominal versus Interacting Group Processes for Committee Decision-Making Effectiveness," *Academy of Management Journal* 14 (June 1971): 203–12.

31. Ibid.

32. Charles D. Pringle and Sue E. Neeley, "Nominal vs. Interacting Groups: Further Evidence," *The Mid-Atlantic Journal of Business* 21 (Summer 1983): 25–34.
33. Min Basadur, George B. Graen, and Stephen G. Green, "Training in Creative Problem Solving: Effects on Ideation and Problem Finding and Solving in an Industrial Research Organization," *Organizational Behavior and Human Performance* 30 (August 1982): 41–70.
34. "Are You Creative?", *Business Week*, 30 September 1985, p. 81.

SUPPLEMENTARY READING

Ackoff, **Russell L.** *The Art of Problem Solving: Accompanied by Ackoff's Fables.* New York: Wiley, 1978.

Arkes, **Hal R.,** and **Blumer, Catherine.** "The Psychology of Sunk Cost." *Organizational Behavior and Human Performance* 35 (February 1985): 124–40.

Bowen, **Michael G.** "The Escalation Phenomenon Reconsidered: Decision Dilemmas or Decision Errors." *Academy of Management Review* 12 (January 1987): 52–66.

Camillus, **John C.,** and **Lederer, Albert L.** "Corporate Strategy and the Design of Computerized Information Systems." *Sloan Management Review* 26 (Spring 1985): 35–42.

Carroll, **Archie B.** "Behavioral Aspects of Developing Computer-Based Information Systems." *Business Horizons* 25 (January/February 1982): 42–51.

Couger, **J. Daniel.** "E Pluribus Computum." *Harvard Business Review* 64 (September-October 1986): 87–91.

Drucker, **Peter F.** "The Discipline of Innovation." *Harvard Business Review* 63 (May-June 1985): 67–72.

Einhorn, **Hillel J.,** and **Hogarth, Robin M.** "Decision Making: Going Forward in Reverse." *Harvard Business Review* 65 (January-February 1987): 66–70.

Franz, **Charles R.,** and **Robey, Daniel.** "Organizational Context, User Involvement, and the Usefulness of Information Systems." *Decision Sciences* 17 (Summer 1986): 329–56.

Galbraith, **Jay R.,** "Designing the Innovating Organization." *Organizational Dynamics* 10 (Winter 1982): 5–25.

Jones, **Jack William,** and **McLeod, Raymond Jr.** "The Structure of Executive Information Systems: An Exploratory Analysis." *Decision Sciences* 17 (Spring 1986): 220–49.

Kanter, **Rosabeth Moss.** "The Middle Manager as Innovator." *Harvard Business Review* 60 (July-August 1982): 95–105.

Northcraft, **Gregory B.,** and **Neale, Margaret A.** "Opportunity Costs and the Framing of Resource Allocation Decisions." *Organizational Behavior and Human Decision Processes* 37 (June 1986): 348–56.

Porter, **Michael E.,** and **Millar, Victor E.** "How Information Gives You Competitive Advantage." *Harvard Business Review* 63 (July-August 1985): 149–60.

Ross, **Jerry,** and **Staw, Barry M.** "Expo 86: An Escalation Prototype." *Administrative Science Quarterly* 31 (June 1986): 274–97.

Rutigliano, **Anthony J.** "An Interview with Peter Drucker: Managing the New." *Management Review* 75 (January 1986): 38–41.

Sinetar, Marsha. "SMR Forum: Entrepreneurs, Chaos, and Creativity—Can Creative People Really Survive Large Company Structure?" *Sloan Management Review* 26 (Winter 1985): 57–62.

Whyte, Glen. "Escalating Commitment to a Course of Action: A Reinterpretation." *Academy of Management Review* 11 (April 1986): 311–21.

DELTA MANUFACTURING COMPANY

Over the past ten years, Delta Manufacturing Company had grown both in market share and human resources. The company was initially staffed with five people who formed a tightly knit and cohesive work group. Harold Baker, the company's president and founder, had always performed the personnel function for the company, since he knew every employee as well as their families.

The company had grown to a staff of over eighty people comprising several major departmental units. Consequently, Baker made the decision to hire a personnel director to handle the human resources function for the company. He selected Robert Carson, a young business graduate from a local university, as his director of human resources. Rather than place Robert in a direct reporting relationship with himself, Baker decided to have Robert report through Jim Copper, the company's vice-president in charge of manufacturing.

All went fairly smoothly for the first several months of Robert's employment. He seemed to be making the correct employment decisions and kept the company clear of any discrimination or wrongful-discharge complaints. The fact that

Case prepared by Donald R. Myers, vice-president of Dominion Trust Company.

his boss, Jim Copper, had a close working relationship with the president pleased Robert, since Robert felt this made his future secure.

One afternoon Jim Copper called Robert to his office and told him that it would be necessary to fire a clerk who was responsible for incorrect billings to several customers. Robert realized that this decision was possibly a result of a personality conflict between the billing clerk and Jim, since the billing clerk had spoken confidentially with Robert on two occasions about problems with Jim, the clerk's immediate supervisor. Because these discussions were confidential, there was very little Robert could tell Jim other than that it was necessary for Jim to provide documented reasons for firing a person. According to the firm's probationary policy, unless an employee was guilty of dishonesty or malfeasance, he or she had to be given a written warning concerning the poor job performance and a sixty-day probationary period in which to improve performance to a satisfactory level.

When Robert explained his position to Jim, Jim simply retorted with the demand, "Fire the bum!" When Robert tried to explain the legal reasons for documentation, Jim abruptly stated that if Robert did not comply with his directive, it could mean Robert's job also.

Questions

1. List three possible courses of action which Robert could take at this point. What is the probable outcome of each course of action?
2. What possible effect might the close working relationship between Harold Baker and Jim Copper have on Robert's decision?
3. Based on the facts stated in this case, what would be the action you would take as personnel director?

THEN AND NOW

Procurement of good quality raw materials at a minimum price is the goal of any Materials Management Department. This goal takes on great importance for one *Fortune* 500 pharmaceutical company, for these reasons:

- □ The raw material quality is constantly changing, since it is considered a by-product for the normal operations of the supplier. Trends in the quality are detectable.
- □ The raw material cost is at commodity prices ranging from $.06 to $.15 per pound.
- □ Suppliers are located far enough from the plant site that shipping expense is an important cost component.
- □ The final effect on the manufacturing process is severely impacted by the quality of the raw material.
- □ Once a quality trend is detected in the raw material, there are only twenty-four hours to purchase and properly store the lot before quality declines significantly.

Case prepared by Robert J. Pengelly of James Madison University.

Development of pharmaceutical drugs having unique properties can take ten years or more. To protect this immense investment, patents are actively sought. Once the drug gains federal approval and enters the market, price mark-ups of several thousand percent are not uncommon. There is little incentive to control or reduce production costs: the primary goal is to be certain that enough product is available to meet demand. By the time the patent expires, the next generation of the drug is normally ready for the market.

In one case, a particular drug became preferred by doctors for treatment of certain ailments. That product became a major source of income for the company. Yet the "cash cow" days of the product were quickly ending because the patent was to expire in the coming months. The company would then face generic competition; other manufacturers would be free to use the patent information in developing their manufacturing processes.

At this point, management decided to change its usual strategy of being a "premium producer of drug therapy" to that of being a "low cost producer." All departments were expected to introduce a crash program of cost reduction. It was obvious that Materials Management would have an important role in this endeavor.

The program developed by Materials Management relied on personal computers to provide an increase in the speed of data collection, the dissemination of information by modems, the manipulation and trend analysis of data, and the graphic capabilities of spread-sheet software.

Laboratory tests of the raw material were conducted daily at each potential supplier's location. The data from a battery of tests for each supplier were transferred to Materials Management by modem each day by 9 A.M. An equation that weighted each component test of the battery provided a ranking factor. This ranking factor for the specific supplier would be processed by the software program to detect a trend. Trends of all suppliers were examined. Based on a qualifying trend and the last ranking factor, an expected process yield could be estimated with a corresponding cost per kilogram. Transportation cost and availability were then determined. Normally, rail service was the most cost effective form of transportation, but rail service was not available each day from each supplier. If a "back-haul" was available for a trucking line, its price would be competitive with rail service. (Trucking lines normally charge a reduced rate when they can carry goods in both directions, as opposed to carrying goods in one direction and returning with an empty trailer.) On-line data links were developed between key contract transportation lines to determine availability of service and back-haul possibilities to minimize costs.

The combination of the estimated raw-material price and the transportation cost per projected product produced was determined for each supplier by using the spreadsheet. The supplier that maximized quality and minimized cost was selected and the material captured and shipped. This system reduced the raw material costs by almost 50 percent and raised productivity of the process by 20 percent.

Question

1. How would this problem/opportunity have been handled before management had access to computers?

THE NATURE OF QUANTITATIVE METHODS
Development of Management Science □ Definition and Scope of Management Science

THE METHODOLOGY OF MANAGEMENT SCIENCE
The Use of Models □ Mathematical Models □ Advantages of Models

MANAGEMENT SCIENCE TECHNIQUES
Linear Programming □ Probability Theory □ Program Evaluation Review Technique

EVALUATION OF MANAGEMENT SCIENCE
Limitations of Management Science □ Future of Management Science

Summary □ Key Concepts □ Discussion Questions □ Notes □ Supplementary Reading

CASES: Liquid Assets Company □ The Micromesh Decision

This chapter will enable you to

☐ Define management science and explain how managers can use it to reduce risk in decision making.

☐ Explain model building and discuss the advantages of using mathematical models to analyze problem situations.

☐ Describe specific management science techniques and illustrate their use in managerial decision making.

☐ Delineate the limitations of management science and discuss the prospects for its future use.

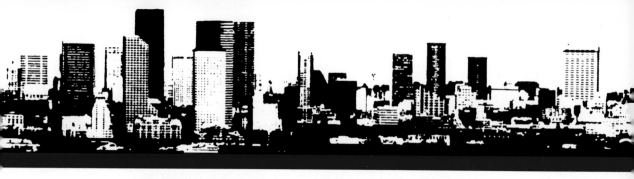

CHAPTER 7
QUANTITATIVE METHODS IN DECISION MAKING

In recent years, managers, managerial literature, and management theorists have emphasized the use of *quantitative techniques* in decision making. Some experts feel that the manager of the future who has an understanding of mathematical concepts will have a marked advantage over one who has little or no knowledge of such techniques. This chapter examines quantitative methods, some of the specific techniques used, and the advantages and limitations of a quantitative approach to decision making.

THE NATURE OF QUANTITATIVE METHODS

Development of Management Science

Managers have used quantitative techniques in decision making for decades. For instance, such factors as the rate of inventory turnover, quality control limits, and return on investment involve quantitative concepts, and all have been used for many years. However, the modern emphasis on quantitative methods involves a much different concept known as *management science*, or *operations research*.

Although these modern techniques are, in some cases, based on mathematical principles dating back as far as the eighteenth century, the specific body of knowledge known today as management science did not emerge until

World War II. During the war, both British and American military leaders enlisted teams of scientists and mathematicians to aid them in solving complex military problems, such as assigning targets and scheduling bomb strikes or determining the safest method of transporting personnel and supplies across the oceans. The value of such systematic, mathematical analysis quickly became evident, and following the war those who had served on operations research teams began to realize that the same basic concepts could be applied to other areas, such as managerial decision making.

Perhaps the major impetus to the growth of management science, however, was the invention of the electronic computer. Since management science is designed to deal with a complex set of interrelated factors, a tremendous amount of data is necessary for maximum effectiveness. Such large volumes of data can practicably be processed only by computer.

Definition and Scope of Management Science

The intent of management science is to improve organizational effectiveness by reducing the risk involved in decision making. Basically, it supplements the manager's experience and intuition with rigorous quantitative analysis. Many nonroutine decisions are so complicated that it would be quite difficult, or even impossible, for one person to visualize all of the significant interrelated factors. Without some sort of systematic, logical method of analysis, these problems would be solved subjectively. Management science, then, provides an objective supplement to the decision process, helping managers clarify their logic and thereby improve the quality of their decisions.

Management science is a mathematical application of the scientific method to the solution of organizational problems. Its distinguishing characteristics are the following:

1. A systems view of the problem—a viewpoint is taken which includes all of the significant interrelated variables contained in the problem.
2. The team approach—personnel with varied backgrounds and training work together on specific problems.
3. An emphasis on the use of formal mathematical models and statistical and quantitative techniques.

Few major nonroutine problems can be limited to only one functional area. Analysis of a complex production problem, for example, might involve not only the production department but also representatives from marketing and personnel—other functional areas interdependent with production. A typical team might include the manager(s) of the department(s) being studied, a superior who understands the total system being analyzed and has authority over various interrelated subsystems, a management science specialist, and a computer professional. The team members, using statistical and quantitative methods, develop a mathematical model of the relationships among the signif-

A SYSTEMS VIEW

Author Barry Shore reports what one team found when studying a small part of a large company:

> There is an interesting story about an inventory manager who prided himself on *never* running out of stock. Only on rare occasions were any of his shelves empty. Late in his career a team composed of representatives from production, inventory control, finance, and marketing was asked to study this inventory system, which had been so "successful" for 30 years. What they found was astonishing. His shelves were overflowing with stock. Millions of extra dollars were tied up in inventory for the purpose of preventing any possibility of an out-of-stock position. They quickly recommended a drastic reduction that would on occasion subject the organization to stockouts but would release much-needed funds for other investments. The team pointed out that the inventory manager viewed his function in very narrow terms and completely ignored the financial considerations of inventory control. Fortunately for the company, the team took a systems point of view.

SOURCE: Barry Shore, *Quantitative Methods for Business Decisions: Text and Cases* (New York: McGraw-Hill, 1978), pp. 7–8.

icant problem elements and then arrive at recommendations based upon their analysis of the model.

This methodology can be profitably applied to a variety of organizational problems. The following list of practical applications, while not exhaustive, indicates the widespread usefulness of management science techniques:

1. Production scheduling
2. Warehouse and retail-outlet location selection
3. Portfolio management
4. Product-and-marketing mix selection
5. Air and highway traffic control
6. Credit management
7. Hospital menu planning
8. Drug abuse treatment and rehabilitation

It must be emphasized that the team neither replaces the manager nor takes over managerial decision-making responsibility. The group merely attempts to formulate objective criteria upon which managers can base their decisions.

Managers do not need to be mathematicians to benefit from management science. However, they do need some understanding of quantitative tools—at least enough to enable them to appreciate the potential of quantitative analysis and to be aware of its limitations. Such an understanding will place them in a much better position to undertake the scientific analysis of problems and to communicate intelligently with management science specialists.

THE METHODOLOGY OF MANAGEMENT SCIENCE

The Use of Models

The essence of the management science approach to decision making is *model building*. A model is basically a simplified representation of an actual situation or subject. Some types of models are quite common—model airplanes or automobiles built to scale are physical models; a road map is a geographic model; and the diagrams used in elementary economics textbooks to describe the concept of supply and demand are graphic models.

A model contains only the most important and basic features of the real system it represents. It is not necessary, for example, that a road map show houses, buildings, and trees. Such a map would be completely unwieldy. But a model can also be too abstract. A map showing only interstate highways would be of little use to a traveler going to a town fifty miles from such a highway.

Mathematical Models

The models used in management science are mathematical, but their fundamental concept is no different from that of the road map—a simplified representation of a real system. Mathematical models are constructed by devising a set of equations which represent the significant variables that must be considered and the relationships among those variables. Any important variable that would affect the decision must be included. Some models are highly complex and are, therefore, very difficult to construct. But underlying this complexity is always the basic equation that a measure of the system's overall performance (P) equals the relationship (f) between a set of significant controllable aspects of the system (C_i) and a set of uncontrollable aspects (U_j). Expressed symbolically, it would appear as follows:[1]

$$P = f(C_i, U_j)$$

Examples of controllable aspects of variables are product prices, size and frequency of production runs, and departmental budgets. For the model to be realistic, limitations or constraints must be placed on these variables. Product prices, for instance, can fluctuate only within certain limits. A ridiculously high price would cause sales to drop to zero, and an extremely low price would fail to cover production costs. The uncontrollable variables—those not subject to the manager's control—would include such factors as competitors' prices and raw-materials costs.

Mathematical models may be either deterministic or probabilistic. In a *deterministic model*, all variables are assigned exact values. A product price, for instance, may be exactly $56, or the distance between two warehouses in a transportation problem may be 131 miles. In a *probabilistic model*, the values of some variables are uncertain. This uncertainty requires the use of probability concepts. The probability of striking oil when drilling, for instance, may be 10 percent. This figure might be based on past experience—the company, over a period of years, has discovered oil one of every ten times it has drilled.

Advantages of Models

Construction of a model requires the manager and the management science team to consider carefully which aspects of the real system are significant, how much weight should be assigned to each, and how they are all interrelated. These preliminary decisions are valuable in themselves, because they force the manager to analyze in detail the problem situation.

Once the model is constructed, the manager can analyze, manipulate, and modify it without disturbing the real system. As in the physical sciences, some variables are held constant while others are manipulated to determine how the real system would be affected by certain changes. This process, called *simulation*, is used to answer "what if" questions.

A model can simulate the operation of an entire firm or of a single department. Production in GM's Saturn plant, for instance, was simulated two years before the plant was constructed.[2] Computers can also simulate a selected geographic or demographic market to determine probable customer reaction to a change in marketing strategy, such as packaging or advertising.

A further advantage of using models is that it provides excellent managerial training. A manager's decision-making ability can be greatly enhanced by dealing with simulated situations involving different aspects of the job. In a few weeks or months, a manager can observe problem situations which would ordinarily occur over a period of years.

A widespread use of simulation is the *business game*, developed in the mid 1950s and now used extensively in universities and management-training programs. Participants make corporate strategy decisions that are likely to yield profits in a competitive environment—increasing the firm's share of the market by lowering prices, increasing advertising expenditures, improving product quality, or investing in employee training programs. The game participant does not know what competitors may do or what changes may occur in the environment. Certain assumptions must be made as a basis for action. Such "play" is helpful in training managers.

The advantages of simulation depend on the degree to which a model realistically represents the actual system. A drastically oversimplified model

SIMULATION IN ACTION

Using a mathematical model developed by researcher Narendra Karmarkar, the Bell Labs division of AT&T has been able to solve unbelievably complex problems. For example, the Karmarkar algorithm was used to develop plans for linking twenty countries bordering the Pacific Ocean into a fiber-optic and satellite transmission network. The problem contained some 43,000 variables involving transmission capacity, location, and construction schedules, as well as numerous political considerations. The Karmarkar algorithm solved the problem in four minutes.

SOURCE: Based on "Karmarkar Algorithm Proves Its Worth," *The Wall Street Journal*, 18 July 1986.

will certainly not be realistic, but one which attempts to duplicate the real system in every detail will be unmanageable. And some problems contain intangible and human factors which may be of paramount importance yet may be difficult or impossible to quantify and, therefore, to include in the model.

MANAGEMENT SCIENCE TECHNIQUES

Three widely used management science techniques are linear programming, probability theory, and the program evaluation review technique. Each has a different purpose. Which technique is used depends on the specifics of a situation.

Linear Programming

Linear programming is a deterministic model that aids the manager in deciding upon the optimal allocation of a firm's limited resources. Such resources include money, capital equipment, raw materials, and personnel. Because they are limited, the manager wishes to use them in the most profitable combination; and their allocation is based upon an objective selected by management, such as maximum profit or minimum cost. Linear programming is one of the most widely used management science tools.

To be solvable by this technique, a problem must have the following characteristics:

☐ A specified objective criterion.
☐ Limited resources with alternative uses.
☐ Quantitative measurement of the problem elements.

□ Linearity—all of the relationships in the problem must be precisely proportional. For instance, a 10 percent increase in shipping distance must cause a commensurate rise in shipping costs.

Once it is evident that the problem meets the linear programming requirements, the mathematical model can be formulated. Such a model is basically a set of linear equations describing the problem in mathematical terms. The equations are then solved simultaneously by a specific linear programming technique, such as the graphic method, simplex method, dual simplex method, or the modified distribution (MODI) method. The method selected would depend upon the nature of the problem.

A simple illustration will help to demonstrate the basic procedure. Assume that a company which has manufactured and sold box spring and mattress sets for years has recently decided to diversify its product line by manufacturing love seats. The process used to produce love seats is similar to that employed in constructing box springs, and the profit margin for love seats is higher.

Management is now faced with a decision: How many mattress/box spring sets should it produce and how many love seats should it manufacture? Demand for both products appears high and relatively stable. Each mattress/box spring set sold contributes $100 to net profit, while each love seat sold will contribute $150. Each product must go through two processes: (1) framework construction with a total of 100 hours' capacity per month and (2) assembly with a total capacity of 80 hours per month.

Each love seat requires 4 hours in framework and 2 hours in assembly. Each mattress/box spring set requires 2 hours in framework and 2 hours in assembly. What combination of mattress/box spring sets and love seats should management produce in order to maximize its profits? Summarizing the situation in tabular form, as shown in Table 7–1, helps to visualize the problem more clearly.

The problem can now be transformed into the following mathematical model:

$$\text{Profit}_{\text{max}} = \$100M + \$150L$$

TABLE 7–1 The linear programming problem

Processes	Hours Required/Product		Monthly Capacity in Hours
	Mattress/Box Spring Set	Love Seat	
Framework	2	4	100
Assembly	2	2	80
Contribution to profit	$100	$150	

Subject to:

$$2M + 4L \leqslant 100 \text{ (Framework)}$$
$$2M + 2L \leqslant 80 \text{ (Assembly)}$$
$$\text{where } M, L \geqslant 0$$

The top line in the model, called the *objective function*, tells us that the goal or objective of this problem is to maximize profits when each mattress/box spring set (M) contributes \$100 to profits and each love seat (L) contributes \$150.

This objective function is subject to the following *constraints*: the framework process has a maximum monthly capacity of 100 hours and each M requires 2 hours of this capacity while each L requires 4 hours; and in the assembly process, which has a total capacity of 80 hours, each M requires 2 hours and each L requires 2 hours. In no case can total production time in either process exceed the monthly capacity of the process although production time may be less than capacity (i.e., $\leqslant$). Finally, the designation "$M, L \geqslant 0$" indicates that negative production (i.e., less than zero units) of either item is not possible.

We can now construct a graph of production combination possibilities, where the production of M is shown on the vertical axis and the production of L on the horizontal axis. Let us now graph the first constraint, which indicates the capacity of the framework process and the time required to construct the framework of both M and L:

$$2M + 4L \leqslant 100$$

This simple function can be shown as a straight line on the graph in Figure 7–1. The shaded area is called the *feasibility space* because any production combination of M and L within this space is feasible (i.e., any combination of M and L within the shaded area can be produced without violating the capacity constraints of the framework process). Any production combination outside the feasibility space is not possible because it would violate the capacity constraints of the framework process.

Now we can add to the graph the second constraint—the assembly process ($2M + 2L \leqslant 80$)—as shown in Figure 7–2. Our feasibility space has now been reduced slightly. Although the framework process capacity permits construction of $50M$, the capacity of the assembly process would be exceeded by that level of production. So the assembly process capacity has limited our feasible production combination possibilities.

The question now is: What is the most profitable combination within the feasibility space? Fortunately, we do not have to test all possible production possibilities within this space. In a two-dimensional problem like this, the optimum solution must always be at one of the corners of the feasibility space, as shown in Figure 7–3.

FIGURE 7–1 The framework constraint

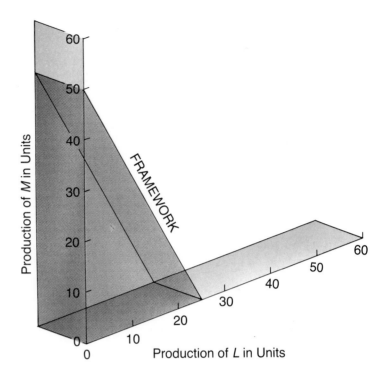

FIGURE 7–2 The framework and assembly constraints

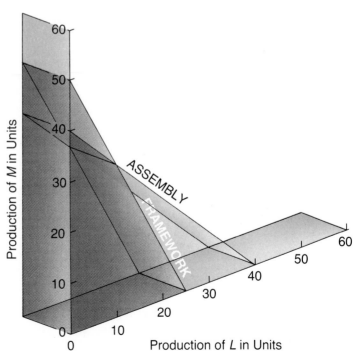

FIGURE 7–3 Possible solutions

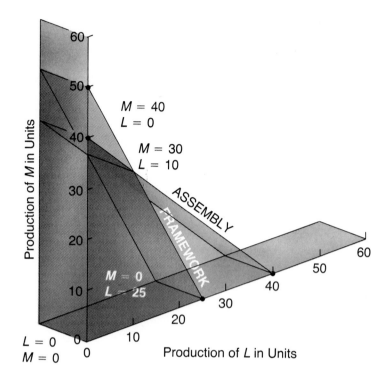

Each corner can now be tested using the objective function:

$$\text{Profit}_{max} = \$100M + \$150L$$

Where $M = 0, L = 0$

$$\$100(0) + \$150(0) = \$0 \text{ profit}$$

Where $M = 40, L = 0$

$$\$100(40) + \$150(0) = \$4,000 \text{ profit}$$

Where $M = 30, L = 10$

$$\$100(30) + \$150(10) = \$4,500 \text{ profit}$$

Where $M = 0, L = 25$

$$\$100(0) + \$150(25) = \$3,750 \text{ profit}$$

The optimum product mix, then, is to produce 30 mattress/box spring sets and 10 love seats every month, given current capacity. No other combination would yield more profit than $4,500.

This simple example illustrates how to construct and solve a mathematical model. Even a problem containing a small number of variables, such as this one, is difficult to solve without the help of a systematic technique. Although realistic linear programming problems are considerably larger and more complex (requiring the use of a computer and a technique called the simplex method), the basic concepts used to solve such problems are similar to those in this example.

This illustration is based on a product mix problem, one of the many applications of linear programming. Other important uses are to determine distribution schedules to minimize transportation costs and to solve production scheduling, machine loading, and blending or mixing problems. Airlines use linear programming to decide which of their pilots and flight personnel to assign to which planes and when and where to do refueling and maintenance on their daily flights. Linear programming is also used to plan menus in university dormitories and hospitals. The objective is to minimize cost, and the various constraints relate to protein content, calories, cholesterol, and so on.

Although linear programming is applicable to a number of managerial problems, many problems do not fall within its requirements and cannot, therefore, be solved through this method. But progress is being made. Exxon and other oil companies, for instance, solve nonlinear refining problems through a sequence of linear programs termed Successive Linear Programming.[3]

Probability Theory

The use of probabilistic models becomes necessary when the values of some variables are uncertain. In such situations, knowledge of *probability theory* becomes quite useful. Probabilistic estimates of the occurrence of future events may be either *objective* or *subjective*. Objective probability estimates are derived from analyses of historical data, while subjective probabilities are based on the manager's intuition and often fall under the heading of formal "educated guesses." The more experienced managers are, the more nearly accurate their subjective probability estimates are likely to be. The concept of probability can best be illustrated by the use of an example.[4]

Assume that a company must make a decision whether to drill a wildcat oil well. Normally, this would be considered a type of decision involving a great deal of subjective judgment or intuition. But considering the problem in a systematic manner, the manager can formulate a procedure to aid in the decision by incorporating the following steps:

1. Identify alternative courses of action
2. Determine the possible outcomes of each alternative
3. Assign probabilities to the various outcomes
4. Calculate the expected value of each alternative
5. Choose the alternative with the highest expected value

TABLE 7–2 Payoff table (new values after costs)

	Outcomes			
Alternatives	Dry Hole	Small Well	Big Well	Expected Value
	.6 Probability	.3 Probability	.1 Probability	
Don't drill	$ 0	$ 0	$ 0	$ 0
Drill	– 500,000	300,000	9,300,000	720,000
Farm out	0	125,000	1,250,000	162,500

Step 1 reveals three alternatives: (1) don't drill, (2) drill, or (3) farm out for a royalty. Step 2 shows three possible outcomes or consequences of drilling or farming out: (1) dry hole, (2) small well, or (3) big well. The expected gain that would be associated with each outcome may then be estimated on the basis of past experience or the judgment of the oil operator.* In step 3, an estimate must also be made, on the basis of past experience or judgment, of the probability of experiencing each of three possible outcomes or consequences (dry hole, small well, big well). Table 7–2 summarizes these factors and shows the expected value calculated for each alternative course of action.

It can be seen that the first alternative offers no prospects of gain or loss, inasmuch as it is a decision not to drill. The second alternative, drilling, leads to a loss of $500,000 (cost of drilling) if no oil is found. A small well will produce $300,000 over and above drilling and operating costs. A big well will produce $9,300,000 on the same basis. If the drilling is farmed out (third alternative), a dry hole will avoid the $500,000 loss, but striking oil will produce a smaller return based on the royalty agreement.

The estimated probabilities appear below each outcome. The chances of hitting a dry hole, for example, are thought to be 6 out of 10. The expected value of each alternative is computed by adding the products of the probability and expected gain for each outcome or consequence. The alternative of drilling has an expected value of $720,000 in contrast to $162,500 and $0 for the other two alternatives. The solution is the alternative with the highest expected value—in this case, the decision should be to drill.

In this problem, then, the decision maker has reached a conclusion by assigning or assuming specific dollar values for each outcome and estimating the probability of each consequence. The process differs from one in which the decision maker is somewhat aware of differences but uses subjective judgment without trying to assign specific values for each variable.

---

*In this illustration, the figures for gain in the event of success are really *present value* figures. The cash income from production will not be fully realized for many years, and the figures represent present value equivalents.

The same problem can be analyzed graphically in the form of a *decision tree*, as shown in Figure 7–4. The rectangular node preceding the first three branches at the left of the decision tree indicates a decision situation. The manager must choose one of the three possible alternatives. The branches to the right indicate the possible outcomes of each alternative decision.

Probability theory has increasingly been put to practical use in industry. Ford, for example, used decision tree analysis to decide whether to produce its own tires. The grocery products division of Pillsbury employed probability theory to determine whether to change a product container from a box to a bag. Honeywell uses decision tree analysis to determine which new weapons programs to pursue. Prominent companies in such industries as manufacturing, oil, and railroads have also used probability theory to aid in decision making.[5]

Program Evaluation Review Technique

A model used to plan and control a complex project of many interrelated activities is the *program evaluation review technique* (PERT). PERT was developed in 1958 as a system for planning and monitoring the development of the Polaris ballistic missile to be carried on nuclear submarines. The technique,

FIGURE 7–4 Analysis by decision tree

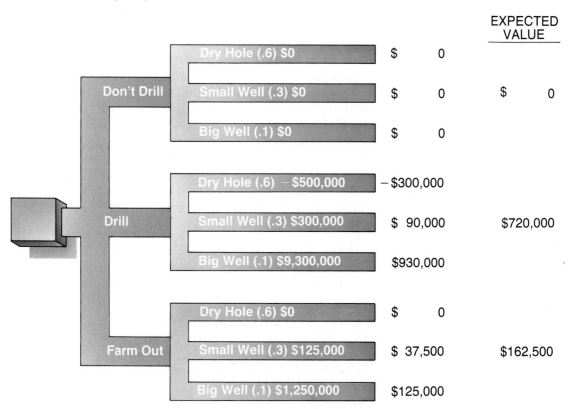

widely credited with saving years in making the Polaris operational, was developed by the Navy in collaboration with Booz, Allen, and Hamilton—a management consulting firm—and Lockheed Aircraft Corporation. The focus of PERT is the scheduling and coordinating of the sequence and timing of activities within complex, nonroutine projects.*

The first step in using PERT is to construct the network of activities which must be completed for the project as a whole to be finished. The network shows what activities must await completion of other tasks and what activities can be performed concurrently with other tasks. In short, PERT represents an application of the systems concept to managerial planning.

The PERT network in Figure 7–5 shows in highly simplified form the basic steps that would be followed by a firm in marketing a new product. (The illustration assumes that the preliminary design work has been completed and that a well-organized plant and distribution setup are available). Activities, represented by arrows on the network diagram, are the tasks or operations that must be performed. The circles denote events, which mark the beginning or end of activities. Numbers on the arrows show the number of days estimated for each activity. These estimates are provided by the organizational departments which will be involved in the various activities. Note that the length of the arrows is not proportional to their time duration.

Proceeding from left to right, examination of the network reveals the total time it will take to complete the project. For example, the lower path will require 90 days for completion, the middle path will require 79 days, and the top path will require 112 days. The time required to complete the entire project is determined by the longest path. Although the middle path requires a time of only 79 days, it cannot be completed until activity B——→D has first been finished. Even though the middle path can reach event D in only 27 days, the sequence of activities on the top path requires 60 days before event D is reached. Likewise, while the lower path can reach event E in 68 days, further work cannot proceed until sequence A——→B——→D——→E is completed, which takes 90 days. Hence, the top path, requiring 112 days, constrains or prevents the earlier completion of the other two shorter paths. The top path, therefore, is termed the *critical path*. Any delay in this path will delay completion of the project. The other two paths have *slack* time, and it may be possible to transfer personnel or other resources from these paths in order to speed up work on the critical path.

The transferability of resources depends on two major constraints. First, some resources simply do not have alternative uses. Although the employees preparing the financial plan (activity A——→C in Figure 7–5) will finish five

---

*PERT is similar to the Critical Path Method (CPM) devised by the Du Pont Company. The primary difference between the two techniques is that PERT was designed for planning and controlling new, nonroutine activities with which the planners had little previous experience. CPM, however, was intended for projects with which the planners had prior experience. As a result, the time estimates for activities in PERT are probabilistic, while those in CPM are more exact. Our discussion will stress features that are common to both techniques.

FIGURE 7–5   Simplified PERT network to introduce a new product

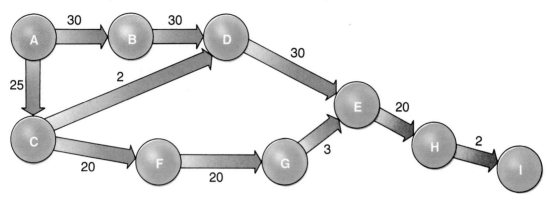

Events:

A. Decision to introduce
   product

B. Completion of engineering
   and design

C. Completion of financial
   planning

D. Purchase orders placed
   for materials

E. Beginning of
   production

F. Completion of marketing
   planning

G. First order
   received

H. Completion of
   production

I. Shipment of
   product

Path Completion Times:

Top path (A-B-D-E-H-I)   = 112 days
Middle path (A-C-D-E-H-I)   = 79 days
Lower path (A-C-F-G-E-H-I) = 90 days

Slack Time:

112 − 112 =   0 days
112 − 79 = 33 days
112 − 90 = 22 days

days before the engineers complete the design plans (activity A——→B), financial planners cannot be transferred to activity A——→B to speed up the design process. Likewise, many types of equipment or other physical facilities can be used for only one purpose. Second, the presence of labor unions may constrain the transfer of human resources. Although plumbers may finish their part of a project before carpenters do, plumbers are not permitted to saw wood or hammer nails, though they are capable of doing so. Such work rules are designed to protect the jobs of union members.

In practice, the network would be infinitely more complex than in Figure 7–5, requiring the use of a computer. Periodically, managers in charge of each activity would report on their progress, and the network would be recalculated to determine if the critical path had been altered.

PERT has several advantages. It requires the manager to take a systems approach in planning all of the activities needed to complete a major project, and it helps the employees involved think in terms of the entire project, the task relationships, and their roles in the mission. Identification of the critical path allows the manager to shorten project completion time by adding resources—temporary personnel, new full-time employees, equipment, overtime—to this path to decrease the time required to perform critical activities.

Because of its advantages, PERT is used extensively in planning construction projects, installing computer systems, manufacturing a variety of products, and establishing marketing and advertising campaigns for new products. One of the major users of PERT is the National Aeronautics and Space Administration (NASA), which has employed PERT to plan and coordinate such overwhelmingly complex projects as sending men to the moon and making the space shuttle operational. PERT is not confined to large projects; its advantages in planning smaller undertakings are becoming increasingly evident. Many organizations place considerable value on this systematic, logical planning technique.

EVALUATION OF MANAGEMENT SCIENCE

Limitations of Management Science

The use of management science is increasing, though not as rapidly as once predicted.[6] The improvement in decision-making effectiveness attributable to management science can be impressive. A survey of 47 major U.S. banks, for instance, indicated that, for each dollar spent implementing management science recommendations, an average of $2.61 was saved.[7]

A NONQUANTIFIABLE VARIABLE

A limitation of management science is that nonquantifiable variables cannot be considered. For example:

> One bus company carried out a major routing exercise and as a result closed down a number of its routes and started several new ones. The company believed that this would lead to a substantial reduction in total costs while still maintaining the same level of service. They did not take full account of the resistance to change of existing bus users. As a result of public pressure one of the closed routes had to be started up again. This wiped out most of the predicted savings.

SOURCE: John Hull, John Mapes, and Brian Wheeler, *Model Building Techniques for Management* (Westmead, England: Saxon House, 1976), p. 170.

THE DIFFERENCE BETWEEN PRECISION AND ACCURACY

Before the *Challenger* disaster, estimates varied greatly about the likelihood that a booster rocket used to put U.S. space shuttles into space would explode. For example, note the following estimates:

Source	Estimated Probability of Explosion
NASA consultant	1/57
Same consultant reacting to pressure from NASA to revise the estimate	1/1,000–1/10,000
U.S. Air Force	1/70–1/210
Low-level NASA engineers	1/100
NASA management	1/100,000

Richard P. Feynman, a Nobel Prize–winning physicist who served on the Rogers Commission investigating the *Challenger* disaster, indicated his belief that NASA greatly overestimated the safety of the shuttle booster rockets. Had NASA accepted the estimates developed independently of its own management, it would have had to acknowledge that the loss of a space shuttle was almost a statistical certainty given that 500 shuttle flights were planned.

SOURCE: Based on "Booster Safety 'Exaggerated,' Expert Charges," *The Houston Post*, 11 June 1986; and "NASA Rejected Shuttle Warning, Report Says," *The Houston Post*, 1 June 1986.

Managers are aware, however, that management science is not a panacea for all organizational problems. Its practical use in decision making is subject to a number of constraints. Perhaps the chief limitation is that some variables in business decisions are simply not quantifiable. Yet to use management science properly, all variables must be assigned quantitative weights. Computers "think" only in mathematical terms. A variable such as creativity cannot be expressed mathematically. Screening out all nonquantifiable variables in a complex system oftentimes greatly reduces understanding of that system.[8]

Another problem is the spurious accuracy that may be associated with quantitative analysis. The use of numbers and equations gives an appearance of scientific accuracy. The resulting willingness to place too much confidence in quantitative methods may be dangerous. Too often we are more concerned with numbers than with the reality the numbers are supposed to represent. There is an "all-important difference between *precision* (which is a measure of how many zeroes and decimal places the number has) and *accuracy* (which is how correct the number is)."[9]

For instance, one manager admitted that he has "many times" modified the value of probability estimates in decision analysis in order to justify to corporate headquarters an alternative that he and his superiors desired.[10] If unrealistic estimates are used in making a decision, the results will be undependable. Yet managers often hesitate to question quantitative reports generated by computers for fear of revealing their own ignorance. Many executives still automatically assume that work done on a computer is correct.[11]

Publishing companies, for instance, have developed computer models to determine how much to bid for a book. The models forecast the future sales revenue from the book and the income from the sale of various rights. But one executive concedes that "a certain passion can develop in the course of an auction that makes a publisher willing to go beyond what makes sense because they want the book so badly."[12]

Finally, note that the use of quantitative tools is concerned with only one phase of the decision-making process. Quantitative analysis is not ordinarily used to identify the problem or to develop the alternative possibilities that are open. It is only after groundwork of this nature has been performed that the adoption of quantitative analysis becomes appropriate.

Future of Management Science

The field of management science is steadily developing. How rapidly new techniques and new applications will be devised can only be surmised, but the outlook is optimistic. As computer technology continues to improve, new quantitative methods probably will be designed to enable the manager to attack even poorly structured business problems and to analyze the results of thousands of alternatives combining complex relationships.

The current state of knowledge is already such that many of the present routine decision-making activities of lower and middle managers, such as inventory control and production and distribution scheduling, can be programmed. As planning and decision making become more complex in an increasingly dynamic environment, well-managed companies will tend to rely more heavily on scientific methods of analysis to help reduce the concomitant risk and uncertainty.

SUMMARY

The application of quantitative techniques to managerial decision making can greatly reduce the risk and uncertainty managers must confront daily. Although managers have used some quantitative tools for decades, the emphasis in recent years has been on *management science*, a concept which emerged during World War II. Management science is the mathematical application of the scientific method to the solution of business problems.

At the center of this approach is the *mathematical model*—a set of equations representing the actual problem situation. The model is constructed by a *team* composed of management science and computer specialists and managers representing the departments being studied. Construction of models enhances understanding of the system being studied and enables the manager to experiment without affecting the system. Experimentation, known as *simulation*, is used to answer "what if" questions. The specific techniques used to construct and solve the model depend on the nature of the problem.

Linear programming, for instance, is used to determine the optimal allocation of a firm's limited resources. *Probability theory* is a systematic and logical method of solving a problem which would otherwise involve substantial judgment. PERT aids the manager in scheduling and coordinating a complex series of activities and also helps reduce the time required for project completion by drawing attention to the project's *critical path*.

Management science does have definite limitations, the major one being that some aspects of decisions are simply not quantifiable. But the field is still relatively new and its practical applications are already numerous. Although management science will certainly never replace the manager or eliminate the manager's decision-making responsibility, it should become an increasingly valuable management tool.

KEY CONCEPTS

Management science	Feasibility space
Operations research	Probability theory
Model	Expected value
Deterministic model	Decision tree
Probabilistic model	PERT
Simulation	Critical path
Linear programming	Slack time

DISCUSSION QUESTIONS

1. *Management science* occasionally has been called "quantitative common sense." Do you agree with this designation? Why or why not?
2. Discuss the advantages of constructing and using a *mathematical model*.
3. Since the manager cannot affect *uncontrollable variables*, why should these variables be included in the *mathematical model* of the problem?
4. Is management science more useful in making routine or nonroutine decisions?
5. Would a *decision tree* be considered a deterministic or probabilistic model? Explain why.
6. What is the *critical path* in PERT? What is its significance?

7. In your opinion, why is management science not being more widely used in business decision making today?

8. Company A wishes to maximize its profit by manufacturing two products, Model A and Model B. A wholesaler has signed a contract promising to purchase at a predetermined price all the company can manufacture over the next 30 days. The basic question is how many units of each product to manufacture. Each Model A contributes $400 to net profit; each Model B contributes $300 to net profit. Information concerning the production of the two products is as follows:

Processes	Labor Hours Required		Labor Hours Available Next 30 Days
	Model A	Model B	
Manufacturing	15	10	15,000
Painting	1	1	1,200
Assembly	3	2	3,000

9. A public official must select only one of four available options (choosing more than one option would make too many political "waves") for controlling urban air pollution: (1) ban outdoor fires, (2) restrict auto traffic, (3) close coal-burning power plants, or (4) reroute aircraft takeoffs. Each of these alternatives will provide a given number of Air Quality Points (AQPs), assuming certain climatic conditions are present. A higher AQP rating means better air. The AQPs for the various conditions have been estimated as below:

Decision Alternatives	States of Nature			
	Inversion	Onshore Wind	Calm	Fog
Ban fires	12	9	6	14
Restrict traffic	14	15	5	10
Close plants	3	11	9	9
Reroute aircraft	18	2	8	6

Determine the appropriate decision if the weather bureau certifies the probability of inversion as .2, onshore wind as .3, calm as .4, and fog as .1.

10. Develop a PERT chart for the following activities. Calculate the time required to complete the entire project. Identify the critical path and calculate slack time.

Activity	Days		Activity	Days
A⟶B	3		D⟶F	3
B⟶C	5		E⟶G	4
B⟶D	6		E⟶F	2
C⟶E	2		F⟶H	6
D⟶E	4		G⟶H	3

NOTES

1. Russell L. Ackoff and Patrick Rivett, *A Manager's Guide to Operations Research* (New York: Wiley, 1963), pp. 24–26.
2. "Detroit Stumbles on its Way to the Future," *Business Week*, 16 June 1986, p. 104.
3. Thomas E. Baker and Leon S. Lasdon, "Successive Linear Programming at Exxon," *Management Science* 31 (March 1985): 264–74.
4. This example is adapted from material prepared by Dr. C. Jackson Grayson, Jr., and is used with his permission.
5. Jacob W. Ulvila and Rex V. Brown, "Decision Analysis Comes of Age," *Harvard Business Review* 60 (September-October 1982): 133–34.
6. Mel E. Schnake and Yunus Kathawaca, "The Application of Quantitative Techniques in Large Corporations: Preliminary Findings of a National Survey," in Dennis F. Ray (ed.), *Southern Management Association Proceedings*, 1986, pp. 337–39.
7. Edwin L. Heard and Jerry E. Wheat, "Management Engineering in Large U. S. Banks," *Journal of Bank Research* 10 (Winter 1980): 221–27.
8. See Russell L. Ackoff, "On the Use of Models in Corporate Planning," *Strategic Management Journal* 2 (October-December 1981): 358.
9. John Cobbs, "A Misplaced Faith in Numbers," *Business Week*, 19 November 1979, p. 17.
10. F. L. Harrison, "Decision Making in Conditions of Extreme Uncertainty," *Journal of Management Studies* 14 (May 1977): 172.
11. "How Personal Computers Can Backfire," *Business Week*, 12 July 1982, pp. 58–9.
12. Laura Landro, "Publishers' Thirst for Blockbusters Sparks Big Advances and Big Risks," *The Wall Street Journal*, 3 February 1986.

SUPPLEMENTARY READING

Ackoff, Russell L. "On the Use of Models in Corporate Planning." *Strategic Management Journal* 2 (October-December 1981): 353–59.

Anderson, John C., and Hoffmann, Thomas R. "A Perspective on the Implementation of Management Science." *Academy of Management Review* 3 (July 1978): 563–71.

Baker, Thomas E., and Lasdon, Leon S. "Successive Linear Programming at Exxon." *Management Science* 31 (March 1985): 264–74.

Brightman, Harvey, and Noble, Carl. "On the Ineffective Education of Decision Scientists." *Decision Sciences* 10 (January 1979): 151–57.

Fuller, Jack A., and Atherton, Roger M. "Fitting in the Management Science Specialist." *Business Horizons* 22 (April 1979): 14–17.

Graham, Robert J. "The First Step to Successful Implementation of Management Science." *Columbia Journal of World Business* 12 (Fall 1977): 66–72.

Grayson, C. Jackson, Jr. "Management Science and Business Practice." *Harvard Business Review* 51 (July-August 1973): 41–48.

Green, Thad B.; Newsom, Walter B.; and Jones, S. Roland. "A Survey of the Application of Quantitative Techniques to Production/Operations Management in

Large Corporations.'' *Academy of Management Journal* 20 (December 1977): 669–76.

Hertz, David B. ''Does Management Science Influence Management Action?'' *Columbia Journal of World Business* 12 (Fall 1977): 105–12.

Levitt, Theodore. ''A Heretical View of Management 'Science.''' *Fortune*, 18 December 1978, pp. 50-52.

MacGregor, John M. ''What Users Think About Computer Models.'' *Long Range Planning* 16 (October 1983): 45–57.

Naylor, Thomas H. ''Effective Use of Strategic Planning, Forecasting, and Modeling in the Executive Suite.'' *Managerial Planning* 30 (January-February 1982): 4–11.

Neuhauser, John J. ''Business Games Have Failed.'' *Academy of Management Review* 1 (October 1976): 124–29.

Richman, Eugene, and Coleman, Dennis. ''Monte Carlo Simulation for Management.'' *California Management Review* 23 (Spring 1981): 82–91.

Sullivan, William G. ''The Use of Decision Trees in Planning Plant Expansion.'' *Advanced Management Journal* 40 (Winter 1975): 29–39.

Ulvila, Jacob W., and Brown, Rex V. ''Decision Analysis Comes of Age.'' *Harvard Business Review* 60 (September-October 1982): 130–41.

Zanakis, Stelios H.; Maurides, Lazaros P.; and Roussakis, Emmanuel N. ''Applications of Management Science in Banking.'' *Decision Sciences* 17 (Winter 1986): 114–28.

LIQUID ASSETS COMPANY

You are the manager of Liquid Assets. Your company produces two grades of solvent, regular and premium. When sold at retail, each barrel of premium-grade solvent will return a net profit of $120, while each barrel of regular-grade solvent will return a $40 profit. The two grades are produced by heating the basic chemical in a pressure tank and then heating the fluid in an open tank. Each barrel of premium requires four hours under pressure and ten hours in the open tank, while each barrel of regular requires two hours in the pressure tank and two hours in the open tank. Because of budget constraints (and a cheap management), only forty hours of pressure-tank time and seventy hours of open-tank time are available during the coming week.

Question

1. As the person responsible for production, you must decide which combination of barrels of premium- and regular-grade solvent will return the maximum net profit to the Liquid Assets Company. Naturally, your decision about the best (or optimal) mix of barrels of premium and of regular must be made with the limitations imposed by the available number of hours in each of the tanks. Solve this problem using the graphic method of linear programming.

Case prepared by Gerald Perselay of Winthrop College.

THE MICROMESH DECISION

During a period of uncertain economic times, the Micromesh Company finds itself with a significant amount of excess cash. Top management believes that there are three feasible ways of investing these funds: expand the company's production and distribution facilities, buy a smaller competitor whose stock is undervalued, or simply invest the funds in three-year certificates of deposit at a 12 percent annual return. Management believes that if the economy becomes stronger, buying the company will yield a 20 percent return on investment, whereas expanding its own facilities will return only 15 percent to Micromesh. If the economy stays the same, expansion is predicted to yield 12 percent, while buying the company will return only 9 percent. If the economy worsens, the return on expansion will probably be only 4 percent, and the return on buying the company only 3 percent. The firm's economic forecaster believes that there is a 50 percent chance that the economy will improve, a 30 percent chance that it will stay the same, and a 20 percent chance that the economy will further decline.

Questions

1. Draw a decision tree for this problem.
2. What decision should the Micromesh Company make?

PART THREE

ORGANIZING FOR EFFECTIVE PERFORMANCE

JOB DESIGN
The Concept of Job Design □ Technology and Job Design □ Techniques of Job Design

IMPORTANCE OF ORGANIZING
Basic Parts of Organizations □ The Systems Approach to Organizing □ Benefits of Proper Organization

UNDERLYING FORCES THAT SHAPE ORGANIZATIONS
Contingency Theory □ Technology and Structure □ Size and Structure □ Environment and Structure □ Strategy and Structure

PATTERNS OF ORGANIZATIONAL DESIGN
The Functional Pattern □ The Product Pattern □ The Geographical Pattern □ The Matrix Pattern □ Networking—A New Pattern?

Summary □ Key Concepts □ Discussion Questions □ Notes □ Supplementary Reading

CASES: State Prison Industries □ Super Discount Stores

This chapter will enable you to

□ Understand how individual jobs are designed.

□ Understand the value of good organization.

□ Explain the underlying situational forces influencing the shape of organizations.

□ Distinguish the various patterns for grouping jobs and activities and explain the reasons for using particular patterns in particular situations.

CHAPTER 8
JOB DESIGN AND ORGANIZATIONAL STRUCTURE

Organizations have an assortment of tasks that must be carried out to meet organizational objectives. How should jobs be designed so that these tasks can be accomplished? Once the jobs are designed, how should they be related or grouped? This chapter examines these structural aspects of organizational life.

JOB DESIGN

A basic part of managing human resources is deciding what activities will constitute individual jobs. A job encompasses a set of duties, functions, and responsibilities and is usually denoted by a title. Vice president, plant manager, supervisor, electrician, and secretary are all examples of job titles.

The Concept of Job Design

By deciding the duties to be included in a specific job, the manager specifies the role of the individual selected to fill that job. A *role* may be defined as the behavior or set of activities expected of a particular individual, the *focal* person. A secretary, for example, may be expected to do word processing, answer the telephone, obtain supplies for the office, and perform other specified duties. The technology of the organization and its overall structure and policies have much to do with the nature of individual jobs. Many groups and individuals, the *role set*, have expectations about the behavior of any one person. Figure

FIGURE 8–1 Role set and role expectations

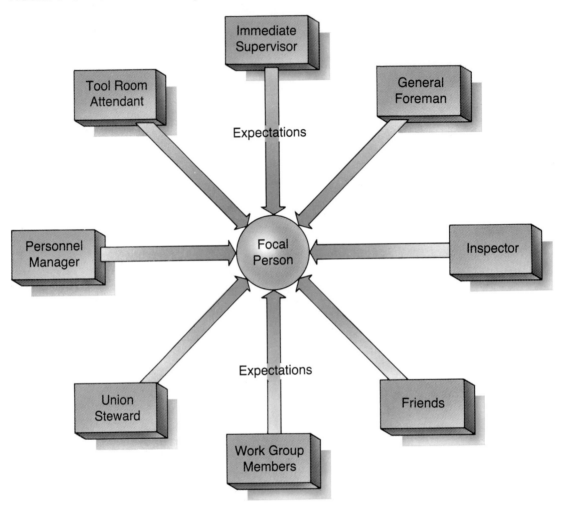

8–1 shows these relationships. Fellow employees and subordinates, for example, also expect the focal employee to behave in particular ways.

Management's definition of job requirements, then, establishes the formal
organizational expectations concerning the focal person. These expectations are
often expressed in written form as a job description (discussed in chapter 10).
This becomes a critical expectation as far as the employee's relationship with
the employer is concerned. The employee must presumably fulfill these role
requirements in some reasonable degree in order to continue employment and
receive the normal rewards for satisfactory performance.

Technology and Job Design

The particular technology that is used in an organization affects the way jobs are designed. *Technology* refers to the machinery, methods, and techniques (both physical and mental) used in converting inputs into outputs. Jobs can be designed using one of two approaches—fitting jobs to people or fitting people to jobs.[1]

Fitting people to jobs is the traditional way of designing jobs as a country industrializes. This approach involves the selection of the economically most efficient technology and the requirement that certain jobs be filled. People are viewed as extensions of machines, which dictate the design of jobs. In fitting jobs to people, on the other hand, the capabilities of available employees take precedence over the technology used. Jobs are designed to be consistent with the available skills and abilities of the labor force.

Some theorists, particularly Eric Trist and his colleagues at London's Tavistock Institute of Human Relations, have argued for a combination of these two approaches, called the *sociotechnical approach* (Figure 8–2). Management is concerned neither with adjusting people to technology nor technology to people but with "organizing the interface" so that the best match possible can be made.[2]

Techniques of Job Design

A major problem is the tendency for jobs to become narrow and specialized. The primary reason for specialization is to increase efficiency, but employee

FIGURE 8–2 The sociotechnical approach

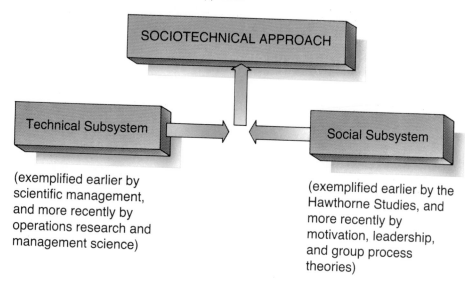

satisfaction and motivation are likely to suffer when jobs become specialized. Low employee job satisfaction can cause increased absenteeism and greater turnover, resulting in decreased organizational performance. Managers use various techniques in designing jobs to avoid the problems of specialization, including job enrichment, job enlargement, job rotation, and work redesign.[3]

In *job enrichment*, the employee's sense of responsibility is promoted by removing some controls from the job, delegating more authority to the employee, and structuring the work in natural units. *Job enlargement* involves increasing the number of tasks each employee performs. *Job rotation* is a procedure that systematically moves employees from one job to another. *Work redesign* improves the characteristics of a job. The best known work redesign model was developed by J. Richard Hackman and Greg R. Oldham.[4] They proposed that job characteristics and employee motivation are related in the manner shown in Figure 8–3.

The middle section of Figure 8–3 deals with three important psychological states. The model suggests that these states must be present if there is to be high internal motivation. First, the work must be perceived as meaningful in

FIGURE 8–3 The complete job characteristics model

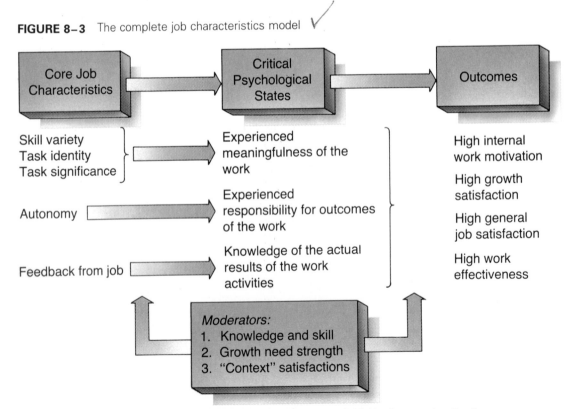

SOURCE: Hackman and Oldham, WORK REDESIGN, © 1980, Addison-Wesley Publishing Company, Inc., Reading, Massachusetts. Pg. 90, Fig. 4.6 & Pg. 73, Fig. 4.1. Reprinted with permission.

terms of the person's background and values. Second, the person must feel some responsibility for the work. Third, there must be some knowledge of results.

As shown in the section entitled Core Job Characteristics, certain properties of the work itself contribute to these psychological states. Research has shown that three characteristics (skill variety, task identity, and task significance) are related to meaningfulness of work, that autonomy is related to feelings of responsibility, and that feedback is necessary for knowledge of actual results.

Because people differ, they do not respond identically to core job characteristics. These differences, or *moderators*, relate to individual variations in knowledge and skill, the need for growth, and so-called context satisfactions with the work environment (such as physical working conditions).

Evidence for the validity of the model is somewhat lacking. Hackman and Oldham believe that the available evidence shows the model to be more right than wrong.[5] But they suggest it is best viewed as a guide for further research and as an aid in planning for changes in work systems.

A different approach to job design involves modification of the job context or environment, including the design of flexible work schedules, job sharing arrangements, and a compressed workweek.[6] *Flexible work schedules* allow employees more flexibility in which hours are worked. A firm may have certain periods in which all employees must be present and other periods in which employees choose their own schedules. *Job sharing* is when two or more people share one job. One person might work half a day, and another could work the other half. The *compressed workweek* involves working forty hours in less than five days. For example, an employee could work ten hours per day for four days. The object of these efforts is to improve the quality of work life by adapting the work schedule to meet the needs of the individual.

IMPORTANCE OF ORGANIZING

A manager must devise some pattern that relates each job to the others within the organization. Without some such pattern of coordination, chaos would result. This section examines the nature and benefits of *formal organization*, the structure intended to provide coordination.

Basic Parts of Organizations

To better understand the nature of organizing, consider a generalized description of organizations and their component parts. Think in terms of a medium or large organization—whether it be a business firm, university, hospital, or some other institution. Figure 8–4 presents a sketch of such an organization and its basic parts as visualized by Henry Mintzberg. This sketch should not be

FIGURE 8–4 Basic parts of an
organization

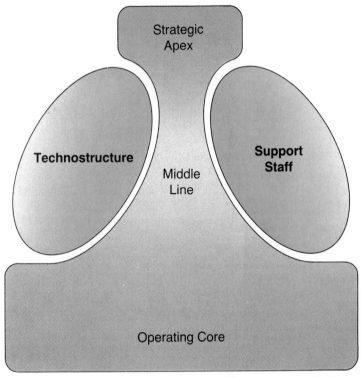

SOURCE: Henry Mintzberg, THE STRUCTURING OF ORGANIZATIONS: A Synthesis of the Research, ©
1979, p. 20. Reprinted by permission of Prentice-Hall, Inc., Englewood Cliffs, New Jersey.

confused with an organization chart. It merely shows the activities that all
organizations have in common.

At the bottom of the diagram is the *operating core*, consisting of the people
who produce the primary goods and/or services of the organization. These are
the assemblers in a manufacturing plant, the faculty in a university, and the
nurses in a hospital. Apart from the contribution of the operating core, the
organization has no reason for existence.

Coordination of work in the operating core is provided by two management groups. The *strategic apex* is the top management group, and the term
emphasizes the strategy-determining role which relates the organization to its
environment. Within the strategic apex is the chief executive officer, who
serves as the ultimate coordinating unit in the organization.

The *middle line* links the operating core with the strategic apex. Divisional
managers, department heads, foremen, and supervisors are all part of this middle line.

Two types of auxiliary functions are identified. One of these, the *technostructure*, includes analysts who assist the middle line and the strategic apex in

performance of their managerial functions. Accountants, production schedulers, and corporate planners are all part of the technostructure. Another type of assistance is provided by the *support staff*. Their contributions include such activities as housekeeping services, cafeteria operation, public relations, and payroll preparation. In contemporary organizations, staff offices often combine activities of both the technostructure and the support staff.

The Systems Approach to Organizing

In the light of systems theory, organizing may be visualized as a design function—creating the structure or framework of the system. Managers establish those relationships among component parts that will provide the most effective system.

If managers approach organizing without a systems point of view, they may adopt organizational rules of thumb or follow conventional practice with little regard for the unique requirements of the particular system. As Jay R. Galbraith points out, operating organizations "are designed to efficiently process the millionth loan, produce the millionth automobile, or serve the millionth client."[7] If a corporation also wishes to design new products and bring them to market, it may need a different type of organization—one which protects innovators and their ideas from operating managers whose quest is efficiency in processing the millionth loan, producing the millionth automobile, or serving the millionth client.

Organizing on a systems basis logically begins with a consideration of the nature of the system—its activity or function or purpose. What is it expected to do and how should it operate? A sound systems-organizing approach has been suggested by Peter F. Drucker.[8] He stresses the importance of identifying *key activities* as a basis for building the organization structure. Questions that help identify these key activities are the following:[9]

1. In what area is excellence required to obtain the company's objectives?
2. In what area would lack of performance endanger the results, if not the survival, of the enterprise?
3. What are the values that are truly important to us in this company?

After the key activities provide the basic framework, the organizer uses decision analysis and relations analysis for group tasks. *Decision analysis* asks questions about the types of decisions that must be made and the levels at which they can appropriately be made. Can the system function more effectively by delegating broad decision-making authority to lower levels of management? *Relations analysis* examines the points of contact among activities and personnel. The structure must facilitate cooperative relationships among people whose functions are intertwined. Once again, the focus is on the working relationship of components of the system.

Benefits of Proper Organization

The benefits of good organizing are those related to what a theorist calls *sound organization*. Charting an organization, for example, brings to light and helps eliminate weaknesses, including gaps in responsibility, overlapping of functions, duplication of effort, and working at cross purposes. Patterns of relationships in large organizations are extremely complex.

The organizer attempts to create a logical structure—that is, a structure designed to work efficiently through careful work specialization, a well-defined hierarchy, and a set of rules and procedures. In addition, a clearly outlined structure provides the employee with a clearer understanding of management expectations. It also stresses unity of command, thus eliminating confusion and identifying the line of responsibility for each individual. The planned organization also specifies the authority assigned to each position, so that everyone will know the scope and limits of authority of that position.

UNDERLYING FORCES THAT SHAPE ORGANIZATIONS

Contingency Theory

The dynamic nature of modern organizations produces repercussions in organizational relationships. For example, business firms which diversify their product line may find it necessary to modify their structure in order to produce and sell the new products efficiently. If the products are drastically different from those in the existing line, completely new departments may be required.

Personnel changes also lead to structural modifications. This is particularly true of replacements at the top-management level. Personal abilities differ among executives, and modifications of organization are made to accommodate the strengths or weaknesses of particular executives. New executives also have their own ideas of organization, and these frequently differ from those of their predecessors.

Since organization structures reflect the functions and purposes of organizations, it is not surprising to find that structures differ because of the basic differences among organizations.

Contingency theory stresses the unique nature of situations and the impact of situational variables on management and organizational performance. It thus helps to explain variations in structure. We would not expect a church, a business corporation, and a college football team to use identical patterns of organization and management. Nor would we expect an organization to retain the same structure over time while it was changing in other ways.

Although many organizational situations may logically call for variations in structure, scholars find it difficult to isolate the most important variables and to understand their implications for design of organizations. (See Figure 8–5 for underlying forces affecting the choice of structure.) The forces discussed in

FIGURE 8–5 Underlying forces affecting choice of structure

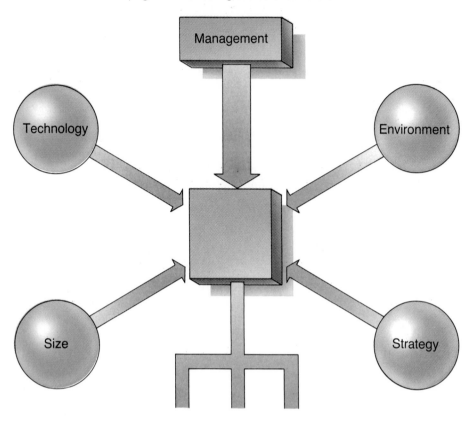

the following sections—technology, size, environment, and strategy—should be taken as tentative explanations of differences in structure, subject to refinement as they are studied further.

Technology and Structure

A few decades ago, writers generally assumed that organizational concepts were universally applicable. Today, this assumption is questioned because of the drastic differences in industrial technology. Perhaps the best-known research in this area was the study of about 100 British manufacturing plants conducted by a university research team and reported by Joan Woodward.[10] The researchers gathered extensive data about the features of formal organization of each plant but experienced difficulty in discerning a logical pattern. The type of structure did not initially appear to be significant in explaining differences in degrees of success. But differences did become sharp when the plants were grouped according to type of production technology, such as unit production, batch production, mass production, and process production. Within these technological groupings, the study revealed a connection between type of structure and successful performance. Thus, it appeared that given types of structures were more appropriate for given technologies.

The Woodward study has been extended and its results corroborated to some extent in other settings. In spite of such investigations, however, knowledge about the nature of the technology-organization relationship and its implications is limited.[11]

The Woodward study was quite broad in relating the structure of entire manufacturing plants to the technology of those plants. However, today's organizations frequently use many different technologies in their operation. More recent studies, therefore, have extended this concept and increased its practicality by focusing upon the technology of individual units and the structure of those individual units.

Size and Structure

The size of organizations also appears to affect their structure. In general, research studies have compared organizations of varying size in terms of a number of organizational variables. One such variable is *formalization*—the extent to which rules, procedures, and instructions are written. Another variable is *concentration of authority*—that is, the degree to which authority for given types of decisions is concentrated at higher levels or delegated to lower levels.

One of the earliest and most famous studies was conducted by the Aston group, a group of scholars associated with the University of Aston in Birmingham, England.[12] They concluded that organization size played an important role in determining structure, especially when compared to technology. The correlation of organization size with specialization, standardization, formalization, and centralization was consistently stronger than the correlation of technology with these same factors.

Other studies have subsequently investigated the relationship of size and structure, and the findings have varied.[13] Although size has been rather consistently related to structure in these studies, the precise nature of the relationship is unclear. And even the Aston study did not suggest that size was the only variable affecting structure. It appears that organizational size influences its structure, but the precise nature of this influence remains a question.

Environment and Structure

Organizations exist in different environments. We recognize, for example, that steel producers, residential builders, private universities, and public utilities face substantially different external situations. Some environments are described as stable and predictable, whereas others are characterized by shifting conditions, uncertainty, and difficulty in predicting the course of events. Uncertainty in a business environment is created by the existence of many competitors and competitive products, broad price ranges and price instability, numerous changes in product design, frequent innovations, and rapid growth in the underlying body of knowledge. Do such differences in environments affect organization structure? The answer is yes, although research is only slowly unraveling the nature of the environment-organization relationship.[14]

As one example of environment-organization research, Lorsch and Morse examined differences in the environments of selected manufacturing plants and research laboratories.[15] They found the environments of manufacturing plants to be relatively stable and certain. Once production was scheduled, the automated nature of plant facilities took over. Rate of change in knowledge was slow. New products required only minimal changes in manufacturing and assembly operations. Feedback was immediate, with regular inspection of product quality during the manufacturing process and prompt reports of customer dissatisfaction. Strategic concerns centered on cost, quality, and delivery.

Managers of the industrial research laboratories, on the other hand, faced uncertain and rapidly changing environments. Problems could be approached in a variety of ways with various possible solutions. Information necessary to work out research problems was ambiguous, open to varied interpretations, and apt to become obsolete. Knowledge was changing rapidly, and feedback was long term—for example, five years from laboratory idea to manufacturing success.

The research of Lorsch and Morse indicated that the more successful manufacturing organizations emphasized formal structure, using formal job descriptions, rules, and procedures, detailed control systems, and greater centralization of decision making. Two Scottish researchers, Burns and Stalker, describe this form of organization as a *mechanistic* structure.[16]

The high-performing laboratories, on the other hand, displayed greater flexibility in management, with only general job descriptions, a minimum of rules, reliance on self-discipline, and greater participative decision making. This Burns and Stalker would describe as an *organic structure*. Later researchers have characterized innovative organizations as having features similar to organic structures, with decentralized decision making, flexibility, and the absence of rigid rules and regulations.[17]

In summary, research has shown that environmental differences are significant in shaping organization structures. Successful performance seems to require an appropriate fit between the type of external environment and the type of formal organization.

Strategy and Structure

As environments change, organizations devise new strategies and adapt their structures to pursue those strategies. To discover the influence of strategy on organization, one must analyze the organization changes that accompany or follow strategy changes. A major study by Alfred D. Chandler, Jr., demonstrated the connection between business strategy and organization structure.[18]

Chandler examined the administrative histories of almost 100 large industrial enterprises, and he analyzed in detail the organizational development of Du Pont, General Motors, Standard Oil (New Jersey), and Sears, Roebuck. His general thesis may be stated as follows:[19]

> Strategic growth resulted from an awareness of the opportunities and needs—created by changing population, income, and technology—to employ existing or expanding resources more profitably. A new strategy required a new or at least refashioned structure if the enlarged enterprise was to be operated efficiently. The failure to develop a new internal structure, like the failure to respond to new external opportunities and needs, was a consequence of overconcentration on operational activities by the executives responsible for the destiny of their enterprises, or from their inability, because of past training and education and present position, to develop an entrepreneurial outlook.

Raymond Miles and Charles Snow have reported studies of strategy and structure in four industries: college textbook publishing, electronics, food processing, and hospitals.[20] They found it possible to classify organizations in these various industries according to their strategic orientation—"defenders," "prospectors," "analyzers," and "reactors"—and to predict with some reliability the structural characteristics associated with a given strategy. Defenders, for example, tend to rely on functional organization structures which group specialists with similar skills into similar units. They also tend to use an extensive division of labor and a high degree of formalization. Miles and Snow's research thus supported the connection between strategy and structure.

PATTERNS OF ORGANIZATIONAL DESIGN

The significance of each of the forces that affect the shape of organizations, as well as their separate and collective impact on organizational structure, is not yet fully understood.[21] Clearly, therefore, managers have discretion in choosing an appropriate structure for their organization. There are a number of basic structural patterns, including the functional pattern, two divisional patterns (product and geographical), and the matrix pattern. A new pattern gaining some acceptance is the network pattern.

The Functional Pattern

The *functional pattern* is one in which functions or activities, such as sales or finance, serve as the basic organizational building blocks. Small manufacturing enterprises find the functional pattern particularly appropriate. This pattern is not limited to the top level of the organization, however. Within the manufacturing department (a functional department), work may be further subdivided on the basis of function. Organizational components at this level may include drilling, grinding, painting, and so on. Different office units similarly may per-

FIGURE 8-6 Functional pattern of organization

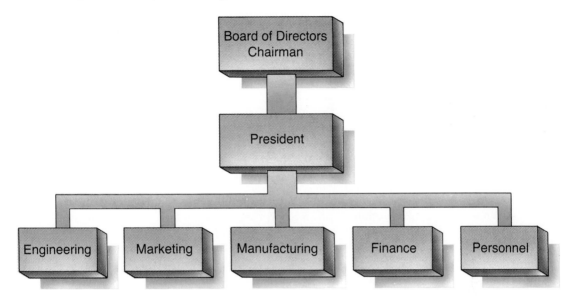

form typing, filing, and messenger service. An example of the functional pattern is shown in Figure 8–6.

Efficiency and economy are among the more important advantages of functional organization, especially for relatively small companies. All selling, for example, is concentrated in one department. A potential weakness in the functional pattern is its tendency to encourage a narrowness of viewpoint. It is easy for functional executives and personnel to look at problems from the standpoint of selling or manufacturing or some other functional specialty rather than seeing them from the standpoint of the company as a whole.

Growth may produce strains on the functional organization. Extreme product diversification and widespread territorial expansion, in particular, contribute to the difficulty of successfully operating according to a simple functional pattern. Hence, growth in the product line or in geographical territory may require a change to a type of *divisional pattern*, either the product pattern or the geographical pattern.

The Product Pattern

A *product pattern* can be used not only at the top level (product divisionalization) but also at lower levels. In a functional sales department, for example, sales personnel may be specialized on the basis of product lines. Similarly, the grouping of college professors into such departments as English, philosophy, and economics provides an example in the field of education. An example of the product pattern in a business corporation is presented in Figure 8–7.

FIGURE 8–7   The product pattern of PacifiCorp

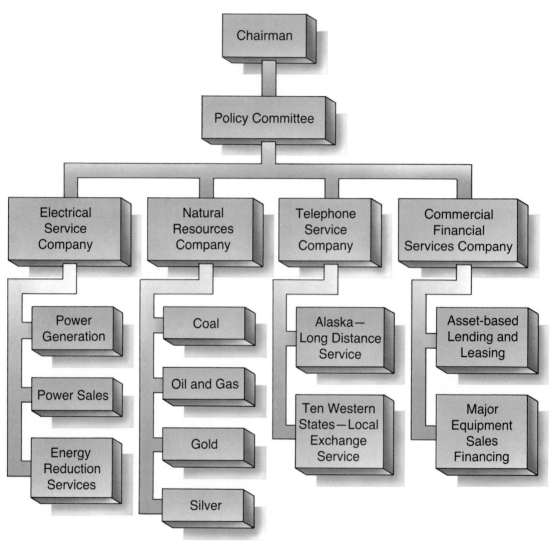

SOURCE: PacifiCorp. Annual Report, 1986, pp. 2–4.

The advantages of product divisionalization are particularly significant in the case of a highly diversified product line. The work of manufacturing or sales personnel in a consumer products division, for example, is drastically different from the work of similar personnel in an industrial equipment division. Product patterns permit specialization in terms of the product or group of products.

Executive development is another attractive feature of product organization. In the functional organization, executives are trained in functional areas

REORGANIZATION AT GENERAL MOTORS

To become more competitive with a greater emphasis on small cars, GM has reduced the company's automobile divisions from five to two. Previously, the five divisions included Chevrolet, Oldsmobile, Buick, Pontiac, and Cadillac. Under the old arrangement, the marketing, design, and engineering functions for the five divisions were directed by central staffs assigned to the corporate level. This structural arrangement made it difficult to pinpoint blame for engineering and design errors, poor sales, or declining profit margins, because many of the cars being developed for all five divisions were virtually identical. For instance, the Chevrolet Monte Carlo, Pontiac Gran Prix, Oldsmobile Cutlass, and Buick Regal all shared the same chassis and engine.

Under the reorganization plan, the key functions of marketing, design, and engineering have been reassigned to each of the two new divisions. One new division consists of a combined Buick-Oldsmobile-Cadillac group that handles only GM's larger cars, while the new Chevrolet-Pontiac division handles only smaller cars. For example, Chevrolet retained its Chevette, Cavalier, and Citation but lost the larger Monte Carlo, Caprice, and Malibu.

Each new divisional manager, called an executive vice president, is now accountable to GM's executive committee for that division's performance.

SOURCE: Adapted from "GM Plans A Great Divide," *Newsweek*, 9 January 1984, 68–69.

and imbued with a functional viewpoint. Only by position rotation or service in different functional areas do they acquire experience outside their own field of specialization. In contrast, the general manager and assistant manager of a product department are responsible for dealing with problems in various functional areas, including production, sales, and research and development.

The Geographical Pattern

Some organizations use a *geographical* pattern rather than a product pattern as their primary structure. This includes some business corporations, even though most divisionalized business firms follow the product pattern. A structure based on geographical divisions is shown in Figure 8–8.

Geographical divisionalization has certain advantages in common with the product pattern. Breadth of managerial experience is secured in the administration of regional areas. Financial control of operations is also facilitated, because managers can prepare a separate income statement for each geographical area and determine its contribution to corporate profits. The locational format is also used at lower levels—in organizing sales activities, for example.

FIGURE 8–8 The geographical pattern of Kelly Services

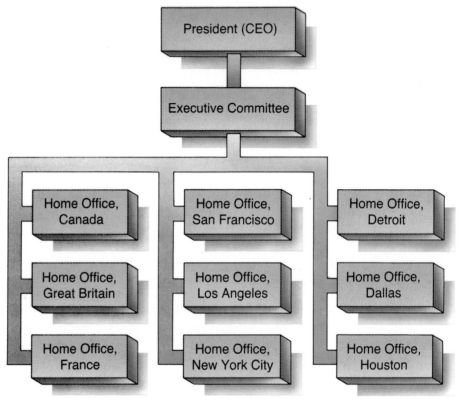

SOURCE: Kelly Services, Inc., Annual Report, 1986, pp. 20–21.

Adaptation to local situations and knowledge of customer needs peculiar to a given area are facilitated by the geographical pattern.

The Matrix Pattern

The growing complexity of environments, markets, and technology has led to the development of a special form of organization called the *matrix pattern*. This type of organization originated with Procter and Gamble in 1927 and was later widely adopted by firms in the aerospace industry. It is currently used in such areas as government, banking, insurance, hospitals, and higher education.

In its most basic form, the matrix pattern is a combination of a functional pattern and a divisional pattern. As such it contains a dual line of control, forsaking the concept of a unified command advocated by traditional management theory. This departure is prompted by a complexity of operations, which requires decisions that incorporate both functional and project thinking.

Figure 8–9 presents an outline of a matrix structure in the aerospace industry. The traditional functional departments of production, engineering, materials, and accounting continue to exist and are headed by managers whose primary orientation lies in their respective functional specialties. A second line of command appears, however, as project managers are appointed to coordinate work on particular projects. These projects are analogous to divisions. The Airplane A project manager, for example, oversees production, engineering, and other work of Airplane A and has some measure of control over those activities. Some personnel within functional departments, therefore, report to both a functional manager and a project manager.

The dual line of command is imposed because management wishes to emphasize particular projects as well as functional specialties. Production specialization and expertise are important, but concentration on production problems and production efficiency may lead to neglect of project priorities. What

FIGURE 8–9   The matrix pattern of an aerospace company

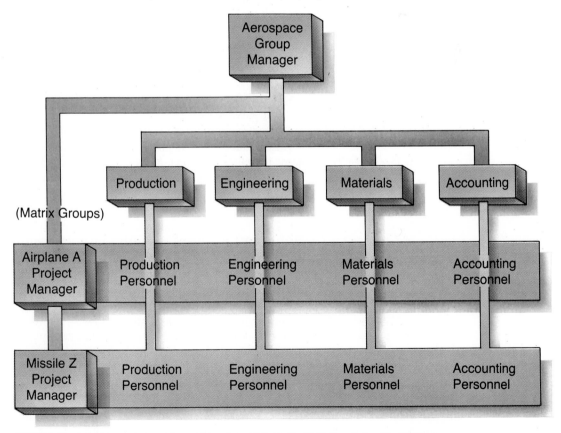

A MATRIX STRUCTURE AT JOHNSON WAX

S. C. Johnson and Sons, manufacturer of Johnson Wax, Raid bug spray, Pledge furniture polish and other products, is a $2 billion consumer products company. In 1984, top management reorganized the company into four "enterprise" units—personal care, home care, specialty chemicals, and insecticides—with an emphasis on motivating managers to act as "owners" of the various products and businesses. Markets had matured and costs had escalated. A matrix pattern was instituted to coordinate the activities of product managers, functional managers, and product-development managers in order to increase product development and lower costs. Before the change, product managers had no control over either research and development or manufacturing.

SOURCE: Adapted from "Trying To Bring Out The Old Shine At Johnson Wax," *Business Week,* 13 August 1984, pp. 138–45.

is most logical in terms of the production function is not necessarily most logical in terms of the Airplane A or Missile Z projects.

In traditional structures, project coordination is performed by the general manager who oversees the various functional departments. In a matrix organization, however, the general manager delegates a part of his or her coordinating function to the various project managers. The project managers can give much more detailed attention to the many specific projects than can one general manager.

The matrix structure modifies the relationships that exist among managers in a traditional organization. The functional manager—in production or engineering, for example—can no longer unilaterally establish work priorities, assign subordinates to particular projects, or evaluate employee performance. These management decisions are shared with one or more other project managers. Consultation on such matters is essential, and many matrix structures require dual "sign-offs" on performance evaluations and on pay and promotion decisions. In view of the strong emphasis upon lateral relationships and the need for negotiations and trade-offs in reaching decisions, project managers must exercise skills that are less essential in traditional organizations.

The role of the employee, the one who must take orders from both a functional manager and a project manager, is also difficult. Theoretically, project managers should achieve such excellent coordination that their subordinates face no conflicting demands. In practice, however, such perfection in management is unlikely to occur. Consequently, the employee must somehow deal with the frustrations of trying to reconcile directions coming from the dual lines of supervision. As it becomes necessary in specific cases to choose be-tween legitimate but competing interests, the employee may face rejection or even punishment from the "losing" side of the matrix.

An impetus for adopting a matrix pattern develops with new products, customers, technologies, product lines, or strategies to existing activities. Prod-uct managers, functional managers, new venture managers, and other manag-ers are created from the new sources of diversity, and all have a strategic re-sponsibility. If at least two of the variables of customer, product, technology, geography, market segmentation, and functional area have equal strategic priorities, a matrix pattern can be an effective organization structure.[22]

Networking—A New Pattern?

Scholars have predicted that a new international economy will develop in which mass production will shift to third world countries while developed countries will perform such specialized services as distribution and marketing on a contract basis. These scholars envision a "solar-system" organization, in which external suppliers "orbit" a small central headquarters.[23] Figure 8–10 shows this type of organization. A *network pattern* is a form of disaggregation, in which one company contracts out certain functions (such as production, marketing, billing, or distribution) to other companies. The contracting com-pany acts as a small central headquarters and communicates what actions are to be taken by the various functions. A network is different from a joint ven-

FIGURE 8–10   A network pattern

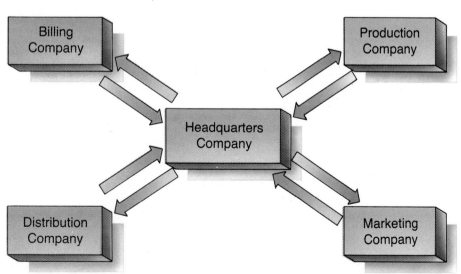

SOURCE: Adapted from John Wilson and Judith Dobrzynski, "And Now The Post-Industrial Corporation." Reprinted from the March 3, 1986, issue of *Business Week* by special permission. © 1986 by McGraw-Hill, Inc.

NETWORKS: FARMING OUT FUNCTIONS

Networks involve securing specialized services from other companies to perform a particular function, with the contracting company acting as a small
central headquarters. For example, Galoob Toys had sales of $58 million in
1985, yet employed only 115 people. Independent engineers and designers
develop the toys sold by Galoob. Manufacturing and packaging are performed
by firms in Hong Kong and shipped to commissioned manufacturers' representatives, who market the toys. Accounts receivable are sold to a financial
services company, which establishes credit policies, bills customers, and collects payment.

SOURCE: Adapted from John Wilson and Judith Dobrzynski, "And Now The Post-Industrial
Corporation," *Business Week*, 3 March 1986, pp. 64–71.

ture. In a joint venture, two or more companies collaborate on a new enterprise. A network involves securing specialized services from other companies
to perform a particular function.

The concept of a network pattern is not entirely new. Such firms as publishers, garment makers, and construction companies have contracted work
out for years. The network concept is spreading to many other firms because
advances in communication have made it easier to coordinate suppliers and
customers.

Despite this increased use of network systems, scholars are uncertain
about the extent to which networks will grow. Some predict that the network
structure will be broadly adopted and will become a major organizational innovation. Others argue that networks constitute a transition stage and will not
be the wave of the future.[24]

SUMMARY

Job design involves deciding what tasks or activities constitute individual jobs.
Managers attempt to promote job satisfaction—and ultimately productivity—
by various techniques. Organizing involves the grouping of jobs into a framework for coordination and direction. This organizational framework, the *formal
organization*, may be portrayed by use of an organizational chart.

The systems approach to organizing emphasizes the essential relationships of component parts of the organization. The organizer must begin with a
consideration of the nature of the system—its function or purpose. Key activities, decisions, and relations must be analyzed in the process of designing the
organization structure.

Contingency theory helps explain variations in organization structure by emphasizing situational differences among organizations. Some of the underlying forces that shape organizations include the firm's *technology, size, environment*, and *strategy*.

Once job content is determined, jobs and activities must be grouped to devise an overall structure. At the top organizational level are a number of basic options—a *functional pattern*, a *divisional* (either *product* or *geographical*) *pattern*, or a *matrix pattern* (a combination of functional and divisional patterns). Some scholars argue that a new form of organization structure, a *networking pattern*, is evolving.

KEY CONCEPTS

Job enlargement	Relations analysis
Job enrichment	Contingency theory
Job rotation	Mechanistic structure
Work redesign	Organic structure
Compressed work week	Divisional pattern
Flexible work schedules	Functional pattern
Strategic apex	Geographical pattern
Operating core	Matrix pattern
Technostructure	Network pattern
Decision analysis	

DISCUSSION QUESTIONS

1. How does technology affect job design?
2. Explain what is meant by *work redesign*. Refer to the Hackman and Oldham job characteristics model.
3. How does the systems point of view affect the manager's organizing function?
4. What specific benefits should result from good organization?
5. How is *contingency theory* related to variations in organization structure? What are the major forces involved in a contingency view of organizations?
6. What is meant by the *pattern* of organization? Why is a mixture of patterns customary?
7. Give several examples, including some based upon your own observations, of organization changes caused by the dynamic nature of organizations.
8. What advantages are found in the *product pattern* of organization that do not exist in the *functional pattern*?
9. What special difficulties are experienced by managers and employees in a *matrix pattern*?
10. Explain the concept of a *network pattern*. Do you think this pattern will become more common in the future?

NOTES

1. B. J. Hodge and William P. Anthony, *Organization Theory*, 2nd ed. (Boston: Allyn and Bacon, 1984), p. 144.

2. Eric Trist, "A Socio-Technical Critique of Scientific Management," in *Meaning and Control: Essays in Social Aspects of Science and Technology*, D. O. Edge and J. N. Wolfe, eds. (London: Tavistock, 1973), p. 103.

3. For a review of these topics, see J. Richard Hackman, "The Design of Work in the 1980s," *Organizational Dynamics* (Summer 1978): 3–17; J. Richard Hackman and Greg R. Oldham, *Work Redesign* (Reading, Mass.: Addison-Wesley, 1980); and Ricky Griffin, *Task Design—An Integrative Work* (Glenview, Ill.: Scott, Foresman, 1982).

4. J. Richard Hackman and Greg R. Oldham, *Work Redesign* (Reading, Mass.: Addison-Wesley, 1980).

5. Ibid., pp. 95–97. See also Karlene H. Roberts and William Glick, "The Job Characteristics Approach to Task Design: A Critical Review," *Journal of Applied Psychology* 66 (April 1981): 193–217.

6. For a more detailed discussion, see John M. Ivancevich and Herbert C. Lyon, "The Shortened Workweek: A Field Experiment," *Journal of Applied Psychology* 62 (1977): 15–37; Allan R. Cohen and Herman Gadon, *Alternative Work Schedules: Integrating Individual and Organizational Needs* (Reading, Mass.: Addison-Wesley, 1978); and Simcha Rosen, *Flexible Working Hours: An Innovation in the Quality of Work Life* (New York: McGraw-Hill, 1981).

7. Jay R. Galbraith, "Designing the Innovating Organization," *Organizational Dynamics* 10, no. 3 (Winter 1982): 6.

8. Peter F. Drucker, *Management: Tasks, Responsibilities, Practices* (New York: Harper & Row, 1974), chapters 42 and 43.

9. Ibid., pp. 530–31.

10. Joan Woodward, *Industrial Organization: Theory and Practice* (London: Oxford University Press, 1965).

11. For a review of this topic, see Louis W. Fry, "Technology-Structure Research: Three Critical Issues," *Academy of Management Journal* 25 (September 1982): 532–52.

12. David J. Hickson, D. S. Pugh, and Diana C. Pheysey, "Operations Technology and Organization Structure: An Empirical Reappraisal," *Administrative Science Quarterly* 14 (September 1969): 378–97.

13. See John R. Kimberly, "Organizational Size and the Structuralist Perspective: A Review, Critique, and Proposal," *Administrative Science Quarterly* 21 (December 1976): 571–97; and John H. Jackson and Cyril P. Morgan, *Organization Theory: A Macro Perspective for Management* (Englewood Cliffs, N.J.: Prentice-Hall, 1978), chapter 7.

14. One of the widely acclaimed statements of theory in this area appears in James D. Thompson, *Organizations in Action* (New York: McGraw-Hill, 1967), chapter 6.

15. Jay W. Lorsch and John J. Morse, *Organizations and Their Members* (New York: Harper & Row, 1974). The research project described here also examined the significance of personal characteristics of organization members as related to environment and internal organization.

16. Tom Burns and G. M. Stalker, *The Management of Innovation* (London: Tavistock, 1961).

17. This relationship has been developed by Richard L. Daft and Selwyn Becker, *Innovation in Organizations: Innovation Adoption in School Organizations* (New York: Elsevier, 1978); Henry Mintzberg, *The Structure of Organizations* (Englewood Cliffs, N.J.: Prentice-Hall, 1979); and Tom Peters and Robert Waterman, *In Search of Excellence* (New York: Harper & Row, 1982).
18. Alfred D. Chandler, Jr. *Strategy and Structure* (Cambridge, Mass.: The MIT Press, 1962). The complexities of this issue are explored in James W. Fredrickson, "The Strategic Decision Process and Organizational Structure," *Academy of Management Review* 11 (April 1986): 280–97.
19. Chandler, *Strategy and Structure*, pp. 15–16.
20. Raymond E. Miles and Charles C. Snow, *Organization Strategy, Structure, and Process* (New York: McGraw-Hill, 1978).
21. An excellent overview of this area is given in W. Alan Randolph and Gregory G. Dess, "The Congruence Perspective of Organization Design: A Conceptual Model and Multivariate Research Approach," *Academy of Management Review* 9 (January 1984): 114–27.
22. Arthur Thompson and A. J. Strickland, *Strategic Management: Concepts and Cases*, 3rd ed. (Plano, Tex.: Business Publications, 1984), 214.
23. Michael Piore and Charles Sabel, *The Second Industrial Divide* (New York: McGraw-Hill, 1984).
24. John Wilson and Judith Dobrzynski, "And Now The Post-Industrial Corporation," *Business Week*, 3 March 1986, pp. 64–71.

SUPPLEMENTARY READING

Bobbitt, H. Randolph, Jr., and Ford, Jeffrey D. "Decision-Maker Choice as a Determinant of Organization Structure." *Academy of Management Review* 5 (January 1980): 13–23.

Bottger, Preston C., and Chew, Irene K. H. "The Job Characteristics Model and Growth Satisfaction: New Effects of Assimilation of Work Experience and Context Satisfaction," *Human Relations* 39 (June 1986): 575–94.

Child, John. "Organizational Design and Performance: Contingency Theory and Beyond," *Organization and Administrative Sciences* 8 (Summer-Fall 1977): 169–83.

Collins, Paul D., and Hull, Frank. "Technology and Span of Control: Woodward Revisited," *Journal of Management Studies* 23 (March 1986): 143–64.

Cordery, John L., and Wall, Toby D. "Work Design and Supervisory Practice: A Model," *Human Relations* 38 (May 1985): 425–41.

Dalton, Dan R.; Todor, William D.; Spendolini, Michael J.; Fielding, Gordon J.; and Porter, Lyman W. "Organization Structure and Performance: A Critical Review." *Academy of Management Review* 5, no. 1 (January 1980): 49–64.

Delbecq, Andre L., and Mills, Peter K. "Managerial Policies That Enhance Innovation," *Organizational Dynamics* 14 (Summer 1985): 24–34.

Donaldson, Lex. "Divisionalization and Diversification: A Longitudinal Study," *Academy of Management Journal* 25 (December 1983): 909–14.

Fredrickson, James W. "The Strategic Decision Process and Organizational Structure," *Academy of Management Review* 11 (April 1986): 280–97.

Fry, Louis W. "Technology-Structure Research: Three Critical Issues," *Academy of Management Journal* 25 (September 1982): 532–52.

Galbraith, Jay R., and Kazanjian, Robert. "Organizing to Implement Strategies of Diversity and Globalization," *Human Resource Management* 25 (Spring 1986): 37–54.

Jonsson, Berth, and Lank, Alden G. "Volvo: A Report on the Workshop on Production Technology and Quality of Working Life," *Human Resource Management* 24 (Winter 1985): 455–65.

Kanter, Rosabeth Moss, and Buck, John D. "Reorganizing Part of Honeywell: From Strategy to Structure," *Organizational Dynamics* 13 (Winter 1985): 5–25.

Kolodny, Harvey F., and Dresner, Barbara. "Linking Arrangements and New Work Designs," *Organizational Dynamics* 14 (Winter 1986): 33–51.

MacMillan, Ian C., and Jones, Patrice E. "Designing Organizations to Compete," *Journal of Business Strategy* 4 (Spring 1984): 22–6

McDonough, Edward F., III, and Leifer, Richard. "Using Simultaneous Structures To Cope With Uncertainty," *Academy of Management Journal* 26 (December 1983): 727–35.

Miles, Raymond E., and Snow, Charles C. "Organizations: New Concepts for New Forms," *California Management Review* 28 (Spring 1986): 62–73.

Pearce, John A., II, and David, Fred R. "A Social Network Approach to Organizational Design-Performance," *Academy of Management Review* 8 (July 1983): 436–44.

Randolph, W. Alan. "Matching Technology and the Design of Organization Units." *California Management Review* 23, no. 4 (Summer 1981): 39–48.

Randolph, W. Alan, and Dess, Gregory G. "The Congruence Perspective of Organizational Design: A Conceptual Model and Multivariate Research Approach," *Academy of Management Review* 9 (January 1984): 114–27.

Spencer, Daniel G. "Employee Voice and Employee Retention," *Academy of Management Journal* 29 (September 1986): 488–502.

Staines, Graham L., and Pleck, Joseph H. "Nonstandard Work Schedules and Family Life," *Journal of Applied Psychology* 69 (August 1984): 515–23.

Weisbord, Marvin R. "Participative Work Design," *Organizational Dynamics* 14 (Summer 1985): 24–34

Woodward, Joan. *Industrial Organization: Theory and Practice*. London: Oxford University Press, 1965.

Zuboff, Shoshanna. "Automate/Informate: The Two Faces of Intelligent Technology," *Organizational Dynamics* 14 (Autumn 1985): 4–28.

STATE PRISON INDUSTRIES

State Prison Industries (SPI) is a prison work program of the department of correction in a southern state. Products manufac-

This case was prepared by Professor Tammy Hunt of Baylor University.

tured by SPI are purchased by the state for use in state institutions. The primary operation is located at the state penitentiary, with secondary operations at other men's, women's, and juvenile centers throughout the state. Prison industries programs are differentiated from work release programs, in which inmates go to civilian jobs during the day but return to the prison each evening. Participants in prison programs remain at the prison, though they are allowed to work off sentence time, earn small amounts of money, and learn work skills. Inmates are not required to participate in the industries program, and in fact the majority do not.

The technology of SPI involves nine different operations, each one autonomous of the others. Except for the data processing division, the machines and procedures are quite crude and outdated. Because each operation is designed to make maximum use of the available inmate labor, all operations are labor intensive. Typical goods produced include highway paint, school desks, prison uniforms, and license plates. Most laborers repeat the same task, such as sanding a desk, day after day without rotation to learn different job skills.

The official goal of SPI is to provide inmates with a meaningful work program that will give them marketable skills upon release and thus keep them out of jail in the future. In practice, though, the program seems to be aimed at two lesser goals. First, the program keeps prisoners busy and out of trouble. Second, when run properly the program helps reduce the state's cost to incarcerate inmates, because state institutions can buy from SPI at lower than market prices. SPI can sell only to the state, and therefore does not seek to earn a profit.

Since the main purpose of SPI is to provide inmates with marketable skills, the program must be successful in meeting that goal to be deemed effective. Yet, evidence shows that this goal has not been attained. About 80 percent of released prisoners are reincarcerated, and the proportion of prisoners who have participated in SPI is not significantly different. Why is SPI not effective in meeting its stated goal?

Effectiveness depends on individual outcomes, such as performance, job satisfaction, and involvement. Before an inmate can become integrated into the outside society, the inmate must feel capable of performing useful work, and must gain a sense of accomplishment from doing that work. When managers provide subordinates with feedback, autonomy, and task identity, the result is an achievement-oriented climate in which members feel responsible for the attainment of group objectives. But when managers emphasize standardized procedures and job specialization, the result is a climate unconducive to responsibility, creativity, or feelings of competence.

The latter is the case at SPI. Inmates do not develop a sense of responsibility or self-confidence. Apparently, the supervisors at SPI are not aware of the official goal: each supervisor is concerned only with meeting production schedules. No attempt is made to make the inmate feel like an important part of the organization. The job is just another task the inmate must do rather than an important element in rehabilitation.

Poor performance and poor job satisfaction are indications that the inmate has not developed marketable skills, a sense of confidence, or sense of responsibility. In short, the inmate will not be able to function well upon release, and therefore the program of SPI is ineffective.

Questions

1. What stakeholder groups have a strong impact on the programs offered by SPI?
2. How could SPI jobs be designed to be more rewarding and meaningful?

SUPER DISCOUNT STORES

Super Discount is an apparel chain owned by a major retailing company consisting of thirty-five stores located in the Southeast. These stores sell men's, ladies', and children's clothing, as well as other items, at 35–60 percent below department store prices. Stores are located in strip centers close to major malls or within newer "discount malls."

Exhibit 1 depicts the existing organization pattern. Buyers, merchandise managers, and district managers all report to the vice-president of operations. District managers supervise five to seven stores within a district, depending on the geographic area.

At the store level, responsibilities are divided and delegated by the store manager, who is responsible for the store operating efficiency. Each store manager uses his or her own system for assigning duties. Usually, each store will have two assistant managers, each responsible for part of the selling floor and the staff. After six to nine months, duties of the assistant managers are alternated, thereby providing training in all areas of store operations. An important aspect of the store manager's job is to train each assistant to eventually become a store manager.

During the past year, several problems have resulted. Buyers have not been properly supervised. In some instances, shortages in some merchandise have occurred, though excessive amounts of other items are in inventory. Buyers complain that they don't know which lines of merchandise should be carried. Three district managers have resigned, stating that the vice-president of operations is not well organized. Other district and store managers concur with the comments of one manager, who said, "Suddenly, decisions are made to either discontinue or add a line of merchandise very quickly. These decisions are never really justified or explained, and customers find the sudden merchandise changes to be frustrating." For example, one manager reported that right before Christmas "domestics" (sheets, towels, and so forth) had been discontinued. Sales of those items following Christmas had always been exceptional. This manager stated that when he questioned the decision, he was "called on the carpet" about the performance of his store. This particular manager has announced his resignation.

After being questioned about these problems by the president of Super Discount Stores, the vice-president of operations commented:

> My job really contains two distinct areas of responsibilities. The merchandise managers and buyers need a lot of direction in their activities. The district managers need to be prodded to ensure that their stores are operating efficiently. Frankly, on the one hand I am dealing with day-to-day problems, and on the other hand I am involved in long-range planning.

An outside consultant has suggested that the present organization structure needs to be revised.

Question

1. What organizational changes would you recommend?

EXHIBIT 1 Organizational chart of Super Discount Stores

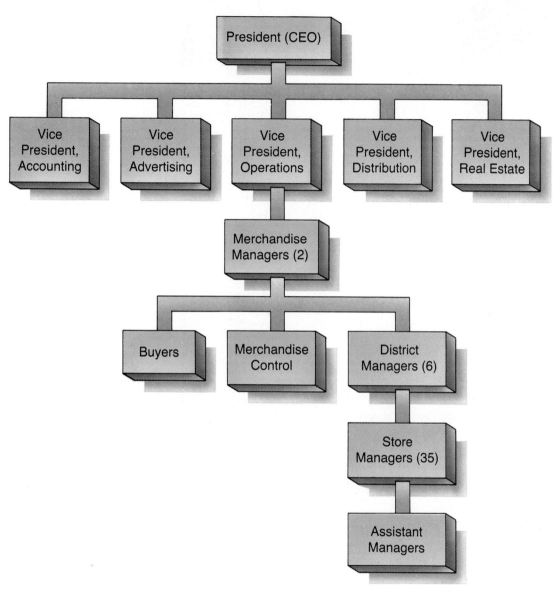

ORGANIZATIONAL DESIGN
Design vs. Structure □ Vertical and Horizontal Relationships

AUTHORITY
Limits to Authority □ Delegation of Authority □ Barriers to Delegation

CHAIN OF COMMAND
Difficulties in Adhering to the Chain of Command □ Dangers in Not Adhering to the Chain of Command □ Unity of Command

SPAN OF CONTROL
Limiting or Broadening the Span of Control □ Variables Affecting Optimum Span Size

DECENTRALIZATION
Advantages of Decentralization □ Disadvantages of Decentralization

LINE AND STAFF RELATIONSHIPS
Line and Staff Functions □ Traditional View of Line Authority □ Increasing Staff Authority

LATERAL COORDINATION
Need for Lateral Relationships □ Forms of Lateral Relationships

Summary □ Key Concepts □ Discussion Questions □ Notes □ Supplementary Reading □

CASES: Delta Fertilizer (A) □ Jacksonville Packaging

This chapter will enable you to

□ Distinguish the differences between organizational design and organizational structure and become familiar with the forms of interdepartmental collaboration.

□ Understand the nature of authority and how authority may be delegated.

□ Recognize the reasons for adhering to a chain of command.

□ Understand the variables that affect the optimum size of the span of control.

□ Realize the advantages and disadvantages associated with decentralization.

□ Understand the importance of lateral relationships.

CHAPTER 9
BASIC CONCEPTS IN
ORGANIZATIONAL DESIGN

Chapter 8 described how jobs can be designed and then arranged in certain structures. Organizational structure is like a human skeleton: it is the framework on which all the parts of an organization are attached. All of these parts, however, must be arranged in such a manner that they work together to accomplish the organization's objectives. Organization design is the process of arranging the various elements in a meaningful fashion. In this chapter, we examine the differences between organizational design and organizational structure, as well as the various techniques for achieving coordination and integration of effort.

ORGANIZATIONAL DESIGN

Design vs. Structure

Organizational structure has been defined as "the sum total of the ways in which an organization divides its labor into distinct tasks and then achieves coordination among them."[1] An organization's structure can be described by a formal organization chart. This chart describes the allocation of tasks and responsibilities to individuals and departments within the organization, designates formal reporting relationships, defines the number of levels in the hierarchy, and groups individuals together into departments.[2]

Organizational design is a broader concept than structure.[3] A design integrates decision making, planning and control, policies and procedures, accountability, and other abstract concerns in order to make the organization work.

Vertical and Horizontal Relationships

Managers ensure that coordination of effort is achieved by designing vertical and horizontal relationships. *Vertical relationships* describe how activities between upper and lower levels of the organization are coordinated. By issuing orders, managers provide the necessary direction and coordination. The nature of authority, chain of command, span of control, decentralization, and line and staff relationships are aspects of vertical relationships and are examined in this chapter.

Managers use *horizontal relationships* to "ensure that the right and left hands of the organization know what the other is doing."[4] For example, decisions made by the marketing department that affect the production department should be known by both departments.

The defining distinction between vertical and horizontal relationships concerns the concept of control. In vertical relationships, linkages are used to facilitate communication, while in horizontal relationships, one department is

HORIZONTAL COMMUNICATION

Hewlett-Packard was the world's largest producer of electronic instruments in 1978, the year John Young became its chief executive. Young pushed for computers to become the company's main product. Despite his emphasis, Hewlett-Packard continued to lag behind its competitors in computer sales, primarily because the company's three computer divisions developed and marketed products that were incompatible and technically inferior to competitors' machines.

In 1984, to solve the problem, Young centralized computer research efforts and required that functional managers in the three divisions work together with engineering and design personnel in the centralized division. These various managers and technicians communicated horizontally across Hewlett-Packard's structure and developed a central computer technology that is used in all three computer divisions.

SOURCE: Adapted from "Can Hewlett-Packard Put The Pieces Back Together?" *Business Week*, 10 March 1986, pp. 114–16.

FIGURE 9–1 Factors that affect the design of vertical and horizontal relationships

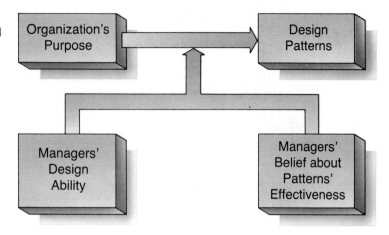

not controlled by another because the departments are on equal hierarchical footing.

The extent that vertical and horizontal linkages are used within an organization depends on the organization's purpose, the design ability of its managers, and those managers' beliefs about the effectiveness of design patterns.[5] Figure 9–1 describes these factors.

AUTHORITY

In a formal organization, authority flows through a system of command. This official system does not control every aspect of organizational activity, because individual members can respond to directions in many ways. Nevertheless, the order-giving system has a great deal to do with what happens in organizations. *Authority* may be defined as a superior's capacity, on the basis of formal position, to make decisions affecting subordinates. Authority is evident in all areas of society. In the family, the parent makes decisions for minor children. At a busy intersection, a police officer gives directions to motorists. In football, the quarterback calls plays for the team. In organizational life, managers act as decision makers.

Authority might be called *institutionalized power* to emphasize its connection with the formal organization and to distinguish it from other types of power. In contrast to authority, *power* requires no formal position to be recognized as power. It refers to the ability to make things happen, to get results. Only a part of the total power found in an organization is institutionalized. This means that others besides managers have power. Output quotas, for example, may be established and enforced by informal work groups, as described in chapter 2.

Limits to Authority

Members of organizations may choose to resist managerial authority. In a notable challenge to traditional views, Chester I. Barnard drew attention to the possibility of a subordinate's rejection of direction by higher authority. "It is surprising," said Barnard, "how much that in theory is authoritative, in the best of organizations in practice lacks authority—or, in plain language, how generally orders are disobeyed."[6] Acceptance of the order, then, becomes an important step or part of making the authority of the order-giver effective.

Many directions are accepted without question. Barnard suggests the existence of a *zone of indifference* that determines which orders will be accepted:[7]

> The phrase "zone of indifference" may be explained as follows: If all the orders for actions reasonably practicable be arranged in the order of their acceptability to the person affected, it may be conceived that there are a number which are clearly unacceptable, that is, which certainly will not be obeyed; there is another group somewhat more or less on the neutral line, that is, either barely acceptable or barely unacceptable; and a third group unquestionably acceptable. This last group lies within the "zone of indifference." The person affected will accept orders lying within this zone and is relatively indifferent as to what the order is so far as the question of authority is concerned.

The authority of a superior's order is seldom so absolute that the subordinate has no choice whatever. As Herbert Simon has expressed it, "the leader, or the superior, is merely a bus driver whose passengers will leave him unless he takes them in the direction they wish to go."[8]

Delegation of Authority

Delegation of authority is a process through which managers assign part of their duties to subordinates. Managers delegate so that more work can be done. This process involves authority, responsibility, and accountability, as shown in Figure 9–2. The manager assigns responsibility for a certain job to a

FIGURE 9–2 Authority, responsibility, and accountability

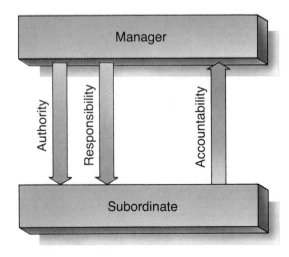

subordinate, and the subordinate is granted authority to accomplish the job. Such authority may involve planning activities, directing the work of others, or securing needed resources. In turn, the subordinate is held accountable for the job.

A significant difference exists between "just running the business" and "building an organization." Managers who can entrust authority to others cre-

DELEGATION AND ACCOUNTABILITY: PROBLEMS IN THE WHITE HOUSE

In the delegation process, authority and responsibility are transferred from manager to subordinate. The subordinate then becomes accountable to the manager. Accountability is an important element of the process. But what happens when a manager delegates but then fails to follow through on the accountability of subordinates? Such a failure to follow through in the White House made front-page news in 1987.

President Ronald Reagan was known for having a management style that concentrated primarily on setting broad outlines of policy and then delegating the details to trusted subordinates. Although officials in Washington reported that Reagan sometimes revealed his ignorance of details about various policies, his first-term chief of staff served the president well. This man made sure that policies were implemented in such a manner that Reagan was never embarrassed.

During the president's second term, Reagan appointed a new chief of staff and continued his same style of delegation. In an attempt to free hostages from Middle East terrorists, the White House staff engaged in a swap of arms for hostages with Iran. The policy was a failure and created a political debacle. An independent commission that investigated the matter reported that "every top U.S. official involved in the affair failed to act responsibly. The President failed to keep himself informed of how the Iran operation was being handled and his Chief of Staff failed to make the President focus on the risks." The chairman of the three-member commission reported that "this is really a story of people whose performance was, perhaps, somewhat short of heroic."

Later, the secretary of state, George Schultz, reported to a congressional committee that other top officials had used "lies and deceit" to keep him ignorant and that those who had kept facts from the president hoped that the president's "skills as a communicator" would "bail them out."

SOURCE: Adapted from "Tower Report Faults Reagan, Aides," *Dallas Morning News,* 27 February 1987; "Managerial Style Fails—Reagan in the Dark," *The Wall Street Journal,* 27 February 1987; and "Secretary's Testimony Staggering," *The Wall Street Journal,* 24 July 1987.

ate opportunities within their organizations.[9] For example, subordinates will mature as decision makers and will be able to manage more effectively.

Barriers to Delegation

Potential barriers to the delegation of authority include the design of an organization and the psychological make-up of the manager or the subordinate.

Organizational Design Barriers. In some organizations, decision making is traditionally allowed at lower levels of the hierarchy. But in other organizations, decision making is tightly centralized. For example, educational institutions typically operate in a decentralized manner. A military organization operates at the other extreme—tightly controlled and centrally managed. Most business organizations tend to fall somewhere in the middle.

The type of function or work being managed may determine how much authority can be delegated. A manager may find it impossible to "stay on top" of work performed by subordinates if the subordinates have a variety of duties. The manager's only recourse may be to allow them greater freedom. One study compared the predictability of hospital work—the extent to which unexpected events disturb work routine—with closeness of supervision. A strong, positive correlation was discovered between predictable work and close supervision. Apparently, managers were unable to follow closely those jobs having unexpected variations in their day-to-day content.[10]

The training and ability level of subordinates can limit the manager's ability to delegate. Employees may be so inexperienced that their work requires constant checking. On the other hand, if employees are educated and experienced, the manager can delegate relatively more authority.

Psychological Barriers for Managers. Many managers experience difficulty in delegating because of psychological barriers. Generally, there are four problem areas: exercise of power, feelings of insecurity, loss of identity, and time to complete the task.[11]

Managers' egos are involved in the exercise of power. Their own importance can be enhanced when subordinates come to them with questions and with problems needing resolution. Their importance and significance can be seen as diminished when decision-making power is turned over to others. Delegation often means letting others become the experts.

Insecurity can cause a manager to be a poor delegator. Surveys of managerial attitudes indicate that even in well-managed organizations, a substantial percentage of management personnel are quite unsure about where they stand with the company that employs them. The insecure manager is fearful of the consequences if all tasks are not carefully performed. This manager feels it necessary to keep in close touch with work for which he or she is responsible, making it difficult to allow a subordinate to perform a task without careful supervision.

DOING IT ALL

Much has been written about the reluctance of subordinates to assume delegated authority, but a problem also exists when supervisors fail to delegate.

Sakowitz, Inc., a company with seventeen department stores in Texas, Arizona, and Oklahoma, filed for Chapter 11 reorganization in 1985. Certainly, the depressed oil economy of those states had some effect on Sakowitz, which had the reputation for serving fashion-conscious, oil-rich women. But the management style of the owner, Robert T. Sakowitz, also probably created some of the problems.

Sakowitz, who began managing the business in 1981 after his father's death, was evidently uncomfortable delegating authority. He attempted to do nearly everything himself. A former associate recalls that Sakowitz "would spend hours pondering the color of the changing rooms for a new store." Because he was heavily involved in civic affairs, served on the boards of directors of other companies, and even bought part of the store's high-fashion merchandise, Sakowitz was often not in the store. His absence created problems. Said one former employee, "We couldn't decide on the wall coverings for a new store until he came back from Europe." His reluctance to delegate slowed organizational decision making considerably.

SOURCE: Based on Alison Cook, "The Fraying Empire of Bobby Sakowitz," *Texas Monthly* 13, no. 2 (December 1985): 132–36; 232ff (quotes are from pp. 237 and 238); and "How Bobby Sakowitz Took An Escalator to the Basement," *Business Week*, 19 August 1985, pp. 54–55.

Managers may be reluctant to delegate because they tend to lose their identity in the delegating process. In delegating, a manager sometimes has to shift from the role of specialist (finance, engineering, etc.) to that of a generalist. Delegation involves giving up particular skills that provided recognition and acquiring new ones that may not be familiar.

A frequent complaint heard from managers who do not delegate is that they can do the work faster and better than their subordinates.[12] Such managers tend to become frustrated while the subordinate is "getting up to speed" in learning the new tasks.

Psychological Barriers for Subordinates.   Not all of the barriers to delegation are found in the delegator. Frequently, subordinates are visualized as eagerly reaching out to grasp any decision-making authority that is offered them. In reality, some subordinates are apathetic and lack motivation. Others are apprehensive about accepting authority. These apprehensions can be explained, in part, by research into the delegating process. Several studies, for example, have investigated what happens in dyadic decision making when delegation occurs. *Dyadic decision making* involves a manager and subordinate working together to reach a decision.[13] Generally, the decision is made by a democratic process in which alternatives are reviewed, discussed, and adopted or discarded. When the manager and subordinate make decisions together, power is shared. Delegation changes the relationship. Although the subordinate now has autonomy to make decisions that have been delegated, power is no longer shared. The manager, alone, determines what decisions the manager will make and which ones will be delegated to the subordinate.[14] The social relationship that previously existed between manager and subordinate is changed. The effect of delegation in this situation is that subordinates can no longer be "just one of the group." The satisfaction of being a group member is lost.[15]

CHAIN OF COMMAND

In its simplest form, a *chain of command* is the relationship between a superior and a subordinate. Starting at the top with the chief executive, we may visualize a series of lines connecting the executive with the next layer of management. An organization chart diagrams these organizational relationships with lines fanning down from the chief executive and increasing in number at lower levels of the organization.

The phrase "chain of command" implies an authoritative relationship, but the chain has at least three distinguishable characteristics, namely, *authority*, *responsibility*, and *communication*. In an authoritative chain, the manager's status is that of order-giver. The chain is an official channel, and the superior's communications are authoritative (Figure 9–3).

FIGURE 9–3 The chain of command

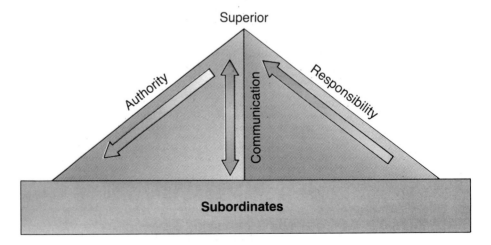

The chain of command is also a line of responsibility which holds subordinates accountable for their performance. If satisfactory performance is the rule, there may be little or no mention of accountability. In many cases, however, managers conduct formal performance reviews in which they evaluate and discuss the performance of subordinates.

Classical management theory says that authority should be commensurate with responsibility. This means that there is a basic unfairness involved in holding an individual responsible for that which he or she lacks authority to accomplish. Unfortunately, higher management sometimes fails to see the limitations confronting a subordinate or neglects to confer upon him or her the necessary authority. Even in well-managed organizations, however, authority is seldom spelled out as carefully as implied by traditional management theory. In practice, employees are expected to ''get the job done'' as well as possible even though their authority may be limited or unclear.[16]

Difficulties in Adhering to the Chain of Command

In practice, adherence to the chain of command can never be complete. Almost any manager is known personally and evaluated by two or three levels of supervision. Relationships of this type are not confined to *joint conferences*, in which several layers of management are present, but also include ''leapfrogging'' that runs counter to the chain-of-command concept.

Several forces contribute to this flexibility of the chain of command. One is the need for speed in communications. Clearing a communication through several levels of management is time consuming even if the matter is given reasonably prompt treatment. For example, if D (in Figure 9–4) wishes to communicate with G through channels, D must go through C, B, A, E, and F.

Dangers in Not Adhering to the Chain of Command

''Short-circuiting'' the chain of command occurs whenever certain levels of command are bypassed. A top manager may go around an immediate supervisor to deal with lower-level employees. Conversely, lower-level subordinates may bypass their superiors and report to higher-level managers. Short-circuiting the official chain of command quickly undermines the position of a bypassed manager. In contacts between the bypassed manager and that manager's subordinates, the effectiveness of leadership is impaired. Subordinates may well reason, ''If the boss does not take our supervisor seriously, why should we?'' In addition, these subordinates are subjected to multiple supervision, an arrangement that is often unsatisfactory for the subordinate.

The seriousness of short-circuiting depends on the circumstances. Emergency situations, for example, provide greater tolerance of contacts outside the chain of command. No one considers it necessary to shout ''fire'' through channels! In the absence of emergencies, the willingness of intermediate management levels to tolerate leapfrogging depends on the importance of the sub-

FIGURE 9–4 Communication through the chain of command

ject discussed, the nature of the contact (whether it is confined to discussion or involves decisions), and the extent to which intermediate levels are kept fully informed.

In some instances, short-circuiting by subordinates is justified as a protection against unfairness in supervision. Although managers may be reasonable and fair most of the time, they occasionally take arbitrary and harsh administrative action. In such cases, the subordinate has little recourse except to "go over the head" of the superior. Several companies, such as IBM and Armstrong World Industries, have "open-door" policies that permit employees to bring problems of unfair treatment to top management.

Researchers have found that managers whose decision-making authority is undercut by their superiors experience a high level of stress. Some managers deal with that stress by relying on alcohol or pills. Others may quit their jobs, have high absenteeism rates, do shoddy work, or even engage in industrial sabotage.[17]

On the other hand, strict adherence to the chain of command can block a top manager's understanding about the workings of lower levels of the hierarchy. The top manager may not be familiar with the bright young people in those lower levels. The more rigidly higher-ranking executives follow the chain of command, the less they see lower-ranking personnel in action. Top managers can occasionally relax the chain of command by conducting casual conversations with lower-level employees and providing direct supervision when immediate managers are absent.

Unity of Command

The concept of *unity of command* holds that no individual should be subject to the direct command of more than one superior at any given time. In practice, this precept is often violated. In some cases, a subordinate reports to two or more superiors of approximately equal status. In other situations, one manager exercises administrative control, while another manager provides technical control over work. Sometimes organizational relationships are vague, and the subordinate finds that two or more superiors are behaving as though the subordinate reports to each of them.

The reasoning supporting the desirability of unity of command is that two or more superiors are unlikely to agree perfectly in their instructions to the same subordinate. The individual subject to multiple supervision is also subject to role conflict and is likely to be dissatisfied with the supervisory situation.[18] The subordinate is in a strategic position, furthermore, to play off one supervisor against another, inasmuch as neither superior has complete knowledge of the total assignment.

SPAN OF CONTROL

Thus far, we have looked at authority and its exercise through the chain of command. A related question concerns the breadth of a manager's reach—that is, the number of subordinates whom he or she can effectively manage. The *span of control* refers to the number of immediate subordinates reporting to a given manager. If the president gives orders to only one executive vice-president, the president's span of control is one.

FIGURE 9–5 Spans of different sizes

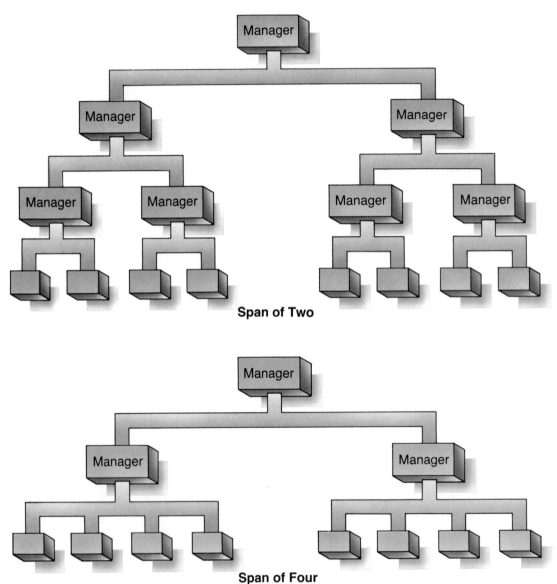

The size of the span of control is inversely related to the number of *echelons,* or layers, in an organization. As the span is broadened, there is a tendency to flatten the structure. In Figure 9–5 we can see that a span of two would require four echelons to direct eight operative employees, whereas a span of four would require only three echelons.

Limiting or Broadening the Span of Control

The reason for limiting the span of control is plain enough. The strength and time of any manager are limited. One manager, for example, could not personally direct the work of a thousand employees. The logic supporting smaller spans—or "tall" organizations—is sometimes extended far beyond the obvious case. A manager who can in some way direct the activities of twelve subordinates, it is reasoned, should be able to direct eight or six or four even more effectively. Extremely small spans are costly, however, and may also be defective by encouraging overly close supervision.

Broadening the span, as noted earlier, produces a flatter organization by reducing the number of echelons. This facilitates vertical communication by eliminating organizational levels that can become communication bottlenecks.

By broadening the span of control, organizations may also experience an increase in morale. The evidence is far from conclusive, however. A well-known study of this type concerns Sears, Roebuck and Company.[19] In this company, some managers were assigned relatively large numbers of subordinates. These managers were unable to direct and control their subordinates in a detailed manner. The management concluded that the flat organization with a wide span of control resulted in "not only a higher level of accomplishment but, at the same time, a more satisfying type of supervision and a higher level of employee morale."

In another study, Lyman Porter and Edward Lawler measured the job satisfaction of almost 2,000 managers in companies of various sizes.[20] They found no overall superiority of flat over tall organizations in providing satisfaction for the needs of managers. Another study of 467 trade salespeople from three large national organizations has shown a relationship between flatness and organizational behavior.[21] Trade salespeople in the flat organization perceived more self-actualization, more autonomy satisfaction, and lower amounts of stress and performed more efficiently than salespeople in medium and tall organizations. However, another study of sales representatives indicated that role conflict and role ambiguity increased as the span of control widened.[22] From these studies, it is evident that the relationship between flatness and morale is not clear.

Another obvious advantage of a broad span of control is the reduction of administrative overhead cost. By having each manager direct a large number of subordinates, the necessary number of management officials is substantially reduced in any sizable organization.

Variables Affecting Optimum Span Size

Although the topic of span of control is widely discussed in management textbooks, there is little agreement about what variables affect optimum span size.[23] Certain researchers have stated that the variables affecting one level of the hierarchy may not affect other levels.[24] In other words, variables affecting span of control may be level specific. For example, the number of specialties supervised was found to affect managerial control more in middle and lower levels of the hierarchy than in upper levels.[25]

A number of variables have been identified that have an impact on the optimum span of control. These include the nature of work performed, managerial characteristics, methods of management, and the capacity and training of subordinates.[26]

DECENTRALIZATION

As organizations grow, they become more difficult to manage. When they become huge—with tens of thousands or hundreds of thousands of employees—they become unwieldy and require new types of organizational and management practices.

About 1920, General Motors pioneered an approach to management of large organizations that was to become famous. Introduced by Alfred P. Sloan, Jr., this management approach became known as *decentralized management*. Decentralization facilitated, or at least permitted, the tremendous growth that made General Motors one of the leading industrial concerns in the world.

Decentralized management basically involves the subdivision of a large organization into components of more manageable size. The key to decentralization, however, is the autonomy accorded to the separate divisions. They are directed by divisional heads who function much like chief executives. Decentralization thus necessitates delegation of authority, but it is not synonymous with delegation. Even in more centralized organizations, individual managers may delegate freely. Decentralization occurs when delegation is practiced systematically throughout an organization by the creation of relatively autonomous divisions.

Decentralization of authority and decision making is often centered about product or territorial divisions that receive grants of authority from company headquarters. As noted in chapter 8, such organization structures are described as divisionalized. It should be noted, however, that decentralization is not the same as divisionalization. In a company organized along functional lines, lower-level officials may be granted either substantial or minor authority. And even in a company having product or territorial divisions, there is no guarantee that divisions are free from close control by headquarters.

Research indicates that there is no one best way for an organization to structure itself to implement a given strategy. Many good design alternatives exist.[27] In an investigation of the relationship between the effectiveness of strategic business units (SBUs) and decentralization, evidence suggests that firms should employ different degrees of decentralization depending on the strategy of the individual SBU.[28] For example, the mission of an SBU of a multibusiness organization may be to build market share, and its competitive strategy may be to differentiate itself in the marketplace by unique product features, brand image, special services, and so forth. The mission of another SBU with the same company might also be to build market share, but the competitive strategy used by the second SBU may be to have the lowest cost. Neither of these two SBUs should have the same degree of decentralization because each uses a different competitive strategy. The first SBU should be more decentralized; the second should be more centralized.[29]

Advantages of Decentralization

One advantage of decentralization is that managerial ability may be developed throughout the organization. Another advantage of decentralized corporate management is the principle of the *profit center*. The division manager who is given freedom in management can be held responsible for the profitable operations of the division. Managers of such profit centers can be highly motivated to operate productively. Their effectiveness or ineffectiveness is no longer obscured by blending the operating results of all divisions into one overall financial report.

In some cases, lower-level decisions are better than higher-level decisions. The manager on the ''firing line'' is close to the problem and often has insights that higher-level management lacks. In addition, the immediate manager is in a position to move quickly if not required to check constantly with headquarters. One study showed that firms facing strong competitive pressures, with the accompanying market turbulence, tend to have more decentralization and more participative decision making.[30]

Decentralization is also good for product diversification. It is difficult, if not impossible, for a company having a highly diversified line of products to operate with tightly centralized management. Centralized control over the

DIFFICULTIES IN DECENTRALIZING

The failure of the Penn Square Bank of Oklahoma City in 1982 affected many larger banks, such as Continental Illinois National Bank and Trust Company of Chicago, Seattle-First National Bank, and New York's Chase Manhattan Bank. These larger banks suffered because they had joined with Penn Square in some of its loans. Chase's difficulties could be explained because of decentralization. Reportedly, Chase's Institutional Banking Division was very aggressive in hunting for quick profits. This division participated in a number of loans with Penn Square without having them reviewed by Chase's highly respected energy lending group.

SOURCE: Adapted from ''The Stain from Penn Square Keeps Spreading,'' *Business Week*, 2 August 1982, pp. 60–64.

units of a food chain, for example, is simpler than centralized control of a company producing such diverse equipment as water heaters, electronic equipment, and farm implements.

Disadvantages of Decentralization

Decentralization can also involve disadvantages. In some instances, autonomous divisions may be allowed to function without adequate control. For example, divisions of banks eager to improve divisional performance may approve loans involving excessive risk.

The lack of ability of lower-level personnel may also limit the options of top management to decentralize. This may become a vicious circle, however, with the lack of ability an effect as well as a cause of failure to decentralize. Such a case spotlights a serious weakness in higher-level management.

Some functions are more easily decentralized than others. Manufacturing has traditionally been one of the first to be decentralized, while finance has remained centralized even in many large companies that are otherwise decentralized.

LINE AND STAFF RELATIONSHIPS

The chief executive officer of a large U.S. corporation was asked to explain the difference between line and staff employees. "Line employees search the market place, develop new products, get raw materials and equipment into the factory, make the products, and then sell them," he said. "Staff employees try to stop them."

Line and Staff Functions

In most organizations, a simple distinction can be made between activities that accomplish the basic purposes of the organization and activities that are indirectly helpful. In colleges and universities, for example, the teaching faculty provides educational services, whereas student financial aid offices contribute indirectly by helping students finance their education. In manufacturing plants, production departments make products for customers, whereas personnel offices recruit employees for production and other departments. In department stores, selling departments sell merchandise to customers, whereas credit departments evaluate the financial capacity of customers.

From an operational point of view, *line functions* are those that contribute directly to accomplishment of the organization's primary objective. The primary or line functions of a manufacturing concern, for example, include producing and selling a product. The firm exists to make and sell products, and customers pay for this service. Employees in production and sales, accordingly, are line personnel, and the manufacturing and sales departments are line departments of the enterprise. In basic economic terms, line departments produce "time, place, and form" utility for customers.

Staff functions, on the other hand, are supporting functions. Their performance facilitates the accomplishment of primary objectives by line departments. The nature of staff work is often described as advisory to other departments. In addition, the staff may be used for investigation, fact gathering, and service. In fact, many nonline departments provide a combination of advice and service.

One weakness of this classification is that it does not distinguish between important and unimportant activities. We can, for example, classify finance or accounting as a staff function, but it is dangerous to assume that either is unimportant. In classifying specific functions as line activities, therefore, we must avoid the error of considering staff functions as unimportant.

Traditional View of Line Authority

Much of the line and staff problem in a typical organization concerns the question of authority between line and staff departments or personnel. Who decides questions of mutual interest to both line and staff departments? According to the traditional view of management, line managers are the proper decision makers and their authority must be maintained. To preserve unity of command, staff must be denied command authority. Only in this way, presumably, can line managers be held responsible for results.

How then can staff managers perform the functions for which they are responsible? Although they may seek to enforce their judgment by appealing to the chain of command, they cannot expect higher-level managers to solve all their problems for them. For the most part, they must use horizontal relationships and provide advice and service which is perceived by the line to be competent and practical. Figure 9–6 illustrates the relationship between line and staff departments.

FIGURE 9–6 Line-staff organization

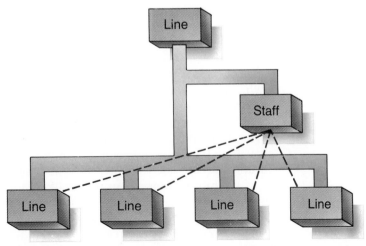

NOTE: According to the traditional view, staff has a "dotted-line" or advisory relationship, not a command relationship, to other departments.

Discussion of the traditional staff role and the degrees of staff authority tends to understate its extensive influence—an influence that often exceeds its formal authority. Some reasons for the power of staff are identified in the following statement:[31]

> Since they are experts in their respective areas, staff people can withhold valuable advice or slow down service to pressure a manager to heed their influence attempts. A cooperative staff can be an important asset, but because staff people are experts in areas in which line managers are not, they can sometimes overwhelm the line manager with their specialized knowledge. They may have more influence with higher levels of line management because these managers depend on them to provide information about line performance.

Increasing Staff Authority

The supposedly ideal authority relationships between line and staff are difficult to observe. Situations arise in which it appears desirable from the standpoint of the organization as a whole to delegate to staff some degree of decision-making authority. A deliberate decision may place certain issues or decisions in the hands of staff.

Various degrees or types of staff authority have been established.[32] One type, *compulsory staff consultation*, requires operating managers to confer with appropriate staff personnel before taking action. They are not required to follow the advice but presumably must listen before acting.

Another type of staff authority, *concurrent authority*, substantially increases the power of staff. The line manager must obtain staff agreement before taking action. By requiring concurrent authority, the organization makes sure that staff knowledge is used in reaching a decision. As an example, the line manager may be required to get the concurrence of the legal department before signing a contract.

An even greater limitation is placed on the authority of line managers by granting *functional authority* to staff. This gives staff some specified authority over line activities. One of the most common forms of functional authority is the assignment to specialized staff of controls pertaining to their own areas. Often these are of a routine or procedural nature—"how to do it" rather than "what to do." The accounting office establishes accounting procedures, and the personnel department specifies personnel procedures. As another example, a dangerous industrial production process may require functional authority for safety inspectors. Although safety management is a staff function, management may grant the safety inspector authority to shut down an operation in order to insure adequate safety for personnel and equipment.

We can see from the examples of an attorney's approval of contracts and a safety inspector's approval of safety conditions that staff authority is limited to particular issues or conditions. Such arrangements restrict the line manager's independence in specific areas, but they do not create full-fledged dual or multiple lines of command.

STAFF THREATS TO LINE AUTHORITY

To function as contemplated in traditional theory, the staff must tread softly to avoid threats to line authority. Accordingly, a chief executive officer who builds up the power of staff offices makes life difficult for line managers. Harold S. Geneen's almost legendary managerial style as CEO of International Telephone and Telegraph (ITT) (until his retirement in 1977) created intense pressure for line managers. Part of this pressure was exerted through the ITT staff, whose surveillance was described as follows:

> An equal source of managerial terror in the Geneen years was the mammoth corporate staff. Line managers worked with the unsettling knowledge that they were being scrutinized by teams at headquarters who could advance their own careers by finding problems and perhaps exaggerating their importance. Like most bureaucracies, the staff in time became bloated and unwieldy. But Geneen stuck faithfully to the system.

A later CEO cut back the huge staff, thereby changing the balance of power—a move widely applauded by ITT's operating managers.

SOURCE: Geoffrey Colvin, "The De-Geneening of ITT," *Fortune* 105 (11 Janauary 1982): 34–39.© 1982 Time Inc.

LATERAL COORDINATION

After the formal organization chart has been developed to describe the tasks, responsibilities, and reporting relationships, certain horizontal mechanisms must be designed that will integrate the various individuals and departments as well as promote the chain of command. Employees may be physically separated or may not talk with one another on a regular basis. *Lateral coordination* involves the use of various mechanisms that can be used to improve information flow and horizontal cooperation.

Need for Lateral Relationships

A department typically interacts with a number of other departments, although the pattern and volume of interaction are not uniform. A sales department, for example, may interact with manufacturing, personnel, advertising, accounting, legal, research, and other departments. Many of these interactions involve direct contacts, as sales personnel and managers confer directly with peers in other departments.

To function effectively, therefore, organizations must use horizontal forms of communication and decision making.* They can avoid an overload in the chain of command by working directly with other departments at the same level in solving problems and coordinating their respective activities. If every difficulty or point of friction between departments were taken upward to a mutual superior, that superior would need to devote an unreasonable amount of time to peacemaking and integrative activities.

Suppose that Departments F and G in Figure 9–7 experience a problem that affects their respective operations and overall organization performance. Department F, for example, may encounter delays which affect the flow of output from Department F to Department G. If this problem can be resolved laterally, it avoids delays and also minimizes the managerial burden placed on managers of A, B, and C.

The extent of lateral coordination varies with the nature of work operations and particularly the degree of task uncertainty. *Task uncertainty* refers to variability in work—for example, the sameness of work from day to day, the number of exceptions, frequency of delays in deciding how to solve problems, and so on. One research study has shown that as tasks increase in uncertainty, more horizontal communication and group meetings are used in lieu of the chain of command.[33]

FIGURE 9–7 Lateral coordination

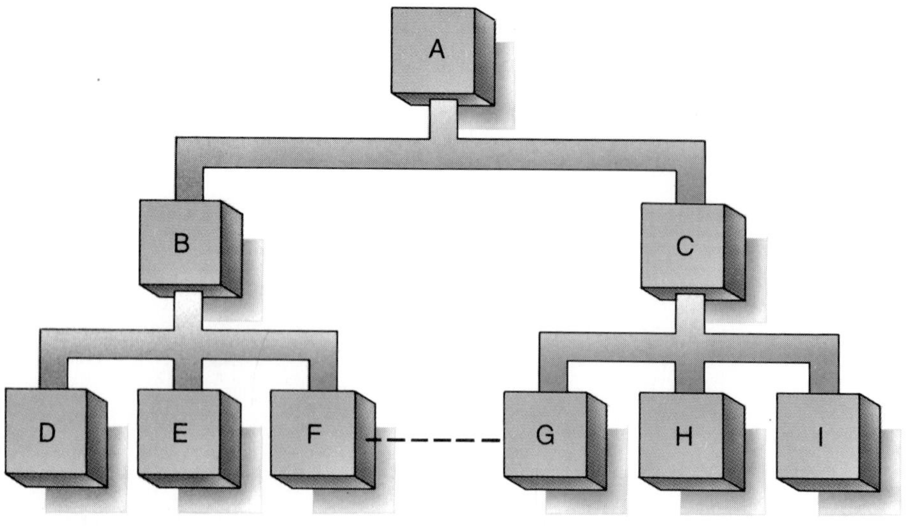

---

*Management theorists have long recognized the need for horizontal communication and decision making, but, in earlier years, treated it as a limited, exceptional relationship needing careful control. The noted French writer Henri Fayol emphasized the need for supervisory authorization prior to lateral contacts and prompt reporting of any lateral agreements to higher-level supervisors. See Henri Fayol, *General and Industrial Management*, trans. Constance Storrs (New York: Pitman, 1949).

Forms of Lateral Relationships

Collaboration among departments takes various forms. The simplest approach involves *direct contact* between managers who have a mutual problem. Suppose, for example, that two departments in a university school of business prepare tentative schedules that would overload limited facilities or that would offer required seminars at the same hour. Instead of referring such problems upward to the dean for resolution, the department chairpersons can simply get together and work out a solution.

In some organizations, the volume of interdepartmental contacts is so great that a special *liaison role* is created to assist in coordination. This may be illustrated by the product design and process design groups of a manufacturing plant.[34] The product design group prepares new product designs, and the process design group works out the manufacturing processes necessary to produce them. To aid in coordination, a group of process designers is physically stationed in the product design area. This liaison group performs a variety of integrative activities such as working with product designers to find design alternatives which allow less costly manufacturing processes. In addition, close contact with product designers enables the process designers to schedule their own manufacturing process design work efficiently. They have discovered that design of a new product does not need to be 100 percent complete before the manufacturing process design can begin.

TASK FORCES AT PROCTER AND GAMBLE

Procter and Gamble (P&G) has been rated as a well-managed company by a number of observers. John Smale, chief executive of P&G, plans to maintain the firm's quality by using task forces to stimulate innovation. Creative employees are formed into business teams or task forces to evaluate projects still in the formative stage. All disciplines within a given division, as well as key corporate staff areas, are included on the task force. Although the respective division manager has the responsibility for determining the strategic direction of the division, the task force provides a broad range of input into both the decision-making process and how the decisions will be implemented.

Smale comments that project proposals previously had to go through a sequence of reviews and discussions. Certain functional area managers were not involved until a final review. The task force not only eliminates these lengthy reviews but allows all of the functional areas to provide input before the project plan is completed.

SOURCE: Adapted from Priscilla Petty, "Behind the Brands at P&G: An Interview with John Smale," *Harvard Business Review* (November-December 1986): 78–90.

As more general problems arise or projects become more complex, management may create a *task force* or *team* of representatives from various departments to provide coordination. A task force might be created within a college or university, for example, to coordinate efforts to achieve academic accreditation. Formation of teams has also been proposed as a mechanism for guiding market-research projects.[35] These teams would bring together personnel from such diverse areas as manufacturing, finance, accounting, advertising, sales, product planning, and market research in order to define market-research needs and guide research projects.

As lateral decisions become increasingly important, a need for still stronger leadership often arises. This leads to the creation of an *integrating role*.[36] Someone is assigned specific leadership responsibility for integrating or coordinating interdepartmental efforts. These integrative positions carry such titles as product manager, program coordinator, business manager, project leader, and so on. A product manager, for example, becomes the representative for a given product in all departments having any relationship to that product. If such a pattern continues to grow and the coordinator acquires formal authority, it becomes a matrix pattern (as described in chapter 8).

SUMMARY

Organizational design, a broader concept than structure, involves weaving together various factors to make the organization work. *Horizontal* and *vertical relationships* are mechanisms that ensure adequate integration and coordination of effort by linking together the various individuals and departments, as well as the chain of command.

Authority is defined as the capacity to make decisions affecting the behavior of subordinates. Limitations exist in the extent to which formal authority is accepted by subordinate members of an organization. Chester I. Barnard has suggested the concept of a *zone of indifference* within which employees are willing to accept orders. Forms of resistance include both open defiance and subtle disobedience.

By *delegation of authority*, a manager conveys to a subordinate the right to make decisions that would otherwise be made by the delegator. Barriers to delegation include both *organizational barriers* and *psychological barriers*. Inexperience of personnel, for example, constitutes an organizational barrier. Psychological barriers include deeply ingrained habit patterns, a sense of individual importance, feelings of insecurity, and an enjoyment of exercising power. Another barrier to delegation takes the form of the subordinate's reluctance to assume delegated authority. Among the advantages of delegation are the relief of the delegator from time-consuming work, development of subordinate personnel, and improvement of morale.

Adherence to the *chain of command* strengthens the organization by preserving the status of management officials and avoiding confusion among subordinate personnel. Subordinates often find it distressing to receive multiple supervision, whether this results from short-circuiting the chain of command or from conflict with the concept of *unity of command.*

Although there are difficulties in extending the size of the span of control, some have found advantages, particularly in terms of communication, productivity, and morale, in the use of broader spans that result in flatter organizations. Some of the variables affecting the desirable span size include the nature of the work, the qualities of the manager, managerial methods and procedures, and the ability of subordinates. Certain variables tend to have a greater impact on one level of the hierarchy than on another.

Decentralization occurs when delegation is used systematically and extensively throughout an organization. Decentralization aids control through the principle of the *profit center*, facilitates product diversification, and improves some decisions by permitting them to be made closer to the problem level. Difficulties in decentralizing include uneconomical duplication of some operations and limited capability of lower-level personnel. Strategic business units with distinct competitive strategies will require different degrees of decentralization to become more effective.

Line functions, those directly concerned with the accomplishment of an organization's primary objectives, are aided by *staff functions*, which support line activities in the form of service and advice. According to traditional theory, staff should generally occupy an advisory rather than a command relationship to line. As a practical matter, however, staff is frequently granted some authority, such as *compulsory staff consultation, concurrent authority*, or *functional authority.*

Lateral relationships are necessary to achieve interdepartmental coordination without overloading the chain of command. They take such forms as direct contact, liaison role, task force, team, and integrating role.

KEY CONCEPTS

Organizational design	Chain of command
Horizontal relationship	Span of control
Vertical relationship	Decentralization
Authority	Profit center
Institutionalized power	Divisionalization
Functional authority	Staff functions
Delegation of authority	Liaison role
Zone of indifference	Task force
Organizational barriers to delegation	Integrating role
Psychological barriers to delegation	

DISCUSSION QUESTIONS

1. How does the concept of organizational design differ from organizational structure?
2. What is the difference between *horizontal* and *vertical* relationships from a design perspective? How do they ensure adequate integration and coordination of effort?
3. What is the *zone of indifference* suggested by Barnard, and how is this related to a superior's authority?
4. Suppose a top-level executive feels it is necessary to go outside channels in contacting a manager two or three levels below. How can adverse effects be minimized?
5. What pressures encourage short-circuiting of the *chain of command*? Do these factors constitute valid reasons or are they merely excuses for short-circuiting?
6. How is the *span of control* related to the number of *echelons* in an organization?
7. What seems to be the greatest advantage resulting from expanding the span of control?
8. If the staff lacks *authority*, how can it provide any guidance or control? Won't its suggestions be disregarded by line managers? Should it, therefore, be given some degree of authority?
9. Distinguish between *decentralization* and *divisionalization*.
10. "There is a one best way for managers to structure their organizations to implement a given strategy." Agree? Disagree? Discuss.
11. Discuss the relationship of the *delegation of authority* and the morale of employees. Do subordinates really want authority and the responsibility that accompanies it?
12. Have you ever worked for a supervisor who delegated very little authority? For one who delegated extensively? Describe as carefully as possible your reactions and the reactions of your fellow employees to either or both types of supervision.

NOTES

1. Henry Mintzberg, *The Structuring of Organizations* (Englewood Cliffs, N.J.: Prentice-Hall, 1979), p. 2.
2. John Child, *Organization* (New York: Harper & Row, 1977), p. 10.
3. Jay Galbraith, *Organizational Design* (Reading, Mass.: Addison-Wesley, 1977), p. 72.
4. Richard L. Daft, *Organization Theory and Design*, 2nd ed. (St. Paul, Minn.: West, 1986), p. 217.
5. Harvey F. Kolodny and Barbara Dresner, "Linking Arrangements and New Work Designs," *Organizational Dynamics* (Winter 1986): 33–51.
6. Reprinted by permission of the publishers from Chester I. Barnard, *The Functions of the Executive*, Cambridge, Mass.: Harvard University Press. Copyright, 1938, by the President and Fellows of Harvard College, 1966, by Grace F. Noera Barnard, p. 162.
7. Ibid., pp. 168–69.

8. Herbert A. Simon, *Administrative Behavior*, 3d ed. (New York: The Free Press, 1976), p. 134.
9. Glenn H. Matthews, "Run Your Business Or Build An Organization?" *Harvard Business Review* 62 (March-April 1984): 34–44.
10. Gerald D. Bell, "The Influence of Technological Components of Work Upon Management Control," *Academy of Management Journal* 8 (June 1965): 127–32.
11. This discussion is based on Timothy W. Firnstahl, "Letting Go," *Harvard Business Review* 64 (September-October 1986): 14–18.
12. David M. Schweiger and Carrie R. Leana, "Participation in Decision Making," in Edwin Locke (ed.), *Generalizing From Laboratory to Field Settings: Research Findings From Industrial-Organizational Psychology, Organizational Behavior, and Human Resource Management* (Lexington, Mass.: D.C. Heath, 1986): 147–66.
13. Robert C. Liden and George Graen, "Generalizability of the Vertical Dyad Linking Model of Leadership," *Academy of Management Journal* 23 (September 1980): 451–65.
14. Benjamin Schneider, "Interactional Psychology and Organizational Behavior," in Larry L. Cummings and Barry M. Staw (eds.), *Research in Organizational Behavior* 5 (Greenwich, Conn.: JAI Press, 1986): 1–31.
15. Carrie R. Leana, "Predictors and Consequences of Delegation," *Academy of Management Journal* 29 (December 1986): 754–74.
16. For a research study that supports this position, see J. Kenneth White and Robert A. Ruh, "Effects of Personal Values on the Relationship between Participation and Job Attitudes," *Administrative Science Quarterly* 18 (December 1973): 506–14.
17. Morley D. Glicken and Katherine Janka, "Executives Under Fire: The Burnout Syndrome," *California Management Review* (Spring 1982): 56–72.
18. Confirmation of this negative attitude effect of multiple supervision in bureaucratic organizations is reported in Martin J. Gannon and Frank T. Paine, "Unity of Command and Job Attitudes of Managers in a Bureaucratic Organization," *Journal of Applied Psychology* 59 (June 1974): 392–94.
19. James C. Worthy, "Organizational Structure and Employee Morale," *American Sociological Review* 15 (April 1950): 169–79.
20. Lyman W. Porter and Edward E. Lawler III, "The Effects of 'Tall' Versus 'Flat' Organization Structures on Managerial Job Satisfaction," *Personnel Psychology* 17 (Summer 1964): 135–48.
21. John M. Ivancevich and James H. Donnelly, Jr., "Relation of Organizational Structure to Job Satisfaction, Anxiety-Stress, and Performance," *Administrative Science Quarterly* 20 (June 1975): 272–80.
22. Lawrence B. Chonko, "The Relationship of Span of Control to Sales Representatives' Experienced Role Conflict and Role Ambiguity," *Academy of Management Journal* 25 (June 1982): 452–56.
23. David D. Van Fleet, "Span of Management Research and Issues," *Academy of Management Journal* 26 (September 1982): 452–56.
24. Robert D. Dewar and Donald P. Simet, "A Level Specific Prediction of Spans of Control Examining the Effects of Size, Technology, and Specialization," *Academy of Management Journal* 24 (March 1982): 5–24.
25. Ibid.
26. Jon G. Udal, "An Empirical Test of Hypotheses Relating to Span of Control," *Administrative Science Quarterly* 12 (December 1967): 420–39.

27. Larry J. Bourgeois, "Strategic Management and Determinism," *Academy of Management Review* 9 (April 1984): 586–96.

28. Vijay Govindarajan, "Decentralization, Strategy, and Effectiveness of Strategic Business Units in Multibusiness Organizations," *Academy of Management Review* 11 (October 1986): 844–56.

29. For a more comprehensive discussion of these relationships see Michael E. Porter, *Competitive Advantage* (New York: Free Press, 1985); and Raymond E. Miles and Charles C. Snow, *Organizational Strategy Structure and Process* (New York: McGraw-Hill, 1978).

30. Pradip N. Khandwalla, "Effect of Competition on the Structure of Top Management Control," *Academy of Management Journal* 16 (June 1973): 285–95.

31. John H. Jackson and Cyril P. Morgan, *Organizational Theory: A Macro Perspective for Management* (Englewood Cliffs, N.J.: Prentice-Hall, 1978), p. 145.

32. For a fuller discussion of various types of staff authority, see Jackson and Morgan, *Organizational Theory*, pp. 144–45.

33. Andrew H. Van de Ven, Andre L. Delbecq, and Richard Koenig, Jr., "Determinants of Coordination Modes within Organizations," *American Sociological Review* 41 (April 1976): 322–28.

34. This example is cited by Galbraith, *Organizational Design*, p. 194.

35. William B. Locander and Richard W. Scamell, "A Team Approach to Managing the Market Research Process," *MSU Business Topics* 25 (Winter 1977): 15–26.

36. Paul R. Lawrence and Jay W. Lorsch, "New Management Job: The Integrator," *Harvard Business Review* 45 (November-December 1967): 142–51.

SUPPLEMENTARY READING

Biggart, Nicole W., and Hamilton, Gary G. "The Power of Obedience." *Administrative Science Quarterly* 29 (December 1984): 540–49.

Child, John. "Organizational Design and Performance: Contingency Theory and Beyond." *Organization and Administrative Sciences* 8 (Summer-Fall 1977): 169–83.

Chonko, Lawrence B. "The Relationships of Span of Control to Sales Representatives' Experienced Role Conflict and Role Ambiguity," *Academy of Management Journal* 25 (June 1982): 452–56.

Hawley, John A. "Transforming Organizations Through Vertical Linking." *Organizational Dynamics* (Winter 1984): 68–80.

Mansfield, Roger. *Company Strategy and Organizational Design.* New York: St. Martin's Press, 1986.

Mintzberg, Henry. "Structure in 5's: A Synthesis of the Research on Organization Design." *Management Science* 26 (March 1980): 322–41.

———. "Organization Design: Fashion or Fit?" *Harvard Business Review* 59 (January-February 1981): 103–16.

Petty, Priscilla H. "Behind the Brands at P&G: An Interview with John Smale." *Harvard Business Review* 63 (November-December 1985): 78–90.

Podsakoff, Philip M.; Williams, Larry J.; and Todor, William D. "Effects of Organizational Formalization on Alienation Among Professionals and Non-professionals." *Academy of Management Journal* 29 (December 1986): 826–31.

Slocum, John W., Jr., and **Hellriegel, Don.** "Using Organizational Designs to Cope with Change." *Business Horizons* 22, no. 6 (December 1979): 65–76.
Vancil, Richard F. *Decentralization: Managerial Ambiguity by Design.* New York: Financial Executives Research Foundation, 1980.
Van de Ven, Andrew H., and **Walker, Gordon.** "The Dynamics of Interorganizational Coordination." *Administrative Science Quarterly* 29 (December 1984): 598–621.

DELTA FERTILIZER (A)

Hughes Brown, certified public accountant, has recently been offered the job of controller for Delta Fertilizer. Hughes is twenty-nine, married with two children, and presently employed as an auditing supervisor with a "big-eight" accounting firm. Hughes has just completed an audit of Delta Fertilizer and has reported a number of irregularities in the corporate books. The president of Delta has mentioned that the vice-presidents of sales and production have been dissatisfied with the way that accounting information has been provided to them. Delta's present controller, who is sixty-four, has just retired.

Hughes is interested in the controller's position for several reasons. For example, the new job has a higher salary, is close to his parents' and his home, and the demanding travel associated with his present job will be eliminated. The new job also offers some challenging opportunities. The accounting department at Delta needs to be revitalized. The president of Delta has stated that he wants the "accounting problems corrected within four months."

There are twelve staff accountants, four clerical employees, and three secretaries in Delta's accounting department. Hughes believes that these employees are capable and qualified but have not been properly supervised or challenged. As an auditing supervisor, Hughes directed the activities of six professional accountants.

Hughes wonders if his span of control will be too broad at Delta. He was able to give the accountants in his auditing group a great deal of autonomy in performing their duties. Hughes also has other concerns: How will Delta's accounting staff respond to his proposed changes? Is the staff really competent? Should he recommend that an assistant controller be hired to assist him in providing supervision?

Hughes hesitates to discuss these concerns with Delta's president because they might be interpreted as an indication that Hughes will not be able to handle the job.

Questions

1. Should Hughes immediately attempt to improve performance before attempting any structural changes in the accounting department? Why or why not?
2. How does the competency of subordinates affect considerations about the span of control?
3. If you were Hughes, what would you do now? Why?

JACKSONVILLE PACKAGING

Jacksonville Packaging manufactures corrugated containers from rolls of Kraft paper. A corrugated container is simply a paper box with several plies of paper glued together. The manufacturing process at Jacksonville is a 24-hour-per-day, seven-day-a-week operation and consists of the following:

☐ *Corrugated Department* A large high-speed machine glues the plies of paper together in a continuous roll and then cuts various size blanks from the roll.

☐ *Printing and Folding Department* The multi-ply blanks of paperboard are joined, folded, and printed using a high speed printer-folder. Completed corrugated containers or paper boxes are made ready for shipment by banding them in units using plastic strapping. The finished containers are produced in various sizes and banded together based on customer specifications. For example, one customer may specify 50 boxes per bundle, another specifies 80, and so forth.

☐ *Shipping Department* Particular customers may order many different sized boxes and request that they be shipped together. Jacksonville's customers are located within a 50-mile radius of the plant and shipments are made by truck.

The paper box business in Jacksonville is very competitive. Firms compete on the basis of price and delivery time. Jacksonville Packaging has achieved a competitive advantage by having a price that meets the competition and by having a policy to ship finished boxes to customers three days after receipt of an order. No other competitor offers this service.

A normal day of shipping at the Jacksonville plant involves the loading of approximately fifty trailer-trucks (trailers are 10 feet wide and 40 feet long). All of the trailer-trucks and drivers are contracted from other firms. Jacksonville does not use any of its own trucks in order to avoid the high cost of owning a trucking fleet. Firms providing the trucks and drivers have to be notified prior to 4:00 P.M. on the preceding day.

A manufacturing and shipping schedule is prepared weekly by the planning department of the Jacksonville plant. The shipping department manager is responsible for scheduling the proper number of trucks and drivers each day to meet the shipping schedule. Whenever deviations occur in the manufacturing and shipping schedule, the planning department prepares an "exceptions" list and then distributes it.

Serious problems have developed. Orders are not completed on time. Too many trucks and drivers are being scheduled. Shipping costs have increased and customers have become dissatisfied.

Jacksonville's plant manager asked the industrial engineering manager for a report determining the causes of these problems. Industrial engineering reports that the shipping manager is strictly following the manufacturing and shipping schedule and that the "exceptions" report is not being properly prepared. The planning department reports that they are not always notified when the deviations occur. For example, the corrugating and printing and folding departments can experience machine breakdowns causing delays. Other problems may force these two departments to change the order production sequence. The two departments do not always inform planning when these events happen. The planning department has requested that five additional employees be hired to resolve the problem.

Question

1. As plant manager, how would you solve this problem?

HUMAN RESOURCE PLANNING AND RECRUITING
Job Analysis □ Process of Recruiting

SELECTION AND ORIENTATION
Application Blank/Résumé □ Background Checks □ Tests □ Interviews □ Compensation □ Orientation and Socialization

PERFORMANCE APPRAISAL
Techniques of Performance Appraisal □ Improving Performance Appraisal

MANAGEMENT DEVELOPMENT
Management Development Methods □ Evaluating Development Programs

Summary □ Key Concepts □ Discussion Questions □ Notes □ Supplementary Reading

CASES: Accountants Must Be Good Looking? □ Challenge

This chapter will enable you to

□ Explain the process of human resource planning and recruiting.

□ Comprehend the process organizations use to select and hire new employees, and the role management plays in orienting newcomers to their surroundings and in helping them become integral parts of the organization.

□ Understand the purpose of performance appraisal and the contributions and limitations of certain appraisal techniques.

□ Identify the various methods of management development.

CHAPTER 10
HUMAN RESOURCE MANAGEMENT

A competent, motivated team of organization members can make the difference between an effective and an ineffective organization. Building and maintaining this team require careful management of the organization's human resources. This process begins with *human resource planning* and the subsequent recruitment of job applicants. Through a process involving a number of hurdles such as application blanks, background checks, tests, and interviews, qualified applicants are selected for positions within the organization. These new employees must be appropriately compensated, oriented to their jobs and surroundings, and socialized into organizational membership. Performance appraisal not only helps new employees understand organizational expectations, but measures how effectively the organization's human resources are being used. Finally, any effective organization must have an able, competent cadre of managers. Building such a team requires a well-planned management development program.

HUMAN RESOURCE PLANNING AND RECRUITING

Determining the firm's human resource requirements is the first step in staffing the organization. The process of *personnel forecasting* enables management to answer such questions about the future as the following:

1. How many additional personnel will we require over the next year? The next five years?

2. What types of positions must we fill?
3. What qualifications are required for these positions?

In estimating staff requirements, a number of factors must be considered. Probable losses from retirements, deaths, resignations, and other reasons must be calculated. Estimates of this kind require attention to age distribution of present staff, historical rate of attrition, and so on. Any expansion plans of the business similarly affect estimated requirements. This factor requires a forecast of future trends, as discussed in earlier chapters.

Human resource planning has become increasingly important in recent years. Rapid technological change, combined with an uncertain economy, has made planning more necessary, yet more difficult, than ever. As a former chairman of General Electric put it, "I didn't realize it [in 1970], but we were a company with 30,000 electromechanical engineers becoming a company that needed electronics engineers. We didn't plan for this change in 1970, and it caused us big problems by the mid-1970s."[1] This experience was instrumental in GE's developing a formal human resource planning process.

Federal Equal Employment Opportunity (EEO) programs have caused management to plan and develop more rational career paths and job requirements, and more objective procedures for matching candidates with jobs. Some EEO regulations that affect management are shown in Figure 10–1. The Civil Rights Act and the Affirmative Action Program have had great impact on organizational staffing. Other acts prohibit discrimination on the basis of age or

FIGURE 10–1 Major equal employment opportunity requirements for organizations

Title VII of Civil Rights Act (1964, amended in 1972)—applies to all private employers with at least fifteen employees, governments at all levels, and labor unions with at least fifteen members. States that *race, religion, national origin, sex,* or *color* may not be used to

1. Refuse to hire or to discharge an individual or discriminate against a person with respect to pay, conditions of employment, or privileges of employment.
2. Classify employees in such a way as to deprive anyone of employment opportunities.
3. Refuse entrance into training programs or apprenticeship programs.

Executive Order 11246 (1965, expanded in 1968 and 1970)—established an *affirmative action program* which applies to all organizations with federal contracts or subcontracts. Goes further than the Civil Rights Act by stating that an employer can no longer be passive, but must actively attempt to reduce unequal employment opportunities through recruitment, selection, placement, performance evaluation, wage programs, and so on. In short, all personnel activities must foster affirmative action.

EMPLOYEE LOYALTY?

In just two years in the mid-1980s, almost half a million white-collar employees lost their jobs as large companies restructured their operations in attempts to become more competitive. Many of these workers had assumed that as long as they performed well they would have a job with their company for as long as they wished. Not only are they now disillusioned, but the survivors of the cutbacks are beginning to wonder if their jobs are secure. It is difficult for a company to eliminate as much as 20 percent of its work force and still retain a commitment among those who remain.

One notable exception to this trend is IBM. During the depression of the 1930s, Thomas J. Watson, Sr., indicated that the company should not lay off its employees, and his wishes have been followed ever since. But maintaining its full workforce has not been easy. During tough economic times, IBM restricts hiring, cuts overtime, asks employees to use any saved vacation days, limits work to subcontractors, moves work among its plants, and retrains, reeducates, and redeploys its employees so that they might be used more efficiently.

SOURCE: "The End of Corporate Loyalty?", *Business Week*, 4 August 1986, pp. 42–9; Thomas F. O'Boyle, "Loyalty Ebbs at Many Companies As Employees Grow Disillusioned," *The Wall Street Journal*, 11 July 1985; and "IBM's Fancy Footwork to Sidestep Layoffs," *Business Week*, 7 July 1986, pp. 54–5.

pregnancy, or require federal contractors and the federal government to practice affirmative action toward the physically or mentally handicapped and veterans.

Although surveys reveal that most organizations prepare a long-term business plan, fewer than half of the companies fully integrate their human resource planning with the strategic business plan.[2] Of those organizations that conduct human resource planning, the activities that receive the most emphasis are recruiting job applicants, selecting new employees, training and developing employees, and planning for managerial succession. One researcher concluded that the companies that engage in human resource planning "do it because their top executives are convinced it gives them a competitive advantage in the marketplace."[3]

Job Analysis

Effective personnel planning requires detailed knowledge of the positions in the organization. The process of compiling this information is termed *job analysis*. A job analysis includes two elements: (1) a *job description*, which contains

FIGURE 10–2 Sample job description and specification

TITLE OF POSITION: **Personnel Manager, Plant**

Basic Purpose

To develop and maintain an employee relations climate that creates and permits a stable and productive workforce. To manage and coordinate all functions of employee relations, including employment, labor relations, compensation and benefit services, manpower planning, training and development, affirmative action, and security.

Duties and Responsibilities

1. Selects, trains, develops, and organizes a subordinate staff to perform and meet department responsibilities and objectives effectively.

2. Provides leadership in the establishment and maintenance of employee relations that will assist in attracting and retaining a desirable and productive labor force.

3. Manages the interpretation and application of established corporate and division personnel policies.

4. Directs the preparation and maintenance of reports necessary to carry out functions of the department. Prepares periodic reports for the Plant Manager; Director, Employee Relations; Manager, Labor Relations; and/or Manager, Compensation and Benefits, as necessary or requested.

5. Directs and maintains various activities designed to achieve and maintain a high level of employee morale.

6. Plans, implements, and maintains a program of orientation for new employees.

7. Provides and serves as the necessary liaison between the location employees and the location Plant Manager.

8. Supervises the labor relations staff in administration of the labor agreements and interpretation of contract language and ensures that the Supervisor, Labor Relations is well informed to administer the provisions effectively and in accordance with management's philosophy and objectives.

9. Strives to establish an effective working relationship with union representatives to resolve and minimize labor problems more satisfactorily and to avoid inefficient practices and work stoppages.

10. Determines, or in questionable cases recommends, whether grievance cases appealed to the arbitration stage should be settled by

concessions or arbitrated. Prepares and presents such cases or supervises subordinates in same.

11. Manages and coordinates planning for plant labor contract negotiations; ensures that labor cost aspects are defined and that major position papers are prepared. Supervises the preparation and publication of contract language and documentation. Serves as chief spokesman or assists in negotiations at the operating unit level.

12. Establishes operative procedures for ensuring timely compliance with notice, reporting, and similar obligations under agreements with labor organizations.

13. Supervises the compensation and benefits staff in the administration and/or implementation and communication of current and new compensation and benefit programs, policies, and procedures.

14. Directs the development and implementation of approved location affirmative action plans to achieve and maintain compliance in accordance with the letter and intent of equal employment opportunity laws and executive orders.

15. Plans, implements, and maintains supervisory and management development activities.

16. Provides leadership in the establishment and maintenance of a plant security force.

17. Represents the company in the community and promotes the company's goodwill interests in community activities.

Organizational Relationships

This position reports directly to the Plant Manager and functionally to the Director, Employee Relations. Directly supervises Supervisor, Labor Relations; Supervisor, Employment; Supervisor, Compensation and Benefits; and Supervisor, Security; and indirectly supervises additional nonexempt employees. Interfaces daily with management and division employee relations.

Position Specification

Bachelor's Degree, preferably in Personnel Management or equivalent plus 6–8 years related experience, including supervisory/managerial experience in a wide range of employee relations activities. Must possess an ability to understand human behavior and be able to lead and motivate people. Must have mature judgment and decision-making ability.

SOURCE: Reprinted, by permission of the publisher, from *Job Descriptions in Manufacturing Industries* by John D. Ulery, pp. 24–26. © 1981 by AMACOM, a division of American Management Association, New York. All rights reserved.

240

the specific duties and responsibilities of the position; and (2) a *job specification*, which defines the education, experience, skills, and behaviors required of the position holder. A representative job description and specification for the personnel manager of a plant are shown in Figure 10–2.

Besides its obvious use in human resource planning, the job analysis document has a number of other important uses, including the following:[4]

- □ It serves as the basis for recruitment advertisements in newspapers and other publications.
- □ It helps interviewers match applicants to job openings.
- □ It helps orient and train new employees.
- □ It serves as a basis for performance appraisal.

Since jobs change as the organization changes, frequent updating of job descriptions and specifications is required. Although the initial job analysis is usually performed by the personnel department, it is the responsibility of line managers to notify the personnel department of changes in the jobs under their supervision.

Process of Recruiting

Once management has determined the number and types of positions to be filled over some span of time, the process of the *recruitment* of qualified applicants to fill those positions begins. In some cases, job seekers initiate the process themselves by walking in and filling out applications or by mailing unsolicited résumés to the personnel department. Current employees may even recommend individuals they know to fill particular job openings. Although these are inexpensive means of garnering a pool of applicants, it is unlikely that unsolicited applications will match the organization's specific needs. Then, too, most organizations are required to conduct an objective recruiting process in order to comply with EEO guidelines.

Most organizations, then, must actively seek job applicants, usually from a number of sources. Each source has its own advantages and disadvantages. As an example, consider three common sources of applicants for entry-level managerial positions—colleges and universities, other organizations, and the organization itself.

College Recruitment. Most large firms, many government agencies, and some small companies send recruiters to college campuses on annual or semiannual quests for job candidates. This process allows organizations to choose to recruit only from those colleges with academic programs that fit their needs and to specify the types of applicants—by major or degree—whom they will interview. Some organizations even indicate that they will not interview students who have cumulative grade point averages below a certain point. Table 10–1 ranks characteristics organizations find important.

TABLE 10-1 Important characteristics in hiring entry-level college graduates

Rank	Résumé Characteristics	Personal Characteristics
1	Concentration or major	Intelligence
2	Outside work experience (e.g., part-time jobs)	Work motivation (personal work standards)
3	Grade point average	Initiative
4	Field experience (e.g., internships)	Oral communication skills

SOURCE: Survey results from 101 companies. Adapted by permission of the publisher from "College Recruitment: The View from Both Sides," by Eileen Kaplan, *Personnel*, November 1985, 45, 47, © 1985 American Management Association, New York. All rights reserved.

On the other hand, campus recruiting is an expensive means of forming an applicant pool. The direct cost of recruiting and selection is relatively high. The recruiter must travel to the campus to interview between eight and twelve applicants. Out of the eight to twelve applicants, only one or two may actually meet the organization's needs. And since these one or two individuals may also receive competing job offers from other firms, the company may actually hire only one individual after recruiting at, say, ten different universities. The expected turnover rate of these employees is also great. One source indicates that, within three-and-a-half years, 32 percent of engineering majors and 27 percent of accounting/business administration majors had quit their first job.[5]

Recruitment from Other Organizations. Other organizations—often competitors—also may be used to train or supply managerial talent. Employees of other organizations have been seasoned by experience and, hence, may be superior to employees of the same caliber without work experience. Some factors contributing to this increasingly common practice are the trend toward professional management (with an emphasis on administrative ability and loyalty to the profession as well as the employer) and the emergence of specialized executive recruiting firms. Unfortunately, some organizations known for their excellent managerial training programs are often used as "training grounds" by other organizations. A recent college graduate, after completing the expensive training provided by one organization, may be recruited by other organizations lacking quality training programs.

Internal Recruitment. The organization itself is another source of executive personnel. In filling vacancies, many corporations emphasize promotion from within. This has the advantage of rewarding outstanding performance on the part of the existing staff. It also secures executive personnel who have experience with the organization and its methods of operation. Some organizations maintain computerized *skills inventories* for this purpose. Such an inventory can provide detailed information on the present performance, strengths, weaknesses, and potential for promotion of each of the organization's employees.

Assessment centers may also be used to locate potential managerial talent within the organization. According to the typical format, one or more six-person groups are brought together to participate in group exercises for two or three days. During this time, they take part in interviews, psychological tests, and simulation exercises such as in-basket tests.* A trained staff of line managers, personnel specialists, and psychologists observes and rates the applicants during the exercises.

A danger in internal recruitment, or at least in extensive reliance upon this source, is the inbreeding that may occur. This is particularly serious in positions requiring originality and new ideas.

SELECTION AND ORIENTATION

Once a pool of applicants is available, the process of the *selection* of individuals to fill the appropriate positions begins. Many organizations use a *multiple-hurdles* model of selection, such as the one illustrated in Figure 10–3. Under this system, the size of the applicant pool diminishes after each step or hurdle. Only those applicants who pass all of the hurdles may be offered jobs. Each hurdle should help distinguish between individuals who are likely to perform well and those who probably will not.

Application Blank/Résumé

The first step in the selection process for individuals applying for operative work is filling out an application blank. Candidates for managerial jobs are usually screened through information on their résumés, and those who appear qualified are often asked to complete a standardized application blank. This initial step in the selection process, as is true of subsequent steps, must be conducted in such a way as to minimize the possibility that the organization will discriminate against applicants. For instance, organizations usually cannot request such information from job applicants as the following:

□ Race, national origin, or religion (although these data must be gathered to meet EEO/affirmative action requirements, they should be kept separate from the applicant's file)

---

*An in-basket test is a simulated situation in which the candidate is given a set of memoranda, telephone messages, letters, notes, and requests that he or she must organize and respond to within a limited period of time. The exercise tests the individual's ability to set priorities, relate items, request additional information, make decisions, and so on.

FIGURE 10–3 Steps in the multiple-hurdles selection process

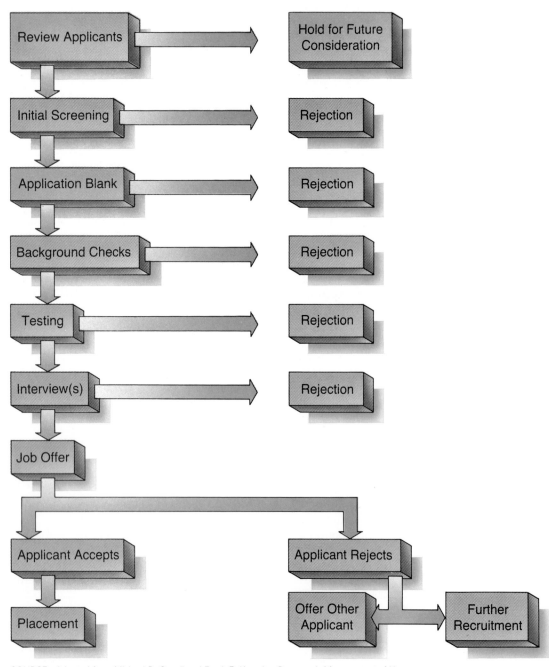

☐ A photograph of the individual (it can identify the individual's sex, race, or national origin)
☐ Height or weight (unless they are bona fide occupational qualifications)
☐ Date of birth or age (except when a minimum age is required by child work laws)
☐ Marital status or number of children (may discriminate against women)

Application blanks and résumés not only give the organization pertinent data on applicants' qualifications and background, but also "test the candidates' abilities to write, to organize their thoughts, and to present facts clearly and succinctly."[6]

Background Checks

Background checks are necessary to validate the information the candidate has given on the application blank. If sufficient lead time is available, the checks may be made through the mail. Telephoning references, however, not only provides greater speed but also a higher probability of eliciting a frank response, since the reference is not required to put his or her assessment of the candidate in writing.

If the candidate has previous work experience, the most useful references are likely to be previous supervisors and even coworkers. Again, legal restrictions on requesting information apply. It is legal, however, for an employer to release the following information about ex-employees: dates of employment; job progression; job titles, duties, and responsibilities; performance appraisals by employees' supervisors; and other objective measures of employee performance, such as absenteeism, quantitative production, or sales.[7]

Tests

Many organizations use some form of testing in selection because they believe that it introduces a needed element of objectivity into what is essentially a subjective process. Tests may attempt to measure such characteristics as the applicant's general intelligence or aptitudes. To ensure that tests do not discriminate against certain groups of applicants, organizations must validate their tests. A valid test is one that measures the individual's ability or potential ability to perform in a particular type of job. Among the more realistic tests are those derived through a systematic job analysis in which measures of the actual knowledge, skills, and abilities required by the job are developed. The job applicant is then given a test that simulates situations to be encountered on the job. Not only does the organization learn whether the applicant is capable of handling—or learning to handle—the job requirements, but the applicant gains a clear understanding of the job itself.[8]

Interviews

Although interviews may be used at various stages of the selection process, job candidates are inevitably interviewed after all of the previous hurdles have been cleared. Although it is, by far, the most widely used selection tool, interviewing is at best an inexact "science."

The essence of the interview's basic subjectivity is portrayed in Figure 10–4. In this conceptualization, the outcome of an interview depends upon three factors: (1) the applicant's experiences, background, characteristics, perceptions, and behavior; (2) the situation, which includes variables ranging from current economic conditions to the physical setting of the interview; and (3) the interviewer's own experiences, background, characteristics, perceptions, and behavior. It is the unique interaction of these variables, which will differ from one interview to the next, that determines the outcome. From this perspective, it is not surprising that the interview is unscientific.

FIGURE 10–4 The employment interview

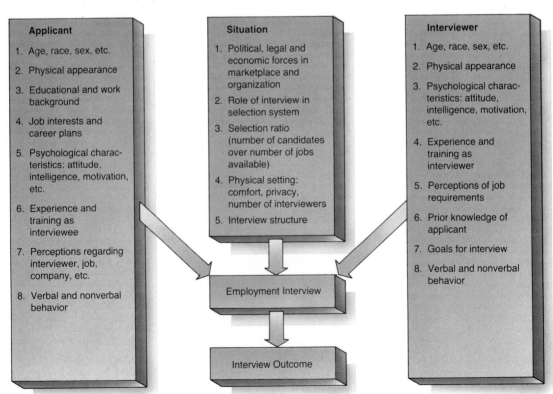

SOURCE: Richard D. Arvey and James E. Campion, "The Employment Interview: A Summary and Review of Recent Research," *Personnel Psychology* 35 (Summer 1982): 283.

A WEEK IN THE LIFE OF A JOB APPLICANT

A student reports that he had widely varying experiences during his first week of interviews with job recruiters in the university placement center. At the first interview, the recruiter monopolized the entire twenty-five minutes with a monologue describing the company and its products, structure, and career paths. With no time remaining, the recruiter asked the student: "Do you have any questions?"

By contrast, the second recruiter began the interview by hurling the following question at the student before he was even seated: "If you were suddenly made president of this company, what two changes would you make first?" The question, of course, tested the student's knowledge of the company, his preparation for the interview, and his ability to think quickly and articulate a response.

The third interview was virtually unstructured. The recruiter began by conversing about the university's football team and other non-job-related matters. Finally turning to the task at hand, the recruiter asked two questions: "What can you tell me about yourself?" and "What would you like to know about our company?"

In spite of its subjectivity, however, the interview continues to be widely used. It is, for instance, the only way management has to judge an applicant's ability to present his or her ideas to others. It is also the primary means the organization has of selling itself to applicants who may have alternative job opportunities.

Three recently developed techniques hold some promise for making the interview more objective. One is the *panel interview*, in which the applicant is interviewed by a panel of individuals. It may be that "sharing different perceptions with the different interviewers forces interviewers to become more aware of irrelevant inferences made on non-job-related variables."[9]

The second technique is the *situational interview*, made up of objectively scored questions derived from a systematic job analysis. The questions are composed by the job supervisors themselves and require applicants to indicate how they would behave in representative job situations. For example, in developing questions for individuals applying for sawmill worker positions, supervisors wrote the following question:

> Your spouse and two teenage children are sick in bed with colds. There are no relatives or friends available to look in on them. Your shift starts in three hours. What would you do in this situation?

INTERVIEW BY COMPUTER

Some companies are using computer interviews to screen job applicants. The computer uses a voice system to ask questions, and applicants respond by using a keyboard. According to users of this system, the computer is unbiased, asks each question to each applicant in exactly the same way, and never forgets to ask any of the questions.

SOURCE: Based on Selwyn Feinstein, "Computers Replacing Interviewers For Personnel and Marketing Tasks," *The Wall Street Journal*, 9 October 1986.

Based on their own experience, the supervisors devised the following three benchmark responses to evaluate the application:[10]

I'd stay home—my spouse and family come first (1 point).
I'd phone my supervisor and explain the situation (3 points).
Since they only have colds, I'd come to work (5 points).

A third technique that holds potential for improving the predictive validity of interviews is the *patterned behavior description interview*. This technique requires the interviewer to be trained to: (1) assemble a set of questions that probe how applicants have behaved in situations similar to those found in the job at hand, (2) question applicants in a way that ensures that they do not evade or stray from the questions, (3) record the applicants' responses rather than the interviewer's preconceived judgments, and (4) rate the applicants relative to each of the responses.[11]

Compensation

Decisions to hire an applicant must be coupled with decisions concerning the applicant's compensation. In its broadest sense, compensation refers not only to the individual's salary or wages but also to group benefits such as health, life, and dental insurance; pension plans; vacation time; food services; profit sharing; and stock ownership.

Compensation systems should not simply evolve; they should be carefully planned. Because they represent a significant portion of the organization's total cost of doing business (perhaps as high as 40 percent in manufacturing organizations to over 70 percent in service organizations) and because pay is one of the most important job factors to individual employees, management must decide on the goals of its compensation system.[12] Among the more common objectives are the following:[13]

- □ *Attract employees*—organizations must pay competitive salaries to attract qualified applicants.
- □ *Retain good employees*—although high-quality employees may leave the organization for a number of reasons, the most frequent cause is inadequate compensation.
- □ *Motivate employees*—although pay has limited value in motivating all employees (see chapter 13), management can help encourage high job performance by tying financial rewards to employee performance levels.
- □ *Meet legal requirements*—federal (and some state) laws govern such areas of compensation as minimum wages, overtime pay, and equal pay for men and women who do equal work on jobs requiring equal skill, responsibility, and effort being performed under similar working conditions.

Wages and salary levels are usually set through the process of *job evaluation*—the systematic analysis of jobs to determine their relative worth to the organization. Job evaluation systems usually assign points to all the jobs in the organization, based on such variables as working conditions and the responsibility the job involves. These points are then converted into pay scales for each job in the organization. Jobs which are less important to the company receive lower levels of compensation than those that are more important. The characteristics of the person holding the job (such as skill level or educational attainment) may be used to adjust the pay rate of some individuals.

Edward E. Lawler III argues that, in some cases, such *content-based job evaluation systems* have dysfunctional consequences.[14] If, for instance, evalua-

THE COMPARABLE WORTH ISSUE

The concept of comparable worth involves paying the same salaries to all workers who perform jobs that require comparable skills. Proponents contend, for instance, that the level of skills required of secretaries is comparable to that required of truck drivers, yet secretaries are paid significantly less because most secretaries are women and most truck drivers are men. Opponents argue that it is a plentiful supply of secretaries that keeps their pay down.

Although the first major legal battle was lost by comparable worth advocates in a 1985 U.S. Appeals Court decision, a large number of lawsuits are currently in litigation, and over half the states have comparable worth legislation in process.

tion systems measure responsibility rather than skills, individuals may be encouraged to seek supervisory jobs, even though they lack managerial skills. Or they may attempt to increase the size of their budget and their span of control.

On the other hand, *person-based job evaluation systems*, which pay individuals according to their skill levels, can encourage individuals to learn new skills and further develop the ones they already possess. This system can be useful, for instance, in encouraging technical specialists to remain in their specialization by providing attractive levels of compensation to them. Currently, for instance, engineers in many chemical companies must eventually enter the managerial ranks if they expect to advance significantly in compensation and career standing, because these forms of advancement are based on budgetary and people responsibilities.

Orientation and Socialization

Once an individual has accepted a job offer, the employing organization has the responsibility of orienting the newcomer to the new surroundings and helping him or her become a part of the organization. These processes, illustrated in Figure 10–5, are respectively referred to as *orientation* and *socialization*.

Some organizations, mostly large ones, conduct formal orientation programs for new employees. Other organizations orient the employee more informally. Whatever form orientation takes, it should focus on two levels: (1) information about the organization in general, such as its values and policies, and (2) information concerning the newcomer's own department and job. Some of this information may even be conveyed during earlier job interviews. Evidence indicates that a modest but significant reduction in turnover among new employees can be achieved by giving them a "realistic job preview" during the interview stage.[15]

The socialization process, culminating with the employee's transformation from "outsider" to organizational "insider," may require anywhere from a month to a year, depending on the particular organization and individual. Socialization encompasses such formal and informal activities as learning the job and developing appropriate skills, forming new interpersonal relationships, and accepting the organization's culture and norms. From the organization's perspective, effective socialization results in order and consistency in behavior. "The aim of socialization is to establish a base of attitudes, habits, and values that foster cooperation, integrity, and communication."[16]

Meryl Reis Louis suggests that three features characterize the newcomer's entry experience:[17]

□ *Change*—the external, objective differences in moving from one organization to another (e.g., a change in such factors as physical location, title, and salary).
□ *Contrast*—differences between prior and present experiences the newcomer regards as personally significant (e.g., recent college graduates may con-

FIGURE 10–5 Orientation and socialization

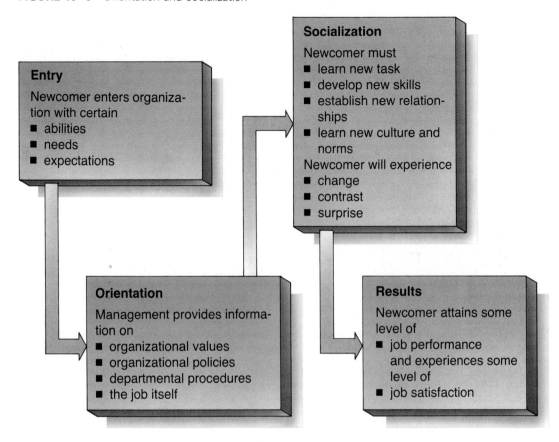

trast the frequent and relatively objective feedback about their performance in college courses with the less frequent and relatively subjective performance appraisals in their first job).

☐ *Surprise*—the difference between the newcomer's expectations about the new organization and job and what he or she actually experiences in the new setting.

Surprises are often interpreted in the light of the newcomer's prior experience, which may be inappropriate to the new setting. Yet these interpretations, correct or incorrect, can lead to feelings of commitment to the organization or alienation from it. Individuals who expect to be competent job performers and perceive that they are not may experience considerable dissatisfaction with their job, the new organization, and even themselves. On the other hand, individuals who perceive themselves to be competent performers but who are disappointed with other aspects of the organization may spend more energy looking for a new employer than performing well on their job.

Such dysfunctional consequences for the newcomer and organization alike can be lessened through appropriate supervisory behavior. As Daniel C. Feldman points out, "The supervisor can make or break a newcomer's early career in an organization."[18] The supervisor, for instance, can facilitate socialization by training newcomers in job specifics; fostering links between newcomers and their coworkers; buffering newcomers from demands outside the work group so they can learn the job more quickly; and conducting early and frequent performance appraisals which give newcomers accurate assessments of their performance and help them channel their efforts in the proper direction.[19]

Evidence suggests that different patterns of socialization lead to different forms of newcomer adjustment. For instance, mass socialization techniques lead to passive role orientations, whereas individualized socialization techniques produce innovative role orientations.[20]

PERFORMANCE APPRAISAL

Aside from its obvious utility in helping new employees understand the expectations of their supervisor and the organization, *performance appraisal* measures how effectively the organization's human resources are being used. As such, it is a form of control which compares measured performance with an established standard, resulting in corrective action, if necessary. Specifically, performance appraisal should:[21]

□ Provide feedback to each individual in the organization on his or her job performance. Most of us desire to know exactly "where we stand" and how our job performance is rated by our supervisor.

□ Link rewards such as promotions or merit raises to actual performance. In this vein, performance appraisal serves as a motivational tool.

□ Show the employee how to improve his or her performance. This use of performance appraisal has applications in training and developing the organization's human resources.

□ Help the organization comply with EEO programs.* EEO actions and judicial decisions have emphasized the need for organizations to maintain "accurate, objective records of employee performance to defend themselves

---

*One analysis of sixty-six court cases involving alleged discrimination in performance appraisal indicates that successful defenses of the charges were enhanced if: the appraisal criteria were based on a job analysis; specific, objective performance criteria were used; specific written instructions had been given to the supervisors who conducted the appraisals; and the supervisors personally reviewed the appraisal results with the employee. See William H. Holley and Hubert S. Feild, "Will Your Performance Appraisal System Hold Up in Court?" *Personnel* 59 (January-February 1982): 61–3. Another analysis revealed that communicating performance standards to employees, training supervisors to use the rating instrument, and documenting all evaluations and reasons for personnel actions also should decrease the probability of legal action. See Shelley R. Burchett and Kenneth P. De Meuse, "Performance Appraisal and the Law," *Personnel* 62 (July 1985): 37.

against possible charges of discrimination in discharges, promotions, and/or salary increases.''

In most organizations, the immediate supervisor conducts a formal, systematic performance appraisal of subordinate employees. Some organizations supplement this evaluation, however, with appraisals by other managers familiar with the subordinate's performance or by the subordinate's peers in an attempt to reduce subjectivity.[22]

The performance of most employees is evaluated on an annual basis. Although organizations should, logically, make the evaluation follow the completion of a major product—so that the appraisal is tied naturally to task completion—many schedule performance evaluations on arbitrary dates because it is more convenient. Hence, all employees may be evaluated after their first three months on the job and, thereafter, at yearly intervals.

REALISM IN PERFORMANCE APPRAISAL

There is some evidence that without an accurate performance appraisal system employees hold distorted views of their own job performance. Herbert H. Meyer, manager of personnel research for General Electric for twenty years, reported the following results of a survey asking employees to rate their own performance:

□ 46 percent of workers in a blue-collar group, 29 percent of engineers in a research lab, and 37 percent of accountants in several firms ranked themselves in the ''top 10 percent'' of performers in their organization.
□ Only 1 percent of the blue-collar workers, none of the engineers, and 3 percent of the accountants placed themselves in the ''bottom 50 percent'' of performers in their organization.

Such a situation cries out for realistic performance appraisal. But data from a recent study by Jone L. Pearce and Lyman W. Porter indicate that caution is required. Pearce and Porter found that employees who received ratings of ''satisfactory'' on a new formal appraisal system subsequently had a distinct and significant drop in their attitudes toward the organization. The researchers recommend that supervisors be helped to anticipate and manage the possible negative reactions of employees who receive less than highly positive feedback.

SOURCE: Herbert H. Meyer, ''The Pay-for-Performance Dilemma,'' *Organizational Dynamics*, 3 (Winter 1975): 44; and Jone L. Pearce and Lyman W. Porter, ''Employee Responses to Formal Performance Appraisal Feedback,'' *Journal of Applied Psychology*, 71 (May 1986): 211–18.

Techniques of Performance Appraisal

The specific techniques of appraisal vary from organization to organization. Usually the appraisal is recorded on a form and shown to the employee. In some organizations, the superior and subordinate discuss the evaluation; in others, the subordinate simply signs the form, acknowledging having seen it. Some of the more widely discussed techniques of appraisal are examined here.[23]

Conventional Rating Scale. The oldest and most often used appraisal technique is the *conventional rating scale,* illustrated in Figure 10–6. Although the exact form varies among organizations and among departments within an organization, the conventional rating scale usually contains a list of qualities, characteristics, or traits upon which the employee is to be rated on a scale ranging from "poor" to "outstanding." A common example is the instructor evaluation form filled out by students at the end of each term at most universities. The instructor may be rated on such qualities as "presentation of material" and "preparation for class."

The major advantage of the conventional rating scale is the ease of developing it. The scale may be designed by the raters themselves, consultants, or the personnel department. Obviously, the qualities upon which the individual is to be rated must be directly related to effective performance. Personal appearance or initiative, for instance, is not equally important in all positions and may not even be necessary for effective performance in some jobs.

Aside from the difficult problem of deciding which qualities are essential to effective job performance, conventional rating scales are subject to a number of *rater weaknesses.* Raters, for instance, differ in their interpretations of "out-

FIGURE 10–6 Example of a conventional rating scale

Name_____ Position_____

	(5) Outstanding	(4) Good	(3) Satisfactory	(2) Fair	(1) Poor	Not Observed
Job Knowledge						
Quality of Work						
Relationships with Subordinates						
Initiative						
Personal Appearance						
Cooperation						
Reliability						
Career Potential						

standing'' and the standards they mentally establish for evaluating subordinates. Some may be lenient graders (such as the teacher who assigns As to 40 percent of the class), whereas others may be tough graders. If the rating period is one year, some raters may evaluate based on only the past few weeks' or months' performance (the *recency effect*). Some may fall victim to the *halo effect*, assigning the same rating to each quality being assessed.

Ranking. To overcome some of these difficulties, some organizations have turned to *ranking*, a technique that requires the rater to rank his or her subordinates from highest to lowest, based on some criterion. The criterion, for instance, may be job performance, promotion potential, or ability to relate to clients. This technique makes it impossible for the rater to assign all subordinates an ''outstanding'' or an ''average'' rating. In other words, the rater is forced to compare subordinates and differentiate among them.

The use of this technique makes it difficult to give concrete feedback to employees, however. It may be hard to explain to an individual why he or she is ranked eighth instead of fifth. Also, the technique gives no consideration to the extent of differences between ranks. Is the difference between the top two employees the same as the difference between the ninth and tenth? Finally, ranking makes it difficult to compare employees in department A with those in department B. The top employee in department A, for example, might rank only fourth if he or she were in department B.

Behaviorally Anchored Rating Scales. In recent years, a new technique termed *behaviorally anchored rating scales* (BARS) or *behavioral expectation scales* (BES) has been devised to measure actual specific job behavior.[24] The scales are devised by the raters themselves and are intended to reduce subjective rater judgment. To develop the scales, the raters give examples of subordinate job behavior which is particularly effective or ineffective. Then specialists place these ''critical incidents'' into a smaller number of job dimensions. Another group of raters is then asked to categorize the incidents within each dimension from highly effective to grossly ineffective forms of behavior. An example of the incidents within the dimension ''meeting day-to-day deadlines'' for a department manager in a retail store is shown in Figure 10–7. When numerically scaled, the behavior might range from one at the bottom to nine at the top.

The advantages of this technique are as follows:

□ BARS possesses the distinct legal strength of being based on an extensive job analysis.
□ The scales refer to observable job behavior that is related to effective performance.
□ The scales make clear what effective performance is and, hence, can be used to help employees improve their performance.
□ The scales are designed by the raters themselves and, therefore, should be more acceptable to them.

FIGURE 10–7 Department manager job behavior rating scale for the dimension "meeting day-to-day deadlines"

	Could be expected never to be late in meeting deadlines, no matter how unusual the circumstances.
Could be expected to meet deadlines comfortably by delegating the writing of an unusually high number of orders to two highly rated selling associates.	
	Could be expected always to get his associates' work schedules made out on time.
Could be expected to meet seasonal ordering deadlines within a reasonable length of time.	
	Could be expected to offer to do the orders at home after failing to get them out on the deadline day.
Could be expected to fail to schedule additional help to complete orders on time.	
	Could be expected to be late all the time on weekly buys for his department.
Could be expected to disregard due dates in ordering and run out of a major line in his department.	
	Could be expected to leave order forms in his desk drawer for several weeks even when they had been given to him by the buyer after calling his attention to short supplies and due dates for orders.

SOURCE: John P. Campbell et al., *Managerial Behavior, Performance, and Effectiveness* (New York: McGraw-Hill, 1970), p. 122.

Additionally, there is some evidence that employees whose performance is evaluated on BARS scales view the appraisal process more favorably than do those who are rated on conventional rating scales.[25]

Unfortunately, BARS is expensive to develop (costing as much as $3,000 for a single job category) and requires a substantial number of employees performing the same job (for instance, department managers in a large retail chain) before the technique becomes cost feasible.[26] Research indicates that the extra cost may not be warranted for many organizations since the accuracy of BARS over other techniques has not yet been clearly demonstrated.[27]

Other Techniques. Other appraisal techniques include *MBO* (discussed in chapter 5), *essay evaluation* (the evaluator is asked to describe the employee's strong and weak points), and *checklist* (the rater checks which descriptive statements apply to the employee). Each has its own particular strengths and weaknesses. The most appropriate method depends upon the purpose of the evaluation, the nature of the job, preferences of the organization's members, and the history of the organization.

Improving Performance Appraisal

Although most organizations do not have rater training programs, evidence suggests that training improves rater accuracy. The most effective means of reducing rating errors may well be to concentrate on training the rater rather than refining the rating instrument. Alerting raters to the dangers of leniency and halo effect, for instance, leads to significant decreases in these forms of error. Rater participation in developing the appraisal instrument, too, seems to improve accuracy, perhaps because studying the job to develop the scales increases the rater's understanding of the job components. Furthermore, some supervisors believe that recording behavioral observations regularly in a formal diary enhances their observation skills and retention. Finally, training in interviewing and counseling techniques seems likely to improve the tone and effectiveness of the appraisal session in which the superior and subordinate discuss the evaluation.[28]

MANAGEMENT DEVELOPMENT

One objective of performance appraisal is to determine the developmental needs of the organization's managers. *Management development* is the process of increasing the effectiveness of managers in their present jobs and preparing them for promotion. This is accomplished through formal and/or informal means. Although probably no two companies use identical approaches to management development, one survey indicates that "the vast majority of actual development occurs on the job, through the handling of progressively more responsible assignments and problems under fire."[29] The respondents agreed, however, that formal development programs are valuable supplements to job experience.

Organizations can provide opportunities for management development, but cannot actually develop managers. The managers themselves must accomplish their own development. Sending a manager to a training conference, for example, is no guarantee of improved performance. If any real development is to occur, managers must assume some responsibility for their own progress. Of course, the organization can create the proper atmosphere, provide opportunities for development, and encourage interest in activities of this kind.

A study of management development programs in four leading corporations revealed that the impetus for a successful development program must come from top management. In these corporations, senior managers were involved in designing the program and even in teaching part of the courses. The programs had clear objectives, emphasized implementing the companies' strategies and attaining goals, and were custom designed for each firm.[30]

Management Development Methods

Job-Centered Training. The most basic or fundamental approach to management development is that of managerial experience. The manager learns to manage by managing. Such experience may be more or less productive depending on the type of direction and guidance provided by higher management. Extensive delegation of authority, for example, seeks to maximize development through managerial experience.

Job Rotation. One method of expanding direct job experience is to broaden that experience through a system of rotation. Such a job rotation plan seeks to enhance experience by shifting managers periodically from one job to another. Individuals selected for such programs are moved at the end of a stipulated period—say, one year—and the positions they hold at any given time are viewed as training positions.

A less formalized variation of job rotation is also used by many organizations. In promotion and transfer decisions, an attempt is made to move individuals to facilitate their development. This system does not operate on a calendar basis, however, and there is no planned series of steps or transfers. A manager, for example, may fill a position in engineering for two or three years. If a vacancy occurs in sales or production management at the end of that time, consideration is given to shifting the engineering manager into such a position.

Supervisory Coaching. The supervisory manager is expected to provide guidance to subordinates and serve as their role model. This function is considered so important that many firms evaluate their middle- and upper-level managers on their abilities to develop subordinates.[31]

If coaching can be conducted in the right atmosphere, it provides an excellent type of developmental experience. Its major limitation is its dependence upon the skills of the coach. It has the practical advantage of being centered in the "real world"—the manager's work activities—and provides guidance from the one best able to evaluate performance and to supply help—the employee's superior. The requirement poses a problem for the superior, however, in that appraising and coaching may easily be viewed as critical and destructive rather than as helpful and motivating to the subordinate.

Training Conferences.   Managerial personnel are often brought together for training conferences. The purpose of such conferences is to impart knowledge or to improve skills of participants through lectures, case studies, role playing, and videotaped simulations which allow participants to view and critique their own behavior. Conferences of this type are particularly appropriate in cases in which a number of managers have similar training needs.

Outside Developmental Activities.   Some organizations use outside activities or schools in supplementing inside development or in providing training not available within the firm. Of particular interest are the management development programs conducted by university schools of business. These programs typically range from one to six to eight weeks in length and deal with general aspects of administration. They have the advantage of exposing managers to two perspectives that may differ from their own—the academic perspective of the university faculty and the perspective of peers from other organizations.[32]

Professional associations also provide training conferences for professional management personnel. Some are limited to such technical fields as engineering or accounting, whereas others deal with general problems of management. Participation in such conferences exposes a manager to current thinking and also provides contact with personnel from other organizations with similar problems.

Organizations that use such outside programs must carefully ensure that the returning managers are given the opportunity to use their training. A survey of 312 participants in university executive development programs revealed that 66 percent of the managers reported no systematic effort by their organizations to incorporate the development into their job or the company.[33] The firm must provide a facilitative environment to utilize the manager's newfound knowledge and enthusiasm.

Evaluating Development Programs

A survey of some of the largest companies in the United States indicates that the most common means of evaluating the effectiveness of development programs in forty-seven firms are, in order, the following: (1) the judgment of higher-level management; (2) the judgment of participants either *after* the program was over, or (3) *at* the program's conclusion; and (4) the measurement of changes in on-the-job behavior or performance.[34] Although the judgments of upper-level managers and the perceptions of program participants are useful in evaluating program effectiveness, more objective job performance-related criteria are desirable. Participants can "feel good" about a program, yet fail to change their behavior on the job. Development is worth its cost if the job performance of the program participants improves significantly or if the participants are better prepared for promotion.* Management needs to develop evaluation techniques which reflect the extent of these changes.

SUMMARY

Building an effective organizational team requires planning and control of its human resources. This process begins with a forecast of the organization's future personnel needs based upon an *analysis* of its job requirements, projections of turnover, and plans for growth. Once management has determined the number and types of positions to be filled over some span of time, the process of *recruiting* qualified applicants from a variety of sources to fill those positions begins. From the resulting applicant pool, those individuals estimated (through application blanks, background checks, tests, and interviews) to have the appropriate ability or potential ability are *selected*. Applicants are offered a certain level of *compensation*—salary and benefits—reflecting the relative worth of their jobs to the organization.

Once an individual has accepted the job offer, the employing organization is responsible for *orienting* the newcomer to the job and new surroundings and helping him or her become a part of the organization. The individual's *socialization* process can be aided through appropriate managerial actions, many of which depend upon the skill of the newcomer's supervisor.

Performance appraisal is a control technique designed to measure how effectively the organization's human resources are being used. Specifically, it provides feedback to employees concerning their performance and how it may be improved. A number of appraisal techniques are available to organizations. These include *conventional rating scales, ranking, behaviorally anchored rating scales*, and *MBO*—each with its own advantages and disadvantages.

Once the developmental needs of the organization's managers have been determined through performance appraisal, *management development*, the process of increasing managerial effectiveness and preparing managers for promotions, is begun. The most fundamental type of development is that which occurs in the actual performance of managerial duties. Regardless of what formal training opportunities may be provided by management, development must ultimately be *self-development*.

---

*For a report of a management training program in which the benefits to the organization outweighed the costs by a ratio of 6:1, see W. J. Cascio and G. R. Gilbert, "Making Dollars and Sense Out of Management Development," in R. C. Huseman (ed.), *Proceedings of the 40th Annual Meeting of the National Academy of Management, 1980*, pp. 95–98.

KEY CONCEPTS

Personnel forecasting	Compensation
Equal employment opportunity	Job evaluation
Job analysis	Orientation
Job description	Socialization
Job specification	Performance appraisal
Recruitment	Conventional rating scale
Assessment center	Ranking
Multiple-hurdles selection model	Behaviorally anchored rating scale (BARS)
Panel interview	
Situational interview	Management development
Patterned behavior description interview	Job rotation
	Supervisory coaching

DISCUSSION QUESTIONS

1. What role does *job analysis* play in human resource planning?
2. Compare the advantages and difficulties in *recruiting* managerial personnel from competitive organizations.
3. Explain the *multiple-hurdles* model of selection.
4. Why is *interviewing* a subjective process? How can this subjectivity be reduced?
5. Besides paying employees "a fair day's wages for a fair day's work," what ends do organizations seek to attain through their *compensation* systems?
6. Distinguish between *orientation* and *socialization*. What role might the immediate supervisor play in facilitating both processes?
7. What are the purposes of *performance appraisal?*
8. How do *conventional rating scales* and *behaviorally anchored rating scales (BARS)* differ?
9. How might performance appraisal be improved?
10. Explain the reasoning underlying the concept of *self-development* in managerial growth.
11. Describe the ideal conditions for effective on-the-job management development.

NOTES

1. D. Quinn Mills, "Planning with People in Mind," *Harvard Business Review* 63 (July-August 1985): 97.
2. For representative surveys, see the following: Ibid., pp. 97-105; Elmer H. Burack, "Corporate Business and Human Resources Planning Practices: Strategic Issues and Concerns," *Organizational Dynamics* 15 (Summer 1986): 73–87; and Stella

M. Nkomo, "The Theory and Practice of HR Planning: The Gap Still Remains," *Personnel Administrator* 31 (August 1986): 71–84.

3. Mills, "Planning with People in Mind," p. 99.

4. Based on Michael R. Carrell and Frank E. Kuzmits, *Personnel: Management of Human Resources* (Columbus, Oh.: Merrill, 1982), p. 88.

5. Frank S. Endicott, *The Endicott Report 1980* (Evanston, Ill.: The Placement Center, Northwestern University, 1979), p. 8.

6. George Strauss and Leonard R. Sayles, *Personnel: The Human Problems of Management*, 4th ed. (Englewood Cliffs, N.J.: Prentice-Hall, 1980), p. 371.

7. Carrell and Kuzmits, *Personnel*, p. 213.

8. Neal Schmitt and Cheri Ostroff, "Operationalizing the 'Behavioral Consistency' Approach: Selection Test Development Based on a Content-Oriented Strategy," *Personnel Psychology* 39 (Spring 1986): 91–108.

9. Richard D. Arvey and James E. Campion, "The Employment Interview: A Summary and Review of Recent Research," *Personnel Psychology* 35 (Summer 1982): 293.

10. Gary P. Latham, Lise M. Saari, Elliott D. Pursell, and Michael A. Campion, "The Situational Interview," *Journal of Applied Psychology* 65 (August 1980): 424.

11. Tom Janz, "Initial Comparisons of Patterned Behavior Description Interviews Versus Unstructured Interviews," *Journal of Applied Psychology* 67 (October 1982): 577–80; and Christopher Orpen, "Patterned Behavior Description Interviews Versus Unstructured Interviews: A Comparative Validity Study," *Journal of Applied Psychology* 70 (November 1985): 774–76.

12. Edward E. Lawler III, *Pay and Organization Development* (Reading, Mass.: Addison-Wesley, 1981), pp. 4–5, 31.

13. Carrell and Kuzmits, *Personnel*, pp. 426–35.

14. Lawler, *Pay and Organization Development*, pp. 34–5.

15. Steven L. Premack and John P. Wanous, "A Meta-Analysis of Realistic Job Preview Experiments," *Journal of Applied Psychology* 70 (November 1985): 706–19; Glenn M. McEvoy and Wayne F. Cascio, "Strategies for Reducing Employee Turnover: A Meta-Analysis," *Journal of Applied Psychology* 70 (May 1985): 342–53; and Stephen M. Colarelli, "Methods of Communication and Mediating Processes in Realistic Job Previews," *Journal of Applied Psychology* 69 (November 1984): 633–42.

16. Richard Pascale, "The Paradox of 'Corporate Culture': Reconciling Ourselves to Socialization," *California Management Review* 27 (Winter 1985): 37.

17. Meryl Reis Louis, "Surprise and Sense Making: What Newcomers Experience in Entering Unfamiliar Organizational Settings," *Administrative Science Quarterly* 25 (June 1980): 226–51.

18. Daniel C. Feldman, "A Socialization Process That Helps New Recruits Succeed," *Personnel* 57 (March-April 1980): 22.

19. Ibid.; and Louis, "Surprise and Sense Making," p. 247.

20. Gareth R. Jones, "Socialization Tactics, Self-Efficacy, and Newcomers' Adjustments to Organizations," *Academy of Management Journal* 29 (June 1986): 262–79.

21. Alan H. Locher and Kenneth S. Teel, "Performance Appraisal—A Survey of Current Practices," *Personnel Journal* 56 (May 1977): 245. For the authoritative overview of this area, see *Uniform Guidelines on Employee Selection Procedures* (Washington, D.C.: U.S. Government Printing Office, 1978).

22. An intriguing departure from the traditional appraisal format is a system in which the supervisor evaluates "what" the employee has done and the subordinates of the employee evaluate "how" the work was done. See Paul R. Reed and Mark J. Kroll, "A Two-Perspective Approach to Performance Appraisal," *Personnel* 62 (October 1985): 51–7.

23. For a thorough review of the issues involved in performance appraisal, see Gary P. Latham, "Job Performance and Appraisal," in C. L. Cooper and I. Robertson (eds.), *Review of Industrial and Organizational Psychology* (Chichester, Eng.: Wiley, 1986).

24. A technical variation of this technique is known as behavioral observation scales (BOS). For an explanation of the differences, see Gary P. Latham, Charles H. Fay, and Lise M. Saari, "The Development of Behavioral Observation Scales for Appraising the Performance of Foremen," *Personnel Psychology* 32 (Summer 1979): 299–311.

25. John M. Ivancevich, "A Longitudinal Study of Behavioral Expectation Scales: Attitudes and Performance," *Journal of Applied Psychology* 65 (April 1980): 139–46.

26. "Appraising the Performance Appraisal," *Business Week*, 19 May 1980, p. 153.

27. Rick Jacobs, Ditsa Kafry, and Sheldon Zedeck, "Expectations of Behaviorally Anchored Rating Scales," *Personnel Psychology* 33 (Autumn 1980): 630; and Paul O. Kingstrom and Alan R. Bass, "A Critical Analysis of Studies Comparing Behaviorally Anchored Rating Scales (BARS) and Other Rating Formats," *Personnel Psychology* 34 (Summer 1981): 263–64.

28. For a discussion of rater training, see the following: David E. Smith, "Training Programs for Performance Appraisal: A Review," *Academy of Management Review* 11 (January 1986): 22–40; and Frank J. Landy and James L. Farr, "Performance Rating," *Psychological Bulletin* 87 (January 1980): 71–107.

29. Lester A. Digman, "How Well-Managed Organizations Develop Their Executives," *Organizational Dynamics* 7 (Autumn 1978): 68.

30. James F. Bolt, "Tailor Executive Development to Strategy," *Harvard Business Review* 63 (November-December 1985): 169.

31. Digman, "How Well-Managed Organizations Develop," p. 68.

32. Albert W. Schrader, "How Companies Use University-Based Executive Development Programs," *Business Horizons* 28 (March/April 1985): 53–62.

33. Ibid.

34. Lester A. Digman, "How Companies Evaluate Management Development Programs," *Human Resource Management* 19 (Summer 1980): 9–13.

SUPPLEMENTARY READING

Adler, Philip, Jr.; Parsons, Charles K.; and Zolke, Scott B. "Employee Privacy: Legal and Research Developments and Implications for Personnel Administration," *Sloan Management Review* 26 (Winter 1985): 13–22.

Beer, Michael. "Performance Appraisal: Dilemmas and Possibilities." *Organizational Dynamics* 9 (Winter 1981): 24–36.

Bewayo, Edward D. "What Employees Look For in First and Subsequent Employers." *Personnel* 63 (April 1986): 49–54.

Burack, Elmer H. "Corporate Business and Human Resources Planning Practices: Strategic Issues and Concerns." *Organizational Dynamics* 15 (Summer 1986): 73–87.

Cederblom, Douglas. "The Performance Appraisal Interview: A Review, Implications, and Suggestions." *Academy of Management Review* 7 (April 1982): 219–27.

Davies, Julia, and Easterby-Smith, Mark. "Learning and Developing from Managerial Work Experiences." *Journal of Management Studies* 21 (April 1984): 169–83.

Dipboye, Robert L. "Self-Fulfilling Prophecies in the Selection-Recruitment Interview." *Academy of Management Review* 7 (October 1982): 579–86.

Gallagher, Daniel G., and Veglahn, Peter A. "Arbitral Standards in Cases Involving Testing Issues." *Labor Law Journal* 37 (October 1986): 719–30.

Heilman, Madeline E., and Stopeck, Melanie H. "Attractiveness and Corporate Success: Different Causal Attributions for Males and Females." *Journal of Applied Psychology* 70 (May 1985): 379–88.

Katz, Marsha; Lavan, Helen; and Malloy, Maura Sendelbach. "Comparable Worth: Analysis of Cases and Implications for HR Management." *Compensation and Benefits Review* 18 (May-June 1986): 26–38.

Kroll, Mark J., and Dolan, Janet A. "Cafeteria Benefit Plans: A Concept That Fits the Changing Face of Work." *SAM Advanced Management Journal* 50 (Summer 1985): 4–9.

Latham, Gary P., and Saari, Lise M. "Do People Do What They Say? Further Studies on the Situational Interview." *Journal of Applied Psychology* 69 (November 1984): 569–73.

Lawler, Edward E., III; Mohrman, Allan M., Jr.; and Resnick, Susan M. "Performance Appraisal Revisited." *Organizational Dynamics* 13 (Summer 1984): 20–35.

Lee, Cynthia. "Increasing Performance Appraisal Effectiveness: Matching Task Types, Appraisal Process, and Rater Training." *Academy of Management Review* 10 (April 1985): 322–31.

Moskowitz, Milton. "Lessons from the Best Companies to Work For." *California Management Review* 27 (Winter 1985): 42–7.

Pearce, Jone L., and Porter, Lyman W. "Employee Responses to Formal Performance Appraisal Feedback." *Journal of Applied Psychology* 71 (May 1986): 211–18.

Prince, J. Bruce, and Lawler, Edward E., III. "Does Salary Discussion Hurt the Developmental Performance Appraisal?" *Organizational Behavior and Human Decision Processes* 37 (June 1986): 357–75.

Wexley, Kenneth N., and Baldwin, Timothy T. "Management Development." *Journal of Management* 12 (Summer 1986): 277–94.

ACCOUNTANTS MUST BE GOOD LOOKING?

Herb Gentry, director of personnel for the Transcontinental Railroad, walked toward his department's conference room, shaking his head. He had just come from his boss's office after spending thirty minutes listening to the vice-president of finance complain about the quality and turnover of junior-level accountants. Sure, he thought, the 37 percent attrition in this year's crop was high, but was that his fault? He wondered if he was just being made a scapegoat for someone else's problem. Recruiting is recruiting—no big deal. His interviewers were all top-notch and selected the best people available.

As Herb entered the conference room, he forced a smile as he met the gaze of his staff of twelve full-time interviewers. "Well, boys and girls," he said, "accounting has done it to us again! Why we're getting blamed for inefficiency is beyond me! After all, the whole process is such a simple procedure: they tell us how many junior-level replacements they need, we go out and cull the wheat from the chaff, send them our nominees, and they do the rest."

Herb continued on in this manner for several more minutes and then, with a frown, asked if anyone could think of anything that could be done to improve the situation. After a moment's silence, Ann Balke, one of the newer recruiters, nervously shifted in her chair and quietly said, "Herb, I agree with what you have been saying, but I've always wondered about our interview form. I mean to say, does it really help us in the selection process?"

Herb rocked his head back as if he had been struck a blow and condescendingly replied, "Ann, honey, we've been using this checklist for the past fifteen years. It is ideal to use regardless of the type of employee we are looking for." Turning to his secretary, he said, "Mary, get a handful of those checklists and pass them around to everybody." When this was done, he then looked over at Ann and continued, "OK, missy, tell us all about what's wrong with this here piece of paper."

Question

1. Given that Ann needs this job and that "chauvinistic" Herb actually means well, what improvements should Ann recommend concerning this interview checklist (Exhibit 1)?

Case prepared by Professor Paul R. Reed of Sam Houston State University.

EXHIBIT 1 Transcontinental Railroad interview checklist

TRANSCONTINENTAL RAILROAD
"Serving the Nation"
College Interview Checklist

Name (last name first) _____   College Name _____

Source:	Race:	Sex:	Degree:	Average	Class Rank:
Campus ☐	White ☐	Male ☐	Bachelors ☐	(A = 4.0)	Top 10% ☐
Walk-in ☐	Black ☐	Female ☐	Masters ☐	Overall ☐	Top 25% ☐
Intern ☐	Asian ☐		Law ☐	Major ☐	Top half ☐
Agency ☐	Hispanic ☐		Major:		Bottom half ☐
	Am. Indian ☐		_____		

Interviewers must ascertain the answers to the following items. Each is deemed to be equally important in selecting a candidate for employment by our company. (Five "no" answers disqualifies applicant from further consideration.)

Appearance

	yes	no		yes	no
Freshly bathed	☐	☐	Clean shaven (M)	☐	☐
Neat hair	☐	☐	Handsome (M)	☐	☐
Dark suit	☐	☐	Appropriate make-up (F)	☐	☐
Shined shoes	☐	☐	Good looking (F)	☐	☐

Activities

	yes	no		yes	no
Varsity sports	☐	☐	Fraternity/Sorority	☐	☐
Intramural sports	☐	☐	Part-time work	☐	☐
Professional society	☐	☐	Honor society	☐	☐

Attitude—Motivation—Goals

(positive, cooperative, energetic, motivated, successful, goal-oriented)
Poor ☐   Average ☐   Good ☐   Outstanding ☐
Comments:
_____
_____
_____

Intellectual Abilities

(insightful, creative, curious, imaginative, understands, reasons, intelligent, scholarly)
Poor ☐   Average ☐   Good ☐   Outstanding ☐
Comments:
_____
_____

Leadership

(self-confident, takes charge, effective, respected, management minded, grasps authority)
Poor ☐   Average ☐   Good ☐   Outstanding ☐
Comments:
_____
_____
_____

_____
Interviewer signature

CHALLENGE

Delaware Community College is a small, state-supported school situated in a quiet, rural area just south of the state capitol. Chartered in 1911, it has become an integral part of the community with programs aimed primarily at preparing students to enter four-year colleges and universities, though a few are two-year paraprofessional programs. Like most schools, Delaware uses a traditional grading system. Karen Mayes, an instructor at Delaware, was soon to find herself seriously questioning this time-honored tradition.

Karen took her teaching seriously, working hard to balance the demands of her doctoral studies at the university with her teaching duties at the community college. In the classroom, Karen was "relationship oriented," trying to involve the students in active discussions of the material. The students seemed to respond well.

Today she had taught her Intro to Management class. The class became energetic and she too got caught up in their enthusiasm. The cause of the excitement was a case study about grading and the problems it caused at a particular university. The case itself was complicated because the class had been subjected to three different teachers during a term. Predictably, these teachers had different styles and different expectations.

The class discussion quickly became a discussion of grading at Delaware Community. Here, too, many teachers had different styles. Some lectured exclusively; others, like Karen, lectured and led class debate; others relied almost entirely upon class participation. Professors used different testing methods—objective tests, essay tests, or both. Nevertheless, despite these varied inputs, practically all teachers used the traditional grading system, and in the opinion of the class members it left a lot to be desired.

"Grades, grades, grades, why do we need them anyway?" Leroy Mark asked.

"You don't like them because you can't get good ones—that's why you complain," Pamela Johnson said.

"It's not that at all; they just aren't fair. They don't measure what I've learned. You mean to tell me that when I can answer questions well in class, but not on some test, I should only get graded for my test answers? That's not fair!" Leroy retorted.

"That's true, Leroy's got a point. Plus we know teachers use the old A, B, C scale. Somebody's got to get the Ds and Fs. But what happens if the whole class is pretty smart?"

"Well, why don't they give all As and Bs, then nobody's hurt," Richard Green suggested.

Peggy Vandero chimed, "Now that idea I like!"

And so the discussion raged, back and forth, back and forth. Alternatives were suggested and rejected. Even when the bell rang the discussion went on; no one in the class moved! Finally, Karen stopped them. Reflecting on what she'd suggested, she was beginning to wonder if she'd let things go too far.

"I hate to interrupt this lively discussion," she said, "but the bell's rung, and there's another class coming in. To

This case was prepared by George E. Stevens and Penny Marquette when they were at Kent State University. All names are disguised. Copyright © 1977, George E. Stevens.

summarize, I hear you saying that there are a number of grading systems being used, including our traditional A, B, C, D, F system. Furthermore, you believe the traditional system is not fair and does not always reflect the quality of your work. Here today you've discussed some alternatives, including Pass/Fail and blanket grades, yet these appear to have faults as well. Let me make a proposition. I challenge you to put your money where your mouth is. We're only in the second week of class and if *you* can come up with a grading system that meets the dual criteria of being fair and reflecting the quality of work done, I'll implement it. You have from now until Friday to prepare your proposals either individually or in groups. During Friday's class, the proposals can be presented and voted on, and the one deemed most acceptable will be instituted."

Questions

1. Grading is a form of performance appraisal with which all students can readily identify. What are some of the more common types of grading systems?
2. What factors influence the grade a student may be assigned?
3. How might the grades and grading systems used affect people after graduation?
4. Does the problem go beyond just grading? What are the social implications of coping with varying grading systems and of dealing with the existence or nonexistence of equity in the university environment?
5. If a university changed its grading system from an A, B, C, D, F scale to Pass/Fail, what might be some of the behavioral implications?

FORCES FOR CHANGE
External Forces □ Internal
Forces □ Motivation to Change

THE PROCESS OF CHANGE
Realization of Need for Change □
Organizational Examination and
Diagnosis □ Goal Setting □ Choice and
Implementation of Change Methods
□ Evaluation and Control of Change

ORGANIZATION DEVELOPMENT
Assumptions Underlying OD □ OD
Methods □ OD Research

THE GOAL OF CHANGE:
ORGANIZATIONAL EFFECTIVENESS

Summary □ Key Concepts □ Discussion
Questions □ Notes □ Supplementary
Reading

CASE: National Insurance Company

This chapter will enable you to

□   Understand the pressures and
opportunities that create the need for
organizational change.

□   Identify and discuss the steps involved
in a program of planned organizational
change.

□   Explain organizational development, a
type of change program that focuses
on human behavior and interaction.

□   Become familiar with the concept of
organizational effectiveness.

CHAPTER 11
ORGANIZATIONAL CHANGE AND DEVELOPMENT

As anyone who has lived through the turbulent times of the past few decades can attest, change resulting from an increasingly dynamic environment is an inescapable part of our lives. Organizations, affected by the same forces, must change in order to remain effective. This chapter examines the forces that provide the impetus for organizational change and the programs for introducing such changes. The third section of this chapter introduces you to the field of organization development and the role it plays in planned organizational change. Finally, we examine the ultimate goal of planned change—maintaining the organization's effectiveness.

FORCES FOR CHANGE

A number of basic *forces,* individually or in combination, can lead to significant change within an organization. One broad set of forces consists of *external forces,* pressures or opportunities which arise from outside the firm. Another set is composed of internal forces. Figure 11–1 illustrates many of the major external and internal forces for change that affect contemporary organizations.

External Forces

The purpose of monitoring the environment is to help management detect events which require some form of organizational change. In some cases, environmental *pressures* adversely alter the "fit" between the organization and its

FIGURE 11–1 Internal and external forces for change

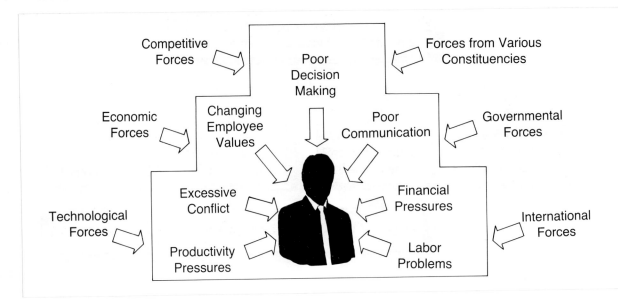

environment. For example, U.S. Steel (now USX) remained profitable for seven decades despite an emphasis on short-term profits and preservation of the status quo. By the 1970s, however, the environment of the steel industry was changing rapidly. Not only was foreign competition increasing, but also small domestic "minimills" were capturing a larger share of the market. U.S. Steel found its domestic market share dropping to less than 16 percent (compared with a share of over 50 percent in earlier years). By 1982, estimates indicated that the company was losing $154 on every ton of steel shipped. Management initiated significant changes in personnel, organizational structure, product lines, and marketing in an attempt to "fit" the new dynamic environment more effectively.[1] Such actions constitute *reactive change*: the organization reacts, or responds, to environmental pressures.

In other situations, management's monitoring activities may reveal environmental *opportunities* which can be exploited. In such cases, management initiates change by leading the organization in new directions to maintain its competitive edge. Such actions reflect a strategy of *proactive change*.

Any number of external forces can lead to reactive or proactive organizational change. Undeniably, one of the most prominent forces in recent years has been technology. Increasing knowledge and technological advances in semiconductors and microcircuitry, for instance, have provided the opportunity for enterprising inventors and entrepreneurs to create a new industry in personal computers. This development, in turn, is enabling progressive banks, retail stores, and real estate agencies to devise means by which their customers can transfer funds, make purchases, or shop for new houses without having to

PROACTIVE CHANGE

For almost a century and a half, Dun & Bradstreet, a wide-ranging information services company, has been a financially successful firm. Among its many products and services, D&B provides financial and credit information; collection services; market research and electronic data processing systems development; group insurance and benefit plans to small business; "Yellow Pages" sales representation; management, marketing, and information processing consulting; official airline guides; encyclopedias; and travel services. The firm has successfully weathered business cycles and wars, and today dominates many of its markets.

Some companies in such an enviable position might relax and become complacent—not Dun & Bradstreet. As its chief executive once explained:

> Our goal is to be in a state of continuous transition so we can always accommodate the changing environment of our clients. . . . Instead of concentrating on new ways to package and sell information we happen to have on hand, we are beginning to look at the changing needs of the marketplace and to devise ways to fill those needs.

In response to this mandate, D&B introduced some 200 new products in 1985 alone.

SOURCE: Based on "How D&B Organizes for a New Product Blitz," *Business Week*, 16 November 1981, p. 87; and "That Purring You Hear is Dun & Bradstreet's Money Machine," *Business Week*, 13 October 1986, pp. 90–94.

leave their homes. Technological change, in some cases, has proceeded with unbelievable rapidity:[2]

> One firm built a new plant to make transistors and moved in a work force from another location but was forced to close the plant six months later because the "bottom had fallen out" of the transistor market due to newly developed microminiature circuitry.

There are numerous other environmental forces that influence organizational change. Depressed economic conditions have provided the impetus for significant organizational changes in some industries. A constant force for managers in virtually any organization is competitive pressure. And the government, the international arena, and such pressures from various constituencies as consumer interest groups, the community, and stockholders all create forces for organizational change.

Internal Forces

Events occurring within the organization can also create change. Labor problems, such as strikes, high grievance rates, or the threat of unionization, often cause management to modify its personnel policies. High turnover among employees or excessive absenteeism are also instrumental in causing management to reassess its operations. Such "people pressures" may result in changes in job design, organization structure, wage rates, hiring policies, supervisory styles, and so on.

Managers have been particularly concerned about the problems of stagnant productivity and changing employee values. The search for ways to improve productivity has led to the adoption of new forms of technology, motivation systems, and participative decision making. Increasing participation in decision making, for instance, is not only an attempt to improve productivity, but also a response to demands by employees that they be permitted a voice in decisions that affect their work.

Motivation to Change

Most organizational change is probably reactive rather than proactive. Few organizations, for reasons we shall examine shortly, are likely to create significant change on their own in the absence of any immediate pressure to modify their operations. As Michael Beer has pointed out: "If there is one thing of which researchers are very certain, it is that organizations do change when they are under pressure and rarely when they are not."[3]

Beer believes that crisis is often required to get the attention of top management. Although all organizations do not require crisis to change, it is undeniably a powerful force. Its role may be to raise "dissatisfaction with the status quo [in order] to overcome resistance caused by the costs of change to organizational members."[4]

Managers must place more emphasis on proactive strategies. The assumption that pressure is required for organizations to change should be altered to create a new emphasis: rather than simply reacting to environmental change that has already occurred, managers should be encouraged to create change. These changes often generate pressures to which other organizations must then respond. Certainly, some organizations practice proactive change. The best examples are often pioneers in emerging industries—such companies as Wang Laboratories in the word processing field or Apple Computer in the personal computer market. But managers in any field have the opportunity to create change. What is required is creativity and a major modification in management's way of thinking about organizational-environmental relationships.

THE PROCESS OF CHANGE

Once management's monitoring activities have detected significant pressures for—or opportunity to—change, management can begin the necessary process

FIGURE 11–2 Planned organizational change

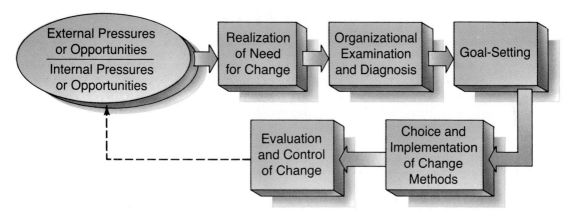

of modifying the organization with *planned organizational change*, a procedure that consists of the steps illustrated in Figure 11–2.

Realization of Need for Change

Even intense forces for change do not automatically lead to organizational adaptation. The reason for this delay in management's response is illustrated in Figure 11–3. Although the forces for change may be great, the forces opposing change may be equally powerful.[5]

Reasons for Resisting Change.   Change is not always resisted. Few of us would refuse a gift of a million dollars even though accepting it would likely lead to significant changes in our life style. But change is often not viewed positively, either because the benefits of the proposed change are unclear or because organization members perceive that the benefits of the change are outweighed by its costs. Such costs include the following:

☐   Many individuals resist change because they fear it may adversely affect their job security. In truth, organizational changes often involve extensive

FIGURE 11–3 Forces for and against change

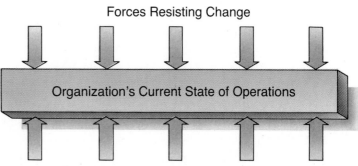

POLITICAL RESISTANCE TO CHANGE

After a number of years of rapid growth, the president of an organization decided that its size demanded the creation of a new staff function—New Product Planning and Development—to be headed by a vice president. Operationally, this change eliminated most of the decision-making power that the vice presidents of marketing, engineering, and production had over new products. Inasmuch as new products were very important in this organization, the change also reduced the vice presidents' status which, together with power, was very important to them.

During the two months after the president announced his idea for a new product vice president, the existing vice presidents each came up with six or seven reasons the new arrangement might not work. Their objections grew louder and louder until the president shelved the idea.

SOURCE: Reprinted by permission of Harvard Business Review. Excerpt from "Choosing Strategies for Change" by John P. Kotter and Leonard A. Schlesinger (March-April 1979). Copyright © 1979 by the President and Fellows of Harvard College; all rights reserved.

layoffs as organizations attempt to cut costs and increase operating efficiency. The problem, of course, is that what is good for the organization is not necessarily good for each of its members.

☐ Since change, by definition, alters the status quo, some individuals are likely to lose political power or status while others stand to gain. Even such simple changes as moving individuals from one set of offices to new quarters in another part of the same building can create considerable anxiety.

☐ Organizational change usually modifies the organization's informal network of relationships. The introduction of new technology or the transfer of personnel can break up cohesive work groups and threaten friendships and norms. Few of us are anxious to change familiar, comfortable ways of working with others.

☐ Some individuals resist change because they fear that they will be unable to acquire the necessary new skills and behaviors. This fear is particularly prevalent in organizations undergoing technological change.

Resistance to change may not always be conscious. Organizational culture, a concept discussed in chapter 12, can make change difficult even for those individuals who desire change. For example, Data General Corporation found itself foundering badly several years ago. Its first microcomputer had been a market failure, and it had entered the superminicomputer market three years later than its competitors. The company attempted a structural change but found many of its managers unwilling or unable to develop the new skills required to transform the firm from its entrepreneurial orientation into a more professional marketing-oriented systems company. To make a break with its culture, Data General began replacing its veteran managers with executives from IBM and other firms.[6]

Reducing Resistance to Change. Figure 11–3 indicates that resistance to change can be overcome either by increasing the forces for change or by reducing the forces resisting change. Organizational change specialists generally prefer the latter approach because increasing the forces for change often leads to a strengthening of the resistance to change. In practice, however, both approaches are used to "unfreeze" resistant attitudes and behaviors. The following discussion presents a sample of various methods for overcoming, or reducing, resistance to change:[7]

□ If the resistance is based on poor or misleading information, a program of education and communication concerning the purpose and benefits of the change may help reduce the resistance. Such a program obviously requires that the resisters trust top management. Additionally, it may be necessary for management to guarantee organization members that neither their job security nor their income will be adversely affected by the change.

UNFREEZING AT BLACK LAKE

Resistant attitudes can be "unfrozen" in a variety of ways. As an example of a nontraditional technique, consider the unfreezing process employed by General Motors and the United Auto Workers (UAW) as they began a change program to improve GM/UAW relations.

Each week during the winter, about 300 managers and union members traveled to a remote area near Black Lake, Michigan, for a week-long session. During the week, which was filled with classes and seminars, each management and union person shared a room together, taught together, and participated evenly in all classes:

> People who have never interacted with their union/management counterpart spend the week rooming, eating, working, talking, and walking with each other. . . . People who have taken their assumptions and behaviors for granted over many years spend the week thinking about and discussing new values and new behaviors.

SOURCE: Sydney L. Solberg, "Changing Culture Through Ceremony: An Example from GM," *Human Resource Management* 24 (Fall 1985): 330–32.

□ Resistance can sometimes be reduced by encouraging the resisters to become involved in the change program and to participate in designing and implementing it. In many cases, such participation can lead to increased member commitment to the change program.

□ Management can sometimes facilitate the change by offering support such as training employees in the new technology or aiding them in developing the behavioral skills that will be required. Such support can reduce the anxieties that cause resistance to certain types of change.

□ Because all three of these forms of reducing resistance can be time consuming, management may turn to coercion. In this case, organization members are forced to change through threats (of job loss, for instance), firings, or transfers of resisters. The outcomes of this strategy may include anger and lingering bitterness. "But in situations where speed is essential and where the changes will not be popular, regardless of how they are introduced, coercion may be the manager's only option."[8]

Certainly the appropriate approach depends upon the magnitude and type of change, the characteristics of the members who will be affected, the expected time frame, and the reasons for opposition to the change. The wise manager analyzes the situation carefully before deciding upon a means of reducing or overcoming resistance. As Kurt Lewin, one of the pioneers of organizational change theory, pointed out: "Managers rushing into a factory to raise production by group decisions are likely to encounter failure. In social management as in medicine, there are no patent medicines and each case demands careful diagnosis."[9]

Organizational Examination and Diagnosis

Once organizational attitudes are "unfrozen" and members realize that change is needed, it is necessary to examine the organization in order to diagnose the specific areas that require change. Some organizations term this phase *self-study*. Often, a consultant, or *change agent*, is brought in from outside the organization to aid in the examination and diagnosis. Although the organization's own managers can—and do—serve as change agents, an outside consultant may be able to view the organization more objectively. Management must be aware, however, that a consultant often arrives with his or her own set of biases and selective ways of viewing organizational problems. Hence, it is advisable for the consultant, after collecting information on the organization's operations, to compare his or her problem definition with that of management. Both organization members and consultants are likely to understand the problems better by comprehending how and why the other arrived at a particular diagnosis.

Optimally, the focus of the self-study is each of the organization's four major subsystems and their interactions, as shown in Figure 11–4. Change may be required in the organization's *technology* (how it changes inputs into out-

FIGURE 11–4 Interactions among organizational subsystems

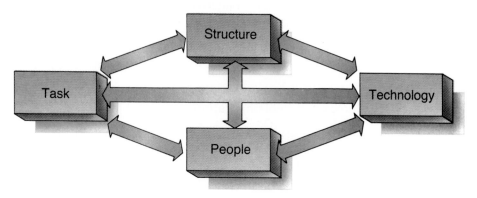

SOURCE: From Harold J. Leavitt, "Applied Organizational Change in Industry: Structural, Technological and Humanistic Approaches," in James G. March, ed., *Handbook of Organizations.* Copyright © 1965 by Rand McNally College Publishing Co., p. 1145.

puts), its *tasks* (the way specific jobs are designed), its *structure* (the way the tasks are grouped), or its *people* (the way in which organization members behave and interact). By taking a systems view, management will realize that a change in any one of these subsystems will affect the others.

Goal Setting

Upon completion of the self-study, organization members must formulate the goals they wish to establish for the change program. In other words, they must explicitly answer the question, What changes do we desire in our organization?

David A. Nadler and others emphasize the importance of communicating a clear image of the future to organization members.[10] Change programs are likely to be more effective if those involved have a clear idea of the direction in which they are going and what their ultimate destination will be:[11]

> While there is no concrete future state on which to focus, some picture of the future can be constructed and communicated. In this case, it is more likely to be a vision or a set of principles or guidelines for doing business than a concrete structure or set of organizational arrangements. It may simply be a statement of "what we will be and what we won't be," or a description of "why we are where we are, and where (in general terms) we're headed."

Without clear goals, organization members may misinterpret the change program and its results. Although a three-year organization-wide change program within the Tennessee Valley Authority was deemed largely successful, the lack of a clear statement of goals created some misunderstanding among employees:[12]

Since it was unclear what was to be accomplished, expectations among division employees varied considerably. Unrealistically high initial expectations were tempered by participation as more direct participants learned that change is a slow and sometimes cumbersome process. Those employees who were less involved retained their high expectations and began to see the [change program] as ineffective since they could not see anything tangible being accomplished.

Choice and Implementation of Change Methods

Once the goals of the change program are established, the specific methods to be used must be selected. The techniques available to management, as implied by Figure 11–4, may focus upon changing the following: the task (through job enrichment, for example), the structure (by developing profit centers, for instance), the technology (through increasing the level of computerization, for example), the people (such as by reducing destructive intergroup conflict), or any combination of these.

There is some evidence that a shared approach—one involving individuals at all levels of the hierarchy in choosing and implementing change methods—is characteristic of successful programs.[13] Participation, which requires much time and some relinquishing of managerial control, can create such new problems as conflict. In some cases, these costs are overshadowed by the benefits. In a study of change in a public utility, those employees who directly participated in planning and implementing the change perceived themselves as having more influence over work-related decisions, were more likely to feel that their contributions were accepted by those above them, and had more favorable attitudes toward their jobs and the organization than did employees who did not directly participate. These results were maintained over a three-year period.[14]

A danger in participative programs is that the managers may feel that, if they play an active role, their power might interfere with the change process. In reality, the "backing off" of a leader may be perceived by lower-level participants as noncommitment. Such behavior may imply that employee participation is not important. Managers must provide a role model and should be visible enough so that employees feel that their ideas are being received and acted upon by those who have the authority to implement change.[15]

The evidence from one study strongly suggests that change programs be actively managed. The most effective change consistently occurred in programs where managers carefully monitored the entire change process, regulating and controlling social and political issues as they arose. These managers were active in developing and justifying new definitions of acceptable performance and showing how present practices could be improved.[16] Without careful monitoring, managers may fall into the trap of focusing most of their attention on the future they desire while assuming that the implementation stage is simply a mechanical process.

Evaluation and Control of Change

Evaluation of the change involves frequent monitoring of organizational performance and employee performance and attitudes to ensure that the change is proceeding as planned. Such monitoring requires the development of feedback mechanisms to provide the necessary information:[17]

> There is a huge amount of anecdotal data about senior managers ordering changes and assuming those changes were made, only to find out to their horror that the changes never occurred. Such a situation develops because managers lack feedback devices to tell them whether actions have been effective or not. During stable periods, effective managers develop various ways of eliciting feedback. During the transition state, however, these mechanisms often break down because of the turbulence of the change or because of the natural avoidance of providing "bad news." Thus it becomes important for transition managers to develop multiple, redundant, and sensitive mechanisms for generating feedback about the transition.

A MONUMENTAL CHANGE EFFORT

What has been described as "the biggest single planned organizational change in the country in the second half of the century" began at American Telephone & Telegraph in 1982 when the U.S. Justice Department ordered AT&T to divest itself of its Bell System telephone companies. Moving from a regulated world with guaranteed earnings and little competition into highly competitive markets required significant changes.

Those changes did not occur overnight. As an executive at a rival firm said, "Their people just didn't grow up in an environment where they had to sell to feed their families. They can't be transformed into a lean and mean marketing organization in a few years."

To encourage change and to "refreeze" individuals into new ways of performing, AT&T devised a stock-option plan for managers, changed sales-force compensation from straight salary to partial commission, and began measuring the performance of individual managers and products. It also was forced to drop its commitment to lifetime job security for its employees: by 1987, over 40,000 jobs had been eliminated at AT&T.

SOURCE: Based on "Conversation with Charles L. Brown," *Organizational Dynamics* 11 (Summer 1982): 30–33; "The New AT&T Struggles to Get to its Feet," *Business Week*, 3 December 1984, p. 92; "A Leaner AT&T Could Cost Thousands of Jobs," *Business Week*, 15 September 1986, p. 50; and "Can Jim Olson's Grand Design Get AT&T Going?", *Business Week*, 22 December 1986, pp. 48–49.

Feedback is essential because change programs, even though successful, often have side effects—the creation of new problems. As Gerald I. Susman puts it, "We never quite solve our problems, rather we navigate through sets of interdependent problems guided by the vision of a more desirable future."[18] Certainly, a perspective which evaluates the change from a systems viewpoint is required.

Finally, it is important to realize that significant change takes time. "Refreezing" individuals into the new ways of working and interacting requires a new reward system. Since people are likely to behave in ways that lead to the rewards they desire, rewards such as pay increases and promotions should be linked to the types of behavior that are required to make the organization change effective. Aaron J. Nurick recommends that if the organization benefits financially from the change program, then its members should share in the gains. The connection between organizational improvement and the employees' well-being thus becomes clear. Without such rewards, employees are unlikely to see involvement as worthy of their efforts.[19]

ORGANIZATION DEVELOPMENT

This section examines more closely one particular approach to organization change which has been widely adopted in recent years. Long-term, system-wide organization change that focuses primarily on the ways that organization members behave and interact is termed *organization development* (OD). Encompassing a wide range of programs, OD attempts to improve organizational relations and encourage teamwork. The following statement by Richard Beckhard provides a useful working definition:[20]

> Organization development is an effort (1) *planned,* (2) *organization-wide,* and (3) *managed* from the *top,* to (4) increase *organizational effectiveness* and *health* through (5) *planned interventions* in the organization's "processes," using *behavioral-science* knowledge.

OD is planned in the sense of involving (1) a systematic diagnosis of the way an organization functions and (2) a prescription of certain organization development methods to improve its functioning. The analysis involves an entire organization, although this may be a corporation, an autonomous division, or even a local unit.

In saying the development is managed from the top, Beckhard is stressing the desired commitment of top leaders. Increasing effectiveness and health of an organization would entail improvements in intergroup and interdepartmental collaboration, development of undistorted communication, identification of shared values, and reduction of interpersonal friction.

Through planned intervention, managers and other organizational members step back and analyze the way the organization is functioning and look at alternative ways of working together. The behavioral science knowledge deals with such features of organizations and management as "motivation, power, communications, perception, cultural norms, problem-solving, goal-setting, interpersonal relationships, intergroup relationships, and conflict management."[21]

A central figure in most types of organization development is the change agent who provides the technical or professional leadership necessary to improve the functioning of the organization. The change agent must inspire confidence; to do so requires an ability to understand and diagnose organizational problems as well as a knowledge of behavioral science and OD methodology. The client organization, however, must accept responsibility for the program and for its implementation if the program is to be taken seriously.

Assumptions Underlying OD

The basic assumption underlying OD is that it is possible for "the goals and purposes of the organization [to be] attained at the same time that human values of individuals within the organization are furthered."[22] Human beings are viewed as desiring growth, development, and the opportunity to contribute to organization goals if permitted. Such human development requires effectively functioning work groups and an organization characterized by a high degree of interpersonal trust, support, and cooperation.[23]

Beyond this basic assumption, OD is founded on other fundamentals, which include the following:[24]

□ The level of interpersonal trust, support, and cooperation is lower than is desirable in most organizations.
□ Most people wish to make—and are capable of making—a greater contribution to organization goal attainment than the organization permits.
□ People wish to be accepted by others and to work in groups. Work effectiveness increases through joint problem solving and task collaboration.
□ The culture in most organizations suppresses the feelings people have about each other, and these suppressed feelings adversely affect problem solving, personal growth, and job satisfaction.
□ Viewing personal feelings as important to the organization can open up avenues for improved goal setting, leadership, communications, problem solving, intergroup collaboration, and job satisfaction.
□ Organization structure and job design can be modified to meet the needs of individuals, groups, and the organization better.

OD Methods

Change techniques include MBO, job enrichment, and various conflict-resolution tools. OD consultants have also developed a number of other methods to effect change. A sampling is presented here.

Survey Feedback. As a first step, many OD methods require collecting data through questionnaires which explore the feelings and attitudes of all organization members toward their jobs, their supervisors, their peers, and the organization in general. The results of the survey are presented to the organization members as an aid in diagnosing where change is needed. This feedback process occurs in a session attended by the supervisor, subordinates, and change agent, who acts as a facilitator. Survey feedback can serve as the first step of a program designed to change individuals, groups, or the entire organization. The primary differences between survey feedback and the traditional employee survey process are shown in Figure 11–5.

Individual Change. An example of a method developed to change individuals is *sensitivity* (or *T-Group*) *training.* Its purpose is to develop interpersonal skills among organization members. Through participation in group projects and exercises, managers are taught to look at their behavior as it may affect others and to attempt to understand the behavior and attitudes of others. Emphasis is placed on the way that individuals "come across" in their face-to-face interactions with others.

Group Change. *Team-building* conferences are intended to improve the functioning of groups or work teams. A conference begins with a review of team purposes and priorities and areas in which improvement may be helpful. After this self-diagnosis, group members attend several sessions, guided by the change agent, in which they discuss possible ways of solving problems and making their group function more effectively:[25]

> Team-building methodology is based on what behavioral scientists call an action research paradigm. This paradigm directly applies Kurt Lewin's three-stage process of change (i.e., unfreezing, changing, and refreezing). The key aspects include collection of data, diagnosis of problems, feedback to the work group, discussion of the data by the work group, action planning, and action. The sequence tends to be cyclical, with the focus on new or advanced problems as the group learns to work together more effectively. . . .

Organizational Change. One of the most widely discussed means of changing organizations is Robert Blake and Jane Srygley Mouton's *Grid organization development.*[26] *The Managerial Grid®*, a key tool in this program, shows managerial orientation in terms of two variables—concern for people and concern for production (Figure 11–6).

A series of exercises is used to permit managers to analyze their own positions on the Grid and to work toward the ideal 9,9 position. The complete program involves additional steps designed to carry the Grid approach to all parts of the organization.[27]

FIGURE 11–5 Two approaches to the use of attitude surveys

	Traditional Approach	Survey Feedback or OD Approach
Data collected from	Rank and file, and maybe foreman	Everyone in the system or subsystem
Data reported to	Top management, department heads, and perhaps to employees through newspaper	Everyone who participated
Implications of data are worked on by	Top management (maybe)	Everyone in work teams, with workshops starting at the top (all superiors with their subordinates)
Third-party intervention strategy	Design and administration of questionnaire, development of a report	Obtaining concurrence on total strategy, design and administration of questionnaire, design of workshops, appropriate interventions in workshops
Action planning done by	Top management only	Teams at all levels
Probable extent of change and improvement	Low	High

SOURCE: Wendell L. French and Cecil H. Bell, Jr., *Organization Development: Behavioral Science Interventions for Organization Improvement,* 3rd Edition, © 1984, p. 182. Reprinted by permission of Prentice-Hall, Inc., Englewood Cliffs, New Jersey.

FIGURE 11–6   The Managerial Grid®

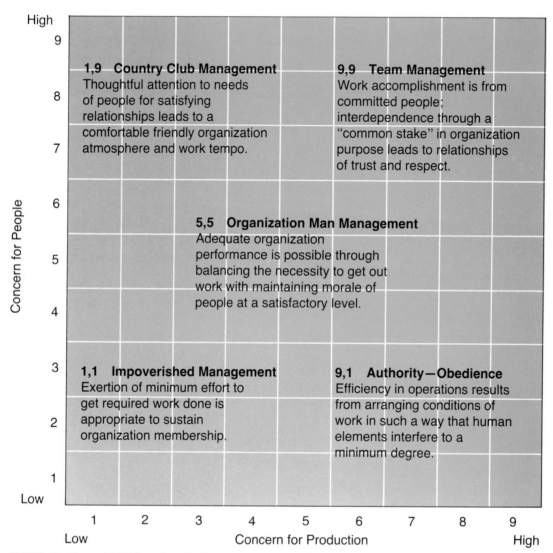

SOURCE: The Managerial Grid figure from *The Managerial Grid III: The Key to Leadership Excellence,* by Robert R. Blake and Jane Srygley Mouton. Houston: Gulf Publishing Company, Copyright © 1985, page 12. Reproduced by permission.

OD Research

Much of the research on the effects of OD interventions is poorly documented, though research quality is improving.[28] One of the clearest findings is that no single OD method works well in all situations.[29] Different programs are required for different kinds of employees, for different organizational levels, and for different desired results (i.e., the goal may range from decreasing turnover and absenteeism to helping the organization attain a better "fit" with its environment).

OD research must be properly designed and reported because managers need a sound base to "make informed decisions regarding the choice, continuance, expansion, or curtailment of OD programs."[30] If OD practitioners wish to fulfill their potential for helping organizations interact more effectively with their environment and for improving the quality of work life, they must substantially enhance their methods of program evaluation. Thus, the goals of the change effort must be explicitly stated before the program begins, multiple measures of both the process and the results must be used, and cause-and-effect relationships must be fully documented.[31]

THE GOAL OF CHANGE: ORGANIZATIONAL EFFECTIVENESS

The purpose of organizational change is to ensure that the organization operates effectively. Precisely, what is an effective organization? As is the case with a number of thorny issues, the exact definition of *organizational effectiveness* is the focus of considerable debate and could be the subject of several chapters. Many theorists, however, would probably agree that an effective organization is one that attains its goals, if goals are defined broadly. Such goals are of two basic types:[32]

□ *Primary goals*—those tied directly to satisfying the needs of the organization's primary client group (those people the organization was established to serve).
□ *Secondary goals*—those tied to the satisfaction of the needs of secondary beneficiary groups (organization members, the general public, suppliers, creditors, regulating agencies, and so on).

The actual weight, or importance, assigned to these various goals by top management will vary over item and across situations. Also, goals may conflict with one another.

This conceptualization of organizational effectiveness is useful for profit and nonprofit organizations alike. A business, for instance, must satisfy the needs of its customers (primary client group) without ignoring the needs and requirements of its employees, stockholders, bondholders, suppliers, OSHA, EPA, IRS, and so on (secondary beneficiary groups). A company which is able to perform adequately in the eyes of each of these groups is considered more effective than one which does not. And it seems probable that an effective business organization is a profitable one. Profitability in itself, however, does not indicate effectiveness. Profit may be attained by polluting the environment or selling illegal products. Effectiveness, then, encompasses considerably more than profitability.

A nonprofit organization, such as a university, must satisfy the needs of its students (primary clients) for education and personal development as well as such secondary beneficiary groups as faculty, administration, community, EEOC, the state legislature, employees, and so on. Although no well-accepted measure such as profit exists, the university is effective to the extent it satisfies these various and often conflicting needs.

Management's task, then, is to make the organization effective and maintain that effectiveness over time. To attain this end, managers must take a balanced, systems view of their organization, realizing that its multiple goals may conflict and that emphasis on particular goals may change or fade as conditions change. Effectiveness, once attained, is not a constant state. Careful and continued monitoring of the organization and its environment will enable management to plan and carry out the organization changes that are required to maintain effectiveness.

SUMMARY

A number of basic forces may create the need for significant change within an organization. These precipitating factors consist of *external* forces—environmental *pressures* or *opportunities*—and/or *internal* forces—events occurring within the organization. Although most organizational change is a reaction to these forces, many organizations could improve their performance by emphasizing proactive strategies which create—rather than simply respond to—environmental change.

The process of *planned organization* change begins with the realization of the need for change. Organization members often resist change because the benefits of the proposed change are unclear or because they perceive that the benefits of the change are outweighed by its costs. Even the culture of some organizations makes change difficult. Change can be facilitated either by increasing the forces for change or reducing the forces resisting change.

Once organizational attitudes are "unfrozen" and members realize that change is needed, it is necessary to examine the organization in order to diagnose the specific areas that require change. Upon completion of this *self-study*, organization members must formulate the goals they wish to establish for the change program. Then, the specific methods to be used in attaining these ends must be selected and implemented. Finally, the change program must be evaluated—through feedback mechanisms—and controlled by "refreezing" individuals into the new ways of working and interacting.

One popular approach to changing organizations that focuses primarily on the ways in which organization members behave and interact is termed *organization development* (OD). This approach assumes that it is possible for organization goals to be attained at the same time that human values of organization members are being furthered. OD change techniques may concentrate on changing individuals, as with sensitivity training, for instance; on changing groups, as in team building; or on changing the entire organization system, by using the *Managerial Grid®,* for example. Different change programs are required for different situations or results. It is essential that each program's effectiveness be evaluated through appropriate research methodology.

The purpose of organization change is to improve *organizational effectiveness.* An effective organization is one that attains its goals, where goals are broadly defined. These include the organization's *primary* goals (those tied directly to satisfying the needs of the people the organization is established to serve) and *secondary* goals (those tied to the satisfaction of the needs of various secondary beneficiary groups such as organization members, the general public, owners, suppliers, creditors, regulating agencies, and so on).

KEY CONCEPTS

External forces	Participation
Internal forces	Refreezing
Reactive change	Organization development
Proactive change	Survey feedback
Planned organizational change	Sensitivity training
Resistance to change	Team-building
Unfreezing	Managerial Grid
Self-study	OD research
Change agent	Organizational effectiveness

DISCUSSION QUESTIONS

1. Identify some *external* and *internal forces* that could create the need for change in your university.
2. Distinguish between *pressures* and *opportunities* for change.
3. What are some of the reasons why organization members *resist* change even when it is needed?
4. How might resistance to change be *reduced* or *overcome?*
5. What is an organization *self-study* and what is its purpose?
6. What are the advantages and disadvantages associated with using a participative approach to organization change?
7. What is the OD approach to changing organizations?
8. How does *survey feedback* differ from the traditional employee attitude survey?
9. What role does research methodology play in OD?
10. Reply to this question: "Is your university an effective organization?" Justify your answer based on the definition of *organizational effectiveness* presented in this chapter.

NOTES

1. "The Toughest Job in Business," *Business Week,* 25 February 1985, pp. 50–6.
2. Edgar F. Huse, *Organization Development and Change,* 2d ed. (St. Paul, Minn.: West, 1980), p. 19.
3. Michael Beer, *Organization Change* and *Development: A Systems View* (Santa Monica, Calif.: Goodyear, 1980), p. 47.
4. Ibid.
5. Kurt Lewin, *Field Theory in Social Science: Selected Theoretical Papers,* ed. D. Cartwright (New York: Harper & Row, 1951).
6. "How Data General Started Humming Again," *Business Week,* 30 January 1984, pp. 53, 57.
7. This discussion is based on John P. Kotter and Leonard A. Schlesinger, "Choosing Strategies for Change," *Harvard Businesss Review* 57 (March-April 1979): 109–12.
8. Reprinted by permission of Harvard Business Review. Excerpt from "Choosing Strategies for Change" by John P. Kotter and Leonard A. Schlesinger (March-April 1979). Copyright © 1979 by the President and Fellows of Harvard College; all rights reserved.
9. Kurt Lewin, "Studies in Group Decision," in *Group Dynamics,* ed. D. Cartwright and A. Zander (New York: Row, Peterson, 1953), p. 300.
10. David A. Nadler, "Managing Organizational Change: An Integrative Perspective," *Journal of Applied Behavioral Science* 17 (April-May-June 1981): 202.
11. David A. Nadler, "Managing Transitions to Uncertain Future States," *Organizational Dynamics* 11 (Summer 1982): 44.
12. Aaron J. Nurick, "The Paradox of Participation: Lessons from the Tennessee Valley Authority," *Human Resource Management* 24 (Fall 1985): 345.
13. Larry E. Greiner, "Patterns of Organization Change," *Harvard Business Review* 45 (May-June 1967): 119–28; and Richard E. Walton, "From Control to Commitment in the Workplace," *Harvard Business Review* 64 (March-April 1985): 77–84.
14. Aaron J. Nurick, "Participation in Organizational Change: A Longitudinal Field Study," *Human Relations* 35 (May 1982): 413–29.
15. Nurick, "The Paradox of Participation," pp. 349–50, 354.
16. Paul C. Nutt, "Tactics of Implementation," *Academy of Management Journal* 29 (June 1986): 230–61.
17. Nadler, "Managing Organizational Change," p. 294.
18. Gerald I. Susman, "Planned Change: Prospects for the 1980s," *Management Science* 27 (February 1981): 150.
19. Nurick, "The Paradox of Participation," pp. 354–55.
20. Richard Beckhard, *Organization Development: Strategies and Models* (Reading, Mass.: Addison-Wesley, 1969), p. 9.
21. Ibid., p. 13.
22. Wendell L. French and Cecil H. Bell, Jr., *Organization Development: Behavioral Science Interventions for Organization Improvement* (Englewood Cliffs, N.J.: Prentice-Hall, 1973), p. xiii.
23. Ibid., chapter 6.
24. This discussion is based on Huse, *Organization Development and Change,* pp. 29–30; and Wendell L. French, "Organization Development Objectives, Assumptions, and Strategies," in *Organization Development: Theory, Practice and Research,*

ed. W. L. French, C. H. Bell, Jr., and R. A. Zawacki (Dallas: Business Publications, 1978), pp. 28–9.

25. S. Jay Liebowitz and Kenneth P. De Meuse, "The Application of Team Building," *Human Relations* 35 (January 1982): 3.

26. Robert R. Blake and Jane Srygley Mouton, *The Managerial Grid III* (Houston: Gulf, 1985).

27. The basic goal of the Grid—developing a 9,9, style of management—has been criticized by many scholars. The contingency approach to leadership (see chapter 14) indicates that under certain circumstances a behavioral pattern emphasizing both concern for people and production may not always be ideal or desirable. An argument for the 9,9 style may be found in Robert R. Blake and Jane Srygley Mouton, "A Comparative Analysis of Situationalism and 9,9 Management by Principle," *Organizational Dynamics* 10 (Spring 1982): 20–43.

28. John M. Nicholas and Marsha Katz, "Research Methods and Reporting Practices in Organization Development: A Review and Some Guidelines," *Academy of Management Review* 10 (October 1985): 747.

29. John M. Nicholas, "The Comparative Impact of Organization Development Interventions on Hard Criteria Measures," *Academy of Management Review* 7 (October 1982): 540.

30. David E. Terpstra, "Relationship between Methodological Rigor and Reported Outcomes in Organization Development Evaluation Research," *Journal of Applied Psychology* 66 (October 1981): 541.

31. Melvin Blumberg and Charles D. Pringle, "How Control Groups Can Cause Loss of Control in Action Research: The Case of Rushton Coal Mine," *The Journal of Applied Behavioral Science* 19, no. 4 (1983): 409–25.

32. This classification is based on B. J. Hodge and William P. Anthony, *Organization Theory*, 2d ed. (Boston: Allyn and Bacon, 1984): pp. 282–84.

SUPPLEMENTARY READING

Blumberg, Melvin, and **Pringle, Charles D.** "How Control Groups Can Cause Loss of Control in Action Research: The Case of Rushton Coal Mine." *The Journal of Applied Behavioral Science* 19, no. 4 (1983): 409–25.

Cameron, Kim S. "Effectiveness as Paradox: Consensus and Conflict in Conceptions of Organizational Effectiveness." *Management Science* 32 (May 1986): 539–53.

Carnall, C. A. "Toward a Theory for the Evaluation of Organizational Change." *Human Relations* 39 (August 1986): 745–66.

Eden, Dov. "OD and Self-Fulfilling Prophecy: Boosting Productivity by Raising Expectations." *The Journal of Applied Behavioral Science* 22, no. 1 (1986): 1–13.

Greenhalgh, Leonard. "Maintaining Organizational Effectiveness during Organizational Retrenchment." *Journal of Applied Behavioral Science* 18 (1982): 155–70.

Kaplan, Robert E. "Is Openness Passé?" *Human Relations* 39 (March 1986): 229–43.

Kotter, John P., and **Schlesinger, Leonard A.** "Choosing Strategies for Change." *Harvard Business Review* 57 (March-April 1979): 106–14.

Liebowitz, S. Jay, and **De Meuse, Kenneth P.** "The Application of Team Building." *Human Relations* 35 (January 1982): 1–18.

March, James G. "Footnotes to Organizational Change." *Administrative Science Quarterly* 26 (December 1981): 563–77.

Nadler, David A. "Managing Organizational Change: An Integrative Perspective." *Journal of Applied Behavioral Science* 17 (April-May-June 1981): 191–211.

Nicholas, John M., and Katz, Marsha. "Research Methods and Reporting Practices in Organization Development: A Review and Some Guidelines." *Academy of Management Review* (October 1985): 737–49.

Nurick, Aaron J. "The Paradox of Participation: Lessons from the Tennessee Valley Authority." *Human Resource Management* 24 (Fall 1985): 341–56.

Pasmore, William, and Friedlander, Frank. "An Action-Research Program for Increasing Employee Involvement in Problem Solving." *Administrative Science Quarterly* 27 (September 1982): 343–62.

Schuster, Michael. "The Scanlon Plan: A Longitudinal Analysis." *Journal of Applied Behavioral Science* 20, no. 1 (1984): 23–38.

Solberg, Sydney L. "Changing Culture Through Ceremony: An Example from GM." *Human Resource Management* 24 (Fall 1985): 329–40.

Susman, Gerald I. "Planned Changes: Prospects for the 1980s." *Management Science* 27 (February 1981): 139–54.

Walton, Richard E. "From Control to Commitment in the Workplace." *Harvard Business Review* 63 (March-April 1985): 77–84.

Weisbord, Marvin R. "Participative Work Design: A Personal Odyssey." *Organizational Dynamics* 13 (Spring 1985): 5–20.

Woodman, Richard W., and Wayne, Sandy J. "An Investigation of Positive-Findings Bias in Evaluation of Organization Development Interventions." *Academy of Management Journal* 28 (December 1985): 889–913.

Woodworth, Warner; Meyer, Gordon; and Smallwood, Norman. "Organization Development: A Closer Scrutiny." *Human Relations* 35 (April 1982): 307–19.

NATIONAL INSURANCE COMPANY

For nearly 30 years, the National Insurance Company had operated their Investment Division as shown in the organization chart (Exhibit 1). Aaron Jackson, executive vice-president for investments, was responsible for all company investments, including mortgage loans, securities (stocks, bonds, etc.), and the small amount of company-owned real estate.

In the last ten years National had significantly increased its sales of large group insurance policies and was administering several large trust funds, such as state teachers' retirement funds. These changes resulted in great sums of money which had to be invested, in accordance with various legal and fiduciary restrictions, in treasury bills, bonds, other securities, and real estate. Also, top management had decided to decrease its involvement with residential mortgages because of their relatively low yields in relation to the costs of processing and servicing these loans. It now appeared that the commercial loans and real estate were more promising investment alternatives.

Two major problems had developed with

Case prepared by Professors Thomas R. Miller and James M. Todd, Memphis State University.

EXHIBIT 1   National's organization chart

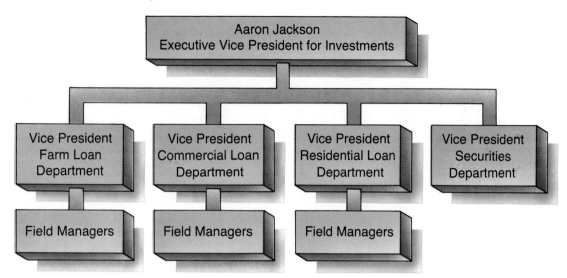

the existing organization given the changing needs of the Investment Division. Mr. Jackson was concerned that he had too many people reporting directly to him. His day-to-day involvement with the Securities Department was rather extensive, as he had formerly headed this department and had maintained a close association with it in his current position. He felt that he could not keep up with the operations under him. Furthermore, with the de-emphasis on residential loans, there were now too many employees in the Residential Loan Department with not enough work to do, both at the headquarters in Chicago and at the field-level offices in the smaller cities.

In an effort to deal with the changing demands on the Investment Division, Mr. Jackson appointed a committee to conduct a study of the current organization and submit its findings and recommendations to him for submission to the board of directors. Six months later the organization plan shown in Exhibit 2 was recommended to and then later approved by the board for implementation early in the following year.

Under the reorganization plan, there was to be a change from three vice-presidents reporting on mortgage loans to one senior vice-president in charge of all mortgages. This made it necessary to consolidate the three mortgage departments into one. With the increased activity in real estate investment, a new real estate section was to be placed under the senior vice-president.

Early in January the management team of the Investment Division, including the field managers, was called to a meeting in Chicago. This had been billed as the announcement of the reorganization of the Investment Division. In presenting the restructure, the executive vice-president for investments stated that there were two major reasons for the organizational change: (1) there had been too many people reporting directly to him, and (2) the investment market today made it necessary to have an organization that was fluid enough to shift its efforts to the most desirable investment opportunities. He explained that the reorganization would require retraining and recycling some

EXHIBIT 2 The recommended organization chart

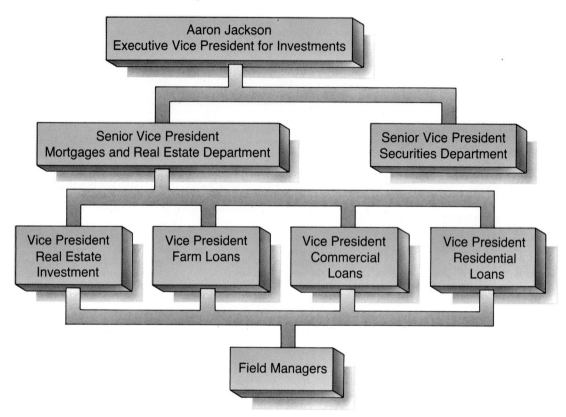

employees in order for them to meet their new responsibilities effectively. However, in accordance with established company policy, no employees would lose their jobs nor would anyone receive a cut in pay. (In fact, many of the employees affected actually received increases in pay, partly due to inflation and partly because it was thought this would promote their acceptance of the new organization.) He announced the appointments of the two senior vice-presidents and the four vice-presidents and wished them well in their new positions.

Although everything was worked out "on paper," soon problems began to emerge in the mortgage loan units. The three vice-presidents who had formerly been

department heads were now only vice-presidents reporting to a department head. They did not relish their reduced status. At the level of the field organization there were also subsequent changes. Where before there had been a field manager for each of the Farm, Commercial, and Residential Loan units, there was now only one field manager for all mortgage loans. Thus, where there had been three field offices in each major city, there was now one office per city for all mortgage loans. Some former field managers were now only field representatives reporting to a field manager. As the field offices were consolidated, there were also shifts among the administrative and clerical employees. With the change to one field office, there was a need for just one office manager, not three, and this was not well accepted by those who were no longer managers. In several instances in the company, employees who had worked together as peers for many years were now cast into the roles of superior and subordinates with restructured jobs and reporting relationships.

For some employees the restructure seemed to offer expanded opportunities, and they were eager to ''get the show on the road.'' However, others felt that they were not getting ''their share of the grapes'' and were resistant and even uncooperative. Although earnest efforts were made to convince the personnel that the new organization would ultimately provide greater opportunities, for various reasons they were not all convinced.

Some of the managers affected by the reorganization had spent many years with National and were approaching retirement age. They felt that they had paid their dues, and they knew that National would not terminate them after long faithful service. Some of them had spent 15 to 20 years doing the same job and doing it very well. They had become comfortable with the status quo and wanted everything to stay as it was. Gradually, some discontented workers adjusted and continued to make excellent employees with their new assignments. Others withstood their dissatisfaction until they could retire, while a few younger managers left the organization.

Specific forms of resistance to the reorganization were varied. One senior appraiser who had previously worked in a small field office did not like it because his new office didn't open into the reception area. Certain long-time residential appraisers felt it ''beneath their dignity'' when now called upon to appraise farm property. A farm appraiser left the company because he felt farm loans would eventually

be cut out. Others resented the loss of status of their job functions under the new organizational pattern.

As certain key positions were filled with people from Commercial Loans, it was rumored ''this is not a reorganization but a Commercial Loan Department takeover.'' One of the reasons for the reorganization was to make better use of the large Residential Loan workforce by transferring them to work with Commercial Loan units which were now understaffed. The rumor then started that the same thing would happen to the Farm Loan employees unless they worked harder and produced a high volume of farm mortgages. This proved to be unsettling to the Farm group.

In retrospect, one thing that National apparently overemphasized was the belief that existing personnel could be retrained to assume all positions in the new structure. While some employees were successfully retrained, such as residential appraisers who became competent to do commercial appraisal work, it was found that outside specialists had to be brought in to fill certain key positions, particularly in the Commercial Loan and Real Estate Investment units.

Questions

1. What forces caused Aaron Jackson to perceive the need for organizational change?
2. Note the positive aspects of the firm's approach to the organizational change. What actions did the firm take in planning and implementing change that you would disagree with?
3. Why was the change resisted by some?
4. Would coercion have been more effective in reducing resistance in this case?
5. Could organization development (OD) have been useful in this situation? Why or why not?

THE SOCIAL STRUCTURE OF ORGANIZATIONS
The Human Side of Organizations □ The Organization as a Social System

POWER AND POLITICS
Sources of Power □ A Contingency View of Power □ The Managerial Power Structure □ Power-Oriented Behavior and Job Dependency □ Techniques of Building and Using Political Power □ Informal Power and Organizational Effectiveness

ORGANIZATIONAL CULTURE
What Is Culture? □ Implications of Culture in Management

THE NATURE AND FUNCTIONS OF STATUS
Status Differences in Organizations □ Functions of the Status System □ Symbols of Status □ Problems of Status

Summary □ Key Concepts □ Discussion Questions □ Notes □ Supplementary Reading

CASES: The Token Woman □ Coolaire Corporation

This chapter will enable you to

☐ Explain the human side of organizations and the nature of organizations as social systems.

☐ Understand the nature of informal power and the political processes involved in building and exercising such power.

☐ Analyze the effect of culture on the functioning and management of organizations.

☐ Describe the nature of status differences and contributions of status systems to organizational life.

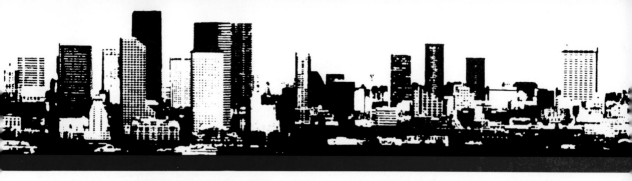

CHAPTER 12
ORGANIZATIONS AS SOCIAL SYSTEMS

An organization can be visualized as a series of productive operations and activities integrated by the organization's structure. This is a correct but incomplete notion of organized behavior. Although the formal structure specifies important relationships, it is merely the skeleton of the organization. The organization is a *social system,* and all formal and informal human relationships are important parts of the system. In this chapter, we broaden our view of organizations to emphasize the various aspects of human relationships which supplement the formal structure. Special attention is given to the informal, power-oriented behavior of managers and also to the concepts of culture and status as they relate to organizational life.

THE SOCIAL STRUCTURE OF ORGANIZATIONS

The Human Side of Organizations

An organization requires people to provide the mental and physical services necessary to accomplish its objectives. The official responsibilities and relationships of these people are indicated in a general way by an organization chart. The lines on such a chart represent *interpersonal* relationships, and these relationships provide the skeleton for the social structure. When we say that a laboratory supervisor reports to a department manager, this involves more than one box on a chart reporting to another box. It means that the individuals in these positions personally interact, with varying degrees of cooperation, conflict, and respect.

The *social structure* of an organization encompasses more than the formal superior-subordinate relationships. Any member of the organization also has contact with other members of the same organization. Two employees work side by side in a shop or share adjoining desks in an office. All of these informal relationships, if they continue over time, are a part of the social structure of the organization (Figure 12–1).

An organization, therefore, is more than a collection of individuals. To understand its nature, we must recognize social relationships and their significance. The highly personal nature of organizations became painfully clear to one college student on a summer job:

> I was employed as a forklift driver for one long, frustrating summer. Soon after being introduced to my work group, I knew I was in trouble. A clique had formed and, for some reason, resented college students. During lunch breaks and work breaks, I spent the whole time by myself. Each morning I dreaded going to work. The job paid well, but I was miserable.

Fortunately, most interpersonal relationships are less unpleasant, and many contribute positively to attainment of organizational goals.

FIGURE 12–1 Formal and informal relationships

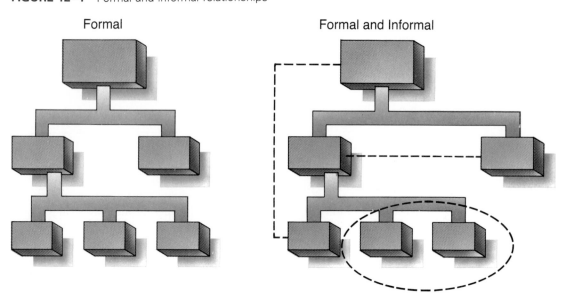

Formal

Formal and Informal

THE IMPORTANCE OF PEOPLE

Consider these recent comments:

> People don't fail due to lack of technical skills and energy. They are most often derailed because of people problems.

> In business, as in anything else, personalities and cultural norms, not P/E ratios and maximizing shareholder value, sometimes rule the game.

> It makes me sick to hear economists [tell students] that their job is to 'maximize shareholder profits.' Their job is going to be managing a whole host of constituencies: bosses, underlings, customers, suppliers, unions, you name it. Trying to get cooperation from different constituencies is an infinitely more difficult task than milking your business for money.

> I'd consider taking another [network television sports announcing] job, but it can be a very political situation, and I don't know if I want to deal with that again. If you don't want to have drinks with someone you don't like, it can be a tough business. There are a lot of people behind the scenes to deal with and they all demand some attention. If you don't give it to them, it can work against you, no matter how good you are on the air.

SOURCE: These comments, in order of appearance, were found in: statement by R. Peter Mercer, a human resources executive at General Electric, from "Fast-Track Kids," *Business Week,* 10 November 1986, p. 92; Mary Cunningham, *What Really Happened at Bendix* (New York: Fawcett Gold Medal, 1984), p. 313; statement by John Kotter, professor at the Harvard Business School, from "Playing Office Politics," *Newsweek,* 16 September 1985, p. 54; and statement by Kyle Rote, former pro football announcer for NBC, in "Kyle Rote: TV 'Politics' Not His Style," *The Houston Post,* 28 July 1985.

The Organization as a Social System

The effect of the Hawthorne Studies, described in chapter 2, was to turn a spotlight on the social structure of organizations. Using the insights of these experiments and of much subsequent research, management theorists now visualize organizations as social systems. According to this view, the social system of a hospital, store, or university has as its component parts the employees of those organizations. The component parts—that is, the people—function or work together through patterns of interaction that develop among the members. One part of an organization—say a drafting room or typing pool—is a social system, and the entire organization is also a social system. In other words, there are subsystems within social systems.

The functioning of a social system, however, is only partially prescribed by the formal organization. Employees devise arrangements and procedures that supplement or conflict with that formal structure. One important area, for instance, in which informal organizational processes differ significantly from the relationships described in the organization chart is *power*. In virtually all organizations, considerable power is wielded in an unofficial or informal way by certain employees or groups.

POWER AND POLITICS

Sources of Power

Many members of the organization—not just managers—possess power to some degree. This section explores why some people have more power than others. One well-known classification of the sources of power indicates that an individual can derive power from one or more of the following bases:[1]

☐ *Reward power*—an individual can influence the behavior of others because he or she has the ability to reward them for their cooperation.
☐ *Coercive power*—others cooperate with an individual because they fear that he or she will punish them for not cooperating.
☐ *Legitimate power*—cooperation occurs because the individual has been formally appointed or elected as the leader, and the followers have been conditioned to accept orders from the formal leader. The title of manager or supervisor automatically confers legitimate power (also known as authority) upon an individual.
☐ *Referent power*—an individual's charismatic personality is instrumental in causing others to cooperate because they admire the individual and wish to identify with him or her.
☐ *Expert power*—others cooperate with an individual because they believe that he or she is more expert or knowledgeable about a task than they are.

Subsequent additions to this list include the following:

☐ Power derived from one's access to important individuals and information.[2]
☐ Power through exchange (such as ingratiation or praise).
☐ Power by manipulation (where the recipient is not aware of being influenced).
☐ Power from persistence or assertiveness.
☐ Power by banding together to form a coalition.[3]

Examination of these lists indicates that power, unlike authority which is reserved for managers only, can be accumulated by virtually anyone in the organization. A computer programmer or secretary may, under some conditions, have considerably more power than a divisional manager. Regardless of who is wielding the power, the more bases of power the individual can draw upon, the greater will be his or her ability to influence the behavior of others.

Evidence about the relative effectiveness of various power bases is unclear. There is a positive relationship between the use of expert or referent power and subordinate satisfaction with supervision. Use of coercive power, on the other hand, is negatively related to or has no relationship with subordinate satisfaction. Beyond this knowledge, the evidence does not permit any generalizing.[4]

A Contingency View of Power

A somewhat more complex explanation of the origins of power is known as *strategic-contingencies theory.*[5] This view holds that the power of an individual or of a particular department or unit within an organization is contingent upon the problems and uncertainties facing the organization as a whole. According to this theory, power accrues to individuals and organizational components which cope with critical organization problems:[6]

> In its simplest form, the strategic-contingencies theory implies that when an organization faces a number of lawsuits that threaten its existence, the legal department will gain power and influence over organizational decisions. . . . In time, the head of the legal department may become the head of the corporation, just as in times past the vice-president for marketing had become the president when market shares were a worrisome problem and, before him, the chief engineer, who had made the production line run as smooth as silk.

In Figure 12–2, the greatest threat to the organization is posed by environmental force C. The impact of environmental forces varies; some create more critical threats than others. If force C constitutes the most critical threat, unit H, which must cope with force C, will tend to obtain necessary scarce resources and wield much power. To the extent that power develops as suggested by the strategic-contingencies theory, therefore, the various parts of an organization become more or less powerful.

In the insurance industry, for instance, the dominant environmental requirement is product/market adjustment and innovation. Insurance executives who are in marketing or product development have been found to have relatively great power within their management teams. By contrast, hospital executives who are in accounting, process improvement, or operations have relatively great power because they are situated to cope with their firm's dominant environmental requirement of efficiency/cost control.[7]

Strategic contingencies are not always associated with environmental forces. Problems and uncertainties can also arise from an organization's strategy, technology, or information flows. The organizational subsystems that cope with these contingencies are likely to accumulate power.

FIGURE 12–2 The impact of critical contingencies

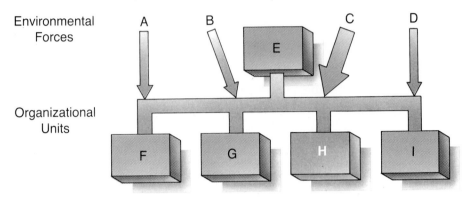

The Managerial Power Structure

The combination of formal authority and the informal, power-oriented activities of managers creates centers of power or influence in an organization. The framework incorporating these centers of influence might be called the *power structure*.

The power structure differs from the formal structure to the extent that the influence of particular units and individuals does not correspond perfectly to the formal structure. In view of variations in both situational and personal factors, some such discrepancy between formal position and power is to be expected. Rarely would six vice-presidents each have precisely the same influence over company policy.

Differences in relative power are readily recognized by people who work in various organizations. People generally agree about who is most powerful. The following comments reflect the view of two researchers who have analyzed perceptions of organizational power:[8]

> So far we have studied over 20 very different organizations—universities, research firms, factories, banks, retailers, to name a few. In each one we found individuals able to rate themselves and their peers on a scale of influence or power. . . . Their agreement was unusually high.

One of the classic studies of organizational power is Melville Dalton's analysis of the political activities and power structure in the Milo Fractionating Center, a fictitiously named industrial organization having 8,000 employees.[9] As a part of his study, Dalton rated the relative influence of various members of the management team. Their influence did not always correspond to their formal positions. As an example, he found that the assistant plant manager (Hardy) held power equal to that of his boss, the plant manager (Stevens). Following is Dalton's explanation of the Hardy-Stevens relationship:[10]

In executive meetings, Stevens clearly was less forceful than Hardy. Appearing nervous and worried, Stevens usually opened meetings with a few remarks and then silently gave way to Hardy who dominated thereafter. During the meeting most questions were directed to Hardy. While courteous, Hardy's statements usually were made without request for confirmation from Stevens. Hardy and Stevens and other high officers daily lunched together. There, too, Hardy dominated the conversations and was usually the target of questions. This was not just an indication that he carried the greater burden of *minor* duties often assigned to assistants in some firms, for he had a hand in most issues, including major ones. Other items useful in appraising Hardy and Stevens were their relative *(a)* voice in promotions, *(b)* leadership in challenging staff projects, *(c)* force in emergencies, *(d)* escape as a butt of jokes and name-calling, *(e)* knowledge of subordinates, *(f)* position in the firm's social and community activities.

It is clear from Dalton's study that centers of power are not always evident on the surface and cannot be read with assurance from the organization chart. Only careful observation of the functioning of the organization reveals the true power centers and the extent to which they differ from the formal structure.

Power-Oriented Behavior and Job Dependency

Managers engage in various types of power-oriented behavior to augment their official authority. Their activities are often described as "political." Unfortunately, the word *politics* has a connotation of unethical conduct. As used here, however, the word describes the manner in which positions of power are established and influence is exerted in the administrative process; that is, there is no implication of the use of power for undesirable ends. Any intentional action that an individual or group takes to promote or protect self-interest is considered political behavior.

The extent to which a person engages in political activity depends upon that person's vulnerability. The nature of such vulnerability is not always evident. The following account by a manager describes his own feelings of dependency on others:[11]

> In retrospect (after a year and a half on the job), it is hard to believe how little I really did know. For example, Helen Wagner wasn't in any picture book or on any organization chart, but she is about as important as anyone to the success of the acquisition that I'm working on now. Helen is (Executive VP) Phil Peter's secretary. Phil is my boss on this project. A variety of key decisions that I have to clear through him come up occasionally and demand a reasonably quick or very quick response. Phil's office is in Manhattan in our headquarters building, and so my access to him on the phone or by memo is through Helen. And as you can imagine, he is very busy and gets lots of phone calls and mail. Helen is responsible for making judgments regarding priorities. She's got the power to make my life very difficult.

Managers who are highly dependent on many others for success must spend more time building relationships and "mending fences" than managers who can personally control their own resources. Figure 12–3 portrays the contrasting circumstances of a plant manager X with few dependencies and a hospital manager Y with many dependencies. The two managers differ sharply in the time they spend to make sure that others "cooperate" with them. John Kotter described the contrast as follows:[12]

> Whereas Y spent close to 80 percent of her day in activities that related directly to acquiring and maintaining power or to using it to influence others, X spent about 25 to 30 percent of his time in those activities.

Kotter concluded that "the larger the number of job-related dependencies, the more time and energy the management incumbent tends to put into power-oriented behavior to cope with those dependencies."[13]

Vulnerability may also arise out of organizational change. Evidence indicates that political behavior increases during periods of organizational instability.[14] A dramatic move by competitors, a significant change in top management, a new technological development, or a reduction in sales revenue can all disturb the equilibrium of an organization and increase the vulnerability of a manager. To reduce that vulnerability, the manager attempts to accumulate power.

Techniques of Building and Using Political Power

Managers use various methods of building power and exerting that power to achieve their goals. For example, they create obligations by doing favors for others, as in this case:[15]

> Most of the people here would walk over hot coals in their bare feet if my boss asked them to. He has an incredible capacity to do little things that mean a lot to people. Today, for example, in his junk mail he came across an advertisement for something that one of my subordinates had in passing once mentioned that he was shopping for. So my boss routed it to him. That probably took 15 seconds of his time, and yet my subordinate really appreciated it. To give you another example, two weeks ago he somehow learned that the purchasing manager's mother had died. On his way home that night, he stopped off at the funeral parlor. Our purchasing manager was, of course, there at the time. I bet he'll remember that brief visit for quite a while.

Not all favors are personal favors. The manager's role in the organization may involve the provision of official services—the personnel manager who recruits capable personnel, for example. Such services may be performed in such a way that the recipient correctly perceives his or her dependence upon the personnel manager. In various ways, a manager may "take care" of others, who will respond with feelings of loyalty.

FIGURE 12–3 Dependence (high, medium, or low) inherent in two managerial jobs

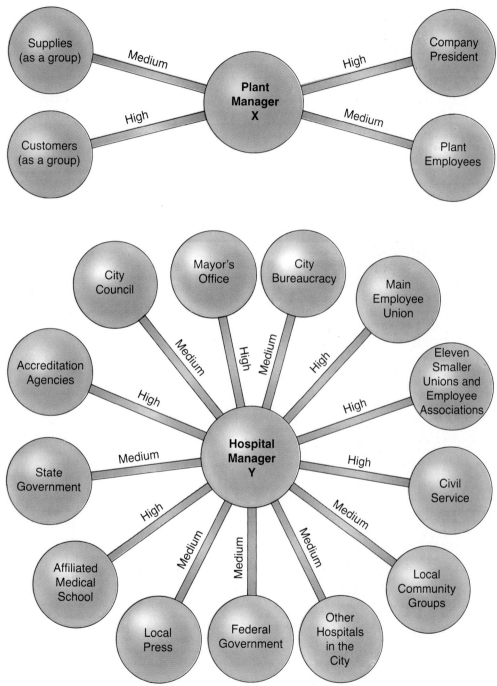

SOURCE: Reprinted, by permission of the publisher, from "Power, Success, and Organizational Effectiveness," John P. Kotter, *Organizational Dynamics* 6 (Winter 1978), p. 29. © 1978. American Management Association, New York. All rights reserved.

A manager's political activities may be directed toward control of subordinates, colleagues, and even superiors. Mintzberg has identified a number of political "games" that managers might play. For instance, a manager might build a power base with a superior by closely associating with the boss, trading loyalty in return for power (i.e., the "sponsorship game"). Managerial peers might negotiate implicit contracts of support for one another to advance themselves in the organization (i.e., the "alliance building game"). Managers and nonmanagers alike can exploit their technical skills and knowledge, emphasizing their uniqueness, criticality, and irreplaceability to build power bases (i.e., the "expertise game").[16]

Managers engage in various forms of informal activity, therefore, to supplement the power of their organizational positions. Managers' total power,

DEMONSTRATING ONE'S POWER

When young Tim Babcock was put in charge of a division of a large manufacturing company and told to "turn it around," he spent the first few weeks studying it from afar. He decided that the division was in disastrous shape and that he would need to take many large steps quickly to save it. To be able to do that, he realized he needed to develop considerable power fast over most of the division's management and staff. He did the following:

☐ He gave the division's management two hours' notice of his arrival.
☐ He arrived in a limousine with six assistants.
☐ He immediately called a meeting of the forty top managers.
☐ He outlined briefly his assessment of the situation, his commitment to turn things around, and the basic direction he wanted things to move in.
☐ He then fired the four top managers in the room and told them that they had to be out of the building in two hours.
☐ He then said he would personally dedicate himself.to sabotaging the career of anyone who tried to block his efforts to save the division.
☐ He ended the 60-minute meeting by announcing that his assistants would set up appointments for him with each of them starting at 7:00 A.M. the next morning.

Throughout the critical six-month period that followed, those who remained at the division generally cooperated energetically with Mr. Babcock.

SOURCE: Reprinted by permission of Harvard Business Review. Excerpt from "Power, Dependence, and Effective Management" by John P. Kotter (July-August 1977). Copyright © 1977 by the President and Fellows of Harvard College; all rights reserved.

then, involves a combination of their formal authority and their unofficial power developed and exerted in less obvious, informal ways.

Informal Power and Organizational Effectiveness

Informal power-oriented activities of managers can contribute to or interfere with the achievement of organizational goals. Authority is granted to those in positions of leadership so they can function effectively in coordinating organizational activities. Informal power may be used for the same purpose and thereby contribute to organizational effectiveness.

Organizational politics, for instance, can be used to overcome vested interests and promote change that will enhance the effectiveness of the organization. Politics can also be instrumental in correcting the irresponsibility or inefficiency of superiors or in ensuring that all sides of an issue are effectively aired. Senior managers can use political alliances to gain acceptance of their decisions.[17]

On the other hand, informal power may damage organizational relationships and reduce overall effectiveness. The company politician may be more concerned with the advancement of personal interests than those of the organization[18] To prevent such situations from getting out of hand to the extent that political activities dominate rather than supplement normal management processes and personal ambition supplants organizational goals, top management must sense and prevent extreme or self-seeking forms of political action. A program of objective evaluation of subordinates is one essential safeguard against the destructive company politician. Political intrigue that subordinates organizational goals to narrow personal objectives must be rejected. The climate must prevent an abuse of political power. This is difficult to accomplish, because political action is often carefully camouflaged and rationalized.

ORGANIZATIONAL CULTURE

The way an organization functions is affected not only by the power of managers but also by underlying cultural forces. Organizational culture regulates the way in which the firm's members go about their work and even the way in which managers build and exercise power.

What Is Culture?

In a general sense, *culture* consists of the behavior patterns and values of a social group. These are patterns of belief and behavior that have been learned from other members of the society. They are, as the cultural anthropologist would say, socially transmitted.

An organization functions within the cultural system of the society in which it is located. The expectations of the surrounding community about the establishments located within it are based on the community's cultural traditions. Employees bring into the firm the cultural values they have assimilated from the community. Both the community and the employees are inclined to expect some conformity to prevailing cultural values.

But organizational culture is more than simply a reflection of broader social values and expectations. Organizations within the same industry and city often exhibit distinctly different ways of operating:[19]

> All one has to do to get a feel for how the different cultures of competing businesses manifest themselves is to spend a day visiting each. Of course there are patterns in the trivia of variations in dress, jargon, and style—but there is something else going on as well. There are characteristic ways of making decisions, relating to bosses, and choosing people to fill key jobs.

Over time, each organization evolves its own culture, the basis of which lies in the assumptions about success that were held by the founders of the organization. With the passage of time, these assumptions are modified as organization members learn from experience. An organization's current set of values, beliefs, and behaviors, then, reflects an interaction between the founder's assumptions and the organization's subsequent history.[20]

Organizational culture is reflected not only in the behavior of employees but also in the artifacts created by the organization. The physical design of a building and its offices and furnishings, for example, reflect the organization's culture:[21]

> A building gives occupants and visitors messages about what the company does, how it works, and what it believes in. . . . [Buildings] tell people how the company operates, what it values, and where it has been and is going.

For example, the belief that open communication and close working relationships are important is reflected in the open designs of the headquarters of such companies as Levi Strauss in California and Corning Glass Works in New York.[22]

An important value at PepsiCo, for instance, is winning. New employees quickly learn that the fastest path to success lies in beating their competition—both inside and outside the company. A "creative tension" is fostered among departments, and "careers ride on tenths of a market share point." Furthermore, "consistent runners-up find their jobs gone. Employees know they must win merely to stay in place—and must devastate the competition to get ahead."[23]

These values are consistent with PepsiCo's strategic direction. Managers are given considerable autonomy and are encouraged to move quickly to take advantage of opportunities. These quick reflexes are of paramount importance in marketing consumer products and have made PepsiCo one of the premier marketing firms in the world.[24]

Implications of Culture in Management

Organizational culture can facilitate or hinder the firm's strategic actions. Because culture reflects the past, periods of environmental change often require significant modification of the organization's culture. It is essential that changes in strategy be accompanied by corresponding alterations in organizational culture. Otherwise the strategy is likely to fail. Conservative organizations do not become aggressive, entrepreneurial firms simply because they have formulated new goals and plans.

For example, the success of General Foods owed much to an emphasis on cost control and earnings improvement. In the 1980s, the company found it necessary to develop a strategy that emphasized diversification and growth. To facilitate the change, the organization revised its compensation system (to link bonuses to increases in sales volume rather than just to increased earnings); decentralized decisions on spending for new products, advertising, and some capital investments; increased its emphasis on product development; and sent its managers to marketing and product seminars.[25]

Culture can even provide an excuse for inaction. Whorton and Worthley suggest that the culture of management in the public sector is composed of "if-onlys" and "thems." These may be offered as excuses for nonperformance or failure.[26] Such excuses reflect the numerous constraints under which managers in government operate. "If-onlys" are illustrated by such statements as:

□ "If only I could fire Jones, then we could get this department in shape." (reflects Civil Service constraints)
□ "If only the budget division would stop setting expenditure ceilings." (reflects legislative constraints)

"Thems" refer to the adversaries of public managers—that is, those groups which influence or set the constraints, including politicians, the press, consumer groups, and so on. As Whorton and Worthley explain:[27]

> ["If onlys" and "thems"] foster an elaborate myth that insulates the organization from its environment by creating the expectancy that performance will always be something less than it could be.
> When fully institutionalized as part of the culture, if-onlys and thems can produce a wholly negative focus and become defense mechanisms for resisting change and denying the possibility that new technologies might improve organizational performance.

Continuing organizational performance and success depend heavily upon the organizational culture appropriate for the current environment. What was, at one time, a facilitative culture vis-à-vis the environment may because of changing conditions become a barrier to continued organizational effectiveness.

A CLASH OF CULTURES

Mergers between two organizations often seem easier to accomplish on paper than in reality. Reality often reveals that the cultures of the organizations and the personalities of their top executives fail to mesh as easily as corporate assets. In no case has this situation been more dramatically illustrated than in the 1984 merger of Electronic Data Systems (EDS) into General Motors.

The merger brought together two disparate cultures. Bureaucratic, tradition-bound, "by-the-book" GM found itself attempting to absorb a far smaller firm best characterized as possessing a "can do, anything is possible," entrepreneurial spirit.

A cultural clash was inevitable. Dallas-based EDS, a nonunion firm, had an extremely stringent hiring and selection process followed by a grueling trial and training period that could last as long as two years. Those who survived displayed unusually high morale and a devotion for doing whatever was required to accomplish the task.

GM's white-collar workers, accustomed to automatic pay raises and cost-of-living adjustments, felt threatened by the EDS practice of rewarding only job performance. GM employees were taken aback by the hard-driving competitiveness of the EDS workers with their unquestioning adherence to rigid dress and personal grooming codes. As reported in *The Wall Street Journal*, "In some ways, EDS merging with GM is like a Green Beret outfit joining up with the Social Security Administration."

Frustrated by GM's slowness to change, top-level executives at EDS—particularly its founder and chairman, H. Ross Perot—began to criticize GM publicly. Finally, GM's management and board had had enough. Perot was about to publicly chastise the GM board for considering paying end-of-the-year (1986) bonuses to senior management following a $338.5 million operating loss in the preceding quarter and a decision to lay off 29,000 workers. To forestall that criticism, the board voted unanimously to pay Perot about $700 million to leave EDS, and an additional $50 million to buy out three other EDS executives. As part of the agreement, Perot faced a fine of up to $7.5 million if he continued to criticize GM in public.

SOURCE: Based on Laurie P. Cohen and Charles F. McCoy, "Perot's Singular Style Raises Issue of How He'll Fit at GM," *The Wall Street Journal,* 2 July 1984 (source of quotation); Damon Darlin and Melinda Grenier Guiles, "Some GM People Feel Auto Firm, Not EDS, Was the One Acquired," *The Wall Street Journal,* 19 December 1984; "How Ross Perot's Shock Troops Ran Into Flak At GM," *Business Week,* 11 February 1985, pp. 118–22; "GM Boots Perot" and "Perot to Smith: GM Must Change," *Newsweek,* 15 December 1986, pp. 56–62; and "GM Hasn't Bought Much Peace" and "The Risks of Running EDS Without Perot," *Business Week,* 15 December 1986, pp. 24–27.

THE NATURE AND FUNCTIONS OF STATUS

One aspect of culture involves judgments of the relative importance of various individuals, roles, and groups. *Status* is concerned with an entity's prestige or standing within some larger entity. Examples are the standing of a person within a department or the standing of a department within an organization. Deference is generally shown to the person or group with higher status.

Different people use different weights or values in their individual judgments regarding status. Technically, therefore, there are as many different status systems as there are individuals making judgments of this variety. We often simplify this process, however, by making generalizations about status. These generalizations express a consensus regarding the status of particular persons, positions, occupations, or groups.

Status Differences in Organizations

Two kinds of status have been suggested by Chester I. Barnard.[28] The first of these, *functional* status, is based upon the type of work or activity performed. The professional, such as an engineer or attorney, enjoys greater prestige than nonprofessional members of the organization. The craftsperson has a higher status than the unskilled employee. There may also be status differences between line and staff positions or between jobs at the headquarters and those in branch offices.

Scalar status, on the other hand, is concerned with the level in the organization's hierarchy or chain of command. Positions near the top of the organization chart generally have higher status than those that are lower.

Barnard's two types of status are both descriptive of the position, regardless of the incumbent. A third variety might be designated as *personal* status. Although formal position, by virtue of its scalar and functional qualities, goes a long way in determining an individual's status, status may be augmented or reduced by the individual's personal characteristics. When a brilliant or distinguished person replaces a lackluster incumbent, the replacement enjoys higher status even though the position is unchanged. Some presidents of the United States, for instance, have had higher status than others; that is, they were perceived to be more competent and were held in greater esteem. Although neither functional nor scalar status is changed, a new president's energy, appearance, or personality may produce greater personal status than the predecessor's.

Functions of the Status System

Although status systems often seem undemocratic, they are a reality in organizations and sometimes play constructive roles. Two of their positive contributions relate to communication and motivation.

Communication. The existence of a status system makes possible effective and authoritative communication. Someone must provide direction and coordination to members of work organizations. The status system permits an understanding of who is to lead and who is to follow.

Motivation. The status system and the symbols of status that pervade society also provide strong motivation. Few individuals are content with the status quo, and aspirations for advancement are as linked with conceptions of status as with hopes of material gain. Most people think it is important to live in the "right" section of the city and drive a type of car befitting their positions.

The rise in the standard of living may have changed the nature of the status symbols, but it has hardly eliminated status distinctions. No matter how much we may disparage status differences, we must recognize their powerful influence as a motivational force. Achievement in society results from such motivation.

Symbols of Status

Status levels are indicated by various indicators closely connected with the individual. These *symbols* permit an observer to understand the status of the person in question.

Vice-presidents have offices that are not only private but larger than those of lower officials. Office furnishings similarly reveal status distinctions. At some level, offices are carpeted, and metal desks give way to wooden desks. Draperies at the window and paintings on the wall are also symbolic of prestige. Potted plants, lounge chairs, private washrooms, and adjoining private conference rooms all suggest the prestige of the person occupying the office.

Various privileges also indicate status level. Many employees, for example, punch a time clock, but higher-level employees are not required to do so.

Status symbols communicate the consensus of the organization regarding status, providing cues to both organization members and visitors concerning the relative status of employees. The result is predictability and order in interpersonal relationships throughout the organization.

Problems of Status

Although status performs constructive functions, it can also create problems. Indeed, some observers are so conscious of its weaknesses that they refer to the *pathology* of status. One important negative feature concerns the *social distance* between organization levels. When social distance is great, a subordinate may feel that the superior is detached or aloof or "living in another world." Even though some authoritative communication is desirable, organization levels must work together in achieving the objectives of the organization. It is possible, consequently, that status distinctions may be emphasized to the point that active cooperation is reduced. The subordinate may follow orders but find it difficult to work closely with higher levels. An individual may also become so preoccupied with status symbols that the entire system is run into the ground. Getting a private office or a staff assistant or a desktop computer becomes important in and of itself, and little regard is paid to the need for these symbolic trappings.

Members of an organization may also experience feelings of anxiety as a result of status considerations. One's status may appear undesirable, and the person may feel powerless to change it. Whatever the reason, the inability to improve one's status may produce a sense of frustration within that individual. This feeling may be described as *status anxiety. Status inconsistency* may also lead to anxiety. The title of the position may be right, for example, but the incumbent may lack a private office that seems appropriate for the particular level. Such status problems can create unhappiness and reduce organizational efficiency.

SUMMARY

The Hawthorne Studies increased our understanding of the social nature of business organizations. These experiments demonstrated that organizations are *social systems* in which relationships among people are extremely significant in determining organizational behavior. As social systems, organizations include not only *formal* groups and relationships but also *informal* groupings and relationships that supplement the formally prescribed structure.

Formal authority conferred by the organization is supplemented by informal, power-oriented activity of organization members. Not only do managers possess power to varying degrees, but nonmanagerial members may also accumulate power. The more bases of power an individual can draw upon, the greater will be his or her ability to influence the behavior of others. According to the *strategic-contingencies theory,* the greatest organizational power accrues to individuals and organizational components which cope with the most critical threats or problems confronting organizations.

The *power structure* of an organization may be similar to the formal organization, but differences exist in the case of those who hold more or less power than the formal structure confers upon them. Organizational power is derived not only from a formal position of authority, but also from informal and political relationships and activities.

Organizational culture reflects not only societal values and expectations but also the unique set of values, beliefs, and behaviors that characterizes each organization. Organizational culture can facilitate or hinder the firm's strategic actions. Because culture reflects the past, periods of environmental change often require significant modification of the organization's culture.

Status refers to gradations in standing or rank that exist in any group. Status is *scalar, functional,* and *personal* and is determined by a combination of organizational and personal factors. The status system performs useful functions in organizations and in society generally. Status levels are communicated by means of *symbols*, which include not only official titles but also such privileges and physical trappings as private offices and lunchroom privileges. Although it performs useful functions, the status system also involves problems of *social distance* between organizational levels, preoccupation with status symbols, and *status anxiety*.

KEY CONCEPTS

Social system	Organizational culture
Power	Status
Authority	Functional status
Strategic-contingencies theory	Scalar status
Power structure	Personal status
Politics	Status symbols
Dependency	

DISCUSSION QUESTIONS

1. Refer to some organization with which you are familiar. Describe both its formal structure and informal structure.
2. Explain the concept of an organization as a *social system.*
3. Explain how a nonmanagerial member of an organization might accumulate *power.* Is there any base of power not available to a nonmanager?
4. How does *strategic-contingencies theory* explain the relative power of various organization components?
5. What is the *power structure,* and why may it differ from an accurately drawn organization chart?
6. The term "playing politics" is often used in a negative sense. Is playing politics inherently bad or unethical?
7. Explain carefully the concept of *organizational culture.*
8. What is the relationship between organization *strategy* and *culture?*
9. What is the basic distinction between *functional* status and *scalar* status?
10. Do you believe that the average American works more for money (and the goods and services that money will buy) or for status and the symbols that signify status?

NOTES

1. John R. P. French, Jr., and Bertram Raven, "The Bases of Social Power," in *Studies in Social Power,* ed. D. Cartwright (Ann Arbor, Mich.: University of Michigan Press, 1959): pp. 150–67.

2. David Mechanic, "Sources of Power of Lower Participants in Complex Organizations," *Administrative Science Quarterly* 7 (December 1962): 353.

3. For an overview of the literature in this area, see Warren K. Schilit and Edwin A. Locke, "A Study of Upward Influence in Organizations," *Administrative Science Quarterly* 27 (June 1982): 304–16.

4. Philip M. Podsakoff and Chester A. Schriesheim, "Field Studies of French and Raven's Bases of Power: Critique, Reanalysis, and Suggestions for Future Research," *Psychological Bulletin* 97 (May 1985): 387–411.

5. D. J. Hickson et al., "A Strategic Contingencies Theory of Intraorganizational Power," *Administrative Science Quarterly* 16 (June 1971): 216–29.

6. Gerald R. Salancik and Jeffrey Pfeffer, "Who Gets Power—And How They Hold On To It: A Strategic-Contingency Model of Power," *Organizational Dynamics* 5 (Winter 1977): 5.

7. Donald C. Hambrick, "Environment, Strategy, and Power within Top Management Teams," *Administrative Science Quarterly* 26 (June 1981): 253–75.

8. Salancik and Pfeffer, "Who Gets Power," p. 4.

9. Melville Dalton, *Men Who Manage* (New York: Wiley, 1959).

10. Ibid., p. 23.

11. Reprinted, by permission of the publisher, from "Power, Success and Organization Effectiveness," John P. Kotter, *Organizational Dynamics* 6 (Winter 1978), p. 31. © 1978. American Management Association, New York. All rights reserved.

12. Ibid., p. 30.

13. Ibid.

14. Henry Mintzberg, "The Organization as Political Arena," *Journal of Management Studies* 22 (March 1985): 142–32; and Kenneth D. MacKenzie, "Virtual Positions and Power," *Management Science* 32 (May 1986): 629.

15. Reprinted by permission of Harvard Business Review. Excerpt from "Power, Dependence, and Effective Management" by John P. Kotter (July-August 1977). Copyright © 1977 by the President and Fellows of Harvard College; all rights reserved.

16. Mintzberg, "The Organization as Political Arena," pp. 134–39.

17. Ibid., pp. 148–50.

18. For an examination of the ethics of organizational politics, see Gerald F. Cavanagh, Dennis J. Moberg, and Manuel Velasquez, "The Ethics of Organizational Politics," *Academy of Management Review* 6 (July 1981): 363–74.

19. Howard Schwartz and Stanley M. Davis, "Matching Corporate Culture and Business Strategy," *Organizational Dynamics* 10 (Summer 1981): 30.

20. Edgar H. Schein, "The Role of the Founder in Creating Organizational Culture," *Organizational Dynamics* 12 (Summer 1983): 14.

21. John A. Seiler, "Architecture at Work," *Harvard Business Review* 62 (September-October 1984): 114, 120.

22. Reported in Tim R. V. Davis, "The Influence of the Physical Environment in Offices," *Academy of Management Review* 9 (April 1984): 273.

23. "Corporate Culture: The Hard-to-Change Values That Spell Success or Failure," *Business Week,* 27 October 1980, pp. 148; 151; 154 (quotes are from pp. 151 and 148).

24. "Pepsi's Marketing Magic: Why Nobody Does It Better," *Business Week,* 10 February 1986, pp. 52–57.

25. "Changing the Culture at General Foods," *Business Week,* 30 March 1981, pp. 136; 140.

26. Joseph W. Whorton and John A. Worthley, "A Perspective on the Challenge of Public Management: Environmental Paradox and Organizational Culture," *Academy of Management Review* 6 (July 1981): 359–60.

27. Ibid., p. 360.

28. Chester I. Barnard, *Organization and Management* (Cambridge: Harvard University Press, 1948), pp. 209–10.

SUPPLEMENTARY READING

Astley, W. Graham, and Sachdeva, Paramjit S. "Structural Sources of Intraorganizational Power: A Theoretical Synthesis." *Academy of Management Review* 9 (January 1984): 104–13.

Barney, Jay B. "Organizational Culture: Can It Be a Source of Sustained Competitive Advantage?" *Academy of Management Review* 11 (July 1986): 656–65.

Biggart, Nicole Woolsey, and Hamilton, Gary G. "The Power of Obedience." *Administrative Science Quarterly* 29 (December 1984): 540–49.

Blackburn, Richard S. "Lower Participant Power: Toward a Conceptual Integration." *Academy of Management Review* 6 (January 1981): 127–31.

Brass, Daniel J. "Being in the Right Place: A Structural Analysis of Individual Influence in an Organization." *Administrative Science Quarterly* 29 (December 1984): 518–39.

Buono, Anthony F.; Bowditch, James L.; and Lewis, John W., III. "When Cultures Collide: The Anatomy of a Merger." *Human Relations* 38 (May 1985): 477–500.

Cavanagh, Gerald F.; Moberg, Dennis J.; and Velasquez, Manuel. "The Ethics of Organizational Politics." *Academy of Management Review* 6 (July 1981): 363–74.

Collins, Eliza G. C. "Managers and Lovers." *Harvard Business Review* 61 (September-October 1983): 142–53.

Davis, Tim R. V. "The Influence of the Physical Environment in Offices." *Academy of Management Review* 9 (April 1984): 271–83.

Farrell, Dan, and Petersen, James C. "Patterns of Political Behavior in Organizations." *Academy of Management Review* 7 (July 1982): 403–12.

MacKenzie, Kenneth D. "Virtual Positions and Power." *Management Science* 32 (May 1986): 622–42.

Mintzberg, Henry. "The Organization as Political Arena." *Journal of Management Studies* 22 (March 1985): 133–54.

Murray, Victor, and Gandz, Jeffrey. "Games Executives Play: Politics at Work." *Business Horizons* 23 (December 1980): 11–23.

Schein, Edgar H. "Coming to a New Awareness of Organizational Culture." *Sloan Management Review* 25 (Winter 1984): 3–16.

Schilit, Warren Keith. "An Examination of Individual Differences as Moderators of Upward Influence Activity in Strategic Decisions." *Human Relations* 39 (October 1986): 933–53.

Schwartz, Howard, and Davis, Stanley M. "Matching Corporate Culture and Business Strategy." *Organizational Dynamics* 10 (Summer 1981): 30–48.

Vredenburgh, Donald J., and Maurer, John G. "A Process Framework of Organizational Politics." *Human Relations* 37 (January 1984): 47–66.

Wiley, Mary Glenn, and Eskilson, Arlene. "The Interaction of Sex and Power Base on Perceptions of Managerial Effectiveness." *Academy of Management Journal* 25 (September 1982): 671–77.

THE TOKEN WOMAN

The Mainstream Life Insurance Company, to forestall possible affirmative action pressure because of the lack of women in the insurance industry's managerial ranks, decided to actively recruit a woman to fill a recent opening in the Research Division of the company's Trust Department. The vacant research analyst position is one of several middle-management jobs at Mainstream that traditionally have been the stepping-stone for promotion to the executive rank.

The required credentials for this particular opening in the Research Division are an MBA degree (or a comparable graduate degree with a major emphasis in finance), at least two years of academic or business experience, and proven research capability in the investment field. An exhaustive search and meticulous screening resulted in the hiring of Claire Meredith, an attractive 27-year-old single woman whose MS degree in finance was awarded "with distinction" (i.e., with high honors) and whose master's thesis was published by a prestigious university press. Meredith was previously employed as a broker in a highly respected Wall Street investment banking firm. In addition, she had written numerous articles as a result of extensive theoretical and applied research projects. Mainstream was able to hire Meredith only after John Forbes, her potential immediate boss, assured her of equal opportunity on all possible levels. Additional inducement was supplied by the starting salary, $2,000 higher than her other recent employment offers.

Case prepared by Professor Linda Pickthorne Fletcher of Louisiana State University and Professor Susan M. Phillips of the University of Iowa.

At the end of her third month on the job, Meredith privately acknowledged a pervasive feeling of frustration in connection with her new position. She began reviewing the activities of the past three months to determine the basis of her negative reaction.

During the first day on the job, each of Meredith's colleagues had expressed enthusiastic delight at having her "on board." One colleague observed that "it's high time the company hired a woman for our section—we've needed some beautification of the office for a long time now." Another chimed in with the remark that "we better tell our wives that Claire is married so they won't think we're researching monkey business!" When Meredith in reply suggested that they all have lunch together, Roy James, a division programmer, told her that "each of the guys brings a brown bag for lunch and we eat and talk shop in one or the other's office." Accordingly, she decided to emulate her colleagues and announced that she was joining the brown bag league. She was surprised, therefore, when at noon the following day Roy James opened his office door and urged, "Come on, you guys, let's research our brown bags—Frank, you and Jim get the coffee while David and I get the ice cream, and don't forget Don wants double cream in his coffee." Since Claire's name was not mentioned specifically, she decided—after some hesitation—to eat alone in her office. Meredith did not feel she should join the secretaries and clerks for lunch although she knew she would be welcome. This routine, with minor variations, was then the established pattern.

Breaks for coffee in the company cafeteria were no exception to the seemingly established separation principle—only once in that three-month interval had Meredith been invited to join her colleagues for coffee. At that particular coffee break, she remembered, she felt particularly uncomfortable. Although she felt she had an excellent working relationship with her associates, she had little in common with them outside of the work environment. In addition, it was quite obvious that the men in the division seemed to plan social gatherings for both after work and the week-ends. Although her colleagues were very friendly in the office, they never seemed to think to include her in their plans.

Having reviewed the informal social structure of her employment, Claire recognized similar frustrations with respect to various functions of her position. She recalled John Forbes, head of the Research Division, explaining the operational features of the section: "We meet once a week in committee to determine the status of current projects, discuss proposals for the future, and make individual assignments of new research projects to be initiated. Any ideas you have—write them up in memo form for distribution to everyone prior to the next meeting, and we'll all go over your suggestion at the earliest possible meeting to determine the feasibility of your idea."

Because she was the most recent addition to the staff, Meredith deliberately maintained a low profile during the first few weekly committee meetings of the Research Division. The other members of the committee appeared to endorse her strategy by seeking her opinions only infrequently and by failing to draw her into their policy deliberations. At the fourth gathering, John Forbes noted that his secretary was unable to be present to record the minutes of the meeting. Frank Howard suggested sending for a replacement from the secretarial pool, but Forbes shook his head and casually

replied that "a replacement is unnecessary since the logical substitute is Ms. Meredith—besides, brushing up on her shorthand will give her something to do during the meeting." Meredith hastened to observe that "since I do not know shorthand, I must decline the honor of this additional responsibility." At this point, she recalled, she decided to abandon her sideline role at the next meeting by presenting a research proposal she had been developing in the area of commission reduction through utilization of regional exchanges.

To date, her specific assignments include responsibility for several ongoing projects which require little attention. The major portion of her time, however, is spent on Cost Allocation, a computer system which will, when completed, provide complete investment information for each of Mainstream's trust customers. All trust funds are pooled for investment purposes. The pooling is necessary since some of the trust accounts are so small that investment income would be difficult to generate for these accounts. Any income would virtually be "wiped out" by the commission expenses of such small transactions.

The current method of determining investment income for each trust account is to apply the average new investment rate to the pro rata portion of each account's share of the total investment funds. Consequently, several of Mainstream's larger trust accounts had complained that their investment income was "supporting" the smaller accounts. Threatened with the loss of these large accounts, the financial vice-president of Mainstream, Bill Newbit, instructed John Forbes to develop some type of allocation system so that each account could be properly charged with expenses while simultaneously enjoying the income of the pooled investment.

John Forbes developed the specifications for the system and then turned over the design and programming to a research analyst, who resigned several months before Meredith joined the division. She later found out through the grapevine that he had quit because he felt he was getting nowhere with Cost Allocation. Claire recalled that when she was hired, she was told she would have full responsibility for the completion of the system, including supervising the programming by Roy James, developing comprehensive test data, and ultimately getting the system on line. Since investment income for each account was currently calculated by hand under the supervision of Frank Howard, Meredith anticipated the usual problems of employee resistance to a new computer system. She therefore had begun some orientation classes for the personnel involved. Meredith had determined that the existing personnel, with training, would be adequate to use and run the new system effectively. No personnel displacement would be necessary.

Meredith was currently in the final stages of testing the system with Roy James. When she took the first run of test data into John Forbes, he expressed complete surprise. He admitted, "I can't believe that Cost Allocation has ever gotten off the ground.

This system has been knocking around for three years—we had just about counted the $800,000 developmental costs spent so far as sunk. In fact, we were going to write them off this year. I guess we'll have to start thinking about moving on this thing . . . manpower planning and so on."

When Meredith left John Forbes's office, she was shocked and disappointed by his reaction. As she reviewed his comments, she began to wonder just what she was supposed to be doing at Mainstream and how she could go about doing it.

Questions

1. Describe and evaluate the informal structure of the Research Division of the Trust Department and its effect on Meredith's relationships.
2. Why was Meredith hired?
3. Discuss Meredith's role in the weekly policy committee meetings. How might she change her established role in these meetings?
4. Why was Meredith disappointed at Forbes's reaction to the first run of test data?
5. What should Meredith do about her feelings of job frustration?

COOLAIRE CORPORATION

Phil Waverly was just beginning to figure it all out. Somehow he had become caught in the middle of something he sensed as

From Daniel Robey, *Designing Organizations*, 2nd ed. (Homewood, Ill.: Richard D. Irwin, 1986), pp. 571–74. © Richard D. Irwin, Inc., 1986. All rights reserved.

impending disaster. There was no way he could fulfill the biggest service contract his branch had ever seen with the personnel and resources allocated to the project. His service technicians were already working 12 hours of overtime each week, and the office staff had fallen three weeks behind in its paperwork. On top of this, three senior technicians, each with over 10 years of service, had just resigned because of job pressures. Two of the branch's most competent clerks had also quit recently. With profits rapidly eroding, Phil felt powerless to change anything. But at least he was beginning to see how it all began.

Phil Waverly is the manager of one of the Coolaire Corporation's largest regional branches. The Coolaire Corporation, one of the world's major manufacturers of air conditioning and refrigeration equipment, surpassed $2 billion in gross sales for the first time in 1987. In 1988, Coolaire was acquired by means of an unfriendly takeover by a large multinational conglomerate, Allied Industrials. Coolaire became the fourth major section of the Allied empire, the other three being the Allied Power Group, the Allied Electronics Group, and National Elevators.

Coolaire's Machinery and Systems Division comprises two departments with parallel structures: sales and service. The service department's role in the organization is to maintain large-capacity industrial refrigeration and air-conditioning equipment manufactured by Coolaire, and some of that manufactured by the organization's competitors as well. At the local branch level of the service department are the technicians, clerks, and secretaries. These people report to service supervisors. The service supervisors report to branch managers who are responsible for 10 to 40 employees and from $1 to $4 million of Coolaire's business. Anywhere from three to six branch managers report to each district manager, each of whom is, in turn, responsible to a zone manager, of which there are only four in the nation. Zone managers report to the national manager, who is a company vice president. This hierarchy is shown in Exhibit 1.

EXHIBIT 1 Coolaire service hierarchy

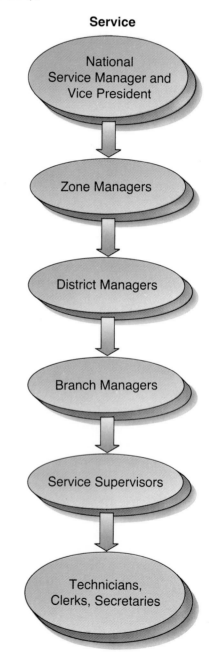

Service

- National Service Manager and Vice President
- Zone Managers
- District Managers
- Branch Managers
- Service Supervisors
- Technicians, Clerks, Secretaries

The Service Contract

Recently, Coolaire was one of a handful of companies invited to bid on a large service contract. A meeting was held of all Coolaire's branches in the Birmingham district (as this is where the contract would be executed), to come up with ideas on how to manage the contract in the event it was awarded to Coolaire. Three major possibilities were explored: (1) to treat the contract as an extension of ordinary business, with several branches participating on the basis of geographic location; (2) to create a new branch to manage this contract exclusively; and (3) to manage the whole contract from a single existing branch. This third proposal was adopted by the group, and Phil Waverly's branch was chosen to manage the contract if the bid was won.

Phil recalled his feelings after the meeting was over.

> This was the first time that the branch managers really provided input for a big decision, and I felt that we did it very well. Each alternative was evaluated systematically, taking into account the extra work and the extra personnel required to manage the contract. Everyone left the meeting with a feeling of contribution and accomplishment. I was really pumped up just imagining myself running such a big contract.

Coolaire's bid was more than 30 percent lower than its closest competitor's, and Coolaire was awarded the contract. The bid itself was prepared by the Southeast zone manager in consultation with the national service vice president with no input from the branch managers who had attended the meeting in Birmingham. At the time Phil thought little of this exclusion because he was accustomed to administering contracts rather than preparing bids. He never guessed the extent to which he had become a pawn in someone else's chess game.

Strategy Behind the Bid

Coolaire's exceedingly low bid was part of an emerging struggle between Coolaire's service group and National Elevator's service group. Coolaire's takeover by Allied Industrials left many of Coolaire's top service managers uncertain about their future with the organization. A cold war of sorts was the result, with the service departments of Coolaire and National Elevator battling to become the core of Allied's planned consolidated service department, with the majority of the managers in the new centralized service organization coming from the ranks of the surviving department. As Coolaire had recently lost three large contracts, success on their latest bid was crucial.

Responsibility for fulfillment of this contract was delegated to Phillip Waverly's branch in hopes that giving one branch full responsibility for the contract would provide a tighter rein on expenditures and simplify managerial accounting and paperwork. Phil recalled, "Part of the deal was that additional office and field personnel would be an absolute necessity for any branch attempting to fulfill the contract on its own." But as he researched the problem further Phil uncovered a particularly dismaying bit of information. Three years earlier, Coolaire had bid on and lost the same contract. At that time, 4 branch managers, 9 supervisors, 52 service technicians, and 6 clerks had been allocated to the contract. Under Waverly there would be only 3 supervisors, 23 service technicians, and 2 clerks—a reduction in staff size of over 50 percent to fulfill a contract that had increased in size during the three-year period.

The air-conditioning equipment being maintained by the branch has rapidly deteriorated as the field personnel have become overtaxed just doing emergency repairs, with no time for routine preventive maintenance. Profit margins have become microscopic, and since the contract contained no allowances for inflation during its three-year term, profits will continue to erode and probably disappear altogether. Phil privately wondered if the next scene in the unfolding drama would be one called scapegoat. If so, he surmised that those pulling the strings would have no trouble identifying the actor to play that role.

Questions

1. How can the bid on the service contract be understood from a formal organization perspective?
2. Phil fears that he will become a scapegoat. Help him map out a strategy that would avoid this outcome.

PART FOUR

LEADING AND MOTIVATING

NATURE OF MOTIVATION
Elements of a Motivation System □
Managerial Assumptions Underlying
Motivation

THEORIES OF MOTIVATION
Content Theories □ A Process Theory:
Expectancy Theory □ A Process Theory:
Behavior Modification □ Expectancy
Theory vs. Behavior Modification □ Issues
in Motivation

JOB SATISFACTION
Job Satisfaction and Performance □
Effects of Job Satisfaction

Summary □ Key Concepts □ Discussion
Questions □ Notes □ Supplementary
Reading

CASES: Value of Recognition □ "Things
Are Different Around Here"

This chapter will enable you to

□ Understand the concept of motivation
and identify the primary elements of a
motivational system.

□ Explain the major theories of motivation
and recognize how each can be applied
in organizations.

□ Become familiar with the concept of
job satisfaction and understand its
relationship to organizational
effectiveness.

CHAPTER 13
MOTIVATION AND JOB SATISFACTION

A major responsibility of managers at all organizational levels is to direct and inspire the work of others. High performing employees can make the difference between a marginal organization and a highly effective one. To fulfill this responsibility, the manager should understand individual and group behavior and be able to motivate, lead, and communicate. This chapter begins our section on the interpersonal processes involved in management by examining the topic of motivation and the related concepts of individual needs and job satisfaction.

NATURE OF MOTIVATION

Motivation refers to (1) the *direction* of an individual's behavior, that is, what one chooses to do when several alternatives are available; (2) the *strength* of the behavior once the choice is made; and (3) the *persistence* of the behavior.[1] For an organization to be effective, its members must direct their behavior toward high job performance in a strong, persistent way. How management can encourage this type of behavior is the subject of much of this chapter.

Elements of a Motivation System

A number of elements affect the usefulness of any particular motivational approach. Because of the interrelationships among such elements, motivation is more complex than often assumed. The three general elements of a motiva-

FIGURE 13–1 Elements of a
motivational system

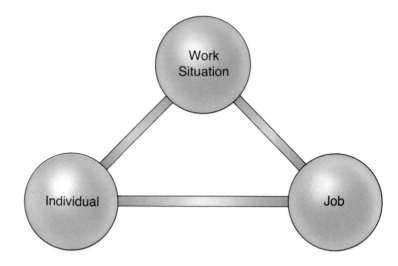

FIGURE 13–1 Elements of a motivational system

tional system, as portrayed in Figure 13–1, are (1) the individual being motivated, (2) the job, and (3) the work situation.

The Individual.   Organization members, whether managerial or nonmanagerial, differ in intelligence, ability, attitudes, and needs. Hence, they are unlikely
to react uniformly to particular motivational forces. A recent study of the differences in priorities between managers and computer specialists is particularly
revealing. Managers valued responsibility, autonomy, and job title more than
computer specialists. The computer specialists had higher needs than managers
for security, location, better hours, and learning new skills.[2] Certainly, different
motivational programs would be required for these two groups.

The Job.   Job design has the potential to motivate, as was seen in chapter 8.
Some people are highly motivated by enriched, challenging tasks. Others prefer
more routine, structured tasks. Managers must try to match the person with
the task in a way that brings forth the best performance.

The Work Situation.   The third general element affecting work motivation
involves the environment in which the work occurs. Many aspects of the work
situation appear significant. Relationships with other members of the work
group or organization, depending on the circumstances, may stimulate or retard performance because of group norms or peer approval. Supervisory behavior is likewise relevant in the establishment of work standards, regulation
of work processes, and dispensation of rewards.
    The interaction of the three general elements—the individual, the job,
and the work situation—produces the motivational appeal to individual members of the organization. As we realize that each of these three might be broken
into still more specific elements, we can gain an appreciation of the overall
complexity of work motivation.

Managerial Assumptions Underlying Motivation

Motivational approaches reflect an underlying set of assumptions about the nature of people and their probable response to various types of motivation. The best-known classification of assumptions was provided by Douglas McGregor under the labels of *Theory X* and *Theory Y*.[3] Although these concepts are often regarded as leadership approaches, they are more appropriately described as assumptions.

Theory X represents a relatively pessimistic view of human nature and holds that most people, and employees in particular, tend to be lazy, lack ambition, and require supervision to "keep them moving." The opposite assumptions of Theory Y may be explained as follows:[4]

> Theory Y states, in essence, that man is capable of integrating his own needs and goals with those of the organization; that he is not inherently lazy and indolent; that he is by nature capable of exercising self-control and self-direction, and that he is capable of directing his efforts toward organizational goals.

These assumptions tend to produce different motivational approaches. A manager's view of the nature of human beings influences his or her methods of motivating subordinates. Theory X managers tend to rely to a greater extent on disciplinary methods and penalties, while Theory Y managers tend to place more emphasis on positive motivation and self-management.

THEORIES OF MOTIVATION

Because motivation is unobservable—we can observe job performance but not the reasons underlying the level of performance—various theories have been developed to explain it. Even a perfunctory discussion of these theories is far beyond the scope of a single chapter. Hence, the following presentation of selected theories focuses on those ideas which continue to have the greatest impact on managerial practice.

Motivation theories may be divided into two groups.[5] *Content theories* emphasize the specific factors that motivate an individual. These factors may reside within the individual (human needs, for instance) or within the individual's environment (job characteristics, for example). *Process theories*, on the other hand, focus on the dynamics of motivation, from the initial energization of behavior, through the selection of behavioral alternatives, to actual effort.

Content Theories

Need Hierarchy.   One of the earliest and most enduring content theories is the *need hierarchy* proposed by A. H. Maslow.[6] The stairstep diagram in Figure 13–2 ranks five categories of human needs in accordance with Maslow's theory.

FIGURE 13-2   Maslow's need hierarchy

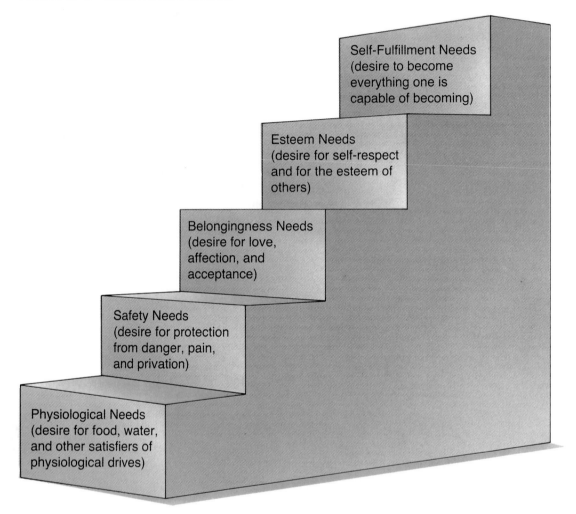

Self-Fulfillment Needs
(desire to become
everything one is
capable of becoming)

Esteem Needs
(desire for self-respect
and for the esteem of
others)

Belongingness Needs
(desire for love,
affection, and
acceptance)

Safety Needs
(desire for protection
from danger, pain,
and privation)

Physiological Needs
(desire for food, water,
and other satisfiers of
physiological drives)

If needs are viewed in this way, it is the physiological needs—inherited drives directly connected with the physical body—that must be satisfied first. Once these needs are reasonably well satisfied, the next level—the need for safety and security—assumes priority. Only after our physical and safety needs are being met do we begin to desire companionship and close interpersonal relationships. Partial satisfaction of the belongingness needs activates the need to respect ourselves and to have others think well of us. Finally, if all four of these needs are reasonably satisfied, we are then driven by the need to self-actualize—to fulfill our potential.

Some have questioned Maslow's assertion that needs are arranged in a hierarchy.[7] Maslow appropriately emphasized that much human behavior is directed toward the satisfaction of unfulfilled needs. Furthermore, it seems likely that Maslow is at least partially correct, particularly in distinguishing between lower-level needs—that is, the physiological and security needs—and higher-level needs:[8]

> There is a strong evidence to support the view that unless the existence needs are satisfied none of the higher-order needs will come into play. There is also some evidence that unless security needs are satisfied, people will not be concerned with higher-order needs. . . . There is, however, little evidence to support the view that a hierarchy exists once one moves above the security level.

A two-level hierarchy can, therefore, be supported on the basis of present knowledge.*

Contemporary organizations satisfy needs in varying degrees. Physiological and safety needs are at least partially satisfied for many U.S. workers through wages and salaries, medical and life insurance benefits, retirement plans, safety regulations, and so on. In some organizations, labor unions have provided additional need satisfaction through seniority protection clauses, strike benefits, and cost of living allowances. The lack of fulfillment of higher-level needs poses a significant problem for millions of employees, however.

Two-Factor Theory. Perhaps the most widely discussed content theory is Frederick Herzberg's *two-factor theory* of motivation.[9] Herzberg proposed that two major categories of job factors—*hygiene factors* and *motivators*—affect employee attitudes and behavior, as suggested in Figure 13–3.

Hygiene factors are associated with the job *context* or environment and serve to keep employees from becoming dissatisfied. Examples are organizational policy and administration; interpersonal relationships with superiors, peers, and subordinates; job security; and salary. If employees feel that the organization's policies are appropriate, that their salaries are fair, that they have adequate job security, and that their working relationships are pleasant, they are unlikely to be dissatisfied. These factors, however, are insufficient to satisfy them or to motivate them to high performance.

The motivational role is filled by the second type of job factor. Examples of motivators are achievement, recognition, responsibility, and advancement.

---

*There are at least two other well-known need theories. One identifies three basic drives which vary from individual to individual: (1) the need for *achievement*, (2) the need for *power*, and (3) the need for *affiliation*. Another classifies human needs into three basic categories: (1) *existence* needs (material and physiological desires), (2) *relatedness* needs (relationships with significant others), and (3) *growth* needs (desires to create and produce). For information on the former, see John W. Atkinson and Joel O. Raynor, *Personality, Motivation, and Achievement* (Washington, D.C.: Hemisphere Publishing Corp., 1978) and David C. McClelland and David H. Burnham, "Power Is the Great Motivator," *Harvard Business Review* 54 (March-April 1976): 100–10. The latter is described in Clayton P. Alderfer, *Existence, Relatedness, and Growth: Human Needs in Organizational Settings* (New York: The Free Press, 1972).

FIGURE 13-3 Two-factor theory

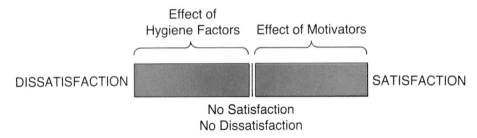

These factors are associated with the job *content* and, if present, make individuals satisfied with their jobs and help to motivate them. According to Herzberg, then, if management can enrich employees' jobs by giving them more responsibility, a chance to advance, and feelings of achievement and recognition, the employees will perform better. In other words, job enrichment should help employees satisfy their upper-level needs.

Research evidence on Herzberg's theory is mixed, and the theory's foundations have been criticized on a number of grounds.[10] The theory has had a significant impact on job design. Much of the recent work in job enrichment, reported in chapter 8, is an outgrowth of Herzberg's earlier efforts.

A Process Theory: Expectancy Theory

A motivational formulation that explicitly accounts for individual differences is *expectancy theory,* which, unlike Maslow's or Herzberg's conceptualizations, is a process theory.[11] Expectancy theory holds that motivation begins with a desire for something—perhaps self-actualization, higher status, a feeling of accomplishment, or more leisure time. The degree to which an individual desires a particular *outcome* is termed the *valence* (or psychological importance) of that outcome. Outcomes may be either *extrinsic*—external rewards such as pay or promotion—or *intrinsic*—internal rewards such as feelings of increased self-esteem or self-actualization.

The individual seeks to determine how the desired outcomes can be attained. Feelings of accomplishment, for instance, may be attained in a variety of ways—performing well on one's job, going to work for another organization, or even engaging in off-the-job activities. Management hopes that the employee will engage in high job performance. But the means the employee will use to gain the desired feelings of accomplishment depends upon the factors illustrated in Figure 13–4.

Expectancy is the individual's estimate of the likelihood that his or her effort will result in performance. Effort is not the same as performance, as any student who has studied all night for an exam only to make a D will testify. Performance depends not only on effort but also on (1) having the appropriate

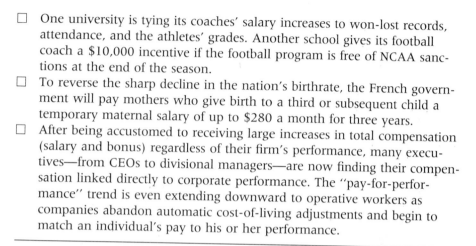

EXPECTANCY THEORY IN ACTION

☐ One university is tying its coaches' salary increases to won-lost records, attendance, and the athletes' grades. Another school gives its football coach a $10,000 incentive if the football program is free of NCAA sanctions at the end of the season.

☐ To reverse the sharp decline in the nation's birthrate, the French government will pay mothers who give birth to a third or subsequent child a temporary maternal salary of up to $280 a month for three years.

☐ After being accustomed to receiving large increases in total compensation (salary and bonus) regardless of their firm's performance, many executives—from CEOs to divisional managers—are now finding their compensation linked directly to corporate performance. The "pay-for-performance" trend is even extending downward to operative workers as companies abandon automatic cost-of-living adjustments and begin to match an individual's pay to his or her performance.

SOURCE: Glen Macnow, "Eastern Michigan's Plan to Tie Coaches' Pay to Performance Derided on Other Campuses," *The Chronicle of Higher Education*, 17 July 1985, p. 27; "Sidelines," *The Chronicle of Higher Education*, 8 January 1986, p. 29; "Europe's Population Bomb," *Newsweek*, 15 December 1986, p. 52; Amanda Bennett, "More Managers Find Salary, Bonus Are Tied Directly to Performance," *The Wall Street Journal*, 28 February 1986; and Carrie Dolan, "Many Companies Now Base Workers' Raises On Their Productivity," *The Wall Street Journal*, 15 November 1985.

abilities and traits and (2) channelling behavior in the proper direction rather than engaging in unfocused effort. *Instrumentality* is the relationship the individual perceives between performance, once it is attained, and the desired outcome.

Assume that an employee desires a greater feeling of accomplishment and feels there are two possible means of attaining it: performing well on the present job or taking a new job with another organization. The individual will first

FIGURE 13–4 Expectancy theory

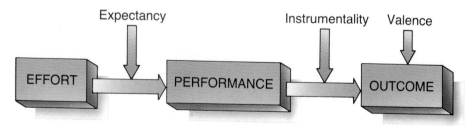

estimate the probability that effort will lead to high performance on the present job and will compare this estimate with the expectancy that effort directed toward finding a new job (another type of performance) will result in an appropriate position. Next, the individual will assess the likelihood that job performance will lead to feelings of accomplishment and compare this with the probability that a job change will result in the desired feelings of accomplishment.

The alternative the employee will choose is a multiplicative function of valence, instrumentality, and expectancy.[12] As shown in Figure 13–5, the employee is likely to quit the present position to go to work for another organization. Why? Because the person places a high value (10, say, on a scale of 10) on accomplishment, perceives a job change as being highly instrumental (.8 probability) in attaining the desired outcome, and believes that job-seeking efforts are reasonably likely (.6 probability) to lead to a new job. Although the probability of performing well on the present job is higher (.8 probability), the present job is not seen as being instrumental (.2 probability) in attaining feelings of accomplishment.

Expectancy theory, then, accounts for individual differences by showing that each of us is motivated by differing outcomes to which we assign our own valences. Additionally, our perceptions of instrumentality and expectancy are also likely to differ. In the example of Figure 13–5, for instance, job enrichment would probably be beneficial for that employee because it should increase the employee's estimate of the instrumentality between performance and feelings of accomplishment.

FIGURE 13–5 Assessment of behavioral alternatives

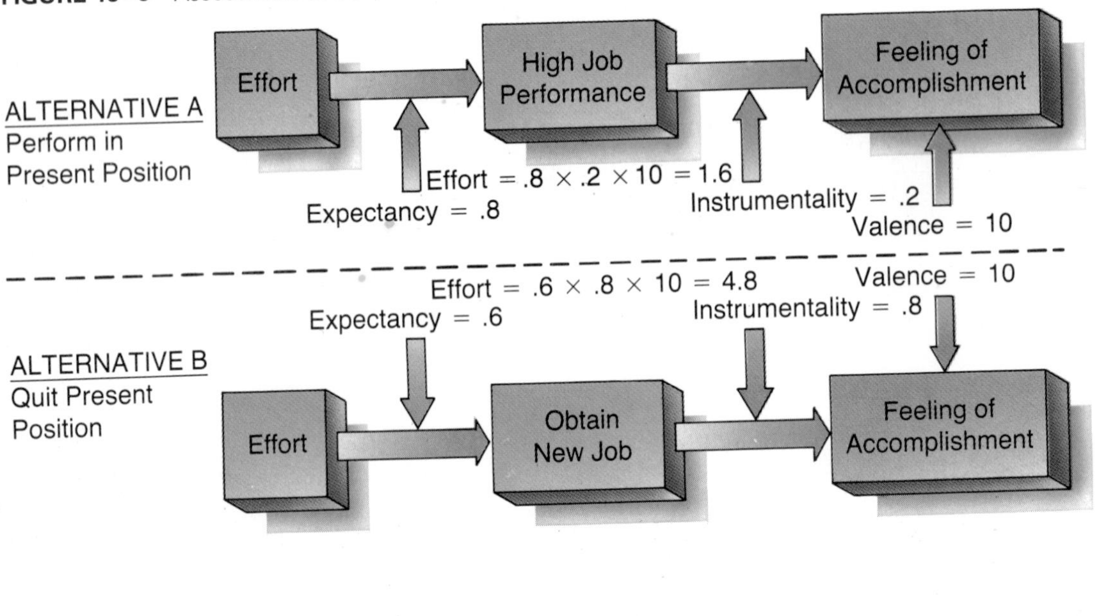

ALTERNATIVE A
Perform in
Present Position

Effort → High Job Performance → Feeling of Accomplishment

Effort $= .8 \times .2 \times 10 = 1.6$
Expectancy $= .8$
Instrumentality $= .2$
Valence $= 10$

Effort $= .6 \times .8 \times 10 = 4.8$
Expectancy $= .6$
Instrumentality $= .8$
Valence $= 10$

ALTERNATIVE B
Quit Present
Position

Effort → Obtain New Job → Feeling of Accomplishment

Management's Role. Management's task is to (1) ensure that employees perceive high instrumentalities between job performance and the outcomes they desire and (2) increase employee expectancies that effort will result in performance. The first requires management to learn what outcomes employees value, since the outcomes that motivate one individual may differ from those that motivate another person. This may be done through questionnaires or interviews. It also requires managers to be alert and consistent in providing such extrinsic rewards as recognition and salary increases. The second—increasing expectancies—can be accomplished through training and development programs, which improve employee abilities, and through the setting of clear, specific job goals, which help employees channel their efforts in the proper direction.[13]

REWARDING *A* WHILE HOPING FOR *B*

Managers of organizations must ensure that they reward the type of performance they desire. As Steven Kerr has so aptly pointed out, some universities *hope* that their professors will teach well, but *reward* them for research and publications. Hence, many instructors are more likely to spend time writing then preparing for class because they perceive a low instrumentality between teaching well and the outcomes they desire, such as promotions, pay raises, and national recognition. Administrative encouragement of excellent teaching will have little effect until a higher instrumentality is perceived between teaching and rewards.

In spite of this reward system, some professors at those universities teach well. Why? Because they perceive a high instrumentality between their performance and the particular set of outcomes that they desire—helping students learn, being recognized as one of the school's premier teachers, fulfilling the need for esteem and self-satisfaction, and so on.

In a related example, a 1985 survey of managers in the federal government indicated that top government officials *hoped* that managers would cut costs, but the officials failed to reward such behavior. Supervisors reported that cutting nonproductive workers from a department would actually reduce a supervisor's own pay grade, because a supervisor's pay grade in part reflected the number of subordinates in the department. The intent of the recent merit-pay reform act is to eliminate this type of problem.

SOURCE: Steven Kerr, "On the Folly of Rewarding A, While Hoping for B," *Academy of Management Journal* 18 (December 1975): 769–83; and Donald J. Devine, "Giving Incentive Leverage to Our Government's Bosses," *The Wall Street Journal,* 8 April 1985.

When an individual is relatively certain that his or her effort will result in high performance and is equally certain that performance will be rewarded with desirable outcomes, that person is likely to be a high performer, according to expectancy theory. Conversely, when individuals perform well but observe that their rewards do not differ significantly from employees who are poor performers, their estimates of instrumentality—and hence their efforts—are likely to decrease in the future. If an organization rewards seniority rather than performance, it can scarcely hope to have a work force composed of high performers.

Assessment of Expectancy Theory.   The complexity of expectancy theory poses a problem for researchers and practitioners alike.[14] Research findings have been mixed, partially because of varying methods of measuring the theory's concepts. Implementation of the theory in an organization requires that motivational programs be tailored to individual needs and that they recognize that these needs change over time. A manager who is aware of subordinates' needs and desired outcomes can use expectancy theory concepts to motivate those subordinates, provided the manager has control over the necessary rewards.

The value of expectancy theory lies in its emphasis on individual differences and its explication of how one's goals and desires influence one's behavior. Human beings are viewed as thinking individuals who reason and make conscious behavioral choices based on their expectations about the future.

A Process Theory: Behavior Modification

A considerably different philosophy of motivation is derived from principles of *behavior modification,* based upon operant conditioning theory.[15] A well-established area of study in psychology, operant conditioning has only recently been formally applied in organizations.

Operant behavior—unlike instinctual behavior such as sneezing—is behavior that is followed by an event (called *reinforcement*) which affects the probability that the behavior will occur again in the future. The closer the reinforcement follows the behavior, the greater the likelihood that future behavior will be affected. The major types of reinforcement available to the manager are:

□ *Positive reinforcement* increases the probability that the behavior will be repeated in the future. An employee who has just performed some task superbly may be praised, recognized publicly, given a raise or promotion, or handed an attractive job assignment.

□ *Negative reinforcement* or *avoidance* strengthens behavior by providing an avenue of escape from an unpleasant event. An individual might perform well to avoid being chewed out by the boss.

□ *Punishment* decreases the probability that undesirable behavior will be repeated. An employee who arrives at work late may be reprimanded by the boss or have his or her pay docked.

□ *Extinction* is also used to reduce undesirable behavior. Positive reinforcement is withheld following the behavior. An individual's inane comments at a meeting may simply be ignored.

"The objective of each of the four reinforcement types is to modify an individual's behavior so that it will benefit the organization."[16] Of course, the effectiveness of a given form of reinforcement upon behavior may vary from individual to individual. Praise, for instance, does not work with all people.

Probably the most common form of reinforcement used by managers is positive reinforcement. When desirable behavior is positively reinforced each time it occurs, a *continuous reinforcement* schedule is being used. *Partial reinforcement* occurs when the desired behaviors are reinforced occasionally rather than continuously. In practice, most reinforcement is partial, since continuous reinforcement is often impractical. Salary, for instance, is paid on a *fixed interval* schedule, such as monthly or weekly. Praise is often bestowed at *variable intervals*, that is, not at regularly scheduled times.

Operant conditioning theory holds that partial reinforcement is more effective in sustaining behavior than is continuous reinforcement. Particularly effective is a *variable ratio* schedule under which behavior is reinforced, on the average, following every *x* number of desired responses.[17] For example, reinforcement might occur after three responses, then after twenty responses, then after seven, for an average of ten. (Gambling is a common example of variable ratio reinforcement, and the gambling habit is notoriously hard to break.) Results of controlled research on variable ratio reinforcement in organizations, however, are not clear.[18] For instance, in a comparison of programs to reduce absenteeism, employees in one plant who received personal recognition at the end of each quarter in which they had no more than one absence (i.e., positive reinforcement on a fixed interval schedule) had significantly lower absenteeism rates than employees in another plant who were eligible for a lottery at the end of each quarter in which they did not exceed one absence (i.e., positive reinforcement on a variable ratio schedule).[19]

Punishment, though used frequently in organizations, has been examined less than positive reinforcement.[20] The act of punishment itself is often postponed by managers for as long as possible because of the likely aftermath. The potential negative outcomes of punishment may include resentment, hostility, apathy, formal grievances, reduced performance, and an uncomfortable relationship between manager and subordinate.

A nonpunitive approach to discipline has been suggested as a means for minimizing these negative outcomes while simultaneously enhancing the subordinate's commitment to the job and organization.[21] The first step consists of a meeting between the manager and subordinate in which the manager reminds the employee of his or her responsibility to meet the department's standards of performance and behavior. The manager secures the employee's agreement to solve the problem, though no written record of the meeting is placed in the employee's file. If the problem continues, the manager again meets with the employee to review the employee's failure to abide by the agreement and the reasons underlying the rule or behavioral standard. Together, the manager and subordinate create a plan to eliminate the problem. This meeting is documented in writing with a copy to the employee's personnel file. No reprimand for past misbehavior or warning about the future is given; instead, the focus is on the plan to improve behavior or performance.

Should the employee's behavior fail to improve, then he or she is given a paid, one-day "decision-making leave." The time off is to be used for the employee to decide whether to change behavior or to quit. The employee must meet with the manager the next day. If the employee elects to stay, an action plan with specific goals is jointly drawn up by the subordinate and manager.

BEHAVIOR MODIFICATION IN ACTION

□ Sales clerks in eight departments in a large department store were positively reinforced for engaging in the following behaviors: (1) being present in the department, (2) assisting a customer within five seconds (or if already waiting on a customer, acknowledging the new customer's presence and promising assistance momentarily), and (3) keeping the display shelves at least 70 percent filled. Those who behaved in the desired fashion received time off with pay, or the cash equivalent, and an opportunity to compete in a drawing for a paid week's vacation for two. Their performance showed a significant improvement compared to the performance of clerks in eight other departments whose undesired behavior was punished but whose desired behavior was ignored (extinction).

□ In Hungary, to reduce the chances for undesirable hitchhikers to get rides, the government has begun issuing official hitchhiker cards to individuals who have a permanent job and residence. Attached to the card are twenty lottery tickets, and cardholders are asked to give one to a driver who gives them a lift. The cards are turned in by the drivers, and an annual drawing awards a car to the driver who has the winning card (positive reinforcement on a variable ratio schedule).

SOURCE: Fred Luthans, Robert Paul, and Douglas Baker, "An Experimental Analysis of the Impact of Contingent Reinforcement on Salespersons' Performance Behavior," *Journal of Applied Psychology* 66 (June 1981): 314–23; and "Helping a Hitchhiker Could Lead to New Car," *The Houston Post*, 26 May 1984.

This step is also documented in writing. If the subordinate should still fail to improve, employment is terminated.

This process focuses on the positive ways in which employee performance can be improved rather than on punishing an employee for poor performance. As such, it requires individual employees to accept responsibility for their own behavior.

Expectancy Theory vs. Behavior Modification

The primary, and highly significant, difference between expectancy theory and behavior modification is the relative emphasis placed upon the thought processes of the individual. Expectancy theory is firmly based on the view that one's present behavior is a function of one's expectations about the future and the connection one perceives between present behavior and future outcomes. In other words, we choose to act as we do because we believe our actions will result in some desirable future outcome.

Behavior modification, on the other hand, proposes that our present behavior results from our past experiences. We engage in certain behaviors because they have been positively reinforced, and we avoid actions that have been punished:[22]

> Notice that there are no references to any internal cognitive processes. Reinforcers do not feel good or bad, they simply change the frequency of the behavior. The true behaviorist believes that operant behavior is caused by environmental events. This philosophy is called *environmental determinism*. It is our past history of reinforcement that causes our current behavior.

Although both theories explain present behavior in considerably different ways, both strongly emphasize the essential linkage between performance and rewards. Behavior desired by management must be rewarded while undesirable behavior should not be rewarded:[23]

> Indeed, it may be that the two models are not entirely incompatible. Combining [behavior modification and expectancy theory] influences on effort and performance may increase our ability to structure rewarding environments to the benefit of both organizations and their employees.

Issues in Motivation

The Opportunity to Perform.   Of the three general elements in motivation identified earlier in this chapter—the individual, the job, and the work situation—most of the emphasis in motivational research has been on the individual and job design. Only recently have scholars begun to emphasize the importance of broader situational factors.[24]

It is the manager's responsibility to provide an *opportunity* for willing and capable subordinates to perform well. "In many work situations, persons who are both willing and able to successfully accomplish a task may be either inhibited in or prevented from doing so due to situational characteristics beyond their control."[25] The role that opportunity plays in influencing job performance is illustrated in Figure 13–6. For high performance to occur, an employee must have the *capacity* to perform (i.e., must have the requisite ability, intelligence, health, etc.), must have the *willingness* (or the motivation) to perform, and must have the *opportunity* to perform. The capacity of subordinates to perform can be improved through better recruitment and selection techniques and by training and development programs, as discussed in chapter 10. Willingness to perform can be enhanced by the motivational programs discussed in this chapter.

Creating the opportunity to perform requires the manager to analyze such factors as the organization's (or subsystem's) technology, planning/scheduling systems, and delegation practices. For instance, improvements in performance brought about through technological change are probably more dramatic than are increases resulting from emphasis on rewards or job design. Also, efficient

FIGURE 13–6 Dimensions of job performance

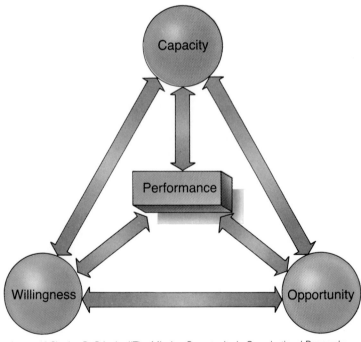

SOURCE: Melvin Blumberg and Charles D. Pringle, "The Missing Opportunity in Organizational Research: Some Implications for a Theory of Work Performance, "*Academy of Management Review* 7 (October 1982): 565.

planning for the delivery of raw materials and parts and for the scheduling of workflow and coordination of activities provides the opportunity for higher performance than does an inefficient planning system. Even delegation of challenging and important tasks to able individuals helps them realize their full potential and is likely to pay dividends in higher performance.

Other actions that can encourage higher performance include placing able newcomers into a formal work group of high performers, the sponsorship of aspiring managers by higher-level executives in a mentor relationship, and protecting employees from interruptions and unnecessary meetings.[26]

Role of Pay in Motivation. Although the precise effect of pay on individual motivation is debated, pay can motivate under certain conditions.[27] The primary requirement for strong motivation is that pay be explicitly tied to individual job performance. But this condition is not as simple as it appears. Performance must be directly, objectively measurable. Even if performance is measurable, the individual must be able to control those aspects of performance on which he or she is to be evaluated. (Profit-sharing plans typically fail to meet this criterion, for instance, because the work of one individual has so little impact on overall profit performance.) If the foregoing conditions are met, management must then ensure that the pay increases awarded to high performers are sufficiently large to be meaningful. Unless all of these conditions are met—and in many situations, they cannot be—pay is unlikely to encourage more than average performance.

Ethical Considerations in Motivation. The use of motivational techniques prompts a number of ethical considerations. For instance, does motivation at some point become manipulation?[28] To what extent do managers have the right to control the behavior of subordinates? Since we have only limited knowledge of human motivation, is management's application of such concepts as expectancy theory or behavior modification premature? Further, some motivation systems—such as expectancy theory—require the probing of employee values relating to the desirability of various outcomes. How far should management go?

> Most people are sensitive to the privacy of individual values in the context of other social behaviors such as voting, yet no one seems bothered by the possibility that the worker may not want his or her values explored, or that line supervisors may not be competent to perform such an assessment accurately.[29]

The answers to issues such as these are neither easy nor simple. But managers must be aware of the issues. Programs intended to enhance organizational effectiveness must not disregard the individual's freedom, dignity, and right to privacy.

JOB SATISFACTION

As suggested earlier, motivation, performance, and job satisfaction are inter-twined. *Job satisfaction* is a multidimensional concept, encompassing the atti-tudes an individual has toward such important dimensions as the organization, immediate supervision, financial rewards, fellow employees, and job design. Specific attitudes need not be uniformly favorable or unfavorable. An em-ployee, for example, may enjoy performing the task and take pride in the or-ganization yet may feel that the boss is incompetent.[30]

Most people have experienced situations in which job satisfaction has temporarily declined or increased as a result of a new boss or a change in pay, organizational policies, or job design. Yet some evidence indicates that job at-titudes remain rather consistent for each individual employee. Even when peo-ple change employers and/or occupations, their prior attitudes are a stronger predictor of subsequent job satisfaction than are changes in pay or status.[31]

Job Satisfaction and Performance

A perplexing question concerning job satisfaction is the extent of its relation-ship to performance. Intuitively, we are inclined to expect a strong positive correlation. Yet, a moment's reflection reminds us that a happy, sociable em-ployee may spend time socializing rather than working, and a college student may be satisfied with a part-time job because the task is not demanding and allows the student to study on the job. In short, little substantive evidence supports the idea that a "happy worker is a hard worker."[32]

SATISFACTION AND PERFORMANCE

□ Pressure to produce often leads to low job satisfaction but high job per-formance. One New York City publishing firm is described by a former sales representative as a firm that "runs a sales contest every year. The winners get to keep their jobs."

□ Little evidence indicates that high job satisfaction results in high job per-formance. An employee who made ten personal telephone calls each working day was admonished by his supervisor. His reply? "My professor at the community college said that a happy employee is a good employee. I am not happy unless I talk to my close friends every day."

SOURCE: "The Bastion of Best Sellers," *Newsweek,* 2 July 1984, p. 61; and Larry Stessin, "Cut-ting the Cord of Office Bell Ringers," *The Wall Street Journal,* 30 January 1984.

Recent evidence suggests that both satisfaction and performance are related to rewards.[33] Rewards provide satisfaction to the subordinate if he or she values those particular rewards and if the rewards are provided in sufficient magnitude. But the rewards are not likely to influence performance unless the subordinate perceives that his or her effort will result in high performance and that the performance will be rewarded. If a subordinate who performs poorly is rewarded with the same salary increase as that given to high performers, the subordinate is likely to be satisfied with the reward, but little improvement in individual performance is likely. "A properly designed reward system . . . dissatisfies low performers because it doesn't give them the rewards they want."[34] It is then the manager's responsibility to help them translate their dissatisfaction into improving their effort and performance.

Likewise, high performers will be more satisfied when their performance is explicitly rewarded and will be significantly less satisfied when rewards are unrelated to performance.[35] At the extreme, a reward system that ignores performance will likely end up with low performers who are satisfied and high performers who are dissatisfied. Furthermore, the latter group will probably search for employment opportunities where high performance is rewarded.

Effects of Job Satisfaction

Even though it appears that favorable job satisfaction may not inspire high productivity, other beneficial effects occur. Favorable employee attitudes, according to different studies, are associated with a lower rate of personnel turnover and less absenteeism.[36] Possibly, high performers in particular will have higher turnover rates when job satisfaction declines because of their ability to find other employment. Average employees, on the other hand, because of their inability to leave, may exhibit little relationship between job satisfaction and turnover.[37]

A high morale level probably also represents a plus in terms of public relations. In addition to general benefits accruing from a favorable public relations image, recruitment may be easier. A favorable public attitude encourages the best applicants to apply, and this is particularly significant in times of short labor supply.

Union relationships may also be helped or hindered by the general attitudes of personnel. Grievances and work stoppages can result from negative attitudes. No doubt the task of supervision is also less burdensome if job satisfaction is high. A manager, therefore, has a number of reasons for seeking positive attitudes.

SUMMARY

The topics of *motivation* and *job satisfaction* are central to organizational effectiveness. Motivation refers to the direction, strength, and persistence of an individual's behavior. The motivation process is complex, involving three major groups of variables: the individual, the job, and the work situation.

Early ideas about motivation took the form of *content theories*, focusing on the specific factors that motivate people. Two of the better-known theories in this area are Maslow's *need hierarchy* and Herzberg's *two-factor theory*. Maslow suggests that individuals are motivated by the desire to fulfill needs and that these needs range, hierarchically, from physiological needs to self-fulfillment needs. Herzberg proposes the factors associated with the job context *(hygiene factors)* can keep employees from becoming dissatisfied while factors associated with the job content *(motivators)* are capable—through job enrichment—of making individuals satisfied with their jobs and motivated.

A more complex formulation that recognizes the differences among individuals is *expectancy theory*. This theory hypothesizes that individuals will direct strong effort toward their jobs when (1) they believe that high performance will lead to outcomes they desire, and (2) when they expect that their efforts will indeed result in high performance. Human beings are viewed as thinking individuals who make conscious behavioral choices based on their expectations about the future.

A significantly different view of motivation is based on *behavior modification* principles, derived from operant conditioning theory. These principles predict that behavior which is *positively reinforced* is likely to be repeated in the future, while behavior which is *punished* is likely to decrease in occurrence. Present behavior, then, is a function of past reinforcement experiences. Although this is nearly the opposite view presented by expectancy theory, both ideas emphasize the essential linkage between performance and rewards.

Although most of the emphasis in motivational research has been on the individual and job design, managers are also responsible for providing an *opportunity* for willing and capable subordinates to perform well. Creating a facilitative environment requires an analysis of factors such as technology, planning/scheduling systems, delegation practices, placement, and mentorship.

Pay can be used to motivate employees if (1) the pay is explicitly tied to the individual's job performance, (2) the performance is objectively measurable, (3) the individual can control those aspects of performance which are being evaluated, and (4) the pay increases awarded to high performers are large enough to be meaningful.

Job satisfaction is a multidimensional concept composed of the attitudes a person has toward such task dimensions as the organization, immediate supervision, financial rewards, fellow employees, and the job. Although many individuals expect job satisfaction and performance to be positively related, there is no necessary relationship between the two. Evidence suggests that both are influenced by rewards. Valued rewards can increase employee satisfaction but will influence performance only if they are directly tied to performance criteria.

KEY CONCEPTS

Motivation	Behavior modification
Individual differences	Reinforcement
Theory X	Positive reinforcement
Theory Y	Negative reinforcement
Content theory	Punishment
Need hierarchy	Extinction
Two-factor theory	Continuous reinforcement
Hygiene factors	Fixed interval reinforcement
Motivators	Variable interval reinforcement
Expectancy theory	Opportunity to perform
Outcome	Capacity to perform
Valence	Willingness to perform
Expectancy	Job satisfaction
Instrumentality	

DISCUSSION QUESTIONS

1. What is meant by the general elements of a motivational system?
2. Explain the distinction between *Theory X* and *Theory Y* and indicate the type of leadership or motivation that might be associated with each.
3. Explain carefully the concept of a *need hierarchy*. What is the significance of this concept in terms of motivation?
4. What is the difference between a *hygiene factor* and a *motivator?* Specifically, how are individuals motivated, according to the *two-factor theory?*
5. Define the following concepts: *outcome, valence, instrumentality,* and *expectancy,* and explain how individuals are motivated according to *expectancy theory.*
6. How does *expectancy theory* account for individual differences?
7. Explain how *behavior modification* may be used to motivate individuals to high performance.
8. What is the major difference between *expectancy theory* and *behavior modification?* How are they similar?
9. Explain how a properly trained, highly motivated employee may not be able to perform well due to a lack of *opportunity.*
10. What are some of the difficulties involved in using pay as a tool for motivation?
11. Is a "happy worker" likely to be a "hard worker"? Why or why not?
12. What types of benefits may result from favorable employee attitudes?

NOTES

1. John P. Campbell et al., *Managerial Behavior, Performance, and Effectiveness* (New York: McGraw-Hill, 1970), p. 340.

2. "When Money and Rank Are Not Enough," *Business Week,* 20 February 1984, p. 72.

3. Douglas McGregor, *The Human Side of Enterprise* (New York: McGraw-Hill, 1960).

4. Edgar H. Schein, "In Defense of Theory Y," *Organizational Dynamics* 4 (Summer 1975): 20.

5. Campbell et al., *Managerial Behavior,* p. 341.

6. A. H. Maslow, "A Theory of Human Motivation," *Psychological Review* 50 (July 1943): 370–96.

7. John Rauschenberger, Neal Schmitt, and John E. Hunter, "A Test of the Need Hierarchy Concept by a Maslow Model of Change in Need Strength," *Administrative Science Quarterly* 25 (December 1980): 654–70; and Mahmoud A. Wahba and Lawrence G. Bridwell, "Maslow Reconsidered: A Review of the Research on the Need Hierarchy Theory," *Organizational Behavior and Human Performance* 15 (April 1976): 212–40.

8. Lyman W. Porter, Edward E. Lawler III, and J. Richard Hackman, *Behavior in Organizations* (New York: McGraw-Hill, 1975), p. 43.

9. Frederick Herzberg, Bernard Mausner, and Barbara Block Snyderman, *The Motivation to Work* (New York: Wiley, 1959). A succinct discussion of Herzberg's theory with an accompanying practical application may be found in Frederick Herzberg, "One More Time: How Do You Motivate Employees?" *Harvard Business Review* 46 (January-February 1968): 53–62.

10. See, for instance, Robert J. House and Lawrence A. Wigdor, "Herzberg's Dual-Factor Theory of Job Satisfaction and Motivation: A Review of the Evidence and a Criticism," *Personnel Psychology* 20 (Winter 1967): 369–89.

11. Two of the better-known formulations are found in Victor H. Vroom, *Work and Motivation* (New York: Wiley, 1964) and Lyman W. Porter and Edward E. Lawler III, *Managerial Attitudes and Performance* (Homewood, Ill.: Richard D. Irwin, 1968).

12. Evidence from laboratory experiments indicates that adding—rather than multiplying—valence, instrumentality, and expectancy is sufficient to explain an individual's choice of behavior. For a review of the literature on the "multiplicative versus additive" issue, see Adrian Harrell and Michael Stahl, "Additive Information Processing and the Relationship Between Expectancy of Success and Motivational Force," *Academy of Management Journal* 29 (June 1986): 424–33.

13. Anthony J. Mento, Robert P. Steel, and Ronald J. Karren, "A Meta-Analytic Study of the Effects of Goal Setting on Task Performance: 1966–1984," *Organizational Behavior and Human Decision Processes* 39 (February 1987): 52–83.

14. A representative review of the research on expectancy theory may be found in Terence M. Mitchell, "Expectancy-Value Models in Organizational Psychology," in *Expectancy, Incentive and Action,* ed. N. Feather (Hillsdale, N.J.: Erlbaum, 1980).

15. See B. F. Skinner, *Science and Human Behavior* (New York: The Free Press, 1953); and C. B. Ferster and B. F. Skinner, *Schedules of Reinforcement* (New York: Appleton-Century-Crofts, 1957).

16. Andrew D. Szilagyi, Jr., and Marc J. Wallace, Jr., *Organizational Behavior and Performance,* 2d ed. (Santa Monica, Calif.: Goodyear, 1980), p. 125.

17. An interesting application of variable ratio reinforcement in a small manufacturing plant is described in John G. Carlson and Kenneth D. Hill, "The Effect of Gaming on Attendance and Attitude," *Personnel Psychology* 35 (Spring 1982): 63–73.

18. Robert D. Pritchard et al., "The Effects of Varying Schedules of Reinforcement on Human Task Performance," *Organizational Behavior and Human Performance* 16 (August 1976): 205–30; and Robert D. Pritchard, John Hollenback, and Philip J. De Leo, "The Effects of Continuous and Partial Schedules of Reinforcement on Effort, Performance and Satisfaction," *Organizational Behavior and Human Performance* 25 (June 1980): 336–53.

19. K. Dow Scott, Steven E. Markham, and Richard W. Robers, "Rewarding Good Attendance: A Comparative Study of Positive Ways to Reduce Absenteeism," *Personnel Administrator* 30 (August 1985): 72–83.

20. For an extensive review of the variables that affect the supervisor's use of rewards and punishments, see Philip M. Podsakoff, "Determinants of a Supervisor's Use of Rewards and Punishments: A Literature Review and Suggestions for Further Research," *Organizational Behavior and Human Performance* 29 (February 1982): 58–83.

21. David N. Campbell, R. L. Fleming, and Richard C. Grote, "Discipline Without Punishment—At Last," *Harvard Business Review* 63 (July-August 1985): 162–78. For a contrasting view in which eighty-four managers reported better resolution of subordinate performance problems when more punitive control tactics were used, see Stephen G. Green, Gail T. Fairhurst, and B. Kay Snavely, "Chains of Poor Performance and Supervisory Control," *Organizational Behavior and Human Decision Processes* 38 (August 1986): 7–27.

22. Terence R. Mitchell, *People in Organizations: Understanding Their Behavior* (New York: McGraw-Hill, 1978), p. 167.

23. Richard M. Steers and Lyman W. Porter, eds., *Motivation and Work Behavior*, 2d ed. (New York: McGraw-Hill, 1979), p. 213.

24. Melvin Blumberg and Charles D. Pringle, "The Missing Opportunity in Organizational Research: Some Implications for a Theory of Work Performance," *Academy of Management Review* 7 (October 1982): 560–69; and Lawrence H. Peters and Edward J. O'Connor, "Situational Constraints and Work Outcomes: The Influences of a Frequently Overlooked Construct," *Academy of Management Review* 5 (July 1980): 391–97. For empirical support, see Robert P. Steel and Anthony J. Mento, "Impact of Situational Constraints on Subjective and Objective Criteria of Managerial Job Performance," *Organizational Behavior and Human Decision Processes* 37 (April 1986): 254–65; and Edward J. O'Connor, Lawrence H. Peters, Abdullah Pooyan, Jeff Weekley, Blake Frank, and Bruce Erenkrantz, "Situational Constraint Effects on Performance, Affective Reactions, and Turnover: A Field Replication and Extension," *Journal of Applied Psychology* 69 (November 1984: 663–72.

25. Peters and O'Connor, "Situational Constraints," pp. 391–92.

26. Blumberg and Pringle, "The Missing Opportunity," pp. 567–68.

27. Edward E. Lawler III, *Pay and Organizational Effectiveness: A Psychological View* (New York: McGraw-Hill, 1971); and Edward E. Lawler III, "Merit Pay: Fact or Fiction?" *Management Review* 70 (April 1981): 50–53. A study in which merit pay for managers had no effect on organizational performance is reported in Jone L. Pearce, William B. Stevenson, and James L. Perry, "Managerial Compensation Based on Organizational Performance: A Time Series Analysis of the Effects of Merit Pay," *Academy of Management Journal* 28 (June 1985): 261–78. For an excellent review of merit pay and other pay issues, see Rosabeth Moss Kanter, "From Status to Contribution: Some Organizational Implications of the Changing Basis for Pay," *Personnel* 64 (January 1987): 12–37.

28. These and other issues are raised in Craig C. Pinder, "Concerning the Application of Human Motivation Theories in Organizational Settings," *Academy of Management Review* 2 (July 1977): 384–97.

29. Ibid., p. 386.

30. Gender and job satisfaction appear to be unrelated. Recent studies show no significant difference between men and women in overall work satisfaction at either upper- or lower-level job categories. See Clifford Mottaz, "Gender Differences in Work Satisfaction, Work-Related Rewards and Values, and the Determinants of Work Satisfaction," *Human Relations* 39 (April 1986): 359–78.

31. Barry M. Staw and Jerry Ross, "Stability in the Midst of Change: A Dispositional Approach to Job Attitudes," *Journal of Applied Psychology* 70 (August 1985): 469–80. For a report of how prior attitudes predicted job satisfaction over a span of almost fifty years, see Barry M. Staw, Nancy E. Bell, and John A. Clausen, "The Dispositional Approach to Job Attitudes: A Lifetime Longitudinal Test," *Administrative Science Quarterly* 31 (March 1986): 56–77.

32. A meta-analysis (i.e., the statistical analysis of a large collection of results from individual studies) of seventy articles in this area found the average correlation between satisfaction and performance to be .146 (corrected to .17). See Michelle T. Iaffaldano and Paul M. Muchinsky, "Job Satisfaction and Job Performance: A Meta-Analysis," *Psychological Bulletin* 97 (March 1985): 251–73.

33. Charles N. Greene and Robert E. Craft, Jr., "The Satisfaction-Performance Controversy—Revisited," in *Motivation and Work Behavior,* 2d ed., ed. Steers and Porter, pp. 270–87.

34. Lloyd Baird, "Managing Dissatisfaction," *Personnel* 58 (May-June 1981): 18.

35. Philip M. Podsakoff, William D. Todor, and Richard Skov, "Effects of Leader Contingent and Noncontingent Reward and Punishment Behaviors on Subordinate Performance and Satisfaction," *Academy of Management Journal* 25 (December 1982): 810–21.

36. The most often-referenced review in this area is found in Vroom, *Work and Motivation,* 1964. Also see K. Dow Scott and G. Stephen Taylor, "An Examination of Conflicting Findings on the Relationship Between Job Satisfaction and Absenteeism: A Meta-Analysis," *Academy of Management Journal* 28 (September 1985): 599–612.

37. Ellen F. Jackofsky, "Turnover and Job Performance: An Integrated Process Model," *Academy of Management Review* 9 (January 1984): 74–83.

SUPPLEMENTARY READING

Arvey, **Richard D.,** and **Ivancevich, John M.** "Punishment in Organizations: A Review, Propositions, and Research Suggestions." *Academy of Management Review* 5 (January 1980): 123–32.

Baird, **Lloyd.** "Managing Dissatisfaction." *Personnel* 58 (May-June 1981): 12–21.

Blumberg, **Melvin,** and **Pringle, Charles D.** "The Missing Opportunity in Organizational Research: Some Implications for a Theory of Work Performance." *Academy of Management Review* 7 (October 1982): 560–69.

Campbell, **David N.;** Fleming, **R. L.;** and **Grote, Richard C.** "Discipline Without Punishment—At Last." *Harvard Business Review* 63 (July-August 1985): 162–78.

Deci, Edward L. "The Hidden Costs of Rewards," *Organizational Dynamics* 4 (Winter 1976): 61–72.

Dowling, William. "Are Workers Pigeons?" *Across the Board* 15 (November 1978): 26–33.

Hamner, W. Clay, and Hamner, Ellen P. "Behavior Modification on the Bottom Line." *Organizational Dynamics* 4 (Spring 1976): 3–21.

Haynes, Robert S.; Pine, Randall C.; and Fitch, H. Gordon. "Reducing Accident Rates with Organizational Behavior Modification." *Academy of Management Journal* 25 (June 1982): 407–16.

Iaffaldano, Michelle T., and Muchinsky, Paul M. "Job Satisfaction and Job Performance: A Meta-Analysis." *Psychological Bulletin* 97 (March 1985): 251–273.

Lawler, Edward E., III "Merit Pay: Fact or Fiction?" *Management Review* 70 (April 1981): 50–53.

Locke, Edwin A. "The Myths of Behavior Mod in Organizations." *Academy of Management Review* 2 (October 1977): 543–53.

Lockwood, Diane L., and Luthans, Fred. "Contingent Time Off: A Nonfinancial Incentive for Improving Productivity." *Management Review* 73 (July 1984): 48–52.

Loher, Brian T.; Noe, Raymond A.; Moeller, Nancy L.; and Fitzgerald, Michael P. "A Meta-Analysis of the Relation of Job Characteristics to Job Satisfaction." *Journal of Applied Psychology* 70 (May 1985): 280–89.

Mitchell, Terence R. "Motivation: New Directions for Theory, Research, and Practice." *Academy of Management Review* 7 (January 1982): 80–88.

Murphy, Kevin J. "Top Executives Are Worth Every Nickel They Get." *Harvard Business Review* 64 (March-April 1986): 125–32.

Peters, Lawrence H., and O'Connor, Edward J. "Situational Constraints and Work Outcomes: The Influences of a Frequently Overlooked Construct." *Academy of Management Review* 5 (July 1980): 391–97.

Porter, Lyman W., and Lawler, Edward E., III. *Managerial Attitudes and Performance.* Homewood, Ill.: Irwin, 1968.

Pringle, Charles D., and Blumberg, Melvin. "What Really Determines Job Performance?" *SAM Advanced Management Journal* 51 (Autumn 1986): 9–13.

Staw, Barry M. "Organizational Psychology and the Pursuit of the Happy/Productive Worker." *California Management Review* 28 (Summer 1986): 40–53.

Vroom, Victor H. *Work and Motivation.* New York: Wiley, 1964.

VALUE OF RECOGNITION

The Purity Chemical Corporation (all names have been changed) was a large American manufacturing company. The plant involved

Case prepared by Professor Leon C. Megginson of University of South Alabama. Reprinted with permission from Megginson, *Personnel: A Behavioral Approach to Administration,* rev. ed. (Homewood, Ill.: Richard D. Irwin, Inc., © 1972), pp. 592–94.

in this case was one of the largest in the corporation and had been established to fill the needs of a growing market. The primary product of the plant sold well because quality was high, and the capacity of the plant, though large, was continually oversold. In the manufacturing process a by-product was produced and was "drawn off the stream" in such quantities that it was thought of as a co-product rather than a by-product; it also required a high degree of purification.

A large technical department was headed by a technical director who had several assistants, each in charge of a given phase of the department's activities. One of these assistants, Mr. Roberts, was in charge of a group of chemists and chemical engineers whose primary duties related to the important by-product. The men in this group reported directly to Mr. Roberts. He, in turn, reported to the technical director. Research problems, product development, quality, and the like were handled by the personnel in this group, reviewed by Mr. Roberts, and passed along to the technical director. Since the purification operations and quality control associated with the by-product were so technical, the group members also served as supervisors for the operating crews of the by-product plant.

Joe Brown, a chemical engineer, was a member of the technical group under Mr. Roberts' supervision. He became completely absorbed in the research work in that area and set out to "learn everything there was to know about it."

At the start of the project, he was pleased with the potential it held and would half-jokingly say, "I'm going to make myself an expert in this field."

Elaborate research was conducted for about a year, and Joe thought the results he achieved were well worth the effort. However, about six months after he started, Joe sensed that his work was being taken for granted and that his superiors had not given the project the importance it deserved. Joe did not let this lack of recognition affect his work, however, and the quality and value of his work and research findings remained high. He expressed his feelings to some of his associates, but since they were

not as close to the problem as he, their replies were more humorous than serious. This reaction did not help Joe's feelings one bit, but he increased his efforts and did an excellent research job.

He reported the results completely and thoroughly in a well-written, well-documented report. As was the practice in the group, all copies of the report were delivered to Mr. Roberts, who was to review the report, present it to the technical director, and arrange for necessary meetings to discuss practical applications of the findings.

Joe waited about a month for action on his work, but none came. He was given some other minor assignments, and he helped on routine work. He found it difficult to approach Mr. Roberts concerning the report and was put off time after time when he inquired about the project.

Mr. Roberts was called out of town on a business trip, and Joe was assigned the duty of "pinch-hitting" for him while he was gone. One day the technical director gave Joe the key to Mr. Roberts' desk and asked him to get a file which he knew was there. When Joe opened the desk, he saw all the copies of his report lying there, apparently unread. This discovery caused Joe considerable trauma, since he was confident that by this time some of the copies of the report had been delivered to the technical director and other company officials.

Joe's feeling of worth was reduced to nothing, and with it went his feeling of pride in his work. He was so shaken by this experience that he resigned from the company.

He was immediately hired by a competitive concern, where his success in his chosen field has been outstanding. He is now an outstanding authority in pollution control.

Questions

1. Evaluate Joe Brown's behavior by using expectancy theory. What was the significance of Joe's finding his reports in Roberts' desk?
2. Evaluate Joe's behavior by using behavior modification theory.
3. Does this case illustrate management's failure to motivate properly or an employee's failure to adopt reasonable attitudes concerning his projects?
4. If you were in Mr. Roberts' position, how would you attempt to motivate Joe Brown's replacement?

"THINGS ARE DIFFERENT AROUND HERE"

"Things are different around here" were the first words that Jill was told by the new manager. Mr. Tyler was welcoming Jill back to another summer of working at Trams, a nationwide discount store. Jill was not at all thrilled with the prospect of another summer at Trams.

Reluctantly, Jill had returned to Trams, where she worked in the ladies' and children's apparel department. Her job consisted of folding clothes, fixing the racks, and going to the registers for "price checks." In the summer after her sophomore year in college, Jill had hoped to find something a bit more stimulating or better paying. But jobs were hard to find, so Jill had returned to Trams to work the 2–8 P.M. shift.

Her past memories of Trams were filled with strong disdain. She was originally hired because the management found that college students work hard, and work hard she did. Under the regime of Mrs. Williams, Jill began her employment at Trams. Mrs. Williams had strict rules that were to be adhered to or else you were fired.

Jill's stomach tied in knots as she remembered Mrs. Williams and her rules.

There was to be no talking between employees, or to friends or family who entered the store. Since the department was located by the main doors and the store was only a block from Jill's house, it was a difficult rule to comply with. Each of the four who worked the night shift were assigned a section of the department and would be held responsible for it. With the clientele and the number of price checks, it was nearly impossible to finish. Yet each night, Jill would do the impossible as she would race against the clock to finish her section. Exhausted at the end of the night, Jill would gaze at her completed job and think of the fruitlessness of it all. For the next day, the customers would ruin it all and she would again do it over.

It seemed from the minute she got there until the minute she left, there was not even time to breathe. She did have a fifteen-minute break, but it could not be a second more than that. Mrs. Williams would look through a one-way mirror, so everyone was alert at all times. The pressures of being silent in front of friends and relatives who did not know there was a silence rule, trying to beat the clock, and trying to keep her mind occupied as the taped music droned on repetitiously made Trams an unpleasant place for Jill to work.

This case was prepared by Ann Marie Calacci, student at St. Mary's College in Notre Dame, Indiana, under the direction of Professor Frank Yeandel.

As she talked to Mr. Tyler, she sensed that things really were different. He seemed like such a nice man. One by one the employees she would be working with were introduced to her. Surprisingly, they all seemed to know each other well. Jill was shocked to see them actually smiling as they came in to work. Jill was anxious to see how things were now run. Mr. Tyler then left at 6 P.M., leaving the night crew under no supervision. Jill asked Tara, one of the only remaining old employees, who was in charge. Tara explained that no one was in charge of assigning sections any more, they all worked together as a team.

Jill noticed how the talking ban was lifted. There was a constant chatter among the workers and they eagerly asked Jill about college and how Trams was under Mrs. Williams. Jill was hesitant in talking at first, but after a while she became comfortable talking and working, a thing she had never attempted in the past. Everyone teased her for working so quickly. They reminded her they were a team, and they would all pitch in to complete the section. At break time, Jill became very uncomfortable when after some twenty minutes no one was moving back to work. Her past training was making her very uncomfortable in the new way of working. That night, amazingly to Jill, all the work was finished with time to spare. All the employees sat around or ate popcorn, while Jill nervously double checked to make sure everything was done.

At first Jill was appalled at the amount of goofing around the other sales clerks did, but as time passed Jill found herself enjoying it and participating, too. She actually enjoyed coming in to work. It was so different for her to get to know the people she worked with, especially because they were so different from those she went to school with. The night crew was a team.

They had so much fun, Jill felt guilty, as if she were getting paid to do nothing. She still was good naturedly teased about being a worrier, a clockwatcher, and a workhorse. They reminded her that the kind Mr. Tyler was in charge and Mrs. Williams was long gone. Jill began to act more and more like the others.

Then one day the district manager came to the store and said that things were to be done much neater, because sales had taken a turn for the worse. Suddenly Jill was thrown back into the time-watching method. As the other employees complained, Tara and Jill saw how little they had been doing before. Mr. Tyler enforced this new method for a week and then, slowly but surely, the looser ways started to surface, and then came out with a bang.

Breaks turned into forty-five minute affairs. Eating was done after and during work. The employees became sloppier than ever in their work. They started calling in sick often. Jill liked the relaxed atmosphere but thought that this was ridiculous.

Jill felt responsible for the decline in sales, since the department was so untidy. She hated to see inefficiency and for the sake of the store wanted to do something about it. She began to make suggestions, but the others rejected her ideas. She knew she was in a bad position to suggest things, since they were wary of her education. They resented her level of education, sometimes referring to her language as "college talk" and too difficult for them to understand. So that they would not call her a college snob, Jill made her suggestions to Mr. Tyler. He agreed that they were excellent, but he never mentioned them to the others. Jill was frustrated.

The behavior became even more lax, with no comments from Mr. Tyler. Jill enjoyed this freedom less and less. One day,

Sue did not come in to work or call in sick. This meant that three had to do all the work that four were to do. After this kept up for a week, the employees were sure that Sue would be fired. But Mr. Tyler could not bring himself to fire Sue, so he gave her a warning. The others were outraged.

In rebellion, the breaks became an hour long. They reasoned that if Sue could miss days and not be fired, certainly ten minutes here or there would not make a difference. They did not do their job completely, and what they did was done sloppily. Jill participated in the breaks and the quality of her work went down, but she still tried to do her job and the job of the others. Again Trams became a nightmare for her.

Then one day, Tara approached Jill and asked her to ring up a dress for $2. Jill replied that the tag was $25 and not $2. Tara said that Jill was right, that was what the tag said, but it made no difference. Tara explained how she worked hard for years, did her job and never received any reward.

She reasoned the store owed her this "discount." Jill adamantly refused to ring it up. Tara went to the register and rang up $2. Jill knew now it was time for her to act.

Questions

1. Analyze the relationship between Jill's job satisfaction and job performance last summer under Mrs. Williams' supervision.
2. Analyze the relationship between the sales clerks' job satisfaction and performance at the beginning of this summer under Mr. Tyler.
3. What is the current relationship between job satisfaction and performance among the department's employees? Why has it changed since the beginning of the summer?
4. What style of leadership is Mr. Tyler using? Why is this style inappropriate in this situation?
5. What can be done to improve both job performance and satisfaction?

THE MANAGER'S LEADERSHIP FUNCTION

Leadership Traits □ Leadership Style □ Substitutes and Neutralizers

LEADERSHIP IN A SITUATIONAL SETTING

Contingency Model of Leadership □ Path-Goal Theory of Leadership

PARTICIPATIVE LEADERSHIP

Benefits of Participation □ Constraints on Participation □ Model of Participative Leadership

Summary □ Key Concepts □ Discussion Questions □ Notes □ Supplementary Reading

CASE: Liberia Ain't Louisiana!

This chapter will enable you to

□ Understand the manager's leadership function and identify the various leadership styles that managers use.

□ Recognize the situational nature of leadership by identifying situations in which certain leadership styles are more appropriate than others.

□ Discuss participative leadership and understand its benefits and limitations.

CHAPTER 14
LEADERSHIP

Organizational performance is closely related to quality of *leadership*. Although competent leadership is not the only important ingredient for successful operation, it is an essential one. A bungling leader can wreck morale and destory efficiency. Strong leadership, on the other hand, can transform a lackluster group into a strong, aggressive, successful organization. This chapter examines leadership and its contribution to organizational performance.

THE MANAGER'S LEADERSHIP FUNCTION

Through leadership a manager secures the cooperation of others in accomplishing an objective. Managers at all hierarchical levels have a leadership role to perform. Although some people equate leadership with management, the two concepts differ significantly. A number of management activities—such as determining strategy, budgeting, or monitoring environmental information—are not directly related to leadership. Likewise, leadership differs from supervision. Whereas supervision involves the influence of subordinates through the use of formal rewards and punishments, leadership involves influencing group members through interpersonal processes that do not resort to formal authority.[1] Leadership is the social talent of getting the best effort of an organization's employees.

Leadership Traits

Early theorists believed that the primary factors in leadership effectiveness were the leader's personal characteristics or *traits*. In other words, these theorists explained leadership ability in terms of some property possessed in different amounts by different people. Effective leaders were, at one time or another, hypothesized to be intelligent, tall, self-confident, and so on.[2] From such a perspective, leadership exists primarily in the characteristics of the leader.

A leader's effectiveness, however, usually depends on considerably more than personal characteristics. For instance, the weak relationship found between leader intelligence and group performance may result from a "screening process."[3] The effect of the leader's intelligence on the group's performance may be "screened" by such variables as the leader's motivation to complete the task successfully, the leader's prior experience with this type of task, how the leader relates to his or her superior, and the leader's relationship with the work group. A very intelligent leader with little motivation or experience may perform less effectively than one who is less intelligent but highly motivated and enjoys the close cooperation of group members.

Although the leader's traits cannot be used to predict the performance of the work unit, such personality traits as intelligence, dominance, and masculinity or femininity have been found to be associated with subordinates' perceptions of leadership. Being perceived as a leader may allow one to exert greater influence over the behavior of subordinates.[4]

TRAGIC TRAITS

Unfortunately, the most dramatic leader of modern times was probably Adolf Hitler. Although not very imposing physically, he seems to have mesmerized audiences with "his ability to sense what a given audience wanted to hear and then manipulate his theme in such a way that he would arouse the emotions of the crowd."

> There is something almost magical about the power of his oratory. . . . When he is at a climax and sways to one side or the other his listeners sway with him; when he leans forward, they, also, lean forward, and when he concludes, they are either awed or silent or on their feet in a frenzy.

SOURCE: Walter C. Langer, *The Mind of Adolf Hilter: The Secret Wartime Report* (New York: Basic Books, 1972), p. 46; and Stanley High, "The Man Who Leads Germany," *The Literary Digest,* 21 October 1933, p. 42.

Leadership Style

The inability of trait concepts to account adequately for leadership effectiveness led to a focus on the leader's behavior or *leadership style*. In other words, the emphasis shifted from the personal qualities of the leader to how the leader behaved.

Initiating Structure and Consideration Styles. Although a number of leadership classification schemes have been developed, the most widely accepted scheme distinguishes between leadership behavior that emphasizes task accomplishment and leadership behavior that emphasizes building a strong relationship between leader and subordinates. Researchers at the Ohio State University termed these two dimensions of leader behavior *initiating structure* and *consideration*.[5] Initiating structure (or task-oriented style) describes the leader's actions that define leader-follower relationships, establish definite standards of performance, specify standard operating procedures, and determine who does what. Consideration (relationship-oriented style) describes the leader's attitude toward followers, the warmth of leader-follower relationships, the leader's willingness to listen, and the degree of mutual trust between leader and followers. Since the two dimensions are relatively independent, a leader's behavior may be characterized by either or both. Figure 14–1 indicates four possible combinations of the two dimensions.

Intuitively, we expect employee-centered, considerate leadership to be more effective than initiating structure in producing superior group performance, though research results have been inconclusive. Some studies have reported significant correlations, but they are offset by other studies with conflict-

FIGURE 14–1 Four possible leadership styles

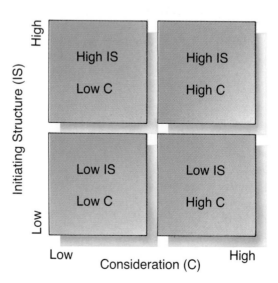

ing findings. No consistent pattern of research results can be used to establish this relationship with any certainty. It seems that significant relationships are being obscured by situational differences in various studies. Under particular circumstances, one leadership approach may lead to higher productivity, while in other circumstances, a different type of leadership may be necessary for enhancing performance. Evidence indicates that the relative effectiveness of consideration and initiating structure depends on such situational factors as the type of organization, the size and cohesiveness of the group, the attitudes of subordinates, and how much influence the leader has with higher-level executives.[6]

LEADERSHIP STYLES

□ The chairman of one conglomerate begins management meetings with an hour of aerobics. The managers wear blue athletic clothes and are led in fight songs such as "no scrap, no scrap: we're for quality."

□ The chairman of an airline defined leadership as "not pandering to what people say they need. It's defining what . . . people need. It's not saying, 'Oh yeah, you want another candy bar? Here, rot your teeth.'"

□ The new chief executive of a small high-tech company is described as deliberate and results-oriented. Says one subordinate, "If you don't agree with something he says, he'll just stare at you and repeat his sentence." Says another, "People don't feel they can just wander into his office."

□ The chairman of one of the stock exchanges is admired for his diplomatic dealings with his constituents and his sixteen-hour work days. But some subordinates find him difficult to work for. One former employee describes him as an autocrat who "likes to give conflicting orders and watch people run around like maniacs." The boss concedes that sometimes he will "hit" high-ranking subordinates hard "just to see if they'll back away."

□ The chief executive of a large computer company is characterized as charming, with the ability to make subordinates feel comfortable, and as possessing a thorough grasp of the business. He is decisive but not stubborn, demanding without being a tyrant, and involved yet able to delegate. One former subordinate recalls, "I'd walk into a meeting, lose the argument, and still walk out smiling, thinking it was a good meeting."

SOURCE: "Northwest Industries: The Acid Test for Bill Farley's Offbeat Style," *Business Week,* 9 September 1985, p. 69; "Up, Up and Away?", *Business Week,* 25 November 1985, p. 91; "How Tom Vanderslice is Forcing Apollo Computer to Grow Up," *Business Week,* 25 March 1985, pp. 96, 98; "Can the Big Board Compete?" *Newsweek,* 15 July 1985, p. 59: and "Akers Remolds IBM in His Image: Friendly But Dominant," *Business Week,* 18 February 1985, p. 86.

A positive correlation does seem to exist between employee-oriented, considerate leadership and employee morale, but even this relationship does not hold in all situations. In those cases showing positive correlations between person-centered leadership and productivity or satisfaction, we are often unsure which is the "chicken" and which is the "egg." There is some evidence to indicate, for instance, that low-performing subordinates cause their superior to behave less considerately, more punitively, and more autocratically toward them. Conversely, high subordinate performance results in greater consideration and less task orientation on the part of the leader.[7] Overall, most such studies show that a leader's behavior and attitudes vary as a function of the subordinates' performance and that the behavior and attitudes of subordinates reflect the leader's behavior.[8] This phenomenon might be termed *reciprocal causation*.

Transactional and Transformational Styles. A recent classification scheme distinguishes between *transactional* and *transformational* leaders.[9] A transactional leader motivates followers by exchanging rewards for performance. By contrast, a transformational leader inspires involvement in a mission, giving followers a "dream" or "vision" of a higher order than the followers' present reality. In effect, the transformational leader motivates followers to do more than they originally expected to do by stretching their abilities and increasing their self-confidence.

One formulation of these styles holds that a single leader can exhibit both transactional and transformational behavior but is likely to emphasize one over the other.[10] The ultimate difference is that leaders who are largely transactional continue to move their organizational systems in line with historical tradition, resulting in marginal improvements. Transformational leadership, however, results in significantly different processes and levels of performance.[11]

Substitutes and Neutralizers

A complicating variable in any analysis of the effect of leadership style on group performance and member satisfaction is a phenomenon known as leadership *substitutes*. These substitutes are variables that weaken the leader's ability to improve or retard the performance or satisfaction of subordinates.[12] The extensive training and experience of subordinates, for example, may make a leader's task-oriented behavior irrelevant. Similarly, such factors as an intrinsically satisfying task or the interaction among cohesive group members may eliminate the need for employee-centered behavior by the leader.

Also complicating analysis of leadership style are leadership *neutralizers*, which interrupt the predictive relationship between a leader's behavior and a subordinate's performance or satisfaction. For instance, a hostile climate between workers and top management may neutralize the effects of initiating structure.[13]

Leadership style is not equally relevant to all situations. Some situations appear to contain variables that influence subordinate performance or satisfaction more strongly than does the leader's behavior.

LEADERSHIP IN A SITUATIONAL SETTING

In an attempt to incorporate the complexities of situational variables into our understanding of leadership effectiveness, current theorists have turned to contingency theories. This section discusses the two major attempts in this direction.

Contingency Model of Leadership

The most ambitious effort to date is Fred Fiedler's *contingency model of leadership*.[14] Fiedler and his associates propose that the most effective leadership style depends on the particular situation. Situations are classified in terms of their "favorableness" for the leader; that is, the degree to which the situation permits the leader to influence the behavior of group members.

Situational Factors. The following three factors define any situation:

□ *Leader-member relations*—the most important factor in a situation is the relationship between the leader and the group members. The trust and confidence members place in their leader depend, to a large extent, upon the leader's expert and referent power, as discussed in chapter 12.
□ *Task structure*—the degree to which the requirements of the subordinates' task are clearly specified.
□ *Leader position power*—the extent of the leader's legitimate, reward, and coercive powers.

The most favorable situation combines close leader-member relations, well-defined tasks, and strong formal position power. Various combinations of these factors yield eight possible leadership situations, which range from highly favorable to highly unfavorable, as shown in Figure 14–2.

Leadership Styles. Fiedler classifies leadership styles into the traditional task-oriented and relationship-oriented categories with one important difference: these two styles of leadership are considered to be opposite ends of a single continuum rather than independent dimensions, as the Ohio State theorists suggest. Leadership style, according to Fiedler, reflects an individual's underlying need structure, which consistently motivates his or her behavior in various leadership situations. Consequently, one's leadership style depends upon one's personality and cannot be readily changed. Leadership style is measured by the leader's responses to a test instrument called the *least-preferred*

FIGURE 14–2   The situational favorableness dimension

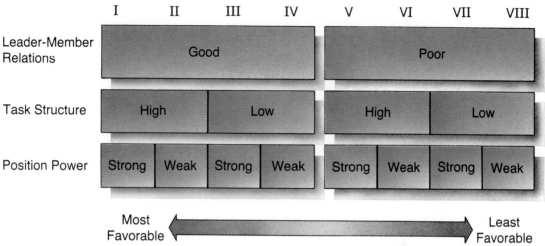

SOURCE: From *Leadership and Effective Management* by Fred E. Fiedler and Martin M. Chemers. Copyright
© 1974 by Scott, Foresman and Company. Reprinted by permission.

coworker scale. This short questionnaire requires the leader to think of the person at work with whom he or she can work least well and to describe that person along such dimensions as the following:

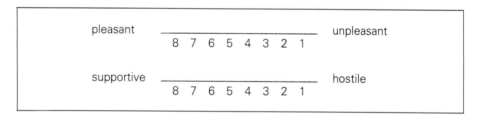

Individuals who describe their least-preferred coworker in relatively favorable terms (that is, pleasant, supportive, and so on) are relationship-oriented leaders. Task-oriented leaders, those who obtain major satisfaction from completing the task successfully, give their least-preferred coworker a relatively unfavorable description.[15]

Combining Leadership Style and the Situation.   Fiedler's findings, based on over three decades of research, are summarized in Figure 14–3. Task-oriented leaders are more effective (in terms of group performance) in the "most favorable" and "least favorable" situations. Relationship-oriented leaders perform best in "mixed situations"—those which are moderately favorable or unfavorable.

In other words, Fiedler's results indicate that task-oriented leaders are likely to have high-performing groups when the leader has either a great deal

FIGURE 14–3   How the style of effective leadership varies with the situation

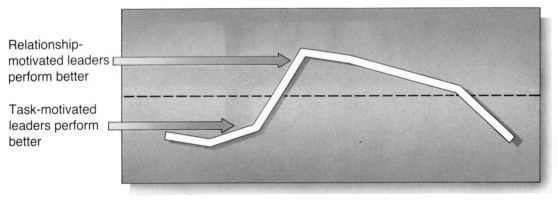

Relationship-motivated leaders perform better

Task-motivated leaders perform better

Leader-Member Relations	Good	Good	Good	Good	Poor	Poor	Poor	Poor
Task Structure	Structured		Unstructured		Structured		Unstructured	
Leader Position Power	Strong	Weak	Strong	Weak	Strong	Weak	Strong	Weak
	I	II	III	IV	V	VI	VII	VIII

of influence (columns I, II, and III) or very little influence (octants VII and VIII). In these situations, a leader who concentrates primarily on the task is required. In situations (octants IV, V, and VI) in which the leader has only moderate influence, a leader who focuses on interpersonal relationships is more likely to have a high-performing group.[16]

Leadership Training.   These conclusions influence Fiedler's recommendations concerning leadership training. If a leader's style depends on personality, then changing a leader's style would require a personality change. Fiedler contends it is more feasible to alter the situation to fit the leader's style.

This may be accomplished through a self-administered, programmed technique which requires the leader to complete the least-preferred coworker scale and determine his or her leadership style. Then the leader is shown how to diagnose a situation and change or modify the situation to match the leader's style:[17]

These changes in situational control might involve requests by the leader to be given routine assignments or to be given the less structured and unusual tasks; the leader might attempt to develop a closer, more supportive relationship with subordinates or to maintain more formal and distant relations; the leader might try to be "one of the gang" or emphasize rank and prerogatives.

Fiedler believes that the *Leader Match* program is cost-effective because it requires no instructor time and only four to six hours of the trainee's time. Initial results indicate that the performance ratings of leaders two to six months after their training are significantly higher than those of leaders who did not receive the training.[18]

Assessment of the Contingency Model. The contingency model has weaknesses. The three situational factors proposed by Fiedler are probably only a partial listing of important factors. Such factors as the organization's reward system, the cohesiveness of the group, and the skill and training of group members may affect group performance. Also, the model predicts the conditions under which a given leadership style will be effective, but it fails to provide a clear explanation of the leadership process. Finally, from a practical standpoint, altering situational factors to match a leader's style may be difficult:[19]

> Leadership effectiveness cannot be the only concern of administrators as they make decisions about job assignments. They must consider other aspects of the organization's operations which may conflict with their attempts to make good use of leadership talent. Some characteristics of the job, task, or organization simply may not be subject to change, at least in the short run.

LEADERSHIP STYLE AND THE SITUATION

The importance of matching the style of the leader to the situation is illustrated by the following experiences of corporate executives who left industry for academia. One individual, who went from a position as chairman and CEO of a railroad to become dean of a business school, found that his leadership style was not transferable. Accustomed to giving unquestioned orders, he discovered that trying to rule independent faculty members by fiat did not work. The faculty and students became so alienated by his autocratic style, among other factors, that he resigned a year later.

By contrast, the former CEO of a large corporation who became dean at another business school used his "thoughtful and participatory management style" to make a number of major curriculum changes with little faculty resistance.

SOURCE: Based on "Executive Suite: A Rough Ride through Academia," *Business Week,* 17 August 1981, p. 37.

Despite its limitations, the contingency model has emphasized the situational nature of leadership and helped us realize that almost anyone can succeed—or fail—as a leader. Leadership involves more than a person's traits or behavior. Contemporary leadership theories must consider not only the leader, but also the leader's subordinates and the task to be accomplished.

Path-Goal Theory of Leadership

A second effort to characterize leadership is the *path-goal theory* of leadership which grew out of attempts to explain the mixed findings of the Ohio State studies.[20] At its outset, this theory deviates from the contingency model by holding that the traditional means of characterizing leadership style as either task-oriented or relationship-oriented is insufficient. Instead, the same leader can engage in any of the following leadership styles:

□ *Directive leadership*—lets subordinates know what is expected of them and how the task should be accomplished.
□ *Supportive leadership*—shows concern for the needs of subordinates, makes the work more pleasant, and is friendly and approachable.
□ *Participative leadership*—consults with subordinates and takes their suggestions into consideration when making decisions.
□ *Achievement-oriented leadership*—emphasizes excellence in performance and displays confidence that subordinates will assume responsibility and accomplish challenging goals.

The most appropriate style is the one that has the greatest impact on the subordinates' performance and satisfaction:[21]

> The motivational functions of the leader consist of increasing the number and kinds of personal payoffs to subordinates for work-goal attainment and making paths to these payoffs easier to travel by clarifying the paths, reducing road blocks and pitfalls, and increasing the opportunities for personal satisfaction en route.

The major situational variables to be considered are (1) the subordinates' personal characteristics and (2) the environmental pressures and demands with which subordinates must cope to accomplish work goals and attain satisfaction. Both variables must be taken into account by the leader in determining the most appropriate leadership style.

Research Results. As an example of subordinates' personal characteristics, research indicates that individuals who believe that they control their own destiny (internals) are more satisfied under a participative leadership style than are individuals who are more fatalistic (externals). Conversely, externals are more satisfied under directive leadership than are internals.[22] In other words, a person with a strong internal locus of control prefers situations where he or she has some voice in decision making, whereas those who feel that their behavior is externally determined are more likely to feel comfortable under directive leadership.

In the area of environmental demands, the most studied variable has been task structure. Research has indicated that when the task is ambiguous and unstructured, a directive leadership style is most effective because it imposes structure upon the task, thereby permitting subordinates to deal with it more successfully.[23] Supportive leadership is most effective when subordinates are working on stressful, frustrating tasks and, hence, need the understanding and concern of their boss.

Assessment of Path-Goal Theory.   Although path-goal theory and the contingency model both emphasize the situational nature of leadership, they also differ significantly. The most obvious difference—that path-goal theory proposes that a leader can engage in more than one style of behavior—was noted earlier.

Another major difference is that, unlike the contingency model, path-goal theory does not attempt to identify all of the variables that influence a leadership situation. The theory holds that the major situational variables are subordinate characteristics and environmental demands, but this perspective provides a research direction rather than a guideline for practitioners. Specific characteristics and demands have been identified by research and incorporated into the theory, and future studies will doubtless modify the theory further.

Finally, as path-goal theory evolves, it not only proposes the most effective style of leadership for a particular situation, but it also explains the reasons underlying the proposition. Unlike the contingency model, which primarily predicts the best style for a given situation, path-goal theory attempts to predict and explain.

Only a few of the path-goal theory's possible predictions have been tested. The results have been "only moderately supportive."[24] One explanation for the mixed results is not only that the variables are difficult to measure, but also that various studies measure them in different ways, reducing comparability of the results. Then, too, leadership substitutes, which negate the need for certain leader behaviors, may be present in some situations.[25]

Each of the schools of thought examined here approaches leadership from a somewhat different perspective.* Each has its supporters and its detrac-

---

*Another view of situational leadership is provided by Paul Hersey and Kenneth H. Blanchard. According to this perspective, a manager should employ a task-oriented style with subordinates who are not "mature" in relation to the specific task they are to perform (that is, they have low willingness or ability to take responsibility for the task, and/or they lack the necessary experience or education to perform it). As subordinates mature, the leader's behavior should change in the following sequence: (1) high-task/low-relationship orientation; (2) high-task/high-relationship orientation: (3) low-task/high-relationship orientation; and (4) low-task/low-relationship orientation. Hence, highly motivated and well-trained subordinates need neither strong direction nor strong supportive behavior. See Paul Hersey and Kenneth H. Blanchard, *Management of Organizational Behavior: Utilizing Human Resources,* 4th ed. (Englewood Cliffs, N.J.: Prentice-Hall, 1982), pp. 150–75. For a critique of this theory, see Claude L. Graeff, "The Situational Leadership Theory: A Critical View," *Academy of Management Review* 8 (April 1983): 285–91.

tors. ''Because at least some empirical support is available for each perspective, leadership appears to be a far more complex set of cause-and-effect relationships than suggested by any one of the comparatively simple theoretical models offered to date.''[26] Much remains to be learned.

PARTICIPATIVE LEADERSHIP

One particular leadership style that has received emphasis in recent years is *participative leadership*. Participation refers to joint decision making between a manager and a subordinate or group of subordinates. Participation is primarily concerned with a sharing of the decision-making process, in contrast to delegation, in which the subordinate makes the decision alone. The continuum of leadership behavior, shown in Figure 14–4, illustrates various degrees of par-

FIGURE 14–4 Continuum of leadership behavior

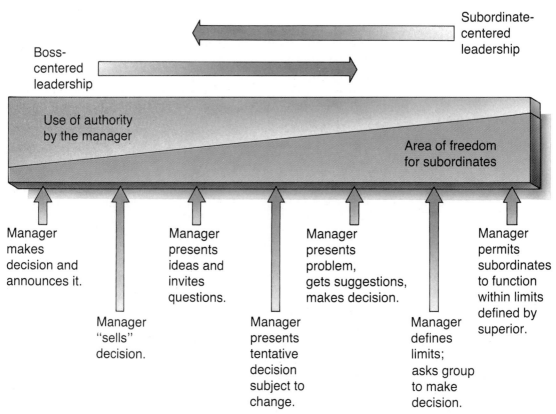

SOURCE: Robert Tannenbaum and Warren H. Schmidt, ''How to Choose a Leadership Pattern,'' *Harvard Business Review* 36 (March-April 1958): 96. Reprinted with permission. Also see the authors' ''Retrospective Commentary,'' *Harvard Business Review* 51 (May-June 1973): 166–68.

ticipative leadership. To the left of the continuum, the manager makes a decision unilaterally, without allowing subordinates to participate. Toward the other end, the manager uses less authority while granting subordinates a greater voice in decision making.

Benefits of Participation

Properly used, participative leadership may yield a number of benefits. For subordinates, participation in decision making can add meaning to their work and enhance their sense of accomplishment. Furthermore, subordinates who are active participants in departmental decision making probably develop faster than those who simply take orders. Also likely, decisions arrived at jointly will be accepted and implemented more effectively by those who have participated in making the decisions. Finally, participation allows management to tap the creativity of all its employees.

The basis for these benefits is aptly summarized in the three principles upon which the widely known Participative Management Program at Motorola is founded:[27]

- □ Every worker knows his or her job better than anyone else.
- □ People can and will accept the responsibility for managing their own work if that responsibility is given to them in the proper way.
- □ Intelligence, perspective, and creativity exist among people at all levels of the organization.

PARTICIPATION AT FORD

What *Business Week* characterized as perhaps "the most extensive and successful worker participation process in a major, unionized company" is Ford's "Employee Involvement" program. This voluntary program involves up to 30 percent of Ford's work force and includes union and worker participation in such wide-ranging decisions as work scheduling and technological changes.

As one example of the program's approach, Ford has equipped work stations on the assembly line with stop buttons to halt the line when a machine malfunctions or a defect is spotted. Within four months after the stop buttons were introduced into one plant, defects per car dropped from seventeen to fewer than one. Ford has truly come a long way since Henry Ford stated, years ago, that "the assembly line is a haven for those who haven't got the brains to do anything else."

SOURCE: Based on "What's Creating an 'Industrial Miracle' at Ford," *Business Week,* 30 July 1984, pp. 80–81.

PARTICIPATION: A THREAT?

Operative employees, whose ideas have generally been ignored for years, and top managers, who may be willing to try almost any program that promises to make their companies more competitive, are often strong supporters of participative management concepts. Resistance to such programs is most likely to come from between those two levels.

Many middle managers and supervisors fear a loss of their authority if workers are allowed to participate in decision making. Managers who were trained to believe that management has all the answers are not likely to share their "information power" with operative employees. As one human resource vice-president said, "Management still assumes its role is to tell—and not tell." In this view, worker participation encroaches on management's own decision-making perogatives. Any participation program that is to be successful must first lessen this managerial resistance.

SOURCE: Leonard M. Apcar, "Middle Managers and Supervisors Resist Moves to More Participatory Management," *The Wall Street Journal*, 16 September 1985; and Bill Saporito, "The Revolt Against 'Working Smarter,'" *Fortune*, 21 July 1986, pp. 58–65.

Constraints on Participation

Evidence on the effectiveness of participation indicates, as path-goal theory would predict, that participative management is not equally effective in all situations.[28] Participation appears to have some effect on both satisfaction and productivity, but overall its effect on subordinate job satisfaction is somewhat stronger than its effect on productivity.[29]

There are a number of reasons why participative leadership is not effective in all situations or for all groups. For instance, the length of time an employee has been in a particular position affects the ability to participate. Personality differences make some more or less interested in participation. There is also a danger in overdoing participation. In one study, project engineers who were asked to participate more than they desired shared certain characteristics—low performance and high stress—with engineers who were not allowed to participate as much as they desired.[30] The optimal level of participation evidently varies from individual to individual and from situation to situation.

Model of Participative Leadership

A model intended to clarify when subordinates should be allowed to participate in decision making has been developed by Victor Vroom and Philip Yetton.[31] Depending on the situation, a leader may make a decision alone or may

FIGURE 14–5   Decision methods for group problems

AI. You solve the problem or make the decision yourself, using information available to you at the time.

AII. You obtain the necessary information from your subordinates, then decide the solution to the problem yourself. You may or may not tell your subordinates what the problem is in getting the information from them. The role played by your subordinates in making the decision is clearly one of providing the necessary information to you, rather than generating or evaluating alternative solutions.

CI. You share the problem with the relevant subordinates individually, getting their ideas and suggestions without bringing them together as a group. Then *you* make the decision, which may or may not reflect your subordinates' influence.

CII. You share the problem with your subordinates as a group, obtaining their collective ideas and suggestions. Then you make the decision, which may or may not reflect your subordinates' influence.

GII. You share the problem with your subordinates as a group. Together you generate and evaluate alternatives and attempt to reach agreement (consensus) on a solution. Your role is much like that of chairman. You do not try to influence the group to adopt "your" solution, and you are willing to accept and implement any solution which has the support of the entire group.

A = autocratic
C = consultative
G = group

SOURCE: Reprinted from *Leadership* and *Decision-Making* by Victor H. Vroom and Philip W. Yetton by permission of the University of Pittsburgh Press. © 1973 by University of Pittsburgh Press.

involve subordinates in the decision process to varying degrees, as shown in Figure 14–5.

The relevant situational variables are defined by seven questions, shown in the top of Figure 14–6. The first three questions focus on the quality of the decision, while the last four are concerned with the acceptance of the decision by the subordinates. The lower part of Figure 14–6 presents a decision tree (or flowchart) the manager may use to determine which decision method or methods are appropriate for a given situation. As an example, look at the lowest branch of the decision tree. This represents a situation in which:

A. the problem has a quality requirement
B. the manager does not have sufficient information to make a high-quality decision

C. the problem is unstructured
D. subordinate acceptance of the decision is important for effective imple-
    mentation
E. if the manager makes the decision alone, he or she cannot be reasonably
    certain that it will be accepted by the subordinates
F. the subordinates do not share the organizational goals to be attained in
    solving the problem

In this situation, the manager should use decision method CII (Figure
14–5)—share the problem with subordinates in a group meeting, obtaining
their ideas and suggestions, and then make the decision alone.

As may be seen from the chart in Figure 14–6, some situations permit a
choice of alternative decision methods. In those cases, the choice would depend upon the leader's personality, the subordinates' qualifications, and the
time available.

Research on the model has been fairly encouraging. Vroom and Arthur
Jago, using self-report measures, found that of 181 actual decisions made by
96 managers, 68 percent of the decisions conforming to the model were successful while only 22 percent of the decisions failing to conform to the model
were successful.[32] Another study of 47 owners of small franchises and 241 of
their employees found that employees of managers who made decisions in
accordance with the model were more "satisfied with supervision" and had
higher productivity than employees of managers whose decisions failed to conform to the model.[33]

The Vroom-Yetton model deals with only one aspect of leadership, participative decision making. But, like the contingency model and the path-goal
theory, it emphasizes the situational nature of the leadership function. An effective leader is one who is able to match his or her style to the situation in an
appropriate way.

SUMMARY

Through the function of *leadership*, a manager secures the effort and teamwork
of organization members. Early theorists believed that the leader's *traits* or personal characteristics induced others to follow. But the inability of trait concepts
to account adequately for leadership effectiveness led to a focus on the leader's
style or behavior. Most of this research has examined the effects of task-oriented styles versus relationship-oriented styles on group performance and satisfaction. Mixed findings have resulted, indicating that leadership effectiveness
cannot be understood through analysis of the leader's style alone.

Current theories take a broader approach by including the interaction
between the leader's style and various situational factors. The most complete
formulation to date is Fiedler's *contingency model of leadership* which predicts the
leader style that is most effective depending upon the particular combination

FIGURE 14–6 Decision process flowchart

A. Does the problem possess a quality requirement?
B. Do I have sufficient information to make a high-quality decision?
C. Is the problem structured?
D. Is acceptance of the decision by subordinates important for effective implementation?
E. If I were to make the decision by myself, am I reasonably certain that it would be accepted by my subordinates?
F. Do subordinates share the organizational goals to be attained in solving this problem?
G. Is conflict among subordinates likely in preferred solutions?

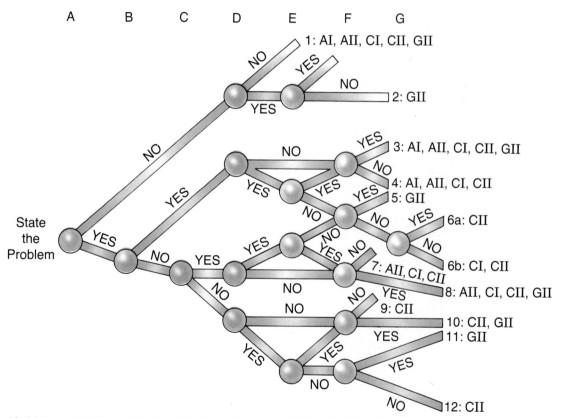

SOURCE: Reprinted from *Leadership and Decision-Making* by Victor H. Vroom and Philip W. Yetton by permission of the University of Pittsburgh Press. © 1973 by University of Pittsburgh Press.

of three situational factors: *leader-member relations, task structure,* and *leader position power.* A different approach is taken by the *path-goal theory,* an attempt to explain which of four leadership styles is most effective, depending upon the subordinates' personal characteristics and the environmental pressures and demands with which subordinates must cope to accomplish work goals and attain satisfaction.

One of the most widely discussed leader behaviors is *participative leadership,* a style which involves subordinates in the managerial decision-making process. Although participative leadership is not effective in all situations or for all groups, research indicates a positive relationship between participative leadership and employee productivity and satisfaction in many cases. The *Vroom-Yetton model* attempts to clarify situations in which participative leadership can be used effectively.

KEY CONCEPTS

Leadership	Task structure
Supervision	Leader position power
Leadership traits	Task-oriented leadership
Screening process	Relationship-oriented leadership
Leadership style	Least-preferred coworker scale
Initiating structure	Leader match
Consideration	Path-goal theory of leadership
Transactional leadership	Directive leadership
Transformational leadership	Supportive leadership
Leadership substitutes	Participative leadership
Leadership neutralizers	Achievement-oriented leadership
Contingency model of leadership	Vroom-Yetton Model of Participative Leadership
Leader-member relations	

DISCUSSION QUESTIONS

1. Why are "trait theories" insufficient explanations of leadership effectiveness?
2. Distinguish between a supervisor who is high in consideration and one who is high in initiating structure. On the basis of your own experience, describe the leadership approach of one manager (or teacher) in each category.
3. Disregarding situational factors, what general relationship exists between leadership style and group effectiveness? What is the most obvious explanation for this relationship?
4. In those cases which do show a positive correlation between relationship-oriented leadership and productivity, how can one know which is the cause and which is the effect?

5. Is *leadership style* important in all situations? Why or why not?
6. An organization characterized by poor quality products and declining revenues is searching for a new chief executive. Should it attempt to hire a *transactional* or *transformational* leader? Explain.
7. What is the significance of the *leadership situation* in choosing a pattern of leadership?
8. Explain Fiedler's *contingency model of leadership.*
9. Compare and contrast the *contingency model of leadership* with the *path-goal theory of leadership.*
10. Does evidence show that *employee participation* contributes to productivity?
11. How might the *Vroom-Yetton model of leadership* be useful to a practicing manager?

NOTES

1. Arthur G. Jago, "Leadership: Perspectives in Theory and Research," *Management Science* 28 (March 1982): 330.
2. Studies in organizations have consistently shown that the leader's sex has little effect on the way subordinates perceive leader behavior or on subordinate satisfaction. See Gregory H. Dobbins and Stephanie J. Platz, "Sex Differences in Leadership: How Real Are They?" *Academy of Management Review* 11 (January 1986): 118–27.
3. Fred E. Fiedler and Albert F. Leister, "Leader Intelligence and Task Performance: A Test of a Multiple Screen Model," *Organizational Behavior and Human Performance* 20 (October 1977): 1–14.
4. Robert G. Lord, Christy L. De Vader, and George M. Alliger, "A Meta-Analysis of the Relation Between Personality Traits and Leadership Perceptions: An Application of Validity Generalization Procedures," *Journal of Applied Psychology* 71 (August 1986): 407–8.
5. Bernard M. Bass, *Stogdill's Handbook of Leadership: A Survey of Theory and Research,* rev. ed. (New York: The Free Press, 1981), pp. 358–92.
6. Ibid., pp. 382–90.
7. Jago, "Leadership: Perspectives in Theory and Research," p. 321.
8. Aaron Lowin and James R. Craig, "The Influence of Level of Performance on Managerial Style: An Experimental Object-Lesson in the Ambiguity of Correlational Data," *Organizational Behavior and Human Performance* 3 (November 1968): 440–58; and David M. Herold, "Two-Way Influence Processes in Leader-Follower Dyads," *Academy of Management Journal* 20 (June 1977): 224–37.
9. This distinction was first made by James MacGregor Burns, *Leadership* (New York: Harper & Row, 1978).
10. Bernard M. Bass, *Leadership and Performance Beyond Expectations* (New York: The Free Press, 1985), p. 22.
11. Bernard M. Bass, "Leadership: Good, Better, Best," *Organizational Dynamics* 13 (Winter 1985): 26–40; and Noel M. Tichy and David O. Ulrich, "SMR Forum: The Leadership Challenge—A Call for the Transformational Leader," *Sloan Management Review* 26 (Fall 1984): 59–68.
12. Steven Kerr and John M. Jermier, "Substitutes for Leadership: Their Meaning and Measurement," *Organizational Behavior and Human Performance* 22 (Decem-

ber 1978): 375–403. Results of a test of this concept can be found in Jon P. Howell and Peter W. Dorfman, "Substitutes for Leadership: Test of a Construct," *Academy of Management Journal* 24 (December 1981): 714–28; and Jon P. Howell and Peter W. Dorfman, "Leadership and Substitutes for Leadership Among Professional and Nonprofessional Workers," *Journal of Applied Behavioral Science* 22, no. 1 (1986): 29–46.

13. Jon P. Howell, Peter W. Dorfman, and Steven Kerr, "Moderator Variables in Leadership Research," *Academy of Management Review* 11 (January 1986): 88–102.

14. This theory of Fred E. Fiedler is widely discussed in the literature. For one comprehensive source, see Fred E. Fiedler and Martin M. Chemers, *Leadership and Effective Management* (Glenview, Ill.: Scott, Foresman, 1974).

15. The meaning and interpretation of the least-preferred coworker score have been much debated. Two representative analyses can be found in Chester A. Schriesheim, Brendan D. Bannister, and William H. Money, "Psychometric Properties of the LPC Scale: An Extension of Rice's Review," *Academy of Management Review* 4 (April 1979): 287–90; and Robert W. Rice, "Reliability and Validity of the LPC Scale: A Reply," *Academy of Management Review* 4 (April 1979): 291–94.

16. A meta-analysis of published studies of Fiedler's theory resulted in "a generally positive conclusion regarding the validity of the Contingency Theory." See Lawrence H. Peters, Darrell D. Hartke, and John T. Pohlmann, "Fiedler's Contingency Theory of Leadership: An Application of the Meta-Analysis Procedures of Schmidt and Hunter," *Psychological Bulletin* 97 (March 1985): 274–85.

17. Albert Leister, Donald Borden, and Fred E. Fiedler, "Validation of Contingency Model Leadership Training: Leader Match," *Academy of Management Journal* 20 (September 1977): 466.

18. See Jago, "Leadership," p. 323; and Fred E. Fiedler and Linda Mahar, "The Effectiveness of Contingency Model Training: A Review of the Validation of Leader Match," *Personnel Psychology* 32 (Spring 1979): 45–62.

19. Chester A. Schriesheim, James M. Tolliver, and Orlando C. Behling, "Leadership Theory: Some Implications for Managers," *MSU Business Topics* 26 (Summer 1978): 38.

20. The path-goal theory is explained in a number of sources. One of the most complete discussions can be found in Robert J. House and Terence R. Mitchell, "Path-Goal Theory of Leadership," *Journal of Contemporary Business* 3 (Autumn 1974): 81–97.

21. Ibid., p. 85.

22. Terence R. Mitchell, Charles M. Smyser, and Stan E. Weed, "Locus of Control: Supervision and Work Satisfaction," *Academy of Management Journal* 18 (September 1975): 623–31.

23. Mark J. Kroll and Charles D. Pringle, "Path-Goal Theory and the Task Design Literature: A Tenuous Linkage," *Akron Business and Economic Review* 17 (Winter 1986): 75–84.

24. Janet Fulk Schriesheim and Chester A. Schriesheim, "A Test of the Path-Goal Theory of Leadership and Some Suggested Directions for Future Research," *Personnel Psychology* 33 (Summer 1980): 350.

25. Ibid., pp. 367–68.

26. Jago, "Leadership," p. 330.

27. William J. Weisz, "Employee Involvement: How It Works at Motorola," *Personnel* 62 (February 1985): 29.

28. Edwin A. Locke, David M. Schweiger, and Gary P. Latham, "Participation in Decision Making: When Should It Be Used?", *Organizational Dynamics* 14 (Winter 1986): 65–79.
29. Katherine I. Miller and Peter R. Monge, "Participation, Satisfaction, and Productivity: A Meta-Analytic Review," *Academy of Management Journal* 29 (December 1986): 748.
30. John M. Ivancevich, "An Analysis of Participation in Decision Making among Project Engineers," *Academy of Management Journal* 22 (June 1979): 253–69.
31. Victor H. Vroom and Philip W. Yetton, *Leadership and Decision-Making* (Pittsburgh: University of Pittsburgh Press, 1973).
32. Victor H. Vroom and Arthur G. Jago, "On the Validity of the Vroom-Yetton Model," *Journal of Applied Psychology* 63 (April 1978): 151–62.
33. Charles Margerison and Richard Glube, "Leadership Decision-Making: An Empirical Test of the Vroom and Yetton Model," *Journal of Management Studies* 16 (February 1979): 45–55.

SUPPLEMENTARY READING

Barnes, Louis B., and Kriger, Mark P. "The Hidden Side of Organizational Leadership." *Sloan Management Review* 28 (Fall 1986): 15–25.

Bass, Bernard M. *Stogdill's Handbook of Leadership: A Survey of Theory and Research,* rev. ed. New York: The Free Press, 1981.

————. *Leadership and Performance Beyond Expectations.* New York: The Free Press, 1985.

Boyle, Richard J. "Wrestling with Jellyfish." *Harvard Business Review* 62 (January-February 1984): 74–83.

Fiedler, Fred E. *A Theory of Leadership Effectiveness.* New York: McGraw-Hill, 1967.

————. "The Leadership Game: Matching the Man to the Situation." *Organizational Dynamics* 4 (Winter 1976): 6–16.

Gordon, Gil E., and Rosen, Ned. "Critical Factors in Leadership Succession." *Organizational Behavior and Human Performance* 27 (April 1981): 227–54.

Grunwald, Wolfgang, and Bernthal, Wilmar F. "Controversy in German Management: The Harzburg Model Experience." *Academy of Management Review* 8 (April 1983): 233–41.

Halal, William E., and Brown, Bob S. "Participative Management: Myth and Reality." *California Management Review* 23 (Summer 1981): 20–32.

House, Robert J. "A Path-Goal Theory of Leadership Effectiveness." *Administrative Science Quarterly* 16 (September 1971): 321–38.

Howell, Jon P.; Dorfman, Peter W.; and Kerr, Steven. "Moderator Variables in Leadership Research." *Academy of Management Review* 11 (January 1986): 88–102.

Jago, Arthur G. "Leadership: Perspectives in Theory and Research." *Management Science* 28 (March 1982): 315–36.

Kroll, Mark J., and Pringle, Charles D. "Path-Goal Theory and the Task Design Literature: A Tenuous Linkage." *Akron Business and Economic Review* 17 (Winter 1986): 75–84.

Kuttner, Robert. "Sharing Power at Eastern Air Lines." *Harvard Business Review* 63 (November-December 1985): 91–101.

Locke, Edwin A.; Schweiger, David M.; and Latham, Gary P. "Participation in Decision Making: When Should It Be Used?" *Organizational Dynamics* 14 (Winter 1986): 65–79.

Meindl, James R.; Ehrlich, Sanford B.; and Dukerich, Janet M. "The Romance of Leadership." *Administrative Science Quarterly* 30 (March 1985): 78–102.

Pfeffer, Jeffrey. "The Ambiguity of Leadership." *Academy of Management Review* 2 (January 1977): 104–12.

Weisz, William J. "Employee Involvement: How It Works at Motorola." *Personnel* 62 (February 1985): 29–33.

LIBERIA AIN'T LOUISIANA!

Charles Simmons was a fast-rising star in the Tomas Oil Company. He had joined the firm some twelve years ago straight out of college and had immediately begun to make his mark. Charles was a character and a hard drinker who cursed at every opportunity. Nevertheless he excelled in getting the job done, usually well under budget. He had little patience with incompetence, and his public temper tantrums were the dread of every offending subordinate. Yet Simmons was quick to praise and reward those who met his exacting standards. As one former subordinate said, "I like him and he knows the business, but it's sometimes hard to know where you stand with him. One minute he is yelling at you and the next he is inviting you to join him at a local pub."

In late 1983, Charles was promoted to be superintendent of a trouble-plagued refining facility in Louisiana. Tomas Oil had expanded rapidly during the previous few years and had run short of qualified lower-level managers. As a result, the Louisiana plant was being operated with a small cadre of very inexperienced supervisors. Functionally, the facility differed little from others of its type. The workers' duties consisted mainly of monitoring the operations of various types of machinery. Managerial functions included the scheduling of production, quality control, and storage of the many derivatives of petroleum.

Charles's reputation preceded his arrival, and the Louisiana work force greeted the news of his coming with a mixture of awe and foreboding. If anyone could straighten out the operation, it would be him, but there would be some "hell to pay" too.

Charles didn't waste a minute. One dazed first-line supervisor summed up the work force reaction: "Charles Simmons is the George S. Patton of Tomas Oil. In the space of forty-eight hours, I was called every name in the book, patted on the back twice, and taught more about my job than I could have learned on my own in five years. You either produced or else!" In the space of two months, Simmons moved the Louisiana plant from last in productivity and among the highest in cost to one of the leading profit centers in the company. The facility stayed that way for the remainder of his eighteen-month tenure as superintendent.

In early 1985, Nelson Lawler, president of Tomas, called Charles and, after praising his usual outstanding performance, asked

Case prepared by Professor Paul R. Reed of Sam Houston State University.

Charles for a personal favor. Would he agree to transferring overseas for no longer than one year, to head the remote Lagos, Liberia, refining facility? To make the offer more tempting, Lawler discussed bringing Charles up to corporate headquarters as his personal assistant after his tour in "little Siberia." Needless to say, Charles was on the next transatlantic flight.

Most of the conditions at the Lagos facility were quite different from those in the United States. All of the U.S. employees served their one-year tour without their families. They lived in company-supplied living quarters in a small but attractive compound. The nearest town of any size, over 100 miles away, offered few diversions. As a result, the U.S. plant crew spent the majority of their spare time in the compound recreation room reading, watching old movies, and patronizing the small bar.

The U.S. work force comprised veterans and several mid-level managers who had been with Tomas for fifteen years or longer. The previous superintendent had been a low-key, easygoing type much admired by the men. The Lagos refinery was almost identical to the Louisiana facility, and the difference in job requirements was minimal.

As might be expected, Charles arrived with his usual flourish. Although the facility had been operating satisfactorily, he decided it did not meet his standards. On several occasions, his displeasure with subordinates was carried from the work site into the compound recreation room. Even the bar small talk began to be interrupted by his sharp tongue. Charles's attempts to raise production and lower costs met with some

success but were accompanied by an increasingly strained atmosphere at the plant and in the compound. The recreation room crowd began to thin out, and many men began spending their leisure time in the privacy of their rooms. Charles noticed that many of his subordinates had begun to avoid him, but he attached no great importance to it.

Four months after his arrival in Lagos, Charles was notified that an old friend, Ross Kroll, V.P. for Personnel, would be making a brief visit in a few days. Charles scheduled the usual briefings and looked forward to Ross's coming. Ross was all smiles when he stepped out of the helicopter and asked that all briefings and other plans be canceled— this was just an unofficial stopover. Upon arrival at the compound, Ross asked Charles to lead the way to his room. After twenty minutes of small talk, Ross got to the reason for his coming: "Charles, we both know that with your ability and a little luck you can someday be running this company." Then after a short pause, he continued, "But if you hope to do that, there is one thing you've got to get straightened out right now—Liberia ain't Louisiana!"

Questions

1. What is Ross trying to tell Charles?
2. Why was Charles successful in Louisiana?
3. Why was he being less successful in Liberia?
4. Analyze Charles's past two years using Fiedler's contingency model of leadership. Does it explain his situation? Why or why not?

NATURE OF GROUPS
Types of Groups ☐ Functions of Groups

ATTRIBUTES OF GROUPS
Activities, Interactions, and
Sentiments ☐ Norms ☐ Conformity
☐ Cohesiveness

THE USE OF COMMITTEES
Nature of Committees ☐ Reasons for
Committees ☐ Dangers and Difficulties

OTHER COOPERATIVE ENDEAVORS
Quality Circles ☐ Autonomous Work
Groups

GROUP CONFLICT
Managing Controversy ☐ Managing
Conflict of Interests

Summary ☐ Key Concepts ☐ Discussion
Questions ☐ Notes ☐ Supplementary
Reading

CASES: The Company Training Program
☐ Al's Exhausting Dilemma

This chapter will enable you to

☐   Identify the types of organizational
    groups and the functions they perform.

☐   Define the major attributes of
    organizational groups.

☐   Explain the reasons for the formation of
    committees and the dangers inherent
    in their use.

☐   Become familiar with such cooperative
    group endeavors as quality circles and
    autonomous work groups.

☐   Recognize the role that conflict plays in
    an organization, and understand how
    to manage it effectively.

CHAPTER 15
GROUP PROCESSES

Much of the work in organizations is accomplished through group effort. Departments, committees, and task forces are collections of individuals who interact to accomplish some common objective. An understanding of how groups affect organizational performance and individual behavior is essential to management.

NATURE OF GROUPS

A *group* is composed of two or more persons who interact to a significant degree in the pursuit of a common goal. Through interaction, persons become "psychologically aware of one another" and "perceive themselves to be a group."[1]

Types of Groups

Groups in organizations can be classified as formal or informal. A *formal group* is created by management and charged with the responsibility of contributing to the organization. An *informal group* is a natural outgrowth of human interaction and develops without formal management sanction.

Formal Groups. The most common formal group is the *command group,* composed of a manager and his or her immediate subordinates. Command groups are often formally designated as departments or work units. The purpose of such groups is "to perform some task more efficiently through the pooling and coordination of the behavior and resources of a collection of individuals."[2]

Another formal group is the *problem-solving group,* which combines the knowledge and resources of several individuals to solve a problem or exploit an opportunity. The most common problem-solving group is the *committee,* a relatively permanent collection of individuals who are responsible for specific assignments or activities. A *task force* is a less permanent form of problem-solving group, often established to deal with a particular nonroutine decision that cuts across functional or departmental lines.

Informal Groups.   Informal groups arise spontaneously throughout the organization and are found at all hierarchical levels. "Whenever individuals associate on a fairly continuous basis there is a tendency for groups to form whose activities may be different from those required by the organization."[3] Such groups may form because individuals receive satisfaction from their association with others or because they wish to advance some common interest. Although our concern in this chapter is the formal group, such groups cannot be studied in isolation. Formal interaction is inevitably modified by formal activities and attitudes.

Functions of Groups

The primary function of a formal group is to attain some goal or goals which contribute to overall organizational effectiveness. These goals vary from group to group. One group may have the responsibility of keeping accurate account-

GROUP LOYALTY

Under extreme circumstances, the desire to be with the members of one's group exceeds even the desire for physical safety. As one officer in the Royal Air Force during World War II wrote:

> Everyone looked forward to the completion of his tour, but so strong was the crew spirit in the Bomber Command that it was not an uncommon occurrence for a man to volunteer to do as many as 10 extra trips so that he and his crew could finish together. . . .

SOURCE: D. Stafford-Clark, "Morale and Flying Experience: Results of a Wartime Study," *Journal of Mental Science* 95 (January 1949): 15.

ing records, another planning future strategy, and still another training and developing managers. The rationale under lying group formation is termed *synergy;* that is, the whole is greater than the sum of its parts. In other words, people working together, combining their diverse talents and perspectives and exchanging varied ideas and methods, can accomplish significantly more than could the same individuals working alone.

Formal and informal groups also provide satisfaction for the social needs of members of the organization. Opportunity for social interaction and satisfaction can make a job or organization bearable even though it may have undesirable features. Membership in groups not only provides opportunities for enjoyable social interaction but also contributes to the emotional well-being of employees. Employees are aided in maintaining their emotional equilibrium, particularly in times of crisis or difficulty, by the support they receive from fellow workers.

Group membership also helps to satisfy other needs. Group members who are accepted by their peers may feel more secure than isolated individuals. Group membership also provides a form of recognition and identity far more personal than that bestowed upon the individual by the organization. Finally, membership in an elite group helps fulfill a person's need for esteem.

ATTRIBUTES OF GROUPS

Activities, Interactions, and Sentiments

One approach to understanding work group behavior draws attention to three attributes which characterize virtually any group: *activities, interactions,* and *sentiments.*[4] Activities are those physical acts the employee is required to engage in to perform the job, such as driving a truck, typing invoices, or mapping out an advertising campaign. These activities typically require the employee to engage in interactions with other people during the work day, such as consulting with a superior or coordinating one's work with the work of other employees. Sentiments are the feelings and attitudes the employee has about job, peers, supervisor, the organization's policies, the meaning of work, and so on.

As employees engage in these required activities and interactions, nonrequired activities and interactions emerge. Interaction between some employees, for instance, may lead to sentiments of liking which result in the taking of breaks together, talking with each other on the job more than is required, and so on. Activities such as football pools or horseplay may likewise emerge. Similarly, sentiments of dislike may emerge, causing employees to avoid interaction, even though it may be required.

Hence, activities, interactions, and sentiments are interrelated, as shown in Figure 15–1. As an illustration of these attributes in a practical situation,

FIGURE 15–1 Activities,
interactions, and sentiments

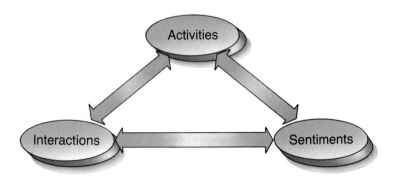

consider a change in production technology that takes employees out of small work teams and distributes them along an assembly line. In all probability, the scope of the job (required activities) would be narrowed. Furthermore, a reduction in interactions would occur. As a result of changes in activities and interactions, sentiments would likewise be affected. If the individual enjoys interaction and the opportunity for performing a varied job, the change to assembly-line work would create dissatisfaction. This, in turn, might affect interaction with the line supervisor and could lead to such emergent activities as trying to find employment elsewhere.

Norms

Over time, the interrelationships among activities, interactions, and sentiments within a group result in the evolution of group norms. A *norm* is a generally agreed-upon standard of behavior to which every member of the group is expected to adhere. The strongest norms are related to those forms of behavior considered most significant by the group members. The workers in the Bank Wiring Observation Room in the Hawthorne plant, described in chapter 2, established a daily production norm and enforced that norm through a number of informal means.

Work-group norms may develop in one or more of several ways. The supervisor, for instance, may explicitly set some norms. Examples are the form in which reports are to be presented and the rules concerning the making of personal phone calls on company time. Norms may also be set by primacy, so that the original behavior pattern that emerges in a group sets subsequent expectations. Examples include where people sit at committee meetings and how formally the first meeting of a committee is conducted. Still other norms emerge because people bring expectations with them from other work groups. Students and professors, for example, carry their mutual expectations of the other's behavior from one class period to another, from one semester to another, and even from one university to another.[5]

Norms allow the group to control some of the more important aspects of behavior, thereby increasing predictability and order within the group, The success and continuity of a group may well depend upon adherence to norms. Groups without strong norms are unlikely to be as stable, long-lasting, or satisfying to their members as are groups with well-developed norms receiving strong member support.

Conformity

Adherence to group norms as a result of perceived group pressure is termed *conformity*. Since significant nonconformity threatens the group's standards, stability, and longevity, the pressure placed on a member to conform to important norms can be intense. Persistent nonconformity may be punished in a variety of ways, the most common being social rejection that results in isolation.

Conformity takes two forms:

☐ *compliance*—a change in behavior resulting in closer adherence to group norms
☐ *private acceptance* or *internalization*—a change in both behavior and beliefs to conform more closely to group norms

Most work group norms apply primarily to behavior, though a statement of beliefs may be required for acceptance by certain groups, such as religious or charitable organizations. Compliance is heavily emphasized because behavior is visible—while beliefs are not—and it is often necessary that a group behave in a united way if it is to succeed.

Not all individuals conform to the same extent. Persons with low status in the group, for instance, are more likely to conform closely to all of the group's norms in order to be accepted by the other members. Persons with low self-confidence are more likely to conform since they may feel that the group's decisions are superior to their own. Individuals are also likely to conform when they perceive that the group's goals are similar to their personal goals. Conformity increases in ambiguous situations (when individuals are not certain how to behave and must look to the group for guidance) and during crises (when the stability of the group is threatened).

Cohesiveness

Cohesiveness refers to how closely the group members "stick together" and act as a single unit rather than as individuals. A cohesive group is attractive to its members, causing them to desire to maintain their membership in the group. As a group becomes more attractive to members, therefore, it becomes more cohesive, and group members derive considerable satisfaction from their interactions and activities.

Cohesiveness also may have powerful effects on group performance. Since membership in a cohesive group is valued by its members, conformity to group norms will be high, reflecting the desire of the members to remain in the group. Hence, if the group develops low performance norms, the members will produce at a low level, and the opposite behavior will occur in groups with high performance norms. The level of a cohesive group's production norms may reflect the group's sentiments toward management.[6] Mutual trust between management and the work group, fostered by members' perceptions of fair treatment by management, is likely to be more conducive to high performance goals than are conditions characterized by distrust and a "we-versus-them" attitude.

As Figure 15–2 indicates, every manager should be aware of the various group attributes. A new manager, particularly, must attempt to determine how cohesive subordinates are, what norms they consider important, and how closely they conform to those norms. Without prior assessment of the group's interactions, activities, and sentiments, a new manager might change the group's structure or work methods and in the process inadvertently violate the group's central norms. In such situations, the puzzled manager may be faced with resistance to the change or even outright rebellion.

Groups can have both positive and negative effects on organizational performance. "There are still major gaps in our understanding of the reasons why some groups function effectively—and why others turn out to be a source of continual difficulty and dismay for both group members and organizational management."[7]

FIGURE 15–2 Attributes of groups that affect group performance and member satisfaction

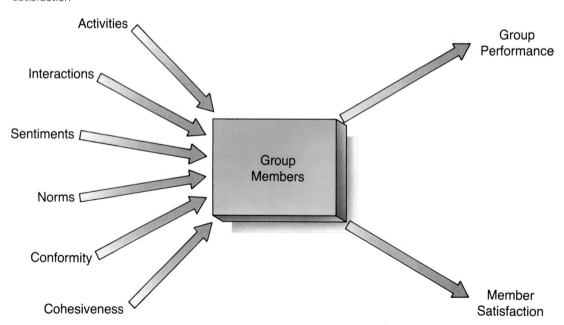

THE USE OF COMMITTEES

Aside from the command group—composed of a manager and immediate subordinates—the most common formal group in many organizations is the committee. A *committee* involves a meeting of two or more individuals who are officially drawn together to identify problems, develop recommendations, or make decisions.

Nature of Committees

Committees multiply as organizations grow in size and complexity. In large governmental, educational, charitable, and business institutions, committees are an integral part of the administrative structure. In the business field, they are not limited to large corporations but are also found in relatively small concerns. Nor are they limited to top management levels—they function at middle and lower levels of the organization as well.

Committees are infinite in their variety. In duration, for example, there are standing committees maintained permanently and *ad hoc* (or special purpose) committees appointed to serve only temporarily. Committees range from those that meet rarely to those that meet regularly on a weekly, or even a daily, basis.

The highest-level committee within most organizations is the board of directors. This group acts as a policy-making committee, working through appointed managers, but it may also overlap the top administrative levels through the use of an executive committee. (That is, the membership of an executive committee may include individuals who serve as both directors and managers of the corporation.)

Many chief executives rely for advice and counsel on at least one formal committee of senior managers. Some of these committees deal with a single recurring issue, such as new product development, capital appropriations, or compensation. Others, chaired by the chief executive, deal with a wide range of matters. Such committees serve to bind the senior officers into a cohesive management team.[8]

Reasons for Committees

For decades, the strengths and weaknesses of committees—described in Figure 15–3—have been debated. In spite of the weaknesses, however, the general consensus among administrators is that committees are useful, and often essential.

Better Decisions through Group Deliberation. The committee can be used to pull together the different abilities and knowledge of its members. No two individuals approach solution of a complex problem in precisely the same way, and varied analytical abilities may, through committee deliberation, be brought

FIGURE 15-3   Strengths and weaknesses of committees

Strengths	Weaknesses
Better decisions through group delib- eration	Danger of compromise
	Difficulty in placing responsibility
Coordination of work	Delay and indecision
Securing cooperation in execution	Domination by one member
Training of participants	

to bear upon the same problem The various departments and functional areas of the organization also involve different points of view which may be discovered and applied to the question at hand.

Committee analysis of a problem represents a kind of insurance against a decision based on faulty reasoning or personal bias. This implies that the committee is more than a rubber stamp and that members can speak out on issues under consideration. (A cartoon has depicted the chairperson putting the question to vote with "All who object, say 'I resign.' ")

Coordination of Work.   Specialization of work, both operative and managerial, makes the problem of synchronization of activities difficult. Many functions of one department are intertwined with those of other departments. As an example, a decision in research and development may have repercussions affecting the sales, production, finance, personnel, public relations, and legal departments. In a large organization, the left hand does not always know what the right hand is doing unless active steps are taken. The committee provides one way to achieve coordination of effort.

Securing Cooperation in Execution.   Certain barriers interfere with effective implementation of plans and policies. Among these are misunderstanding of a given plan or policy and the feeling that one must follow a policy or plan without an opportunity to express opinions about it. A committee may be used as a means of attacking both problems. For example, discussion in a committee meeting can bring to light mistaken ideas and answer questions concerning the matter under consideration. A committee member who is involved in the discussion of a problem and its solution is more likely to be aware of why certain alternatives were rejected and others accepted. This knowledge is likely to lead to better understanding of the decision.

Likewise, a member's resistance to a committee decision is likely to be lessened if the member is allowed to express objections to the decision. Even if some members disagree with the committee's final decision, it is difficult for them to oppose the decision as violently as they might if it were simply handed to them without explanation or opportunity for comments.

HOW TO BE AN EFFECTIVE COMMITTEE MEMBER

☐ Never go to a meeting unprepared.

☐ If you are joining a group that has met previously, ask before taking a seat. Group norms concerning who sits where form early in the life of the group.

☐ Note that the dominant figures at the meeting usually sit at the head and foot of a rectangular table.

☐ Note that individuals with power usually sit in a relaxed position, rather than leaning forward expectantly.

☐ Pick an appropriate time to make your point—when it fits smoothly into the discussion.

☐ Present your idea not as yours alone but as an outgrowth of the group's discussion.

☐ Never get defensive or press prematurely for a group decision.

☐ Never sulk if the decision goes against you.

☐ When disagreeing, remember the need for everyone to save face.

☐ Volunteer to do follow-up work so that your report at the next meeting can lead to your getting some credit for the outcome.

SOURCE: Adapted from Walter Kiechel III, "How to Take Part in a Meeting," *Fortune,* 26 May 1986, pp. 177–80.

Training of Participants. Development of personnel for all levels of management is one of the important responsibilities of administrators. Committee members are exposed to ideas and knowledge outside their usual areas of responsibility. In addition, committee members may engage in study in the process of preparing for committee participation, particularly if they are given some special responsibilities in connection with committee projects and performance. Perhaps the greatest training value comes from the give-and-take of committee sessions. In this atmosphere, committee members gain experience in speaking before a group, expressing ideas, and defending points of view.

Dangers and Difficulties

Committees have their detractors. Have you heard the quip that a camel is a horse that was put together by a committee? Such comments refer to the dangers inherent in committee use.

Danger of Compromise. One of the greatest weaknesses of committees is their tendency toward compromise decisions. One hears such statements as "committee solutions simply represent the lowest common denominator of the thinking of the members on that committee." The thought is that a group lacks the will or forcefulness to reach the same sound conclusion that might be achieved by one individual acting alone.

Reviews of the evidence lend some support to this position. Although the quality of group judgments is generally superior to the quality of the judgments made by the average member of the group, group decisions are often inferior to the decisions of the most competent group member.[9] Even though most of the research has been conducted in laboratory rather than in organizational settings, these findings suggest potential weaknesses in using groups for decision making.

Compromise is often the result of conformity. One who disagrees with the majority may well decide to comply—and vote with the majority—rather than risk alienating the other members for the sake of a losing cause. Irving L. Janis has used the term *groupthink* to refer to excessive conformity:[10]

> The symptoms of groupthink arise when the members of decision-making groups become motivated to avoid being too harsh in their judgments of their leaders' or their colleagues' ideas. They adopt a soft line of criticism, even in their own thinking. At their meetings, all the members are amiable and seek complete concurrence on every important issue, with no bickering or conflict to spoil the cozy, "we-feeling" atmosphere.

Another pressure that contributes to a spirit of compromise is the personal work load of committee members. Because executives typically have full schedules, they attempt to reach a committee decision quickly in order to resume their regular responsibilities. Also, most committee members do not wish to embarrass other members of the same committee. To save face for all participants, the group may accept a conclusion or solution that is not violently opposed by any of the members.

Difficulty in Placing Responsibility. Committee activity can be a shield behind which an individual manager can take refuge. Holding any one manager responsible for the group's decision becomes difficult. Proceeding against a group of executive personnel is almost impossible. As a result, responsibility may be diffused through committee activity in such a way that it is difficult to say that any one member should answer for the group's decision.

Delay and Indecision. Committee action takes time. Meetings require reconciliation of the time demands of the committee with the personal schedules and other official responsibilities of the members. Speed of action in an organization is often important, particularly if it is not achieved at the expense of a proper evaluation of alternatives. Opportunities may be lost by failure to act quickly. Smaller concerns are often recognized as having advantages over larger competitors for this very reason. An organization honeycombed with committees moves more slowly than a streamlined organization acting on the basis of individual judgment and decision.

Domination by One Member.   Occasionally a committee operates under the thumb or domination of one person. This person's reaction provides the key to action by the group. An expression of disapproval, for example, whether verbal or by facial expression, may start the entire group on a negative approach or evaluation. In its most extreme form, such domination results in a committee that simply rubber stamps the pet ideas of the dominant member.

Such deterioration contrasts sharply with the values that are believed to exist in committees. Committees are presumably characterized by the give-and-take of equals. Committee deliberation represents a pooling of ideas in an atmosphere of mutual respect and tolerance. One member builds upon suggestions of another member. All participants sense a freedom to correct, to question, and to suggest modifications to the ideas and purposes of others.

The dominant individual is ordinarily the chairperson of the committee. Frequently, this person is also the superior of other members of the committee, and the committee may therefore be inclined to show deference for this reason alone. If the chairperson is a driving, dominant type of leader, it is difficult to change the atmosphere when the scene shifts to a committee room.

OTHER COOPERATIVE ENDEAVORS

Quality Circles

A special type of group (or committee) that has been much discussed in recent years is the *quality circle (QC)*. A typical QC consists of six to twelve operative employees who volunteer to meet for an hour each week on company time to recommend ways of improving productivity and product or service quality in their area of responsibility. Members may have received training in problem-solving techniques. They are led by a facilitator who is a specially-trained member of management (and may be the group's supervisor).

Besides recommending improvements in productivity and quality, QCs fulfill a psychological function. They promote the participation of lower-level employees in organizational decision making and thereby enhance the development of those employees.

Mixed Reviews of QCs.   The extent to which QCs have been successful in improving efficiency and increasing the quality of working life is not clear.[11] Both successes and failures have been reported. For several reasons, QCs have not attained overwhelming success in U.S. organizations.

QUALITY CIRCLES IN JAPAN

Hitachi Corporation of Japan has a highly developed quality circle program. Such groups operate in twenty-seven of its factories in the following fashion:

- □ 29 percent of the groups work on improving and controlling product quality
- □ 67 percent focus on improving and refining operations management
- □ 4 percent concentrate on improving work safety

A typical group is composed of eight to ten people. Participants include production workers, clerical and support personnel, and certain managerial personnel.

In Hitachi's Musashi Semiconductor Works plant, for instance, each group commits itself to filing a certain number of improvement proposals per month and is asked to submit a monthly review of its activities. The program began in 1977. By 1978, 26,543 proposals were submitted, and over 112,000 suggestions were filed in the last six months of 1980 alone, for an average of 45 proposals per group each month. Of those proposals, almost 88 percent were implemented. Over 25 percent of those dealt with reducing standard times at individual work stations, 27 percent with reducing inventory, almost 25 percent with increasing office efficiency, and 6 percent with improving safety or saving overhead costs.

SOURCE: Based on William H. Davidson, "Small Group Activity at Musashi Semiconductor Works," *Sloan Management Review* 23(Spring 1982): 3–14.

Although QCs were first conceived in the United States, their first widespread implementation was in Japan. QCs fit nicely into the fabric of life in large organizations in Japan, a country in which:[12]

- □ Collective responsibility is emphasized over individual rewards
- □ Lifetime employment creates a commitment to the firm and its goals
- □ Management and labor share common interests
- □ Employees often possess a wide range of skills because of job rotation and skill development programs

QCs do not fit as nicely into the fabric of life in organizations in the United States, a country in which most employees:[13]

- □ Espouse individualism
- □ Desire rewards for individual performance

□ Form only transitory, work-oriented relationships with most fellow employees

In fact, one large Japanese company, considered a leader in QCs in Japan, did not institute QCs in its U.S. plant because it did not consider the American worker suited to QC activities.[14]

Aside from cultural transition difficulties, QCs in U.S. organizations face other obstacles. One study indicates that the first threat most QCs encounter is resistance to their ideas. Those who would implement QC recommendations are middle managers, who do not participate in QCs and are often uncomfortable responding to ideas from subordinates. Many times, these managers see little reason to implement ideas which are not theirs and which may change their own work activities.[15] Another study observed that supervisors tend to dominate QC meetings and that the circles have difficulty limiting problems to their department's area of responsibility.[16]

Improving QC Effectiveness. Because Japanese and American cultures are so different, it seems unlikely that QCs—as used in Japanese firms—can operate effectively in U.S. organizations.[17] But the cultural difference does not mean that QCs should not be used at all. Edward E. Lawler III and Susan A. Mohrman propose three appropriate uses of QCs in U.S. companies.[18]

First, QCs can be used to capture the ideas of the individuals closest to the operative work of the organization. Once the knowledge of some workers has been tapped, circle membership should be rotated in order to maintain enthusiasm. The circle program itself should move from department to department, working on the most obvious problems in each. This way, the approach should not get stale, savings should result, and employees should become more aware of productivity and quality. On the other hand, workers may feel manipulated and can become frustrated if their ideas are not implemented. One study of seventy-four workers concluded that the primary reason workers join QCs is to make their departments better and more productive places. QC members have little patience with simply going through the motions. They want results.[19]

Second, QCs can be used to deal with one-time issues that arise, such as the introduction of new technology. The QC in that case would develop a method for workers to acquire the appropriate new skills. The problem at hand would define the circle's lifetime.

Third, QCs can be used to make a transition a more participative management system. For instance, QCs can evolve into task forces composed of people from different departments and different levels. Because such a group can often implement its own recommendations, it is more stable than a group that can only offer suggestions. Ultimately, some QCs may be transformed into self-managing work groups, known as autonomous work groups. But the transition to an institutionalized participative system is difficult, requiring changes in job design, organizational rewards, and personnel policies. Some organiza-

AUTONOMOUS WORK GROUPS AT WESTINGHOUSE

Westinghouse has designed its "factory of tomorrow" in College Station, Texas, around autonomous work groups. Each group, composed of eight to twelve members, makes electronic assemblies for military radar, with the help of Seiko robots. The employees, paid salaries rather than hourly rates, compare their individual performances with that of other team members and compare the group's overall performance with that of other groups. Peer pressure to produce is high.

Applicants for jobs at the plant must take tests that measure their initiative, creativity, skills, and ability to take advice. Only about one in twenty applicants is hired.

SOURCE: "The Plant of Tomorrow Is in Texas Today," *Business Week,* 28 July 1986, p. 76.

tions may find it easier simply to begin with the formation of autonomous work groups and bypass the QC stage altogether.

Autonomous Work Groups

Autonomous work groups are an outgrowth of the sociotechnical systems approach to designing jobs and organizations. The aim is to mesh fulfillment of the workers' needs for social satisfaction with the technical requirements of the organization so that both satisfaction and organizational performance are enhanced.

Basically, an autonomous work group is a small team given the responsibility for planning and carrying out a whole task. A group of coal miners, for instance, might be given responsibility for an entire geographic section of a mine. The duties of the foreman would be assumed by the group, which would be responsible for its own production. Each miner might be required to learn all of the tasks involved in mining coal so that the members could switch jobs whenever an individual became tired or bored or was absent.[20] Compensation and feedback about performance would be based on the group's accomplishments, rather than on individual contributions.

J. Richard Hackman has suggested the following conditions under which a "self-managing" group design is appropriate:[21]

□ When the best possible job design for individuals would involve only a narrowly defined task
□ When the setting requires high interdependence among workers
□ When the workers have strong needs for social interaction

□ When the motivating potential of the jobs is expected to be considerably higher if arranged as a group task rather than as a set of individual tasks

Autonomous work groups are inappropriate if the workers' tasks are not interdependent, if the workers have higher needs for personal growth and development than for social interaction at work, or if the potential for conflict within or between groups is high.

The evidence on the effectiveness of autonomous work groups is mixed.[22] Hence, a wholesale movement to the use of such groups is not recommended. Instead, such self-managing teams should be selectively used in those situations known to be appropriate until it is better understood how to install and maintain them.[23]

GROUP CONFLICT

All group processes are not necessarily smooth and cooperative. *Conflict* arises, not only between the members of a group, but also between groups themselves. The destructive aspects of conflict are well known: a lack of cooperation, the withholding of information, the avoidance of interaction, the loss of trust, the desire to take revenge, and so on. But conflict is not inevitably destructive. In recent years, we have begun to speak of *managing conflict* so that it yields beneficial results.

The proposed relationship between conflict and organizational effectiveness is illustrated in Figure 15–4. Some amount of conflict is essential in an

---

THE NEED FOR COORDINATION

Lee Iacocca took the job as president of Chrysler in 1978, just as the company announced a quarterly loss of almost $160 million. He later commented:

> Chrysler in 1978 was like Italy in the 1860s—the company consisted of a cluster of little duchies, each one run by a prima donna. . . . What I found at Chrysler were thirty-five vice-presidents, each with his own turf. There was no real committee setup, no cement in the organizational chart, no system of meetings to get people talking to each other. I couldn't believe, for example, that the guy running the engineering department wasn't in constant touch with his counterpart in manufacturing. . . . I took one look at that system and I almost threw up.

SOURCE: Lee Iacocca with William Novak, *Iacocca: An Autobiography* (New York: Bantam Books, 1984), p. 152.

FIGURE 15–4 Proposed relationship between organizational effectiveness and conflict

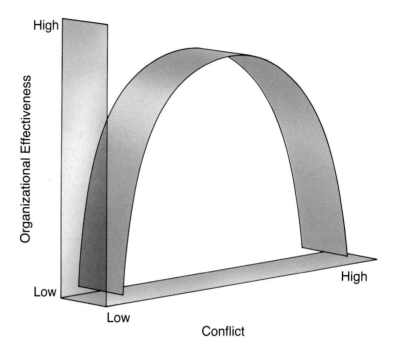

organization; otherwise, the organization stagnates. But too much conflict reduces organizational effectiveness. The question is how to manage conflict so that organizational effectiveness is enhanced.

Conflict is considered to be appropriately managed when it does not substantially interfere with the professional (as opposed to the personal) relationships between the parties involved.[24] The particular way in which a situation is managed depends on the type of conflict.

One useful way of categorizing conflict is to distinguish between controversy and conflict of interests.[25] *Controversy* involves differences of opinion that can prevent or interfere with reaching a decision. Such conflict, for instance, is common in committee meetings. *Conflict of interests* occurs when an individual or a group, in pursuing its own ends, interferes with or blocks the actions of others who are pursuing their own interests. Such conflicts are common between departments pursuing greater budgetary resources, more physical space, or better task assignments, for example.

Managing Controversy

Controversy, if managed carefully, can yield a number of benefits.[26] One review of the literature suggests that controversy can promote interest, communication, and understanding, all necessary for effective problem solving. Nevertheless, group members often avoid controversy, preferring to smooth over differences. When such norms as "don't rock the boat" or "be a team player" prevail, controversy can be intentionally introduced in a number of ways. A single group, for instance, can be divided into two or more subgroups with each assigned different positions to defend. Or one group member can be assigned the role of "devil's advocate."

When conflict causes dysfunction, on the other hand, the leader must help group members learn to feel that even though their ideas are disputed their personal competence is not being questioned. Additionally, the leader must emphasize the group members' cooperative interdependence:[27]

> "We are all in this together" and "Let's seek a solution that is good for everyone" should characterize the group, rather than "I am right and you are wrong." Financial rewards, evaluations, and prestige should be given for group success, not for independent work or for appearing better than everyone else. The group members should seek to find, not winners and losers, but a successful, productive solution to the common problem. All group members should share the rewards of success and the responsibility for failure.

Managing Conflict of Interests

Perhaps the most common means of managing a conflict of interests between two persons or two groups is an *appeal to authority.* One of the functions of the chain of command is to resolve disputes. A decision from higher authority, however, may only reduce the manifestations of the conflict without alleviating the actual cause of dispute. Managers who order their subordinates to stop arguing or who "settle" an issue by creating a winner and a loser may indeed have quieter subordinates but will have done little to address the root cause of the conflict.

Another common conflict management technique is for the disputants to engage in *negotiation* and *bargaining,* in an attempt to reach a compromise resolution. In compromise settlements, both parties lose something and no distinct winner emerges. For example, union representatives may give up the right to decline overtime work, and management may offer a higher wage settlement in return. In some cases, the bargaining approach to resolving conflicts is blended with an appeal to the chain of command. A common superior oversees the bargaining process.

A more powerful conflict management tool is *integration.* The manager who uses integration brings together the conflicting parties so they might discuss the issues face to face. The parties themselves talk through their disagreements and then begin to collaborate in developing a mutually agreeable solution. Such an approach is useful in resolving the real cause of the conflict, and integration sessions often result in a significant reduction in tension.

Integration has been described as a *win-win* method, in contrast to *win-lose* and *lose-lose* methods. Both parties, in other words, can be winners by imaginatively working out a mutually satisfactory solution. In a lose-lose com-

MODIFY THE ORGANIZATIONAL SITUATION

To reduce the chances for conflict among its divisions, Gould, Inc., a high-tech electronics manufacturer, modified the organizational situation. Its chief executive consolidated twenty-two semi-autonomous divisions into four tightly integrated businesses, selling off those that did not fit. Within each division, manufacturing, marketing, and service are closely coordinated, and an incentive system rewards divisional results—not the performance of individual units within the division.

SOURCE; "McDonald's the Name, Fixing Gould is the Game," *Business Week,* 28 July 1986, pp. 77–78.

promise, both parties give up something for a settlement. A major advantage of integration is the shared commitment of both parties to the solution. Integration also provides a strong foundation for further collaboration and resolution of future conflicts.

Finally, some conflicts of interest have their roots in dysfunctional structural arrangements of poorly designed reward systems. These conflicts require management to *modify the organizational situation.* For example, a company that rented construction equipment had a reward system that paid the rental manager a bonus based on increases in rental revenue. By contrast, the service manager's bonus was based on holding maintenance and repair costs down. In essence, the rental manager was being rewarded for renting as much equipment as possible, regardless of its condition. The service manager, on the other hand, was rewarded for keeping the equipment from being rented, because less wear and tear would occur if the equipment simply sat on the lot. No wonder the two managers quarreled constantly! The solution to such a problem required a modification in the bonus system so that only by working together could both managers earn a bonus.

SUMMARY

Groups are essential to the accomplishment of organizational goals. In fact, the organization chart illustrates the *formal* grouping of individuals who are charged with the responsibility of contributing to the organization's goals. Within these formal groups arise *informal* collections of individuals who interact to satisfy their social needs or advance some common cause.

Group behavior may be analyzed by examining the *activities, interactions,* and *sentiments* of the group members. The interrelationships among these variables over time result in the evolution of group *norms.* Members are expected to *conform* to these norms in order to preserve the group's order, stability, and existence. Groups with a high rate of conformity are termed *cohesive.* Members of cohesive groups derive satisfaction from their group membership and often develop important norms regarding work performance.

Committees have become an integral part of the administrative structure of most modern organizations. Advantages resulting from the use of committees include the improvement of decisions through group deliberation, coordination of work, facilitation of cooperation in the execution or application of plans and policies, and training of participants. Among the offsetting dangers and limitations are the danger of undesirable compromise in decision making, difficulty in placing responsibility for decisions, delays and indecision in administrative action, and domination of the committee by one person.

Aside from committees, other cooperative group endeavors include *quality circles,* groups consisting of operative employees who develop recommendations for improving productivity and quality in their area, and autonomous work groups, small teams which are given the responsibility for planning and carrying out a task with the team members assuming the manager's duties.

Not all group processes are cooperative. *Conflict* arises between group members and between groups. Although conflict can be destructive, the emphasis today is on managing conflict so that it yields beneficial results. One form of conflict, *controversy,* involves differences of opinion. Properly managed, controversy can facilitate effective solutions to problems by promoting interest, communication, and understanding. *Conflict of interests* occurs when the interests of one party interfere with the interests of others. Such conflict may be managed by appealing to authority, negotiation and bargaining, integration, or modifying the organizational situation.

KEY CONCEPTS

Group	Compliance
Formal group	Private acceptance
Informal group	Cohesiveness
Command group	Committee
Problem-solving group	Groupthink
Task force	Quality circle
Activities	Autonomous work group
Interactions	Conflict
Sentiments	Controversy
Norms	Conflict of interests
Conformity	Integration

DISCUSSION QUESTIONS

1. Explain this statement: *"Formal group* interaction is inevitably modified by *informal* activities and attitudes."

2. What are the implications of the statement in question 1 for the manager of a formal work group?

3. Think of a group to which you belong. What are the central *norms* which govern behavior in the group? What functions do these norms perform?

4. In the area of *conformity,* why do most groups require only *compliance,* rather than *private acceptance,* from their members?

5. Is it better for a supervisor to deal with subordinates as individuals or to encourage development of a *cohesive* work group? Explain.

6. Which of the suggested dangers or difficulties in the use of committees appears most serious? What is the basis for your answer?

7. Why have *quality circles* not been overwhelmingly successful in U.S. organizations? Is success attainable?

8. Under what conditions might the formation of *autonomous work groups* be appropriate?

9. Describe the probable relationship between *conflict* and organizational effectiveness.

10. Describe an actual *conflict of interests* you have observed in an organization. Suggest how the conflict might be managed to yield beneficial results.

NOTES

1. Edgar Schein, *Organizational Psychology,* 2d ed. (Englewood Cliffs, N.J.: Prentice-Hall, 1970), p. 69.

2. Dorwin Cartwright and Alvin Zander, eds., *Group Dynamics: Research and Theory,* 3d ed. (New York: Harper & Row, 1968), p. 54.

3. James L. Gibson, John M. Ivancevich, and James H. Donnelly, Jr., *Organizations: Behavior, Structure, Processes,* 3d ed. (Dallas: Business Publications, 1979), p. 138.

4. William Foote Whyte, *Organizational Behavior: Theory and Application* (Homewood, Ill.: Richard D. Irwin and The Dorsey Press, 1969), chapters 4 and 5; and George Homans, *The Human Group* (New York: Harcourt, Brace, 1950).

5. This paragraph is based on Daniel C. Feldman, "The Development and Enforcement of Group Norms," *Academy of Management Review* 9 (January 1984): 50–2.

6. A classic study of the effects of cohesiveness on group performance and member satisfaction is reported in Stanley E. Seashore, *Group Cohesiveness in the Industrial Work Group* (Ann Arbor, Mich.: University of Michigan Press, 1954).

7. J. Richard Hackman, "The Design of Self-Managing Work Groups," in *Managerial Control and Organizational Democracy,* ed. B. King, S. Streufert, and F. Fiedler (Washington, D.C.: Winston, 1978), p. 62.

8. Richard F. Vancil and Charles H. Green, "How CEOs Use Top Management Committees," *Harvard Business Review* 62 (January-February 1984): 65–73.

9. Gayle W. Hill, "Group versus Individual Performance: Are $N + 1$ Heads Better Than One?" *Psychological Bulletin* 91 (May 1982): 517–39; and John Rohrbaugh, "Improving the Quality of Group Judgment: Social Judgment Analysis and the Delphi Technique," *Organizational Behavior and Human Performance* 24 (August 1979): 73–92.

10. Irving L. Janis, "Groupthink," *Psychology Today* 5 (November 1971): 43.

11. Robert P. Steel and Guy S. Shane, "Evaluation Research on Quality Circles: Technical and Analytical Techniques," *Human Relations* 39 (May 1986): 449–68; Gregory P. Shea, "Quality Circles: The Danger of Bottled Change," *Sloan Management Review* 27 (Spring 1986): 33–46; Mitchell Lee Marks, Edward J. Hackett, Philip H. Mirvis, and James F. Grady, Jr., "Employee Participation in a Quality Circle Program: Impact on Quality of Work Life, Productivity, and Absenteeism," *Journal of Applied Psychology* 71 (February 1986): 61–9; and Gerald R. Ferris and John A. Wagner III, "Quality Circles in the United States: A Conceptual Reevaluation," *Journal of Applied Behavioral Science* 21, no. 2 (1985): 155–67.

12. K. Bradley and S. Hill, "After Japan: The Quality Circle Transplant and Productive Efficiency," *British Journal of Industrial Relations* (November 1983): 291–311.

13. Ferris and Wagner, "Quality Circles in the United States," p. 161.

14. Robert E. Cole, "Made in Japan—Quality-Control Circles," *Across the Board* 16 (November 1979): 77.

15. Edward E. Lawler III and Susan A. Mohrman, "Quality Circles After the Fad," *Harvard Business Review* 63 (January-February 1985): 68.

16. Gordon W. Meyer and Randall G. Stott, "Quality Circles: Panacea or Pandora's Box?" *Organizational Dynamics* 13 (Spring 1985): 38.

17. Shea, "Quality Circles," pp. 33–46; and Ferris and Wagner, "Quality Circles in the United States," pp. 155–67.

18. Lawler and Mohrman, "Quality Circles After the Fad," pp. 69–71.

19. James W. Dean, Jr., "The Decision to Participate in Quality Circles," *Journal of Applied Behavioral Science* 21, no. 3 (1985): 326.

20. See Melvin Blumberg, "Job Switching in Autonomous Work Groups: An Exploratory Study in a Pennsylvania Coal Mine," *Academy of Management Journal* 23 (June 1980): 287–306.

21. Hackman, "The Design of Self-Managing Work Groups," pp. 85–87.

22. See Toby D. Wall, Nigel J. Kemp, Paul R. Jackson, and Chris W. Clegg, "Outcomes of Autonomous Workgroups: A Long-Term Field Experiment," *Academy of Management Journal* 29 (June 1986): 280–304; and Melvin Blumberg, *Job Switching in Autonomous Work Groups: A Descriptive and Exploratory Study in an Underground Coal Mine* (Palto Alto, Calif.: R & E Research Associates, 1978).

23. Hackman, "The Design of Self-Managing Work Groups," pp. 88–89.

24. Leonard Greenhalgh, "SMR Forum: Managing Conflict," *Sloan Management Review* 27 (Summer 1986): 45.

25. This classification is based on Dean Tjosvold, "Implications of Controversy Research for Management," *Journal of Management* 11 (Fall/Winter 1985): 22–3.

26. This discussion is based on Tjosvold, "Implications of Controversy Research," pp. 21–37.

27. Ibid., p. 32.

SUPPLEMENTARY READING

Altier, William J. "SMR Forum: Task Forces—An Effective Management Tool." *Sloan Management Review* 27 (Spring 1986): 69–76.

Blumberg, Melvin. "Job Switching in Autonomous Work Groups: An Exploratory Study in a Pennsylvania Coal Mine." *Academy of Management Journal* 23 (June 1980): 287–306.

Davidson, William H. "Small Group Activity at Musashi Semiconductor Works." *Sloan Management Review* 23 (Spring 1982): 3–14.

Feldman, Daniel C. "The Development and Enforcement of Group Norms." *Academy of Management Review* 9 (January 1984): 47–53.

Ferris, Gerald R., and Wagner, John A., III "Quality Circles in the United States: A Conceptual Reevaluation." *Journal of Applied Behavioral Science* 21, no. 2 (1985): 155–167.

Fotilas, Panagiotis N. "Semi-autonomous Work Groups: An Alternative in Organizing Production Work?" *Management Review* 70 (July 1981): 50–54.

Greenhalgh, Leonard. "SMR Forum: Managing Conflict." *Sloan Management Review* 27 (Summer 1986): 45–51.

Hackman, J. Richard. "The Design of Self-Managing Work Groups." In *Managerial Control and Organizational Democracy*, edited by Bert King, Siegfried Streufert, and Fred E. Fiedler. Washington, D.C.: Winston, 1978, pp. 61–91.

Klein, Gerald D. "Implementing Quality Circles: A Hard Look at Some of the Realities." *Personnel* 58 (November-December 1981): 11–20.

Lawler, Edward E., III, and Mohrman, Susan A. "Quality Circles After the Fad." *Harvard Business Review* 63 (January-February 1985): 65–71.

Maier, Norman R. F. "Assets and Liabilities in Group Problem Solving: The Need for an Integrative Function." *Psychological Review* 74 (July 1967): 239–49.

Meyer, Gordon W., and Stott, Randall G. "Quality Circles: Panacea or Pandora's Box?" *Organizational Dynamics* 13 (Spring 1985): 34–50.

Munchus, George, III. "Employer-Employee Based Quality Circles in Japan: Human Resource Policy Implications for American Firms." *Academy of Management Review* 8 (April 1983): 255–61.

Rahim, M. Afzalur. "A Strategy for Managing Conflict in Complex Organizations." *Human Relations* 38 (January 1985): 81–9.

Schwenk, Charles R. "Devil's Advocacy in Managerial Decision-Making." *Journal of Management Studies* 21 (April 1984): 153–68.

Shea, Gregory P. "Quality Circles: The Danger of Bottled Change." *Sloan Management Review* 27 (Spring 1986): 33–46.

Steel, Robert P., and Shane, Guy S. "Evaluation Research on Quality Circles: Technical and Analytical Techniques." *Human Relations* 39 (May 1986): 449–68.

Tjosvold, Dean. "Implications of Controversy Research for Management." *Journal of Management* 11 (Fall/Winter 1985): 21–37.

Vancil, Richard F., and Green, Charles H. "How CEOs Use Top Management Committees." *Harvard Business Review* 62 (January-February 1984): 65–73.

Wall, Toby D.; Kemp, Nigel J.; Jackson, Paul R.; and Clegg, Chris W. "Outcomes of Autonomous Workgroups: A Long-Term Field Experiment." *Academy of Management Journal* 29 (June 1986): 280–304.

THE COMPANY TRAINING PROGRAM

Widget Manufacturing Company believed in providing every possible aid and encouragement to the development of its management personnel. Among the many extras that it provided was attendance for thirty or forty people each year at the Industrial Management Conference. These conferences were held in a college town and were widely attended, with as many as 1,200 people from various companies present at the annual three-day sessions. The sessions were divided into workshops and discussion groups, with a liberal sprinkling of speakers—experts in various phases of industrial management. The meetings concluded with a major speech and banquet, followed by entertainment.

When John Hamilton joined the staff of Widget, he was greatly impressed by the efforts of top management to provide such continuous development of its supervisory staff. He took advantage of the extension courses offered, was present at all foremen's classes, and generally considered himself lucky to be part of such an organization. When one of the supervisors approached him and asked if he would like to attend the conference, he was delighted. It seemed to him that it would be an excellent opportunity to sample some of the best thinking of men who were specialists in their fields.

Customarily the men were sent down in several cars to the conference. John Hamilton found himself in a car with three other men, one of whom was Jim Warner, an old line supervisor. John noted the

holiday atmosphere from the beginning of the trip and felt that the men must indeed get a great deal out of the conferences because of the enthusiasm with which they greeted the prospect of attending. Several times on the ride to the conference John tried to draw out Jim on the subject matter of the conferences. All he got was remarks such as " You're sure to enjoy yourself, John—just relax."

Following the registration, John told Jim that he was going to his room and freshen up. He wanted to be sure and catch the first speaker. Before John could leave. Jim said, "Sure, John, just stop in room 325 before you go."

A little while later John knocked on the door of room 325 and was admitted to the smoke-filled room. Two of the desks had been pushed together and a blanket thrown over them. The supervisors he knew were sitting around in their shirt sleeves, playing poker and drinking. Before John could say anything, someone put a paper cup of lukewarm whisky and ginger ale into his hand. "There's plenty of time before the first speaker," said Jim. "Why don't you play a couple of hands."

Hamilton didn't want to miss the speech; neither did he want to antagonize the other foremen by refusing a few friendly hands of poker with them. "Okay," he said. "But I'm only going to play one deal around; then I'm taking off." Five hands later Jim asked him, "How do you like the conference?"

"Look, Johnny boy," said Jim, "this is the conference. That speech making and all the other stuff is hogwash. The whole purpose of these conferences is to give the boys a three-day vacation for a little drinking and poker playing."

Case prepared by Professor Kenneth A. Kovach of George Mason University. Copyright © 1980 by Kenneth A. Kovach.

"That doesn't sound right to me," said John. "From the look of the program, a lot of people have worked hard to line up a very good conference. It doesn't make sense to me to drive all the way down here to hear these experts speak and stay in our rooms and play poker."

"This is the way the company wants it," said Jim. "The main idea is for the foremen to get together and get to know each other better. It makes a closer spirit among the foremen."

Hamilton was in a quandary. He wanted to attend the program, but he knew that if he spurned the poker session more than half of the foremen he knew would think him a "square."

Questions

1. Weight the costs and benefits of (a) conforming to the foremen's behavior and (b) refusing to conform.
2. Should John somehow let his supervisor know what went on when he returns and take the chance of being "blackballed" by the rest of the foremen?

AL'S EXHAUSTING DILEMMA

Al Munn had promised to take his wife and two sons on a sight-seeing tour of the beautiful Shenandoah Valley in Virginia. They reviewed maps and made the necessary motel reservations along their intended route. They would leave in four days, plenty of time to have their mechanic, John, ready the family station wagon for the long drive south. Al had to be back at work in one week and could not risk having car trouble so far from home.

John, an excellent mechanic and trusted friend, had checked over the wagon on several other occasions. This time, his inspection revealed one problem: small holes in the exhaust system. The muffler and tailpipe would have to be replaced to ensure a safe and quiet car ride. Luckily for Al, the exhaust system carried a lifetime guarantee, so it could be replaced at no

charge by any authorized dealer. Yet the nearest shop that could make good on the guarantee was sixty miles away in another city.

Al reasoned that he had to have the work done. His family's safety was too important to let the repairs wait. He made a few calls over the next couple of days to verify that the muffler company had the parts in stock and could do the repairs on Saturday morning, the day before the Munns would leave for Virginia.

Al felt pretty good as he gave his keys to the muffler shop desk clerk. The sixty-mile drive had passed quickly as he thought about leaving the headaches of his job for a vacation with his family. However, the situation changed abruptly when the mechanic came out of the shop area and said to Al, "There's nothing wrong with your muffler or tailpipe. You just want us to put a new exhaust system on your car for free. Well, I'm *not* going to do it!"

Case prepared by Professor Philip B. DuBose of James Madison University.

Al was stunned by such aggressive behavior and was not sure what to do. He certainly did not want to get into a fight with this man, but he also did not want to leave the area without having the necessary repairs made. Al motioned towards the desk clerk, whom he assumed was in charge, and commented to the mechanic, "Maybe your boss over there could look at the muffler and pipes and see if he can find the holes?" At that point, the mechanic looked menacingly at Al and exclaimed, "He's *not* my boss! *Nobody* is my boss!!"

Questions

1. What is Al's objective in this situation?
2. What hidden agendas might have caused the muffler shop mechanic to act in such a way?
3. What alternative approaches might Al attempt in order to resolve this conflict with the mechanic?
4. If you were Al, what alternative approach would you select and why?
5. Interpersonal conflicts often arise unexpectedly. Is there any way to be prepared for such encounters?

NATURE OF COMMUNICATION
Management Through
Communication □ Methods of
Communication □ Communication and the
Systems Viewpoint

CHANNELS OF COMMUNICATION
Formal Channels of Communication
□ Informal Channels of
Communication □ Communication
Channels Within Groups

BARRIERS TO COMMUNICATION
Perceptual Barriers □ Semantic
Barriers □ Serial Transmission
Barriers □ Information Overload

DEVELOPING EFFECTIVE
COMMUNICATION
Two-Way Communication □ Listening
□ Aggressively Sharing Information
□ Need for Honesty and Sincerity
□ Channel Selection

Summary □ Key Concepts
□ Discussion Questions □ Notes
□ Supplementary Reading

CASES: The Empty Sleeper □ Has the
Worm Turned?

This chapter will enable you to

□   Explain the communication process and
identify various methods of transmitting
messages.

□   Understand an organization's formal
and informal channels of
communication.

□   Analyze the major barriers to effective
communication.

□   Become familiar with some techniques
for developing effective
communication.

CHAPTER 16
COMMUNICATION

The process of communication is an integral part of the functioning of any organization. Leadership is exerted and coordination is achieved through communication. As managers improve their understanding of communications problems and increase their skill in communication, therefore, organizational performance will become more effective.

NATURE OF COMMUNICATION

Management Through Communication

The manager's world is a world of words. Much, perhaps most, of a manager's time is spent in communicating with others. Any type of organized activity, in fact, demands communication. The direction of the communication may be *downward* (such as giving instructions or passing along policy changes), *upward* (as in reporting results or asking for additional information), or *horizontal* (such as coordinating the activities of two or more departments). The need for good communication permeates every activity and department in an organization.

   Communication is an interactive process between two or more people, as illustrated in Figure 16–1. A *sender* initiates the process by transmitting a message to a *receiver* or group of receivers. The message conveys not only facts but also the sender's feelings and attitudes about those facts and, often, the send-

FIGURE 16–1 The communication process

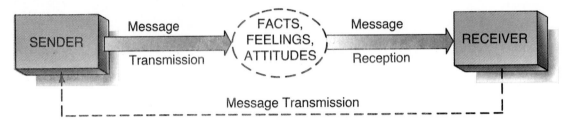

er's feelings and attitudes toward the receiver. The receiver is not passive; he or she often transmits a return message through a nod, a frown, a question, or some other form of behavior to indicate reception and understanding of the message. Feelings and attitudes may also be conveyed by this return message. Ideally, this sending-receiving-sending process continues until both parties fully understand the messages transmitted.

Without reception, communication does not occur, but this logic is not as obvious as it seems. The manager who writes several memos per week to a subordinate believes that he or she is communicating even though the subordinate may routinely discard the messages without reading them. The personnel manager who posts a written explanation, full of legal jargon, of the changes in the organization's health insurance policy is not communicating, since many employees may never see the notice and those who do are unlikely to expend the time and effort required to read it. The goal of the sender should be to transmit a message which is received, so that it may be understood and acted upon.

Methods of Communication

Messages are transmitted in a variety of forms. We all know that language—written and spoken—provides tools for communication. What we sometimes overlook is that language may be supplemented by other less obvious forms of communication. Nonverbal behavior may well be more important than words in conveying meaning.

Consider common physical expressions. A supervisor's scowl when speaking may lead a subordinate to conclude that "she's unhappy about my performance, and my future is clouded." If the supervisor wears a smile, the same words may carry quite a different message. Instinctively, a subordinate picks up such signals. By looking at the boss's behavior and facial expressions, a subordinate may know whether the time is ripe to ask for a raise or to request a day off.

Not only physical expressions and gestures but also voice inflections may tell the listener more than the words themselves reveal. The term *paralanguage* refers to an individual's "tone and quality of voice, pitch, pacing of speech, and sounds such as sighs or grunts," which add meaning to the spoken word.[1]

NONVERBAL COMMUNICATION BETWEEN THE SEXES

When men and women meet under clearly romantic circumstances, such as parties or candlelight dinners, they can be observed exchanging "courtship cues." But these cues are often unconsciously carried over into clearly nonromantic settings, such as the office. Although both males and females may be unaware of the cues, such communication undermines the status and power of female managers and triggers negative responses from male colleagues. Take, for instance, the following examples of miscommunication:

□ *Personal space*—in our society, women allow men or other women to stand closer to them than men do. When a female manager allows a male colleague to stand a bit closer than she prefers, she is acting in accordance with her societal sex role, but she is also undermining her status and power by indicating that she need not be taken seriously.
□ *Body size*—when sitting, men generally take up significantly more space than is physically necessary. They often extend their legs and arms, for example. But women keep their limbs close to their bodies. Since societal sex roles emphasize large male body size and small female body size, the female executive who habitually makes her body appear smaller leaves herself open to a misinterpretation of her status and power.
□ *Touching*—the initiator of a touch generally possesses greater power and status than the recipient. In our society, men touch women about twice as much as women touch men during an average conversation. Pats on the back or such protective gestures as a man taking a woman's arm to "help" her cross the street reinforce the perception that the female manager has less power and status than the male executive.

SOURCE: These and other nonverbal cues are discussed in Lynn Renee Cohen, "Nonverbal (Mis)Communication Between Managerial Men and Women," *Business Horizons* 26 (January-February 1983): 13–17.

The tone of voice, for instance, can transform words of praise into sarcasm. Even silence, the absence of language, can communicate! If an employee performs exceptionally well or completes a project in an outstanding manner, he or she might logically expect some word of commendation. Silence, however, communicates indifference or disrespect, whether intended or not.

Perhaps the most forceful method of communication is not language at all. There is an old saying that "Actions speak louder than words." We observe an individual's behavior and infer something about the person. Even the choice of a meeting place can communicate:[2]

When a boss and a subordinate meet, whose office do they use? If the boss is sensitive to place as territory, the purpose of the meeting will decide the question. To conduct an adversary discussion, to emphasize hierarchy and authority, or to give direction, the boss should hold the meeting in his or her office. If, however, the boss wants to reach out to the subordinate—to have a conversation more on the other's terms—he or she might well consider traveling to the subordinate's office.

From the standpoint of employees, such actions provide the most eloquent expression of management policy and values.

Communication and the Systems Viewpoint

The organization has been pictured throughout this text as a system of interrelated parts functioning together to accomplish certain objectives. Communication provides the means for directing and blending all system and subsystem activities.

The process of communication may be visualized as the functioning of an organizational subsystem that brings problems and related information to man-

---

COMMUNICATING EXPECTATIONS

A manager's expectations of subordinates' job performance may be communicated in a variety of ways. John Gabarro reports the impressions of a corporate vice-president observing the behavior of the firm's newly appointed president:

> I knew immediately, the first day, he was going to be different from [his predecessor]. Everyone knew he was going to be more demanding. A lot of little things—he spends no time on small talk and whenever someone else does he changes the subject back to business. He sat behind his desk while [his predecessor] always sat in the easy chair. [His predecessor] was very informal, **vague**, kind of a "good Joe" seat-of-the-pants-type guy. [The new president] was **prepared to the teeth.** We all knew it was the start of a new era.

Even a manager's working hours communicate expectations to subordinates. A subordinate, observing his boss's work schedule, commented:

> He was the first one in the office. His car was in the lot by 7:00 every morning, and he never left before 6 P.M. That told people a lot about what he expected from us.

SOURCE: John Gabarro, "Socialization at the Top—How CEOs and Subordinates Evolve Interpersonal Contracts," *Organizational Dynamics* 7 (Winter 1979): 14.

agers who must make decisions in solving those problems. The communication system also takes overall system plans and objectives, as formulated by top management, and carries them downward through the various echelons to the operative level. In fact, the organizational structure is an elaborate system for gathering, evaluating, and disseminating information.

Design of the formal organizational structure provides a set of officially established and approved communication channels, though the total communications system is not limited to this formal network. An informal network is also a part of the system, though it is less susceptible to control.

The systems viewpoint stresses the critical role of communication in the functioning of the total system and the importance of a free flow of information throughout the firm. Although we focus here on the organization's internal communication system, the open systems view also includes external communication channels. Through these channels the organization communicates with its environment. Advertising and public relations would be common examples of external communication.

CHANNELS OF COMMUNICATION

Formal Channels of Communication

Every organization has a formally sanctioned communication structure—or network of channels—through which messages move from senders to receivers. These channels may be downward, upward, or horizontal, as shown in Figure 16–2. The entire network of formal channels within an organization is depicted by the firm's organization chart.

Downward Communication Channels. Effective downward communication—from superior to subordinate—is crucial to an organization's success. Plans, policies, and procedures originating at upper management levels must be communicated accurately to lower levels of the organization to ensure effective performance. Daniel Katz and Robert Kahn enumerate five basic types of downward communication:[3]

- □ *Job instructions*—specific task directives
- □ *Job rationale*—information designed to produce understanding of the task and its relation to other organizational tasks
- □ *Procedures and practices*—information about the organization
- □ *Feedback*—to the subordinate about his or her performance.
- □ *Indoctrination of goals*—information of an ideological character to inculcate a sense of mission

Overall, the intent of downward communication is to increase the subordinate's understanding of the organization and his or her job. "If people

FIGURE 16–2 Formal channels of communication

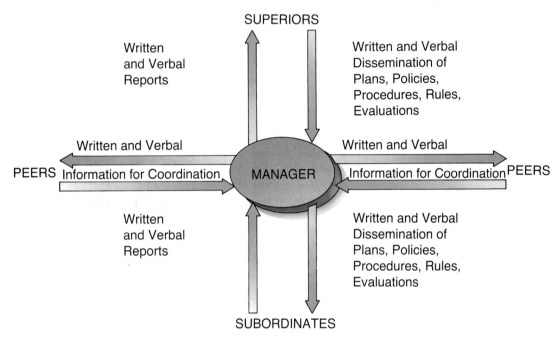

SUPERIORS

Written and Verbal Reports

Written and Verbal Dissemination of Plans, Policies, Procedures, Rules, Evaluations

PEERS Written and Verbal Information for Coordination MANAGER Written and Verbal Information for Coordination PEERS

Written and Verbal Reports

Written and Verbal Dissemination of Plans, Policies, Procedures, Rules, Evaluations

SUBORDINATES

know the reasons for their assignment, this will often ensure their carrying out the job more effectively; and if they have an understanding of what their job is about in relation to their subsystem, they are more likely to identify with organizational goals."[4]

Downward communication is not only informational, but also "relational." Although supervisors may view communication with subordinates as primarily informational (content-oriented), subordinates often consider other types of messages to be important in defining a relationship with the boss. For instance, a subordinate may care about the extent to which the boss gives career advice, how well the boss listens to suggestions and comments, and even how often the boss discusses family and non-work-related interests.[5]

Downward communication may take a number of different forms. The most direct method consists of face-to-face verbal interaction. Although less personal, written instructions, explanations, and evaluations are commonly used to reach a wider audience or to provide a permanent record of the message. Many organizations also use periodicals or newspapers (known as "house organs"), employee manuals, public address systems, and bulletin boards to communicate downward.

Research indicates that managers do not communicate with their subordinates as well as they believe they do. Although subordinates desire information from superiors, a dramatic reduction in information content occurs as messages are transmitted from higher to lower organization levels. Superiors, unaware of this decline in information content, consistently overestimate the amount of information their subordinates have received.[6] Surveys involving some 48,000 employees indicated that fewer than half rated downward communication favorably in their organizations.[7] The reasons for these and other organizational communication problems will be examined in a later section of this chapter.

Upward Communication Channels. Upward communication consists of reports from lower level participants about their job performance, their problems, the performance of others, and their attitudes toward organizational policies and procedures. Without such information, upper management could not accurately monitor organizational performance and make decisions about future programs and activities. Upward communication also provides feedback through which the superior can determine whether downward communication has been received and understood. Finally, some forms of subordinate-superior communication, such as participative management or management by objectives, encourage subordinates to participate in organizational planning and decision-making processes, thereby strengthening their commitment to the organization.

The most basic form of upward communication, the performance report to higher levels, can be the most troublesome. Problems in this area are rooted in the unique nature of the superior-subordinate relationship. The subordinate occupies a position of dependency with respect to the superior. To a great extent, the subordinate's future depends upon the superior's judgment. If the subordinate is to advance, earn pay increases, or receive choice work assignments, the decision must be that of the superior.

In view of the critical importance of the superior's opinion, it is only natural for the subordinate to wish to control all factors serving to influence supervisory judgment. In communication, therefore, the subordinate desires to transmit a message and *also* to influence the superior favorably. Achieving the goal of favorably influencing the supervisor may require some alteration of the communication itself. In its extreme form, this could involve misrepresentation of facts. But, perhaps more likely, this simply involves a subtle, perhaps almost unconscious, adaptation of the subordinate's communication. If the communication goes upward through several levels, it may become increasingly rosy and at the same time farther and farther from reality. For instance, a survey of 150 human resource professionals in a variety of industries indicated that fewer than 50 percent believed that subordinates often shared information about their own mistakes with their superiors. Only 21 percent felt that subordinates often gave feedback to their superiors concerning their superiors' mistakes.[8]

Research indicates that subordinates may be more open and honest with managers who are strongly relationship-oriented.[9] Such openness may also be more common in organic (flexible, decentralized) settings than in mechanistic (less flexible, centralized) structures.[10] Other studies report that openness of communication is enhanced when the subordinate trusts his or her supervi-

THE SPACE SHUTTLE DISASTER: A LACK OF UPWARD COMMUNICATION

Without upward communication, top management becomes increasingly divorced from operational reality. One of the most tragic examples of this process was revealed by the fatal launch of the space shuttle *Challenger*.

The icy conditions on the morning of the launch and their possible effect on the booster rocket's O-rings were behind the refusal of the senior engineer present at the launch site for Morton Thiokol (the manufacturer of the booster rocket) to agree to the launch, even after a lengthy argument. At that point, the managers of the Marshall Space Flight Center made a conference call to Thiokol executives. The result was an override of the engineer's decision. That this argument took place—unprecedented in the history of the National Aeronautics and Space Administration (NASA)—was never passed up the chain of command to the head of the shuttle program or to the associate administrator for space flight, who had the final say. The decision to launch, therefore, was made by individuals who did not have all the facts.

One of the problems appears to have been management at the Marshall Center in Alabama, responsible for the shuttle's booster rocket, main engines, and external fuel tanks. Theoretically, Marshall was to coordinate its operations with the Kennedy Space Center in Florida, responsible for assembling, servicing, and launching the shuttle, and with the Johnson Space Center in Houston, responsible for overseeing the entire shuttle program.

Marshall's management had arrogantly isolated themselves from the other centers, operating in a semi-independent fashion. The Rogers Commission, which investigated the disaster, recommended that NASA should take "energetic steps" to eliminate the tendency of management isolation at Marshall, "whether by changes of personnel, organization, indoctrination or all three. . . ."

SOURCE: Based on "The Report on Challenger," *The Houston Post*, 10 June 1986; and Michael Brody, "NASA's Challenge: Ending Isolation at the Top," *Fortune*, 12 May 1986, pp. 26–32.

sor.[11] And evidence indicates that modifications to important messages are unlikely to occur when the subordinate knows that the superior can obtain the correct information from another source.[12]

Furthermore, research shows that subordinates often experience greater job satisfaction, less turnover, and better performance when they perceive that their superiors welcome upward communication. Hence, the willingness of subordinates to pass information to their superiors can play an important role in increasing the quality of managerial decision making, improving subordinate attitudes and behavior, and enhancing overall organizational effectiveness.[13]

Horizontal Communication Channels. Although vertical communication channels have received greater emphasis in management theory than have horizontal channels, both are equally important to organizational effectiveness. Lateral flows of information help to:

☐ Coordinate the activities of different departments through dispersal and sharing of pertinent information
☐ Solve interdepartmental problems and conflicts by providing a direct means of communication
☐ Provide emotional and social support to employees through interaction focusing on common task concerns

The horizontal flow of information also serves to reduce the strain on vertical communication channels. If the production manager wishes to communicate with the marketing manager, he or she may do that directly without first going through their common superior, the vice-president of operations, unless it is necessary that the superior be involved. This "short-circuiting" of the chain-of-command avoids some of the problems involved in vertical communication, such as distortion and slowness.

As organizations become more diversified and their employees more specialized, the need for coordination, and hence horizontal communication, increases. Many organizations have responded to this need by creating committees composed of representatives from different departments and areas of specialization. The interchange of information among the committee members often results in greater awareness and understanding of the functions and problems of other areas.

Informal Channels of Communication

Much of the communication within organizations is transmitted through nonformal channels. These "nonofficial" messages comprise the organization's informal communication system, often referred to as the *grapevine.*

Functions of the Grapevine. The grapevine involves a normal, rather than an abnormal, set of relationships. Informal communication occurs naturally wherever individuals are thrown together in work or social contacts. Such spontaneous communication can help satisfy the social needs of many individuals.

In addition, the grapevine is often more informative than the formal communication system. Official channels may report that the organization's president has resigned for "reasons of health," or "family and personal considerations," but the grapevine supplements this pronouncement by reporting the inside details of the resignation. A third function of the informal communication system is that messages may be transmitted more rapidly through the grapevine than through formal channels.[14]

Accuracy of the Grapevine.   Occasionally, one gets the impression that only false rumors are circulated by the grapevine. It is true that rumors occur and that wild ones may be rapidly transmitted through informal channels. But other, more substantial information is also conveyed in this way. As a matter of fact, research indicates that rumors occur relatively infrequently and that most of the information transmitted through informal channels is fairly accurate.[15]

The grapevine may be so accurate because of the configuration of informal communication channels. The grapevine is often visualized as a long chain, with A telling B, who in turn passes it on so that it eventually reaches Z. Such a pattern of transmission would clearly maximize the chances for error. Studies of the grapevine, however, have provided evidence that conflicts somewhat with this concept. The general pattern, as discovered by one researcher, is that of the *cluster chain*, illustrated in Figure 16–3.[16] One link in the communication network informs a number of people instead of just one person. One or two of each cluster of receivers, in turn, pass the communication on to another group.

Occasional rumors or errors require corrective action. If a manager discovers an unfounded rumor among subordinates, for example, he or she may simply call them together and discuss the matter with them. Whether the facts will be accepted as such depends upon management's reputation for accuracy and candor in previous communication.

Some organizations have established special programs to detect rumors,

FIGURE 16–3   The grapevine

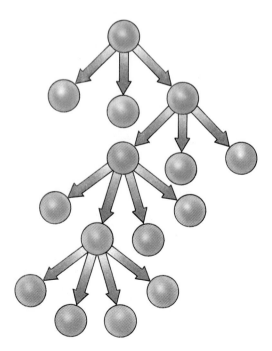

asking employees to bring them to the attention of management. The rumor is then presented along with the facts. The employee newspaper and bulletin boards, among other media, have been used for this purpose.

Constructive Value of the Grapevine. Unless managers wish to multiply their own communication efforts many times, they cannot channel all information through the official chain of command. Informal communications supplement and amplify those emanating from official sources. Much information about work assignments and company policy, for example, is picked up from fellow employees. Also, the grapevine supplies the manager with information about subordinates and their work experiences, thereby increasing the manager's understanding and effectiveness.

Communication Channels Within Groups

Over the past forty years, researchers have experimented with small-group communication networks. The results indicate that the pattern of communication a group uses to solve task problems affects the group's performance and the satisfaction of its members.

Three of the more common communication networks studied are illustrated in Figure 16–4. In the *wheel* network, each member can communicate only with the individual in the center, who in turn may communicate with any of the other members. The *circle* allows each individual to communicate with two other individuals—those on either side. Any member of the *all-channel* network can communicate with any other member.

The following conclusions indicate the effects communication networks have on group performance and member satisfaction:[17]

☐ Simple problems are solved most rapidly by the wheel network. Information is channeled to the central individual in the wheel, who then combines the information to solve the problem.

FIGURE 16–4 Small-group communication networks

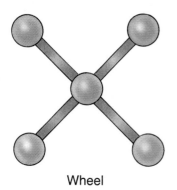

Wheel

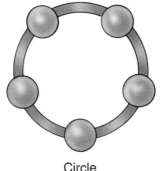

Circle

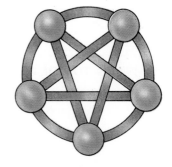

All-channel

☐ The all-channel and circle networks are able to solve complex problems more rapidly. Such problems require considerable two-way communication—answering questions, confirming facts, and seeking additional information.

☐ The satisfaction of members with their tasks is higher in the circle and all-channel networks. Within the wheel network, however, the satisfaction of the individual occupying the central position is much higher than that of the peripheral members. Evidently members of the two "decentralized" networks and the central figure in the wheel feel greater freedom and independence in their positions, while the wheel's peripheral members feel that their behavior is controlled by the central member.

☐ The central individual in the wheel invariably emerges as the group leader, whereas no leader appears consistently in the circle or all-channel networks. The leader of the wheel has greater access to information and the opportunity to coordinate the activities of the other members. The leader, however, often suffers from information overload—particularly in complex problem situations.

Because this research on group communication networks has been conducted in laboratory (that is, artificial) settings, the degree to which the findings can be generalized is debatable. In the experimental settings, each group is viewed as an independent system. But systems theory holds that groups within organizations are not independent. They are connected to other work groups, to supervisors, to incentive systems, and to informal communication channels. Hence, the research in this area has taken a rather narrow view of groups. On the other hand, the results strongly indicate that a group's communication network affects both performance and satisfaction.

Some of these findings have been replicated in field studies of ongoing organizations. For example, a study of forty-four project groups in a research and development laboratory in a large corporation found that project groups with higher performance levels had evolved communication structures appropriate to their tasks. Effective groups dealing with nonroutine or complex tasks used decentralized communication patterns involving extensive peer contact and peer decision making in a form roughly similar to the all-channel network described above. Groups that dealt effectively with more routine tasks evolved centralized communication patterns much like the wheel.[18]

BARRIERS TO COMMUNICATION

Perfect communication would accurately transmit an idea from one mind to another. Unfortunately, transmission is often imperfect. The message received by Person B differs from the message transmitted by Person A, a situation illustrated in Figure 16–5. The circle on the left represents the message (the facts, feelings, and attitudes) that A sends to B. The circle on the right indicates

FIGURE 16–5 Imperfect communication

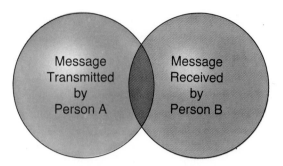

the facts, feelings, and attitudes that B perceives are being transmitted. The overlapping shaded area between the two circles indicates the only part of A's message actually understood by B.

The problem, of course, is that A believes that B understood the entire message sent, and B thinks that he or she understood the message transmitted by A. Both may now proceed on the assumption that perfect communication has occurred, yet both are operating on incorrect premises.

Perceptual Barriers

Considerable differences exist in the way individuals perceive, organize, and understand their environment. These differences stem from different job experiences, educational backgrounds, value systems, and so on. It is not surprising, then, that these differences influence interpretation of messages. A person receives a message and interprets it in the light of previous experiences.

Past experiences may cause an individual to have preconceived ideas of what others are trying to say. If so, it is difficult for the individual to hear anything that differs from his or her preconceptions. Suppose the boss commends a subordinate who is convinced that the supervisor is prejudiced and unfair. The subordinate may think, "The boss must be trying to pull a fast one."

The subordinate in this case is guilty of attributing inaccurate meaning to the boss's message. Individuals often infer that something is being communicated when it is not. This inference then becomes a "fact" upon which the person proceeds. Attributing unwarranted meaning to another's message can be hazardous unless the receiver is conscious of the differences between the facts transmitted by the message and the meaning he or she attributes to those facts. Inferences should be made only in probabilistic terms; that is, "The boss *possibly* commended me because. . . ."

Semantic Barriers

Organizations, departments, functional areas, and members of the same occupational group often devise their own language, or *jargon*, to facilitate communication among members of the same unit. Although such specialized language may increase communication accuracy and understanding among these individuals, jargon is often a source of dismay to outsiders. Individuals use jargon so often that they forget that clients or members of other units or occupations may not understand the special terminology. A person watching a football game on television for the first time, for instance, would have difficulty understanding the announcer's description of what was occurring on the field. Football fans, however, would readily comprehend such terms as "blitz," "sack," "nose guard," and "audible." The description would become protracted and tedious if the announcer had to describe what was happening on the field in everyday language.

Another semantic barrier to communication is that the same words do not always carry the same meaning for both parties. A supervisor, for example, may intend to commend subordinates by commenting upon "satisfactory" performance. Subordinates may take offense at such commendation, however, because they know they are "superior," not *merely* "satisfactory." Similarly, the boss's statement to a subordinate to do something "as soon as possible" may mean that the subordinate should perform the required activity immediately. The subordinate, however, may interpret the request to mean that the required task should be taken care of after everything else the subordinate has to do is completed.

Serial Transmission Barriers

Perceptual and semantic barriers can easily distort communication between two individuals. Imagine, then, the potential for distortion that exists when a

---

DIFFERENT PERCEPTIONS

People interpret the same stimulus in different ways, depending on their previous experience. Take the case of a supervisor who is watching a group of employees laughing:

☐ To the manager who believes that work must be painful in order to be productive, the laughter communicates that time is being wasted, and perhaps assignments are too easy.
☐ To the manager who believes that contented employees work harder, the laughter communicates that he or she is succeeding as a manager.
☐ To the manager who is personally insecure, the laughter communicates that the employees are ridiculing him or her.

SOURCE: Adapted from George Strauss and Leonard R. Sayles, *Personnel: The Human Problems of Management,* 2d ed. (Englewood Cliffs, N.J.: Prentice-Hall, 1967), p. 227.

THE JARGON OF LOBBYISTS

Mark S. Fowler, who met hundreds of Washington lobbyists while serving as chairman of the Federal Communications Commission, has compiled a list of lobbyists' phrases and what the phrases really mean. Some examples:

□ "Do you think I should touch base with the White House on this?" (I'm bluffing. In fact, I'm the sort of person who can't get tickets for the 8 A.M. tour.)
□ "You really need to meet with my people so you can understand their concerns." (My people weigh 350 pounds and hold Golden Glove boxing titles.)
□ "All we are seeking is a fair shake." (Gimme.)

SOURCE: Mark S. Fowler, "An Official's Guide to the Lobbyist Lexicon," *The Wall Street Journal,* 25 January 1985.

message is transmitted through a series of individuals. This *serial transmission effect* is illustrated to most of us at an early age through the game of rumor. A child at one end of a line of children communicates a message verbally to the next child. The receiver then transmits the message to the next child, and so on until the last one in line has received the message. The original message is then compared to the message received by the last person in line. The two usually differ significantly.

In organizations, serial transmission may be either vertical or horizontal. The first receiver may misunderstand or ignore parts of the message, reinterpret parts, or omit some portions of the message that seem irrelevant before transmitting the message to the next link in the chain. If the next receiver likewise modifies the message, the end result will be considerably distorted. The greater the number of links in the chain, the greater the potential for distortion and misunderstanding.

Surprisingly, most people rarely question the accuracy of messages that have been serially transmitted. A survey of 150 human resource professionals indicated that 32 percent almost never questioned downward communications and 24 percent almost never questioned horizontal communications. Fewer than 10 percent often questioned downward communication and only about 16 percent often questioned horizontally transmitted messages.[19]

Information Overload

Communication systems often become defective by providing or permitting a greater volume of communication than the organization can handle—a con-

SERIAL TRANSMISSION DISTORTION

A reporter was present at a [Vietnamese] hamlet burned down by the U.S. Army's 1st Air Cavalry Division in 1967. Investigation showed that the order from the division headquarters to the brigade was: "On no occasion must hamlets be burned down."

The brigade radioed the battalion: "Do not burn down any hamlets unless you are absolutely convinced that the Viet Cong are in them."

The battalion radioed the infantry company at the scene: "If you think there are any Viet Cong in the hamlet, burn it down."

The company commander ordered his troops: "Burn down that hamlet."

SOURCE: James G. Miller, "Living Systems: The Organization," *Behavioral Science* 17 (January 1972): 149, as reprinted from H. Faas and P. Arnett, "Civilians Fear My Lai Is U.S. 'Achilles Heel,'" *Cleveland Plain Dealer*, 8 December 1969, p. 6.

dition termed *information overload.* Managers are not only informed, but deluged with information. A communication network is capable of carrying only so much information, and a manager has only so much time available for reading letters, studying reports, talking on the telephone, and conferring with others. Beyond some point, an attempted increase in communication volume may contribute to inefficiency rather than performing its intended function.

The nature of the manager's job is a major cause of information overload. Managers are required to make decisions and coordinate the activities of others. These role prescriptions demand extensive communication with other subsystems and with individuals and organizations outside the manager's organization. "What seems like a reasonable flow of information from each subsystem or network can easily become a flood when all of these subsystem networks of information converge at one point to form the too often swollen river of information."[20]

This flow of information increases significantly when major changes occur in the organization's environment. An unexpected drop in sales causes management to request information concerning the decline. The resulting statistical data, analyses, and suggested solutions for the problem may amount to a deluge of information, which by its very volume delays processing of the information by the overloaded manager. One study of information overload in two different settings found that overloaded individuals had lower job performance than did employees who reported that they had insufficient information for proper job accomplishment.[21]

DEVELOPING EFFECTIVE COMMUNICATION

Managers can increase the effectiveness of organizational communication by attention to the suggestions presented here. Underlying each suggestion is the need for the sender to empathize with the receiver. Admittedly, a manager may find it difficult to identify with the values or career orientation of subordinates or of more technically oriented individuals. But the more the manager understands the receiver's job and role in the organization, the more likely the manager will be able to communicate appropriately and effectively.

Two-Way Communication

Management literature often emphasizes the importance of two-way communication. An interchange of messages that permits discussion back and forth between two persons, superior and subordinate, for example, presumably communicates with greater effectiveness than a one-way flow. Managers who engage in two-way communication do more than *tell* their subordinates. They *tell* and *listen* or, in other words, engage in conversation with subordinates by encouraging feedback.

Two-way communication offers several advantages, possibly the most significant being greater accuracy. The receiver can check on any unclear matter by asking questions. The give-and-take of discussion may also clarify issues in a general way. In the case of superior-subordinate communication, furthermore, the subordinate gains a sense of greater involvement and self-respect through two-way communication.

The following comments by Harold Leavitt point out strengths and imply weaknesses of a one-way communication flow:[22]

> If speed alone is what is important, then one-way communication has the edge. If appearance is of prime importance, if one wishes to look orderly and business-like, then the one-way method again is preferable. If one doesn't want one's mistakes to be recognized, then again one-way communication is preferable. Then the sender will not have to hear people implying or saying that he is stupid or that there is an easier way to say what he is trying to say.

Although two-way communication is usually preferable, it does not occur automatically. The manager must work at it to make sure it happens.

Listening

Communication involves both transmission and reception. Much of the study of communication has stressed the transmitter and tended to ignore the receiver. Listening requires the active participation of the receiver; it is not simply hearing. A major cause of poor listening is that while the average person speaks at a rate of 100 to 200 words per minute, the average listener can

LISTENING AT SPERRY CORPORATION

Perhaps no organization has done more to emphasize the importance of listening than Sperry Corporation, a manufacturer of machinery, computers, and flight and navigation control systems. Before its takeover by the Burroughs Corporation (the combined company became known as Unisys), Sperry's long-running advertising campaign, based on the slogan "We understand how important it is to listen," stressed the significance of listening as an essential managerial skill. Effective listening enabled Sperry's employees to respond appropriately to people who have direct interest in the products and performance of the company.

In a test of "how well do you listen?" Sperry asked employees such questions as the following:

☐ "On a scale of 0–100 (100 = highest), how would you rate yourself as a listener?" Sperry found the average rating to be 55, with the general range from 35 to 85 and the extreme range from 10 to 90.

☐ "On a scale of 0–100, how do you think [your best friend, your boss, and your spouse] would rate you as a listener?" Sperry reported that most respondents believed that their best friend and their boss would rate them higher than they rated themselves. The spouse rating, however, began at the same high level as the best friend rating but steadily declined as the marriage went on and on.

SOURCE: Adapted from *Your Personal Listening Profile,* a pamphlet (Sperry Corporation); and John Louis DiGaetani, "The Sperry Corporation and Listening: An Interview," *Business Horizons* 25 (March/April 1982): 34–39.

process at least 400 words per minute.[23] This excess listening capacity permits the mind to wander instead of concentrating on the speaker's message.

An active listener learns to use this excess capacity to increase his or her understanding of what the speaker is saying. The following suggestions, for instance, may help you become a more effective listener:[24]

☐ Attempt to identify the main points or central idea the speaker is trying to impart.

☐ Use the lag between speaking and listening rates to review mentally the points the speaker has already made.

☐ Search for deeper meanings by analyzing words for secondary or connotative meanings.

- □ Anticipate what the speaker will say next in order to compare the actual message being transmitted with what you predicted. This mental activity helps reinforce the speaker's ideas in your mind and focuses your attention upon the message.
- □ Do not be distracted by the speaker's unique speaking style; listen for content, not delivery.
- □ Ask questions when you do not understand what is said.
- □ Compensate for emotionally charged words by trying to determine objectively what meaning those words hold for the speaker.
- □ Withhold evaluation of the message until the speaker is finished and you are certain that you understand what was transmitted.
- □ Be flexible in your views. Even ideas that you cannot totally accept may have some merit.

Becoming an active listener, then, requires both concentration and practice. One cannot be an effective communicator without giving conscious attention to the act of listening.

Aggressively Sharing Information

In the typical situation, managers transmit to subordinates those messages that seem necessary in the regular course of business operations. If subordinates need directions or information, the necessary instructions are given. There is no attempt to hold back the facts. Rather, the attention is simply on those communications essential to the operation.

As long as an organization is small and the operation simple, this approach may work reasonably well. Through personal observation, subordinates can supplement that which they learn through formal channels. As the organization grows, however, it may become so compartmentalized that the individual has a very narrow view of the overall operation.

In such situations, an aggressive willingness to share information is required. A survey of 695 employees in a large public-utility firm revealed that those employees who had positive feelings about the sharing of information within the organization also had positive feelings regarding the organization's interpersonal milieu, management in general, and the way employees identify with the organization. Conversely, the withholding of important information by management was negatively related to job satisfaction.[25]

Need for Honesty and Sincerity

A communications program is occasionally used as a type of propaganda effort. An attempt is made to sell or convince employees of some point of view. Attempts at persuasion need not involve deceit—presentation of the organization's point of view may be justified. But an organization or supervisor may slip into the habit of using information as a technique for manipulation. Rather than being forthright and open, information is tailored or withheld to produce the desired effect—"What they don't know won't hurt them."

Such an attitude toward communication is insulting to subordinates, and employees are quick to detect such insincerity. Attempts to manipulate subordinates, therefore, will typically be rejected and produce a negative reaction as well.

Trust and openness on the part of the sender lead to more open, accurate communication since such qualities usually evoke a positive response from the receiver. Likewise, lack of trust or deception on the sender's part may cause the receiver to be cautious and nonsupportive. Effective communication cannot exist in a relationship without trust.

Increasingly strong foreign and domestic competition is forcing companies to try to gain the commitment of their employees. More and more, organizations are having to introduce new technologies, adjust wages, modify work practices, and even close plants. In many cases, workers have rejected pay freezes or cuts because they did not trust management's word that the company was in trouble.[26] The key to gaining worker trust is management's credibility. Credibility is attained only through honesty and the aggressive sharing of information.

Channel Selection

A manager has available a variety of communication channels and methods. Some use the written word, in such varied forms as policy statements, official letters, memos, personal notes, bulletin board announcements, newspaper articles, and employee handbooks. Even oral communications differ greatly in nature and formality. The manager may make a formal address, talk with a colleague over a cup of coffee, hold a committee discussion, or talk on the telephone.

Some channels and methods work better for a given type of communication than do others. An announcement of a change in the retirement program would normally be written rather than being transmitted via the grapevine. In seeking support of a colleague for a proposed policy change, a manager would probably rely on informal discussion rather than send a formal letter. The channel and method are properly tailored to the communication.

Advances in the telecommunications industry have opened new channels of communication to the manager. These channels fit under the generic classification of *teleconferencing,* defined as "interactive group communication through any electronic medium." Included are audio and full-motion video that link two parties in separate geographic locations, and electronic mail from one employee's computer terminal to the terminals of other receivers. Although still in its infancy, teleconferencing is already being used by firms to reduce some forms of travel, to introduce new products to field representatives, and to answer questions from conference participants.[27]

SUMMARY

Communication is an integral aspect of management. Through communication, information, facts, feelings, and ideas are transmitted from one person to another. The communications network, including the formal organizational structure and the supplementary informal channels, may be visualized as an informational system used to direct and coordinate the activities of the various parts (subsystems) of the firm. Communication is accomplished not only through language, but also through voice inflections, physical expressions and gestures, silence, and behavior.

Management establishes a network of *formal communication channels* through which official messages move downward, upward, and horizontally throughout the organization. *Downward channels* transmit plans, policies, and procedures from upper management to lower levels in order to increase subordinates' understanding of their organization and jobs. Downward communication also serves to define the superior-subordinate relationship. *Upward channels* carry reports from lower levels which enable managers at higher levels to monitor organizational performance for future decision-making activities. The actions of various departments are coordinated and conflict among the departments resolved through *horizontal channels.*

The *grapevine,* or *informal communication network,* supplements the formal communication channels. This informal network emerges spontaneously to help satisfy the social needs of organizational participants and to provide information not carried through official channels.

Evidence indicates that particular configurations of group communication networks are more appropriate in certain situations than in others. Simple, routine problems are solved more rapidly by the *wheel* network, while complex, nonroutine tasks should be dealt with through the *all-channel* and *circle* networks.

Communication barriers prevent transmission from a sender to a receiver. The sender's *perceptual world,* for instance, may differ considerably from the receiver's. Organizational or departmental *jargon* hinders accurate communication, as does the *serial transmission effect.* And many managers suffer from *information overload,* a condition in which the volume of information received by the manager is greater than his or her capacity to absorb and use it.

An effective communication program requires the manager to engage in *two-way communication* with subordinates, superiors, and peers. The ability to *listen* must be carefully cultivated, and the manager must attempt to *share information aggressively.* Adequate communication does not develop naturally without effort. In view of the employee's ability to detect insincerity, *openness* and *honesty* are also prime features of effective communication. The proper *channel* and method for most effective communication depend upon the nature of the communication and other factors.

KEY CONCEPTS

Communication	Circle network
Transmission	All-channel network
Reception	Perceptual barriers
Downward communication	Semantic barriers
Upward communication	Serial transmission barriers
Horizontal communication	Information overload
Formal communication channels	Two-way communication
Informal communication channels	Listening
Grapevine	Aggressive sharing of information
Wheel network	Teleconferencing

DISCUSSION QUESTIONS

1. Communication includes more than the transmission of facts. What are the other aspects of communication? Of these, which is most difficult to transmit in writing?
2. "Without reception, communication does not occur." How can a manager determine whether subordinates are receiving the message that he or she is sending?
3. Suppose a state governor or the president of the United States personally inspects a flood-stricken area. Explain the significance of such a visit from the standpoint of communication.
4. What are the purposes of *downward communication? upward communication? horizontal communication?*
5. Why do superiors overestimate the amount of information their subordinates receive?
6. What is the basic reason for distortion in performance reports to higher levels?
7. What are the functions of the informal communication system (the *grapevine*)?
8. Why is the *wheel* network inappropriate for solving complex, nonroutine problems?
9. Explain the major barriers to effective communication.
10. How does one become a more effective listener?
11. What philosophy of management is implied by the phrase *aggressive sharing of information?*

NOTES

1. Michael B. McCaskey, "The Hidden Messages Managers Send," *Harvard Business Review* 57 (November-December 1979): 147.
2. Ibid., p. 138.

3. Daniel Katz and Robert L. Kahn, *The Social Psychology of Organizations,* 2d ed. (New York: Wiley, 1978), p. 440.

4. Ibid., p. 443.

5. Larry E. Penley and Brian Hawkins, "Studying Interpersonal Communication in Organizations: A Leadership Application," *Academy of Management Journal* 28 (June 1985): 309–26.

6. This research is summarized in John E. Baird, Jr., *The Dynamics of Organizational Communication* (New York: Harper & Row, 1977), p. 269.

7. Walter Kiechel III, "No Word From On High," *Fortune,* 6 January 1986, p. 125.

8. Allan D. Frank, "Trends in Communication: Who Talks to Whom?" *Personnel* 62 (December 1985): 42.

9. J. C. Wofford, P. J. Calabro, and Alan Sims, "The Relationship of Information Sharing Norms and Leader Behavior," *Journal of Management* 1 (Fall 1975): 23.

10. Jerald W. Young, "The Subordinate's Exposure of Organizational Vulnerability to the Superior: Sex and Organizational Effects," *Academy of Management Journal* 21 (March 1978): 119–20.

11. These studies are summarized in Jerry C. Wofford, Edwin A. Gerloff, and Robert C. Cummins, *Organizational Communication: The Keystone to Managerial Effectiveness* (New York: McGraw-Hill, 1977), pp. 376–77; and Janet H. Gaines, "Upward Communication in Industry: An Experiment," *Human Relations* 33 (December 1980): 929–42.

12. George Huber, "Organizational Information Systems: Determinants of Their Performance and Behavior," *Management Science* 28 (February 1982): 138–55.

13. Michael J. Glauser, "Upward Information Flow in Organizations: Review and Conceptual Analysis," *Human Relations* 37 (August 1984): 614; and Daniel G. Spencer, "Employee Voice and Employee Retention," *Academy of Management Journal* 29 (September 1986): 488–502.

14. Katz and Kahn, *Social Psychology of Organizations,* p. 449.

15. A brief review of the literature in this area is provided by Baird, *Dynamics of Organizational Communication,* p. 275.

16. Keith Davis, *Human Relations at Work,* 3d ed. (New York: McGraw-Hill, 1967), p. 225.

17. Excellent reviews of the literature in this area may be found in Baird, *Dynamics of Organizational Communication,* pp. 277–85; Wofford et al., *Organizational Communication,* chapter 16; and Brian L. Hawkins and Paul Preston, *Managerial Communication* (Santa Monica, Calif.: Goodyear, 1981), pp. 166–73.

18. Michael L. Tushman, "Work Characteristics and Subunit Communication Structure: A Contingency Analysis," *Administrative Science Quarterly* 24 (March 1979): 82–98.

19. Frank, "Trends in Communication," p. 44.

20. Richard K. Allen, *Organizational Management through Communication* (New York: Harper & Row, 1977), p. 80.

21. Charles A. O'Reilly III, "Individuals and Information Overload in Organizations: Is More Necessarily Better?" *Academy of Management Journal* 23 (December 1980): 684–96.

22. Harold J. Leavitt, *Managerial Psychology,* 3d ed. (Chicago: University of Chicago Press, 1972), p. 118.

23. This and other research findings on oral communication are summarized in Richard C. Huseman, James M. Lahiff, and John D. Hatfield, *Interpersonal Communica-*

tion in Organizations: A Perceptual Approach (Boston: Holbrook Press, 1976), p. 107.

24. These suggestions are based on Larry L. Barker, *Listening Behavior* (Englewood Cliffs, N.J.: Prentice-Hall, 1971), pp. 73–8; and Huseman et al., *Interpersonal Communication,* pp. 112–15.

25. Paul M. Muchinsky, "Organizational Communication: Relationships to Organizational Climate and Job Satisfaction," *Academy of Management Journal* 20 (December 1977): 592–607.

26. "How Companies Are Getting Their Message Across to Labor," *Business Week,* 24 September 1984, p. 58.

27. Robert Johansen and Christine Bullen, "What to Expect From Teleconferencing," *Harvard Business Review* 62 (March-April 1984): 164–65.

SUPPLEMENTARY READING

Baskin, Otis W., and Aronoff, Craig E. *Interpersonal Communication in Organizations.* Santa Monica, Calif.: Goodyear, 1980.

Campbell, Mary Ellen, and Hollmann, Robert W. "ABC = Auditing Business Communications." *Business Horizons* 28 (September/October 1985): 60–64.

Di Gaetani, John L. "The Business of Listening." *Business Horizons* 23 (October 1980): 40–46.

————. "The Sperry Corporation and Listening: An Interview." *Business Horizons* 25 (March/April 1982): 34–9.

Gabarro, John. "Socialization at the Top—How CEOs and Subordinates Evolve Interpersonal Contracts," *Organizational Dynamics* 7 (Winter 1979): 3–23.

Glauser, Michael J. "Upward Information Flow in Organizations: Review and Conceptual Analysis." *Human Relations* 37 (August 1984): 613–43.

Hatfield, John D., and Huseman, Richard C. "Perceptual Congruence about Communication as Related to Satisfaction: Moderating Effects of Individual Characteristics." *Academy of Management Journal* 25 (June 1982): 349–58.

Josefowitz, Natasha. "Management Men and Women: Closed vs. Open Doors." *Harvard Business Review* 58 (September-October 1980): 56–62.

Kikoski, John F. "Communication: Understanding It, Improving It." *Personnel Journal* 59 (February 1980): 126–31.

"Listening and Responding to Employees' Concerns: An Interview with A. W. Clausen." *Harvard Business Review* 58 (January-February 1980): 101–14.

Luthans, Fred, and Larsen, Janet K. "How Managers Really Communicate." *Human Relations* 39 (February 1986): 161–78.

McCaskey, Michael B. "The Hidden Messages Managers Send." *Harvard Business Review* 57 (November-December 1979): 135–48.

Peters, Tom, and Austin, Nancy. "MBWA (Managing By Walking Around)." *California Management Review* 28 (Fall 1985): 9–34.

Rowe, Mary P. and Baker, Michael. "Are You Hearing Enough Employee Concerns?" *Harvard Business Review* 62 (May-June 1984): 127–35.

St. John, Walter. "In-House Communication Guidelines." *Personnel Journal* 60 (November 1981): 872–78.

Sanderlin, Reed. "Information Is Not Communication." *Business Horizons* 25 (March/April 1982): 40–42.

Schein, Edgar H. "Improving Face-to-Face Relationships." *Sloan Management Review* 22 (Winter 1981): 43–52.

Spiller, Rex, and Housel, Thomas J. "SMR Forum: Video Teleconferencing—A New Training Tool." *Sloan Management Review* 27 (Fall 1985): 57–62.

THE EMPTY SLEEPER

Fuzzy Inc., a manufacturer of teddy bears, had always used for-hire transportation. With the onset of the motor carrier deregulation act of 1980, the executive management team at Fuzzy Inc. decided to experiment with its own fleet in hopes of cutting costs. With this concept in mind, the approval was given to purchase a tractor and trailer and to hire two drivers.

After several weeks, a "rig" was purchased, and two drivers were employed. Since the initial trip involved a delivery to a customer who was approximately fourteen hours away, it was decided that the trip should begin at night so that arrival would be during regular working hours. Everyone gathered around the truck, the champagne bottle was smashed against the bumper, the drivers climbed aboard (one in the driver's seat and the other in the sleeper), and they departed on their maiden voyage.

As Adam, the driver, headed down the highway, he realized that they had overlooked a minor detail. In all the excitement, nobody had thought of placing a CB unit in the cab. He made a mental note of the fact and turned on the radio to ease the loneliness.

After approximately four hours of driving, Adam decided to stop at a rest area. He climbed down from the cab and was

about to knock on the sleeper to awaken his partner, Dudley, when he thought, "Let him sleep, I'll wake him at the next stop when it's his turn to drive." With that in mind, Adam went to the rest room. Afterwards, he looked for a phone booth, since company policy dictated that the customer be called at each stop to inform him of the estimated time of arrival.

While Adam was seeking a phone booth, Dudley awoke, realized he was at a rest stop, and decided to go to the rest room. A few minutes later, he emerged from the rest room just in time to see Adam and the rig leaving the rest area. Dudley thought for a moment, and immediately decided to call the traffic manager for a decision. Upon hearing what had happened, Sigmund, the traffic manager, advised Dudley to try to catch Adam further along the route (feeling certain Adam would call when he discovered the mishap). With this advice, Dudley hitched a ride with another truck driver.

After three hours had passed, Adam decided it was Dudley's turn to drive. He turned into a rest area, climbed down and knocked on the door of the sleeper. Getting no answer, he opened the door to find the sleeper empty. Without a bit of hesitation he immediately called Paul, the assistant traffic manager, for a decision. Paul instructed Adam to return immediately and find Dudley. Adam complied.

Case prepared by Professor Marc G. Singer of James Madison University.

Can you imagine the thoughts racing through Dudley's mind as he watched Adam speeding along in the other direction? Can you imagine Dudley's feeling when the driver he hitched a ride with requested fifty dollars for the lift? The mishap cost the company approximately fifteen hundred dollars and an irate customer. Adam and Dudley endure ribbing to this day. But the company did develop a new slogan. Every truck at Fuzzy Inc. has a sign prominently mounted on its dashboard which reads "IS YOUR BUDDY WITH YOU?"

Questions

1. Discuss the communication breakdowns which occurred.
2. What policies could the company institute to prevent similar problems from happening in the future?
3. Could what happened at Fuzzy Inc. really have been prevented?

HAS THE WORM TURNED?

The foreman watched as Alan Boswell, assistant to the factory manager, posted a memorandum on the bulletin board of the management lounge. There had seemingly been an endless stream of memoranda relating to policies, procedures, rules, and regulations since George Parker became factory manager five months ago. In addition, too many of the old department heads and management staff had been replaced by MBA's in vested suits, with Boswell being the worst.

For five months, Parker and his boys had harped on efficiency and by stumbling over one another had managed to drop the plant from second to fifth place in the division. But Parker was a hard man to talk to—and not a man to cross, because of his temper and autocratic style. Poor old Jimmy Collins found out about that after he spoke up in the annual budget meetings last month.

When Boswell had gone, the foremen approached the bulletin board, shaking their heads wearily, to read the message.

Case prepared by John E. Schoen and Jerry L. Crowder.

CONFIDENTIAL

TO: All Department Managers   May 10
    All General Foremen

FRIDAY STAFF MEETING

As mentioned in the last staff meeting, we will devote the last 15 minutes of each weekly staff meeting to a review and an answer period (a chance to get acquainted). Subjects may be presented verbally or in writing; the latter may be in a sealed envelope, unsigned, and directed confidentially to the writer.

The purpose of this discussion is to strengthen our managerial team by communication, affording all managers an opportunity to have their questions concerning plant administration thoroughly analyzed, clarified, and answered.

A well-informed management team is one of our key objectives. This team's knowledge and skill, ability to plan and organize effectively, to direct and control, and to evaluate and critique thoughtfully are requisites for effective and outstanding management.

We deal mostly with people, and we must be adequately prepared to:

1. Set goals and meet quotas
2. Work efficiently and effectively
3. Build sound, effective, and loyal teams
4. Stimulate and motivate
5. Develop others for promotion

Topics for discussion should not be limited, but must be meaningful and objective. They may relate to (1) improving individual performance, (2) clarifying procedures and policies, (3) improving leadership styles, or (4) any appropriate subject of your choice. Let's communicate and direct our efforts toward making the management team outstanding in each of its management responsibilities.

(signed)

George Parker
Factory Manager

Questions

1. Evaluate the probable effectiveness of the message in stimulating two-way communication in the staff meeting and/or generally.
2. Evaluate the content of the message with respect to management principles and/or a participative approach to management.
3. Who has responsibility for establishing communication after managerial succession?
4. Evaluate the method the factory manager has used to communicate instructions regarding the Friday staff meeting.

PART FIVE

CONTROLLING PERFORMANCE

AN OVERVIEW OF CONTROL
Importance of Organizational
Control □ Strategic Control vs. Operational
Control

THE CONTROL PROCESS
Establishing Performance Standards
□Measuring Performance and Comparing It
to Standards □ Taking Corrective
Action □ Timing of Controls

CONTROL STRATEGIES
Market Control □ Bureaucratic
Control □ Clan Control □ Supervisory
Control

CONTROL TECHNIQUES
Financial Statements □ Budgets □
Responsibility Centers □ Performance
Appraisals □ Policies and Procedures
□ Statistical Reports □ Audits

DYSFUNCTIONAL CONSEQUENCES OF CONTROL
The Narrow Viewpoint □ Emphasis on the
Short Run □ Falsification of Reporting
□ Improving Control Effectiveness

Summary □ Key Concepts □ Discussion
Questions □ Notes □ Supplementary
Reading

CASES: Delta Fertilizer (B) □ Specialty
Manufacturing

This chapter will enable you to

□ Explain the differences between
strategic control and operating control.

□ Understand the purpose of
organizational control and how the
control process works.

□ Examine how certain control strategies
can be utilized.

□ Discuss the various control techniques
that managers use.

□ Identify some of the dysfunctional
consequences of control and suggest
how they may be overcome.

CHAPTER 17
THE CONTROL PROCESS

Controls are an ordinary part of life in society. Some are presented in a positive way—"Do this and achieve that." Weight control in the form of exercising is an example of a positive control. Other controls are presented in a negative way—"Don't litter."

Controls are also a part of organizational life. Organizations seldom function perfectly in executing plans. As a result, managers must monitor their operations to ensure that the organization is functioning as intended. Management activities that check on performance and correct it when necessary are a part of the *management control function.*

AN OVERVIEW OF CONTROL

Importance of Organizational Control

Control has a special role in dealing with powerful forces. For example, fire is often destructive, but if confined and directed fire can be a source of great energy.

Employees exhibit various types of behavior. Marketing personnel may write fake orders; accounting personnel may "borrow" from incoming revenues; production personnel may leave the factory with finished products or spare parts. On the other hand, employees can be very creative and can accomplish tasks with effective results.

Managers seek ways both to motivate their employees and to control their employees' actions. Motivated people, when aroused, can be an angry mob or a powerful organization. The crucial aspect is how well their energies are harnessed and controlled.[1]

Strategic Control vs. Operational Control

An organization achieves its long-term objectives by formulating and implementing strategies, as discussed in chapter 4. A control system must be developed that focuses on the gap between strategy development and strategy implementation. This type of control, referred to as *strategic control*, is the concern of the organization's top managers. These managers deal with the relationships between external opportunities and threats and internal performance that are essential to the success of a strategy.

Another type of control system guides, monitors, and evaluates progress toward meeting the objectives of a particular strategy. This type of control, referred to as *operational control*, is the concern of an organization's operating managers. These managers are concerned with controlling how the organization's financial, physical, human, and technological resources are being used.[2] This chapter is primarily concerned with operating control, and from this point on operational control is used synonymously with *organizational control*.

THE CONTROL PROCESS

Organizational control consists of certain basic steps that a manager uses to ensure that actual performance conforms to a pre-determined performance level. The steps in the control process are shown in Figure 17–1.

Establishing Performance Standards

The first step in the control process, establishing standards, emphasizes the inseparability of planning and control, for it is through planning and goal setting that performance standards are established.

Goals at various organizational levels are translated into performance standards by making them measurable. An organizational goal to increase market share, for example, may be translated into a top-management performance standard to increase market share by 8 percent within a twelve-month period. This standard then serves as the basis upon which a middle-management performance standard, such as to increase sales within the southwest region by $13 million within twelve months, is established. Further down the ladder, the standard at the individual sales representative's level might become to increase sales in your district by $400,000 within twelve months. In many cases, these yearly standards will be broken down into quarterly standards so that corrective action may be taken early should performance begin to fall below the standard.

FIGURE 17–1   The control process

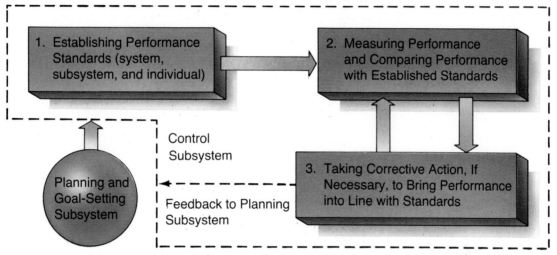

Although this example illustrates growth and sales standards, standards must be established in all areas of the organization. Control, then, requires a systems view. An organization must develop *sets of criteria*, each of which corresponds to some wider system of which the organization is a part. Figure 17–2

FIGURE 17–2   Systems criteria for judging company performance

Superordinate System	Criteria
Stockholders	Price appreciation of securities Dividend payout
Labor force	Wage levels Stability of employment Opportunity
The market: consumers	Value given
The market: competitors	Rate of growth Innovation
Suppliers	Rapidity of payment
Creditors	Adherence to contract terms
Community	Contribution to community development
Nation	Public responsibility

SOURCE: Reprinted by permission of the *Harvard Business Review.* An exhibit from ''The Manager's Job: A Systems Approach'' by Seymour Tilles (January-February 1963). Copyright © 1963 by the President and Fellows of Harvard College; all rights reserved.

presents some suggestions concerning appropriate criteria for a business organization with respect to various superordinate systems.

Quantification of the objective or standard is sometimes difficult. Consider the goal of product leadership, for example. In evaluating product leadership, an organization compares its products with those of competitors and determines the extent to which it pioneers in the introduction of basic products and product improvements. Such standards may exist even though they are not formally and explicitly stated. Inability to quantify the output standard, however, does not indicate the absence of some conception about what constitutes reasonable or standard output or performance. This conception, in effect, constitutes a standard for controlling.

Measuring Performance and Comparing It to Standards

Performance measurement occurs at various stages of the operations process, as indicated in Figure 17–3. Performance may be measured at the input stage (e.g., to determine the quality of materials purchased), during the process stage (e.g., to determine if the product being manufactured meets quality standards), or at the output stage (e.g., to determine how well the product is selling).

Some controls, such as those at the input stage, are *preventive controls*. They measure performance and compare it to standards before the process stage is reached. A poor-quality product resulting from defective raw materials can be prevented through this form of control. Control based on measurement during the process stage is termed *concurrent control* because it occurs as the product or service is being produced. And measurement indicating problems at the output stage results in *corrective control*, or control after the fact.

Performance information is often channelled to the appropriate manager in the form of reports. If reports are to be useful, they should be specifically tailored to each manager's needs and must be timely and accurate. A computer

FIGURE 17–3 Stages of measurement and control

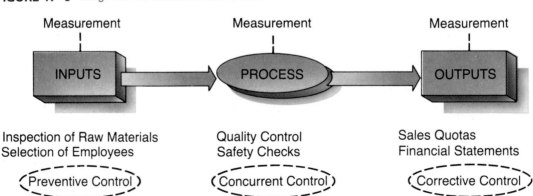

information system can be extremely useful in providing the up-to-date information necessary for effective control.

Not all information is formalized. Personal observation and informal discussions are used extensively in many organizations to keep managers in touch with units under their direction. In fact, informal systems are most appropriate for certain types of control situations. Most first-line supervisors, for example, must rely heavily on such methods to keep in touch with subordinates. At any level of any organization, some feedback is informal.

Taking Corrective Action

Corrective action is required when performance deviates significantly from the standard in an unfavorable direction. To prevent the deviation from recurring, such action must be preceded by an analysis of the cause of the deviation. If a student has established a standard of making a 90 on an exam and makes only a 60, he or she must determine the cause of the unfavorable deviation before taking the next test. To be effective, corrective action must locate and deal with the real cause.

Some deviation from the standard may be justified because of inaccuracies in the standard, changes in environmental conditions, or other reasons. The manager who states "I don't want to hear excuses; I just want to see results!" fails to realize that standards may become unrealistic over time. Extenuating circumstances do occur. The data must be examined in the light of existing conditions. Such an examination may result in more realistic plans, goals, and control standards.

Some processes are self-controlling. A common example is that of a heating system with a thermostat. Assume the thermostat is set at 65 degrees in the winter (the standard). The thermostat measures the temperature in the room and compares it to the standard. If the temperature is significantly less than 65 degrees, the thermostat activates the heating system (corrective action) to warm the room to 65 degrees. As long as the system works properly, no human is required to oversee it. In some industries—oil refining, for instance—computers are programmed to control intricate production processes in this way.

Timing of Controls

Organizations require multiple control systems. An organization cannot just adopt one control technique and expect it to be effective. Figure 17–3 indicates how multiple control systems can be utilized. In the input stage, preventive controls can be developed for raw-material quality, personnel selection, and so forth. A number of concurrent controls can be used to monitor each phase of the organization's process. Finally, several controls can be used to monitor outputs. These controls can provide feedback for future planning and for rewarding employees.

THE VALUE OF INFORMATION

A Pratt and Whitney supervisor of pricing who helped develop confidential bids for Air Force parts contracts later supplied the same information to competitors in return for payments of nearly $300,000. Over a five-year period, this employee sent thousands of bids to competitors, who were then able to underbid Pratt and Whitney. Executives of Pratt and Whitney believe the company lost millions of dollars as a result.

Information crimes are on the increase because of the increasing value of information. Trade secrets—formulas, designs, marketing plans, and customer lists—are the new "gold" of the marketplace.

The legal system has not adapted to the severity of trade-secret crimes. Laws are weak, inconsistent, and outdated. The courts are slow to punish the few who get caught stealing trade secrets, and penalties are usually slight. For example, a Ford engineer pleaded guilty to selling Ford technology to Romania for nearly a million dollars. The engineer was sentenced to a year in jail and fined $1,000.

SOURCE: Adapted from Gregory L. Miles, "Information Thieves Are Now Corporate Enemy No. 1," *Business Week*, 5 May 1986, pp. 120–25.

CONTROL STRATEGIES

Management control varies according to hierarchical level.[3] Control systems for various levels of the organization are described in Figure 17–4. At the top level, managers are concerned with developing a strategic plan for the organization. Emphasis is placed on overall forecasting and objectives, as well as on profit and loss goals. Control at this level is system-wide and uses impersonal reports. Long time periods (quarterly and annually) are involved. Performance measures are aggregated to reflect the overall organization's performance.

Middle-level managers are involved with controlling performance in their respective departments. Impersonal reports are used on a periodic basis (weekly and monthly). Targets are developed and standards are established for the various departments, such as manufacturing or accounting. Information is gathered that allows departmental activities to be measured against the targets or standards.

Lower-level managers control the individual tasks of subordinates. The reports are personal and frequent. Information at lower levels is not aggregated.[4]

Managers at the various levels use different strategies for control. For example, managers at the top and middle levels can adopt three control strategies—market control, bureaucratic control, and clan control. All three types may be present in an organization.[5] Two types of control strategies are available to managers at lower levels who engage in supervisory control strategies—behavior control and output control.[6]

Market Control

Market control involves the use of price competition to evaluate output. Managers compare profits and prices to determine the efficiency of their organization. Market control is appropriate when prices can be assigned to outputs and when competition exists. Market control is not appropriate in controlling functional departments, unless the price for services is set through competition and is representative of the true value of provided services.

An example of market control is when top managers use profit figures to evaluate the performance of various divisions or profit centers of the organization.

Bureaucratic Control

Bureaucratic control involves the use of authority, chain of command, rules, policies, and other bureaucratic devices that managers can employ to standardize behavior and evaluate performance. Bureaucratic control can be used when

FIGURE 17–4 Management control by hierarchical level

Hierarchical Level	Control System	Nature of Control	Methods of Control
Top	Organizational	Strategic plans, overall forecasting and objectives, profit and loss goals	System-wide, impersonal reports, long time period (quarterly, annually)
Middle	Management	Departmental performance, subobjectives, programs, budgets	Department-wide, impersonal periodic reports (weekly, monthly)
Lower	Supervisory	Supervisory operating plans, schedules, activities	Individual tasks, personal, frequent (daily, weekly)

SOURCE: Reprinted by permission from *Organization Theory and Design,* 2nd ed., by Richard L. Daft; Copyright © 1986 by West Publishing Company. All rights reserved.

MULTIPLE CONTROL STRATEGIES AT GALLO

The market share of the U.S. wine market controlled by the E. and J. Gallo Winery of Modesto, California, is more than three times larger than its nearest rival, Seagram and Sons. Gallo even has a larger market share than all combined imports. Its Bartles and Jaymes wine cooler is first in sales. *Fortune* estimates that Gallo, a private company, is extremely profitable.

Most wineries have concentrated only on production, using independent distributors to sell their products. These independents, many of which work for several competing wine producers, are in many states protected by law from being acquired. Several states even regulate the number of distributors.

Gallo has developed a unique relationship with its independent distributors, using multiple control strategies to ensure desired performance. The independents are encouraged to use a separate sales force to sell Gallo products.

Bureaucratic controls are employed by using a 300-page training manual, developed by Gallo, to train the distributor's sales force. The manual describes and diagrams every conceivable angle of the wine business. Subsequent activities of the distributor's sales force are evaluated against the do's and don'ts of the manual.

Market control occurs by evaluating the distributor's accomplishments in selling Gallo products. In the 1970s, Gallo was prohibited by the Federal Trade Commission from punishing distributors for selling competing products and requiring them to disclose sales figures. Later, the FTC set aside the order and Gallo began again to regulate its distributors.

Clan control is achieved by getting the distributors to share the same values and beliefs that Gallo has. Distributors have commented that they behave as if they were family members rather than independents because they owe their success to the winery. The distributors believe that if they execute the marketing strategy developed by Gallo, then they too will become successful.

SOURCE: Adapted from Jaclyn Fierman, "How Gallo Crushes The Competition," *Fortune*, 1 September 1986, pp. 23–31.

behavior cannot be controlled with market or price mechanisms. Almost all organizations use some form of bureaucratic control.

Clan Control

Clan control involves a socialization process to control behavior and assess performance. Taken into consideration are the social characteristics of values, traditions, shared beliefs, and commitment. Organizations that use clan control require trust among their employees. Clan control works well in departments with high uncertainty, such as research and development. Such control is invisible yet very powerful, and can be used to replace bureaucratic control.

An example of clan control is the control exerted in hospitals, where physicians and nurses work together in teams. Task performance is ambiguous, and a precise evaluation of individual contribution is impossible. The doctors and nurses are subjected not only to skill training but also to value training. They are indoctrinated (socialized) with a system of beliefs about their professional activities.[7] Clan rather than bureaucratic control is most important to these professionals. Clan strategies are also used by Japanese managers to keep their employees committed and working hard.[8]

Supervisory Control

Managers use two types of supervisory control in regulating the performance of individual employees—behavior control and output control. *Behavior control* involves actually observing an employee's behavior and work procedures. This type of lower-level control requires a great amount of the manager's time, because each employee requires personal surveillance.[9]

Output control consists of using written records to measure employee productivity and output. This type of control is used when the outputs of individual employees can be easily measured. Piece-rate jobs, in which production per hour is easily calculated, is an example of output control. Many sales jobs can be evaluated and regulated by output control because the quantity of sales can be measured.

CONTROL TECHNIQUES

A number of techniques are available to managers in assuring that various organizational units make good use of available resources. Several of these were presented in Figure 5–6, which described an organization's management control system. Control techniques include the use of financial statements, budgets, responsibility centers, performance appraisals, policies and procedures, statistical reports, and audits.

Financial Statements

Because cash and access to credit are integral to an organization's survival, financial control is often emphasized. Perhaps the most visible accounting control tools are those reports detailing the organization's financial condition. The *balance sheet*, as shown in Figure 17–5, reports the organization's financial position as of the date of preparation. This requires a presentation of *assets* (what is owned), *liabilities* (what is owed), and *net worth* (the difference between assets and liabilities).

FIGURE 17–5   Balance sheet

Sleepy Bedding Company
Balance Sheet
Year Ended December 31

Assets		*Liabilities & Net Worth*	
Current Assets		Current Liabilities	
Cash	$ 50,000	Accounts Payable	$ 90,000
Marketable Securities	170,000	Notes Payable	190,000
Accounts Receivable	250,000	Accrued Taxes	20,000
Inventories	350,000		
Total Current Assets	820,000	Total Current Liabilities	300,000
Fixed Assets		Long-term Debt	700,000
Plant & Equipment		Net Worth	
(less depreciation)	1,200,000	Common Stock	
		(at par)	600,000
		Retained Earnings	420,000
Total Assets	$2,020,000	Total Net Worth	1,020,000
		Total Liabilities and	
		Net Worth	$2,020,000

The Sleepy Bedding Company, which manufactures and sells mattresses and box springs, has current assets (those which are cash or will be converted into cash within a year) of $820,000. Besides cash, these assets consist of marketable securities (stocks and certificates of deposit), accounts receivable (the amount customers still owe the company), and inventories of mattresses and box springs (valued at cost). Fixed assets (those which will not be converted into cash within a year) consist of the organization's manufacturing facilities and tools, minus their depreciated value.

Current liabilities (those the company must pay within a year) amount to $300,000. The amounts owed include accounts payable (owed to suppliers), notes payable (short-term loans from banks), and accrued taxes (the tax liability already incurred). Long-term debt (which does not have to be paid within a year) amounts to $700,000. The difference between total assets ($2,020,000) and total liabilities ($1,000,000) represents the owners' equity or net worth ($1,020,000). This entry consists of the common stock purchased by investors and retained earnings (the firm's cumulative profits over the years after dividends).

FIGURE 17–6 Income statement

Sleepy Bedding Company
Income Statement
Year Ended December 31

Net Sales		$3,500,000
Cost of Goods Sold		2,850,000
Gross Profit		650,000
Less: Selling Expenses	$ 35,000	
General And Administra-		
tive Expenses	50,000	
Depreciation	115,000	
Interest Expense	112,000	312,000
Net Income Before Taxes		338,000
Income Taxes		135,000
Net Income After Taxes		203,000
Cash Dividends to Stockholders		100,000
Increase in Retained Earnings		$ 103,000

The *income statement* (Figure 17–6) presents a more dynamic picture of the organization, showing over some period of time the amount of *revenue* which flowed into the organization less all *expenses* and *taxes* and the resultant *net profit* or *loss*. While the balance sheet indicates the net worth of the organization's owners, the income statement reveals how much money the organization made or lost over a given period of time.

The Sleepy Bedding Company sold $3,500,000 worth of mattresses and box springs during the calendar year. The production costs incurred during that time (raw materials, labor, and so on) amounted to $2,850,000, leaving a gross profit of $650,000. Other expenses, which are shown separately so that they might be compared to previous years' expense levels, amounted to $312,000, leaving net income before taxes of $338,000. Income taxes consumed $135,000 of that amount, resulting in net income after taxes of $203,000. After dividend payments of $100,000 to the stockholders, the retained earnings account increased by $103,000.

Although financial statements reveal such figures as profit, net worth, and so on, these numbers alone provide limited information. Hence, *ratio analysis* is used to interpret the financial statements by giving management more of the information it needs for control purposes.[10]

Examples of some of the more common—and meaningful—ratios are shown in Figure 17–7. Each ratio may be interpreted by comparing it to the firm's ratios from previous years (to discern trends) and/or to standard industry ratios. In Figure 17–7, the median ratios for small firms in the mattress/box springs industry are shown alongside the Sleepy Bedding Company's ratios.

FIGURE 17–7   Selected ratios for Sleepy Bedding Company

Type of Ratio	Ratio for Sleepy Bedding Company	Median Ratio for Industry
Liquidity Ratio (ability to meet short-term financial obligations)		
$\text{Current Ratio} = \dfrac{\text{Current Assets}}{\text{Current Liabilities}} = \dfrac{\$820,000}{300,000} =$	2.73 times	2.42 times
Leverage Ratio (ability to meet long-term financial obligations)		
$\dfrac{\text{Debt-to-Net-Worth}}{\text{Ratio}} = \dfrac{\text{Total Debt}}{\text{Net Worth}} = \dfrac{\$1,000,000}{1,020,000} =$	98.0%	78.7%
Activity Ratios (ability to employ resources effectively)		
$\text{Inventory Turnover} = \dfrac{\text{Sales}}{\text{Inventory}} = \dfrac{\$3,500,000}{350,000} =$	10 times	7.2 times
$\dfrac{\text{Average Collection}}{\text{Period}} = \dfrac{\text{Accounts Receivable}}{\text{Sales/365 days}} = \dfrac{\$250,000}{3,500,000/365} =$	26 days	26.1 days
Profitability Ratios (ability to operate efficiently)		
$\dfrac{\text{Profit Margin}}{\text{on Sales}} = \dfrac{\text{Net Income after Taxes}}{\text{Sales}} = \dfrac{\$203,000}{\$3,500,000} =$	5.80%	2.7%
$\dfrac{\text{Return on}}{\text{Net Worth}} = \dfrac{\text{Net Income after Taxes}}{\text{Net Worth}} = \dfrac{\$203,000}{1,020,000} =$	19.90%	13.4%

SOURCE: Median ratios for the industry are from Dun & Bradstreet's 1987 *Industry Norms and Key Business Ratios*, p. 63. The industry is Mattresses and Bedsprings (SIC 2515), and the ratios are for companies with less than $50,000,000 in net worth.

The median ratio, we should caution, is not necessarily a goal for which Sleepy Bedding Company should strive. Differences in accounting practices among firms may distort direct comparisons. Nevertheless, such evaluations are helpful in acquiring general impressions concerning the organization and its performance. Significant deviations from industry figures indicate that further analysis is required.

Some of the ratio comparisons in Figure 17–7 require further comment. The company's current ratio may be a bit high, probably because its inventory levels are excessive, as shown by its inventory turnover ratio. The debt-to-net-worth ratio of Sleepy Bedding Company is above the industry's median. This comparison indicates that the company would probably be questioned by its creditors if it desired to borrow funds. Collection of accounts receivable appears to be in line with industry practices.

Finally, the profitability ratios indicate that Sleepy Bedding's return on net worth (often considered the final criterion of a firm's profitability) is higher than the industry median. The company also receives more net income per dollar of sales than the industry median. The company is either able to sell at higher prices than the average firm or is able to keep its expenses lower.

To use financial statements with any degree of sophistication, one must have some appreciation of their limitations. As one example of these difficulties, the changing value of the dollar presents continuing problems. Assets are typically shown at cost or, in the case of inventory, at the lower of cost or market. But when general price levels change markedly, the worth of assets as shown on the books becomes unrealistic. Charging depreciation on the basis of cost, therefore, may be insufficient to make possible replacement of fully depreciated assets.

Another related difficulty is associated with the valuation of inventories. Some companies use a FIFO (first in, first out) method, while others use a LIFO (last in, first out) method. The FIFO method, for example, treats inventory costs as if items purchased first are sold or consumed first. When inventory is purchased at different prices over a period of time, asset values and profits

MONITORING FINANCIAL CONTROLS

A 1987 Congressional subcommittee report estimated that white-collar crimes cost American business $67 billion a year. Most of the employees involved in the crimes are "trusted people."

Financial controls have to be maintained and monitored to be effective. One middle-sized company used a simple expedient of having supervisors verify employee time cards and then give out paychecks. The supervisors also gave out W-2 forms each year. These practices made it easy for the supervisors to keep approximately eighteen phantom employees on the payroll, pocket the checks, and endorse them for their own use.

The scheme was discovered after a summer employee was denied a college loan because of excessive earnings. His father complained to the company that it reported to the government far more earnings than his son had actually received. An investigation revealed that the student had been kept on the payroll by a supervisor, who continued to punch the student's time card in and out each day.

Further investigation indicated other supervisors with phantom employees. The payroll scam, which had existed for five years, had cost the company nearly $400,000.

SOURCE: Adapted from Sanford L. Jacobs, "Owners Who Ignore Security Make Worker Dishonesty Easy," *The Wall Street Journal*, 11 March 1985.

differ according to the method of inventory valuation used. Someone's judgment regarding inventory valuation is involved, therefore, in "scientifically" determining profit results.

Many accounting figures must be approximations. As an example, the portion of equipment cost to be charged as an expense in a particular period must be estimated. The useful life cannot be predicted with complete accuracy. A particular machine may last well beyond its expected life or become obsolete earlier than anticipated. Either of these eventualities could prove depreciation estimates inaccurate.

Accounting information, furthermore, supplies only part of the total relevant information for control purposes. Some aspects of business operations are difficult to reduce to a dollar basis for inclusion in financial statements. Suppose, for example, that two managers are being compared on the basis of the profit performance of their respective divisions. That one division suffered the loss of several key executives during the year or that unexpectedly strong competition developed for one division may not be shown on the financial statements.

Budgets

Budgets were discussed in chapter 5 as an aid to planning. As is the case with most planning tools, budgets are also useful control devices. Budgeted figures serve as standards to which actual performance can be compared. As a plan for expenditures, the budget provides preventive control, and as a means of pinpointing areas in which overspending is occurring, it serves as a corrective control tool. Budgeting, however, "should not be thought of as a device for limiting expenditures; the budgeting process is a tool for obtaining the most productive and profitable use of the company's resources."[11]

The overall budgeting process is illustrated in Figure 17–8. The budgets are based on the firm's plans and forecasts. One set of budgets relates to manufacturing. Sales forecasts are translated into budgets for the actual production of goods or services, for materials, for labor, and for expenditures for new plant and equipment (capital expenditures). Budgets for advertising and selling what the firm produces are also needed. Budgets are likewise required for research on new products and the improvement of present products and for the organization's staff of general managers. Finally, budgets for each product, each branch, and each region are also formulated. The double arrow above these budgets indicates that the budgets may also influence the organization's forecasts. For instance, the size of the advertising budget will affect sales.

The bottom of the diagram reveals that the various budgets may be synthesized to yield predicted or *pro forma* financial statements. These statements show the expected financial condition of the organization at the end of the budgetary period.

Budgets can be used to control functional areas, product lines, and subsystems such as branches or regions. They are, therefore, used to establish control standards for revenues, expenses, and profits.

FIGURE 17-8 Overall view of the total budgeting process

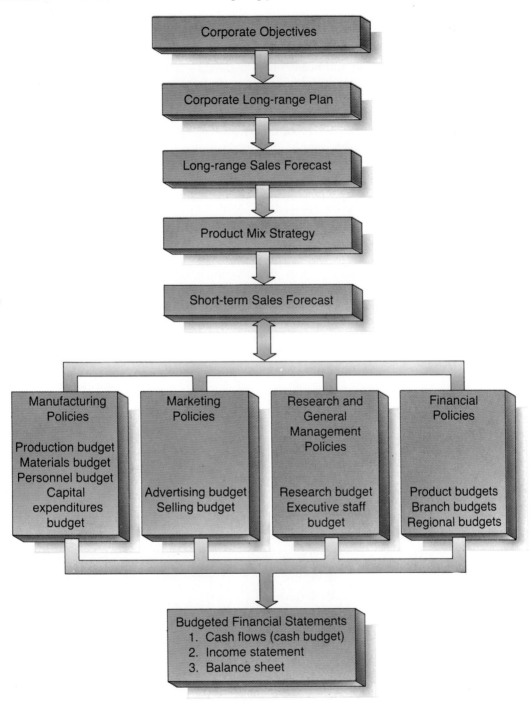

SOURCE: From *Managerial Finance*, 8/e, by J. Fred Weston and Thomas E. Copeland. Copyright © 1986 by CBS College Publishing. Copyright © 1981 The Dryden Press. Copyright 1978, 1977, 1972, 1969, 1966, 1962 by Holt, Rinehart & Winston. Reprinted by permission of Holt, Rinehart & Winston, Inc.

Responsibility Centers

A *responsibility center* is an organizational subsystem charged with a well-defined mission and headed by a manager accountable for the performance of the center. "Responsibility centers constitute the primary building blocks for management control."[12]

The logic behind the concept is straightforward. Assume that an organization has no specific responsibility centers. Assume further that the company's year-end profits are significantly lower than expected. Where does the responsibility for the poor operating performance lie? If the entire organization is the responsibility center, pinpointing the problem(s) would probably be quite difficult, meaning that appropriate corrective action will either not be taken or will be unnecessarily delayed.

If the organization has three product divisions—each headed by a manager accountable for its performance—and an accounting system which measures the performance of each division, then control is considerably enhanced, as shown in Figure 17–9. In this case, management can analyze the operations of Product Division B while allowing Divisions A and C to continue operating normally. This process saves management time and facilitates corrective action.

The types of responsibility centers vary by organization and situation. A *profit center* is responsible for both revenues and expenditures. The manager of a product division may be held accountable for the sales and expenses—and hence profits—associated with the operation of that division. This is a common

FIGURE 17–9 Pinpointing responsibility

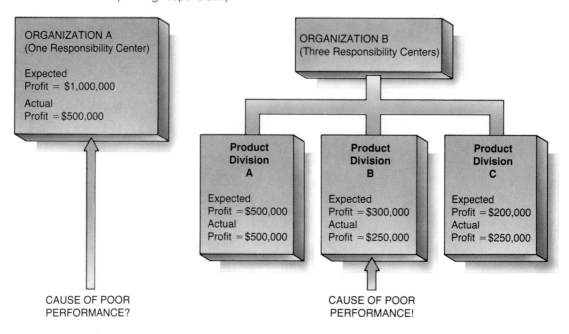

arrangement in the retail industry (individual stores or even departments may be profit centers), in multiproduct (or service) organizations, and in organizations structured along geographic lines.

Many businesses with functional structures and most nonprofit organizations contain *expense centers* responsible for expenditures but not revenues. Business examples would include production departments, staff units, accounting and electronic data processing divisions, purchasing departments, public relations staffs, and so on. Control focuses on measuring the profit or expenses of the responsibility center and comparing it with the figures of other responsibility centers as well as with historical trends. The object is to determine which centers are operating less effectively than others and, therefore, require corrective action.

YOU HAVE TO KNOW THE NUMBERS

For 17 years, Harold Geneen was known as the hard-nosed chief executive of International Telephone and Telegraph (ITT). Geneen's philosophy was that his managers were expected to achieve the earnings that they had committed to earn. ITT had 250 profit centers, and each had its own budget. Controllers from every profit center had to provide headquarters with the figures of their businesses each week. Less than satisfactory results were clearly identified and reviewed during monthly meetings. The identified poor performance was not allowed to be forgotten. Managers had to tell Geneen what was being done to solve the problem. If the manager was stumped, help would be sent from headquarters.

Because of this approach, Geneen was described as having a management style of "managing by the numbers." In some instances, Geneen's subordinates tried to manage by the numbers—pushing sales or receivables from one quarter to another. Geneen argued that the significant difference between well-managed and not-so-well managed companies is the degree of attention that is paid to the numbers. How frequently are numbers reported up the chain-of-command? Are the numbers accurate? To what extent are variations allowed between budget forecasts and actual results before management takes action? How much trouble does management go to in developing a solution for the deviation?

Geneen has suggested that the most important issue in being a successful manager is to develop an understanding of the numbers. The numbers themselves will not tell a manager what to do. What is happening *behind* the numbers, however, is what is important.

SOURCE: Adapted from Harold S. Geneen, "The Case For Managing By The Numbers," *Fortune*, 1 October 1984, pp. 78–81.

Performance Appraisals

Performance appraisals involve a formal method of evaluating managers based on performance and goals. Performance appraisals are more fully discussed in chapter 10.

Policies and Procedures

Policies and procedures are the rules and regulations that prescribe correct behavior. In many organizations these are referred to as *standard operating procedures*. Managers use these to bring activities back into line.[13]

Statistical Reports

Managers use periodic *statistical reports* to monitor and evaluate nonfinancial performance. Such items as the number of employees, number of new customer contracts, delinquent accounts, sales volume received, and other statistics vital to the department or business unit are included. Statistical reports can be issued weekly, monthly, or quarterly and provide feedback about departmental or business unit results.[14]

Audits

Audits, appraisals of an organization's operational, financial, and accounting systems, encompass two forms—the external audit and the internal audit.[15] *External audits* are usually concerned with an independent appraisal of the organization's accounting and financial procedures by a certified public accounting firm. Such an audit determines if the records are accurate and reflect generally accepted accounting practices.

Internal audits differ significantly from external audits. Internal audits are conducted by members of the organization and perform a "number of high level monitoring services" for top management.[16] These include a continuing study and evaluation of internal management control systems as well as a review of operating practices to promote increased efficiency. For some parts of the external audit, internal auditors may have the training, objectivity, and experience to assist the external auditor in gathering certain information. But the external auditor is the only one qualified to make the final judgment about the adequacy of internal controls and the accuracy of statement balances.[17]

DYSFUNCTIONAL CONSEQUENCES OF CONTROL

In designing and applying control systems, unanticipated and undesirable effects are often realized. For example, ambiguity tends to promote innovation, and rules can create unnecessary bureaucratic problems.[18] An illusion of being in control may develop that can lead to a failure of policy.[19] Also, instead of controlling organizational activity as intended, controls can produce side effects, by-products of the control system.

The Narrow Viewpoint

One such undesirable effect is the tendency of some control systems to narrow one's viewpoint unduly. The controls act as a set of blinders to limit the individual's vision or concern to his or her own sphere, with possible disregard for broader organizational values. A pay incentive system in manufacturing, for example, may base the reward on output to the extent that quality suffers. Such a system may give the individual little or no encouragement to think beyond the daily production record to the broader objectives of the organization and the contributions one might make to these.

Many college students—and faculty members, for that matter—complain that grades have similar undesirable effects. Studying for exams and writing term papers become ends in themselves rather than means to learning.

Emphasis on the Short Run

Another possible effect is that the control system may encourage a short-run course of action that is counter to the long-run interests of the organization. Consider, for example, the profit control applied to the different divisions of a decentralized company. The profit goal of the division serves as a powerful incentive for the division manager, who is under tremendous pressure to achieve that objective. Under certain conditions, this presents a strong motivation to win in the short run, even though the long-run effects may be disastrous.

The following decisions by division managers illustrate this type of undesirable short-run reaction to a control system:[20]

> In order to increase his rate of return, a division manager reduced his research costs by eliminating all projects that did not have an expected payout within two years. He believed that if he did not improve his rate of return, he would be replaced.
>
> A division manager scrapped some machinery that he was not currently using in order to reduce his investment. Later, when the machinery was needed, he purchased new equipment.

One study of managers in six major companies indicates that division managers who emphasize the attainment of short-run profits over long-term strategic goals often do so for two reasons.[21] The first is that the manager's performance evaluation (and financial incentives) often stress short-run criteria. The second is that short-term goals are more visible and easily comprehended than long-range objectives. Many lower level managers are not fully aware of their organization's strategic goals.

CONTROLLING FOR SHORT-TERM IMPROVEMENTS

Several chief executives of American firms are concerned that their company may be the next takeover target. Many of these executives report that this situation forces them to focus even more on the short-term. Andrew Sigler, CEO of Champion International, states that merger mania makes managers do all the things considered to be "bad management" practices. Professor William Fruhan of the Harvard Business School reports that takeovers have forced many managers to engage in certain strategies that may not have any long-term benefits. Instead of concentrating on growth and profitability, managers watch the gap between their share price and the break-up estimate of the "wildest maniac." The wider the gap, the greater potential raiders have to make money, reasons Fruhan.

John Rosenberg, dean of the Darden Graduate Business School at the University of Virginia, advises that for some managers who cannot manage effectively, a takeover threat causes them to self-destruct. Other companies, however, have emerged from takeover attempts as much stronger companies. Rosenberg states that the key for surviving a takeover fight depends on the firm's managers and how they control for *both* short-term and long-term improvements.

SOURCE: Adapted from Judith H. Dobrzynski, "More Than Ever, It's Management For The Short Term," *Business Week*, 24 November 1986, pp. 92–93.

Falsification of Reporting

Pressure to achieve standards is an everyday fact of life for employees at all levels. Pressure, of course, can be useful in motivating individuals to high performance, but for some employees, the pressure becomes too intense and they find themselves faced with the choice of either being branded "incompetent" by their supervisors or resorting to falsifying reports.

This ethical issue is most often faced by middle- and lower-level managers, particularly in organizations in which these managers have little voice in setting their own performance goals. For example, middle managers at several divisions of Allegheny International engaged in deceptive accounting practices when they could not otherwise meet profit goals set by top management.[22]

Consider the attitude expressed by one department store salesperson concerning sales quotas:

> Every day we are assigned a quota based on what was sold a year before. No account is taken of economic conditions, whether a holiday (such as Easter)

comes early or late this year, or other such factors. In other words, only one criterion is used. When the quota is either too high or too low, my performance suffers. If it is too low, there is no challenge. If the quota is too high, which is worse, the quota is just out of reach. Management is plain being unrealistic. Why should I try to reach such an arbitrary quota? My attitude is negative.

If management appears unreasonable in the application of controls, the subordinate naturally becomes disturbed. A superior, for example, may refuse to accept reasonable explanations for delays. As a consequence, the subordinate must be content with an unfavorable evaluation by the superior or resort to one or more of the devious means available in combating the situation.

DYSFUNCTIONAL CONTROL AT AMERICAN EXPRESS

In 1983, American Express expected to record its 36th straight year of earnings increases—a record in the financial services industry. The CEO of American Express, James Robinson III, was pressing hard to exceed the earnings of 1982. Controls were in place to monitor performance of the company's different divisions. Robinson was particularly concerned about the performance of an insurance subsidiary, Fireman's Fund, because other property and casualty companies were engaged in fierce price-cutting, which was lowering overall industry profits. Fireman's Fund, however, had continued to show good profits.

Suddenly, in mid-December after weeks of turmoil, American Express announced that 1983 earnings would be $520 million rather than the previously estimated $700 million and below actual 1982 earnings of $581 million. Robinson stated that Fireman's Fund had created bogus millions in pretax profit through a series of accounting transactions that had no business purpose. While Fireman's Fund was expected to earn $215 million in 1983, actual earnings with corrections were approximately $40 million.

Executives at Fireman's Fund reported that they were under enormous pressure to attain the expected earnings amount. One Fireman's Fund executive stated that top executives in American Express were urging us to be "creative—to pull out all of the stops. The pressure to succeed was intense."

After the announcement, American Express stock dropped from $32 to under $29 per share, a 10 percent decrease, which amounted to almost a $700 million loss in market value.

SOURCE: Adapted from Carol J. Loomis, "How Fireman's Fund Singed American Express," *Fortune*, 9 January 1984, pp. 80–81; and Carol J. Loomis, "How Fireman's Fund Stoked Its Profits," *Fortune*, 28 November 1983, pp. 99–104.

Improving Control Effectiveness

Managers, in installing and using controls, obviously do not desire the undesirable effects described. Nor are these effects an inescapable consequence of all control systems. Establishing controls, however, does create pressures that often lead to these undesirable effects. Managers should, therefore, be aware of this tendency and attempt to minimize the harmful effects.

Participative Management. To gain general acceptance, standards must be established so that they are perceived as fair by those whose performance is controlled. The use of participative management, for example, tends to induce acceptance of standards as reasonable. Standards which recognize some range of acceptable performance and which appear to be established objectively, as is the case with statistical quality controls, also encourage acceptance by those whose performance is controlled.

In addition, controls must be recognized as means and not as ends in themselves. Higher level management can assure this only by a reasonable interpretation of results being controlled. If all explanations, regardless of validity, are unacceptable, the control system will almost inevitably become an end in itself.

The Extent of Control. In any situation, the formality and nature of control can be varied. Control may be either loose and general or close and detailed. The concepts of delegation and decentralization, for example, involve a philosophy of only general control. Higher management expects certain results but permits lower levels to proceed without detailed control in accomplishing those results. The extent to which a decentralized approach is adopted, therefore, governs the closeness of control that may be used appropriately.

Improvement in managerial control may thus call for a paradoxical solution. By controlling less, the manager may control better. If a manager follows a natural bent toward overcontrol, on the other hand, the results may be destructive rather than helpful. Within limits imposed by the situation, a manager may lighten control—delegating, avoiding close supervision, and eliminating burdensome control procedures—and still achieve greater success than otherwise.

Management by Objectives. The management-by-objectives (MBO) approach discussed in chapter 5 tends to minimize undesirable behavioral effects. The principal feature of this type of management is the establishment of specific performance goals for each position, particularly for each managerial position. By stressing these objectives, overall control is achieved through self-control by individual participants. Rather than applying control from above, the emphasis is placed on control from within.

Use of Strategic Control Points. The effectiveness of control partially depends upon the selection of the points at which control is applied. Consider a process or activity, for example, starting at point X and proceeding through stages *a, b,* and *c* to reach completion at point Y.

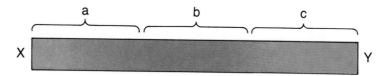

To control the process, checking may be employed at various points. The work may be checked at the end of the process, at the end of each stage, or at various points during each stage. The best combination of control points would keep the process in line with a minimum of cost and control effort.

Management by Exception. Economy of control effort uses the principle of *management by exception.* In using this approach, the manager devotes effort to unexpected or out-of-line performance. Some standard is established, and significant deviations from that standard are the exceptions. If performance conforms to anticipations, time spent in reviewing is largely wasted. Managing by exception permits the manager to isolate nonstandard performance and to concentrate upon it.

Suppose that six sales territories are each expected to produce $50,000 in sales. If one produces $40,000, another $60,000, and four others between $49,000 and $51,000, the manager can focus upon two territories, thereby conserving time which can more profitably be devoted to planning and other managerial functions. The existence of appropriate responsibility centers would facilitate this process.

Expectations Approach. An interesting approach to control, developed in Great Britain by John Machin, is based on managerial "expectations."[23] All managers in the organization are asked to make an extensive list of the expectations they hold of the performance of other managers with whom they interact. Then the managers list the expectations they perceive other managers hold of them. The managers then meet to discuss the lists with each other.

As an example, the two managers illustrated below would discuss variations in their lists.

Manager A's List	*Manager B's List*
Expectations A holds of B ———	— Expectations B perceives A holds of B
Expectations A perceives ——— B holds of A	— Expectations B holds of A

Almost invariably, the expectations that A holds of B differ from B's perceptions of those expectations. Through discussions, managers reach a more accurate understanding of the inputs they expect from others and the outputs they are expected to supply to others. These expectations of performance are formalized and serve as standards to which actual performance may be compared.

SUMMARY

The purpose of control is to solve the problem of directing and evaluating the activities of the overall organization, its departments, and its individual employees. The control process involves establishing standards, evaluating performance, and taking corrective action, if necessary. Controls can be introduced into an organization at one or more of three general points. Generally, organizations require multiple control systems.

The concepts of control strategies—*market, bureaucratic, clan, behavior,* and *output* control—help explain how control can be achieved at each hierarchical level in the organization.

Although financial control techniques, such as *financial statements* and *budgets,* have received a great deal of attention, other control techniques are common. These include *responsibility centers, performance appraisals, policies* and *procedures, statistical reports,* and *external* and *internal audits.*

The control process can stifle innovation and has a tendency to produce certain undesirable effects in the organization that is being controlled. Some of these effects are narrowness of viewpoint, emphasis on the short run, and evasion of controls through falsification of reporting.

A number of possible variations or changes in control systems are available to managers who wish to improve their effectiveness. Harmful consequences may be minimized, for example, by careful development of the elements of the control system and by equitable administration. Improvement is also possible in many situations by reducing the extent of control through delegating authority and avoiding close supervision. *Management by objectives,* use of *strategic control points, management by exception,* and the *expectations approach* may also contribute to a workable control system.

KEY CONCEPTS

Strategic control	Behavior control
Operational control	Output control
Organizational control	Responsibility centers
Preventive control	Profit centers
Concurrent control	Statistical reports
Corrective control	External audits
Timing of controls	Internal audits
Market control	Financial control
Bureaucratic control	Dysfunctional aspects of control
Clan control	Management by exception
Supervisory control	Expectations approach

DISCUSSION QUESTIONS

1. Explain the difference between *strategic control* and *operational control*.
2. What is the relationship between planning and control?
3. Distinguish between *preventive, concurrent*, and *corrective* controls.
4. How does control vary by hierarchical level?
5. How does the use of *ratio analysis* aid in financial control?
6. Explain *market, bureaucratic, clan*, and *supervisory* control strategies.
7. How does *output control* differ from *behavior control?*
8. Explain how the responsibility concept aids in organizational control.
9. Explain *internal* and *external audits*.
10. "Organization control tends to stifle innovation." Agree? Disagree? Discuss.
11. How can controls cause undesirably narrow viewpoints in individual members or departments of an organization?
12. "There is a direct correlation between increasing organizational control and improved organizational efficiency." True or false? Why?
13. An office manager commented: "It is my responsibility to keep up with all aspects of every activity and project that is assigned to this office." Evaluate this statement in the light of managerial control theory.

NOTES

1. These examples are developed from Derek F. du Troit, "Confessions of a So-So Controller," *Harvard Business Review* 63 (July-August 1985): 50–59 and William H. Newman, *Managerial Control* (Chicago: Science Research Associates, 1984).
2. For a more detailed discussion about the various aspects of strategic and operating control see John A. Pearce II and Richard B. Robinson, Jr., *Strategic Management: Strategy Formulation and Implementation*, 2nd ed. (Homewood, Ill; Irwin,

1985); and Arthur A. Thompson, Jr., and A. J. Strickland III, *Strategic Management: Concepts and Cases*, 4th ed. (Plano, Tex.: Business Publications, 1987).

3. Kenneth A. Merchant, *Control in Business Organizations* (Marshfield, Mass.: Pitman, 1985).

4. Richard L. Daft and Norman B. Macintosh, "The Nature and Use of Formal Control Systems for Management Control and Strategy Implementation," *Journal of Management* 10 (Spring 1984): 43–66.

5. William G. Ouchi, "The Relationship between Organizational Structure and Organizational Control," *Administrative Science Quarterly* 22 (March 1977): 95–113; William G. Ouchi, "A Conceptual Framework for the Design of Organizational Control Mechanisms," *Management Science* 25 (September 1979): 833–47; and William G. Ouchi, "Markets, Bureaucracies, and Clans," *Administrative Science Quarterly* 25 (September 1980): 129–41.

6. William G. Ouchi and Mary Ann McGuire,"Organizational Control: Two Functions," *Administrative Science Quarterly* 20 (June 1975): 559–69.

7. Ouchi, "Design of Organizational Control Mechanisms," p. 837.

8. Alfred M. Jaeger and B. R. Baliga, "Control Systems and Strategic Adaptation: Lessons from the Japanese Experience," *Strategic Management Journal* 6 (April–June 1985): 115–34.

9. Peter M. Blau and W. Richard Scott, *Formal Organization* (San Francisco: Chandler, 1962).

10. Excellent discussions of this area may be found in J. Fred Weston and Thomas E. Copeland, *Managerial Finance*, 8th ed. (Hinsdale, Ill.: Dryden Press, 1986); Eugene Brigham, *Fundamentals of Financial Management*, 4th ed. (Hinsdale, Ill.: Dryden Press, 1986); and Robert H. Hermanson, James Don Edwards, and F. Salmonson, *Accounting Principles*, special edition (Plano, Tex.: Business Publications, 1987).

11. Weston and Copeland, *Managerial Finance*, p. 205.

12. Glen A. Welsch, D. Paul Newman, and Charles T. Zlatkovich, *Intermediate Accounting*, 7th ed. (Homewood, Ill.: Irwin, 1986), p. 346.

13. Richard L. Daft, *Organization Theory and Design*, 2nd ed. (St. Paul, Minn.: West, 1986), pp. 320–21.

14. Ibid.

15. C. William Thomas and Emerson O. Henke, *Auditing: Theory and Practice*, 2nd ed. (Boston: Kent, 1986).

16. Ibid., p. 222.

17. Ibid., p. 223.

18. This problem is discussed in greater detail in James D. Thompson, *Organizations in Action* (New York: McGraw-Hill, 1967); and Karl Weick, *The Social Psychology of Organizing*, 2nd ed. (Reading, Mass.: Addison-Wesley, 1979).

19. David A. Whetten, "Organizational Decline: A Neglected Topic in Organizational Science," *Academy of Management Review* 5 (April 1980): 577–88.

20. Bruce D. Henderson and John Dearden, "New System for Divisional Control," *Harvard Business Review* 44 (September-October 1966): 150.

21. Robert L. Banks and Steven C. Wheelwright, "Operations vs. Strategy: Trading Tomorrow for Today," *Harvard Business Review* 57 (May-June 1979): 112–20.

22. Matt Rothman and Gregory L. Miles, "Allegheny's New Chairman Starts Picking Up the Pieces," *Business Week*, 1 December 1986, 116–18.

23. John L. J. Machin, "A Contingent Methodology for Management Control," *Journal of Management Studies* 16 (February 1979), 1–29.

SUPPLEMENTARY READING

Brownell, Peter. "Budgetary Control and Organization Structure." *Journal of Accounting Research* (Autumn 1982): 177–203.

_____, and McInnes, Morris. "Budgetary Participation, Motivation, and Managerial Performance." *Accounting Review* (October 1986): 587–99.

Churchill, Neil C. "Budget Choice: Planning vs. Control." *Harvard Business Review* 62 (July-August 1984): 150–64.

Eccles, Robert G. "Controls with Fairness in Transfer Pricing." *Harvard Business Review* 61 (November-December 1983): 149–161.

Gomez-Mejia, Luis R.; Tosi, Henry; and Hinking, Timothy. "Managerial Control, Performance, and Executive Compensation." *Academy of Management Journal* 30 (March 1987): 51–70.

Hofstede, Geert. "The Poverty of Management Control Philosophy." *Academy of Management Review* 3 (July 1978): 450–61.

Hrebiniak, Lawrence G., and Joyce, William F. *Implementing Strategy.* New York: Macmillan, 1984.

Kamin, Jacob Y., and Ronen, Joshua. "Effects of Budgetary Control Design on Management Decisions: Some Empirical Evidence." *Decision Sciences* 12 (1981): 471–85.

Kaplan, Robert S. "Yesterday's Accounting Undermines Production." *Harvard Business Review* 62 (July-August 1984): 95–101.

Kelly, Charles M. "Effective Communications—Beyond the Glitter and Flash." *Sloan Management Review* 26 (Spring 1985): 69–74.

Klein, Janice A. "Why Supervisors Resist Employee Involvement." *Harvard Business Review* 62 (September-October 1984): 84–91.

Merchant, Kenneth A., and Simons, Robert. "Control in Complex Organizations: An Overview." *Journal of Accounting Literature* 5 (1986): 183–204.

Parker, Lee D. "Control in Organizational Life: The Contribution of Mary Parker Follett." *Academy of Management Review* 9 (October 1984): 736–45.

Peterson, Kent. "Mechanisms of Administrative Control of Managers in Educational Organizations." *Administrative Science Quarterly* 29 (December 1984): 573–97.

Shohet, John R. "Financial Statement Presentation." *Journal of Accountancy* (October 1986): 80–86.

Waller, William S., and Chow, Charles W. "The Self-Selection and Effort Effects of Standard-Based Employee Controls: A Framework and Some Empirical Evidence." *The Accounting Review* (July 1985): 458–76.

Walton, Richard E. "From Control to Commitment in the Workplace." *Harvard Business Review* 63 (March-April 1985): 76–84.

DELTA FERTILIZER (B)

Hughes Brown, CPA and controller of Delta Fertilizer, had just returned from a meeting with Henry Fisher, who had recently been appointed executive vice-president of Delta. During the meeting, Fisher had asked Brown to develop a budget for the research and development department.

Brown had expressed some concern about developing such a budget. Fisher agreed that performance in the research and development department was satisfactory, but research employees seemed to have the freedom to do as they pleased. Many of them worked when they wanted to, during the day or at night. After Fisher had observed research employees leaving early and coming to work late, he decided to visit the research department and discuss his concerns with the department manager, Dr. Leo Herbert. Fisher was appalled to discover that most of the research employees were sitting around drinking coffee and talking when he arrived. Fisher learned that Dr. Herbert had left to watch his daughter play in a tennis match. Later, when Dr. Herbert returned, Fisher related his concerns about behavior in the department. Dr. Herbert

This case was developed from concepts presented in Richard L. Daft, *Organization Theory and Design*, 2nd ed. (St. Paul, Minn.: West, 1986), pp. 323–24.

responded that his employees often worked long hours to complete their projects. Whenever anyone left during the day to attend to personal business, they usually worked at night to make up for lost time. Dr. Herbert mentioned that he and several employees had worked until midnight the night before and appeared to have developed a significant application for one of their projects. In the morning, he had asked his employees to meet informally and discuss the results of the discovery.

Fisher's background had been in manufacturing, where statistical reports and detailed budgets were used. All of the activities in manufacturing were evaluated on a weekly basis. Fisher wanted Brown to develop a detailed budget system for each research project. All expenditures were to be budgeted. Statistical reports were to be issued that identified how employees spent their time and what output was accomplished.

Questions

1. What type of controls should Brown develop? Why?
2. Should Fisher be concerned about developing a budget for research and development?

SPECIALTY MANUFACTURING

John Morgan could not believe the information he had received from his banker. Morgan, president and owner of Specialty Manufacturing, had taken a six-month leave of absence to develop new

accounts in Mexico. His banker had called and advised that payment on a large note had not been made. The banker, who had known Morgan for many years, mentioned that rumors were circulating that Specialty

Manufacturing was behind in payments to many suppliers.

Hurriedly, Morgan called his office to talk with his office manager and accountant, Pete Motal, who confirmed that the problem existed. Motal said that during the past six months many orders had been rejected by customers because of poor quality, and a recent inventory indicated that raw materials valued at half a million dollars were missing. Specialty had not paid any of its suppliers for the past two months and had missed payment on a large bank loan. The company barely had enough money to pay employees for their past week's work.

Morgan had graduated twenty years ago from the state university with a BS in textile engineering and had gone to work for a large textile firm. After ten years, Morgan was a division vice-president of manufacturing, earning a salary in the high five figures. Morgan had suggested that the firm develop a product that could be used as an inside lining for "outerwear" garments. After his suggestion had been rejected, Morgan worked at night in his basement and developed a lightweight fiber lining with superior insulating qualities.

Morgan obtained a small business loan, resigned his job, and started Specialty Manufacturing. The product was a commercial success. Morgan reinvested his profits in Specialty, purchased a larger building, more manufacturing machines, and delivery trucks, and developed other successful products. He paid himself a handsome salary and built a large home for his family. From time to time, Morgan experienced cash flow problems, so he borrowed a large sum of money from a local bank.

Morgan was the driving force behind his business, working long hours and operating with a "lean" staff. Many employees now in responsible positions had worked their way up from entry-level jobs. Although these employees were loyal and worked long hours, they knew very little about managing a business. Motal, who did not have a college degree, had begun working at Specialty as a shipping clerk. Morgan relied on an outside accounting firm to provide various financial assistance as needed. This firm had mentioned on numerous occasions that Specialty needed a formal control system.

Morgan's response was that he could sense what was going on in his plant and that he wanted his employees to "produce products" rather than become bookkeepers. Morgan did keep track of the number of orders processed and focused his attention on bottleneck areas that affected output.

Morgan had never taken a vacation, but recently he felt burned out. He had lost interest in the business despite its financial success. A customer had mentioned starting an operation in Mexico and asked Morgan if he would be interested in becoming a partner. Morgan decided to take off for six months and explore opportunities that might exist in Mexico. Specialty had a backlog of orders, and Morgan believed the business could run itself.

Robert Taylor, Specialty's first employee, was left in charge. Every week Morgan called and asked Taylor about the number of orders processed during the week. Morgan always asked Taylor if any special problems existed, and Taylor had always replied that everything was under control.

Questions

1. What type of control existed at Specialty?
2. What should Morgan have done to ensure control while he was absent?

OVERVIEW OF OPERATIONS MANAGEMENT
Importance of Operations Management ☐ Productivity and Operations Management ☐ Types of Operations

PLANNING AND ORGANIZING OPERATIONS
Capacity Planning ☐ Site Location ☐ Process Planning ☐ Layout Planning ☐ Aggregate Planning ☐ Scheduling ☐ Procurement

CONTROLLING OPERATIONS
Controlling Material Requirements ☐ Controlling Inventory ☐ Controlling Quality ☐ Controlling Output

Summary ☐ Key Concepts ☐ Discussion Questions ☐ Notes ☐ Supplementary Reading

CASES: Madison Electronics ☐ Centex Car Wash

This chapter will enable you to

☐ Understand the nature and importance of operations management.

☐ Describe the basic types of operations in organizations.

☐ Identify the various functions that managers must perform as they plan and organize operations.

☐ Discuss how managers control such operational areas as material requirements, inventory, quality, and output.

CHAPTER 18
OPERATIONS MANAGEMENT

The heart of every organization is its operational subsystem, which is concerned with the conversion of inputs into final products and services. The efficiency with which these operations are managed is a major determinant of the organization's ability to compete and to operate effectively.

OVERVIEW OF OPERATIONS MANAGEMENT

Operations management focuses on the organizational subsystem that is responsible for transforming inputs into outputs. Its basic objective is to ensure that products or services are produced which have a value that exceeds the combined costs of the required inputs and the transformation process.

The first formal analysis of operations management began at the turn of the twentieth century with Frederick W. Taylor's work in scientific management (discussed in chapter 2). In addition to Taylor's "scientific" study of work processes, the emphasis of his school of thought was exemplified by Frank B. and Lillian M. Gilbreth's time-and-motion studies, which helped workers reduce inefficiency and fatigue, and Henry L. Gantt's study of work scheduling. This focus on the technical aspects of organizational operations became known as production or manufacturing management.

In the 1930s, the Hawthorne Studies (see chapter 2) expanded this view of operations to include human and social factors. It was not until the 1950s, however, that the technical and social perspectives of operations management

IGNORING THE SOCIAL SUBSYSTEM

Shenandoah Life Insurance installed a $2 million system to computerize processing and claims operations at its Roanoke, Virginia, headquarters. The results were disappointing. Processing a typical policy conversion still required twenty-seven working days and handling by thirty-two clerks in three departments. Engineers and computer processing experts reevaluated the system and reported that problems were occurring because of a bureaucratic maze rather than any defects in the new technology.

Feedback from operative employees indicated that the new system had fragmented work activities and de-emphasized skill requirements. The new job assignments were narrow and confining, and perceived as separating doing from thinking. Employees, who were supervised using a top-down military approach, were expected to obey many new rules and regulations. As a consequence, they had rebelled against the system and were simply "doing things by the numbers."

The company responded by grouping the clerks into "semiautonomous" teams of five to seven members. Each team now performs all of the functions that were previously spread over three departments. Team members have learned new skills, output has more than doubled, and service complaints have practically been eliminated.

SOURCE: Adapted from John Hoerr and Michael A. Pollock, "Management Discovers the Human Side of Automation," *Business Week*, 29 September 1986, pp. 70–79.

were formally joined into a single school of thought known as the *sociotechnical approach* (see Figure 8–2). Introduced by Eric Trist and his colleagues at the Tavistock Institute of Human Relations in London, this approach emphasizes that operations management is neither concerned with "adjusting" people to technology nor technology to people but with "organizing the interface so that the best match could be obtained between both."[1]

Importance of Operations Management

Generally, there is a tendency to associate operations management with industrial manufacturing processes. But operations management consists of all of the activities that are directly related to producing goods or providing services. Operations management, the core of most business organizations, is responsible for the creation of an organization's products or services. Inputs of labor, materials, energy, and time are used to develop finished goods or services using one or more transformation processes.[2] Figure 18–1 provides examples of inputs, transformation, and outputs.

FIGURE 18–1 Inputs, transformation, and outputs

Inputs	Transformation	Outputs
Human	Processes	Goods
Physical	Cutting, drilling	Houses
Intellectual	Storing	Automobiles
Raw materials	Transporting	Textbooks
Energy	Extracting	Clothing
Water	Farming	Typewriters
Chemicals	Teaching	Machines
Metals	Assembling	Televisions
Lumber	Equipment	Food
Fibers	Machines	Energy
Other	Computers	Furniture
Technology	Typewriters	Services
Information	Trucks	Health care
Time	Buses	Entertainment
	Facilities	Car repair
	Factories	Car wash
	Schools	Transportation
	Hospitals	Delivery
	Service garages	Gift wrappig
	Offices	Banking
	Retail stores	Education
	Warehouses	

SOURCE: William J. Stevenson, *Production/Operations Management,* Second Edition (Homewood, Ill.: Richard D. Irwin, 1986), p. 10.

Employment in industry sectors has changed over time, as shown in Table 18–1. For example, though manufacturing was by far the largest industry in the United States in 1920, it was second to services and close to being overtaken by the wholesale and retail trade industry by 1984. Because nonmanufacturing organizations are so important in our society, we must be aware that operations management concepts and skills apply to the operations of all types of organizations.

Productivity and Operations Management

A large number of factors influence organizational productivity (see chapter 1), but the greatest gains in productivity are often attained by increasing the efficiency of the operations subsystem. Such efforts may focus on improving job performance, updating technology, improving coordination and scheduling processes, and so on.

Organizational emphasis on increasing productivity is directly related to the degree of competition the organization is experiencing. This relationship

TABLE 18–1 Employment (in thousands) in selected industries

Industry	1920	1940	1960	1980	1984	Growth Rate 1920–1984	Estimated 1995
Manufacturing	10,534	10,780	16,369	21,593	20,254	93%	23,491
Transportation, communication, and public utilities	3,998	3,013	3,921	6,393	6,422	61%	6,837
Wholesale and retail trade	4,623	6,940	11,698	19,727	19,509	322%	21,346
Finance, insurance, and real estate	1,110	1,436	2,494	5,860	6,518	487%	7,685
Services	2,142	3,477	6,673	27,983	30,922	1345%	31,920

SOURCE: *Statistical Abstract of the United States*, 1986, p. 405; 1981, p. 390; 1961, p. 207; 1951, p. 175. *Employment Projections for 1995*, Bulletin 2197 of U.S. Bureau of Labor Statistics, 1986.

explains why such significance has been placed on productivity improvements in manufacturing organizations during recent years.

From 1970 to 1985, American industry lost its predominant position in four major industry groups—smokestack, appliance, automotive, and electronics. For example, in 1970 the United States fell behind in such smokestack industries as textiles, steel, and brass. Many believe the problems resulted from the low-cost labor and modern equipment of foreign competitors.[3]

In 1975 U.S. dominance disappeared in televisions, stereos, microwave ovens, and other electrical goods, as products from Japan and other Far East countries flooded U.S. markets. This time the problem was thought to be caused by the dumping and/or copying of U.S. products.[4]

By 1980 the automobile industry was in serious trouble. Japan's automakers could build a small car and then deliver it to the United States for $1,500 less than Detroit's cost to produce a similar car.[5] Although various reasons were cited, Americans began to realize that they were having problems in competing.[6] In 1985 U.S. dominance in electronics was eroded when leadership in producing microchips was lost.[7]

Because of the historical dominance of U.S. manufacturing, the American standard of living has become the envy of the rest of the world. If the U.S. manufacturing base continues to erode, both the United States and the rest of the world are likely to live less well.

Despite these alarming situations, the factory (i.e., manufacturing) is re-emerging as a focal point for developing corporate and business level strategy. Top managers are beginning to realize that the operations subsystem should and can be used to provide a competitive advantage for the organization.[8]

Types of Operations

The specific type of operation an organization uses to transform its inputs into outputs depends on its industry, markets, competitors, strategies, image, available funds, and so on. Yet there are some general types of operations used by both manufacturing and nonmanufacturing organizations alike. The following classification, for instance, is based on the degree of process repetitiveness that characterizes an operation:[9]

□ *Continuous flow production*—characterized by a steady transformation of inputs into outputs. An oil refinery, for example, receives from tankers a fairly continuous input of crude oil which is refined on a round-the-clock basis into products, such as gasoline, which are then pumped into tank trucks and railroad cars for shipment to customers. A hospital intensive care ward is an example from the service sector.

□ *Mass production*—characterized by large production runs of a relatively standardized product requiring very specialized equipment and personnel. An automobile assembly plant is a common example.

□ *Large batch production*—characterized by the grouping of customer orders or products for large production runs. The production of different types of wine (rosé, burgundy, white, and so on) by a winery is an example. Traffic court is another example.

□ *Job lot production*—characterized by production solely to customer order using short production runs and general-purpose equipment and personnel. A manufacturer of church pews, for example, produces no standard pews because each church requires different pew lengths, types of wood, and designs.

□ *Unique item production*—characterized by production of a "one-of-a-kind" product or service tailored to a specific customer so that, once the operation is completed, the same task never arises again. The work of a major repair yard for ships is an example. A house mover is also an example.

Table 18–2 provides examples of all five types of operations in both the production and service sectors of the economy.

PLANNING AND ORGANIZING OPERATIONS

Management must perform a number of functions as it plans and organizes operations. This section identifies these various functions, beginning with consideration of the physical facilities required to transform inputs into outputs.

Capacity Planning

The first function the operations manager performs involves planning the productive *capacity* required to meet the organization's sales forecast. To determine required capacity, the manager must convert forecasted dollar sales into physical units of output. In the automobile industry, for example, capacity is the number of cars that can be produced yearly. An airline's capacity is measured by number of seats, and a library's by number of volumes. The projected output requirements are then compared to the organization's current capacity to determine whether expansion, contraction, or maintenance of capacity at its present size is required.

Long-range planning may indicate that the organization needs to construct additional facilities or, conversely, sell some of its existing facilities or equipment. In the short run, capacity can be expanded through such means as hiring temporary help, paying employees for overtime, renting space, or subcontracting excess orders. Likewise, capacity can be temporarily contracted through such actions as laying off employees, leasing idle space, or instituting shorter work weeks.

Site Location

New organizations and older ones that expand their operations must make decisions regarding the appropriate geographical *location* for physical facilities.

TABLE 18–2 Examples of operations

Degree of Process Repetitiveness	Type of Operation					
	Production			Service		
	Manufacturing	Converting	Repairing	Protection	Logistics	Well-being
Continuous flow	Paper mill	Electrical power plant	Water-treatment plant	Prison	Gas pipeline	Hospital intensive-care ward
Mass	Automobile assembly plant	Open-pit coal mine	Large auto paint shop	U.S. secret service	Airline	Public school
Large batch	Winery	Scrap-metal reduction plant	Road-repair contractor	Traffic court	Grain elevator	Military basic-training camp
Job lot	Furniture maker	Custom slaughterhouse	Auto-body shop	Fire department	Trucking firm	Travel tour guide
Unique item	Office-building construction firm	Ship salvage company	Major ship-repair yard	Lloyds of London insurance	House mover	Management consulting firm

SOURCE: Stephen E. Barndt and Davis W. Carvey, *Essentials of Operations Management*, © 1982, p. 9. Reprinted by permission of Prentice-Hall, Inc., Englewood Cliffs, New Jersey.

Such decisions are complex because multiple factors must be considered (Figure 18–2) and because tradeoffs among these factors are inevitable. No site is optimal in every respect. A location with low land cost and taxes, for instance, may be far removed from a plentiful supply of skilled labor. The complexity of the decision, of course, is magnified when organizations locate branch offices or plants overseas and must deal with such additional complicating factors as different legal systems and cultures.

Although site decisions are important to all organizations, they are crucial for particular types of firms. For instance, organizations that supply other companies with parts or other goods often consider delivery time an important part of their service. Firms that market directly consumed goods or services, such as restaurants, banks, movie theaters, and churches, can rarely succeed without convenient locations.

Process Planning

Once capacity and site decisions are made, management must determine the precise *process* that will be used to transform inputs into outputs. For any operations process, alternative means exist for converting inputs into final products or services. Automobiles, for instance, can be manufactured by mass production (General Motors), by autonomous work groups (Volvo), or by hand (Rolls Royce). The particular process chosen depends largely upon volume or

FIGURE 18–2 Some factors in deciding site location

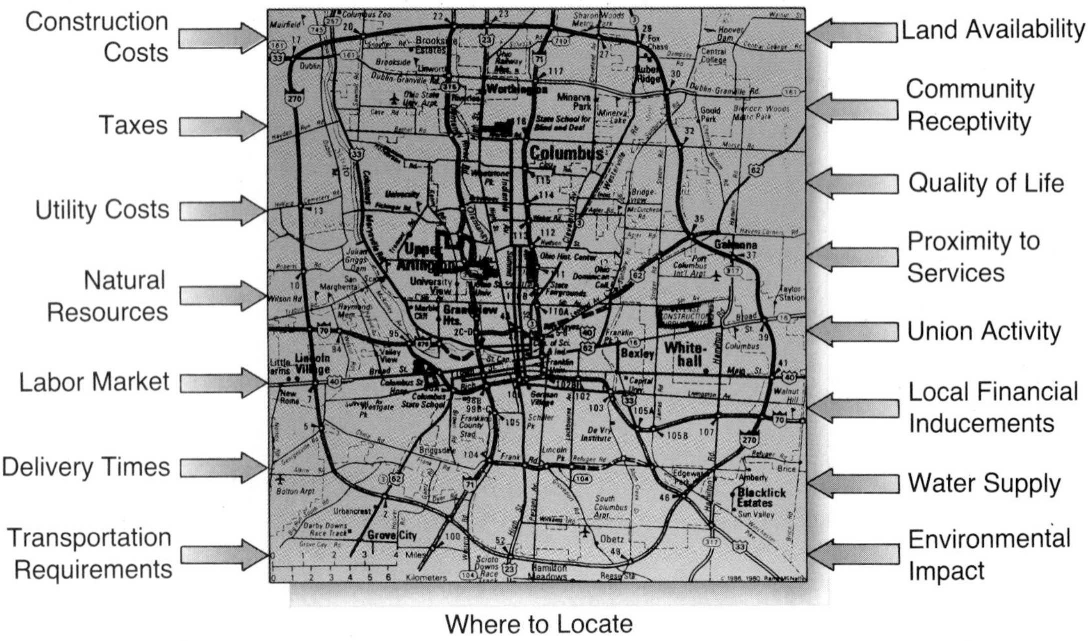

Construction Costs — Taxes — Utility Costs — Natural Resources — Labor Market — Delivery Times — Transportation Requirements — Land Availability — Community Receptivity — Quality of Life — Proximity to Services — Union Activity — Local Financial Inducements — Water Supply — Environmental Impact

Where to Locate

SOURCE: © Rand McNally & Company. Used by permission.

AUTOMATING THE FACTORY

The two to three dozen American companies that are the giants of the aerospace, appliance, automotive, computer, and heavy-equipment industries are using high technology to reinvent the factory. With the new technology, known as computer-aided manufacturing (CAM), computer-controlled machinery performs the work while humans watch from control rooms. For example, material-handling systems, machine tools, test equipment, and robots are now computer controlled and operated. *Business Week* estimates that American companies will increase CAM spending from $15 billion in 1985 to $32 billion in 1990.

Because of the expense and challenges involved in successfully executing a CAM strategy, one might believe that only giant companies participate. Surprisingly, many small companies are adopting a CAM approach. For example, approximately 25 percent of the companies that purchased robots from June, 1985, to June, 1986, had annual sales below $10 million.

SOURCE: Based on Otis Port, "High Tech To The Rescue," *Business Week,* 16 June 1986, pp. 100–103; Richard Brandt and James Treece, "Retool or Die: Job Shops Get A Fix On The Future," *Business Week,* 16 June 1986, pp. 106–8.

capacity decisions, product design and quality, and the skill level of the organization's employees.

In general, any process design requires the following decisions:[10]

□ Determining tasks and their sequence—this requires delineation of every operation, inspection, handling, and required wait (for drying or cooling, for example), and can be determined through assembly and flow process charting.

□ Determining type of process—this requires a decision on whether production should be continuous flow, mass production, large batch, job lot, or unique item.

□ Determining machines and work stations—this involves decisions about the kinds (general or special purpose) and number of machines, materials handling devices, and work stations.

These decisions in manufacturing organizations increasingly involve choices about automation. Although most often associated with continuous flow or mass production operations, automation has begun making inroads into large batch and job lot production in the form of computer-integrated manufacturing systems. In its most advanced state, known as a *flexible manufacturing system,* machine operations are controlled through a central computer, which also provides for automated transfer of parts among the machines in the system.[11]

Layout Planning

More detailed than process planning, *layout planning* involves determining the precise configuration of the departments (and equipment within the departments) that constitute the transformation process. Included in these plans are the specific locations of such peripheral areas as storage spaces, tool rooms, and rest rooms in factories, and customer service areas in such organizations as banks, offices, and supermarkets.

Although an infinite variety of layouts is possible, the following basic types of layouts are common:

- □ Product layout—work centers arranged in such a way as to assemble a product or serve a client through a standardized sequence of activities. This layout is used to produce a large volume of a particular product (an automobile assembly line, for instance) or to serve a large number of clients with similar needs (a cafeteria serving line, for example).
- □ *Process layout*—work centers grouped together by similarity of function. The product being produced or the client being served is transported from one

ROBOTICS

The age of robotics has begun:

- □ A large steel and plastic robot performed as guest organist for a Japanese symphony orchestra
- □ A robot in Australia sheared 200 sheep and bloodied only a few in the process
- □ A ping-pong match occurred in San Francisco between an English robot and an American robot
- □ A large cosmetics firm uses two robots to package 10,000 tubes of lipstick in an eight-hour shift, replacing twenty human workers
- □ Robots are used extensively by Allen-Bradley, a Milwaukee manufacturer of industrial controls, in 26 complex automated assembly stations in its computerized factory
- □ The University of Southern California medical school uses an android with distinctly humanistic features and qualities in training medical students

SOURCE: Based on Patti Hagan, "Once and Future Robots," *Across the Board* 12 (June 1984): p. 21; Noel Perrin, "We Aren't Ready for the Robots," *Wall Street Journal,* 25 February 1986; Gene Bylinsky, "A Breakthrough In Automating the Assembly Line," *Fortune,* 26 May 1986, pp 65–66.

work center to another, depending on the sequence of functions required. This layout is used when a number of different products are produced (a job lot production shop, for instance, has separate areas for lathes, drill presses, and so on) or when clients with different needs are served (an automobile repair shop has different areas for front-end alignments, tune-ups, and oil changes, for example).

□ *Fixed-position layout*—appropriate work centers brought to the location of a stationary product or client. This layout is used when the product or client cannot be moved (a farm, for example) or when it is not feasible to move the product or client (such as consulting on-site for a client).

The layout not only affects the organization's physical operations and financial requirements, but greatly influences the activities, interactions, and sentiments of the organization's employees.* Some of the technical and human consequences of layouts are shown in Table 18–3.

Aggregate Planning

Once capacity requirements have been determined and the facility design completed, management must plan the firm's aggregate (total) production requirements (versus the requirements for a particular item). In its simplest form, aggregate planning involves consideration of the organization's beginning inventory, the forecasted demand for its products, and the desired target figure for ending inventory. From these figures, management can determine the amount of production that will be required for some future period of time. Decisions can then be made concerning the number of workers to be employed for this period.

Since production requirements vary from one period to another due to fluctuations in market demand, management must make choices regarding its work force. Some organizations may hire and lay off workers as production requirements change, while others maintain a steady work force over time but vary the intensity with which it is used. During slack times, for instance, the length of the work week (or work day) might be reduced. During peak demand periods, employees might work overtime. Another common means of maintaining a constant work force size involves producing to inventory; that is, allowing stocks of finished goods to accumulate during slack demand periods and to be depleted during peak sales periods. Each of these alternatives has certain benefits and costs, both human and financial.

---

*In planning for operations, management must consider the safety and health of its employees not only for the obvious ethical and moral reasons but also because such protection is required by law. The Occupational Safety and Health Act of 1970 (OSHA) requires that businesses establish and enforce strict health and safety standards. Failure to comply can result in fines and even jail sentences.

TABLE 18–3 Characteristics of layout designs

Aspect of the Conversion Process	Product-Oriented	Process-Oriented	Fixed-Position
Product characteristics	Layout geared to producing standardized product, in large volume, at stable rates of output	Lay out for diversified products requiring common fundamental operations, in varying volume, at varying rates of output	Low volume, each unit often unique
Product flow pattern	Straight line flow of product; same sequence of standard operations on each unit	Diversified flow pattern; each order (product) may require unique sequence of operations	Little or no product flow; equipment and human resources brought to site as needed
Human skills requirement	Tolerance for performing routine, repetitive tasks at imposed pace; highly specialized work content	Primarily skilled craftsmen; can perform without close supervision and with moderate degree of adaptability	High degree of task flexibility often required; specific work assignments and location vary
Supporting staff	Large administrative and indirect support staff for scheduling materials and people, work analysis and maintenance	Must possess skills for scheduling, materials handling, and production and inventory control	High degree of scheduling and coordinating skills required
Material handling	Material flows predictable, systematized and often automated	Type and volume of handling required are variable; duplication of handling often occurs	Type and volume of handling required are variable, often low; may require heavy-duty general purpose handling equipment
Inventory requirements	High turnover of raw material and work-in-process inventories	Low turnover of raw material and work-in-process inventories; high raw materials inventories	Variable inventories due to lengthy production cycle can result in inventory tie-ups for long periods
Space utilization	Efficient utilization of space, high rate of product output per unit of space	Relatively low rate of output per unit of facility space; large work-in-process requirements	For conversion within the facility, a low rate of space utilization per unit of output may occur
Capital requirements	High capital investment in equipment and processes that perform very specialized functions	Equipment and processes are general purpose and feature flexibility	General purpose equipment and processes that are mobile
Product cost components	Relatively high fixed costs; low unit direct labor and materials costs	Relatively low fixed costs; high unit costs for direct labor, materials (inventory) and materials handling	High labor and materials costs; relatively low fixed costs.

SOURCE: Adam Ebert, *Production and Operations Management: Concepts, Models, and Behavior,* 3rd Edition, © 1986, p. 310. Reprinted by permission of Prentice-Hall, Inc., Englewood Cliffs, New Jersey.

Scheduling

From the aggregate plan, the *master schedule* is derived to indicate which products will be produced, in what quantities, and by what dates. This schedule provides the following:[12]

☐ A basis for estimating the workload of various work centers
☐ A yardstick by which to measure performance
☐ The basis for *detailed schedules*

Detailed schedules, in turn, enable management to:

☐ Assign jobs to work centers
☐ Sequence operations
☐ Determine when each job is to start and finish at each work station, machine, or specialist
☐ Determine the need for special setups, tools, facilities, and equipment
☐ Forecast inventory
☐ Balance machines, work centers, and individuals' availability with jobs

Such planning tools as PERT, discussed in chapter 7, have obvious uses in scheduling.

Procurement

Procurement involves purchasing the materials and equipment required for planned organizational operations. After identifying the needs of operations managers, procurement personnel must evaluate alternative sources of supply to obtain items of the desired quality and quantity at the lowest possible price. Purchasing also involves consideration of raw materials inventories so that the requirement for uninterrupted production is balanced with the need to minimize the size of the inventory. Purchasing personnel also serve as a primary source of information to operations managers concerning the availability of new materials and equipment from suppliers.

While American procurement managers often change suppliers for reasons involving cost, delivery, or quality, some Japanese companies enter into an "everlasting partnership" with their suppliers. Once a supplier has demonstrated its reliability by consistently delivering high-quality raw materials, the relationship between the supplier and the customer takes on a permanence rarely found in the United States:[13]

> One simply does not develop a relationship with an everlasting customer in the same way that one makes a one-time sale—the two require completely different expectations and approaches. Nor does one disappoint an everlasting customer by delivering defective products or by failing to meet delivery schedules. One does not disappoint a supplier-partner by not buying from him if his prices are some-

what out of line, although one certainly works with him to help him get prices back in line with those of competitors.

CONTROLLING OPERATIONS

As we saw in the preceding chapter, control requires standards to which actual performance can be compared. Hence, the actual process of production is controlled through the master and detailed schedules. "Events presented in the schedules, such as 'start assembly of wheels' or 'end interview phase' or 'complete first lot of 500 fire extinguishers' are on the one hand objectives to guide action, and on the other hand standards against which progress is compared."[14] In addition to these time and quantity standards, management establishes standards for the quality of inputs and outputs and for the costs of various aspects of operations, such as direct labor and material, inventory, and maintenance of equipment. This section examines three areas that receive considerable management emphasis—the control of material requirements, inventory, and quality.

Controlling Material Requirements

The number of products or services to be produced in a given period of time may be found on the master schedule. From this figure, the operations manager can derive the demand for the raw materials and component parts required to produce these outputs. Many organizations use computerized *Material Requirements Planning* (MRP) systems, which determine material requirements and purchase schedules from such inputs as the master schedule, the bill of materials (which lists all of the materials and parts required to produce a single product or service), and current inventory levels of materials and parts. Although the MRP concept is useful for virtually any organization that requires materials or parts, its greatest contribution is in the manufacturing of complex products built from numerous components, such as diesel engines or radar equipment.[15]

Computerized systems are particularly useful because they react well to changing conditions. If significant increases or decreases in demand force modification of the master schedule, the MRP system can quickly refigure the organization's need for materials and parts. When these components number in the hundreds, the advantage of this control system becomes clear. Additionally, a good MRP system can help management reduce inventory and production lead time and make more realistic delivery commitments to customers.[16]

Controlling Inventory

In many organizations, inventory is the largest current asset. For this and other reasons, inventory control is essential for success. From a cost standpoint, control of inventory quantity is necessary. If a substantial investment in inventory is required, the expense of maintaining it is considerable. These costs are of several types. The cost of capital invested in excessive or unnecessary inventory represents a waste. Interest costs on such capital may be avoided, or the money may be invested more profitably elsewhere by the use of effective inventory control. Other costs arise from increased warehouse space requirements, insurance, and taxes. In addition, inventory items may be subject to deterioration or obsolescence as well as to loss through price changes. Limitation of the inventory to the smallest practical size serves to minimize these losses.

Effective inventory control also is essential for operating efficiency. If a production tie-up is caused by an out-of-stock part, the resulting costs may be staggering. In a retail store, customer dissatisfaction occurs if the shelf is bare when the customer wishes to buy. The objective of inventory control, then, is an adequate but not excessive inventory.

Effective control of regularly stocked inventory items requires an accurate determination of minimum and maximum inventory levels. In calculating the size of the minimum reserve stock, some judgment is necessary concerning the seriousness of stockouts. If stockouts are extremely dangerous—say a part whose shortage would shut down a production line—the minimum reserve stock must be higher than would otherwise be necessary. The pattern of withdrawals also has a bearing on the proper level. A relatively large stock is required in the case of items in which withdrawals occur irregularly and possibly in large quantities.

Given a specified minimum stock level, the maximum is determined by the amount procured at one time. Buying in large quantities increases both the maximum and average inventory size. To determine the most economical level, the manager must calculate an amount known as the *economic order quantity (EOQ)*. This is the purchase quantity that minimizes total costs by properly balancing costs associated with large orders (such as cost of money tied up in inventory and warehouse space) and costs associated with small orders (such as loss of quantity discounts, cost of stockouts, and overhead clerical cost in placing purchase orders).[17] In Figure 18–3, the optimal order quantity is the point where total cost is at a minimum.*

---

*The economic order quantity may be determined mathematically by the following standard formula:

$$EOQ = \sqrt{\frac{2DC}{I}}$$

where D = expected annual product demand in units
C = procurement costs per order
I = inventory carrying cost in dollars per unit per year

For example, if the expected demand is 1000 units, the cost of placing an order is $20, and the annual inventory carrying cost per unit is $.16, then

$$EOQ = \sqrt{\frac{2 \times 1000 \times \$20}{\$.16}} = 500 \text{ units.}$$

FIGURE 18–3 Inventory costs and economic order quantity

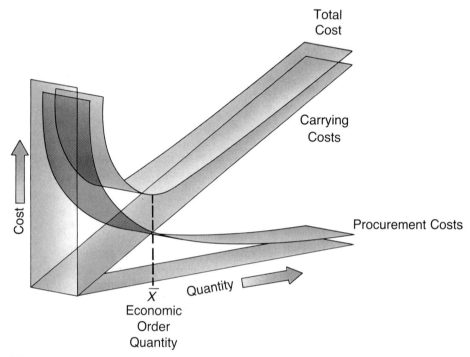

SOURCE: Adapted from Richard J. Hopeman, *Production and Operations Management: Planning, Analysis, Control,* 5th ed. (Columbus, Oh.: Charles E. Merrill Publishing Co., 1984), p. 368.

Controlling Quality

Purpose of Quality Control. Product quality is directly related to the basic objectives of the firm and rests, therefore, upon fundamental policy decisions of management. One manufacturer, for example, may elect to sell to a segment of the market desiring superior quality, while another may decide to sell to the mass market, which accepts a lower-quality product. Such decisions entail evaluation of market potential at various levels as well as evaluation of production capacity to produce at these levels. Production cost is also pertinent. Higher quality typically entails higher production cost. Quality objectives emerge in this way from the general strategy and purposes of the enterprise.

The manufacturer's concept of quality may involve standards for a number of different characteristics, such as physical dimensions, chemical composition, weight, color, strength, freedom from scratches, and so on. In light of market and cost conditions, the manufacturer chooses a specific quality level, not necessarily the best. But, having chosen it, he or she attempts to meet that standard consistently.

DEMING AND QUALITY CONTROL

Dr. W. Edwards Deming, who commanded fees as high as $10,000 a day by 1986, has been a severe critic of quality control efforts in the United States. Dr. Deming, a statistician, was ignored for decades in the United States while he worked to improve the quality of Japanese goods. In fact, the highest award given in Japan each year for industrial quality is named the Deming Award.

Dr. Deming, after returning to the United States, began stressing his "14 points of management," which include using statistical methods to find trouble spots and making employees secure so that they will point out problems and ask for information. Deming also advises doing away with posters and slogans to improve quality—rather, managers should show their employees how to solve problems.

SOURCE: Adapted from Jeremy Main, "Under the Spell of the Quality Gurus," *Fortune,* 18 August 1986, pp. 30–34. For a detailed version of Deming's 14 points see W. Edwards Deming, *Quality, Productivity, and Competitive Position* (Cambridge, Mass: M.I.T. Press, 1982), pp. 16–17.

Inspection.   Although inspection is an integral part of quality control, it is not fully synonymous with control of quality. Inspection provides feedback to management by measuring the product to determine the extent to which it conforms to established standards. Control also includes those steps necessary to regulate and correct the manufacturing process to meet the stipulated standards.

Some type of inspection is required in the quality control process. This inspection may be limited to the finished product and occur at the end of the production process, or it may occur at different stages during the process. A key question, in fact, concerns the number of times the product should be inspected. The ideal is to minimize inspection costs without losing control of the product. Other questions relating to inspection concern the number of items to be inspected—100 percent or some fraction of the items—and the location of the inspection—floor versus central inspection.

Statistical Quality Control.   Statistical quality control applies the theory of probability to the process of inspection and quality control. Even without statistical quality control, inspection is often conducted on the basis of systematic sampling. Rather than using 100 percent inspection, only a part of a lot is singled out for inspection. The assumption is that the quality of the entire lot will be indicated by the inspected items. Lacking statistical methodology, however, there is little knowledge of the degree of risk involved.

By the use of statistical quality control methods, management is able to make a choice as to the degree of risk that can be tolerated—that is, the proportion of below-standard items that can be accepted (such as 1 percent or 5 percent). The extent of risk can be specified by the statistician, and the risk (of accepting defective items) can be reduced with the expenditure of additional time and money. Statistical quality control tells the manager how likely it is that bad products will slip by with a given inspection plan. He or she can then weigh this problem against the increased cost required to reduce that risk.

The same statistical principles can be applied to the production process itself. Machines and various processes can be checked periodically to ensure that they are operating within acceptable limits. If they are "out of control"— as shown on a statistical chart—corrective adjustments can be made immediately.

Figure 18–4 illustrates one type of statistical quality control chart—the *mean chart.* The vertical scale shows gradations for plotting the arithmetic means of random items selected from the production process. In this situation, the items are packed by the case, with 16 items in each case. The mean weight of the cases should be 105.633 grams, with an allowable variation for deviations from the mean ranging from two standard deviations below (the lower control limit) to two standard deviations above (the upper control limit) the mean. The horizontal scale indicates hours of the day at which sample cases are randomly selected and weighed.

The samples taken at 8:00 through 1:00 indicate that the mean is shifting upward and the production process is out of control. If the trend line revealed

FIGURE 18–4 Sample mean chart

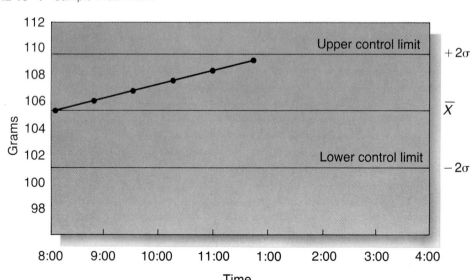

SOURCE: Richard J. Hopeman, *Production and Operations Management: Planning, Analysis, Control,* 5th ed. (Columbus, Oh.: Charles E. Merrill Publishing Co., 1984), p. 477.

only chance variations from the mean, the sample weights would fluctuate both above and below the mean. In this case, the trend is not due to chance but to some assignable cause, such as tool slippage or tool wear, poor raw materials, inattention of the worker, or a gradual malfunctioning of the machine. A quality control manager would take corrective action before the 2:00 report.[18] The emphasis in this case is on correcting the manufacturing process to prevent the production of defective items rather than identifying the defective items after they have been produced.

Controlling Output

A concept called *optimized production technology* (OPT) is increasingly being used in production and inventory control. A growing number of managers believe that OPT could revolutionize manufacturing in the United States. The OPT system involves two parts—a simulated manufacturing program and a set of radical shop-floor management rules. Managers who have used the system contend that OPT enables a company to increase a plant's output while simultaneously lowering its inventory and operating expenses. The OPT system forces managers and employees to coordinate the work and the parts flow with one principle in mind—identifying so-called bottlenecks. According to the proponents of OPT, bottlenecks determine what can be produced and when it can be produced.[19]

SUMMARY

Operations management focuses on the organizational processes that transform inputs into outputs. An outgrowth of early scientific management and the later human relations movement, operations management integrates both technical and human considerations in its emphasis on improving operational efficiency. Although operations management has traditionally been associated with industrial manufacturing processes, its basic principles are today being applied to all types of organizations, including retail and service establishments. Even though specific activities will vary from one type of organization to another, the following general types of operations may be used by both manufacturing and nonmanufacturing organizations: *continuous flow production, mass production, large batch production, job lot production,* and *unique item production.*

Management must perform a number of functions as it plans and organizes organizational operations. These include planning the productive *capacity* of the organization; selecting an appropriate geographical *location* for operations; determining the precise *process* that will be used to transform inputs into outputs; planning the *layout*—or precise configuration—of departments and equipment within those departments; forecasting the firm's *aggregate* (total) production requirements; *scheduling* which products will be produced, in what quantities, and by what dates; and *procuring* the materials and equipment required for organizational operations.

Once actual production begins, the process of controlling various aspects of operations becomes important. An increasing number of organizations are controlling their material requirements through computerized *Material Requirements Planning* (MRP) systems which can determine the organization's material needs for many different products under changing conditions. Other organizations are using a concept called *optimized production technology* (OPT) to increase output while simultaneously lowering inventory and operating expenses.

KEY CONCEPTS

Sociotechnical approach
Job lot production
Capacity planning
Flexible manufacturing system
Layout planning
Aggregate planning

Master schedule
Procurement
EOQ
MRP
OPT

DISCUSSION QUESTIONS

1. Briefly explain the *sociotechnical* view of operations management.
2. Are *operations management* principles transferable from manufacturing to non-manufacturing organizations? Explain.
3. Explain the significance that has been placed on productivity improvements in manufacturing operations during recent times.
4. What types of organizations are more likely to emphasize *productivity* increases? Why?
5. Contrast *mass production* operations with *job lot production*.
6. Distinguish among *capacity planning, process planning,* and *aggregate planning*.
7. Is the *location* for a university important? Why or why not?
8. Is *scheduling* a planning or a control tool? Explain.
9. What are the two major competing types of costs involved in *inventory control?*
10. Explain the concept of *statistical quality control*.
11. Briefly describe the OPT concept.

NOTES

1. Eric Trist, "A Socio-Technical Critique of Scientific Management," in *Meaning and Control: Essays in Social Aspects of Science and Technology,* ed. D. O. Edge and J. N. Wolfe (London: Tavistock, 1973), p. 103.

2. William J. Stevenson, *Production/Operations Management,* 2d ed. (Homewood, Ill.: Irwin, 1986), pp. 8–10.
3. Eliyahu M. Goldratt and Robert E. Rox, *The Race* (Croton-On-Hudson, N.Y.: North River Press, 1986), p. 3.
4. Ibid., p. 2.
5. Russell Mitchell, "Detroit Stumbles On Its Way To The Future," *Business Week,* 16 June 1986, pp. 103–4.
6. Goldratt and Fox, *The Race,* p. 2.
7. Ibid., p. 2.
8. Steven C. Wheelwright, "Restoring the Competitive Edge in U.S. Manufacturing," *California Management Review* 3 (Spring 1985): 26–41.
9. This is a traditional classification of types of operating or technological processes based upon the work of Joan Woodward, *Industrial Organization: Theory and Practice* (London: Oxford University Press, 1965), chapters 3 and 4.
10. Stephen E. Barndt and Davis W. Carvey, *Essentials of Operations Management* (Englewood Cliffs, N.J.: Prentice-Hall, 1982), p. 43.
11. See Melvin Blumberg and Antone Alber, "The Human Element: Its Impact on the Productivity of Advance Batch Manufacturing Systems," *Journal of Manufacturing Systems* 1 (August 1982): 43–52; and Donald Gerwin, "Do's and Don't's of Computerized Manufacturing," *Harvard Business Review* 60 (March-April 1982): 107–16.
12. Barndt and Carvey, *Essentials of Operations Management,* pp. 64–67.
13. Reprinted by permission of *Harvard Business Review.* Excerpt from "Why Japanese Factories Work" by Robert H. Hayes (July-August 1981). Copyright 1981 by the President and Fellows of Harvard College; all rights reserved.
14. Barndt and Carvey, *Essentials of Operations Management,* p. 101.
15. Ibid., p. 78.
16. Everett E. Adam, Jr., and Ronald J. Ebert, *Production and Operations Management: Concepts, Models, and Behavior,* 2d ed. (Englewood Cliffs, N.J.: Prentice-Hall, 1982), p. 522.
17. For a well-reasoned criticism of the economic order quantity concept, see John E. Bishop, "Integrating Critical Elements of Production Planning," *Harvard Business Review* 57 (September-October 1979): 154–60.
18. Example based on Richard J. Hopeman, *Production and Operations Management: Planning, Analysis, Control,* 4th ed. (Columbus, Oh.: Merrill, 1980), pp. 476–77.
19. Robert L. Lundrigan, "What is This Thing Called OPT?" *Journal of Production and Inventory Management* (Second Quarter 1986): 2–12; and Robert F. Jacobs, "OPT Uncovered: Many Production Planning and Control Concepts Can Be Applied With or Without Software," *Industrial Engineering* (October 1984): 25–38.

SUPPLEMENTARY READING

Anderson, John C., and Schroeder, Roger G. "Getting Results from Your MRP System." *Business Horizons* 27 (May-June 1984): 57–64.
Armstrong, David J. "Sharpening Inventory Management." *Harvard Business Review* 63 (November-December 1985): 42–58.
Armstrong, J. Scott. "Forecast by Extrapolation: Conclusions from Twenty-Five Years of Research." *Interfaces* 14 (November-December 1984): 52–66.

Barndt, Stephen E., and Garvey, Davis W. *Essentials of Operations Management,* 2d ed. Englewood Cliffs, N.J.: Prentice-Hall, 1986.

Followell, Robert F., and Oakland, John S. "Research into Methods of Implementing Statistical Quality Control." *Quality Assurance* 11 (1985): 27–32.

Forward, Gordon E. (Interviewed by Alan M. Knatrow) "Wide-Open Management at Chaparral Steel." *Harvard Business Review* 64 (May-June 1986): 96–102.

Haas, Elizabeth. "Breakthrough Manufacturing." *Harvard Business Review* 65 (March-April 1987): 75–81.

Hayes, Robert H., and Clark, Kim B. "Why Some Factories Are More Productive Than Others." *Harvard Business Review* 64 (September-October 1986): 66–73.

Jaikumar, Ramchandran. "Postindustrial Manufacturing." *Harvard Business Review* 64 (November-December 1986): 69–76.

Meal, Harlan C. "Putting Production Decisions Where They Belong." *Harvard Business Review* 62 (March-April 1984): 102–11.

Plenert, Gerhart, and Best, Thomas D. "MRP, JIT, and OPT: What's Best?" *Production and Inventory Management* (Spring Quarter 1986): 22–29.

Ritzman, Larry P.; King, Barry E.; and Kratjewski, Lee J. "Manufacturing Performance: Pulling the Right Levers." *Harvard Business Review* 62 (March-April 1984): 143–52.

Schonberger, Richard J. *Japanese Manufacturing Techniques: Nine Hidden Lessons in Simplicity.* New York: The Free Press, 1982.

———, and Gilbert, James P. "Just-In-Time Purchasing: A Challenge For U.S. Industry." *California Management Review* 26 (Fall 1983): 54–68.

Smith, Albert C., Jr. "Robotics: A Strategic Issue." *SAM Advanced Management Journal* 50 (Spring 1985): 7–11.

Wadhwani, Romesh T. "Integrating Robot Power Into Automated Factory Systems." *Management Review* 73 (June 1984): 8–14.

Walleigh, Richard C. "What's Your Excuse for Not Using JIT?" *Harvard Business Review* 64 (March-April 1986): 38–54.

Wheelwright, Steven C., and Hayes, Robert H. "Competing Through Manufacturing." *Harvard Business Review* 63 (January-February 1985): 99–109.

Whitney, Daniel. "Real Robots Do Need Jigs." *Harvard Business Review* 64 (May-June 1986): 110–15.

MADISON ELECTRONICS

The Madison Electronics Company (MEC) manufactures electrical components for a variety of major U.S. firms. The standards for the components vary with the customer but usually must conform to rather close tolerances. Despite receiving some large orders for components in recent years, MEC is currently being forced to lay off employees.

Part of this layoff can be attributed to an efficiency team brought into the

Case prepared by Professor Joe Thomas of Northeast Missouri State University.

organization one year ago to redesign jobs and workflow to increase productivity and reduce per unit costs. One of the recommendations of this group of consultants was the implementation of a bonus system. MTM (motion and time method) was used to establish rates for the various jobs throughout the facility. While there was initial resistance to using such a system, most employees have discovered that they can exceed the rate and so earn more than their base pay.

One of the jobs which has been unable to meet the rate is trimming the various parts prior to their being assembled and sold to the customers. The parts are sent directly to the trimmer from the casting department. The trimmers insert the part into a shearing machine, which trims away burrs and other irregular formations on the parts. After trimming, the parts are sent to milling, where they are smoothed and prepared for assembly and shipped to the intended customer, as shown in Exhibit 1. If the part does not fit into the shearing equipment, it is rejected and returned to the casting department for possible reworking.

The standard rate for the trimmer is 500 units per hour, or 4,000 units per day. When the casting machines are properly adjusted this rate can be attained by a diligent worker. However, if the trimmer rejects a part because it does not fit the shearing machine, it is not counted as a unit completed and does not count toward the rate set for the operator. Since the dies in the casting department are allowed to become quite worn before replacement, it becomes increasingly difficult for the trimmer to achieve the established rates of production. This creates special problems, since once the parts are trimmed, other workers in assembly and shipping are able to achieve their rates and earn their bonus. Trimmers are quite dissatisfied with the existing system, and turnover for the department is excessive.

The manager of the trimming department has asked the casting manager numerous times to replace the dies before they become so worn. The casting manager is reluctant to replace the dies sooner than is absolutely necessary because this increases the down time for his workers and keeps them from achieving their established rates. Doing maintenance also causes increased operating costs for the department.

The personnel manager has been very reluctant to change the established bonus system. The standard reply has been that the system was developed by specially trained time-and-motion experts and that they knew what they were doing.

Questions

1. What do you believe is the major problem in this case?
2. How might this problem be effectively resolved?

EXHIBIT 1   Workflow of cast components

CENTEX CAR WASH

Bob Paige, owner of Centex Car Wash, is about to make a decision that could possibly lead to an unfavorable outcome. Five years ago Bob started his business with the intention of creating the best full-service car wash in the area. He started in a newly constructed building—designed expressly for state-of-the-art car washing equipment—on one of the most heavily traveled streets in the city. Activity was brisk right from the start, and Bob has been considering adding equipment to the wash line that could increase revenues by providing services some of his customers would value.

The facility is housed in a building 120 feet long and 40 feet wide. Autos are driven to the beginning of the wash line by attendants after the customer's vehicle has been thoroughly vacuumed and filled with gas (if requested), and after a check on the position of external mirrors and antennas has been completed. Once at the head of the line, the attendant thoroughly wets the automobile and sprays the tires with a concentrated cleaning solution. Bob pays particular attention to how clean the customer's tires are after having the Centex treatment—unsightly tires are the primary reason for customer dissatisfaction. The automobile, engaged by a floor-mounted conveyor system, is moved through the car wash system.

The four functions performed with the automatic equipment originally installed at Centex are: (1) prewash soaping, (2) wash, (3) rinse, and (4) forced-air drying. Bob knows that a high-quality wax capability is a feature gaining in popularity, though this is not available at Centex. He did not provide wax initially because he was not convinced that the equipment or waxes available at the time were worthy. Recent advances have changed Bob's mind. After meeting with several vendors of hot wax equipment, he is now trying to decide if he should invest the required $122,500 for an applicator that will mount directly to the rear of the present rinse equipment with no modification to the present wash line.

From October to March, the car wash is open from 7 A.M. until 5 P.M. It stays open until 9 P.M. the rest of the year. It is possible for clean cars to exit the wash line every 100 seconds. On the average, the business operates at 65 percent of its maximum capacity during the winter and at 82 percent during the summer. Bob reports that the current price of $5.49 provides a 44 percent margin for profit. The manufacturer of the wax applicator forecasts that one of every five customers will purchase the wax treatment at a suggested price of $1.89. That suggested price will provide a 30 percent margin for profit. Bob would like to pay for the new equipment during a single season, if possible. He has the cash to pay for the equipment on installation. But he is currently earning an 8.5 percent rate of return on his money through his local bank, and he does not know if he should withdraw these funds or finance the new equipment purchase through a 120-day same-as-cash offer through the vendor.

Questions

1. Should Bob Paige acquire a new wax applicator for Centex? If yes, in which

Prepared by Professor Van Gray of Baylor University.

season should the equipment be operational? Why?

2. If Bob were to purchase the new equipment, should he take advantage of the manufacturer's 120-day same-as-cash offer? Why or why not?

3. What is the maximum revenue that Centex can generate during the winter season? During the summer season?

SOCIAL RESPONSIBILITY

The Changing Social Contract □ The Extent of Social Responsibility □ Profit Maximization and Social Responsibility □ Corporate Responsiveness to Social Performance

ETHICS IN MANAGEMENT

Ethical Decision Making in Organizations □ Foundations for Business Ethics

SOCIAL RESPONSIBILITIES OF SENIOR MANAGERS AND BOARDS OF DIRECTORS

Responsibility of Senior Managers □ Board Responsibility for Ethical Leadership □ Problems in Achieving Strong Board Leadership □ Prospects for Effective Control

Summary □ Key Concepts □ Discussion Questions □ Notes □ Supplementary Reading

CASES: Walter Stanton: Employee Responsibility and the Use of Time □ Preventing Future Price-Fixing— The President's Dilemma

This chapter will enable you to

□ Realize that organizations have social responsibilities and understand the problems that managers face in dealing with such issues.

□ Understand the relationship between social responsibility and profits.

□ Identify a variety of ethical problems in contemporary organizations and explain how ethical decision making occurs in an organizational setting.

□ Explain the responsibility of senior managers and boards of directors for providing ethical leadership in the organization.

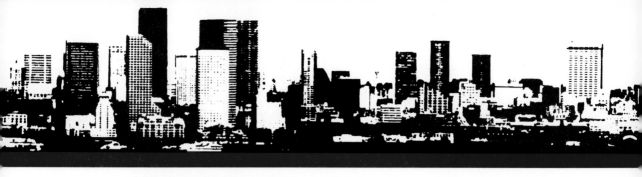

CHAPTER 19
SOCIAL RESPONSIBILITY AND ETHICAL BEHAVIOR

Business and other organizations affect the physical environment, their employees, the local community, and other parts of society. We expect these organizations to do the "right things" and to exhibit "responsible" performance. Managers are recognizing that their organizations have responsibilities to society that extend beyond narrowly defined objectives and strategies. Managers also realize that in an informed society the frequent discrepancy between what organizations can do and what they actually do makes them vulnerable to more public control. In this chapter, we examine the once peripheral but now vitally important areas of social responsibility and ethical behavior.

SOCIAL RESPONSIBILITY

All organizations are open systems that interact with their environments. Managers must be concerned with the public expectations and requirements that affect their organizations. Unless many companies develop a more positive public image, the degree of freedom corporations have come to enjoy may prove only a fleeting phase in the history of American commerce.[1]

The public expects responsible performance from all types of organizations. Governmental agencies, labor unions, hospitals, universities, and business corporations are all institutions whose operation affects the public interest. The public is increasingly demanding that these institutions shoulder responsibility beyond their own specific missions, particularly in areas closely related to their primary fields of operation.

The Changing Social Contract

Justification for a sense of social responsibility is grounded in the freedom accorded by society to business and other organizations—accorded through what is often called a *social contract*. A business corporation, like other legitimate organizations, is given freedom to work toward some legitimate objective. The payment for that freedom is the firm's contribution to society. Terms of the contract, moreover, are not permanently fixed but change over time. Business firms have been expected to assume increasingly broader responsibilities to society.

At one time, business responsibilities were defined narrowly as consisting of those pictured in the center circle of Figure 19–1. These responsibilities for providing jobs, goods, and services are still primary responsibilities, but many, if not most, observers now see business obligations extending to other issues related to business operations—the type listed in the middle circle. The outside circle contains social needs of a more general character—aid to education, urban development, and so on. Public opinion is mixed about business responsibilities in these areas. There is no question, however, that the social contract has been expanding to include more and more obligations outside the center circle.

The Extent of Social Responsibility

As responsible citizens, how should managers respond to the changing social demands of consumers, employees, and the general public? Some demands are mandated by public regulation, through which social responsibility is narrowly defined. For example, legal standards of behavior are prescribed through environmental protection, equal opportunity employment, honesty in advertising, political contributions, product warranties, employee safety, and so on.

Another approach in defining social responsibility is bound up in the notion of "conscience." This approach represents a change from traditional thinking, which regards conscience as an attribute of a person, not an organization. The actions of corporations are now often considered to reflect a kind of moral judgment comparable to that made by individuals.

Still another approach in defining social responsibility is the "what is good for business" argument. Proponents of this approach contend that the future of business is intertwined with the future of society. Societal decay affects business health. Therefore, business organizations have a responsibility to alleviate such decay.

There is evidence that managers are avoiding social responsibility. For example, recent research indicates that from the mid 1970s to the mid 1980s, roughly two-thirds of America's 500 largest corporations were involved in varying degrees in some form of illegal behavior.[2] What can explain these misbehaviors?

Several explanations have been offered regarding the lack of social responsibilities shown by managers. One is that business lacks expertise in solv-

FIGURE 19–1 Areas of social responsibility

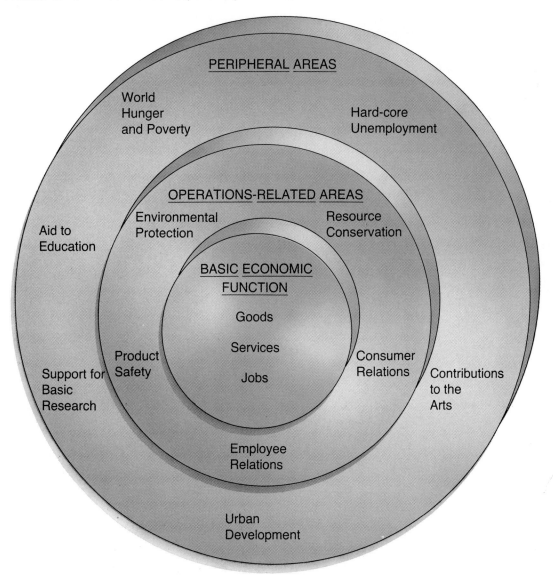

ing social problems, and thus it is improper for corporate executives to spend stockholders' money for public purposes. Stockholders should be permitted to spend their money as they see fit. Furthermore, it is not the place of business to establish social priorities—to decide, for example, whether a new hospital is more important than a little league ball park. After all, the "governing" rule in industry is that something is good only if it pays.[3]

Another explanation is that there are very real limits on managers' discretion in a market economy, and that the individual firm's interest as a com-

EXAMPLES OF UNETHICAL BEHAVIOR

An English judge, Edward Thurlow, writing in the 1700s, inquired "Did you ever expect a corporation to have a conscience, when it has no soul to be damned and no body to be kicked?"

Various lawmakers are looking for a body to kick because of an increasing number of unethical actions committed by many blue-chip companies. Following are examples of reported unethical behavior:

☐ Eighteen *Fortune* 500 firms, each with over $1 billion in defense contracts, are under investigation by the Defense Department because of alleged cost mischarges.

☐ Chase Manhattan sues six former officers for $175 million alleging negligence in buying loans from Penn Square Bank.

☐ Bank of America alleges that former employees engaged in a mortgage-backed securities scandal costing the bank $95 million.

☐ Three executives of Film Recovery Systems of Elk Grove Village, Ill., were each sentenced to twenty-five-year prison terms for an employee's death resulting from unsafe plant conditions.

☐ Exxon is ordered by the Supreme Court to refund $2 billion for overpricing oil from a Texas field.

☐ Dennis Levine pleads guilty to making $12.6 million by trading on non-public information.

SOURCE: The Thurlow quote is from "How To Take A Bite Out of Corporate Crime," *Business Week*, 15 July 1985, p. 122. The examples of unethical behavior were reported in (order of appearance): *Business Week*, 1 July 1985, p. 24; *The Wall Street Journal*, 10 July 1985; *The Wall Street Journal*, 10 July 1985; *Business Week*, 10 February 1986, p. 73; *The Wall Street Journal*, 28 January 1986; *The Wall Street Journal*, 13 May 1986; *The Wall Street Journal*, 21 November 1986; *Houston Post*, 21 October 1983; *Business Week*, 24 February 1986; *Business Week*, 25 November 1985, p. 125; *Business Week*, 28 April 1986; *The Wall Street Journal*, 9 November 1984; *Newsweek*, 4 February 1985; *Fortune*, 13 October 1986.

petitor in the marketplace often diverges from its interest as a part of the wider society.[4] For example, a firm may welcome a cleaner environment for society in general, but as a competitor in the market place it only has an interest in minimizing its own pollution abatement costs. In a market economy, no individual firm can be sure that it is not placing itself at a competitive disadvantage by interpreting its own obligations more strictly than its competitors do. In such circumstances, all firms are likely to shoulder less social responsibility than they would in principle be willing to accept.[5]

Managerial ethical dilemmas occur because social responsibilities often represent a conflict between an organization's economic performance (measured by revenues, cost, and profits) and its social performance (stated in terms

□ Ivan Boesky settles Securities and Exchange Commission's charges of insider trading by paying $100 million in fines. Boesky implicates other Wall Street professionals in the insider-trading scheme.

□ Despite documents from test drivers and other company sources warning of brake locking problems on 1980 X-body automobiles, General Motors went ahead and produced the front-wheel-drive car in 1979 without correcting the problem.

□ E. F. Hutton pleads guilty to 2,000 counts of mail and wire fraud, paying $2 million in fines after the Justice Department uncovers a Hutton branch manager's memo describing a complicated scheme of defrauding banks using check-clearing delays.

□ After killing nearly 2,000 people and injuring many thousands more in Bhopal, India, the chief executive of Union Carbide announces that "early they thought we'd give the store away. Now we are in a litigation mood. I'm not going to roll over and play dead."

□ General Dynamics encourages employees to use new "ethics hotlines" to report misconduct after the company was charged with alleged cost mischarges on defense contracts. Over 400 calls were received the first two months the ethics lines were in operation.

□ Southland Corporation admits that it paid nearly $2 million in kickbacks to big buyers of its dairy products from 1975 to 1977.

□ A reporter for the *Wall Street Journal* allegedly made $675,000 by trading securities of companies that were to be featured in a stock-market column. The reporter was charged with securities fraud and conspiracy for defrauding the *Journal* by making a personal profit on information he gathered as a *Journal* reporter.

□ E. F. Hutton charges that a customer defrauded the company of $48 million using an elaborate stock and commodity trading scam. The customer alleges that Hutton's managers helped him play an enormous "float" game to maintain their commissions.

of obligations to persons both within and outside the organization). Social responsibility can be costly. For example, the salesperson who unethically bribes purchasing agents will probably have a better sales record and will receive higher commissions than the salesperson who refuses to engage in unethical payments.

Profit Maximization and Social Responsibility

Many believe that the business system works best when managers focus almost entirely on maximizing profits, and this belief is also a central part of economic theory.[6] The principle has been well stated by Milton Friedman:[7]

> In a free economy there is one and only one social responsibility of business . . . to use its resources and engage in activities designed to increase its profit, so long as it stays within the rules of the game . . . engaging in open and free competition . . . without deception or fraud.

Friedman assumed his readers understood the concept of Pareto optimality as the basis for his contention.[8] *Pareto optimality* describes a condition in which the scarce resources of society are being efficiently used by producers and in which goods and services are being effectively distributed by competitive markets in such a manner that it is impossible to make any single person better off without harming some other person.[9] Pareto optimality provides a theory for the relationship between profit maximization and social responsibility. The organization should always be truthful, observe its contracts, be competitive, always decide for the greater economic return, and achieve economic equilibrium where it is impossible to make any single person better off without making some other person worse off.[10]

It can be intellectually satisfying to use economic theory to explain the optimal use of scarce material, capital, and labor in the production of the optimal numbers of consumer goods and services. But in considering the ethical dilemmas that result between the conflict of the economic performance and the social performance of an organization, economic theory often fails to provide answers to what is "right" or "just."

Corporate Responsiveness to Social Performance

How aggressive should corporations be in fulfilling their social responsibilities? Within the limits of their financial resources, they may choose too little or much. Figure 19–2 shows a number of responsiveness strategies, ranging from "fight all the way" to "lead the industry."

For instance, when General Dynamics was investigated by the Department of Defense for overcharges and unethical behavior in the company's work for the military, the company's chief executive reacted defensively by stating there was nothing dishonest about the way General Dynamics conducted its business. Johnson and Johnson, on the other hand, showed a much more proactive response regarding its product Tylenol. When Tylenol was reported to have caused several deaths because of either tampering or defective processing, Johnson and Johnson moved quickly to stop production and removed Tylenol from store shelves.[11]

As a result of the growing emphasis on social responsibility, some corporations now attempt to evaluate the quality of their social performance. Such an assessment procedure, often described as a *social audit*, identifies corporate activities believed to have a positive social impact.[12] Some social audits merely describe such corporate activities; others attempt to assign a dollar value to them. Most social contributions are difficult to quantify, however, and even the most rigorous social audits lack the precision of financial audits.

Although social audits may lack rigor, they can serve as information sys-

FIGURE 19–2 Levels of social responsiveness

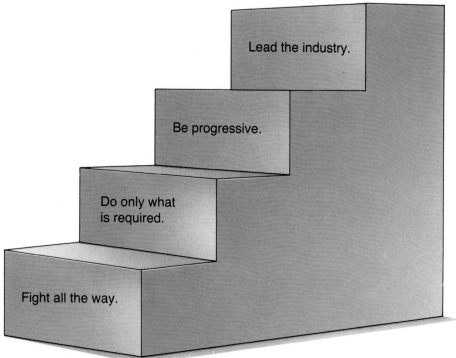

SOURCE: These categories of responsiveness were suggested by Terry W. McAdam, "How to Put Corporate Responsibility into Practice," *Business and Society Review* 6 (Summer 1973): 14.

tems for managers wishing to monitor social performance. As such, they can identify the important social issues facing a specific organization, develop performance measures, and evaluate corporate performance in terms of some standard. A corporation, for example, might compare its contributions to education with those of similar organizations.

ETHICS IN MANAGEMENT

Ethical problems exist for all types of organizations—educational, governmental, religious, business, and so on. The focus of the remainder of this chapter deals with the ethics of management in determining what is right and just in actions and decisions that affect other people. Managerial ethics goes beyond simple questions of bribery, theft, or collusion. Instead, managerial ethics addresses all that is associated with what a manager's relationship should be to the organization's employees, distributors, suppliers, customers, stockholders, creditors, and neighbors. What do we owe a major supplier that provided us with credit years ago and now represents an inefficient source of materials?

What do we owe a customer who purchased one of our products two years ago before we realized that the product may fail, causing inconvenience and perhaps a threat to safety? What do we owe one of our middle managers who has been with the organization for twenty-five years and is now no longer needed? Is there a right and just balance between economic performance and meeting the organization's social responsibilities?

People have a tendency to oversimplify the nature of ethical problems in business organizations. Frequently, they see decisions as involving simple choices between right and wrong, black and white. Yet decisions with ethical overtones are often considerably more complex. The rightness of a decision from an ethical standpoint may not be clear at all. Often there are conflicts in values. Managers have difficulty freeing themselves from bias and prejudice and looking at issues objectively. Despite good intentions, the person becomes involved in the situation and identifies with certain positions or points of view. It is not easy to step back and take a detached view of an issue from an ethical standpoint.

Ethical Decision Making in Organizations

Business leaders have attempted to extend their ethical standards in the decision-making process by using formal ethical codes. A survey of large U.S. corporations (673 responses from 2,000 questionnaires) revealed that 77 percent of respondents had a formal code of conduct.[13] The largest corporations were most likely to use codes—97 percent of those in the largest size category indicating their use of a code. The adoption of codes has been strongly encouraged by the provisions of the federal Foreign Corrupt Practices Act, which requires effective systems of internal control.

Even though most corporations now use codes, there is disagreement regarding their effectiveness. Some managers see codes as mere scraps of paper, unrelated to real behavior. Statements of this kind may cause organizational dysfunction by emphasizing the negative.[14] Clearly, little is gained from preparing a statement of ethics that is not taken seriously.

A code can provide an explicit definition of ethical standards. For example, Electronic Data Systems has a published code of corporate ethics that describes standards of conduct for dealing with prohibited payments, conflicts of interest, proprietary data, insider information about the purchase or sale of securities, antitrust actions, international trade regulations, and record keeping.[15] There is some advantage in being specific, rather than being so vague that the statements are virtually meaningless. Assuming clarity in ethical standards, the next question concerns the seriousness with which a code is communicated. Some organizations, for example, require a signed statement from management employees that they understand and will adhere to the company's code. An annual compliance review is conducted with the results going to the audit committee of the board of directors.

Research indicates that ethical decision making in organizations can be explained by the interaction of situational and individual components.[16] Figure

FIGURE 19–3   Interactionist model of ethical decision making

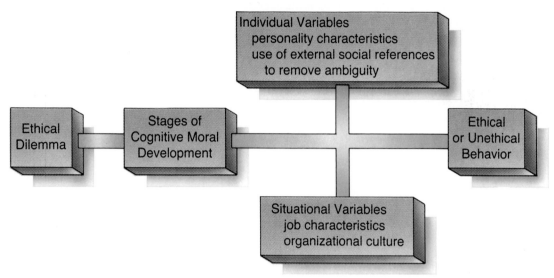

SOURCE: Adapted from Linda K. Trevino, "Ethical Decision Making in Organizations: A Person-Situation Interactionist Model," *Academy of Management Review* 11 (July 1986): 603. Reprinted with permission of the *Academy of Management Review* and the author.

19–3 shows a model adapted from one developed by Linda Trevino.[17] In this model, individuals are viewed as having stages of cognitive moral development. Cognition is the process of knowing or becoming aware.

Figure 19–4 details six stages of moral development, from middle childhood to adulthood. A person moves from stage to stage in an irreversible sequence. Fewer than 20 percent of American adults are believed to reach stage

FIGURE 19–4   Six stages of moral development

	Stage	*What Is Considered to Be Right*
1	Obedience and punishment	Obeying rules to avoid physical punishment
2	Exchange orientation	Obeying rules only when it is in one's immediate interest
3	Mutual expectations	Living up to what people close to you expect
4	Societal contributions	Obeying laws; fulfilling obligations and duties that have previously been agreed upon
5	Individual rights	Upholding nonrelative rights and values regardless of majority opinion
6	Ethical principles	Following self-chosen ethical principles; acting in accordance with principles when laws violate those principles

SOURCE: Adapted from pp. 409–412 In THE PHILOSOPHY OF MORAL DEVELOPMENT: Volume One, Essays on Moral Development by Lawrence Kohlberg. Copyright © 1981 by Lawrence Kohlberg. Reprinted by permission of Harper & Row, Publishers, Inc.

5.[18] Both the existence of these stages and the movement from stage to stage have been supported by a number of studies.[19]

When a member of an organization is confronted with an ethical problem, an interplay exists between thought and action. The individual's level of moral development (the particular stage as described in Figure 19–4) affects his or her thoughts about what is right and wrong. But how the person acts depends on the influence of the individual and situational variables described in Figure 19–3.[20]

Foundations for Business Ethics

Each society has moral standards that are reflected in the ethical values of the business world. One approach to understanding the foundations of business ethics is to assume that the general level of ethical standards in business conduct will not differ substantially from the ethical standards in nonbusiness areas of society. In essence, this approach holds that business ethics are only one part of broader ethical standards.

Figure 19–5 contains a summary of five major ethical systems as developed by LaRue Hosmer. Although these systems do not openly conflict with one another, there are differences among the five. No one system can successfully guide managers in reaching a difficult ethical decision. Hosmer suggests that managers should develop "moral reasoning" that involves the use of all five ethical systems to think through the consequences of their actions.[21] Combining this type of ethical analysis with an economic evaluation and an awareness of legal requirements can provide a foundation for business ethics (Figure 19–6).

SOCIAL RESPONSIBILITIES OF SENIOR MANAGERS AND BOARDS OF DIRECTORS

Various disclosures of corporate wrongdoing have focused attention on America's leading corporations and their chief executive. An obvious question arises: "Where were their senior managers and their boards of directors?" This question points to the underlying issue of the responsibility of both the board and senior management for ethical performance.

Responsibility of Senior Managers

Organizational culture is an important situational variable in ethical decision making (as shown in Figure 19–3). Values are often considered the bedrock of this organizational culture.[22] Peters and Waterman stated that the "real role of the chief executive is to manage the *values* of the organization."[23] Explicit recognition of ethical values by top managers is necessary to correct the myopia that typically accompanies planning for growth and profits.[24] If little explicit

FIGURE 19–5   Summary of five major ethical systems

	Nature of the Ethical Belief	*Problems in the Ethical System*
Eternal Law*	Moral standards are given in an Eternal Law, which is revealed in Scripture or apparent in nature and then interpreted by religious leaders or humanist philosophers; the belief is that everyone should act in accordance with the interpretation.	There are multiple interpretations of the Law, but no method to choose among them beyond human rationality, and human rationality needs an absolute principle or value as the basis for choice.
Utilitarian Theory	Moral standards are applied to the outcome of an action or decision; the principle is that everyone should act to generate the greatest benefits for the largest number of people.	Immoral acts can be justified if they provide substantial benefits for the majority, even at an unbearable cost or harm to the minority; an additional principle or value is needed to balance the benefit-cost equation.
Universalist Theory	Moral standards are applied to the intent of an action or decision; the principle is that everyone should act to ensure that similar decisions would be reached by others, given similar circumstances.	Immoral acts can be justified by persons who are prone to self-deception or self-importance, and there is no scale to judge between "wills"; an additional principle or value is needed to refine the Categorical Imperative concept.†
Distributive Justice	Moral standards are based upon the primacy of a single value, which is justice. Everyone should act to ensure a more equitable distribution of benefits, for this promotes individual self-respect, which is essential for social cooperation.	The primacy of the value of justice is dependent upon acceptance of the proposition that an equitable distribution of benefits ensures social cooperation.
Personal Liberty	Moral standards are based upon the primacy of a single value, which is liberty. Everyone should act to ensure greater freedom of choice, for this promotes market exchange, which is essential for social productivity.	The primacy of the value of liberty is dependent upon acceptance of the proposition that a market system of exchange ensures social productivity.

SOURCE: LaRue Hosmer, "Conclusions on Normative Philosophy," in *The Ethics of Management* (Homewood, Ill.: Irwin, 1987), p. 106. Reprinted by permission.

*Hosmer uses the concept of an Eternal Law as representative of all religious faiths. In the United States, the strongest religious tradition is the Judeo-Christian heritage. For reasoned presentations of the Christian faith, involving a minimum of theological jargon, see the following: C. S. Lewis, *Mere Christianity* (New York: Macmillan, 1960); or Paul Little, *Know Why You Believe* (Downers Grove, Ill.: Inter-Varsity Press, 1968).

†The German philosopher Immanuel Kant argued that the moral basis of ethics must be derived from the inner self by direct perception and intuition. He referred to this reasoning as being an absolute, a "categorical imperative." This phrase has been widely interpreted as meaning that "one must do only what one can will that all others should do under similar circumstances." In other words, categorical imperative is the unconditional command of conscience. For a more detailed discussion, see John Watson, *Selections from Kant's Philosophy* (New York: Macmillan, 1951; or Will Durant, *The Story of Philosophy* (New York: Simon and Schuster, 1953).

FIGURE 19–6 Foundations for business ethics

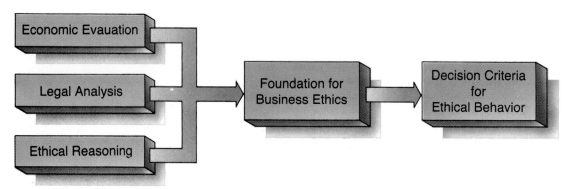

recognition is given to ethics, the resulting organizational culture makes it easy to ignore ethical considerations.[25]

Senior managers who choose to emphasize ethics and who skillfully articulate the importance of ethics promote the integration of social responsibility into the day-to-day operating decisions of the organization. Yet it is not easy to communicate these values in a way that they are clearly understood and consistently followed throughout the organization. Statements by senior managers in support of ethical values must be consistently reinforced by management decisions and management actions if the statements are to be taken seriously.[26]

Board Responsibility for Ethical Leadership

Traditionally, directors have functioned as guardians of the financial interest of stockholders, with a specific concern for earnings and dividends. Even this role has been performed in a largely passive manner. Now, in the aftermath of major business scandals, the system of corporate governance and the role of directors have become subjects of special interest.

To meet such demands, boards must extend their oversight beyond traditional matters of profits to areas of ethics and social responsibility. A concern for ethical performance is not necessarily inconsistent with stockholder interest, of course, but the connection between ethics and profits is often unclear.

We desire moral leadership from the board because as directors, they presumably have the power to require ethical performance by management. The overall organizational impact of a board which demands ethical performance is greater than that of a vice-president who does the same.

Recognition of the growing responsibility of directors is not entirely voluntary. The courts and the Securities and Exchange Commission (SEC) are actively involved in expanding areas of board responsibility. In a number of cases, the SEC has brought legal action against individual outside directors as well as against corporations. For example, the SEC named the outside directors of Wickes, a Los Angeles retailer, as aiding and abetting in frauds perpetrated by management. Stockholder lawsuits against directors and officers of Wickes were settled for $25 million, believed to be the largest claim paid for unethical conduct.[27]

In holding board members responsible, the SEC has taken the position that anyone in a position to know what is going on and to do something about it will be held liable. Overt action or direct participation in a fraud is not necessary for a judgment of liability. Directors presumably have access to the facts, or they should probe sufficiently to get the facts.

Problems in Achieving Strong Board Leadership

There are difficulties in correcting board performance to make it an effective agency for control. In practice, directors often lack the power they have in theory. To be sure, they are not powerless. From time to time, directors act decisively—for example, by dismissing a chief executive or even "blowing the whistle" on management. But the balance of power still favors the senior managers. In large corporations, this group continues to influence the selection of board members and to guide their deliberations. Harold Geneen, former chief executive of International Telephone and Telegraph (ITT), has asserted that directors cannot protect the stockholders. Geneen argues that it is impossible for outside directors to take the necessary time to develop their own solutions. Instead, these directors tend to rely on the recommendations of senior management. Geneen also holds that it is difficult for outside directors to disagree with senior management because of "all the perks heaped on them by the management they are to judge."[28]

Important in building a strong board of directors is the appointment of outside directors. These directors are usually qualified persons capable of asking tough questions and demanding responsible performance. Recently, the increasing number of lawsuits by stockholders against directors has caused insurance companies to cancel the directors' and officers' liability insurance for many firms. Without liability insurance, outside directors are personally liable for any monetary damages awarded against them in a lawsuit. As a consequence, many outside directors are resigning or refusing to serve. Several companies—such as Bank of America and Pacific Gas and Electric—have established their own liability insurance companies. The advantage in establishing an insurance unit is that premiums are tax deductible as a business expense, whereas money simply set aside in case of an eventual claim is not.[29]

Prospects for Effective Control

The prospects for managers to control ethical behavior effectively are promising. For example, many corporate leaders have recognized the importance of organizational values. Researchers have demonstrated strong, positive correlations between the sharing of organizational values and the success of organi-

WHAT IS THE PROPER ROLE FOR BOARDS OF DIRECTORS?

Generally, the responsibility of a board of directors is to review and evaluate plans developed by the organization's senior managers. To what extent should the board become involved?

A number of lawsuits have been filed against directors for failing to protect their stockholders' interests. For example, a Delaware court awarded $13 million in damages against the directors of Trans Union Corporation because of a failure to properly evaluate management's recommendation to sell the company. The Federal Deposit Insurance Corporation filed suit against more than 200 directors of various U.S. banks in 1985, citing board approval of "poor management practices."

Several prominent members of boards have argued that corporations must take risks to become profitable and that it will not be a "healthy" situation for a board to become too assertive in questioning the actions of management. Such a board could usurp the job of the chief executive. For example, Richard Behar and Mark Clifford have noted the following relationships between a visionary chief executive and his board:

□ Henry Luce started *Life* in 1936 with huge losses but continued because his board supported him.
□ Thomas Watson made a success of IBM's system 360 in 1964 without having to justify his innovative strategy to the board.
□ Chrysler's board gave Lee Iacocca a free hand during Chrysler's crisis and did not second guess his every move.

Could these three executives have succeeded with an assertive board acting in a domineering manner?

SOURCE: Adapted from Richard Behar and Mark Clifford, "Kibitzing From the Boardroom," *Forbes,* 10 February 1986, pp. 70–74.

zational strategies. Both managers and researchers have indicated that employees at all levels of the organization are aware that ethical behavior is an important element of "values." A growing number of studies, however, indicate that employees watch to see how stated ethical values are reinforced and how these values influence the actions of senior managers.[30] In other words, senior managers have to practice what they preach. Whether or not senior managers will be successful in promoting ethical decision making will depend on their own ethical orientations, their ability to communicate and reinforce ethical values, and the ethical values of their subordinates.

Certainly the law is clear that the board's responsibility is to oversee the performance of the chief executive and the salaried management team. The appointment of capable outside directors is important in achieving this responsibility. Outside directors may represent the traditional interests of stockholders by monitoring the overall effectiveness of management, rather than giving routine approval to management programs. For example, outside directors can provide a chief executive with some useful advice and counsel. One must be wary, however, of assuming that the appointment of outside directors will in itself greatly improve corporate behavior.

SUMMARY

Society expects a *social responsibility* from business corporations and other organizations in return for the right to exist. These expectations are not fixed, however, and increasing demands are being made on all organizations, especially business corporations. Although some socially desirable activities are profitable, many are costly to the corporation. Profits are essential if a corporation is to invest substantial amounts in programs for the public good. Within the limits of their financial resources, corporations may choose to do little or much. To evaluate their social performance, some firms now use a method of assessment known as a *social audit.*

Ethical decisions are involved in all aspects of organizational life. The ethics of management involves determining what is right and just in actions and decisions that affect other people. Managers are faced with maintaining a balance between an economic performance and meeting the organization's social responsibilities.

Many top managers have attempted to extend ethical standards within their organizations by using *formal ethical codes.* Even though most corporations now use codes, there is disagreement about their effectiveness.

Ethical decision making in organizations involves an interaction among an individual's level of moral development and certain situational and individual variables. Managers can develop ethical reasoning that involves the use of various ethical systems to think through the consequences of their actions. Combining an ethical analysis with an economic evaluation and an awareness of legal requirements can provide a foundation for business ethics.

Both senior managers and boards of directors have major responsibilities for providing social and moral leadership in organizational life. The Securities and Exchange Commission has brought legal action against individual directors and officers who failed to display such leadership. Senior managers can improve the integration of ethics into the day-to-day operating decisions of the organization by emphasizing the importance of ethical behavior. Board membership and the choice of outside directors are important in determining the effectiveness of the board's moral leadership.

KEY CONCEPTS

Social responsibility

Social contract

Pareto optimality

Social audit

Formal ethical code

Cognitive moral development

Ethical dilemma

Eternal law

Distributive justice

Moral reasoning

Outside directors

DISCUSSION QUESTIONS

1. Using Figure 19–1, explain the nature of the *social contract*. How does this concept relate to corporate management?
2. Several approaches have been developed with respect to how managers should respond to changing social demands. Compare and contrast the "conscience" approach and the "what is good for business" approach.
3. What is the profit impact of socially responsible corporate action?
4. How does market competition affect corporate decision making on social issues?
5. Explain how managerial *ethical dilemmas* occur.
6. What is the relationship between profit maximization and *social responsibility?*
7. Explain what is meant by *Pareto optimality*. How can this concept be used in a *social responsibility* sense?
8. How does a *social audit* differ from a financial audit?
9. Is there any value in using a *formal code of ethics?*
10. Explain how ethical decisions can be made in an organization using Figure 19–3.
11. How can managers develop ethical reasoning?
12. What general viewpoint has been expressed by the Securities and Exchange Commission regarding the responsibilities of directors for the ethical conduct of a corporation?
13. How can senior managers influence ethical decision making?
14. Explain the relative strength of an inside versus an outside board in overseeing company morality.

NOTES

1. James R. O'Toole, *Vanguard Management* (New York: Doubleday, 1985), 16.
2. Saul W. Gellerman, "Why 'Good' Managers Make Bad Ethical Choices," *Harvard Business Review* 64 (July-August 1986): 85.
3. Theodore Levitt, "The Dangers of Social Responsibility," *Harvard Business Review* 36 (September-October 1958): 48.
4. Ian Maitland, "The Limits of Business Self-Regulation," *California Management Review* 3 (Spring 1985): 132–47.
5. Ibid., p. 133.

6. Milton Friedman, "The Social Responsibility of Business is to Increase Its Profits," *New York Times Magazine,* 13 September 1970, pp. 33, 122–25.

7. Milton Friedman, *Capitalism and Freedom* (Chicago: University of Chicago Press, 1962): 113.

8. LaRue Hosmer, "Moral Problems in Microeconomic Theory," in *The Ethics of Management* (Homewood, Ill.: Irwin, 1987): 37.

9. The concept of Pareto optimality was developed by Valfredo Pareto, an Italian sociologist and economist. For an expanded discussion see Donald McCloskey, *The Applied Theory of Price* (New York: Macmillan, 1982), 401–5; and Edmund S. Phelps, *Political Economy* (New York: Norton, 1985), 214–15.

10. Hosmer, *The Ethics of Management,* pp. 34–37.

11. James Ellis and Judith Dobrzynski, "General Dynamics Under Fire," *Business Week,* 25 March 1985, pp. 70–76; "What Did Hutton's Managers Know—And When Did They Know It?" *Business Week,* 20 May 1985, pp. 110–12; "Johnson and Johnson Voluntarily Removes Tylenol from Public Use," *Wall Street Journal,* 18 February 1986.

12. Archie B. Carroll and George W. Beiler, "Landmarks in the Evolution of the Social Audit," *Academy of Management Journal* 18 (September 1975): 589–99.

13. Bernard J. White and B. Ruth Montgomery, "Corporate Codes of Conduct," *California Management Review* 23 (Winter 1980): 80–87.

14. Douglas S. Sherwin, "The Ethical Roots of the Business System," *Harvard Business Review* 61 (November-December 1983): 183–92.

15. "EDS: A Code of Conduct," 1986 Company Records. (EDS has maintained this code of conduct while being a part of General Motors.)

16. Linda K. Trevino, "Ethical Decision Making in Organizations: A Person-Situation Interactionist Model," *Academy of Management Review* 11 (July 1986): 601–17.

17. Ibid., p. 603.

18. Ibid., p. 606.

19. James C. Gibbs and Kenneth F. Widaman, *Social Intelligence: Measuring the Development of Sociomoral Reflection* (Englewood Cliffs, N.J.: Prentice-Hall, 1982), p. 215.

20. For a more complete description of how the different variables in the model interact see Trevino, "Ethical Decision Making," 601–15.

21. Hosmer, *The Ethics of Management,* pp. 107–9.

22. Barry Z. Posner, James M. Kouzes, and Warren H. Schmidt, "Shared Values Make A Difference: An Empirical Test of Corporate Culture," *Human Resource Management* 24 (Fall 1985): 293–309.

23. Thomas J. Peters and Robert H. Waterman, Jr., *In Search of Excellence: Lessons from America's Best Run Corporations* (New York: Harper & Row, 1982), p. 26.

24. John I. Reynolds, "Improving Business Ethics: The President's Lonely Task," *Business and Society* 19 (Fall 1978): 14–19.

25. Robert V. Krikorian, "Ethical Conduct: An Aid to Management?" An address to Albion College, printed by Rexnord Corporation (Brookfield, Wis.: 1985).

26. Justin G. Longenecker, "Management Priorities and Management Ethics," *Journal of Business Ethics* 4 (1985): 65–70.

27. David B. Hilder, "Risky Business: Companies Are Finding It Difficult Now to Obtain Liability Insurance for Their Directors," *Wall Street Journal,* 10 July 1985.

28. Harold S. Geneen, "Why Directors Can't Protect the Shareholders," *Forbes,* 17 September 1984, p. 42.

29. David B. Hilder, "Liability Insurance is Difficult to Find Now For Directors, Officers," *Wall Street Journal,* 10 July 1985.

30. D. V. Seibert and William Proctor, *The Ethical Executive* (New York: Simon and Schuster, 1984), p. 122.

SUPPLEMENTARY READING

Andre, Renee. "The Scientist, the Artist, and the Evangelist." *New Management* 2 (1985): 16–21.

Andrews, Kenneth R. "Difficulties in Overseeing Ethical Policy." *California Management Review* 26 (Summer 1984): 133–38.

Auerbach, Joseph. "The Poletown Dilemma." *Harvard Business Review* 63 (May-June 1985): 93–99.

Barach, Jeffrey A. "The Ethics of Hardball." *California Management Review* 27 (Winter 1985): 132–40.

Baruch, Hurd. "The Foreign Corrupt Practices Act." *Harvard Business Review* 57 (January-February 1979): 32–50.

Brody, Michael. "Listen to Your Whistle Blower." *Fortune* (24 November 1986): 77–82.

Dayton, Kenneth N. "Corporate Governance: The Other Side of the Coin." *Harvard Business Review* 62 (January-February 1984): 34–37.

Denison, Daniel R. "Bringing Corporate Culture To The Bottom Line." *Organizational Dynamics* (Autumn 1984): 4–22.

Dierkes, Meinolt, and Antal, Ariane B. "Whither Corporate Social Reporting: Is It Time to Legislate?" *California Management Review* 28 (Spring 1986): 106–21.

Foote, Susan B. "Corporate Responsibility in a Changing Legal Environment." *California Management Review* 26 (Spring 1984): 217–28.

Goodpaster, Kenneth, and Matthews, John B., Jr. "Can A Corporation Have A Conscience?" *Harvard Business Review* 60 (January-February 1982): 128–34.

Hosmer, LaRue T. "The Other 288: Why A Majority of Our Schools of Business Administration Do Not Offer a Course in Business Ethics." *Journal of Business Ethics* 4 (1985): 17–22.

Jackall, Robert. "Moral Mazes: Bureaucracy and Managerial Work." *Harvard Business Review* 61 (September-October 1983): 118–30.

Jones, Peter T. "Sanctions, Incentives, and Corporate Behavior." *California Management Review* 27 (Spring 1985): 119–31.

Klonoski, Richard. "Moral Responsibilities of Stockholders." *Journal of Business Ethics* 5 (October 1986): 385–91.

McCoy, Bowen H. "The Parable of the Sadhu." *Harvard Business Review* 61 (September-October 1983): 103–6.

Mintzberg, Henry. "The Case for Corporate Social Responsibility." *Journal of Business Strategy* 14 (1984): 3–15.

Nader, Ralph. "Reforming Corporate Governance." *California Management Review* 26 (Summer 1984): 126–32.

Paine, Lynn S. "Ethics and Values: Twelve Executives Speak Out." *Directors and Boards* 11 (Fall 1986): 31–34.

Post, James E. "Assessing the Nestle Boycott: Corporate Accountability and Human Rights." *California Management Review* 27 (Winter 1985): 113–31.

Sashkin, Marshall. "Participative Management Is An Ethical Imperative." *Organizational Dynamics* (Spring 1984): 4–22.

Stalnaker, Armand. "Selecting Directors: Outsiders, Insiders, and Conflict of Interest." *The Corporate Board* (November-December 1986): 1–7.

Waters, James; Bird, Frederick; and Chant, Peter. "Everyday Moral Issues Experienced by Managers." *Journal of Business Ethics* 5 (October 1986): 373–85.

Williams, Oliver. "Who Cast the First Stone?" *Harvard Business Review* 62 (September-October 1984): 151–60.

Velasquez, Manuel; Moberg, Dennis; and Cavanagh, Gerald. "Organizational Statesmanship and Dirty Politics: Ethical Guidelines For the Organizational Politician." *Organizational Dynamics* (Autumn 1983): 65–80.

WALTER STANTON: EMPLOYEE RESPONSIBILITY AND THE USE OF TIME

Walter Stanton, in discussing the responsibility of an employee to his or her employer with a group of MBA students at a southwestern business school, was surprised at the number of questions he received and the diversity of opinion he found among his students regarding the use of time on and off the job. To give some focus to the discussion, he asked each student to describe a specific incident in the student's own experience in which this question had arisen. The following are a few of the incidents reported by the students.

Jerry Donaldson

Last summer I was employed in a service station in my home town in Idaho. Besides selling petroleum products, this station had a Big O Tire and Honda motorcycle franchise. My responsibilities included

pumping gas, fixing tires, greasing cars, making minor motorcycle repairs, and assembling new motorcycles which came in crates from Japan. I also assisted the mechanic and the manager whenever they needed me.

Early in the summer, the manager decided that it would be profitable to stay open 24 hours a day. Many tourists traveled through our town during the summer months, and they had no place to purchase gas after 10:00 P.M. The manager also thought that the night man could clean up the station, do the necessary motorcycle repairs, and assemble at least two motorcycles each night shift.

Although I was reluctant to work the 10:00 P.M. to 7:00 A.M. shift, I finally agreed to rotate every other week with another of the employees.

During my first week of working night shifts, I went over the detailed list of duties for the night man to perform and planned how much time I had to accomplish each assigned job. I tried to use all of the time

Case prepared by Professor Clinton L. Oaks of Brigham Young University.

allotted to each job, even if it meant doing the job very slowly. This method allowed me to be busy the whole night and made the time go faster. I also found that if I wasn't busy all the time, I became very bored and drowsy. Therefore I always tried to stay busy.

About the third week of working night shifts, I started to see how fast I could finish all of the assigned tasks. I worked out a whole series of shortcuts for cleaning the station and found that I could do it in an hour less than it had taken me previously. I also found that I could up my efficiency in working motorcycle repairs and in assembling new Hondas. I made a game out of pushing myself and found that I could do all the jobs and still have at least two hours left after they were all completed. At first I did not know what to do during the two hours, and they went by very slowly. I have always enjoyed tinkering with my car, however, so I decided that during this spare time I would wash and wax it, work on the tune-up and make all of the little repairs that it needed. I always felt a little guilty working on my car while I was getting paid, but since I was doing a good job of finishing all the assigned tasks, I felt I was justified in using any spare time on my own projects.

My boss evidently was pleased with my work because he frequently commended me on doing my job well. Several times I heard him "chewing out" the other employee for not doing a good job. I never told him that I worked on my car, but since I had him get some parts for me I was pretty sure he knew what I was doing. He never said anything to me about it.

Towards the end of the summer, my boss announced that the corporation that owned this station had decided that it would be beneficial to the company if every employee in the company received a polygraph test at least once a year. They had all of their employees sign a statement that they agreed to take the test.

Early one Saturday morning when I arrived at work, I discovered that the test administrator was at our station and that I was to take the test that morning. I was not alarmed since I had been honest in putting all money that I had received in the till and making a proper receipt out after each sale.

After putting all of the equipment on me and turning on his tape recorder, the man began asking me some general questions regarding my honesty. I felt very comfortable telling him I had never stolen any money from the till and that I always accomplished tasks that were assigned to me. Towards the end of the test he asked, "Do you make good use of all of your time at work?" Suddenly, I felt very uncomfortable and could feel my heart start to beat a lot faster.

Questions

1. What should Jerry Donaldson tell the polygraph operator?
2. Is the company's use of the polygraph ethical?

Allen Chan

After I finished my undergraduate work in mathematics and computer science, my wife persuaded me to take a job for a couple of years so that we could pay off some of our bills and get ahead a little before I started on my MBA. She was also concerned that I wasn't spending enough time with my two young sons. Between the demands of my course work and a part-time job, I usually left early in the morning and often was not home until after they had been put to bed.

One of my undergraduate professors was instrumental in getting me a job with

Nelson Data Processing. I understood before I started that they were a hard-driving firm with a reputation for high quality work. Once aboard, I found that the company had a large backlog and that management was encouraging everyone to put in overtime, for which they paid a generous hourly rate on top of the employee's salary.

We needed the money and the work was interesting. Before long, I found myself working late almost every night. Barbara, my wife, didn't say much at first, but I could tell she wasn't happy with the way things were working out. Finally one day she said, "Allen, you were spending more time at home when you were in school than you are now." I mumbled something about "trying to cut it down a little" and dropped the subject.

The next day at noon when another employee and I were on our way out to grab a sandwich, I mentioned that my wife was unhappy about all the time I was spending away from home. He said, "Look, Allen, you don't have to punch a time clock on those extra hours. A lot of the guys just take their work home with them. Keep track of your time and turn it in just like you do now. I'm not sure what the company policy is, but I have been doing this every so often for several months now, and nobody has ever said anything about it."

The more I thought about the idea of doing my overtime at home, the better I liked it. I could spend the early evening with the family and then, after the boys were to bed, I could really get some work done. As I had expected, Barbara was elated when I explained to her what I was going to do.

The first few nights I found it hard to get up to speed again after letting down for dinner and roughhousing with the kids. As I got into the swing of it, however, I found

that since there were no distractions, as there often were at the office, I could do a lot more at home in an hour than I was doing at work. Whenever I needed someone to help with the checking or sorting, Barbara was always available and seemed to enjoy working with me. I found that there were some things she could do faster and more accurately than I could. One night after we had finished a particularly long and involved task in about half the time it would ordinarily have taken me, I said, "Barbara, there ought to be some way to put you on the payroll." She laughed and said, "Why don't you just increase the number of hours put in for yourself to cover it?"

Questions

1. Should Allen Chan report his wife's working time as part of his own working time and thereby receive compensation for it?
2. Does the arrangement whereby work is performed at home present any particular ethical problems?

Lupe Diaz

I had been working for Patterson Engineering for nearly a year when I decided to come back and get my MBA. About three weeks before school was to start, I gave my supervisor, Jim, who was really a great boss, my two-week notice. Since he and I had talked a number of times about my going on to school as a preparation for a move into management, he was not at all surprised. He asked me to come in his office for a few minutes later that morning to make plans for my departure. I thought he might be concerned about several things I was working on that would be hard to turn over to anyone until

I completed my present segment. I wasn't too concerned, however, because I had worked out a careful schedule and I figured I would just have time to do it all in those last two weeks.

When I entered my supervisor's office, he said, "Lupe, you have done a great job for us, and when you finish your education, we want you to keep us in mind. You said that school started right after the first of next month?" I nodded, and he went on to say, "I imagine that you have a lot of work to do to get packed and moved, don't you?" I replied, "Boy, I'll say! Moving is always such a hassle. We want to get out of our apartment by the fifteenth so that we can get our deposit back. I would like to have allowed myself a few more days, but when we figured out what we would need for school this year, we found that the money from these last two weeks was really crucial."

My supervisor smiled and leaned back in his chair. "Yes," he said, "I remember how is was. I think, though, that I can help you out. According to my records, you have accumulated about twelve days' sick leave. Is that right?" "Yes," I answered. "Well, as you know, the firm doesn't pay any sick leave unless you are actually sick. In your case, though, you are going to be sick—sick of moving. I want you to spend this afternoon acquainting Tom with where you are on each one of your projects. Then each morning for the next two weeks I want you to call in sick. If there is any question about it, I'll cover for you."

That night I thought a lot about what Jim had said—but I just didn't feel good about it. Tom was a good man, but it would take someone else at least twice as long to finish the things I was working on as it would take me. One of the projects was the kind that someone new would almost have to start over. The executives at Patterson had really been good to me in terms of the kinds of assignments they had given me—and I had been given a pay raise every six months instead of every year, as was typical with new employees.

I went in early the next morning and was right in the middle of my most important project when Jim came by. He frowned when he saw me at my desk. "I thought I told you to take these two weeks off. I don't want to see you in here after today!"

Question

1. Should Lupe Diaz accept her supervisor's offer and take sick leave during the time she is moving?

Lorraine Adams

When I was an undergraduate, I worked summers on an electronic composer for Brown Publishing. This is a typewriter with a memory which enables it to type course material in columns and justified (flush right) margins. Because it is difficult to determine how long it takes to type material into memory and play it back, I often went for four hours without taking the fifteen-minute break we were supposed to have both morning and afternoon. Some of the other women who had the same problem kept track of the breaks they didn't take and then used them as justification for leaving a half hour early or arriving a half hour late, recording their time as if they had left or arrived at the normal time. One woman even saved hers for two weeks and then took an afternoon off to do some shopping. I am sure that this was contrary to company policy, but our supervisor was a very relaxed and friendly woman who never seemed to notice when someone was gone.

Another problem I had with breaks is, what can constitute a break? If a friend, who wasn't an employee of the company, dropped in for a few minutes, I always thought of that as a break. But what if some other employee who is tired, bored, or worried comes by and spends a few minutes talking about her work, her plans for the weekend, her current boyfriend, or some personal problem? Should you count that as a break? One morning our supervisor talked to me for twenty minutes about job opportunities for women with MBAs. Was that a break?

Accounting for my time has always been a problem for me. Last summer, I worked as a department manager in a branch of a large department store in Los Angeles. A number of the department managers would arrive at 8:00, as we were supposed to do, and then take off across the mall to a coffee shop "to make plans for the day." They usually got back just before the store opened at 9:30. I went with them a couple of times and found that if they discussed anything related to their work in the store, it was only an incidental part of their conversation. A couple of these guys would also regularly take up to an hour and a half for lunch and then check out right after five. Since we didn't have to check in and out for breaks or for lunch, their time card would show an eight-hour day. When I said something to one of them about it one day, he answered, "Listen, Lorraine, summer is a slack time around here. You ought to be here during the Christmas rush. We work a lot of hours then that we don't get paid for. The store owes us a chance to relax a little when the heat is off."

Questions

1. What constitutes a legitimate break? Is it ethical to save up breaks and use them at other times?

2. Are the department managers acting ethically in taking extended coffee breaks and lunch hours?

Robert Jeffries

Before I came back to school, I worked for two years for a branch of Jefferson Sporting Goods. Jefferson had five large stores located in different metropolitan areas in the state and did a large volume in men's and women's sports clothes. Our branch wasn't the largest in the chain but would have been second or third.

The store manager, Rand Walker, had been manager since the store was opened. He had previously had soft goods experience with several other stores and really knew that part of the business.

We got along really well. Not long after I came to work, Rand put me in charge of the shoe department. Later he made me manager of the men's clothing department, and, a year later, he made me assistant manager. He always saw that I got a substantial raise after each six month review. He seemed to have a lot of trust in me. I noticed, for example, that even before I had been there for a year, he shared a lot of confidential figures with me that he didn't show to any of the other managers.

One day Rand called me into his office. He had me shut the door so that no one else would hear our conversation. "Bob," he said, "I've got a chance to buy the Blue Hills Pant Depot and I want to know what you think about it." Blue Hills was in a suburb about ten miles north of our store. Rand proceeded to tell me the details of the offer. "It looks like a good deal as far as I can tell," I said, "but would it be as profitable for you as Jefferson's has been?" I was assuming he would quit when he bought the store. "Oh," he said, "I'm not going to quit unless Elliot Jefferson, the owner, tells me to." I was surprised because it looked to me like a clear case of conflict of interest. I knew that Rand had been looking at some outside investments since he had done very well at Jefferson's, but I hadn't thought he would consider buying another clothing store.

I didn't say much after that, trying not to get too involved with what was happening. Many times Rand would come to me to ask my opinion on certain clothing lines. He asked me to give him a list of the top five pant vendors and their salespersons' names and addresses, which I did.

Several weeks later, I asked Rand if he had made a decision on the store. He said he had gone ahead and bought it. He said he put it under his wife's name, and that she was going to run it; that way he felt he could justify continuing his work at Jefferson's.

After that, I noticed that Rand spent a lot more time in his office and less time out on the floor. Occasionally, I would drop into his office to see him and find him paying invoices and doing book work for his pant store. I never asked anything about it and, in fact, tried to keep our conversations on problems that needed attention at Jefferson's.

This situation remained unchanged for several months. I concentrated my attention on doing my job and kept my thoughts to myself. Many of the other employees kept asking me about the Pant Depot. They wanted to know, for example, who really owned it, Rand or his wife. I would just tell them I didn't know.

In October, Rand came to me again and said that he was planning on acquiring a second pant store in another suburb about fifteen miles south of our store. A clothing store in that town was going out of business, and he had a chance to rent the building. This really surprised me. I kiddingly asked if he was planning to open a whole chain. He replied that he would like to open several stores similar to the one he had already and that all he needed was to find good locations where he could rent store space cheaply.

On November 1, Rand opened his second store. It immediately became a success, almost equalling the volume of the first.

After that, I seldom saw Rand on the floor. He was either in his office or gone. I found myself trying to cover for him when we would get calls from the home office. This situation made me very uncomfortable. When he did come in, he seemed a lot more absent-minded about things in our store.

I wondered how much Elliot Jefferson knew (or suspected) about Rand's involvement in these other stores. I wondered, too, if I should tell the home office why our reports were slow and why our sales had stopped increasing as rapidly as they had when Rand spent full time managing the store.

Questions

1. Did Rand Walker experience a sufficient conflict of interest to constitute an ethical problem?
2. Does Robert Jeffries have an obligation to report Walker's outside business involvement to the top management of Jefferson Sporting Goods?

PREVENTING FUTURE PRICE-FIXING—THE PRESIDENT'S DILEMMA

In 1976, twenty-three paper companies were indicted by a federal grand jury for price-fixing in the sale of corrugated containers, the paperboard shipping boxes used to package and protect consumer and industrial goods. Corrugated containers are manufactured primarily from heavy kraft paper, consisting of an inner liner of alternating ridges and grooves laminated to outer liners. The kraft paper is produced at a paper mill and then shipped in large rolls to a corrugated container manufacturing plant. It is difficult to differentiate corrugated boxes on the basis of quality, so most box plants have been designed to provide prompt delivery. As a result, price becomes the basis of competition. During periods of industry overcapacity, prices sink to low levels.

The process of manufacturing corrugated boxes has almost been totally automated, and labor costs are very low. Plant equipment is high speed and technically complex, with the majority of costs being fixed. Cost per corrugated box decreases rapidly as volume increases because of the high degree of fixed costs. Box plant managers are paid a bonus based on plant profitability. The resultant strategy is to keep output as high as possible and to maintain reasonable sales prices. Both box plant managers and their sales personnel are continually tempted to make agreements with their competitors to ensure that sales prices remain at reasonable levels.

Beginning in 1960, various box plant managers of the twenty-three paper companies participated in a conspiracy to allocate customers and fix prices, thereby violating the Sherman Antitrust Act. Following the 1976 indictment, each paper company was liable for a maximum fine of $1 million, and each chief executive officer could be sentenced to a five-year prison term. The individual managers also faced severe fines and jail sentences. Many customers were threatening to sue the paper companies if the prices had indeed been fixed.

Twenty-two of the firms pleaded no contest to the price-fixing charges. A plea of no contest is considered to be equivalent to a guilty plea, but the admission of guilt cannot be used in any subsequent civil lawsuit.

A federal judge fined each of the paper companies $50,000 (considered to be low) and imposed the following strict provision: each year, for ten years, a senior officer from each of the twenty-two companies was required to appear before the judge and demonstrate that the executive's company was not violating any provisions of the Sherman Antitrust Act in selling corrugated boxes. The judge stipulated that if infractions occurred, he would impose maximum sentences on the respective chief executive.

Question

1. As chief executive, what system would you establish to demonstrate that price-fixing no longer occurs in your box plants?

Case adapted from ''Paper Companies Have to Pay For Antitrust Violations,'' *Pulp and Paper* (November 1976): 23–27 and ''Unique Antitrust Settlement Imposed On Paper Companies,'' *Business Week* (29 September 1976): 36–40. Paper company antitrust violations are also described by LaRue Hosmer in *The Ethics of Management* (Homewood, IL: Irwin, 1987), pp. 171–173.

PART SIX

OPPORTUNITIES IN MANAGEMENT

INTERNATIONALIZATION OF BUSINESS

The Nature of International Business □
International Management vs. Domestic
Management □ Impact of International
Business on U.S. Domestic Markets □
Rise of the Multinational Corporation

ENVIRONMENT OF THE
MULTINATIONAL CORPORATION

Political and Legal Elements □ Host
Country Relationships

MANAGEMENT PROCESSES IN
INTERNATIONAL BUSINESS

Development of Global Strategies □
Management Selection □ Technology
Transfer □ Cross-Cultural Management

JAPANESE MANAGEMENT

Japanese Management Techniques □
Japanese vs. American Management

Summary □ Key Concepts □ Discussion
Questions □ Notes □ Supplementary
Reading

CASES: Cuidad Del Carmen Products □
The Road to Hell

This chapter will enable you to

□ Describe the growth of international
business and understand how U.S.
domestic markets are affected.

□ Identify the political, legal, and cultural
environment of international business.

□ Understand the management
processes involved in international
business.

□ Be aware of cross-cultural management
patterns and understand the techniques
of Japanese management.

CHAPTER 20
MANAGEMENT IN THE
INTERNATIONAL ARENA

International business is considered to be those business activities that cross national boundaries. In this chapter, we explore the differences between international and domestic management, consider the impact of international business on U.S. domestic markets, study the environment of international business, and focus on the management processes involved in international business. The various business practices that exist among the many different countries engaged in international business are not compared, but the techniques of Japanese managers are presented in the section on cross-cultural management. This particular topic was chosen because of the success of the Japanese in international business and because the American public and most of the world have become intrigued with Japanese management practices.

INTERNATIONALIZATION OF BUSINESS

The world economy is dominated by the activities of giant companies, usually called *multinationals* or *international enterprises*. In 1985 there were 385 foreign and U.S. companies with annual sales that exceeded $5 billion. Twenty-three of these corporations had sales of over $20 billion.[1] The largest corporations—including Exxon, IBM, General Motors, Royal Dutch/Shell, Mitsubishi, British Petroleum, and Mobil—have annual sales that exceed the gross national products of many nations, as shown in Table 20–1.

TABLE 20-1 A comparison of the annual sales of the largest multinationals and various countries' GNPs

Rank		GNP or Sales (billions)	Rank		GNP or Sales (billions)
1	United States	3915.4	51	Pakistan	36.2
2	USSR	NA	52	Greece	35.3
3	Japan	1366.1	53	Hong Kong	33.8
4	West Germany	667.9	54	Philippines	32.6
5	France	526.6	55	Egypt	32.2
6	United Kingdom	474.2	56	Malaysia	31.9
7	Italy	371.1	57	DuPont*	29.2
8	Canada	347.4	58	General Electric*	28.3
9	China	318.9	59	Amoco*	27.3
10	Brazil	222.0	60	Toyota*	27.1
11	India	194.8	61	Libya	27.0
12	Australia	171.2	62	United Arab Emirates	26.4
13	Spain	168.8	63	Kuwait	24.8
14	Mexico	163.8	64	ENI*	24.5
15	Netherlands	132.9	65	New Zealand	23.7
16	Switzerland	105.2	66	IRI Group*	23.5
17	Saudi Arabia	102.1	67	Hitachi*	22.7
18	Sweden	99.1	68	Unilever*	21.6
19	General Motors*	96.4	69	Chrysler*	21.2
20	Korea	88.4	70	Israel	21.1
21	Exxon*	86.7	71	Matsushita Electric*	20.9
22	Indonesia	86.6	72	Hungary	20.7
23	Belgium	83.2	73	Pemex*	20.4
24	Royal Dutch Shell*	81.8	74	Toyo Menka Kaisha*	20.2
25	Poland	79.0	75	Elf-Aquitaine*	20.1
26	Nigeria	75.9	76	Portugal	20.1
27	Mitsui*	72.1	77	ITT*	20.0
28	Mitsubishi*	70.5	78	Safeway*	19.6
29	Austria	69.1	79	Francaise des Petroles*	19.6
30	South Africa	65.3	80	Atlantic Richfield*	19.5
31	Argentina	65.1	81	Singapore	19.0
32	C. Itoh*	59.6	82	Nissan Motors*	18.9
33	Norway	57.6	83	Nichimen*	18.2
34	Denmark	57.3	84	Phillips Group*	18.1
35	Mobil*	57.1	85	Volkswagenwerk*	17.9
36	Marubeni Group*	56.1	86	Peru	17.8
37	Turkey	56.1	87	Siemens*	17.8
38	Algeria	55.2	88	Daimler-Benz*	17.8
39	Sumitomo*	54.5	89	Kanematsu-Gosho*	17.6
40	Venezuela	53.8	90	USX*	17.4
41	Finland	53.5	91	Ireland	17.3
42	British Petroleum*	53.1	92	Nestle*	17.1
43	Ford*	52.8	93	Syria	17.1
44	IBM*	50.1	94	BASF*	16.2
45	Yugoslavia	47.4	95	Veba Group*	16.1
46	Texaco*	46.3	96	Puerto Rico	15.9
47	Thailand	42.1	97	Samsung*	15.7
48	Chevron*	41.7	98	Bayer*	15.6
49	Nissho Iwai Corp.*	37.7	99	Tennoco*	15.4
50	Columbia	37.6	100	Toshiba*	15.2

SOURCE: *1987 World Bank Atlas* (Washington, D.C.: World Bank), pp. 19–21; and *Forbes*, 28 July 1985, pp. 176–207.

*Multinational corporation

The Nature of International Business

International organizations have existed for a long time. For example, international trade occurred between Egypt and the Phoenician city of Byblos as long ago as 2800 B.C.; the fifteenth-century Venetian city-state was heavily involved in international finance; and many large international trading companies, such as the Hudson Bay Company and the Dutch East India Company, developed commercial operations on many continents during the seventeenth century. But it was not until the late nineteenth and early twentieth centuries that large, specialized corporations appeared that amassed great concentrations of economic resources and near-monopoly power with operations in many countries.[2]

International business, now considered a distinct field of management, deals with business activities that cross national boundaries, including the movement of goods, services, capital, and personnel as well as transfers of technology, data, and information.[3] Two other terms, *foreign business* and *comparative business,* are sometimes used as synonyms for international business. Foreign business refers to domestic operations within a foreign country, such as GM's assembly plant in Mexico City. Comparative business focuses on the similarities and differences among international business systems, such as Japanese management versus American management styles.[4]

There is no universally accepted definition for international business, as evidenced by the number of definitions that can be found in the business literature. At one end of the spectrum, international business is said to occur when organizations buy or sell goods and services across two or more national boundaries, even if management is located in a single country. At the other end of the spectrum, international business is equated with large business firms that have operating units outside of their own country. In the middle are various institutional arrangements, such as joint ventures,* that provide for managerial direction of the activity occurring abroad but exclude an ownership control of the business carrying on the activity.[5]

International Management vs. Domestic Management

Most of this text has focused on management in a domestic setting. International management is not just domestic management on a grander scale. Rather, the differences involve operating effectively in:[6]

- □ National markets that vary greatly in structure, population, and area
- □ Disparate economic and cultural conditions
- □ Circumstances of varying geographical distances
- □ Situations in which people have different languages, expectations, value systems, and laws.

---

*Various international business arrangements are discussed by Richard W. Wright, "Evolving Business Arrangements," edited by K. C. Dhawn, Hamid Etemad, and Richard Wright in *International Business: A Canadian Perspective* (Don Mills, Ontario: Addison-Wesley, 1981), pp. 490–505.

FIGURE 20–1 Variables affecting the international arena

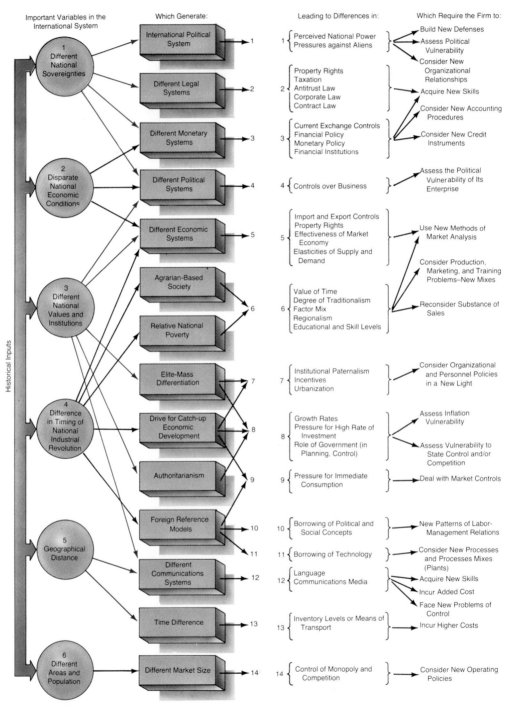

Important Variables in the International System

1 Different National Sovereignties

2 Disparate National Economic Conditions

3 Different National Values and Institutions

4 Difference in Timing of National Industrial Revolution

5 Geographical Distance

6 Different Areas and Population

Historical Inputs

Which Generate:

International Political System — 1

Different Legal Systems — 2

Different Monetary Systems — 3

Different Political Systems — 4

Different Economic Systems — 5

Agrarian-Based Society

Relative National Poverty — 6

Elite-Mass Differentiation — 7

Drive for Catch-up Economic Development — 8

Authoritarianism — 9

Foreign Reference Models — 10

— 11

Different Communications Systems — 12

Time Difference — 13

Different Market Size — 14

Leading to Differences in:

1 { Perceived National Power
Pressures against Aliens

2 { Property Rights
Taxation
Antitrust Law
Corporate Law
Contract Law

3 { Current Exchange Controls
Financial Policy
Monetary Policy
Financial Institutions

4 { Controls over Business

5 { Import and Export Controls
Property Rights
Effectiveness of Market Economy
Elasticities of Supply and Demand

6 { Value of Time
Degree of Traditionalism
Factor Mix
Regionalism
Educational and Skill Levels

7 { Institutional Paternalism
Incentives
Urbanization

8 { Growth Rates
Pressure for High Rate of Investment
Role of Government (in Planning, Control)

9 { Pressure for Immediate Consumption

10 { Borrowing of Political and Social Concepts

11 { Borrowing of Technology

12 { Language
Communications Media

13 { Inventory Levels or Means of Transport

14 { Control of Monopoly and Competition

Which Require the Firm to:

Build New Defenses

Assess Political Vulnerability

Consider New Organizational Relationships

Acquire New Skills

Consider New Accounting Procedures

Consider New Credit Instruments

Assess the Political Vulnerability of Its Enterprise

Use New Methods of Market Analysis

Consider Production, Marketing, and Training Problems–New Mixes

Reconsider Substance of Sales

Consider Organizational and Personnel Policies in a New Light

Assess Inflation Vulnerability

Assess Vulnerability to State Control and/or Competition

Deal with Market Controls

New Patterns of Labor-Management Relations

Consider New Processes and Processes Mixes (Plants)

Acquire New Skills

Incur Added Cost

Face New Problems of Control

Incur Higher Costs

Consider New Operating Policies

SOURCE: From INTERNATIONALIZATION OF BUSINESS: AN INTRODUCTION by Richard D. Robinson.
Copyright © 1984 by CBS College Publishing. Reprinted by permission of Holt, Rinehart & Winston, Inc.
NOTE: Many important relationships are not charted here. This scheme is presented only as an illustration.

Domestic management may be considered merely as a special case within the much larger international system.[7]

Despite these differences in definition, we can still use general management principles in studying international management.[8] Figure 20–1 indicates how certain variables in the international arena require a firm to engage in certain actions. For example, different national sovereignties generate an international political system, different legal systems, different monetary systems, and different political systems.

Different monetary systems lead to differences in current-exchange controls, financial policy, monetary policy, and financial institutions. These differences require the firm to acquire new skills, develop new accounting procedures, and consider new credit instruments.

Impact of International Business on U.S. Domestic Markets

American companies do not have a monopoly on business transacted in the United States. German steel, Japanese autos, and French tires compete with American industry in its own home territory. Furthermore, foreign competition in the domestic market has expanded significantly during recent years, particularly in certain product areas. For example, Table 20–2 reveals how some foreign goods have swamped U.S. industry, Table 20–3 describes the increasing amount of selected commodities imported by the United States, and Table 20–4 presents the twenty-five largest foreign investors in the United States during 1985. All of these figures demonstrate the intensifying foreign competition some American firms face.

In early 1987, the U.S. government imposed 100 percent tariffs on a small portion of Japanese imports because the Japanese were suspected of dumping microchips in the United States. *Dumping* is selling a product for less than the cost of making it. When manufacturers turn out more goods than customers want, they often sell the products in other countries at very cheap prices rather than throw the products away. The Commerce Department, in early 1987, estimated that Japanese microchips were selling in world markets at 40 percent to 60 percent of their costs.

Although many American executives believe that Japanese trade policies are unfair, these managers realize that important trade interdependencies exist between the United States and Japan. For example, 38.5 percent of Japan's exports are consumed by Americans, and 10 percent of the U.S. deficit is financed by Japanese investors. Trade experts state that in an all-out trade war between Japan and the United States, Japan would suffer more. Japan has to import to survive; without American markets, unacceptable levels of unemployment would result. On the other hand, the U.S. economy would be buffeted by higher interest rates and increased inflation. Also, many U.S. executives favor a free trade policy.* The revenues of many major U.S. companies

---

*Many scholars also advocate a free trade policy. For a reasoned argument supporting free trade, see Robert Z. Lawrence and Robert E. Litan, "Why Protectionism Doesn't Pay," *Harvard Business Review* 65 (May-June 1987): 60–66.

TABLE 20–2 Foreign goods as percent of U.S. markets

Product	1972	1985
Blowers and fans	3.6%	29.2%
Luggage and personal goods	20.7	52.4
Converted paper products	10.4	20.1
Men's and boy's outerwear	8.7	26.8
Costume jewelry	10.4	28.6
Musical instruments	14.9	25.2
Dolls	21.8	54.7
Nitrogenous fertilizers	4.3	19.4
Electronic computing equipment	0	14.2
Power-driven hand tools	7.5	23.2
Lighting fixtures	4.2	17.4
Sporting and athletic goods	13.0	23.2
Precious metal jewelry	4.9	24.9
Telephone and telegraph equipment	2.1	12.1
Primary zinc	28.4	51.5
Tires and inner tubes	7.2	15.1
Printing trades machinery	8.5	22.9
Women's blouses	14.9	33.0
Radio and TV sets	34.9	57.5
Women's suits and coats	7.3	24.5
Semiconductors	12.3	30.5
Wool yarn mills	6.1	17.4
Shoes	17.1	50.4

SOURCE: "Import Products," *U.S. Department of Commerce Statistical Report,* 1986, p. 29.

TABLE 20–3 U.S. imports of selected commodities, 1970–1984

Commodity	1970 (millions of dollars)	1984 (millions of dollars)	Percent Increase
Automobiles and parts	5,068	45,284	793
Motorcycles	307	731	138
Rubber tires and tubes	205	1,839	797
Iron and steel mill products	1,952	10,208	423
Clothing	1,269	13,497	963
Footwear	629	5,034	700
Clocks and watches	184	1,254	582

SOURCE: *Statistical Abstract of the United States,* 1986, pp. 816–817.

TABLE 20–4 The twenty-five largest foreign investors in the United States, 1985

Rank	Foreign Investor	Home Country	U.S. Company	Industry	Revenue (millions)
1	Seagram Co. Ltd.	Canada	DuPont	Chemicals	$29,239
			J.E. Seagram	Alcoholic beverages	1,810
2	Royal Dutch/Shell	Netherlands	Shell Oil	Energy	20,477
			Numerous others		1,500
3	British Petroleum	UK	Standard Oil	Energy	17,873
4	Mitsui & Company	Japan	Mitsui (USA)	Conglomerate	10,357
5	B.A.T. Industries	UK	BATUS, Inc.	Retailing	7,569
6	Tengelmann Group	Germany	Great A&P Tea	Retailing	6,615
7	Renault	France	American Motors	Automotive	6,103
8	Nestle	Switzerland	Numerous	Food	5,916
9	Beneficiaries of U.S. Philips Trust	Netherlands	North American Philips	Electronics	4,845
10	Volkswagenwerk	Germany	Volkswagen of America	Automotive	4,326
11	Unilever	Netherlands	Numerous	Food	4,249
12	Hanson Trust	UK	Numerous	Conglomerate	4,025
13	Bayer A.G.	Germany	Numerous	Chemicals	4,010
14	Bell Canada	Canada	Northern Telecom	Telecommunications	3,409
15	Anglo American of South Africa	South Africa	Engelhard	Metals	3,382
16	General Occidentale	France	Grand Union	Retailing	2,612
			Crown Zellerbach	Paper	592
17	Mitsubishi Corp.	Japan	Mitsubishi Int.	Trading	2,950
18	Electrolux AB	Sweden	White Consolidated	Appliances	2,837
19	Franz Haniel & Cie	Germany	Scrivner Inc.	Food distribution	2,800
20	BASF Group	Germany	BASF Corporation	Chemicals	2,568
21	Group Bruxelles Lambert	Belgium	Drexel Burnham Lambert	Finance	2,500
22	Hong Kong and Shanghai Banking Corp.	Hong Kong	Marine Midland Bank	Banking	2,495
23	Canadian Pacific	Canada	Numerous	Conglomerate	2,488
24	Credit Suisse	Switzerland	First Boston	Investment banking	2,452
25	Petrofina SA	Belgium	American Petrofina	Energy	2,409

SOURCE: "The *Forbes* Foreign Rankings." *Forbes*, 28 July 1986, pp. 200–201.

depend partially on exports, and new U.S. tariff barriers could adversely affect trade with Europe.[9]

Rise of the Multinational Corporation

An important development in the expansion of international business has been the growth of the *multinational corporation* (MNC)—a firm with operating components located in other countries.

By operating across national boundaries, MNCs can maximize operating efficiency in terms of the entire world. For example, they can take advantage of low labor costs in one part of the world, sell in countries of strong demand and higher costs, transfer managerial and professional skills from one country to another, and locate financial resources in various countries according to interest costs and taxes.

American firms are not the only MNCs. During the 1970s, MNCs from other countries made dramatic gains to reduce the overall dominance of American corporations. Even though U.S. foreign investment has grown in absolute terms, American firms are facing increasing competitive pressure abroad, particularly from European and Japanese companies. In 1960, for example, seventeen American companies were among the world's largest industrial firms. By 1985, the United States placed only ten.[10] The top twenty-five largest U.S. MNCs in 1985 are presented in Table 20–5.

ENVIRONMENT OF THE MULTINATIONAL CORPORATION

Political and Legal Elements

As an organization's environment expands from domestic to international, management faces not only a larger number of environmental elements, but also far greater environmental complexity. Rather than dealing with one legal system, management may find itself operating under dozens of sets of laws. Conflict among these diverse regulations is inevitable, and since each government controls only a portion of the MNC, the potential for conflict between the company and each nation also increases.

Each country, of course has different regulations regarding requirements for local participation in ownership, labor unions, and distribution of products. This complexity is illustrated in Figure 20–2. The arrows in the figure indicate that the MNC's operations are constrained by both home and host governments. At the same time, however, the MNC may attempt to have various laws modified in its favor through lobbying and other acts of influence. In some cases, the U.S. government, through negotiations, may attempt to persuade the host country to modify certain restrictions, and vice versa. Meanwhile, various constituencies of the corporation in each country may attempt to influence its

TABLE 20–5 The twenty-five largest U.S. multinationals, 1985

| Rank | Company | Industry | Revenues (millions) | | Total Assets (millions) | Foreign Assets as Percent of Total Assets |
			Foreign	Total		
1	Exxon	Petroleum	$59,067	$86,673	$69,160	43.4%
2	Mobil	Petroleum	32,678	57,111	41,752	45.2
3	Texaco	Petroleum	21,864	46,297	37,703	29.6
4	IBM	Computers	21,545	50,056	52,634	41.3
5	GM	Motor Vehicles	16,167	96,372	63,643	21.3
6	Ford	Motor Vehicles	15,995	52,774	31,366	50.1
7	Salomon	Financial Services	15,100	27,896	88,601	8.8
8	Chevron	Petroleum	12,722	41,742	38,899	23.6
9	Citicorp	Financial Services	10,600	22,504	160,505	48.8
10	DuPont	Chemicals	10,551	29,239	25,140	30.0
11	ITT	Conglomerate	7,754	20,007	37,849	31.0
12	Dow Chemical	Chemicals	6,326	11,537	11,830	46.6
13	Amoco	Petroleum	5,984	27,258	25,198	25.9
14	Bank America	Financial Services	5,144	13,390	118,974	35.2
15	Chase Manhattan	Financial Services	5,024	9,733	87,685	46.6
16	Safeway Stores	Retailing	4,261	19,651	4,841	22.9
17	J.P. Morgan	Financial Services	3,684	6,575	69,375	46.8
18	Procter & Gamble	Consumer Goods	3,625	13,552	9,683	20.1
19	Occidental Pet.	Petroleum	3,619	15,644	16,930	23.0
20	R.J.R. Nabisco	Food/Tobacco	3,262	13,533	16,930	25.7
21	Eastman Kodak	Photo Equipment	3,239	10,631	12,135	26.9
22	Xerox	Copy/Office Equpt.	3,187	11,736	17,163	22.9
23	Goodyear	Rubber products	3,148	9,585	6,754	33.4
24	Phillips Pet.	Petroleum	3,125	15,636	14,045	19.1
25	GE	Electronics	3,112	29,272	26,432	14.4

SOURCE: "The *Forbes* Foreign Rankings," *Forbes*, July 1986, pp. 207–8.

FIGURE 20–2 Legal and political environment of the MNC

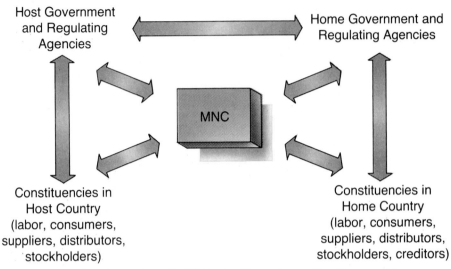

Host Government
and Regulating
Agencies

Home Government and
Regulating Agencies

MNC

Constituencies in
Host Country
(labor, consumers,
suppliers, distributors,
stockholders)

Constituencies in
Home Country
(labor, consumers,
suppliers, distributors,
stockholders, creditors)

SOURCE: Adapted from Anant R. Negandhi, "Multinational Corporations and Host Governments'
Relationships: Comparative Study of Conflict and Conflicting Issues," *Human Relations* 33 (August 1980):
518.

operations, as the MNC in turn affects them. Constituencies unhappy with the
lack of responsiveness of the MNC to their concerns may turn to their government for redress. Obviously, the MNC operates in a complex setting.

Host Country Relationships

As Figure 20–2 makes clear, the quality of the relationship between the host
country and the MNC is crucial. On the surface, it appears that both parties in
this relationship share mutual interests. If the MNC's local subsidiary is able to
operate profitably, the host country's economy will be strengthened, employment will increase, the standard of living will rise, and so on. In reality, however, this view is often not shared.

In a study of 124 subsidiaries of MNCs operating in six developing countries, Negandhi found that host governments and MNCs "had, at best, a most
diffuse understanding of what they were expecting of each other."[11] The
MNC's decision to operate in a host country was based on economic considerations; that is, optimizing the operations of the total organizational system.
The host country expected, on the other hand, specific economic and social
help from the MNC in the form of assistance to local entrepreneurs, the establishment of research and development facilities, and the introduction of products relevant to the local economy. These desires were only noted by the MNC
after the host government had passed regulations to ensure that the expectations were met.[12]

INTERNATIONAL BUSINESS AND TERRORISM

The United States has been relatively free from terrorist attacks against businesses. For example, of the approximately 2300 terrorist incidents that occurred worldwide in 1985, only eight occurred in the United States and only two were directed against business.

Although there were only 21 terrorist attacks on American business firms and executives worldwide in 1984, these attacks were costly. For instance, 28 individuals were killed, 64 were wounded, and property damage was $22 million. Experts who monitor terrorist incidents report that attacks have increased at a 10 to 15 percent annual rate between the mid-1970s and the mid-1980s.

Risks International, a firm that specializes in developing strategies to cope with terrorist attacks, suggests that the following principles should be considered:

☐ *Know where the terrorists are located.* For instance, in Chile the terrorists operate primarily in cities, while in Colombia they operate both in urban and rural areas. A firm that wishes to locate in a rural area in South America would have less trouble in Chile than in Colombia.

☐ *Know the experts who keep track of the terrorists.* The State Department and consulting firms keep track of overseas terrorist activities. In the event of a kidnapping, these experts can help arrange payments.

☐ *Don't count on welfare programs to provide immunity from attacks.*

☐ *Treat your employees well.* Terrorists win points with local employees if they kill or kidnap unpopular managers.

☐ *Consider advice from managers in the subsidiary firm.* Do not just rely on decisions made in corporate headquarters far removed from the scene.

☐ *Carefully consider the prudence of hiring local managers.* While some firms believe that local managers will ward off terrorist attacks, the locals may be more loyal to themselves than to the company. In one instance, an American was murdered by locals when he investigated wrongdoings by local managers who worked for the company in that country.

☐ *Locate in foreign areas relatively free from terrorist attacks.* Almost no risks exist for American or other foreign firms in many Asian countries. The Philippines is a notable exception.

SOURCE: Adapted from Brian O'Reilly, "Business Copes With Terrorism," *Fortune,* 6 January 1986, pp. 47–55 and "Multinational Firms Act to Protect Overseas Workers From Terrorism," *Wall Street Journal,* 29 April 1986.

Because the sales volume of some corporations exceeds the gross national product of many host countries, local governments are highly sensitive to displays of corporate power (see Table 20–1). Besides the obvious economic effects of the MNC's operations, other social changes occur—migration to urban areas, breakup of kinship and family, and change in social and occupational status, for instance.

In an attempt to maintain control over their own national economies, many host governments restrict the strategic freedom of local subsidiaries. For example, before allowing Ford to establish production facilities in Spain, the Spanish government set certain conditions: Ford's sales volume was limited to 10 percent of the prior year's total auto market, and its export volume had to equal at least two-thirds of its Spanish production. Additionally, Ford could not broaden its model line without government approval. Developing countries in South America, West Africa, and the Far East often require some local ownership of MNC subsidiaries in order to control their operations.[13]

The key to peaceful coexistence with the host government has perhaps best been expressed by Reginald H. Jones when he was chairman and chief executive officer of General Electric. Jones indicated that the relationship between an MNC and a host country develops over a period of years based on an understanding of the wants and needs of the host government. It is the responsibility of the corporation to make its operations and products fit local needs and regulations. If this view predominates, then the probability of success increases because both parties want the venture to succeed.[14]

MANAGEMENT PROCESSES IN INTERNATIONAL BUSINESS

Management processes in international business are influenced by the way that organizations conduct their international operations. As shown in Table 20–6, there are a number of ways that organizations can engage in international business. Each approach has a certain organizational form with varying degrees of parent-company control associated with it. The amount of required capital, profit potential, and risk also varies with each approach, creating certain advantages and disadvantages.

Development of Global Strategies

Digman states that most firms operating in foreign countries evolve into international, multinational, or global operations over time.[15] Figure 20–3 describes a three-phase developmental process. The first phase begins with a small stake in a foreign operation, with the primary emphasis on the firm's own domestic operations. The second phase develops as the firm becomes increasingly dependent on foreign operations and evolves both domestic and international divisions. Finally, the last phase occurs when the firm evolves into a global corporate structure.

TABLE 20–6 Organizational form and international business

Organizational Form	Degree of Parent-Company Control	Advantages	Disadvantages
Licensing	Minimal	Minimum capital commitment	Minimum long-term profits Risk of losing license Minimum control over operations
Branch operations	Low	Low capital commitment Easy entry	Risk of losing franchise Long-term profitability is tentative
Joint ventures	Substantial	Easy entry Local commitment Flexible capital commitment Good opportunity for long-term profits Local know-how and management skills can be acquired	Differences in priorities and objectives may occur with venture partners Host countries may engage in discriminatory action
Subsidiary operations	Almost complete	Close control over operation Long-term profit is high but so is risk	Large capital commitment Risk of expropriation or discriminatory action

SOURCE: Information adapted from the following: James G. Hutchinson, *Management Strategy and Tactics* (New York: Holt, Rinehart & Winston, 1971), p. 508; Steven Globerman, *Fundamentals of International Business* (Englewood Cliffs, N.J.: Prentice-Hall, 1986), p. 12–13; Stefan H. Robock and Kenneth Simmonds, *International Business and Multinational Enterprises,* 3rd ed. (Homewood, Ill.: Irwin, 1983), p. 512; and Lester A. Digman, *Strategic Management* (Plano, Tex.: Business Publications, 1986), p. 195.

Once a firm has made the decision to internationalize, an important concern is how to compete internationally. Porter lists the following four alternatives:[16]

□ *Protected niche*—the firm seeks out countries where government restrictions exclude global competitors by requiring local ownership or participation, high tariffs, and so on. The firm works out arrangements to allow it to compete selectively in such protected markets, perhaps through licensing or joint ventures.

□ *National focus*—the firm chooses to outcompete global firms by pursuing an approach focused on the unique needs of individual national markets, taking advantage of differences in national markets.

□ *Global focus*—the firm targets a particular segment of an industry in which to compete on a global basis. A segment is chosen where the impediments

NEW STRATEGIES FOR U.S. MNCs

American MNCs need to develop new strategies to remain competitive in foreign markets. For example, Ingersoll-Rand lost a multimillion dollar contract to supply road-building equipment to the Indonesian government when an Italian rival submitted a bid 44 percent lower. Faced with declining productivity and high labor costs, how can American MNCs compete against foreign rivals?

The strength of the U.S. dollar is a major variable. When the dollar is down, or weak, with respect to foreign currencies, products produced in the United States are cheaper and the U.S. share of export markets increases. The reverse occurs when the U.S. dollar is up, or strong.

To cope with these currency fluctuations, many American MNCs are shifting more and more manufacturing capacity abroad. Others are forming joint ventures in which they act as marketing agents for foreign products. Both General Motors and Chrysler practice "outsourcing" by selling subcompacts in the United States that are produced in Japan and South Korea by foreign firms.

Other American MNCs form joint ventures with foreign companies either to share technologies or to share the costs and risks of developing new products. For instance, Dow Chemical and German's BASF formed a joint venture, Dow-Badisde, in the United States to produce chemical raw materials and fibers. BASF provided the manufacturing technology, and Dow supplied the marketing expertise. Because manufacturing aircraft engines is costly and considerable risks are involved in selling the engines (the engines may not sell), United Technologies and Rolls-Royce of Great Britain formed International Aero Engines to produce and market jet engines.

Joint ventures are not always smooth sailing, however. The corporate objectives of the parent companies often diverge, leading to the venture being terminated. For instance, despite excellent earnings, Dow Chemical and BASF could not agree if Dow-Badisde should be expanded. The venture ended with BASF buying the business.

SOURCE: Adapted from "Drastic New Strategies To Keep U.S. Multinationals Competitive," *Business Week*, 8 October 1984, pp. 168–74; and "Are Foreign Partners Good For U.S. Companies?" *Business Week*, 28 May 1984, pp. 58–60.

to global competition are low and the firm's position in the segment can be defended from incursion by broad line global competitors.

□ *Broad global competition*—the firm competes worldwide in the full product line of the industry, taking advantage of the sources of global competitive advantage to achieve differentiation or an overall low cost position. Imple-

FIGURE 20–3   Typical phases in the internationalization of organizations

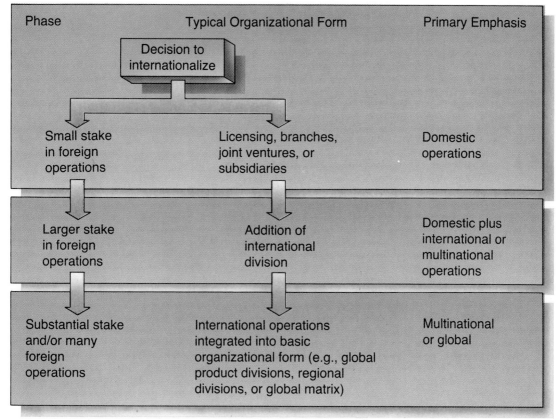

Phase	Typical Organizational Form	Primary Emphasis
	Decision to internationalize	
Small stake in foreign operations	Licensing, branches, joint ventures, or subsidiaries	Domestic operations
Larger stake in foreign operations	Addition of international division	Domestic plus international or multinational operations
Substantial stake and/or many foreign operations	International operations integrated into basic organizational form (e.g., global product divisions, regional divisions, or global matrix)	Multinational or global

SOURCE: Adapted from Lester A. Digman, *Strategic Management* (Plano, Tex.: Business Publications, 1986), p. 197.

menting this strategy requires substantial resources and a long time horizon.

Regardless of which competitive alternative the firm selects, a number of substrategies must be developed. Many of these will be from the firm's domestic strategies (discussed in chapter 4). Robinson suggests that the nine substrategies shown in Figure 20–4 form the basis for functional-area international strategies. These can be grouped into three areas: *basic strategies* (public affairs, sales, and supply), *input strategies* (labor, management, ownership, and financial), and *structural strategies* (legal and control).[17]

Most important in achieving a successful global strategy is to develop a consistent and interrelated set of substrategies that will support the organization's overall international objectives. These substrategies should match the organization's strengths and weaknesses against the environment's opportunities and threats.

FIGURE 20–4   International substrategies

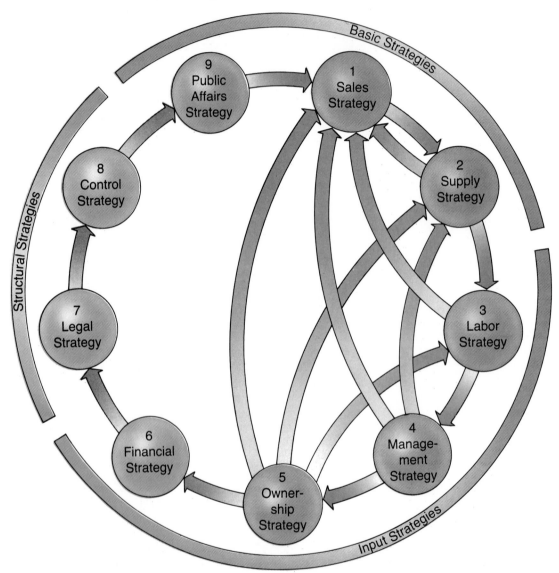

Management Selection

As discussed in chapter 10, an organization's need for a highly qualified staff cannot be overemphasized. This is especially true for international business. A shortage of well-trained managers can be one of the most serious problems affecting a company's international growth.[18] The tasks of international man-

WHAT WORKS IN OHIO MAY NOT IN OSAKA

In the 1970s, several Procter & Gamble products were doing well in Japan. As an example, Pampers had 90 percent of the disposable diapers market, Camay held 3.5 percent of the soap market, and Cheer and Bonus combined had 15 percent of the detergent market.

At the end of 1986, Procter & Gamble's share of the $625-million disposable diaper business had dropped to 15 percent, Camay's share of the $500-million soap market had declined to 2.5 percent, and Cheer and Bonus had slipped to 12 percent of the $1.2-billion detergent market.

What happened?

Procter & Gamble underestimated the technical capabilities and advertising savvy of a Japanese sanitary-napkin maker, Unicharm, that entered the disposable diaper market in 1981. Procter & Gamble used ads that had worked in the United States but did not convince the Japanese to continue purchasing Pampers.

When Cheer and Bonus were first introduced in Japan, Procter & Gamble used a successful U.S. strategy, price discounting. While the strategy worked in the beginning, many Japanese wholesalers were alienated because their profit margins were reduced. Also, 30 percent of all detergent sold in Japan is by "mom and pop" stores with limited shelf space. These stores attempt to make as much as possible on the products they sell and avoid discounted products. As a result, Cheer and Bonus are not sold by the mom and pop stores, excluding Procter & Gamble from almost a third of the detergent market.

Procter & Gamble used the same advertising campaign for Camay in Japan that had worked in South America, Europe, and the Philippines, but the Japanese were insulted. Camay used a commercial with a man comparing a woman's skin to that of a fine porcelain doll. If a Japanese man actually did this, he would be considered rude or unsophisticated or both.

In essence, Cincinnati's Procter & Gamble learned that products and marketing must be tailored to specific markets. What works in Ohio may not in Osaka.

SOURCE: Adapted from Jeffrey A. Trachtenberg, "They Didn't Listen To Anybody," *Forbes*, 15 December 1986, pp. 168–69.

agement are usually more demanding than those of purely domestic management. For example, international managers must have an understanding of the economic, social, and political aspects of the countries in which they serve, as well as those aspects in their headquarters' country.

Managers in foreign subsidiaries usually have broader duties than if they were to manage the same size domestic operation. For instance, many managers of foreign subsidiaries have to perform top-level duties while their domestic counterparts (ones with the same profit or cost responsibilities) perform middle-management tasks. International managers must also do more selling than their domestic counterparts. They must sell themselves, their companies, and the country in which their firms are headquartered. International managers, particularly at top levels, must lead an active social life and often must interact frequently with very high-level foreign authorities. International managers must also cope with communication problems between corporate headquarters and the subsidiaries. And, despite their increased responsibilities, they usually must function with less staff assistance.[19]

The staffing of international management has two distinct requirements. First, people employed at the subsidiary level must be equipped to manage the activities within the countries where they are located. Second, people employed at headquarters must be equipped to coordinate and control the company's worldwide operations.[20]

What characteristics should international managers possess? An important requirement is the ability to think and act in a truly international fashion. Three attitudes of international managers have been identified:

□ Ethnocentric—home-country oriented. This attitude assumes a superiority of home-country nationals over foreigners in headquarters or subsidiaries. Messages of instruction and advice go from headquarters to subsidiaries, and home standards are applied in judging performance.

□ Polycentric—host-country oriented. This attitude recognizes variations in cultures and holds that local people understand local situations better than do foreigners. Foreign segments of the firm are given considerable latitude, and the corporation is held together by financial controls.

□ Geocentric—world oriented. A global view is taken in deciding questions about raising money, building plants, conducting research, and so on. Foreign subsidiaries are parts of a whole, whose focus is on worldwide objectives. A collaborative relationship exists between subsidiaries and headquarters.

A geocentric attitude is naturally best for multinational firms. In practice, though, a geocentric attitude is normally developed over time, and various obstacles can interfere with its development. Until multinational managers accept such an attitude, they may be more provincial than multinational. Patterns of thinking limit the development of management skills in the international arena.

Technology Transfer

Figure 20–4 identified nine international substrategies that can be considered functional areas of management within an international setting. The additional functional area of research and development (R&D), with its implications for technology transfer, can also be important.

Managing technology transfer has become a major part of international business activity.[21] Technology, the organizational process of converting inputs into outputs, includes the knowledge, skills, and other means for the production and distribution of goods and services. Technology should not be thought of as self-contained physical objects stored in a warehouse and then shipped from supplier to user. Rather, technology should be thought of as a body of knowledge that is transferred by a learning process. When the transfer is made from one national environment to another, it can be time consuming, complex, and costly. Many transfer methods are available and many parties may participate in the process.*

Various issues concerning technology can be important for the international firm. For example, if the firm's competitive advantage abroad is based on technology, how is this advantage to be maintained over time once technology is transferred? What price will be charged for the transfer? Are the environmental conditions in the proposed host country such that the transferred technology can be successfully implemented? If the firm chooses to invest its technology directly in a foreign setting, then a strategy must be developed that best fits the foreign environment.[22]

National governments become involved in technology transfers and exert control measures over the process. For instance, home countries exert control for national security reasons and to protect tax revenues. Host countries seek more appropriate technology, reduced payments, and more local R&D.[23]

International businesses are frequently under pressure by host countries to locate R&D facilities abroad, together with production operations. A number of firms have deviated from the usual pattern of keeping R&D operations in the home country. For example, a study of thirty-one American and eighteen European MNCs revealed that the group had more than 200 active foreign R&D units.[24]

Cross-Cultural Management

Business firms are faced with a wide range of cultural differences when they cross national boundaries. These differences affect the achievement of business objectives.

Problems exist in identifying cultural differences because it is natural for people to evaluate behavior of others in terms of the cultural conditioning of their own country. In addition, cultural patterns are not static but constantly change.[25]

There is disagreement on the significance of cultural differences. For instance, Levitt argues that the importance of international cultural differences in developing business strategies is vastly overrated by international managers. He contends that "technology has produced markets for standardized products on

---

*For a more detailed discussion of the various technology transfer methods, see David Teece, *The Multinational Corporation and the Resource Cost of International Technology Transfer,* 2nd ed. (Cambridge, Mass.: M.I.T. Press, 1984) and Stefan H. Robock, *The International Technology Transfer Process* (Washington, D.C.: National Academy of Sciences, 1980).

a previously unimagined scale of magnitude."[26] According to Levitt, if a company "keeps its costs and prices down and pushes quality and reliability up, while maintaining reasonable concern for suitability, customers will prefer its world-standardized products."[27]

Terpstra and David, on the other hand, hold that cultural differences are very significant in achieving a firm's objectives. Part of their argument is that one of the sectors of the firm's environment is societal and includes the patterns of social relationships and cultural definitions of social life. These scholars think that managers face problems involving much more than an intellectual appreciation that cultural differences exist:[28]

> How much should the foreign firm adapt to local business practices? To what extent should the firm refuse to conform to local norms and instead introduce new ways of managing a firm and doing business? Insensitivity to host country customs will not only result in misinformed decisions but may also precipitate local resentment and recrimination.

An important aspect of managing cultural differences is developing a cultural awareness. By achieving cultural sensitivity, international business organizations will be aware of the need to identify cultural variables and to adjust its operation to cultural differences.

JAPANESE MANAGEMENT

As an example of cultural differences, most of the world is intrigued with *Japanese management techniques.* Both scholars and practicing managers are interested in Japan's international business success. In the past few years, many scholars have attempted to isolate distinctive management practices that account for that success. The implications of these analyses are that American companies might do better if they adopted some of the Japanese techniques.

Japanese Management Techniques

In Japan, *manufacturing policies* are developed where a great deal of effort must be devoted to mundane production problems. It is common to see Japanese engineers and managers on the plant floor talking to workers.[29] This deliberate and thorough approach to day-to-day production operations leads to a remarkable absence of crisis management in Japanese plants. The approach yields clean facilities, responsible employees, very little inventory on the plant floor, and almost no rejected products.[30]

Statistical quality control, a management technique widely used in Japan, involves a focus by employees on upgrading the quality level of their products by using statistical concepts developed in the United States. Beginning in the 1950s, considerable effort was made in Japan to reduce the notion that "made in Japan" signaled inferior merchandise.[31]

Ringi (consensus) decision making, another Japanese technique, involves a top-down consultative process rather than a bottom-up consensus process. Japanese managers exert a patronlike exercise of power and influence.[32]

In the *maximization of human resources,* the Japanese utilize an intensive socialization process to create a "company man" identity. Japanese males are hired after their graduation, with the expectation of lifetime employment. Females and part-time workers are used to adjust the size of the work force to varying economic conditions. The socialization process is achieved by under-paying employees in the early stages of their career in favor of higher compensation in later years. The Japanese employee's career path is slow.[33]

Japanese vs. American Management

Theory Z, developed by William Ouchi, emphasizes the ideal Japanese organizational model and compares it against an American model. The Japanese organization is characterized by lifetime employment, slow evaluation and promotion, nonspecialized career paths, implicit control mechanisms, collective decision making, and a holistic concern for employees. The American organization is characterized by short-term employment, rapid evaluation and promotion, specialized career paths, explicit control mechanisms, individual decision making, and segmented concern for workers. Ouchi argues that the characteristics of Japanese management are developed from their culture, which emphasizes interdependence and is more suited to industrialization than the individualism and "expanding frontier" culture of the United States.[34]

Much of the evidence presented for the success of Theory Z is anecdotal in nature and lacks scientific, methodological rigor. Without such rigor, it is difficult to demonstrate that Type Z management is responsible for an organization's success. Furthermore, no specific research program has produced evidence of the ability of Theory Z to increase productivity.[35]

To compare Japanese and American management practices, Pascale and Athos utilized a model consisting of seven management variables developed by McKinsey and Company, a management consulting firm. The model's seven variables are: superordinate goals, strategy, structure, systems, staff, skills, and style. Superordinate goals serve as unifying elements that tie together the interests and activities of the various organizational members. The other six variables are considered to be "levers" that managers can use to influence organizational members and, according to Pascale and Athos, can be divided into "hard Ss" and "soft Ss."

For the hard Ss—strategy, structure, and systems—American management is described as being quite similar to the Japanese. By contrast, the Japanese have advantages in the soft Ss—staff, skills, and style—because of their culture, interdependence, and approach to ambiguity.[36] Pascale and Athos have used broad generalizations based on comparisons drawn between one American and one Japanese chief executive. No specific research program has provided support for their theory.[37]

ZEN AND THE ART OF AMERICAN MOTORCYCLE RESURRECTION

A Japanese instruction manual for assembling bicycles advises the reader that the manual should be read slowly and completely before beginning to assemble the bicycle. This example has been used by some writers to explain holistic approaches to management practices.

One company that emphasized a holistic (or functional relationship) approach to compete against the Japanese is Harley-Davidson. In late 1981, officials of Harley-Davidson complained to the International Trade Commission that the Japanese were engaging in dumping practices by flooding the market with big motorcycles. In early 1983, the Reagan administration imposed stiff tariffs on foreign motorcycles.

Harley-Davidson could have continued doing business using their old methods, since the company was now protected by the tariff. Instead, the company began cutting manufacturing costs, improving product quality, and regaining market share. Harley-Davidson also went one step further, requesting that the tariff be dropped in early 1987. The chief executive of Harley-Davidson, Vaughan Beals, said, "We no longer need the special tariffs to compete with the Japanese."

From 1981 to 1986, Harley-Davidson, modernized its entire motorcycle product line and improved manufacturing and marketing processes. By 1986, productivity had increased 43 percent, market share had improved by 57 percent, scrap and rework had decreased by 68 percent, employee absenteeism had declined by 53 percent, and inventory had been reduced by 61 percent.

Sometimes implementation strategies can be developed using functional relationships that generate outstanding results.

SOURCE: Warren Brown, "Changes Powered Harley To Fend Off Foreign Rivals," *Washington Post,* 3 May 1987. For more about holistic approaches, see Ian Mitroff, "Zen and the Art of Implementation: Speculations on a Holistic Theory of Management," paper presented at the University of Pittsburgh Conference on Strategy Implementation, 1976.

The reality is that Japanese companies also have problems with absenteeism, productivity, profits, and company loyalty.[38] Japan, as a country, faces changes that could significantly affect their management style. For example, currency factors and societal changes will tend to affect Japan's future.

The relationship between the yen and foreign currencies is an important economic issue. When the yen rises, Japanese products become more expensive overseas and exporters have to sacrifice market share or profits or both. Japanese society is becoming more diverse and divisive. For instance, more Asian immigrants will be willing to work at jobs disdained by Japanese, housing shortages will tend to become more acute, the burden of caring for more and more old people will tend to increase, and the concept of lifetime employment will fade away.[39]

Despite the problems facing Japanese companies, studies conducted by Rosalie Tung indicate that American MNCs can learn from Japanese MNCs about training for international assignments. Tung compared the human resource development programs of eighty American and thirty-five Japanese MNCs and found that the failure rate (being dismissed from the company or recalled to headquarters) among U.S. expatriates was significantly higher than that of Japanese expatriates.

American firms reported that the primary reasons American managers failed were because of a lack of relational skills and because of family problems. Relational skills were defined as the ability to deal effectively with suppliers, customers, peers, and business associates. Japanese firms did not report that relational skills or family problems were major issues. Instead, Japanese managers failed because of their inability to cope with the larger responsibilities associated with an international assignment and an inability to adapt to different physical or cultural environments.

Tung suggests that Japanese are better qualified and trained than their American counterparts and that this accounts for the lower failure rates among Japanese MNCs. For instance, Japanese MNCs interview graduates from elite universities where competition has been intense. Aptitude tests are used to determine who is finally selected. Nippon Steel, for example, hired the top 80 candidates from 1,000 applicants.

STRESS AND JAPANESE EXECUTIVES

With all that has been written about how the Japanese concentrate on managing human resources, one might think that Japanese managers are the ultimate team players—happily working for their companies. Recent case histories, however, indicate just the opposite.

Because of the stress to continually improve, Japanese executives are among the most harried, insecure, and frustrated in the world. With the prospects of new technologies facing many Japanese firms, managers are expected to work evenings and weekends to maintain and improve their technical and managerial skills. Many managers feel crushed when they cannot master the new technological advances. The impact of a lower growth rate together with the frustrations of maintaining their competence indicate that in the future even the most talented and dedicated Japanese executives will experience higher rates of alcoholism, absenteeism, and even suicide.

SOURCE: Adapted from Leslie Helm, ''The High Price Japanese Pay For Success,'' *Business Week*, 7 April 1986, pp. 52–54.

After being selected, the candidates receive several years of extensive training before they are given a permanent foreign assignment. Important elements of the training include obtaining fluency in a foreign language, attending graduate programs abroad, and performing one-year training assignments in foreign subsidiaries. Tung argues that the more rigorous the selection and training procedures used, the less the incidences of poor performance in a foreign country will occur. Some American managers argue that their Japanese counterparts can afford to invest in their people because of the system of lifetime employment. Yet the high failure rates among American MNCs are very costly. Tung estimates that it costs $150,000 to $200,000 annually to send an average American family overseas. This includes cost-of-living differentials, base pay, and other adjustments. In considering these six-figure costs together with lost marketing opportunities, training costs for American MNCs may be higher than the costs incurred by the Japanese to train their expatriates.[40]

New insights are being developed about the way in which Japanese manage their companies. Researchers are urging American managers to look beyond the anecdotes, generalizations, and "samurai culture" of Japanese firms, to concentrate instead on the straightforward choices that Japanese managers have made concerning personnel and investment policies. Many of the practices used by Japanese companies can be adopted by American firms to improve productivity. For instance, more resources should be invested in attracting an elite labor force; employees should be supported with investments in equipment, training, and engineering; more frequent contact should occur between engineers and production workers; and pay and promotion policies should reward high performance to motivate employees.[41]

SUMMARY

Although international business was being conducted in 2800 B.C., it was not until the late nineteenth and early twentieth centuries that large, specialized corporations appeared on the world scene. International business is now considered a distinct field of management, dealing with business activities that cross national boundaries.

Significant differences exist between international and domestic management. International management involves operating in national markets that have different economic and cultural conditions, languages, laws, expectations, monetary systems, and political systems. Some American firms face intensifying foreign competition, and increasing amounts of various products are being imported into the United States.

The development of the *multinational corporation* (MNC) allowed business organizations to maximize operating efficiencies on a worldwide scale. MNCs operate in a highly complex environment, with tensions often existing between the firm and its various host governments. The MNC's operations have both positive and negative consequences for its host countries. These governments often place restrictions on the firm's freedom to operate. American firms are not the only MNCs. Beginning in the 1970s, MNCs from other countries made dramatic gains to reduce the overall dominance of American corporations.

There are a number of approaches that organizations can use in conducting international business. Each approach has a distinct organizational form with specific characteristics. *Global competitive strategies* must be developed if the firm is to compete internationally. The firm must also integrate seven basic substrategies as it conducts business. Two other functional management areas—*technology transfer* and *management selection*—present special challenges to the international firm.

International managers should take a *geocentric* attitude. Social and cultural differences compound the difficulty of doing business, and developing a *cultural sensitivity* will allow managers to be aware of the need to identify cultural variables and to adjust to cultural differences.

Because the Japanese have enjoyed such phenomenal economic success since World War II, many U.S. managers have recently become interested in *Japanese management practices,* with specific managerial techniques being widely publicized as *Theory Z.* To better understand the Japanese techniques, American managers and scholars have attempted to isolate distinctive management practices that account for Japan's economic success. Evidence indicates that most of these theories are based on anecdotes and generalizations without any scientific, methodological rigor. The Japanese have taken straightforward steps to improve their manufacturing operations and place heavy emphasis on the development of their human resources.

The practicing managers and scholars who have studied the Japanese indicate that many of the practices used by Japanese companies can be adopted by American firms to improve productivity.

KEY CONCEPTS

Dumping	Polycentric
International business	Geocentric
International management	Technology transfer
Multinational corporation (MNC)	Cross-cultural management
Global competitive strategy	Cultural sensitivity
Ethnocentric	Japanese management

DISCUSSION QUESTIONS

1. Using Table 20–1 as a reference, how do the annual sales of the largest MNCs compare to the GNP of the largest world countries?
2. *International management* is just domestic management on a grander scale. Agree? Disagree? Discuss.
3. What has been the trend of imports as a percent of U.S. markets during recent years?
4. Why do many American executives favor a free trade policy rather than having tariffs to protect their products from foreign competition?
5. Why do the objectives of the host country and those of the MNC often differ? What problems do these differences create for management of the MNC?
6. Discuss how the degree of *parent-company control* varies between the organizational form of *licensing arrangements* and *subsidiary operations*. What are the advantages and disadvantages of each of these organizational forms?
7. What alternatives can a firm use to compete internationally?
8. Discuss how most businesses that operate in foreign countries evolve into international, multinational, or global operations over time.
9. Why are the tasks of international management more demanding than those in purely domestic companies?
10. Explain the difference between an *ethnocentric* attitude and a *geocentric* attitude. How are they related to the MNC?
11. Describe *technology transfer.* What are the implications for international organizations?
12. In what ways does the culture of other countries appear to differ from U.S. culture? If you have traveled or lived abroad, give an example from your own experience.
13. What are some barriers to the wholesale adoption of *Japanese management techniques* by U.S. managers?

NOTES

1. Developed from "The Forbes Foreign Rankings," *Forbes*, 28 July 1986, pp. 176–93; and "The Top 1000 U.S. Companies Ranked By Industry," *Business Week*, 14 April 1986, pp. 113–60.
2. Kurt R. Mirow and Harry Maurer, *Webs of Power: International Cartels and the World Economy* (Boston: Houghton Mifflin, 1982), pp. 150–56; Sabatino Moscati, *The World of Phoenicians* (London: Weidenfeld and Nicholson, 1968), p. 28.
3. Stefan H. Robock and Kenneth Simmons, *International Business and Multinational Enterprises*, 3rd ed. (Homewood, Ill.: Irwin, 1983), p. 3
4. Ibid., pp. 4–5.
5. Steven Globerman, *Fundamentals of International Business Management* (Englewood Cliffs, N.J.: Prentice-Hall, 1986), p. 3.
6. Richard D. Robinson, *Internationalization of Business: An Introduction* (Hinsdale, Ill.: Dryden Press, 1984), p. xi.
7. Richard D. Robinson, *Performance Requirements for International Management: U.S. Management Response* (New York: Praeger, 1983), p. 16.

8. Ibid., p. 27.

9. George Russell, "Trade Face-Off: A Dangerous U.S.-Japan Confrontation," *Business Week*, 13 April 1987, pp. 29–36; Joel Dreyfuss, "The Perils of Pushing Japan," *Fortune*, 11 May 1987, pp. 113–16.

10. *Fortune*, July 1961, p. 168; August 1961, p. 130; 27 April 1986, p. 364; and *Forbes*, 28 July 1986, p. 176.

11. Anant R. Negandhi, "Multinational Corporations and Host Governments' Relationships: Comparative Study of Conflict and Conflicting Issues," *Human Relations* 33 (August 1980): p. 534.

12. Ibid., pp. 534–35.

13. Yves L. Doz and C. K. Prahalad, "How MNCs Cope with Host Government Intervention," *Harvard Business Review* 58 (March-April 1980): 149–57.

14. "The Basic Formula for Business Success," *Harvard Business Review* 58 (November-December 1980): 155; as reprinted from Reginald H. Jones, "The Transnational Enterprise and World Economic Development," a speech delivered at Airlie, Va., July 10, 1980.

15. Lester A. Digman, *Strategic Management* (Plano, Tex.: Business Publications, 1986), pp. 195–96.

16. Michael E. Porter, *Competitive Strategy* (New York: Free Press, 1980), pp. 294–95.

17. Richard D. Robinson, *International Business Management*, 2nd ed. (Hinsdale, Ill.: Dryden Press, 1978), p. 23.

18. Jacques G. Maisonrouge, "The Education of a Modern International Manager," *Journal of International Business Studies* 14 (Spring-Summer 1983): 141–46.

19. Jean E. Heller, "Criteria for Selecting an International Manager," *Personnel* 57 (May-June 1980): 42–51.

20. John D. Daniels and Lee H. Radenbaugh, *International Business*, 4th ed., (Reading, Mass.: Addison-Wesley, 1986), pp. 730–32.

21. *International Approaches to the Acquisition of Technology* (New York: United Nations Industrial Development Organization, 1985), pp. 82–86.

22. Robock and Simmons, *International Business and Multinational Enterprises*, 3rd ed., pp. 464–67.

23. Ibid., pp. 475–76.

24. Jack N. Behrman and William A. Fischer, "Transnational Corporations: Market Orientation and R&D Abroad," *Columbia Journal of World Business* (Fall 1980), pp. 55–60.

25. Nancy Adler, "Cross-Cultural Management Research: The Ostrich and the Trend," *Academy of Management Review* 8 (April 1983): 415–37.

26. Theodore Levitt, "The Globalization of Markets," *Harvard Business Review* 61 (May-June 1983): 97.

27. Ibid., p. 98.

28. Vern Terpstra and Kenneth David, *The Cultural Environment of International Business*, 2nd ed. (Cincinnati, Oh: South-Western, 1985), p. 177.

29. Andrew Weiss, "Simple Truths of Japanese Manufacturing," *Harvard Business Review* 62 (July-August 1984): 119–25.

30. J. Bernard Keys and Thomas R. Miller, "The Japanese Management Theory Jungle," *Academy of Management Review* 9 (April 1984): 342–53.

31. Ibid., p. 344.

32. Charles Y. Yang, "Demystifying Japanese Management Practices," *Harvard Business Review* 62 (November-December 1984): 172–82.

33. Nina Hatvany and Vladimir Pucik, "An Integrated Management System: Lessons From the Japanese Experience," *Academy of Management Review* 6 (July 1981): 469–80.

34. William C. Ouchi, *Theory Z: How American Business Can Meet the Japanese Challenge* (Reading, Mass.: Addison-Wesley, 1981).

35. Jeremiah J. Sullivan, "A Critique of Theory Z," *Academy of Management Review* 8 (January 1983): 132–42.

36. Richard T. Pascale and Anthony G. Athos, *The Art of Japanese Management* (New York: Simon and Schuster, 1981).

37. Ikujiro Nonaka and Johny K. Johansson, "Japanese Management: What About the 'Hard' Skills?" *Academy of Management Review* 10 (April 1985): 181–91.

38. George S. Odiorne, "The Trouble With Japanese Management Systems," *Business Horizons* 4 (July-August 1984): 17–23; and Leslie Helm, "The High Price Japanese Pay For Success," *Business Week,* 7 April 1986, pp. 53–54.

39. "Japan's Troubled Future," *Fortune,* 30 March 1987, pp. 21–24.

40. Rosalie L. Tung, "Human Resource Planning In Japanese Multinationals: A Model For U.S. Firms?" *Journal of International Business Studies* 4 (Fall 1984): 139–48.

41. Weiss, "Simple Truths of Japanese Manufacturing," 1984; and Yang, "Demystifying Japanese Management Practices," 1984.

SUPPLEMENTARY READING

Adler, Nancy J. "Women Do Not Want International Careers: And Other Myths About International Management," *Organizational Dynamics* 13 (Autumn 1984): 66–79.

Amsalem, Michel A. "Technology Choice in Developing Countries: The Impact of Technology Transfer." Washington, D.C.: World Bank, 1983.

Chakravarthy, Balaji S., and Perlmutter, Howard V. "Strategic Planning For A Global Business," *Columbia Journal of World Business* 20 (Summer 1985): 3–10.

Conway, Michael A. "Reducing Expatriate Failure Rates," *Personnel Administrator* 29 (July 1984): 31–38.

Culbertson, John M. "The Folly of Free Trade," *Harvard Business Review* 64 (September-October 1986): 120–28.

Encarnation, Dennis J., and Vachari, Sushil. "Foreign Ownership: When Hosts Change The Rules," *Harvard Business Review* 63 (September-October 1985): 152–60.

England, George W. "Japanese And American Management: Theory Z And Beyond," *Journal of International Business Studies* 14 (Fall 1983): 131–42.

Graham, John L. "The Foreign Corrupt Practices Act: A New Perspective," *Journal of International Business Studies* 15 (Winter 1984): 107–121.

Graham, John L., and Herberger, Roy A., Jr., "Negotiators Abroad—Don't Shoot From The Hip," *Harvard Business Review* 61 (July-August 1983): 160–168.

Hofstede, Geert. "The Cultural Relativity of Organizational Practices And Theories," *Journal of International Business Studies* 14 (Fall 1983): 75–89.

Keys, J. Bernard, and Miller, Thomas R. "The Japanese Management Theory Jungle," *Academy of Management Review* 9 (April 1984): 342–53.

Negandi, Anant R.; Eshghi, Golpira S.; and Yuen, Edith C. "The Management Practices of Japanese Subsidiaries Overseas," *California Management Review* 27 (Summer 1985): 93–105.

Nonaka, Ikujiro, and Johansson, Johny K. "Japanese Management: What About the 'Hard' Skills?" *Academy of Management Review* 10 (April 1985): 181–91

Porter, Michael E. "Changing Patterns of International Competition," *California Management Review* 28 (Winter 1986): 9–40.

Reich, Robert B., and Mankin, Eric D. "Joint Ventures With Japan Give Away Our Future," *Harvard Business Review* 64 (March-April 1986): 78–86.

Sethi, S. Prakash; Namiki, Nobuaki; and Swanson, Carl L. "The Decline of the Japanese System of Management," *California Management Review* 26 (Summer 1984): 35–45.

Shaked, Israel. "Are Multinational Corporations Safer?" *Journal of International Business Studies* 17 (Spring 1986): 83–106.

Shreave, Thomas W. "Be Prepared for Political Changes Abroad," *Harvard Business Review* 62 (July-August 1984): 111–18.

Tung, Rosalie L. "Strategic Management of Human Resources In The Multinational Enterprise," *Human Resource Management* 23 (Summer 1984): 129–43.

Weiss, Andrew. "Simple Truths of Japanese Manufacturing," *Harvard Business Review* 62 (July-August 1984): 119–25.

Young, John A. "Global Competition: The New Reality," *California Management Review* 27 (Spring 1985): 11–25.

CUIDAD DEL CARMEN PRODUCTS

Wood-Mosaic, Incorporated, headquartered in Louisville, Kentucky, produces and markets expensive floorings, which are mosaics of various pieces of wood. Frequently used are certain varieties of mahogany from South America and eucalyptus from Brazil. Mahogany and eucalyptus logs are purchased throughout South America and shipped by boat to Wood-Mosaic's Mexican subsidiary, Cuidad Del Carmen Products (CDCP), located in the Bay of Campeche. At CDCP, the logs are sliced into various sized veneers, or *flitches*. The flitches, dried and cured to prevent warping, are then shipped to Louisville for further processing. CDCP is well known for its excellent quality and workmanship. In fact, many flitches are sold to European firms that produce similar products but do not compete in the same markets with Wood-Mosaic.

Wood-Mosaic has a wood-products manufacturing plant in Canada and distribution facilities in Great Britain and France. The managers of these operations, as well as the manager of CDCP, report to the vice-president of international operations located in Louisville. Wood-Mosaic uses a combination of home-country, host-country, and third-country nationals in top positions in their foreign operations. It is not uncommon for managers to rotate among the foreign operations and the U.S. domestic operation in Louisville.

Recently, the general manager of CDCP, who is a U.S. national, suddenly announced that he will leave within a month to join a

European firm. Wood-Mosaic has a policy that general managers of foreign operations cannot be hired from outside the company. Otherwise, the options are fairly open. The vice-president of international operations formed a committee of various individuals and requested that they recommend five candidates for the job. The vice-president of international operations in consultation with the president of Wood-Mosaic will make the final choice for the CDCP position. The committee quickly narrowed its choice to the following candidates.

Robert Marshall

Aged fifty-six, Marshall has thirty-one years of service with Wood-Mosaic. He is assistant general manager of the Louisville operations and well versed in all of the technical, production, and marketing aspects required in the job. He has never worked abroad for Wood-Mosaic. Neither he nor his wife speaks Spanish. All of their children are grown and live in the United States. He was considered for the general manager's position in Louisville three years ago but was passed over for a much stronger individual. He is considered moderately competent in the management of his duties.

Michael White

Aged forty, he has been with Wood-Mosaic for fifteen years. He is considered highly competent and is viewed as a "fast-track" employee. He has never been permanently assigned to a foreign job but has worked for the last two years as a special assistant to the vice-president of international operations. White has frequently traveled to South America, Mexico, and Europe. Both he and his wife speak adequate Spanish. He has two children, aged sixteen and fifteen, who are just beginning to study Spanish.

His wife is a professional, holding a responsible marketing position with an office systems firm in Louisville.

Rebecca Davis

She has been with Wood-Mosaic for ten years and has an MBA from a prestigious eastern university. At age thirty-five, she has held staff and line positions of increasing responsibility. For three years she was second in command of the French distribution facility, serving with distinction. She has expressed an interest in international operations because her undergraduate major was international management. Presently, she is deputy director of strategic planning for Wood-Mosaic. She speaks Spanish fluently, is divorced, and has no children.

Ian Stewart

Aged forty-five, he is a Canadian citizen and manages the Canadian wood products operation. He joined Wood-Mosaic from a Canadian firm. He worked on the staff of the vice-president of international operations until being promoted to his present job. He is considered an excellent manager, highly respected by his Canadian employees. Stewart has never worked outside of Canada and the United States. Neither he nor his wife speaks Spanish. He has three young children ranging in age from five to eight. His wife does not work outside the home but is very active in local community service organizations. Next year, she is scheduled to become national president of the Canadian Women's Allegiance Against Child Abuse, a well-respected organization. Both she and Ian are excited about her involvement in the organization.

Jose Gomez

Aged thirty, he is assistant to the present general manager of CDCP. He joined Wood-Mosaic two years ago after completing an undergraduate degree in the United States and an MBA from a Mexican university. He is well connected with the local Mexicans and is a member of a prominent Mexican family. He speaks English adequately. His wife does not work outside the home and does not speak English. They have two small children, three years and one year

old. Gomez is considered to be competent but lacking in experience. Two members of the selection committee have indicated that, while he has received excellent evaluations, they are not personally familiar with his performance.

Questions

1. What problems might each candidate encounter in the position?
2. Who should be selected for the assignment and why?

THE ROAD TO HELL

John Baker, chief engineer of the Caribbean Bauxite Company of Barracania in the West Indies, was making his final preparations to leave the island. His promotion to production manager of Keso Mining Corporation near Winnipeg—one of Continental Ore's fast-expanding Canadian enterprises—had been announced a month before, and now everything had been tidied up except the last vital interview with his successor—an able young Barracanian, Matthew Rennalls. It was vital that this interview be a success and that Rennalls should leave encouraged to face the challenge of his new job. A touch on the bell would have brought Rennalls walking into the room, but Baker gazed thoughtfully through the window considering just exactly what he was going to say and, more particularly, how he was going to say it.

John Baker, an English expatriate, was forty-five years old and had served his

Case prepared by Gareth Evans for Shell-British Petroleum Development Company of Nigeria. Used by permission of Professor John J. Gabarro of the Harvard Business School.

twenty-three years with Continental Ore in many different places: the Far East, several countries of Africa, Europe, and for the last two years the West Indies. He hadn't cared much for his previous assignment in Hamburg and was delighted when the West Indian appointment came through. Climate was not the only attraction. Baker had always preferred working overseas (in what were termed the developing countries) because he felt he had an innate knack—better than most other expatriates working for Continental Ore—of knowing just how to get on with regional staff. Twenty-four hours in Barracania, however, soon made him realize that he would need all of this "innate knack" to deal effectively with the problems awaiting him.

At his first interview with Hutchins, the production manager, the whole problem of Rennalls and his future was discussed. It was made quite clear to Baker than one of his most important tasks would be the "grooming" of Rennalls as his successor. Hutchins had pointed out that not only was Rennalls one of the brightest Barracanian prospects on the staff of Caribbean Bauxite—at London University he had taken high honors in earning an engineering degree—but, being the son of the Minister of Finance and Economic Planning, he also had no small political clout.

The company had been particularly pleased when Rennalls decided to work for them rather than for the government, in which his father had such a prominent post. Management ascribed his action to the effect of the company's vigorous regionalization program, which since World War II had produced eighteen Barracanians at mid-management level and given Caribbean Bauxite a lead in this respect over other international concerns operating in Barracania. The success of this regionalization policy had led to excellent relations with the government—a relationship given added importance when Barracania three years later became independent, an occasion which encouraged a critical attitude towards the role foreign interests would have to play in the new Barracania. Hutchins had therefore little difficulty in convincing Baker that the successful career development of Rennalls was of the first importance.

The interview with Hutchins was now two years old, and Baker, leaning back in his office chair, reviewed just how successful he had been in "grooming" Rennalls. What aspects of the latter's character had helped and what had hindered?: What about his own personality? How had that helped or hindered? The first item to go on the credit side would be the ability of Rennalls to master the technical aspects of his job. From the start he had impressed Baker with an ability to tackle new assignments and to offer constructive comments in

departmental discussions. Rennalls was popular with all ranks of Barracanian staff and had an ease of manner which stood him in good stead when dealing with European superiors. These were all assets, but what about the debit side?

First and foremost, there was Rennalls's racial consciousness. His four years at London University had accentuated this feeling and made him sensitive to any sign of condescension on the part of expatriates. It may have been to give expression to this sentiment that as soon as he returned home from London he threw himself into politics on behalf of the United Action Party, which was later to provide the country with its first prime minister.

The ambitions of Rennalls—and he certainly was ambitious—did not, however, lie in politics. Staunch nationalist as he was, he saw that he could serve himself and his country best—for was not bauxite responsible for nearly half the value of Barracania's export trade?—by putting his engineering talent to the best use possible. On this account, Hutchins had found it unexpectedly easy to persuade Rennalls to give up political work before entering the production department as an assistant engineer.

It was, Baker knew, Rennalls's well-repressed sense of race consciousness which had prevented their relationship from being as close as it should have been. On the surface, nothing could have seemed more agreeable. Formality between the two men was at a minimum; Baker was delighted to find that his assistant shared his own peculiar "shaggy dog" sense of humor, so that jokes were continually being exchanged. They entertained each other at their houses and often played tennis together. Yet the barrier remained ever present. The existence of this "screen" between them was a constant source of frustration to Baker, since it indicated a weakness he hated to accept. If successful with all other nationalities, why not with Rennalls?

At least he had managed to break through to Rennalls more successfully than any other European. In fact, it was the young Barracanian's attitude—sometimes overbearing, sometimes cynical—toward other company expatriates that had been one of the subjects Baker had raised last year. He knew, too, that he would have to raise the same subject again in the forthcoming interview because Jackson, the senior draughtsman, had complained only yesterday about the rudeness of Rennalls. With this thought in mind, Baker leaned forward and spoke into the intercom: "Would you come in, Matt, please? I'd like a word with you."

Baker began the interview. "As you know, Matt, I'll be off to Canada in a few days' time, and before I go I thought it would be useful if we could have a final chat together. It is indeed with some deference that I suggest I can be of help. You will shortly be sitting in this chair doing the job I am now doing, but I, on the other hand, am ten years older, so perhaps you can accept the idea that I may be able to give you the benefit of my longer experience." Baker saw Rennalls stiffen slightly in his chair. "You and I have attended enough company courses to remember those repeated requests by the personnel manager to tell people how they are getting on as often as the convenient moment arises and not just the automatic 'once a year' when, by regulation, staff reports have to be discussed."

Rennalls nodded his agreement, so Baker went on, "I shall always remember the last job performance discussion I had with my previous boss back in Germany. He used what he called the 'plus and minus' technique. His firm belief was that when a superior by discussion seeks to improve the work performance of a subordinate, the prime objective should be to make sure that the latter leaves the interview encouraged and inspired to improve. Any criticism must therefore be constructive and helpful. He said that one very good way to encourage a person—and I fully agree with him—is to discuss both the plus factors and the minus factors. So I thought, Matt, it would be a good idea to run our discussion along these lines."

Rennalls offered no comment, so Baker continued. "Let me say, therefore, right away, that, as far as your own work performance is concerned, the plus far outweighs the minus. I have, for instance, been most impressed with the way you have adapted your considerable theoretical knowledge to master the practical techniques of your job—that ingenious method you used to get air down the fifth-shaft level is a sufficient case in point. And at departmental meetings I have invariably found your comments well taken and helpful. In fact, you will be interested to know that only last week I reported to Mr. Hutchins that from the technical point of view he could not wish for a more able man to succeed to the position of chief engineer."

"That's very good indeed of you, John," cut in Rennalls with a smile of thanks. "My only worry now is how to live up to such a high recommendation."

"Of that I am quite sure," returned Baker, "especially if you can overcome the minus factor, which I would like now to discuss with you. It is one which I have talked about before so I'll come straight to the point. I have noticed that you are more friendly and get on better with your fellow Barracanians than you do with Europeans. In point of fact, I had a complaint only yesterday from Mr. Jackson, who said you had been rude to him—and not for the first time either.

"There is, Matt, I am sure, no need for me to tell you how necessary it will be for you to get on well with Europeans, because until the company has trained sufficient people of your caliber, Europeans are bound to occupy senior positions here in Barracania. All this is vital to your future interests, so can I help you in any way?"

While Baker was speaking on this theme, Rennalls had sat tensed in his chair, and it was some seconds before he replied. "It is quite extraordinary, isn't it, how one can convey an impression to others so at variance with what one intends? I can only assure you once again that my disputes with Jackson—and you may remember also Godson—have had nothing at all to do with the color of their skins. I promise you that if a Barracanian had behaved in the same manner I would have reacted in precisely the same way. And again, if I may say it within these four walls, I am sure I am not the only one who has found Jackson and Godson difficult. I could mention the names of several Europeans who have felt the same. However, I am really sorry to have created this impression of not being able to get on with Europeans—it is an entirely false one—and I quite realize that I must do all I can to correct it as quickly as possible. On your last point, regarding Europeans holding senior positions in the company for some time to come, I quite accept the situation. I know that Caribbean Bauxite—as they have been doing for many years now—will promote Barracanians as soon as their experience warrants it. And, finally, I would like to assure you, John—and my

father thinks the same too—that I am very happy in my work here and hope to stay with the company for many years to come."

Rennalls had spoken earnestly and, though not convinced, Baker did not think he could pursue the matter further except to say, "All right, Matt, my impression *may* be wrong, but I would like to remind you about the truth of that old saying, 'What is important is not what is true but what is believed.' Let it rest at that."

But suddenly Baker knew that he didn't want to let it rest at that. He was disappointed once again at not being able to break through to Rennalls and having yet again to listen to a bland denial that there was any racial prejudice in his make-up. Baker, who had intended ending the interview at this point, decided to try another tack.

"To return for a moment to the 'plus and minus technique' I was telling you about just now, there is another plus factor I forgot to mention. I would like to congratulate you not only on the caliber of your work but also on the ability you have shown in overcoming a challenge which I, as a European, have never had to meet.

"Continental Ore is, as you know, a typical commercial enterprise—admittedly a big one—which is a product of the economic and social environment of the United States and Western Europe. My ancestors were all brought up in this environment, and I have therefore been able to live in a world in which commerce (as we know it today) has been part and parcel of my being. It has not been something revolutionary and new which has suddenly entered my life. In your case," went on Baker, "the situation is different because you and your forebears have only had some fifty or sixty years' experience of this commercial environment. You have had to face the challenge of bridging the gap between fifty and some three hundred years. Again, Matt, let me congratulate you—and people like you—once again on having so successfully overcome this particular hurdle. It is for this very reason that I think the outlook for Barracania—and particularly Caribbean Bauxite—is so bright.''

Rennalls had listened intently. ''Well, once again, John, I have to thank you for what you have said, and, for my part, I can only say that it is gratifying to know that my own personal effort has been so much appreciated. I hope that more people will soon come to think as you do.''

There was a pause and, for a moment, Baker thought hopefully that he was about to achieve his long awaited breakthrough, but Rennalls merely smiled back. The barrier was unbreached. There remained some five minutes' cheerful conversation about the contrast between the Caribbean and Canadian climate and whether the West Indies had any hope of beating England in football before Baker drew the interview to a close. Although he was as far as ever from knowing the real Rennalls, he was nevertheless glad that the interview had run along in this friendly manner and, particularly, that it had ended on such a cheerful note.

This feeling, however, lasted only until the following morning. Baker had some farewells to make, so he arrived at the office considerably later than usual. He had no sooner sat down at his desk than his secretary walked into the room with a worried frown on her face. Her words came fast. ''When I arrived this morning I found Mr. Rennalls already waiting at my door. He seemed very angry and told me in quite a peremptory manner that he had a vital

letter to dictate which must be sent off without any delay. He was so worked up that he couldn't keep still and kept pacing about the room, which is most unlike him. He wouldn't even wait to read what he had dictated. Just signed the page where he thought the letter would end. It has been distributed and your copy is in your in tray.''

Puzzled and feeling vaguely uneasy, Baker opened the ''Confidential'' envelope and read the following letter:

From: Assistant Engineer

To: The Chief Engineer, Caribbean Bauxite Limited

14th August, 1986

ASSESSMENT OF INTERVIEW
BETWEEN MESSRS.
BAKER AND RENNALLS

It has always been my practice to respect the advice given me by seniors, so after our interview, I decided to give careful thought once again to its main points and so make sure that I had understood all that had been said. As I promised you at the time, I had every intention of putting your advice to the best effect.

It was not, therefore, until I had sat down quietly in my home yesterday evening to consider the interview objectively that its main purport became clear. Only then did the full enormity of what you said dawn on me. The more I thought about it, the more convinced I was that I had hit upon the real truth—and the more furious I became. With a facility in the English language which I—a poor Barracanian—cannot hope to match, you had the audacity to insult me (and through me every Barracanian worth his salt) by claiming that our knowledge of modern living is only a paltry fifty years old while yours goes back 300 years. As if your materialistic commercial environment could possibly be compared with the spiritual values of our culture. I'll have you know that if much of what I saw in London is representative of your most boasted culture, I hope fervently that it will never come to Barracania. By what right do you have the effrontery to condescend to us? At heart, all you Europeans think us barbarians, or, as you say among yourselves, we are "just down from the trees."

Far into the night I discussed this matter with my father, and he is as disgusted as I. He agrees with me that any company whose senior staff think as you do is no place for any Barracanian proud of his culture and race—so much for all the company "clap-trap" and specious propaganda about regionalization and Barracania for the Barracanians.

I feel ashamed and betrayed. Please accept this letter as my resignation, which I wish to become effective immediately.

cc. Production Manager
    Managing Director

Questions

1. What were John Baker's reasons for holding this final meeting with Matthew Rennalls?
2. What do you think of Rennalls's behavior during the meeting?
3. Analyze Rennalls's behavior following the meeting.
4. What role did "racial consciousness" play in this situation?
5. Can you foresee any short-term or long-term repercussions likely to grow out of this incident?

THE CAREER MANAGEMENT PROCESS
Mutual Interests in Career Planning ☐
Importance of Personal Goal Setting ☐
Preparing a Career Plan ☐ Getting Started:
Selecting a Profession ☐ Getting Started:
Selecting an Organization

STAGES IN PROFESSIONAL CAREERS
Stage 1: Early Career ☐ Stage 2: Mid-
Career ☐ Stage 3: Late Career

ISSUES IN CAREER MANAGEMENT
Mentor Relationships ☐ Professional Lives
and Family Lives ☐ Dual-Career Marriages
☐ Professional Careers for Women ☐ The
Pressures of Time ☐ Stress Management

Summary ☐ Key Concepts ☐ Discussion
Questions ☐ Notes ☐ Supplementary
Reading

CASES: Loyalty ☐ Whose Career Is This
Anyway?

This chapter will enable you to

☐ Appreciate the importance of career
planning and understand the steps
necessary in preparing such a plan.

☐ Outline the stages of professional
careers and point out the distinctive
features of each stage.

☐ Understand the significance of mentor-
protégé relationships in career
progression.

☐ Recognize the special problems
involved in family-career conflicts, dual-
career marriages, and career planning
for women.

☐ Understand the nature of work-related
stress and describe approaches to
stress management.

CHAPTER 21
MANAGEMENT OF PROFESSIONAL CAREERS

As you prepare for a professional career, you can readily appreciate the difficulty as well as the seriousness of career choices. The many decisions involved in commitments to work life are too important to be left to chance. In this chapter, therefore, we discuss the process of professional career planning and the issues related to such planning.

THE CAREER MANAGEMENT PROCESS

Professional work careers begin as students leave college and enter organizational life. *Career planning* or *career management* refers to the decisions involved in career choices, such as entry into the world of work, new job assignments, transfers, promotions, moves to other organizations, and the like. In brief, it concerns the planning of one's life work.

Although entry into organizational life is the career beginning, it is *only* the beginning. Choices and planning are required as the individual starts as a trainee, gains sufficient experience to act independently, moves on to direct others, accepts broader responsibilities, weathers mid-career crises, moves laterally and/or upwardly, and eventually withdraws and retires.

Both the individual and the employing organization participate in the career planning system. First, the individual and/or organization must assess needs, abilities, and interests—a continuing process. Second, the organization and the individual must evaluate on-the-job performance—again a continuing

FIGURE 21–1 Elements of career management

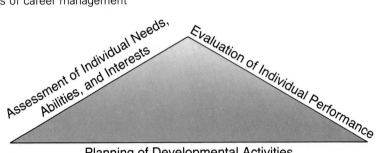

Planning of Developmental Activities

activity. Third, the individual and/or organization must plan activities that will develop the individual for projected positions, a lifelong process (Figure 21–1).

The degree of aggressiveness in career planning varies. Some individuals accept life as it comes and take promotions if and when they come. And some organizations simply assume that "the cream will rise to the top." In contrast, the concept of career planning emphasizes the purposeful mapping of career moves and the proper preparation for those moves. Although little research has been conducted in this area, some evidence indicates that extensive career planning is related to an effective career.[1]

Mutual Interests in Career Planning

The professional may do his or her own career planning without the collaboration of an employing organization. Because of their mutual interests, however, both the individual and the employing organization may become involved in career planning. As shown in Figure 21–2, both the individual and the employing organization must exercise judgment and make choices at all critical points throughout the professional career.

Some organizations ignore career management, and others approach it systematically with formal development programs. One survey of organizational practices discovered the following types of career development activities:[2]

- ☐ Career counseling during the performance appraisal session
- ☐ Special career counseling for high-potential employees
- ☐ Career pathing to help managers acquire experience for future jobs
- ☐ Rotating first-level supervisors through various departments to prepare them for upper-management positions
- ☐ Job posting of open positions and consideration of individual bids
- ☐ In-house advanced management development program
- ☐ Tuition reimbursement program
- ☐ Career counseling and job rotation for women and minorities
- ☐ Preretirement counseling

FIGURE 21–2 Career decisions

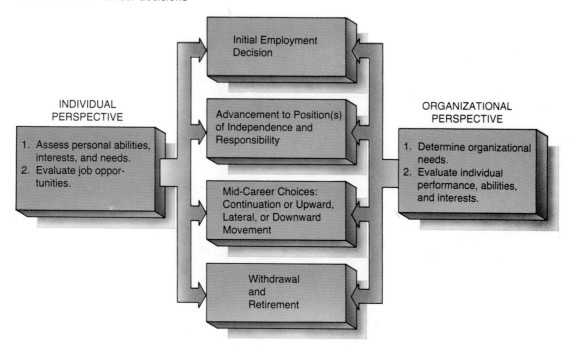

Organizations conduct career management programs in order to increase their operating efficiency. By assessing future needs for professional personnel and monitoring the progression and development of individuals, they attempt to provide a competent staff and avoid shortages in professional talent that might otherwise occur.

One risk of career-management programs is that of unrealistic expectations. If career planning programs create strong aspirations and if the organization cannot deliver the necessary opportunities, professional employees may experience dissatisfaction and anxiety. People who cannot achieve career goals within the organization may become embittered or seek fulfillment in other organizations.

Importance of Personal Goal Setting

Career management involves personal goal setting—the identification of job goals and planning to reach those goals. People who plan their careers in this way can accelerate their development and seize opportunities as they become available.

Everyone has at least vague goals for employment and career. Clear identification of goals and a strong commitment to them, however, can pay rich dividends in career progress. A goal-directed person usually attains more than the person lacking a sense of direction. The implications are clear for the person beginning a career: You can "go further" and enjoy greater personal satisfaction in your achievements by setting and periodically updating career goals.

Setting career goals provides a target and encourages the planning of personal development necessary to goal attainment. In addition, goal setting provides a sound basis for decisions. A person with a goal can better evaluate alternative opportunities as they appear and avoid total reliance on quick weighing of pros and cons.

Preparing a Career Plan

A person can develop a career plan with or without the help of the organization. We can sketch here only the general approach to formulating such a plan. For further assistance, you should consult one of many guides to career planning.*

Step one involves the identification of your long-range career objectives. In view of your abilities, preparation, background, and interests, where do you hope to go professionally? This step requires a balancing of professional goals with those in other areas—family, religious, recreational, and so on. As a student, you may find that career goals are vague because of your lack of knowledge of opportunities coupled with an inadequate basis for evaluating your own potential. Fortunately, your career plans need not be "set in concrete" but can be revised periodically throughout your career.

Step two calls for the establishment of more immediate, short-run goals, goals that might be realized within one to five years. At the time of employment, for example, you might specify completion of the probationary period as one goal, followed perhaps by some assignment of greater independence and responsibility. Precise description of such a goal would depend on the field of employment and the type of assignments young professionals might receive in their first few years of employment.

Step three entails establishment of a timetable for the intermediate goals and even for other more distant points on the route to the ultimate career goal. For example, you might aspire to become comptroller or vice-president by the age of thirty-five. Timetables must obviously be expressed in flexible terms, because much of your progress lies beyond your personal control. Nevertheless, establishing a timetable enables you to monitor your progress. If extensive delays are encountered, you may need to reevaluate career goals, seek employment elsewhere, or take other appropriate action. The important idea is that you should take responsibility, as far as possible, for your own career rather than allowing it to meander along without direction.

---

*Three books offering career-planning assistance are Richard Nelson Bolles, *What Color Is Your Parachute?* (Berkeley, Calif.: Ten Speed Press, 1986); Edmond Billingsley, *Career Planning and Job Hunting for Today's Student: The Nonjob Interview Approach* (Santa Monica, Calif.: Goodyear, 1978); and Marilyn A. Morgan, *Managing Career Development* (New York: Van Nostrand, 1980).

Step four involves deciding what activities are necessary to prepare for the next target position. In some cases, further education is desirable. In other cases, the best preparation is realized through diligent performance in the present job, supplemented perhaps by reading professional and trade journals. Establishing these preparatory steps in measurable terms allows you to obtain reinforcement through achievement of specific goals.

Getting Started: Selecting a Profession

Career planning properly begins with the choice of profession. Speaking of occupational "choice" is somewhat misleading. Rather than a choice at a certain point in time, one's vocational selection is actually a developmental process spanning the years from late childhood to early adulthood. During this process, the individual eliminates some occupational alternatives and retains others. Even after entering a career, many individuals eventually find their work unsatisfactory, their opportunities shrinking, or their interests changing, and feel compelled to make a shift.

Among the various theories which attempt to explain why we choose the occupations we do are the following:

People choose work environments that match their personalities—that is, environments which let them exercise their skills and abilities, express their attitudes and values, and take on agreeable problems and roles.[3]

A person's occupational choice depends upon: (1) factors over which the individual has no control (state of the economy, family background, and chance); (2) the individual's marital status; (3) characteristics specific to the individual (physical and intellectual characteristics, temperament and personality, interests and values, and the individual's sex); and (4) learned skills of various sorts.[4]

A person selects an occupation which reflects his or her self-concept. That is, individuals will choose an occupation which expresses their ideas of the kinds of people they are.[5]

Selecting a field of work necessitates self-evaluation—a determination of who you are and what you want. You must consider what you enjoy doing, evaluate your skills or potential abilities, and think about your basic values. Manuals are available to help you think about vocational choice and suggest steps to follow in selecting a profession.*

Even after you make a choice, however, you are likely to change it. Edgar H. Schein suggests that an individual's basic career "anchor" or orientation is developed gradually over several years of work experience. As people move through their careers, they develop knowledge about their own abilities and talents, motives and needs, and values. This increasing self-awareness enables

---

*The three books cited previously—Bolles, *What Color Is Your Parachute?;* Billingsley, *Career Planning;* and Morgan, *Managing Career Development*—offer practical how-to-do-it guidance.

them to stabilize and guide their careers. Hence, an individual may well change careers after a few years in an attempt to secure a match between career and his or her self-perception.[6]

Getting Started: Selecting an Organization

For those seeking employment—and even for entrepreneurs—the first choice pertains to industry. You must decide whether your interests lie in retailing, banking, oil, utilities, professional services, steel, publishing, education, government, or elsewhere. Some are growing industries, and some offer better average salary levels than others. Retailing and utilities, for example, reportedly offer lower salaries on the average, though the average obviously does not set limits in the individual case.

In selecting a specific organization, the quality of management is more important than the beginning salary. An organization with a well-developed career-management program, therefore, is an attractive prospective employer. A growing, thriving organization has more to offer most individuals than a faltering organization in the process of retrenchment.

One often-overlooked possibility is to form your own organization, to go into business for yourself.[7] Entrepreneurship or launching new ventures offers rich rewards to those with the requisite ability, interest, and courage. In the

THAT FIRST JOB

Many college graduates are concerned about their first job. While some students start with a plum job or a spot in a promising training program, many more have to settle for a mediocre one.

How critical is that first job? The good news is that many top executives began with distinctly humble jobs. Recruiters and human resource executives say that they don't attach much weight to an applicant's first job, so long as he or she doesn't stay in it longer than three or four years.

Some recruiters are encouraged by a crooked career path. "The most effective people usually have had a variety of experiences," reports a human resources vice-president.

Career advisors are now saying that while it is easier and more remunerative to set a career path early and tailor a job search accordingly, most people change their careers at some point in their lives.

One thing to remember: it is easier to succeed in a career if you enjoy the work and are also good at it.

SOURCE: Adapted from Janet Bamford, "Everyone Has to Start Somewhere," *Forbes,* 14 July 1986, pp. 98–100.

last decade, many business schools have launched courses in entrepreneurship and new-venture management at both the graduate and undergraduate levels.

STAGES IN PROFESSIONAL CAREERS

In her best-seller *Passages,* Gail Sheehy describes the predictable crises and stages of adult life.[8] This idea of stages applied specifically to working life can assist our understanding of career development.

At different points in one's working life, a person faces drastically different situations. The neophyte's situation, for example, contrasts sharply with that of the peak performer at mid-career or of the executive awaiting retirement. Different interests, relationships, goals, responsibilities, and emotional responses reflect the varied positions of individuals on career paths. In thinking about career planning, therefore, it is helpful to examine the features of careers at various stages.

Identification of career stages is necessarily arbitrary, and writers differ in the number of stages they recognize. In this discussion, we shall think in terms of three stages: early career, mid-career, and late career (Figure 21–3).

Stage 1: Early Career

The early career begins with entry into the organization and continues through both initial training and a time of broadening work experiences. While the

FIGURE 21–3   Career stages

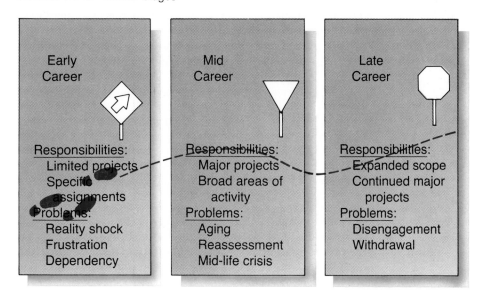

Early Career	Mid Career	Late Career
Responsibilities: Limited projects Specific assignments Problems: Reality shock Frustration Dependency	Responsibilities: Major projects Broad areas of activity Problems: Aging Reassessment Mid-life crisis	Responsibilities: Expanded scope Continued major projects Problems: Disengagement Withdrawal

length of the period varies, we may think of it as lasting roughly until the age of thirty to thirty-five for a person who graduates from college at the usual age.

After the new employee joins the organization, he or she typically works under the close supervision of a more experienced employee. The work itself is generally routine, often a part of a larger project or broader area of responsibility.

The routine and sometimes monotonous nature of initial work assignments often proves frustrating to the person who enters the organization expecting to receive glamorous work assignments, to solve difficult problems, and to make his or her mark in the world. The phrase "reality shock" has been used to describe the beginner's experience of reconciling preemployment dreams with the realities of the work organization. Some managers see this period as a necessary time to get the new employee's head out of the clouds and to acquaint him or her with the "real world." The disillusionment reported by a young professional illustrates this point:[9]

> My first year here was frustrating. I had a good record in graduate school. I was ready to go to work and make a contribution. But for a year, no one paid much attention to my suggestions. I almost left. It took me a year to realize that I didn't yet understand the complexity of the problems we were working on. Now I try to take enough time with new people to help them understand the dilemma of that first year.

Even though entry-level jobs contain less responsibility than higher-level positions, some organizations attempt to make initial job experiences challenging. This practice apparently contributes to career progress. A study of managerial careers at AT&T has shown a strong connection between job challenge and career achievement. At the time of the study, almost six out of ten who had experienced high job challenge had reached middle management. But fewer than one out of ten who had low job challenge had done so.[10]

The newcomer must also adapt to a relationship of dependency. He or she is closely supervised and dependent on a more experienced employee for training and guidance. There is a new world of organizational relationships to learn, and this is also a part of the beginning employee's "reality shock":[11]

> For many new employees, particularly those who entered in staff or managerial roles (as opposed to hourly work), reality shock consisted of the discovery, among other things, that other people in the organization were a roadblock to what they wanted to get done. Others in the organization did not seem as smart as they should be, seemed illogical or irrational, or seemed lazy, unproductive, or unmotivated.

After completing initial training and beginning to "learn the ropes," the trainee often achieves a position of greater independence. He or she may be given responsibility for particular projects or a particular area of responsibility, and supervision becomes less detailed.

COMPANY LOYALTY: THE BEGINNING OF THE END?

Corporate loyalty has had an important role in shaping industry. For example, several advantages occur when employees work hard, protect assets, and stay with the organization. Japanese executives have contended that encouraging worker loyalty is a key to high productivity.

In 1985 and 1986, 300 major companies reduced their work force. For example, AT&T announced layoffs that affected over 35,000 employees, and GE reduced its work force by 26,000. Many other companies are just beginning to "sharpen their knives."

Because a number of the affected employees were experienced managers and professionals with long years of service, many of the cost-cutting programs threaten to kill the concept of corporate loyalty. In a 1986 *Business Week* survey, 65 percent of responding middle managers reported that salaried employees are now less loyal to their companies than they were ten years ago. Many employees now consider working for a big corporation as a short-term contractual relationship. Either side can sever the arrangement on short notice. "People are learning that you only owe allegiance to your own career," reports a career counselor.

While layoffs have cut short-term costs considerably (DuPont has an annual after-tax savings of $230 million from a layoff of 11,200 employees), what are the long-term implications? How important is loyalty?

SOURCE: Adapted from Bruce Nussbaum, "The End of Corporate Loyalty?" *Business Week,* 4 August 1986, pp. 42–49.

Work experiences in the early years following the break-in period enable the person to develop professional abilities. Frequently, this period involves specialization. By specializing, the professional develops a strong foundation for service to the organization, but there is the danger of being "trapped" in a specialized area. This period of development is an important part of the career, however, and danger is involved in trying to escape this stage too quickly because of impatience:[12]

> Time after time in our study, we encountered first-level managers who were not effective in their positions because they did not understand the technical aspects of the work they were supervising. This tended to undermine the manager's self-confidence as well as the confidence of his subordinates.

As John Kotter points out in his study of general managers, the correct criterion for how rapidly one should advance is not the number of functional areas worked in or the number of training courses completed, but growth in business knowledge and in interpersonal and intellectual skills.[13]

Young managers, as might be expected, change jobs more frequently than do older executives. One survey of almost 1200 managers in three major U.S. corporations reveals that the greatest job mobility occurs when managers are under thirty-two years of age.[14] Contrary to popular belief, however, the managers who changed employers made no higher—and, in many cases, lower—salaries than did managers who remained with the same company. It is only when these mobile executives reach mid-career that their jobs in various companies and their background of diversified corporate experience begin to pay off financially.[15]

Stage 2: Mid-Career

Some people remain, by virtue of ability or choice, at the professional level described in Stage 1. They continue to serve as competent, independent performers of significant work. During the Stage 2 years, however, many professionals move on to assume broader responsibilities. This period runs from roughly thirty or thirty-five to fifty or fifty-five years of age. Typically, the in-

PLATEAUING

Mike Morgan, aged 40, wondered how he was going to continue to be motivated. As an executive with a *Fortune* 500 firm, he had been on a fast track, but now things had leveled off. There appeared to be little upward movement for him in the company. Morgan had plateaued.

Judith Bardwick, a clinical psychologist, has studied the experiences of plateauing. She indicates that the only thing separating most people in large, complex companies is not *whether* they will plateau, but *when*. Careers are not always onward and upward.

Bardwick predicts early plateauing for an entire generation of managers for several reasons. For instance, from 1980 to 1990 the number of people aged thirty-five to forty-four (the age for prime management jobs) will increase 42 percent while corporate America is "downsizing"—reducing the number of middle managers. She contends that top management should strive to substitute challenge for promotions. Plateaued employees should be challenged. The question is, how?

SOURCE: Adapted from Scott Burns, "Facing Up To The Reality of Plateaus," *Dallas Morning News*, 17 May 1987; and Judith Bardwick, *The Plateauing Trap* (New York: American Management Association, 1987).

THE REWARDS OF SAVING JOBS

Corporate America faces many competitive pressures. For example, foreign firms have lower costs, Wall Street is mostly concerned with short-term results, and corporate raiders are ready to pounce when stock prices decline. What should a manager do?

Some corporate managers react to these pressures as if they were the captain of a dirigible, lightening the load of costs by throwing a substantial portion of the crew overboard. This tactic often seems to work. Both the stock price and the earnings gain altitude, and the ship rises above the storm clouds. Yet the experience of lightening the load often gives everyone left a case of the shakes, which in the future may cause the corporate ship to fall again.

Some top managers meet such problems in other ways. These managers practice redeployment rather than unemployment. For example, a *Fortune* writer made 100 telephone calls to various companies and located ten that had hunted for "creative approaches" to cost cutting. Despite competitive pressures, the managers of these ten companies elected to improve their operations by using methods other than employee layoffs. The ten companies reduced their costs by changing how the work was done, launched an array of new products, and retrained workers for new jobs.

Perhaps companies that emphasize employee security may find that they are richer in talent than the "lean and trim" firms of the 1980s and 1990s.

SOURCE: Adapted from Bill Saporito, "Cutting Costs Without Cutting People," *Fortune*, 25 May 1987, pp. 26–32.

creased responsibilities involve leadership or direction, formally or informally, of the work of others in the organization.

The Stage 2 professional may also be an "idea person," as indicated by this statement by a Stage 2 scientist:[16]

> I sell ideas. I would describe myself as an innovative scientist. When I work on a problem, it starts to bug me. At some time, I will read something and apply it back to solve the original problem. Others often come to me with problems they cannot solve. Generally I can pull some information from my experience or reading and give them a direction to follow in solving the problems.

Often during Stage 2, the professional moves into or upward in the managerial ranks. It is also a period of reassessment—coming to terms with "aging" and facing the disparity between dreams and accomplishments. Some have referred to it as a "mid-life crisis." It may lead to adjustment in career goals or job changes and possibly to problems in family relationships. If properly coped with, it can also lead to feelings of inner calm.

Stage 3: Late Career

The career directions established in Stage 2 may continue through the final years of a working career. Some persons, however, move on to a more advanced level of career responsibilities. We might think of this period as running from roughly fifty or fifty-five years of age until retirement. Gene W. Dalton, Paul H. Thompson, and Raymond L. Price have described these individuals ("Stage IV" in their frame of reference) as influencing the direction of the organization or some major segment of it:[17]

> A stereotype of organizations pictures this influence as being exercised by only one person—the chief executive officer. But this influence is in fact more widely distributed among key people than is commonly thought. They exercise this influence in a number of ways: negotiating and interfacing with the key parts of the environment; developing the new ideas, products, markets, or services that lead the organization into new areas of activity; or directing the resources of the organization toward specific goals.

For many, late career is a period of relative stability. During this period, of course, the person must face the prospect and eventually the experience of retirement. The details of this period are difficult to summarize because of the highly diverse career patterns that have developed. At some point, the professional must begin a process of disengagement and withdrawal that may require time. The higher the organizational level, the more difficult it is for the employee simply to "lay down his or her tools" and walk off into retirement.

ISSUES IN CAREER MANAGEMENT

Career management involves a number of significant internal and external relationships. Internally, the functions of the mentor are important to career progress. Externally, the professional must balance his or her professional life with family life—an especially challenging task for women professionals and members of dual-career families. Handling the pressures of time and managing the stress of the job are also important in successful career management.

Mentor Relationships

In their early career, young professionals are often aided by older, experienced individuals. These teachers, who also function as protectors and advocates, are known as *mentors*. In some cases they are immediate supervisors, but in other cases they are merely senior employees.[18]

For the young professional who becomes the protégé of a mentor, the implications are clear. For example, by observing and listening to the mentor, knowledge in specific disciplines can be gained and leadership and practical judgment obtained. A survey of 1,250 executives revealed that nearly two-thirds reported once having a mentor, with most of those relationships beginning during the first five years of the career. Those executives who once had mentors earned more money at a younger age and were more likely to follow a career plan than were those who had not had a mentor.[19]

Research indicates that many companies use mentors to reduce turnover among newly hired recruits by building protégé loyalty for the firm.[20] Many protégés have different mentors in various stages of their career, whereas other protégés have only one or two.[21]

Although mentorship is a proven method of effectively developing young executives, the practice can cause significant problems. For example, mentors are usually selected by protégés because of leadership or technical skills with little thought given to personal habits and ethics. Mentors who exhibit unethical behavior—such as cheating on expense accounts, sexual harassment, and racial discrimination—make poor role models. In some cases, the protégé's career depends upon the success or failure of the mentor.[22]

Professional Lives and Family Lives

The stereotype of the fast-track, workaholic manager who sacrifices family for professional success may not be accurate, but it expresses a widespread concern about conflicts between work and family life. Those in professional careers face the problem of integrating these two areas of life. How does the professional,

EMOTIONAL SPILLOVER

In studying the private and professional lives of over 2,000 managers, Fernando Bartolomé and Paul A. Lee Evans have found that some very successful executives have meaningful private lives while others do not.

> What *does* distinguish the two groups is this: the executives whose private lives deteriorate are subject to the negative effects of what we call emotional spillover; work consistently produces negative feelings that overflow into private life. In contrast, the other group of executives have learned to manage their work and careers so that negative emotional spillover is minimized, and thus they achieve a balance between their professional and private lives.

SOURCE: Fernando Bartolomé and Paul A. Lee Evans, ''Must Success Cost So Much?'' *Harvard Business Review* 58 (March-April 1980): 137.

for example, maintain a strong family life while faced with excessive hours, frequent travel, and job worries that do not disappear at night?

One question concerns the relative importance of family versus profession. One might assume that problems occur because career-minded individuals simply forget about their families and place relatively less value on family relationships. This does not seem to be the case with most executives. A study of 532 executives by Fernando Bartolomé and Paul Evans has revealed the dual orientation of most executives.[23] While 7 percent were dominantly career centered and 14 percent were dominantly family centered, an impressive 79 percent expressed a dual orientation. In effect, this majority said that *both* career and family were important and satisfying, though in different ways.

Even though most executives attach a high value to family life, they have difficulty in successfully integrating the two areas. In the study cited, Bartolomé and Evans found that only about one-half of the managers were satisfied with their relative investment of time and energy in professional and family life. This suggests the problem is serious and deserving of serious effort in reconciling the conflicting demands of profession and family.

Dual-Career Marriages

A potentially more serious conflict of professional and family life occurs in the case of dual-career marriages. In such a family, careers are a top priority matter for both husband and wife. The situation differs from that of family units in which the wife works merely to supplement family income. The problems in a dual-career marriage are quite different because the two careers must be reconciled with each other and with family demands. If there are young children, the conflicts obviously become even more severe. A *Fortune* survey indicated that many dual-career parents are seriously troubled about who takes care of their children while both parents are working.[24] More and more parents are asking whether the extra money and prestige compensate for leaving a toddler in tears each morning or returning in the evening to a troubled teenager. Child-care problems also create absenteeism and nonproductive work time. Some researchers report that child care is becoming a predictable factor that influences work performance. For example, 77 percent of women and 73 percent of men questioned in a survey on child care and productivity reported that they had taken time away from work to tend their children. Nearly 30 percent of men and 26 percent of women in the survey said they had refused a new job, promotion, or transfer because it would mean less family time.[25]

Companies are now rethinking their commitment to working parents. For example, nearly 2,000 companies (triple the number in 1982) provide child-care assistance. The 3M Company provides at-home nursing services for sick children of employees. Some 120 firms, such as Wang Laboratories and Hoffmann-LaRoche, provide the ultimate in child-care on-site centers.[26]

Job location and transfer also provide particular difficulties for the dual-career couple. The location that provides the best opportunity for one partner may not provide the best opportunity for the spouse. And a relocation necessary for the advancement of either the husband or the wife can threaten the career of the other.[27]

Merrill Lynch Relocation Management, Inc., the largest relocation firm, surveyed 600 major companies and learned that 60 percent of corporate moves involve dual-career couples, with 75 percent projected for 1990. As a result of the survey, Merrill Lynch Relocation now offers a "trailing-spouse" training service that includes résumé preparation and interviewing techniques. Some companies also provide assistance in relocating dual-career couples by arranging interviews for the spouse at the new location.[28]

Professional Careers for Women

Since 1970, as indicated in Figure 21–4, women have continued to enter managerial and professional careers in increasing numbers. Given that 20 million jobs were created from 1975 to 1985, women are pouring into the job market.[29]

FIGURE 21–4 Women as percent of all workers, by occupation

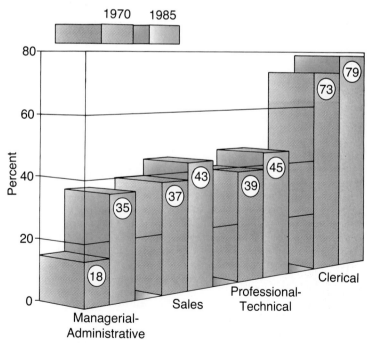

SOURCE: "Workers By Occupation," *Bureau of Labor Statistics* (Washington D.C.: U.S. Government Printing Office, 1972, p. 192; 1986, p. 212). Percentages are rounded.

NOTE: Professional-technical includes accountants, doctors, engineers, lawyers, and teachers.

Women now hold 35 percent of all managerial and administrative jobs in private industry and education.[30] This trend is also reflected in business and professional school enrollments. For instance, one out of every three MBA students is female, compared to one in eight in 1976, and only 3.5 percent in 1971.[31]

Despite these impressive gains, some alarming trends are developing with respect to how long women continue to work as managers. Many of the most educated and motivated women are dropping out of the managerial work force. A 1986 *Fortune* survey revealed that 25 percent of the best women MBAs from the class of 1976 had left their management jobs, whereas only 19 percent of the surveyed men had left. The women who did leave continued to work part-time in a nonmanagerial capacity, stayed at home, or started their own businesses. Research indicates that women's priorities tend to change as they grow older. Marriage overtakes career as what is valued most.[32] Patricia McBroom reports that fewer than one-third of all corporate-level women have children because the corporate life-style does not accommodate professional women with families.[33]

Some companies are trying to help women managers continue in their careers by offering special benefits to ease the stress that full-time jobs can place on families. For example, benefits often include extended maternity leaves with an option to work part-time for a certain period after the baby's birth. Other benefits are flexible work schedules, job sharing, and being allowed to perform certain work duties at home.[34]

SUPERMOM—FADING FAST

A female executive of a major Chicago firm earning more than $50,000 a year suddenly decided to quit, stay home, and raise her children. This executive had been married for a dozen years and had two sons. Good organization was what allowed her to be a wife, mother, and corporate executive. She got up at 5:30 A.M. to be with the kids; by 7:30 she was on a commuter train to the city. On the way home, she established a path from the train station to her home that included stops necessary to run her household. She paid a heavy price, though. Late at night, when her family was asleep, the woman would be awake trying to figure out how to survive. She experienced anger, guilt, and exhaustion in attempting to reconcile the demands of family and work.

"Suddenly I couldn't do it all, anymore—so I just quit."

SOURCE: Adapted from Barbara Kantrowitz and Elisa Williams, "A Mother's Choice," *Newsweek,* 31 March 1986, pp. 46–51.

FIGURE 21–5 Women executives as a percent of all women in the work force

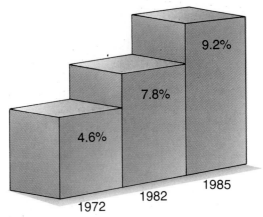

SOURCE: "Managing the Woman's Way," *Newsweek*, 17 March 1986, p. 46.

Sutton and Moore surveyed 1,900 male and female executives in 1985 to replicate a major study conducted in 1965 that investigated attitudes toward women executives. The 1965 study indicated that 54 percent of the men and 50 percent of the women believed that women rarely expected or desired a position of authority. In 1985, only 9 percent of the men and 4 percent of the women surveyed thought that women are not interested in the top job.

In 1965, 90 percent of the male executives reported that a woman had to be exceptional to succeed in business, whereas only 59 percent of male executives held this viewpoint in 1985. Only 9 percent of the men surveyed in 1965 reported they would feel comfortable working for a woman; the number had increased to 21 percent in 1985. In 1965, 40 percent of the women surveyed indicated that they would feel comfortable working for a woman but surprisingly, only 31 percent of the women felt that way in 1985.[35]

A disheartening aspect of the Sutton-Moore study was the finding that salary disparities exist between women and men at every major experience level. For instance, "Men with 21 or more years of experience were more than twice as likely as women with equal experience to earn more than $50,000 annually, and . . . women in the same experience bracket were more than ten times as likely as men to earn less than $30,000 a year."[36]

Figure 21–5 shows the percent of women executives in the U.S. work force. Although the percent of women managers has increased since 1972, the increase has not been as great as some may wish. Social change inevitably takes time. As more and more women succeed in becoming managers, attitudes will continue to change. The women who are in management now must keep the faith for those who will follow.

The Pressures of Time

"How am I ever going to get all of this accomplished?"
"There aren't enough hours in the day!"

These are frequent comments from managers, college students, and people from every walk of life. We have all experienced the stress that comes with the realization that we have more work to do than we have time to complete it. Many of us leave the office, classroom, or library wondering where the time has gone and why we accomplished so little during that time.

Research indicates that a workaholic syndrome among young professionals is intensifying. Many recent graduates are finding that competition for jobs is enormous and that a seventy-hour workweek is the norm.[37]

Some selected time management tools can help you manage your time more wisely:

☐ *Use a written plan.* Set aside the last few minutes of each working day to plan the activities of the following day. These activities can be written down in random order as they occur to you. Analyze each item and assign a priority to it. Some items can be delegated to someone else or need not be done at all. On the following day, begin with the first priority item on your list. After completing it, move to the second item, and so on. Though hardly a revolutionary idea, it is a significant improvement over moving aimlessly from one activity to another, giving attention to interesting items or to whatever happens to come next. A list of activities with assigned priorities provides a systematic daily plan.

☐ *Avoid procrastination.* This is an important aspect of time management because too often, at the end of the day, we find that we have accomplished nothing of consequence and have never gotten to our major tasks. In some instances we delay unpleasant or difficult tasks as long as possible. At other times we justify engaging in trivial or more interesting activities by telling ourselves that we are getting these items out of the way in order to concentrate solely on difficult tasks. Instead, try dividing the dreaded task into small, manageable subtasks, assigning each a high priority. Each subtask, alone, will seem less unpleasant. The feeling of accomplishment derived from completing part of the project may make it easier to work on the remaining parts.

☐ *Use your productive time for high priority items.* Each of us has certain times during the day when we are more productive than at other times. The hours when you feel fresh, alert, and energetic are the hours you should use to work on those items requiring the most creativity. Unfortunately, we often waste these productive times by taking coffee breaks, going through the mail, working on trivial matters, or socializing with others.

Stress Management

Jobs create pressure. Employees are impelled, either by themselves or by their supervisors, to fulfill work assignments and respond to deadlines. The effect of these tensions results in *stress*. The evidence of job stress among managers, professionals, and even blue-collar workers is widespread. Stress adversely af-

NEW WORK HABITS—REWARDS AND PITFALLS

Bruce is an unmarried MBA in his mid-twenties who has a promising future in marketing. He works from 7:00 A.M. till 7:00 P.M., six days a week, and even works later than 7:00 on many nights. Bruce has forsaken romance and many of his former hobbies to accommodate his life-style.

Janet is divorced, in her early thirties, and works as a labor relations consultant. She works twelve hours a day—plus an additional forty hours a week traveling—to advise corporations how to outfox labor unions. She doesn't have time for anything but work.

Charles, a vice-president of a major investment banking firm, earns more than $400,000 yearly. He flies over a million miles a year to deal with anxious clients. Charles considers himself lucky when he can spend one weekday night with his family.

These people are examples of a growing number of management employees, ranging from MBA graduates all the way up to higher executives, who are spending seventy hours or more a week to pursue corporate business. According to management experts, many of them are destined for bitter rewards. Only a few will achieve the goals they seek, and even the winners will find victory empty if they have neglected personal relationships and authentic community involvement.

SOURCE: Examples developed from Richard Thain, *Think Twice Before You Take That Job* (Homewood, Ill.: Dow Jones–Irwin, 1987).

fects their well-being, effectiveness, and health.[38] The consequences of job stress are both physiological and psychological. Numerous physical disorders are related to stress, including cardiovascular disease, gastrointestinal problems, headaches, backaches, skin disorders, and so on. The psychological consequences include feelings of depression, anxiety, and nervousness. As depicted in Figure 21–6, stress is the physiological or psychological state that results from stressors. A *stressor* is the external agent that disturbs the individual's equilibrium. If your supervisor says, "I want that project completed by tomorrow, or I want to know why," you are placed in a stressful situation. Individual differences are obviously important in determining the significance of particular stressors. A threatening comment from a supervisor will more likely

FIGURE 21–6 A stress model

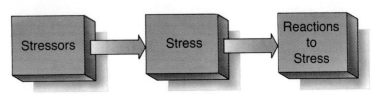

cause stress in an insecure, timid employee than in a self-confident, outgoing type.

Figure 21–7 pictures some of the many types of stressors operating in the organization. Some, such as noise, are related to the physical environment. Others, such as dual supervision, entail role conflict. A number, such as heavy work load, are related to the individual job. Potential stressors are found in all aspects of work, including job demands, group relationships, and organizational policies. In addition, there are many outside sources of stress, such as those associated with family life. Although there are numerous sources of stress in modern life, job-related factors are apparently among the most important.[39]

FIGURE 21–7 Stressors at work

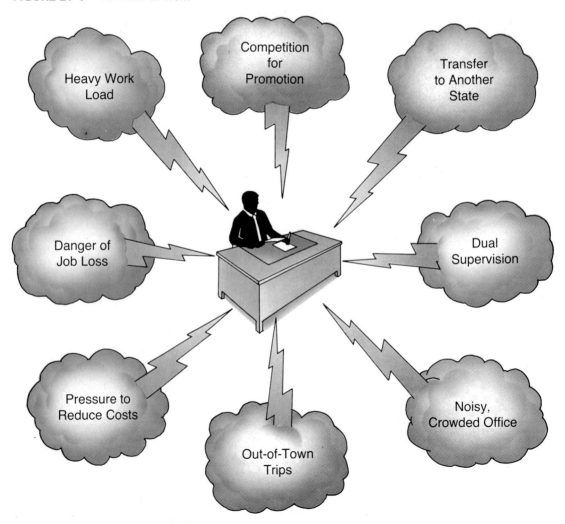

FIGURE 21–8 Relationship of stress to performance

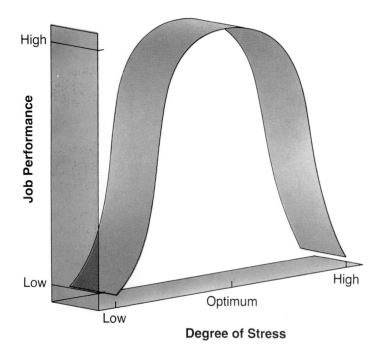

Some stress is clearly beneficial. The stress produced by a college test, for example, may contribute to learning. If the stress is not too extreme, in other words, it can stimulate motivation and achievement. Figure 21–8 shows the relationship of stress to efficient job performance. It is the right-hand half of the curve that involves danger—the extreme stress that leads to less effective performance.

Employees who are working under extreme stress cannot function effectively. They may lose interest in work, experience difficulty in making decisions, become forgetful, find it difficult to concentrate, or resort to alcohol or tranquilizers. Eventually, they may reach a condition described as *burnout*. In burnout, the stress becomes so severe that the victim becomes virtually incapacitated.

A number of researchers consider that a negative or inverse relationship exists between job performance and job stress (Figure 21–9). They argue that by its very nature, stress is harmful to most employees and creates a noxious work environment. Individuals tend to spend a great deal of their time developing coping mechanisms. Noxious conditions may lead to various undesirable job activities, such as goofing off, sabotage, and politicking.[40]

Stress can be managed in several ways. Physical exercise, for example, can be helpful in minimizing stress. Using a variety of relaxation techniques—such as transcendental meditation, yoga, and biofeedback—can reduce stress. One chief executive was quoted in the *Harvard Business Review* as saying that

FIGURE 21–9 An inverted relationship between job performance and job stress

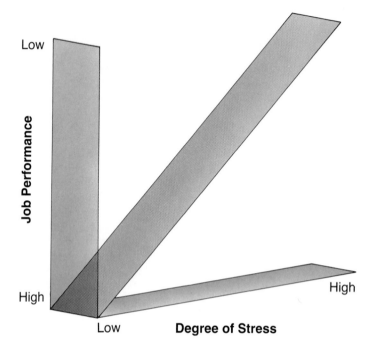

his personal approach to meditation involved prayer and reading the Bible daily.[41]

Management can reduce stress by controlling noise and temperature, minimizing role conflict, providing for effective communication, and outlining career development plans. Some researchers hold that *organizational commitment* may moderate the relationship between performance and job stress. Organizational commitment refers to the nature of an individual's relationship to an organization. Strongly committed employees show a willingness to exert high levels of effort on behalf of the organization. They show an acceptance of the organization's values and goals. Adversities such as high job stress may not keep these employees from performing at reasonable levels.[42]

SUMMARY

Professional career planning or *career management* refers to the decision making involved in choosing and moving through one's working career. The process requires assessing individual needs, abilities, and interests; evaluating work performance; and planning developmental activities. Both the individual and the organization have vital interests in career decisions.

During the *early career*, professionals frequently experience some degree of "reality shock"—a clash of preemployment expectations with the "real world." After beginners progress beyond a training period and acquire expertise, often involving some years of specialization, they move into *mid-career,* a period of expanding responsibilities. Frequently, they also experience a "mid-life crisis," a time of reassessment and reconsideration of career plans established earlier. The third stage of a career, the *late career,* culminates in a time of withdrawal and eventually in retirement.

Mentors play a significant role in the socialization and development of young professionals. They are senior employees (often supervisors) who guide beginners and look out for their interests.

Family interests and professional interests involve some conflict, and many executives experience feelings of frustration in reconciling the two. *Dual-career marriages* provide an especially difficult set of competing interests. Professional careers for women have become much more common in recent years, as women increasingly enter managerial occupations. In spite of impressive gains, however, female executives still earn less than their male counterparts. Nevertheless, their achievements, combined with increasing numbers of women earning business degrees, indicate that they will more and more be filling line positions and entering top-management ranks.

Jobs frequently involve pressures that cause *stress.* Some stress is productive, but excessive stress is harmful to the individual and the organization. Many elements of the job and workplace act as *stressors* on the individual. Reduction of stress is possible through such individual efforts as physical exercise and such organizational efforts as reducing role conflict. *Organizational commitment* may moderate the relationship between performance and job stress.

KEY CONCEPTS

Career management	Fast-track managers
Career stages	Stress
Mentors	Stressors
Dual-career marriages	Burnout
Women and salary disparities	Organizational commitment

DISCUSSION QUESTIONS

1. How does *career planning* differ, if at all, from simply finding a job?
2. What is the risk of "unrealistic expectations," and how is this related to *career planning?*
3. Outline the steps necessary in preparing a *career plan.*
4. Explain the meaning of "reality shock" as applied to careers. Is it helpful or harmful?

5. What are the values of early career specialization, and what is the danger of being trapped in a specialized area?
6. What is the "mid-life crisis," and how does it affect a career?
7. How does a *mentor* contribute to the career development of a young professional?
8. How well do executives appear to reconcile their career and family interests?
9. Identify some of the major problems involved in *dual-career marriages.*
10. How is *stress* related to job performance?
11. Identify a number of *stressors* that exist in most work organizations.
12. How does *organizational commitment* affect the relationship between performance and job stress?
13. Discuss the inverse relationship between job performance and job stress.
14. Describe how *fast-track managers* can become derailed.

NOTES

1. Sam Gould, "Characteristics of Career Planners in Upwardly Mobile Occupations," *Academy of Management Journal* 22 (September 1979): 539–50.
2. Marilyn A. Morgan, Douglas T. Hall, and Alison Martier, "Career Development Strategies in Industry—Where Are We and Where Should We Be?" *Personnel* 56 (March-April 1979): 13–30.
3. John L. Holland, *Making Vocational Choices: A Theory of Careers* (Englewood Cliffs, N.J.: Prentice-Hall, 1973).
4. Anne Roe, "Perspectives on Vocational Development," in *Perspectives on Vocational Development,* ed. J. M. Whiteley and A. Resnikoff (Washington, D.C.: American Personnel and Guidance Association, 1972), pp. 61–82.
5. Donald E. Super, "Vocational Development Theory: Persons, Positions, and Processes," in *Perspectives on Vocational Development,* ed. J. M. Whiteley and A. Resnikoff (Washington, D.C.: American Personnel and Guidance Association, 1972), pp. 14–33.
6. Edgar H. Schein, *Career Dynamics: Matching Individual and Organizational Needs* (Reading, Mass.: Addison-Wesley, 1978).
7. For an extended treatment of this possibility, see Gordon B. Baty, *Entrepreneurship: Playing to Win* (Reston, Va.: Reston, 1974); Clifford M. Baumback and Joseph R. Mancuso, *Entrepreneurship and Venture Management* (Englewood Cliffs, N.J.: Prentice-Hall, 1975); or Karl H. Vesper, *New Venture Strategies* (Englewood Cliffs, N.J.: Prentice-Hall, 1980).
8. Gail Sheehy, *Passages* (New York: Dutton, 1976).
9. Gene W. Dalton, Paul H. Thompson, and Raymond L. Price, "The Four Stages of Professional Careers—A New Look at Performance by Professionals," *Organizational Dynamics,* Summer 1977 (New York: AMACOM, a division of American Management Association), p. 25.
10. Douglas W. Bray, Richard J. Campbell, and Donald L. Grant, *Formative Years in Business: A Long-Term AT&T Study of Managerial Lives* (New York: Wiley, 1974), p. 74.
11. Schein, *Career Dynamics,* p. 95.
12. Dalton, Thompson, and Price, "Four Stages of Professional Careers," p. 28.

13. John P. Kotter, "General Managers Are Not Generalists," *Organizational Dynamics* 10 (Spring 1982): 18.
14. John F. Veiga, "Do Managers on the Move Get Anywhere?" *Harvard Business Review* 59 (March-April 1981): 28.
15. Ibid., p. 36.
16. Dalton, Thompson, and Price, "Four Stages of Professional Careers," p. 30.
17. Ibid., p. 32.
18. Ibid., p. 24.
19. Gerard R. Roche, "Much Ado about Mentors," *Harvard Business Review* 57 (January-February 1979): 14–15, 20.
20. "Formal Mentors Help Junior Staffers Advance at Firms and U.S. Agencies," *The Wall Street Journal,* 15 November 1983.
21. David J. Levinson, *The Seasons in a Man's Life* (New York: Knopf, 1978), p. 123.
22. Donald W. Myers and Neil J. Humphreys, "The Caveats in Mentorship," *Business Horizons* (July-August 1985): 9–14.
23. Fernando Bartolomé and Paul A. Lee Evans, "Professional Lives Versus Private Lives—Shifting Patterns of Managerial Commitment," *Organizational Dynamics* 7 (Spring 1979): 3–79.
24. Fern S. Chapman, "Executive Guilt: Who's Taking Care of the Children?" *Fortune,* 16 February 1987, pp. 30–37.
25. Ibid.
26. Mary Bruno, "Day Care on the Job," *Newsweek,* 2 September 1985, pp. 59–62.
27. Irene Pave, "Move Me, Move My Spouse: Relocating The Corporate Couple," *Business Week,* 16 December 1985, pp. 57–60.
28. Ibid.
29. Karen Pennar and Edward Mervosh, "Women At Work," *Business Week,* 28 January 1986, pp. 80–85.
30. "Workers by Occupation," *Bureau of Labor Statistics* (Washington, D.C.: U.S. Government Printing Office, 1986), 212.
31. "Women and the Executive Suite," *Newsweek,* 14 September 1981, p. 65; and Alex Taylor III, "Why Women Managers Are Bailing Out," *Fortune,* 18 August 1986, p. 16.
32. The survey included 1,039 women and 4,255 men who received an MBA from seventeen of the most selective business schools. For a more detailed discussion see Alex Taylor III, "Why Women Managers Are Bailing Out," *Fortune,* 18 August 1986, pp. 16–23.
33. "Corporate Women Have It All—But A Family Life," *Business Week,* 2 June 1986, pp. 12–14.
34. Taylor, "Why Women Managers Are Bailing Out," *Fortune;* and Aaron Bernstein, "Business Starts Tailoring Itself to Suit Working Women," *Business Week,* 6 October 1986, pp. 50–54.
35. Charlotte D. Sutton and Kris K. Moore, "Executive Women—20 Years Later," *Harvard Business Review* 63 (September-October 1985): 42–66. The earlier study is described by Garda W. Bowman, N. Beatrice Worthy, and Stephen A. Greyser, "Are Women Executives People?" *Harvard Business Review* 42 (July-August 1965): 12–38.
36. Ibid., p. 66.
37. Richard Phillips, "Is There Life After Putting In a 70-Hour Work Week?" *The Dallas Morning News,* 23 December 1986.

38. John M. Ivancevich and Michael T. Matteson, *Stress At Work* (Glenview, Ill.: Scott, Foresman, 1980).

39. Michael J. Davidson and Charles L. Cooper, "A Model of Occupational Stress," *Journal of Occupational Medicine* 23 (1981): 564–74.

40. The researchers are discussed by Muhammad Jamal, "Relationship of Job Stress to Job Performance: A Study of Managers and Blue-Collar Workers," *Human Relations* 38 (1985): 409–24.

41. Herbert Benson and Robert L. Allen, "How Much Stress Is Too Much?" *Harvard Business Review* 58 (September-October 1980): 92.

42. Richard M. Steers, *Introduction to Organizational Behavior* (Santa Monica, Calif.: Goodyear, 1981).

SUPPLEMENTARY READING

Blau, Gary J., and Boal, Kimberly B. "Conceptualizing How Job Involvement and Organizational Commitment Affect Turnover and Absenteeism." *Academy of Management Review* 12 (April 1987): 288–300.

Boeker, Warren; Blair, Rebecca; Van Loo, M. Francis; and Roberts, Karlene. "Are The Expectations of Women Managers Being Met?" *California Management Review* 27 (Spring 1985): 148–157.

Brockner, Joel, and Hess, Ted. "Self-Esteem and Task Performance in Quality Circles." *Academy of Management Journal* 29 (September 1986): 617–23.

Dubno, Peter. "Attitudes Toward Women Executives: A Longitudinal Approach." *Academy of Management Journal* 28 (March 1985): 235–39.

Friedman, Dana E. "Child Care for Employees' Kids." *Harvard Business Review* 64 (March-April 1986): 28–34.

Greenhalgh, Leonard, and Rosenblatt, Zehava. "Job Insecurity: Toward Conceptual Clarity." *Academy of Management Review* 9 (July 1984): 438–448.

Ivancevich, John M.; Matteson, Michael T.; and Richards, Edward P. III. "Who's Liable for Stress on the Job?" *Harvard Business Review* 63 (March-April 1985): 60–72.

Jackson, Susan E.; Zedeck, Sheldon; and Summers, Elizabeth. "Family Life Disruptions: Effects of Job-Induced Structural and Emotional Interference." *Academy of Management Journal* 28 (September 1985): 574–86.

Jones, Edward W., Jr. "Black Managers: The Dream Deferred." *Harvard Business Review* 64 (May-June 1986): 84–93.

Jones, Gareth R. "Socialization Tactics, Self-Efficacy and Newcomers' Adjustments to Organizations." *Academy of Management Journal* 29 (June 1986): 262–79.

Kram, Kathy E. "Phases of the Mentor Relationship." *Academy of Management Journal* 26 (December 1983): 608–25.

———, and Isabella, Lynn A. "Mentoring Alternatives: The Role of Peer Relationships in Career Development." *Academy of Management Journal* 28 (March 1985): 110–32.

Latack, Janina C. "Career Transitions Within Organizations: An Exploratory Study of Work, Nonwork, and Coding Strategies." *Organizational Behavior and Human Decision Processes* 34 (December 1984): 296–322.

_____, and **Dozier, Janelle B.** "After the Ax Falls: Job Loss as a Career Transition." *Academy of Management Review* 11 (April 1986): 375–92.

Lorsch, Jay W., and **Takagi, Harud.** "Keeping Managers Off the Shelf." *Harvard Business Review* 64 (July-August 1986): 60–65.

Luthans, Fred; McCaul, Harriette S.; and **Dodd, Nancy G.** "Organizational Commitment: A Comparison of American, Japanese and Korean Employees." *Academy of Management Journal* 28 (March 1985): 213–19.

Mainiero, Lisa A. "Early Career Factors That Differentiate Technical Management Careers From Technical Professional Careers." *Journal of Management* 12 (Winter 1986): 561–76.

McBroom, Patricia A. *The Third Sex: The New Professional Woman.* New York: Morrow, 1987.

Myers, Donald W., and **Humphreys, Neil J.** "The Caveats in Mentorship." *Business Horizons* 28 (July-August 1985): 9–14.

Near, Janet P. "Reactions To The Career Plateau." *Business Horizons* 27 (July-August 1984): 75–79.

Nelson, Debra L., and **Quick, James C.** "Professional Women: Are Distress and Disease Inevitable?" *Academy of Management Review* 10 (April 1985): 206–18.

Reich, Murray H. "Executive Views From Both Sides of Mentoring." *Personnel* 62 (March 1985): 42–46.

Reichers, Arnon E. "A Review and Reconceptualization of Organizational Commitment." *Academy of Management Review* 10 (July 1985): 465–76.

Slocum, John W., Jr.; Cron, William L.; Hansen, Richard W.; and **Rawlings, Sally.** "Business Strategy And The Management of Plateaued Employees." *Academy of Management Journal* 28 (March 1985): 133–54.

LOYALTY

You are a successful young manager three years out of college, have a good position in the marketing department of a major consumer products corporation, have been happily married for about a year, live in a nice house in a good neighborhood, and are very much involved in your church. You often give thanks for achieving such happiness and success in just three short years.

This Friday morning has been rather slow, and you have been sitting in your office reflecting on some of your good

fortunes: a great job, a great boss, and a reciprocity of respect with the president of the company. You have gained acceptance in the organization, and your subordinates are excellent performers and look to you for leadership. Your thoughts drift to tomorrow (Saturday) and the city tennis tournament. You have been working hard and expect to win the trophy. Especially interested is the president of the company, who is proud of your tennis ability.

Paramount in your thoughts is your first wedding anniversary, also tomorrow. You have a gift purchased and wrapped, hidden at home in the attic. You are filled with

Prepared by Professor Jack Wimer of Baylor University.

love and gratitude when you think of your spouse, who has changed your life and who is responsible to a large degree for your drive to excel. Tomorrow is shaping up to be a great day!

Shortly after lunch, a bombshell drops at a staff meeting in the president's office. It has just been discovered that the company's main competitor has launched a new product far ahead of industry forecasts. Unless your firm reacts immediately, it stands to lose a large portion of market share. The president calls for a crash program to counter the threat, with an advertising blitz ahead of schedule for your company's new competing product. He wants the campaign to be designed and ready for final approval by Monday morning. Sitting there—realizing the impact of this request—you are stunned. Your department is the focal point for the project. It looks like your entire crew will be working long hours all weekend.

Arriving home late Friday evening, you are met by your spouse with a warm and loving greeting and a small, beautifully wrapped gift. As you remove the wrapping, you wonder why you are receiving this a day early. The moment the contents are revealed, you are overcome with love for such a thoughtful gift: a pair of airline tickets to the Bahamas for tomorrow afternoon, with prepaid reservations at your honeymoon hotel of one year ago.

Your mind frantically searches for a solution. What about the boss's mandate for Monday? What about the tennis tournament tomorrow morning? Maybe you can cleverly work in all commitments. Your assistant is good and can lead the group. How can you possibly disappoint your loving spouse, the main person in your life? Only a second or two has passed since you opened the gift, but it seems as though your mind has searched a thousand possibilities.

Question

1. What are you going to say and do?

WHOSE CAREER IS THIS ANYWAY?

Derek was contemplating his college major. He had decided early in his freshman year to choose a major from the business school. In fact, it was the strong reputation of the university's business school that had first attracted him to the campus. The problem now was, which area of business should he select?

Prepared by Professor Tammy Hunt of Baylor University.

Derek has been considering management because he likes working with people and believes he has developed good leadership skills. He was fascinated by most of the topics covered in the principles of management course he took last semester. But Derek's parents have pointed out that the university has a great placement record for accounting and finance majors. His friend Diane just received a job offer with a great starting salary from a Big Eight accounting firm. The starting salaries for management trainees are generally not as high.

In deciding, Derek faces two issues. First, he must make a choice that he can live with, not one his parents or friends desire for him. Second, he must decide what qualities are necessary for a good manager. With a pen and paper, he began listing the characteristics of a manager.

Questions

1. What qualities are needed to become a good manager? Can those qualities be learned or does a person have an inborn aptitude for them?
2. How should Derek deal with his parents' urging that he choose accounting or finance as a major?

GLOSSARY

Achievement-oriented leadership A leadership style that emphasizes excellence in performance, with a confidence that subordinates will assume responsibility and accomplish challenging goals.

Activities Physical acts an employee engages in to perform a task.

Administrative management The early study of management from a top-level perspective. Associated with Henri Fayol, this field of thought identifies the functions of a manager and a set of basic principles or guidelines for management to follow.

Agenda setting Developing a set of loosely connected goals and plans to address a manager's long-, medium-, and short-term responsibilities.

Aggregate planning Determining the firm's total production requirements.

Aggressive sharing of information The process of actively transmitting information to subordinates so they might understand the operations and future directions of their organization.

All-channel network A communications network in which each member can communicate with any other member.

Assessment center A technique of evaluating employees through simulation exercises, interviews, psychological tests, and group exercises to determine the degree to which the employees possess management potential.

Authority The official (institutionalized) right and power to make decisions affecting the behavior of subordinates. It includes the right to give orders and exact obedience.

Autonomous work group A small group that is given the responsibility for planning and carrying out a whole task. The group provides its own leadership and determines the roles each member will play. Compensation and feedback about performance are based on group rather than individual accomplishments.

Barnard, Chester I. An American executive (1886–1961) who analyzed the role of the manager and was the first management theorist to examine the organization as a system.

BARS *see* Behaviorally anchored rating scales.

Behaviorally anchored rating scales (BARS)
A performance appraisal form designed by the raters themselves that uses critical behavioral incidents as points (anchors) on the rating scales.

Behavior control An aspect of supervisory control where the supervisor actually observes an employee's behavior and work procedures.

Behavior modification A motivational concept based on operant conditioning theory. It proposes that certain events which follow particular forms of behavior can affect the probability that those behaviors will be repeated in the future.

Boundary spanning The process of examining the boundary or area of contact between an organizational system and its environment.

Bounded rationality Decision-making conditions under which the manager identifies and analyzes only a few possible alternatives and then selects, from these few, an alternative which he or she predicts will yield a satisfactory return to the organization.

Bureaucracy A concept originated by Weber to refer to a rational organization that performed its task with high efficiency. Managers in a bureaucracy had the right to give orders based on their rational-legal authority.

Bureaucratic control A process of using authority, chain of command, rules, policies, and other bureaucratic devices to standardize behavior and evaluate performance.

Bureaucratic management The management of large organizations in which managers give orders based on rational-legal authority.

Burnout A stressful condition so severe that the victim becomes virtually incapacitated.

Capacity planning Ensuring that the organization has the capability to produce a desired number of output units.

Capacity to perform The physiological and cognitive capabilities that enable an employee to perform a task effectively.

Career management Decisions involved in career choices and the planning of one's life work.

Career stages The idea that working life can

be considered in stages. While various writers recognize a different number of stages, the general view is that three stages exist: early career, mid-career, and late career.

Chain of command The communications and order-giving chain of superior-subordinate relationships in an organization.

Change agent Term for an outside consultant who aids an organization in bringing about planned change.

Circle network A circular communications network in which each individual can communicate with two others.

CIS *see* Computer information system.

Clan control A technique that uses a socialization process to control behavior and assess performance. The process involves the social characteristics of values, traditions, shared beliefs, and commitment.

Classical school of management The earliest formal compilation of management concepts and principles. Stretching from about 1895 until approximately 1920, this school of thought was composed of three related fields—scientific management, administrative management, and bureaucratic management.

Coalition of interests The acceptable consensus that is reached among the numerous parties involved in the process of forming objectives.

Cognitive moral development A six-stage progression of moral behavior that is developed from middle childhood to adulthood.

Cohesiveness The degree to which group members act as a single unit—rather than as individuals—in the pursuit of group objectives.

Command group A formal group composed of a manager and his or her immediate subordinates.

Committee A formal group of individuals who are officially drawn together to consider issues pertinent to the organization or to function in a certain capacity.

Communication An interactive process in which a sender transmits a message—containing facts, feelings, and attitudes—to a receiver, who sends a return message indicating his or her reception and degree of understanding.

Compensation   An employee's salary and fringe benefits.

Compliance   A change in individual behavior resulting in closer conformance to group norms.

Comprehensive plans   The integration of functional-area and divisional plans. Each plan is questioned as to its contribution to established objectives.

Compressed workweek   A work schedule involving more hours per day and fewer days per week.

Computer information system (CIS)   A computerized system which collects data related both to internal operations and the external environment and then transforms the data into usable information.

Conceptual skills   Skills that enable one to deal with abstract concepts. These are particularly useful in creating a vision of what an organization can become and in determining how the organization can realize this ideal state.

Concurrent control   Organizational controls used to monitor products or services as they are being produced.

Conflict   A state of disagreement and disharmony.

Conflict of interests   When an individual or group, in pursuing its own ends, interferes with or blocks the actions of others who are pursuing their own interests.

Conformity   Individual adherence to group norms as a result of perceived group pressure. There are two types of conformity: (1) *compliance*—a change in behavior resulting in closer adherence to group norms; and (2) *private acceptance*—a change in behavior *and* belief resulting in closer adherence to group norms.

Consideration   Leader's actions that enhance the warmth of leader-follower relationships, the leader's willingness to listen to subordinates, and the mutual trust between leader and followers.

Content theory   Any of the theories of motivation that emphasize the specific factors that motivate an individual.

Contingency management   A contemporary school of management thought that attempts to determine the circumstances under which certain managerial actions will yield a particular set of results.

Contingency model of leadership   A leadership theory, formulated by Fiedler, that proposes that the most effective style of leadership depends upon the particular situation.

Contingency planning   The process of developing a set of alternative plans to fit a variety of future conditions.

Contingency theory   A contemporary school of management thought that attempts to determine the circumstances under which certain managerial actions will yield a particular set of results.

Continuous reinforcement   In behavior modification, a reinforcement schedule in which behavior is positively reinforced each time it occurs.

Controversy   Differences of opinion that can prevent or interfere with reaching a decision.

Conventional rating scale   A performance appraisal form containing a list of qualities, characteristics, or traits upon which the employee is rated on a scale ranging from "poor" to "outstanding."

Corrective controls   Organizational controls that monitor outputs and are used to indicate problems occurring after the fact.

Creativity   The development of new ideas, new combinations of existing knowledge, and new approaches to problem solving.

Critical path   In PERT, the sequence of activities that represents the shortest possible time to completion of the entire project. Any delay in this path will delay completion of the project.

Cross-cultural management   Techniques used in identifying cultural variables and adjusting to cultural differences.

Cultural sensitivity   Developing an awareness that cultural differences exist and being responsive to the differences.

Decentralization   The systematic delegation of authority on an organization-wide basis, involving the creation of relatively autonomous divisions.

Decision analysis   An approach used to group

tasks where the organizer considers the types of decisions that must be made and the levels at which they appropriately can be made.

Decision-making style   The way in which a manager defines, analyzes, and solves unstructured problems.

Decision support system   An interactive computer system that provides the manager with easy access to decision models and data in order to support decision-making tasks.

Decision tree   A probabilistic model that depicts the various decision alternatives as branches of a tree.

Delegation of authority   The act of a manager in granting a subordinate the right to act or make decisions.

Dependency   An integral aspect of a manager's job in which the manager's performance is contingent upon the behaviors and activities of other individuals.

Deterministic model   A mathematical model in which all variables are assigned exact values.

Directive leadership   Letting subordinates know what is expected of them and how the task should be accomplished.

Distinctive competencies   The ability of an organization to do some things particularly well in comparison to its competitors.

Distributive justice   Moral standards are based upon the primacy of a single value, which is justice.

Divisionalization   An organizational structure where decentralization of authority and decision making is often centered on product or territorial divisions.

Divisional pattern   An organization structured at the top level in terms of products or geography.

Downward communication   Communication from a superior to a subordinate.

Dual-career marriage   A marriage where both husband and wife pursue professional careers.

Dumping   Selling products in other countries for less than the cost of making it.

Dynamic environment   An environment characterized by rapid change, creating problems for managers who must try to anticipate the direction and magnitude of change.

Dysfunctional aspects of control   Adverse side effects resulting from the reactions of organizational members toward control techniques.

Economic order quantity   The quantity of raw materials, parts, products, or supplies that should be purchased to minimize total inventory costs.

EEO   *see* Equal employment opportunity.

Entrepreneur   An individual who assumes the risks involved in starting a business.

Environmental interface   The boundary or area between an organizational system and its environment.

Environmental scanning   Gathering and analyzing information concerning relevant events and changes in the environment.

EOQ   *see* Economic order quantity.

Equal employment opportunity (EEO)   Various legal requirements mandating that all personnel decisions in covered organizations must be made without regard to such variables as age, race, sex, religion, national origin, or color.

Eternal law   Moral standards which are revealed in scripture or apparent in nature and then interpreted by religious leaders with the belief that everyone should act in accordance with the interpretation.

Ethical dilemma   A situation that occurs when managers, or organizational members, are faced with implementing a costly social obligation that conflicts with the organization's economic performance.

Ethnocentric   A home-country orientation. Nationals from the home country have superior positions in headquarters or subsidiaries and home-country standards are used to judge performance.

Expectancy   In expectancy theory, the employee's estimate of the likelihood that his or her effort will result in performance.

Expectancy theory   A motivation theory which proposes that people make conscious behavioral choices based on their expectations about the future.

Expectations approach   A process where all managers in the organization are asked to make an extensive list of the performance expectations they expect from other managers as well as what they perceive other managers expect of them. Through interpersonal and, later, group discussions, performance expectations are formalized and serve as performance comparison standards.

Expected value   In probability theory, the financial outcome expected from each decision alternative.

Experience curve   The idea that an increase in a company's volume leads to reduction of production costs because practice tends to make perfect.

Expert support system   A computer program that helps solve difficult problems through specialized symbolic reasoning. The program contains a knowledge base of facts and rules related to the problem and a set of reasoning methods.

External audits   An independent appraisal of the organization's accounting and financial procedures by a certified public accounting firm to determine if the records are accurate and reflect generally accepted accounting practices.

External forces   Forces outside the organization that create the need for organizational change.

Extinction   In behavior modification, the act of withholding positive reinforcement following an employee's behavior to reduce the probability that the behavior will be repeated in the future.

Fayol, Henri   A French business executive (1841–1925) who delineated the functions of a manager and formulated a set of principles for managers to follow.

Feasibility space   On a linear programming graph, the area within which any production combination is possible because it meets all of the capacity constraints.

Feedback   The return of environmental information to an organization regarding the results of the organization's process.

Financial control   An aspect of control involving the use of reports detailing the organiza-

tion's financial condition. These include the income statement, balance sheet, financial ratio analysis, and break-even calculations.

Fixed costs   Costs that remain the same over the short run regardless of the organization's level of operations.

Fixed-interval reinforcement   In behavior modification, a reinforcement schedule in which behavior is positively reinforced, not continuously, but at fixed intervals.

Flexible manufacturing system   The use of automation in the form of computer-integrated manufacturing systems into large-batch and job-lot production.

Flexible work schedules   A system for scheduling work which permits individual variation in the hours of the day which are worked.

Follett, Mary Parker   An American author and political philosopher (1868–1933) who was one of the first management theorists to emphasize the importance of human behavior in the workplace.

Formal communication channels   The network designed and sanctioned by management through which messages move from senders to receivers. Such channels may be downward, upward, or horizontal.

Formal ethical code   A published code of corporate ethics which describes standards of conduct.

Formal group   A collection of individuals formed by management and charged with the responsibility of contributing to the organization.

Functional authority   Authority derived from assigning tasks within the organization.

Functional pattern   An organization pattern where jobs and activities are grouped on the basis of function—for example, sales, manufacturing, and finance.

Functional planning   The preparation of functional area plans where the goals of each functional department are related to the overall goals for the entire organization. For instance, production managers prepare production plans, marketing managers prepare marketing plans, and so on.

Functional status   Status derived from one's profession or type of work.

General environment   External conditions that are of concern to all organizations.

Geocentric   A global orientation. Collaborative relationships exist between foreign subsidiaries and headquarters. Control focuses on achieving global objectives.

Geographic pattern   An organizational pattern where jobs and activities are grouped on the basis of geographic location.

Global competitive strategy   Decisions regarding how a firm will compete internationally. Four alternatives exist: seeking a protected niche, developing individual national markets, targeting a particular industry segment, and competing worldwide with a full product line.

Grapevine   The organization's informal communications network, which arises spontaneously without management's sanction.

Gresham's law of planning   Situations in which a manager's daily routine causes planning to be neglected.

Group   Two or more individuals who are psychologically aware of one another, perceive themselves to be a group, and interact to a significant degree in the pursuit of a common goal.

Groupthink   A situation in which the group members emphasize the importance of solidarity over critical thinking.

Hawthorne Studies   A series of experiments conducted in the Western Electric Company's Hawthorne Plant, beginning in 1924, which modified the rational/technical assumptions of the classical school by emphasizing the importance of the human element in management.

Horizontal communication   Communication among individuals at the same hierarchical level.

Horizontal linkages   Lateral relationships among organizational components—that is, direct relationships among units at the same organizational level.

Human relations skills   Skills required to interact effectively with other human beings.

Hygiene factors   In the two-factor theory of motivation, these factors are associated with the job context and serve to keep employees from becoming dissatisfied.

Individual differences   The variation among human beings in terms of needs, aptitudes, abilities, attitudes, interests, and so on.

Informal communication channels   Communication among individuals within an organization that is not transmitted via formal channels but through channels established by the employees themselves.

Informal group   A collection of individuals which arises spontaneously as a natural outgrowth of human interaction and develops without formal management sanction.

Information overload   A condition in which the volume of information being received by an organization or individual is greater than the capacity to handle it.

Initiating structure   Leader's actions that define leader-follower relationships, establish definite standards of performance, specify standard operating procedures, and determine who does what.

Institutionalized power   The connection between authority and the formal organization used to distinguish institutional power from other types of power.

Instrumentality   In expectancy theory, the relationship an employee perceives between performance and the desired outcome.

Integrating role   An individual assigned the specific leadership responsibility for coordinating interdepartmental effort. These positions carry such titles as product manager, project leader, program coordinator, business manager, and so on.

Integration   Bringing conflicting parties together so that they might discuss the issues face-to-face.

Interactions   Behavioral relationships an employee engages in to perform a task.

Internal audits   An appraisal of the organization's internal management control systems as well as a review of operating practices to promote efficiency. Internal audits are conducted by members of the organization.

Internal forces   Forces inside the organization that create the need for organizational change.

International business   Those business activities that cross national boundaries.

International management   A field of management that deals with business activities that cross national boundaries.

Interrelated subsystems   Interdependent parts of a larger system. Each subsystem must mesh its activities with the activities of the other subsystems.

Intuition   The psychological function which transmits perceptions in an unconscious way.

Japanese management   A distinctive management style used by the Japanese. Some essential elements include long-term employment for organizational members, consensus decision making, moderately specialized career paths, and slow evaluation and promotion.

Job analysis   A systematic study of a job which includes the compilation of a job description—containing the specific duties and responsibilities of the position—and a job specification, which defines the education, experience, skills, and behaviors required of the position holder.

Job description   The specific duties and responsibilities of a position.

Job enlargement   An attempt to make jobs more interesting and satisfying by increasing the variety of duties.

Job enrichment   An attempt to make routine jobs more meaningful by providing more challenging tasks, responsibility, and autonomy.

Job evaluation   The systematic analysis of jobs within an organization to determine their relative financial value.

Job lot production   Characterized by production solely to customer orders using short production runs and general-purpose equipment and personnel.

Job rotation   A personnel development technique designed to increase an employee's experience by shifting him or her periodically from one job to another.

Job satisfaction   A multidimensional concept composed of the attitudes a person has toward such work dimensions as the organization, immediate supervisor, financial rewards, fellow employees, and the task.

Job specification   The education, experience, skills, and behaviors required of a position holder.

Just-in-time   An inventory control system where the manufacturer requires suppliers of raw materials and parts to make multiple deliveries daily just as the components are needed in the production process.

Layout planning   Determining the precise configuration of the departments (and equipment within the departments) that will be used to transform inputs into outputs.

Leader Match   In the contingency model of leadership, a self-administered, programmed leadership training program.

Leader-member relations   In the contingency model of leadership, the trust and confidence group members place in their leader.

Leader position power   In the contingency model of leadership, the extent of the leader's legitimate, reward, and coercive powers.

Leadership   The managerial function of securing the cooperation of others in accomplishing an objective.

Leadership neutralizers   Variables that interrupt the predictive relationship between a leader's behavior and subordinate performance or satisfaction.

Leadership style   The way a manager behaves in his or her role as leader. The two most widely discussed leadership styles are task-oriented and relationship-oriented behavior.

Leadership substitutes   Variables that reduce the leader's power to improve or retard the performance or satisfaction of subordinates.

Leadership traits   Personal characteristics of a leader.

Least-preferred coworker scale (LPC)   In the contingency model of leadership, the questionnaire that indicates the leadership style of the respondent.

Liaison role   An organizational unit or individual having the responsibility of coordinating the activities of two or more components of an organization.

Linear programming   A deterministic model which yields the optimal allocation of limited resources having alternative uses—if all of the relationships in the model are linear and all variables can be quantitatively measured.

Listening   To do more than simply receive a message; listening involves the active participation of the receiver in understanding the message he or she is receiving.

Logical incrementalism   The concept that managers in rapidly changing environments may not know precisely their ultimate objective or their entire strategy at a particular point in time, because these managers deal with events in an incremental (or bit-by-bit) fashion.

Long-term results   Outcomes obtained over a long-range time period such as five to ten years.

LPC   *see* Least-preferred coworker scale.

Management   The process of acquiring and combining human, financial, informational, and physical resources to attain the organization's primary goal of producing a product or service desired by some segment of society.

Management by exception   Focusing managerial attention on organizational subsystems in which actual performance deviates significantly from the established standard.

Management development   The process of increasing the effectiveness of managers in their present jobs and preparing them for promotion.

Management functions   The basic activities required of managers in the performance of their jobs. The major management functions include planning and decision making, organizing, leading and motivating, and controlling.

Management principles   Basic guidelines which, if followed, are likely to improve a manager's effectiveness.

Management science   A mathematical application of the scientific method to the solution of organizational problems.

Managerial Grid   An organization development technique, developed by Blake and Mouton, which has as its underlying assumption that the best managers are those who are both highly task-centered and employee-centered.

Managerial roles   The set of behaviors expected of any individual holding a management position.

Market control   A control strategy used by top- and mid-level managers involving the use of price competition to evaluate output. Managers can compare profits and prices to determine the efficiency of their organization.

Master schedule   Derived to indicate which products will be produced, in what quantities, and by what dates.

Material requirements planning   (MRP) A computerized system that integrates the purchase and production of all material and parts needed to produce the required quantity of a good or service.

Matrix pattern   An organizational pattern involving multiple lines of command in which both functional and project managers exercise authority over the same organizational activities.

Maximizing   Decision-making behavior in which the manager selects the *best* alternative (that is, the one that will yield maximum returns to the organization) from all possible alternatives.

Mechanistic structure   An organizational structure based on formality. Formal job descriptions, rules, procedures, detailed control systems, and greater centralization of decision making are used.

Mentors   Older, more experienced individuals who provide guidance and assistance to a newcomer in an organization.

Mission statement   A broadly defined but enduring statement of purpose that distinguishes one firm from other firms of its type and identifies the scope of its operations in product and market terms.

Model   A simplified representation of an actual system, containing only the most important and basic features of that system.

Moral reasoning   A type of moral analysis where individuals use ethical beliefs combined with an economic evaluation and an awareness of legal requirements to provide a foundation for business ethics.

Motivation   A concept that refers to the direction, strength, and persistence of an individual's behavior.

Motivators In the two-factor theory of motivation, these factors are associated with the job content and make employees satisfied with their jobs.

MRP *see* Material requirements planning.

Multinational corporation A corporation having branches, divisions, and/or subsidiaries that straddle national boundaries. An example is an industrial organization with production facilities in many different countries and sales organizations in still other countries.

Multiple-hurdles selection model A process of offering jobs only to applicants who pass all of the organization's selection hurdles (e.g., application blanks, reference checks, tests, and interviews).

Multiple objectives Because many factors can affect organizational outcomes, objectives need to be established in all areas upon which the firm's survival depends.

Multiple scenarios A set of differing assumptions which are used in planning.

Need hierarchy The theory, developed by Maslow, that human needs are arranged in a distinct hierarchy, ranging from physiological needs to self-fulfillment needs. An individual is motivated by the desire to fulfill the lowest-level need which is not yet satisfied.

Negative reinforcement In behavior modification, an event which follows an employee's behavior and strengthens the behavior by providing an avenue of escape from an unpleasant event.

Network building Developing relationships with people whose cooperation is necessary for a manager to perform effectively.

Networking Electronic linking of computers.

Networking pattern A form of disaggregation where one company contracts out certain functions such as production or distribution to other companies. The contracting company acts as a small central headquarters and communicates what actions are to be taken by the various functions. Networks are different from a joint venture in that the focal company secures specialized services rather than collaborating with two or more companies on a venture basis.

New venture division A small organizational subsystem which is guided by entrepreneurial managers and is autonomous of the larger system's daily operations.

Nominal group technique A group decision-making technique in which the members identify alternative solutions to a problem independently without interacting. The alternatives are then discussed, and the members vote on a solution by secret ballot.

Nonroutine decision Decisions which deal with unstructured, nonrecurring problems which have no accepted method of resolution.

Norm A generally agreed upon standard of behavior to which all members of the group are expected to adhere.

OD *see* Organization development.

OD research Research that measures the impact of organization development interventions on organizational effectiveness.

Official objectives The publicly espoused goals of the organization. Less specific than operative objectives.

Open system A system which interacts with its environment.

Operating core The central part of an organization—that part which produces the organization's goods or services.

Operating decisions The day-to-day decisions that involve producing and delivering the organization's goods or services as effectively and efficiently as possible.

Operations research (OR) A mathematical application of the scientific method to the solution of organizational problems.

Operative objectives Goals that the organization actively pursues. More specific than official objectives.

Opportunity to perform The particular configuration of the field of forces surrounding an employee and his or her task that enables or constrains that person's task performance and that are beyond the person's direct control.

OPT *see* Optimized production technology.

Optimized production technology A two-part system that includes a simulated manufacturing program and a set of shop-floor management rules. The system allows managers to identify bottlenecks—thereby increasing output while simultaneously lowering its inventory and operating expenses.

OR *see* Operations research.

Organic structure An organization structure based on flexibility. Only general job descriptions, a minimum of rules, reliance on self-discipline, and greater participative decision making are used.

Organizational barriers to delegation Barriers to the delegation process caused by organizational design elements.

Organizational commitment The nature of an individual's relationship to an organization. Highly committed individuals show a willingness to exert high levels of effort on behalf of the organization and have a definite belief and acceptance of the organization's values and goals.

Organizational control The managerial function that deals with controlling how the organization's financial, physical, human, and technological resources are being used.

Organizational control cycle A process of assuring the effective performance of the organizational system through establishing standards of performance, comparing actual performance with the standards, and taking corrective action, when necessary.

Organizational culture The values and patterns of belief and behavior that are accepted and practiced by the members of a particular organization.

Organizational design The process of arranging the various organizational elements into a meaningful fashion. Involves weaving together such parameters as decision making, planning and control, policies and procedures, as well as accountability to make the organization work.

Organizational effectiveness The degree to which an organization attains its primary goals (those tied to satisfying the needs of the organization's primary client group) and secondary goals (those tied to the satisfaction of the needs of secondary beneficiary groups, such as employees, the public, suppliers, and so on).

Organizational system A system composed of human beings, money, materials, equipment, and so on, which are related in the accomplishment of some goal or goals.

Organization development (OD) A planned, organization-wide effort to increase the organization's effectiveness and health through behavioral science-based interventions.

Orientation The process through which newcomers to an organization are introduced to their jobs and new surroundings.

Outcome In expectancy theory, the reward (either extrinsic or intrinsic) desired by an employee.

Output control An aspect of supervisory control where the supervisor uses written records to measure employee productivity and output.

Outside directors Members of boards of directors who are not employed by the focal firm.

Panel interview A job interview in which the applicant is questioned by a panel of interviewers in an attempt to make the interview more objective.

Pareto optimality A condition where the scarce resources of society are being efficiently used by producers and goods and services are being effectively distributed by competitive markets in such a manner that it is impossible to make any single person better off without harming some other person.

Participation A change program in which employees at all hierarchical levels are involved in choosing and implementing change methods.

Participative leadership Consulting with subordinates and taking their suggestions into consideration when making decisions.

Path-goal theory of leadership A leadership theory which views the leader's function as clarifying the subordinates' paths to work-goal attainment and increasing their opportunities for personal satisfaction.

Patterned behavior description interview A job interview in which the interviewer asks questions that probe how applicants have behaved in situations reflective of the job requirements, records the applicants' responses, and rates the applicants relative to each of the responses.

Perceptual barriers   A hindrance to communication that exists when the sender and receiver interpret a communication from different perceptual states.

Performance appraisal   A form of control designed to measure how effectively the organization's human resources are used. Performance appraisal provides feedback to each person concerning his or her job performance and how performance might be improved.

Personal status   Status derived from one's personal characteristics and accomplishments.

Personnel forecasting   Predicting how many employees an organization will require over some future period, what types of positions must be filled, and what qualifications will be required for each position.

PERT   *see* Program evaluation review technique.

Planned organizational change   A sequence of steps that begins when management realizes that organizational change is needed and then proceeds to diagnose the situation, set goals for the change, choose and implement appropriate change methods, and then evaluate and control the change.

Planning horizon   Includes the organization's interests, goals, and understanding and depends to a large extent upon its environment.

Politics   Any intentional action that individuals or groups take to promote or protect their self-interest.

Polycentric   A host-country orientation. Local individuals are considered to be in a better position to understand situations in their own country rather than foreigners. Financial controls are used to judge performance.

Positive reinforcement   In behavior modification, an event which follows an employee's behavior and increases the probability that the behavior will occur again in the future.

Power   The ability to influence the behavior of others.

Power structure   The positions of influence within an organization. Positions in the power structure exist because of formal authority, in-

formal power, or some combination of the two.

Preventive control   Organizational controls used for monitoring inputs. A poor-quality product resulting from defective raw materials can be prevented through this form of control.

Private acceptance   A change in individual behavior and belief to conform more closely to group norms.

Proactive change   Causing change to occur.

Probabilistic model   A mathematical model in which the values of some variables are uncertain.

Probability theory   A decision-making technique that bases predictions of future events on probabilistic estimates.

Problem-solving group   A group formed to solve a problem or exploit an opportunity.

Procurement   Purchasing the materials and equipment required for planned organizational operations.

Productivity   A measure of economic output per unit of investment.

Program evaluation review technique (PERT)   A sophisticated network technique designed to aid management in scheduling, coordinating, and controlling the sequence and timing of activities in large, complex projects.

Profit center   An organizational unit responsible for both revenues and expenditures. This is a common arrangement in the retail industry, in multiproduct (or service) organizations, and in organizations structured along geographic lines as contrasted with functional structured businesses and most nonprofit organizations that contain expense centers.

Profit center principle   An organizational unit headed by a manager who is responsible for both revenues and expenditures and is accountable for the unit's performance.

Psychological barriers to delegation   Barriers to the delegation process caused by psychological characteristics of both the manager and the subordinate.

Punishment   In behavior modification, an event which follows an employee's behavior and decreases the probability that the behavior will be repeated.

Quality circle   A group of employees who meet regularly on a formal basis to devise means of improving productivity and product or service quality.

Ranking   A type of performance appraisal in which the rater ranks his or her subordinates from highest to lowest, based on some criterion.

Reactive change   Organizational change that occurs as a reaction to changes in the environment.

Reception   The act of receiving a message.

Recruitment   The process of attracting a pool of qualified applicants for position openings.

Refreezing   Stabilizing organizational change at a new state of equilibrium.

Reinforcement   In behavior modification, an event which follows an employee's behavior and affects the probability that the behavior will occur again in the future.

Relations analysis   An approach used to group tasks where the organizer examines the points of contact among activities and personnel. The organization's structure must facilitate cooperative relationships among people whose functions are intertwined.

Relationship-oriented leadership   Leadership style in which the leader's primary motivation is to form strong emotional and affective ties with others in the work situation.

Resistance to change   To oppose an organizational change program.

Responsibility center   An organizational unit charged with a well-defined mission and headed by a manager who is accountable for the unit's performance. Types include profit centers (in which the manager is responsible for both revenues and expenditures) and expense centers (where the manager is responsible for expenditures, but not revenues).

Routine decisions   Decisions which deal with well-structured, recurring problems to which standard decision procedures apply.

Satisficing   Decision-making behavior in which the manager selects an alternative which is "good enough" (that is, one which will yield a satisfactory return to the organization).

Scalar status   Status derived from one's hierarchical level in an organization.

Scientific management   A turn-of-the-century management movement, founded by Taylor, which aimed to increase employee productivity through systematic analysis of work, culminating in "one best way" to perform a task.

Screening process   Variables that weaken the cause-effect relationship between a leader's traits and the group's performance.

Self-study   An examination and diagnosis of an organization by its members in order to identify specific areas that require change.

Semantic barriers   A hindrance to communication that exists when the receiver does not ascribe the same meaning to a word or phrase as the sender.

Sensitivity training   A form of training intended to develop a greater understanding of self, others, and interpersonal relationships.

Sentiments   Feelings and attitudes an employee has about the job and the organization.

Serial transmission barriers   The distortion in communication that occurs when a message is transmitted through a series of individuals.

Short-term results   The outcomes obtained for short-range time periods such as one to two years.

Simulation   A mathematical model which represents the operation of a real system by describing the behavior of individual components of the system and the effects of their interaction. Decisions—and their possible outcomes—may be "simulated" without affecting the real system.

Situational interview   A job interview, based on a systematic job analysis, in which applicants are asked to indicate how they would behave in representative job situations.

Slack time   In PERT, a sequence of activities that has a shorter completion time than the critical path. The difference is termed slack time.

Social audit An identification and evaluation of organizational activities believed to have a positive social impact.

Social contract A model conceptualizing the relationship between an organization and society as a whole, whereby the organization is granted freedom to exist and is obligated to function in the public interest.

Socialization The process through which a newcomer to an organization adjusts to the job requirements and the organization's culture sufficiently to become a full-fledged member of the organization.

Social responsibility The expectation that organizations, particularly business firms, should act in the public interest and contribute to the solution of social and ecological problems.

Social system The system of interpersonal relationships among members of an organization. It includes both formal and informal relationships.

Sociotechnical approach An approach toward designing work in organizations that gives explicit consideration to workers' needs for social and psychological satisfactions and to the technical requirements of the organization.

Span of control The number of subordinates reporting directly to a given manager.

Specific environment External conditions that directly affect an organization's operations.

Stable environment An environment which changes relatively slowly and permits managers to predict the direction and magnitude of change.

Staff functions Service, advisory, or otherwise supportive activities performed by staff units in line and staff organizations.

Stakeholders Various groups that have an interest in how the focal organizational goals are achieved. These groups include customers, suppliers, employees, stockholders, and the general public.

Statistical reports Managers use periodic statistical reports to monitor and evaluate nonfinancial performance. Such items as the number of employees, number of new customer contacts, delinquent accounts and other statistics vital to the department or business are included.

Status The relative standing or prestige of a person or group compared with other persons or groups.

Status symbols External indicators of status, such as private offices and special privileges.

Strategic apex The top-management group which makes strategic decisions for an organization.

Strategic contingencies theory of power A theory which holds that any unit's power is contingent upon that unit's relationship to the problems and uncertainties facing the organization as a whole.

Strategic control The managerial function that deals with the link between external opportunities and threats and internal performance that is essential to the success of a strategy.

Strategic decisions The development of broad or basic programs for the future involving how top management adapts the organization to the external environment.

Strategy evaluation A three-phase process where managers review the external opportunities and threats which are the basis of current strategies, compare expected versus actual results, and take corrective actions when deviations occur between expected and actual performance.

Strategy formulation The process of developing a particular strategic direction from various strategic alternatives. The decision as to which strategy to adopt is difficult and requires much subjective judgment.

Strategy implementation The administrative and behavioral actions used by managers to put the formulated strategy into practice. Every functional area of the firm is involved in implementing the strategy and accomplishing the desired objectives.

Stress The emotional and physiological condition which results from tension and pressure of work as well as from other causes.

Stressors An external agent which disturbs a person's equilibrium and produces stress.

Suboptimization Operating at a less-than-optimal level in one segment of an organization in order to optimize the functioning of the organization as a whole.

Subsystem An interdependent part of a larger system.

Sunk costs Costs that should be irrelevant in decision making because they have already been incurred.

Supervision The lowest level of management. Supervisors direct the work of operative employees.

Supervisory coaching A management development technique in which the supervisor provides guidance to subordinates and serves as their role model.

Supervisory control Strategies used by supervisors to control the performance of individual employees at lower levels of the organization.

Supportive leadership Showing concern for the needs of subordinates, making the work more pleasant, and being friendly and approachable.

Survey feedback An organization development method characterized by the gathering of attitudinal data (via questionnaires) from organization members, followed by a presentation of the results to the members to aid them in diagnosing where change is needed.

System A set of components that are related in the accomplishment of some purpose.

Task force A team of individuals, often representing various departments or interests, which has responsibility for coordinating a study or other efforts involving a number of organizational units.

Task-oriented leadership Leadership style in which the leader's primary motivation is to accomplish a task successfully.

Task structure In the contingency model of leadership, the degree to which the requirements of the subordinates' task are clearly specified.

Taylor, Frederick W. The first person (1856–1915) in history who actually studied work seriously. Often called the "father of scientific management."

Team building An organization development method designed to improve the functioning of groups or work teams through the intensive interaction of group members.

Technical skills Skills required to perform the operative work of an organization.

Technology transfer Where technology is transferred by a learning process. The transfer can be costly, complex, and time consuming when it is made from one national environment to another.

Technostructure Analysts and departments which provide technical assistance and support to line managers.

Teleconferencing Interactive group communication through any electronic medium.

Theory X The assumption that employees are lazy, lack ambition, and require supervision to keep them working.

Theory Y The assumption that employees can integrate their goals with those of the organization, that they can exercise self-control and self-direction, and that they are capable of directing their efforts toward organizational goals.

Theory Z Refers to the style of management characteristic of large Japanese firms and exhibited by a few U.S. corporations. Some of its essential elements include long-term employment for organizational members, consensual decision making, moderately specialized career paths, and slow evaluation and promotion.

Time horizon Time spans for planning range from less than one year to more than twenty. The time horizon tends to lengthen as one moves upward from lower to higher organizational levels.

Timing of controls A number of organizational control systems are required at various stages of the operating process. These controls should provide timely and accurate information.

Transactional leadership Motivating followers by exchanging rewards for performance.

Transformational leadership Motivating followers by inspiring involvement and participation in a mission.

Transmission To convey a message from one person to another.

Two-factor theory   A motivation theory, developed by Herzberg, which proposes that factors associated with the job context (hygiene factors) keep employees from becoming dissatisfied, whereas factors associated with the job content (motivators) make individuals satisfied with their jobs and help to motivate them.

Two-way communication   A communication process in which both parties talk and listen.

Unfreezing   Removing, reducing, or overcoming current attitudes, values, and behaviors as one of the initial steps in organizational change.

Upward communication   Communication from a subordinate to a superior.

Valence   In expectancy theory, the extent to which an employee desires a particular outcome.

Variable budgets   Where an attempt is made to match planned expenditures to varying revenue levels.

Variable costs   Costs that vary with the level of operations.

Variable interval reinforcement   In behavior modification, a reinforcement schedule in which behavior is positively reinforced, not continuously, but at variable intervals.

Verifiable goals   A process of specifying goals in exact terms rather than in general terms and being able to determine if goals have been attained.

Vertical linkages   Vertical relationships that provide direction and coordination between upper and lower levels of the organization.

Vroom-Yetton model of leadership   Theory of leadership that clarifies the conditions under which subordinates should participate in decision making and to what extent.

Weber, Max   A German sociologist and economist (1864–1920) who originated the concept of bureaucracy.

Wheel network   An X-shaped communication network in which each member can communicate only with the individual in the center who, in turn, may communicate with any of the other members.

Willingness to perform   The psychological and emotional characteristics that influence the degree to which an employee is inclined to perform a task.

Women and salary disparities   Research findings indicating that salary differences exist between women and men at every major experience level.

Work redesign   An approach toward job improvement where the characteristics of the job are improved.

Zero-base budgeting   A financial planning tool which requires an assessment and justification of the cost and benefits of all current and proposed organizational activities.

Zone of indifference   A category of subordinate attitudes toward authority in which certain orders are accepted without question.

NAME INDEX

SUBJECT INDEX

WE VALUE YOUR OPINION—PLEASE SHARE IT WITH US

Merrill Publishing and our authors are most interested in your reactions to this textbook. Did it serve you well in the course? If it did, what aspects of the text were most helpful? If not, what didn't you like about it? Your comments will help us to write and develop better textbooks. We value your opinions and thank you for your help.

Text Title _____ Edition _____

Author(s) _____

Your Name (optional) _____

Address _____

City _____ State _____ Zip _____

School _____

Course Title _____

Instructor's Name _____

Your Major _____

Your Class Rank _____ Freshman _____ Sophomore _____ Junior _____ Senior

_____ Graduate Student

Were you required to take this course? _____ Required _____ Elective

Length of Course? _____ Quarter _____ Semester

1. Overall, how does this text compare to other texts you've used?

   _____ Superior _____ Better Than Most _____ Average _____ Poor

2. Please rate the text in the following areas:

	Superior	Better Than Most	Average	Poor
Author's Writing Style	_____	_____	_____	_____
Readability	_____	_____	_____	_____
Organization	_____	_____	_____	_____
Accuracy	_____	_____	_____	_____
Layout and Design	_____	_____	_____	_____
Illustrations/Photos/Tables	_____	_____	_____	_____
Examples	_____	_____	_____	_____
Problems/Exercises	_____	_____	_____	_____
Topic Selection	_____	_____	_____	_____
Currentness of Coverage	_____	_____	_____	_____
Explanation of Difficult Concepts	_____	_____	_____	_____
Match-up with Course Coverage	_____	_____	_____	_____
Applications to Real Life	_____	_____	_____	_____

3. Circle those chapters you especially liked:

1 2 3 4 5 6 7 8 9 10 11 12 13 14 15 16 17 18 19 20

What was your favorite chapter? _____

Comments:

4. Circle those chapters you liked least:

1 2 3 4 5 6 7 8 9 10 11 12 13 14 15 16 17 18 19 20

What was your least favorite chapter? _____

Comments:

5. List any chapters your instructor did not assign. _____

6. What topics did your instructor discuss that were not covered in the text?_____

_____

7. Were you required to buy this book? _____ Yes _____ No

Did you buy this book new or used? _____ New _____ Used

If used, how much did you pay? _____

Do you plan to keep or sell this book? _____ Keep _____ Sell

If you plan to sell the book, how much do you expect to receive? _____

Should the instructor continue to assign this book? _____ Yes _____ No

8. Please list any other learning materials you purchased to help you in this course (e.g., study guide, lab manual).

_____

9. What did you like most about this text? _____

_____

10. What did you like least about this text? _____

_____

11. General comments:

May we quote you in our advertising? _____ Yes _____ No

Please mail to: Boyd Lane
                 College Division, Research Department
                 Box 508
                 1300 Alum Creek Drive
                 Columbus, Ohio 43216

Thank you!